RAISING THE
STANDARD
OF TRUTH

Exploring the History and Teachings
of the Early Restoration

BYU RELIGIOUS STUDIES CENTER

EDITED BY SCOTT C. ESPLIN

RSC
BYU

DESERET
BOOK

Published by the Religious Studies Center, Brigham Young University, Provo, Utah, in cooperation with Deseret Book Company, Salt Lake City.

Visit us at rsc.byu.edu.

© 2020 by Brigham Young University. All rights reserved.

Printed in the United States of America by Sheridan Books, Inc.

DESERET BOOK is a registered trademark of Deseret Book Company.

Visit us at DeseretBook.com.

Any uses of this material beyond those allowed by the exemptions in US copyright law, such as
section 107, "Fair Use," and section 108, "Library Copying," require the written permission of the
publisher, Religious Studies Center, 185 HGB, Brigham Young University, Provo, Utah 84602.
The views expressed herein are the responsibility of the authors and do not necessarily represent
the position of Brigham Young University or the Religious Studies Center.

Cover and interior design by Emily V. Strong.

ISBN: 978-1-9503-0401-1

Library of Congress Control Number: 2020915139

Contents

PART 3. CHURCH HISTORY IN ILLINOIS (1839-1846)

PART 4. CHURCH HISTORY IN SALT LAKE CITY AND BEYOND (1847-PRESENT)

The Grand Tapestry of the Restoration

SCOTT C. ESPLIN

The recorded history of The Church of Jesus Christ of Latter-day Saints documents the opening of the heavens and the ongoing dissemination of divine light. "These were days never to be forgotten," recalled Oliver Cowdery, one early witness to the translation of the Book of Mormon and to angelic visitations (Joseph Smith—History 1:71, note). Later, in 1836, the Prophet Joseph Smith himself added, "The occurrences of this day shall be handed down upon the pages of sacred history to all generations."[1] Writing to John Wentworth, editor of the *Chicago Democrat* in 1842, the Prophet further declared that a "standard of truth has been erected."[2] This standard called on all people to "hearken . . . [to] the voice of the Lord" through "the mouths of [his] disciples, whom [he had] chosen in these last days" (Doctrine and Covenants 1:1–2, 4).

The history of the establishment of the Church and the teachings that emerged from the Lord through these disciples are essential to the faith today. While Latter-day Saints believe in being honest, virtuous, and in doing good (see Articles of Faith 1:13), the theology of the Church is more than a collection of moral teachings. It is rooted in historical accounts of divine dealings in the latter days. Professors Douglas Tobler and George Ellsworth summarized, "History plays a vital role in [Latter-day Saint] thought, where it joins with theology and practical religion to answer many of life's questions and to make daily life meaningful, intelligible, and worthwhile. . . . The foundations of the Church are grounded in a series of historic events, without which the Restoration would be incomprehensible and impotent."[3] For Latter-day Saints, the historical events of the Church, especially those during its earliest decades, are foundational to building faith.

Raising the Standard of Truth explores the events and teachings of the early years of the restoration of the Church. Designed as a companion to personal and family study of the Doctrine and Covenants and Church history, the book is a collection of writings by experts from Brigham Young University, the Church History Department, and the Joseph Smith Papers and also by independent scholars and writers, compiled from materials produced by the Religious Studies Center at BYU. This collection represents some of the center's most frequently requested publications, including seminal works on the history of the Church. The conclusion of each section contains lists of additional resources available at rsc.byu.edu, home to hundreds of books and articles on Latter-day Saint history and doctrine.

The Religious Studies Center was founded in 1975 by Jeffrey R. Holland, then dean of Religious Instruction. Its mission is to encourage, sponsor, and publish serious, faithful, gospel-related materials. In its four decades of existence, the press has produced more than two hundred books and one thousand articles examining the scripture, doctrine, and history of the Church in a scholarly way and from a position of faith. On the occasion of its fortieth anniversary, Elder Holland commented on the Center's future: "I would like this to become known as the scholarly voice of The Church of Jesus Christ of Latter-day Saints on matters that would normally be considered as 'religious studies.' When people think, 'Where do I look to see the real heartbeat of intellectual life and academic contribution for The Church of Jesus Christ of Latter-day Saints,' I want them to think BYU, and at BYU, when the issue is religious scholarship, I want them to think of the Religious Studies Center. . . . I would like it to dive down vertically and really put out first-rate, foundational products, which it seems to me we are beginning to do."[4]

True to that charge, *Raising the Standard of Truth* seeks to present some of these "first-rate, foundational products" on the history of the Church that have been written over the last several years. The volume begins with events in New York and Pennsylvania in the 1820s. Professor Steven C. Harper of Brigham Young University examines Joseph Smith's accounts of his First Vision, demonstrating how a perspective of faith can assist a seeker in responding to criticisms of that pivotal event. Turning attention to the coming forth of the Book of Mormon, fellow professors and Joseph Smith Papers scholars Michael Hubbard MacKay and Gerrit J. Dirkmaat carefully examine eyewitness accounts of the translation process. Professors Amy Easton-Flake and Rachel Cope add the crucial perspectives of female witnesses, and Professor Anthony Sweat describes the witnessing power of the Book of Mormon relics. Together, these articles argue that future studies of the translation of the Book of Mormon should be grounded in the "well-documented religious experience given in the words of those who experienced it." Shining light on one of the most painful episodes early in the Restoration, associate dean of Religious Education J. B. Haws narrates what we know, don't know, and even might know about the loss of 116 pages of Book of Mormon manuscript. Concluding this section of the book, Ronald Barney, retired historian and archivist for the history department of the Church and former associate editor of *The Joseph Smith Papers*, traces the gradual unfolding of the gospel and priesthood authority at the hands of angelic ministers including John the Baptist and Peter, James, and John. He outlines a story that is "far more complex and impressive in scope than is generally recognized."

The book's second section follows the Church as it moves west from New York, with members dividing among Church centers in Ohio and Missouri throughout the 1830s. Here membership expanded while practical applications of gospel teachings began to take root. These include locating and attempting to establish Zion as well as implementing the law of consecration, topics explored by scholars Casey Griffiths and Taunalyn Rutherford. Steven Harper writes of the revelatory process employed by the Prophet, especially as it relates to the numerous revelations in the current Doctrine and Covenants that emerged in this era. Among these revelations are soaring visions of celestial worlds and profound truths regarding redemption available through Jesus Christ, themes explored by Jennifer C. Lane, dean of Religious Education at Brigham Young University–Hawaii. This section of the text concludes with chapters on one of the Church's highest highs, the dedication of the first temple in this dispensation in Kirtland, Ohio, followed by one of its lowest lows, the imprisonment of Latter-day Saint leaders in Liberty Jail and the expulsion of the Church from Missouri.

Following the harrowing experiences of the winter of 1838–39, members and leaders sought refuge in Nauvoo, Illinois, the era discussed in the third section of *Raising the Standard of Truth*. In the City of Joseph, the Church's theology deepened as the Prophet felt an urgency to convey eternal truth even while a temple slowly rose on a bluff overlooking the Mississippi River. Professor and Joseph Smith Papers editor Alexander L. Baugh recounts the teaching and practice of baptism for the dead in Nauvoo, while Rachel Cope challenges us to reclaim the early history of the Relief Society. "If we teach younger generations of students to consider the importance of Relief Society history—to value God's salvific work as engaged in by women," Professor Cope argues, "remembering will inevitably follow." In this section, RSC executive editor Devan Jensen and Professors Michael Goodman and Barbara Morgan Gardner also examine the Saints' growing understanding of the eternity of the family relationship, while Joseph Smith Papers editor and associate dean of Religious Education Andrew H. Hedges discusses the extension of that understanding to the controversial practice of plural marriage. Exploring the animosity this practice created among enemies of the Church, Professor Hedges concludes the Nauvoo section of the volume by probing the antagonists and events that led to the martyrdom of Joseph and Hyrum Smith.

Though the Prophet and Patriarch were gone, no unhallowed hand could stop the work from progressing. The final section of *Raising the Standard of Truth* follows the leadership of Brigham Young in resolving the succession crisis and organizing an orderly exodus across the plains of America. Chad M. Orton, a specialist for the Church History Department, demonstrates not only that the revelations guiding the westward migration provided answers to the Saints' immediate questions, but also that the lessons learned "regarding the importance of keeping sacred covenants and obeying the revealed word of the Lord remain relevant today." Once the Saints were settled in the West, however, opposition continued to rage. Eric Perkins and Mary Jane Woodger discuss John Taylor's leadership of the Church from "the underground" through the tumultuous antipolygamy crusade. Turning to the twentieth century, Professor Richard E. Bennett examines the context for President Joseph F. Smith's profound vision of "the hosts of the dead, both small and great" (Doctrine and Covenants 138:11), including the work of redemption that occurs among them. Continuing the theme of how the work of salvation is expanding on both sides of the veil, historian W. Paul Reeve concludes the volume, examining the challenging story of priesthood and temple restrictions due to race. He argues that President Spencer W. Kimball's 1978 revelation authorizing blessings of the priesthood and the temple for all of God's children was a return to the some of the Church's earliest universalistic roots.

While readers will note that many articles explore well-known episodes from our history in new and insightful ways, the volume examines difficult topics as well. Authors present ways they grapple with some of the challenging aspects of our history in the context of faith. This coincides with what President M. Russell Ballard called "extraordinary efforts" on the part of the Church "to provide accurate context and understanding of the teachings of the Restoration." In fact, he charged gospel teachers, including those featured in this volume, to "be among the first—outside students' own families—to introduce authoritative sources on topics that may be less well-known or controversial so that students will measure whatever they hear or read later against what they have already been taught." Calling this process a "spiritual inoculation," President Ballard continued: "Inoculate them by providing faithful, thoughtful, and accurate interpretation of gospel doctrine, the scriptures, our history, and those topics that are sometimes misunderstood. To name a few such topics that are less known or controversial, I'm talking about plural marriage, seer stones, different accounts of the First Vision, the process of translation of the Book of Mormon or the book of Abraham, gender issues, race and the priesthood, and a Heavenly Mother." It is likely that all readers, at one time or another, have experienced the reality that encountering new information can be initially unsettling. However, chapters in this collection discuss many of these topics because, as President Ballard concluded, "the effort for gospel transparency and spiritual inoculation through a thoughtful study of doctrine and history, coupled with a burning testimony, is the best antidote we have to help students avoid and deal with questions, doubt, or faith crises they may face in this information age."[5]

Through studying early history and teachings in greater depth, Latter-day Saint readers will witness what President Russell M. Nelson called the seeds of "a process of restoration" that continues to expand around the globe.[6] It is a "magnificent tapestry," President Gordon B. Hinckley likewise declared. Strands of suffering and sacrifice entwine with threads of revelation and redemption to form a pattern that persists today. "Weave beautifully your small thread in the grand tapestry, the pattern for which was laid out for us by the God of heaven," President Hinckley charged. "Hold high the standard under which we walk. Be diligent, be true, be virtuous, be faithful, that there may be no flaw in that banner."[7] Indeed, against that banner, "persecutions may rage, mobs may combine, armies may assemble, calumny may defame, but the truth of God will go forth boldly, nobly, and independent till it has penetrated every continent, visited every clime, swept every country, and sounded in every ear, till the purposes of God shall be accomplished and the great Jehovah shall say the work is done."[8]

* * *

As a collection of articles by two dozen scholars and other professionals, this book would not be possible without the help of many people. First, I thank the authors who generously cooperated to share their scholarship and, where necessary, to update portions of its content. Their work is supported by dozens of peers who reviewed these manuscripts before their previous printing and by four additional reviewers who helped select from among our considerable collection what to ultimately include in the volume. The staff of the BYU Religious Studies Center, including managing editor Don Brugger, student editing intern Myla Parke, and lead designer Emily Strong, worked tirelessly to prepare the book for publication. They were assisted by RSC publications coordinator Joany Pinegar, business and production supervisor Brent Nordgren, dean of Religious Education Daniel K Judd, and associate deans J. B. Haws and Andrew Hedges, as well as the staff of Deseret Book Company, with whom we are grateful to partner. In addition to publishing important and impactful content, one of the great joys of working at the Religious Studies Center is to associate with so many people who love and live the message of the Restoration.

NOTES

1. Joseph Smith, Journal, 1835–1836, in *The Joseph Smith Papers, Journals*, 1:216.
2. Joseph Smith, "Church History," *Times and Seasons*, March 1, 1842, 709.
3. Douglas F. Tobler and S. George Ellsworth, "History, Significance to Latter-day Saints," in *Encyclopedia of Mormonism*, ed. Daniel H. Ludlow, 5 vols. (New York: Macmillan, 1992), 2:595–96.
4. Quoted in Thomas A. Wayment, "The RSC Turns Forty: A Conversation with Elder Jeffrey R. Holland," *Religious Educator* 16, no. 2 (2015): 3.
5. M. Russell Ballard, "By Study and by Faith," *Ensign*, December 2016, 25–26.
6. Russell M. Nelson, in "Interview with President Nelson and Elder Stevenson in Chile," Church Newsroom, YouTube video, October 30, 2018, 5:09–6:28, youtube.com/watch?v=hOc2R2IpK7w.
7. Gordon B. Hinckley, "An Ensign to the Nations," *Ensign*, November 1989, 53–54.
8. Smith, "Church History," 709.

Part One

Church History in New England, New York, and Pennsylvania

1805–1830

Chapter One

A Seeker's Guide to the Historical Accounts of Joseph Smith's First Vision

STEVEN C. HARPER

Joseph Smith's First Vision may be the best-documented theophany, or vision of God, in history. The known historical record includes five different accounts in eight statements (three of the statements are nearly identical) of the vision in Joseph's papers, and a few other hearsay accounts in the papers of people who heard him tell of it.[1] Critics contend that the multiple accounts of Joseph Smith's vision are inconsistent with each other or with historical facts and find in them an evolving story that becomes more elaborate over time. The very same evidence sustains a more faithful view that finds Joseph's vision well and richly documented. The multiple accounts do not compel one to disbelieve Joseph Smith. For some the richly documented First Vision is a good reason to believe him.

It is vital to recognize that only Joseph Smith knew whether he experienced a vision of God and Christ in the woods in 1820. He was the only witness to what happened. His own statements are the only direct evidence. All other statements are hearsay. With so much at stake, Joseph's accounts have been examined and questioned. Are they credible? To answer that question satisfactorily, seekers need to know all the evidence and examine it for themselves, independent of anyone else. For several decades now the Church and various scholars have repeatedly published and publicized the known accounts of Joseph's First Vision, and images of the documents containing his own direct statements are available in *The Joseph Smith Papers* (josephsmithpapers.org) and on the Church's website (churchofjesuschrist .org).[2] Despite efforts to publish and publicize the historical record of the vision, relatively few people have learned of these vital historical documents and their contents. Critics, especially with the pervasive use of the internet, prey upon that ignorance to try to undermine faith in the vision. The antidote to that is to study the accounts Joseph left us.

Each of the accounts has its own history. Each was created in circumstances that shaped what it says, how it was recorded, and thus how it was transmitted to us. Each account has gaps and omissions. Each adds detail and richness. For example, Joseph described a highly personalized experience in his earliest account (1832). Using the language of the revivals, he says he became "convicted of my sins," but he could find no place for forgiveness since "there was no society or denomination that built upon the gospel of Jesus Christ as recorded in the new testament and I felt to mourn for my own sins." This account describes how the Lord appeared and filled Joseph "with the spirit of God" and "spake unto me saying Joseph my son thy sins are forgiven thee." It emphasizes the Atonement of Christ and the personal redemption it offered Joseph. He wrote in his own hand that as a result of the vision "my soul was filled with love and for many days I could rejoice with great Joy and the Lord was with me."[3]

Three years later, in 1835, an eccentric visitor from the East inquired of Joseph, whose scribe captured some of Joseph's response in his journal. In this account Joseph cast the vision as the first in a series of events that led to the translation of the Book of Mormon. He emphasized the opposition he felt in the grove, how he made "a fruitless attempt to pray" but couldn't speak until he knelt and was enabled. This account tells that one divine personage appeared in a pillar of fire, followed shortly by another. "I saw many angels in this vision," Joseph added as an afterthought, noting, "I was about 14 years old when I received this first communication."[4] A week later Joseph told another inquirer of the vision, though his scribe recorded only that Joseph gave the fellow an account of his "first visitation of Angels," rather than describing the vision itself.[5] Both of these 1835 accounts were also incorporated into a draft of Joseph's history.

Joseph published two accounts of the vision during his lifetime. The first of these to be written and the best known is in Joseph's manuscript history, written in 1838 or 1839 before being published in the Church's newspaper in 1842 and now excerpted in the Pearl of Great Price. The first to be published is Joseph's response to *Chicago Democrat* editor John Wentworth's request for a "sketch of the rise, progress, persecution and faith of the Latter-day Saints" as source material for a friend, George Barstow, who was writing a history of New Hampshire.[6] The original manuscript of this account is missing. Many of Wentworth's papers are thought to have been destroyed in the 1871 Chicago fire, and there is no known evidence that Barstow used Joseph's account, but Joseph had it printed in March 1842 in the Church's *Times and Seasons* newspaper, making it the first account of the First Vision published in the United States.

Joseph and scribe Frederick Williams wrote the earliest account a decade before those two accounts were published, and the Church's historians brought this document across the plains to Utah, but it became unknown to Latter-day Saints until Paul Cheesman published it in his master's thesis in 1965.[7] Similarly, the two accounts Joseph's scribe Warren Parrish penned into Joseph's journal in November 1835, which were later copied into a draft of Joseph's history, were generally unknown to Latter-day Saints until Latter-day Saint historians published them in the late 1960s.[8]

There is also a handful of contemporary hearsay accounts, meaning that they were written by people who heard Joseph describe his vision. Orson Pratt wrote one of these and published it in Scotland in 1840 as *A[n] Interesting Account of Several Remarkable Visions*. It echoes passages from Joseph's earlier accounts and prefigures passages in later ones. Orson Pratt must have had access to Joseph's tellings, either in person or through the documents of the pre-1840 accounts (or both), and possibly to an unknown document that prefigured the 1842 Wentworth letter. Alternatively, Orson's own rendering of the vision may have shaped the account in the Wentworth letter. The two accounts clearly share phrasing.

Pratt's account of the vision is the most thorough of the third-person accounts. Other hearsay accounts include the first translated publication of a First Vision account, Orson Hyde's 1842 German publication of an account very much like Orson Pratt's. Levi Richards wrote in his journal of hearing Joseph relate the vision in June 1843. David Nye White, editor of the *Pittsburgh Weekly Gazette*, similarly wrote in his paper of his August 1843 interview with Joseph, including an account of the vision. Alexander Neibaur, a German convert to Mormonism, wrote in his journal of hearing Joseph relate the vision in May 1844, just a month before Joseph's death. All of Joseph's accounts and the hearsay accounts have been published, together with scholarly analysis, in *The Joseph Smith Papers* and in the first two chapters of the book *Opening the Heavens: Accounts of Divine Manifestations, 1820–1844.*

Joseph's several accounts tell a consistent story of teenage angst followed by a comforting heavenly vision, a theophany. It is a fact, however, that the accounts vary in emphasis and disagree on some points. In 1832 Joseph declared that "the Lord opened the heavens upon me and I saw the Lord," perhaps referring to two separate heavenly beings each as the Lord, but not explicitly describing two personages as his later accounts declare. His 1835 account says he saw one personage, then another, as well as "many angels." In one account Joseph called the experience his "first visitation of Angels," as noted earlier; in another he "saw two glorious personages."[9] Joseph's 1835 and 1838 accounts emphasize opposition from an unseen power. The other accounts do not mention that part of the experience. In the 1832 account, Joseph's scribe Frederick Williams inserted a clause saying that Joseph was sixteen when the vision came, whereas his 1835 and 1842 accounts and the 1843 hearsay account all say "about 14," and his 1838 account says "in my fifteenth year," or at age fourteen.

Those are the objective facts; interpretations of their meaning vary among subjective interpreters. Suspicious interpreters decide that Joseph is unreliable, perhaps even scheming. Trusting interpreters decide that the variability in the accounts makes sense in terms of the particular ways Joseph remembered and related the experience and the diverse settings and circumstances in which his accounts were communicated, recorded, and transmitted.

Two writers, Fawn Brodie and Wesley Walters, have largely shaped the skeptical interpretations of Joseph's First Vision. They first articulated the criticisms that others have since adopted and published and that circulate widely today. Critical interpretations of Joseph's vision share a common hermeneutic, or explanatory method. They *assume* how a person in Joseph's position must have acted if his story were true and then show that his accounts vary from the assumed scenario. Sometimes they postulate an alternative to Joseph's own explanation. In the first edition of her biography of Joseph, Fawn Brodie cited his 1838 history, the one excerpted in the Pearl of Great Price. She did not draw on Joseph's 1835 journal or the undiscovered 1832 account and therefore concluded that no one had spoken of the vision between 1820 and about 1840. For Brodie, that meant that Joseph concocted the vision "when the need arose for a magnificent tradition."[10]

Fawn Brodie did not change her assumptions when she revised her biography of Joseph after the 1832 and 1835 accounts were discovered and published. She did not reconsider her interpretation in the light of evidence that showed that Joseph had written and spoken openly of the vision on more than one occasion earlier than 1838. Rather, she simply substituted "1830" for "1834" in this sentence about the vision: "It may have been sheer invention, created some time after 1830 when the need arose for a magnificent tradition."[11] She also noted the differences in details between the accounts, suggesting that their inconsistencies evidenced Joseph's invention and embellishment of the story.

Wesley Walters was a Presbyterian minister. Beginning in the 1960s, he published articles claiming that there was no religious revival in Palmyra, New York, in the spring of 1820 and therefore Joseph's claim to have been influenced by such religious fervor must be false.[12] Historians of the First Vision have credited Walters with awakening them to investigate the context of Joseph's accounts, but they fault him for forcing his thesis.[13] Joseph's accounts do not claim that the revivalism centered in Palmyra itself, as Walters argues. Rather, Joseph located the "unusual excitement on the subject of religion" around Manchester, New York, and used a Methodist term to describe a wider geographical scope than Walters's emphasis on the village of Palmyra. Joseph said that "the whole *district* of country seemed affected" by the revivalism (Joseph Smith—History 1:5; emphasis added). To nineteenth-century Methodists, a district was somewhat akin to a Latter-day Saint stake or a Catholic diocese.

It is not hard to empathize with Fawn Brodie or Wesley Walters. Brodie was raised as a Latter-day Saint but chose to leave the faith. For her and like-minded souls, that painful reorientation process requires a reinterpretation of Joseph Smith's First Vision. Walters had just as much at stake. Joseph's most definitive account of his vision relates how he told his mother, "I have learned for myself that Presbyterianism is not true." He also quoted the Savior saying that the Christian creeds "were an abomination" (Joseph Smith—History 1:19–20). Latter-day Saints who feel defensive about Walters's efforts to undermine the vision should be able to empathize with his response to Joseph's testimony. In one sense, his determined and enduring devotion to his cause is admirable. Even so, the critics and some believers lack the open-mindedness that seekers try to cultivate in their quest to learn the veracity of Joseph's accounts.

The critics' preconceived certainty that the vision never happened as Joseph said it did prevents them from exploring the variety of possibilities that the historical documents offer. All of the unbelieving accounts share what is sometimes called the hermeneutic of suspicion. It means, simply, that you don't believe what you're being told. One historian (who doesn't believe Joseph Smith) said that he couldn't trust the accounts of the vision because they were subjective and that it was his job to figure out what really happened. By what power is this historian going to discover what actually happened when he is unwilling to trust the only eyewitness? Such historians give themselves godlike abilities to know. They don't seem to grasp the profound irony that they are replacing the subjectivity of historical witnesses with their own subjectivity. Their method is subjectivity squared. Like it or not, they are limited to the historical documents. But they dismiss the plainest readings of the documents in favor of skeptical interpretations. They severely limit possible interpretations by predetermining that Joseph's descriptions cannot be possible. When Joseph's 1832 account was discovered in the 1960s, opening new interpretive possibilities to Brodie, she did not respond with willingness to consider that Joseph might be telling the truth. She simply fit the new evidence into her previous conclusion.

Similarly, the discovery of considerable evidence of revivalism in and around Palmyra, and especially in the region Joseph described, did not alter the argument Wesley Walters continued to make. No matter what evidence came to light, he interpreted it according to his original conclusion. He chose not to see the possibilities available to those who approach Joseph's accounts on a quest to discover if he could possibly be telling the truth. Even today, though much evidence has been discovered, it is common for some skeptics to contentedly repeat the Walters thesis that Joseph's 1838 account is anachronistic, or out of historical order, because they have long since concluded that no unusual religious excitement occurred to catalyze the vision as Joseph's 1838 account suggested. There is evidence that an intense revival stirred Palmyra in 1816–17 when Joseph moved there with his family. It may have catalyzed Joseph's 1832 description of his mind becoming seriously concerned for the welfare of his soul "at about the age of twelve years."[14] About 1818 Joseph's family purchased a farm in Manchester, a few miles south of Palmyra. A Methodist minister wrote in his diary of attending a camp meeting in Palmyra that June.[15] The next summer, Methodists of the Genesee Conference assembled at Vienna (now Phelps), New York, within walking distance of the Smith farm. The Reverend George Lane and dozens of other exhorters were present. One participant remembered the result as a "religious cyclone which swept over the whole region."[16] Joseph's contemporary and acquaintance Orsamus Turner remembered that Joseph caught a "spark of Methodist fire" at a meeting along the road to Vienna.[17] A Palmyra newspaper documents a revival there in June 1820, which is perhaps not too late to qualify as early spring since it snowed heavily on May 28. The diaries of Methodist minister Benajah Williams show that Methodists and others were hard at work in Joseph's district all the while.[18] They combed the countryside and convened camp meetings to help unchurched souls like Joseph get religion. Joseph's accounts are consistent with this evidence. He said that the unusual religious excitement in his district or region "commenced with the Methodists" and that he became "somewhat partial" to Methodism (Joseph Smith—History 1:5–8). The Walters thesis, though heartfelt and tenaciously defended by him and uncritically accepted and perpetuated by others, no longer seems tenable or defensible.[19]

Similarly, parts of Fawn Brodie's thesis are not as compelling as they once were. The evidence she analyzed in her second edition suggested to her that Joseph embellished each telling of the vision until it matured into the canonized 1838 account. But even later accounts do not continue to become longer, more detailed, or elaborate. Rather, these accounts return to sounding like Joseph's earlier, less-developed accounts. This evidence can be interpreted as Joseph's intention to make his 1838 account definitive and developed for publication, whereas some of the less-developed accounts, including ones later than 1838, were created for other purposes. Some were delivered on the spur of the moment and captured by someone remembering and writing later.

For those who choose to read Joseph's accounts with the hermeneutic of suspicion, the interpretation of choice is likely to remain that Joseph elaborated "some half-remembered dream" or concocted the vision as "sheer invention."[20] Those are not historical facts. They are skeptical interpretations of the fact that Joseph reported that he saw a vision. There are other ways to interpret that fact. Indeed, all of the scholars who have studied the accounts of the vision for decades and written the seminal articles and the earliest scholarly book on the vision share what one of them described as a hermeneutic of trust.[21]

One will arrive at the same conclusions as the skeptics if one shares their assumptions about what the facts mean. But if one is open-minded, other meanings for the same facts are possible. The danger of close-mindedness is as real for believers as for skeptics. Many believers seem just as likely to begin with preconceived notions rather than a willingness to go where Joseph's accounts lead them. They might assume, for instance, that Joseph told his family of the vision immediately or wrote it immediately, that he always understood all of its implications perfectly or consistently through the years, that he would always remember or tell exactly the same story, or that it would always be recorded and transmitted the same. But none of those assumptions are supported by the evidence. Some believers become skeptics in short order when they learn of the accounts and find that their assumptions of what would happen if Joseph told the truth are not supported by the historical record.

There is an alternative approach to the evidence. It is humble, believing, and thoroughly informed. It does not assume that one already knows how Joseph would respond to and tell a heavenly vision. Instead it allows his accounts to shape that understanding. This is the historical method. It is the method of the believing scholars who study all of the accounts and the context in which Joseph lived and wrote or told them. Richard L. Bushman, one such scholar, wrote:

> Behind the simplest event are complex motives and many factual threads conjoining that will receive varying emphasis in different retellings. In all accounts of his early religious experiences, for example, Joseph mentions the search for the true church and a desire for forgiveness. In some accounts he emphasizes one, in some the other. Similarly, in the earliest record of the first vision he attributes his question about the churches to personal study; in the familiar story written in 1838 or 1839 he credits the revival and the consequent disputes as raising the issue for him. The reasons for reshaping the story usually have to do with changes in the immediate circumstances. We know that Joseph suffered from attacks on his character around 1834. As he told Oliver Cowdery when the letters on Joseph's early experiences were about to be published, enemies had blown his honest confession of guilt into an admission of outrageous crimes. Small wonder that afterward he played down his prayer for forgiveness in accounts of the vision. Such changes do not evidence an uncertainty about the events, as Mr. Walters thinks, as if Joseph were manufacturing new parts year by year. It is folly to try to explain every change as the result of Joseph's calculated efforts to fabricate a convincing account. One would expect variations in the simplest and truest story.[22]

Several scholars read Joseph's accounts with a hermeneutic of trust and find them consistent where it counts. These are not bumpkins. They include Ivy League–educated historians who have authored prizewinning books and have studied the documents and their context for decades.

Such scholars are open to historical possibilities. For instance, Joseph may have purposely or unconsciously conflated events. Such compression or blurring is common when people remember and tell their histories. Joseph may have had a hard time remembering exactly when the vision occurred and, thus, how old he was at the time. Some of his accounts use the word *about* to describe his age or when his father moved to Palmyra or later the Manchester farm or other details of the story. As we all do, Joseph may have mixed information from his explicit episodic memory (the kind that consciously recalls events from the past) with semantic memory (the kind that knows what it knows without remembering how it knows, as in remembering one's name or phone number).

It was Joseph's vision and thus the accounts are undeniably subjective. All remembered things are. "Memories," wrote a foremost scholar of memory, "are records of how we have experienced events, not replicas of the events themselves." If two people had witnessed the vision together, their memories of it would be independent and different. Each would remember it a bit differently from the other and a bit differently each time they remembered it. Their memories would be mixtures of past and present. That is, whatever they were thinking about in the present to catalyze their memory of the vision would influence the nature of the memory.[23]

One scholar of memory wrote that "just as visual perception of the three dimensional world depends on combining information from the two eyes, perception in time—remembering—depends on combining information from the present and the past."[24] Another scholar used the same analogy. He explained that "merely to remember something is meaningless unless the remembered image is combined with a moment in the present affording a view of the same object or objects. Like our eyes, our memories must see double; these two images then converge in our minds into a single heightened reality."[25] Another memory scholar calls this heightened reality "insight" and acknowledges that it "may sound a bit magical."[26] Historian Richard Bushman described the process of finding insight in memory. "When we have a strange experience," he said, "something that is new, we have to understand it in terms of what is old. Events and experiences do not carry their meaning on the surface. We have to look around in the inventory of ideas that we have in order to make sense of what has occurred to us. And so [Joseph had] to enlarge his inventories . . . in order to make sense of an experience that he had before."[27]

Some assume that anyone who had such a heavenly experience could not possibly forget the date or his or her age, but who is qualified to make such an assumption? How does one know how a person responds to or remembers a heavenly vision? Those who choose the hermeneutic of trust do not prejudice the issue but rather listen to Joseph carefully with an open mind and make an informed decision about the veracity of his accounts. One who did that was the literary scholar Arthur Henry King. He wrote:

> When I was first brought to read Joseph Smith's story, I was deeply impressed. I wasn't inclined to be impressed. As a stylistician, I have spent my life being disinclined to be impressed. So when I read his story, I thought to myself, this is an extraordinary thing. This is an astonishingly matter-of-fact and cool account. This man is not trying to persuade me of anything. He doesn't feel the need to. He is stating what happened to him, and he is stating it, not enthusiastically, but in quite a matter-of fact way. He is not trying to make me cry or feel ecstatic. That struck me, and that began to build my testimony, for I could see that this man was telling the truth.[28]

Many people who hear or read one or more of Joseph's accounts arrive at the same conclusion. Others, of course, do not. It is not therefore the historical facts or the accounts of the vision that compel the conclusion one makes about it. Believing or not in one of the best-documented theophanies in history is ultimately a conscious, individual decision. One must decide whether to trust or be suspicious of the historical record created by Joseph Smith. That decision reveals much more about the subjective judgments of its maker than it does about the veracity of the claims Joseph made in historical documents.

Steven C. Harper is a professor of Church history and doctrine at Brigham Young University.

Steven C. Harper, "A Seeker's Guide to the Historical Accounts of Joseph Smith's First Vision," *Religious Educator* 12, no. 1 (2011): 165–76.

NOTES

1. The First Vision accounts are available on the Joseph Smith Papers website at https://www.josephsmithpapers.org/site/accounts-of-the-first-vision. They are reprinted and analyzed in John W. Welch, ed., *Opening the Heavens: Accounts of Divine Manifestations, 1820–1844* (Provo, UT: Brigham Young University Press, 2005), 1–75.
2. See Dean C. Jessee, ed., "The Early Accounts of Joseph Smith's First Vision," *BYU Studies* 9, no. 3 (1969): 275–94; *Personal Writings of Joseph Smith*, ed. Dean C. Jessee, rev. ed. (Salt Lake City: Deseret Book; Provo, UT: Brigham Young University Press, 2002); and *Papers of Joseph Smith*, ed. Dean C. Jessee, 2 vols. (Salt Lake City: Deseret Book, 1989–92). See also Milton V. Backman Jr., *Joseph Smith's First Vision: Confirming Evidences and Contemporary Accounts*, 2nd ed. (Salt Lake

City: Bookcraft, 1980), especially the appendixes; Milton V. Backman Jr., "Joseph Smith's Recitals of the First Vision," *Ensign*, January 1985, 8–17; James B. Allen, "Eight Contemporary Accounts of Joseph Smith's First Vision—What Do We Learn from Them," *Improvement Era*, April 1970, 4–13; Richard L. Anderson, "Joseph Smith's Testimony of the First Vision," *Ensign*, April 1996, 10–21. More recently, see Dean C. Jessee, "The Earliest Documented Accounts of Joseph Smith's First Vision," and James B. Allen and John W. Welch, "The Appearance of the Father and the Son to Joseph Smith in 1820," in *Opening the Heavens*, 1–34 and 35–76, respectively. See also https://www.josephsmithpapers.org/site/accounts-of-the-first-vision.

3. Welch, *Opening the Heavens*, 4–7; also Joseph Smith, History, circa Summer 1832, pp. 2–3, *The Joseph Smith Papers*, http://josephsmithpapers.org/.

4. Welch, *Opening the Heavens*, 7–8; also Smith, History, 1834–1836, p. 121, http://josephsmithpapers.org/.

5. Welch, *Opening the Heavens*, 10–11; also Smith, History, 1834–1836, p. 129.

6. Welch, *Opening the Heavens*, 17; also Joseph Smith, History, 1838–1856, volume C-1 [2 November 1838–31 July 1842], p. 1281, http://josephsmithpapers.org/.

7. See Paul R. Cheesman, "An Analysis of the Accounts Relating to Joseph Smith's Early Visions" (master's thesis, Brigham Young University, 1965), 126–32.

8. See James B. Allen, "The Significance of Joseph Smith's 'First Vision' in Mormon Thought," *Dialogue: A Journal of Mormon Thought* 1 (Autumn 1966): 40–41; and Jessee, "Early Accounts of Joseph Smith's First Vision," 275–94.

9. Smith, History, circa Summer 1832, p. 3; History, 1834–1836, p. 129; History, 1838–1856, volume E-1 [1 July 1843–30 April 1844], p. 1715, http://josephsmith papers.org/; and Welch, *Opening the Heavens*, 3–19.

10. Fawn M. Brodie, *No Man Knows My History: The Life of Joseph Smith the Mormon Prophet* (New York: Alfred A. Knopf, 1945), 25.

11. Fawn M. Brodie, *No Man Knows My History: The Life of Joseph Smith the Mormon Prophet*, 2nd ed. (New York: Vintage, 1995), 25.

12. See, for example, Wesley P. Walters, "New Light on Mormon Origins from the Palmyra Revival," *Dialogue: A Journal of Mormon Thought* 4, no. 1 (Spring 1969): 60–67.

13. Dean C. Jessee, James B. Allen (July 27, 2009), Richard L. Anderson (July 29, 2009), Larry Porter (July 30, 2009), Richard L. Bushman (July 31, 2009), Milton V. Backman Jr. (August 12, 2009), interviews by Samuel A. Dodge, video recording, transcriptions in possession of author.

14. Welch, *Opening the Heavens*, 4; also Smith, History, circa Summer 1832, p. 1.

15. Aurora Seager wrote in his diary, "I attended a camp-meeting at Palmyra," in June 1818. He said that over the weekend about twenty people were baptized and forty became Methodists. See E. Latimer, *The Three Brothers: Sketches of the Lives of Rev. Aurora Seager, Rev. Micah Seager, Rev. Schuyler Seager, D.D.* (New York: Phillips & Hunt, 1880), 12, quoted in D. Michael Quinn, "Joseph Smith's Experience of a Methodist 'Camp Meeting' in 1820," *Dialogue* Paperless E-Paper 3, December 20, 2006, 2–3.

16. Quoted in Milton V. Backman Jr., "Awakenings in the Burned-Over District," *BYU Studies* 9, no. 3 (Spring 1969): 308.

17. Orsamus Turner, *History of the Pioneer Settlement* (Rochester, NY: William Alling, 1852), 213. Richard L. Anderson evaluates Turner's credibility as a witness in "Circumstantial Confirmation of the First Vision through Reminiscences," *BYU Studies* 9, no. 3 (1969): 373–404.

18. Diaries of Benajah Williams, in possession of Michael Brown, Philadelphia.
19. See Backman, "Awakenings in the Burned-Over District," 309; and Richard L. Bushman, "The First Vision Story Revived," *Dialogue* 4, no. 1 (1969): 85.
20. Brodie, *No Man Knows My History*, 2nd ed., 25.
21. Richard L. Bushman, interview by Samuel Dodge, July 31, 2009, Provo, Utah, transcription in author's possession.
22. Bushman, "First Vision Story Revived," 83.
23. Daniel L. Schacter, *Searching for Memory: The Brain, the Mind, and the Past* (New York: Basic, 1996), 6.
24. Schacter, *Searching for Memory*, 28.
25. Roger Shattuck, *Proust's Binoculars* (Princeton, NJ: Princeton University Press, 1983), 46–47.
26. Edmund Blair Bolles, *Remembering and Forgetting: An Inquiry into the Nature of Memory* (New York: Walker, 1988), 65.
27. Bushman, interview.
28. Arthur Henry King, *Arm the Children: Faith's Response to a Violent World* (Provo, UT: BYU Studies, 1998), 288.

Chapter Two

The Probation of a Teenage Seer

Joseph Smith's Early Experiences with Moroni

STEVEN C. HARPER

Millennia before Joseph Smith reached his teen years in rural New York, the God of Israel revealed that he would raise a choice seer from among the descendants of Joseph of Egypt and command him and give him "power to bring forth my word" (see 2 Nephi 3:6–13). Although Joseph Smith was foreordained to be a seer, he had to learn and grow through his life experiences and rise to his calling to bring forth the Lord's word—the Book of Mormon. His early experience with seer stones seemed to provide some foundation for this later work, and the angel Moroni offered valuable tutoring through a four-year probationary period.

JOSEPH'S EARLY YEARS

Joseph Smith's 1838–39 history says that after his First Vision in the spring of 1820, he "continued to pursue [his] common vocation" (Joseph Smith—History 1:27), meaning that he farmed with his father and took odd jobs to supplement the family income. Joseph talked about his teenage struggles and sins and his efforts to overcome them. For instance, an early draft of his manuscript history reads:

During the space of time which intervened between the time I had the vision and the year Eighteen hundred and twenty three, (having been forbidden to join any of the religious sects of the day, and being of very tender years, and persecuted by those who ought to have been my friends, and to have treated me kindly and if they supposed me to be deluded to have endeavoured in a proper and affectionate manner to have reclaimed me) I was left to all kinds of temptations, and mingling with all kinds of society I frequently fell into many foolish errors and displayed the weakness of youth and the corruption of human nature which I am sorry to say led me into divers temptations to the gratification of many appetites offensive in the sight of God.[1]

A few years later, while preparing the history for publication under Joseph's direction, Willard Richards clarified Joseph's confession by deleting some words and by adding the following ones:

In making this confession, no one need suppose me guilty of any great or malignant sins. A disposition to commit such was never in my nature. But I was guilty of levity, and sometimes associated with jovial company, etc., not consistent with that character which ought to be maintained by one who was called of God as I had been. (Joseph Smith—History, 1:28)[2]

Joseph was not guilty of sins that unalterably shaped his destiny, but evidence indicates that he was troubled by a nagging covetousness, complicated by his family often being on the verge of, but never finally attaining, a comfortable living. God had work for Joseph Smith to do, but Satan determined to thwart it. Joseph's autobiographies, his mother's memoir, Oliver Cowdery's historical letters, and Joseph Knight's autobiography enable us to watch the teenager struggle to choose between God's plan for him and Satan's efforts to undermine the acquisition and translation of the gold plates. These records make it possible to observe how God sent a messenger (Moroni) to tutor, chasten, and empower Joseph, finally enabling the vulnerable, unlearned farmer to begin a most marvelous work and a wonder: the translation and publication of the Book of Mormon.

To identify Joseph as a tempted—even at times a foolish—teenager may seem antithetical to the justified praises sung to "the man who communed with Jehovah."[3] But this is the story of how he became such, so it must first establish what he candidly admitted about his flawed beginnings and need for development.

Aside from his confession above, he wrote in 1832 that many days after his First Vision in 1820, "I fell into transgressions and sinned in many things which brought a wound upon my soul." He said further, "When I was seventeen years of age I called again upon the Lord and he shewed unto me a heavenly vision for behold an angel of the Lord came and stood before me and it was by night and he called me by name and he said the Lord had forgiven me my sins."[4]

Joseph's faith in Jesus Christ, humility, and resulting repentance, including his choice to respond positively to chastisement, suggest why the Lord called Joseph to be the seer to bring forth the Book of Mormon. Relying on the Lord and responding faithfully to his instructions, he overcame these sins and struggles to bring forth a marvelous work indeed.

CONTEXT FOR JOSEPH SMITH THE SEER

Knowing about Joseph's activities and surrounding culture between 1820 (when he received the First Vision) and 1823 (when Moroni appeared to him) helps to clarify his growth and experiences with the gold plates.

Joseph's world was shifting rapidly from an agrarian economy to an industrialized, capitalistic marketplace. For many, that meant opportunity and wealth. But for many others, including the Smith family, it meant one setback after another. Like the markets, churches were becoming more free and open, competing for converts the same way that shoemakers or whiskey distillers were competing for consumers. Many, including Joseph Smith, struggled with the twin developments of market revolution and the multiplication of churches from which to choose. His family experienced these developments as pressure, an escalation of stress and anxiety about both their home economy and their eternal salvation.

This financial stress drove a substantial group of settlers to "an unconquerable expectation of finding buried treasure in the earth."[5] There is evidence that both Joseph and his father joined in some of the activities of a group of neighborhood treasure seekers who looked for buried riches in nocturnal rituals.[6] For them and many other Christian people, treasure seeking made good sense, though most "respectable" folks, the type Joseph thought ought to have befriended him if they were good Christians, thought treasure seeking was beneath them.[7] But historian Alan Taylor explained why treasure seeking made sense in that time and place: it met the needs of some people who felt pressured by the culture's demand to get more possessions and more religion. In other words, treasure seeking promised "both quick wealth and a sense of power over the supernatural world."[8]

Many treasure seekers appealed to guardian spirits or charted the cycles of the moon to increase their chances of discovering riches. They also "turned increasingly to 'seer stones' or 'peep stones'" in order to find riches.[9] While such a practice may seem odd today, this skepticism is an assumption of modern culture. It has not always been the dominant idea. As the Bible attests, in ancient Israel certain stones were associated with the priestly or prophetic office and considered a means of revelation.[10] The Bible says that Jacob, Moses, and Aaron had powerful rods and that Joseph of Egypt had a cup "whereby indeed he divineth" (Genesis 44:5).[11] In the Book of Mormon, Alma taught his son Helaman a prophecy from the Lord, saying, "I will prepare unto my servant Gazelem, a stone which shall shine forth in darkness unto light" (Alma 37:23). And the Lord prepared two stones for Jared's brother to bury with his records, stones that could be used to translate (see Ether 3:22–24). Perhaps basing their hopes and ideas on biblical precedents like these, several magician-mathematicians, including Isaac Newton, sought after or used marvelous stones in Renaissance and early modern Europe. John Dee, for example, taught algebra and navigation, sought to commune with angels, and used a translucent stone that has been on display in the British Museum.[12]

Joseph evidently discovered one or more seer stones after his First Vision and before he knelt to pray for forgiveness before Moroni's first visit in September 1823.[13] There is no reason to reject the basic assertion that Joseph searched for buried treasure using a marvelous stone, even though the claim is made by some of his antagonists. Joseph did not dispute that claim, and people who loved, trusted, and followed him confirmed that he had such a stone.[14] A man who hired Joseph reported that Joseph's search for a seer stone was inspired by an earlier experience of seeing it through a stone that belonged to a neighbor girl.[15] Another neighbor said that Joseph could see in a stone they found while digging a well.[16] Joseph's mother also acknowledged his gift of seership, saying that Joseph "was in possession of certain means, by which he could discern things that could not be seen by the natural eye."[17] Joseph Knight, who employed Joseph in 1826 and who converted shortly after the Church was organized, wrote that Joseph "looked in his glass," meaning his stone.[18] Brigham Young later used the term *seer stone* to describe this object, called "means" by Lucy and "glass" by Joseph Knight.[19]

However, the most important point here is not the revelatory object, or what the scriptures repeatedly call the "means" (Mosiah 8:18; 28:13; Alma 37; Doctrine and Covenants 8:9; 10:4; 20:8). The point of emphasis here is the gift of revelation itself. As evidenced by the above accounts, Joseph had a gift similar to the one described in this Book of Mormon passage:

> A seer is a revelator and a prophet also; and a gift which is greater can no man have. . . . But a seer can know of things which are past, and also of things which are to come, and by them shall all things be revealed, or, rather, shall secret things be made manifest, and hidden things shall come to light, and things which are not known shall be made known by them, and also things shall be made known by them which otherwise could not be known. Thus God has provided a *means* that man, though faith, might work mighty miracles; therefore he becometh a great benefit to his fellow beings. (Mosiah 8:16–18; emphasis added)

Thus Joseph, as a teenager, had the "means" that, through faith, he could "work mighty miracles." But although he evidently had the ability of seership early on, he was in the process of becoming the Lord's seer, learning how to apply the gift of revelation (see Doctrine and Covenants 8:2–4).

MORONI'S INSTRUCTIONS

On September 21, 1823, Joseph went to bed but not to sleep. "I was verry conscious," he later said of that night, "that I had not kept the commandments, and I repented hartily for all my sins and transgression, and humbled myself."[20] Then light flooded the room, making it brighter than at midday, and an angel appeared, striking, luminous, and standing in the air. Joseph shrank in fear for a moment before the messenger spoke his name, introduced himself as Moroni, and announced that God had work for Joseph to do.[21]

Moroni told Joseph that whoever had the stones and could see in them was a seer, and to Joseph the news was both fascinating and somewhat familiar. He knew that he had the gift of which Moroni spoke because he had already discovered it through his use of seer stones. Now the Lord had sent the angel as a mentor to help Joseph rise to the gift's innate potential to perform a marvelous work.

Moroni launched his first lesson: "He told me of a sacred record which was written on plates of gold," Joseph remembered, adding, "I saw in vision the place where they were deposited."[22] It was the sacred history of a lost civilization, Christians the Savior had visited, Moroni said, and with it were two stones—means God had prepared for its translation. The golden plates were now concealed in a nearby hill with these seer stones.[23]

Then Moroni "commenced quoting the prophecies of the Old Testament," first from Malachi, who described the coming day "that shall burn as an oven" and said that the wicked would be left without root or branch. He then made Malachi's distant prophecy proximate: "I will reveal unto you [Joseph] the Priesthood, by the hand of Elijah the prophet, before the coming of the great and dreadful day of the Lord. . . . And he shall plant in the hearts of the children the promises made to the fathers, and the hearts of the children shall turn to their fathers. If it were not so, the whole earth would be utterly wasted at his coming" (see Joseph Smith—History 1:36–39).

How much Joseph Smith understood is not clear, but over time he learned of Moroni's meaning: God had chosen Joseph to restore the powerful priesthood ordinances in which solemn covenants could bind families to God and, by leading them to eternal lives, fulfill the plan of redemption that this earth was created to facilitate. Otherwise all the effort and energy put forth in creating this earth would be wasted at the Lord's coming.[24]

That was heady stuff for a seventeen-year-old. And there was more. Moroni quoted from Isaiah chapter 11, which foretells that Christ will come in glory, might, and vengeance to separate the righteous from the wicked. But not before setting "his hand again the second time" and gathering "the outcasts of Israel" by setting up an "ensign for the nations," a standard, or in other words, a church with a commission to preach the gospel to the whole world.[25]

Moroni continued by quoting Acts 3:22–23, prophesying that all who failed to hear the Lord's warning voice and gather to his ensign would "be destroyed." He then cited Joel 2:28–32: "I will pour out my spirit upon all flesh; and your sons and your daughters shall prophesy, your old men shall dream dreams, your young men shall see visions." Moreover, cataclysms and terrible judgments would be visited upon all who failed to build Zion. In the end, Zion builders alone would be delivered. Moroni told Joseph "that the fullness of the gentiles was soon to come in," meaning that the large-scale spread of the gospel to all nations loomed imminently in the future. Then, Joseph explains, "[Moroni] quoted many other passages of scripture and offered many explanations which cannot be mentioned here."[26]

Now, standing midair in Joseph's room, Moroni explained that Joseph could not have the plates or seer stones yet and warned that if he showed them to others without permission once he received them, he would be destroyed. Joseph envisioned the hillside in which Moroni deposited the plates over a millennium earlier. Then the light gathered around the messenger and he ascended through a conduit "right up into heaven," leaving Joseph in a dark, still room, "marvelling greatly at what had been told to me by this extraordinary messenger."[27]

"I lay musing on the singularity of the scene," Joseph remembered, "when in the midst of my meditation," Moroni reappeared. He "again related the very same" message, then added more detail on the "great judgments which were coming upon the earth" before ascending again. "Sleep had fled from my eyes," Joseph wrote, "and I lay overwhelmed in astonishment at what I had both seen and heard."[28]

Then Moroni appeared a third time, relayed the same message, and cautioned Joseph "that Satan would try to tempt me (in consequence of the indigent circumstances of my father's family) to get the plates for the purpose of getting rich, This he forbid me, saying that I must have no other object in view in getting the plates but to glorify God, and must not be influenced by any other motive but that of building his kingdom, otherwise I could not get them."[29]

Joseph's mother wrote later that Moroni added "a few words of caution and instruction: thus, that he must beware of covetousness; and he must not suppose the record is to be brought forth with the view of getting gain; for this was not the case; but that it was to bring forth light and intelligence, which had for a long time been lost to the world: and, that when he went to get the plates, he must be on his guard, or his mind would be filled with darkness."[30]

As scholar Terryl Givens summarized Joseph's situation, "He was neither to exhibit the plates to anyone nor to think of alleviating his family's acute impoverishment by selling them" or by selling the book he could publish from them.[31] Seeking fame and fortune—two of the most potent temptations—was explicitly, absolutely forbidden by God's messenger. Warned against the temptations he would face, Joseph had to choose whether or not he would follow God's plan. In fact, during his mortal life, Moroni had written to a young Joseph, chosen to translate the sacred records and potentially covetous of the wealth embedded in a stack of precious metal: "The plates . . . are of no worth because of the commandment of the Lord. For he truly saith that no one shall have them to get gain; but the record thereof is of great worth; and whoso shall bring it to light, him will the Lord bless" (Mormon 8:14–16).

When Moroni ascended again, Joseph "was again left to ponder on the strangeness of what [he] had just experienced" but was interrupted by a rooster announcing the break of dawn. Joseph arose and went to work as usual.[32]

ATTEMPT TO TAKE THE PLATES

Joseph, Alvin, and their father began harvesting together, but Joseph seemed preoccupied. "Joseph," Alvin told him, "we must keep to work or we shall not get our task done." Joseph tried to get back to work, but when his father saw how weak he was, he sent Joseph home.[33] "I started with the intention of going to the house," Joseph wrote, "but, in attempting to cross the fence out of the field where we were, my strength entirely failed me, and I fell helpless on the ground," unconscious. As he woke, Joseph saw "the same messenger" whom he had seen the night before.[34]

According to Joseph's mother, Moroni told Joseph the night before to tell his father what he had heard and seen, but Joseph had not.[35] "Why?" the angel asked him. "I was afraid my father would not believe me," Joseph replied. Moroni then promised that Joseph's father would believe every word.[36] "I obeyed," Joseph wrote, tellingly. "I rehearsed the whole matter to him. He replied to me that it was of God, and told me to go and do as commanded by the messenger."

Joseph reported to a hill, known simply to the Smiths as "a hill of considerable size." There, near the top, on the west side, Joseph found the stone that concealed the box in which the plates were deposited. Joseph found a tree branch, jammed one end of it "under the edge of the stone, and with a little exertion raised it up." He remembered, "I looked in and there indeed did I behold the plates, the Urim and Thumim and the Breastplate as stated by the messenger."[37]

Here Joseph's manuscript history is terse: "I made an attempt to take them out but was forbidden by the messenger."[38] Oliver Cowdery wrote in 1835 that Joseph had experienced "the visions of heaven during the night, and also seeing and hearing in open day; but the mind of man is easily turned, if it is not held by the power of God through the prayer of faith," and as Joseph walked to the hill, "two invisible powers were operating upon his mind . . . one urging the certainty of wealth and ease in this life, [which] had so powerfully wrought upon him" by the time he arrived that the angel's instructions "had entirely gone from his recollection." Oliver didn't blame Joseph. "He was young, and his mind easily turned from correct principles," but also, Oliver acknowledged, he was teachable and ready "to be lead into the great work of God, and be qualified to perform it in due time."[39]

According to Oliver, Joseph "had heard of the power, of enchantment, and a thousand like stories, which held the hidden treasures of the earth, and suposed that physical exertion and personal strength was only necessary to enable him to yet obtain the object of his wish." Oliver had earlier stated, "On attempting to take possession of the records a shock was produced upon his system, by an invisible power, which deprived him in a measure, of his natural strength."[40]

Agonizing that he was powerless to take the plates, Joseph cried out to the Lord, "Why can I not obtain them?" Moroni's reply came: "You have not kept the commandments of the Lord which I gave unto you." He explained to Joseph how succumbing to temptation could teach him of "the power of the advisory [sic]," commanded him to repent, and promised the Lord's forgiveness if he would. Joseph remembered what he had been taught and began to pray, and the Spirit returned.[41]

Joseph was teachable, and Moroni said to Joseph, "Now I will show you the difference between light and darkness and the operation of a good Spirit and an evil one[.] an evil spirit will try to crowd your mind with every evil and wicked thing to keep every good thought and feeling out of your mind but you must keep your mind always staid upon God that no evil may come into your heart."[42] According to Oliver Cowdery, Moroni showed Joseph a vision of "the prince of darkness, surrounded by his innumerable train of associates," and taught that "all this is shown, the good and the evill, the holy and impure, the glory of God and the power of darkness, that you may know hereafter the two powers and never be influenced or overcome by that wicked one."[43]

So Joseph returned home from the hill empty-handed but full of knowledge. He admitted in his 1832 autobiography, "I had been tempted of the advisary and saught the Plates to obtain riches and kept not the command-me[n]t that I should have an eye single to the Glory of God therefore I was chastened."[44] According to Lucy, the angel told Joseph "that he could not take them from the place wherein they were deposited, until he had learned to keep the commandments of God," clarifying that Joseph needed to become "not only willing, but able to do it."[45]

In his later history, Joseph rendered the story more matter-of-factly and said simply that he learned on that first visit to the hill the following:

> [T]he time for bringing them [the plates] forth had not yet arrived, neither would untill four years from that time; but he told me that I should come to that place precisely in one year from that time, and that he would there meet with me, and that I should continue to do so untill the time should come for obtaining the plates. Accordingly as I had been commanded I went at the end of each year, and at each time I found the same messenger there and received instruction and intelligence from him at each of our interviews respecting what the Lord was going to do, and how and in what manner his kingdom was to be conducted in the last days.[46]

Readers of this passage in Joseph's history often assume that he knew at the time that it would be four years before he received the plates, but he did not. All he knew was that the time was not yet, and that he should return in exactly one year and continue faithful until the unspecified time came. Joseph was not simply to pass time until he got the plates regardless of his behavior. He was to prepare himself by gaining experience in keeping the commandments of God and gaining strength to resist temptations; he was to prove himself faithful to the Lord's instructions and get the plates because of his obedience.

A FOUR-YEAR PROBATION

Joseph's four-year probation was characterized not only by divine visitations and adversarial interferences but also by the vicissitudes of everyday family responsibilities as he sought to make ends meet at home and, later, with his bride, Emma Hale. Throughout these years, God, largely through the angel Moroni, mentored Joseph to fulfill his potential as the seer who would obtain and protect the buried golden plates, translate them through the gift of God, and ultimately shepherd the sacred writings into print.

Joseph farmed and helped his brother Alvin build a respectable middle-class frame home for their aging parents. After a day's work Joseph's family gathered, "all seated in a circle . . . listening in breathless anxiety to the religious teachings of a boy eighteen years of age." He urged them not to tell others, fearing rejection and even violence against him.[47] Covetous neighbors—treasure seekers—might get word and demand the treasure. The Smith family members were to keep confidential that which Moroni had revealed in order to prove themselves trustworthy of obtaining further knowledge. "If we are wise and prudent in that which [is] revealed to us," Joseph taught them, "God is able to make all things known to us." His father agreed and promised that they would try to live worthily to be so trusted by God.[48]

But life was not without hardship. "On the 15 of Nov[ember 1823]," Lucy remembered, "Alvin was taken very sick." The family doctor was summoned but unavailable. Another came instead and "administered to him[,] although the patient objected much against it[,] a heavy dose of Calomel." Alvin soon recognized that he would not survive. He charged Hyrum to finish the frame home and take care of his parents in their old age. He spoke to each of his siblings in turn, telling Joseph, now nearly eighteen, "I am going to die now[.] The distress which I suffer and the sensations that I have tell me my time is very short[.] I want you to be a good boy & do everything that lays in your power to obtain the records[.] Be faithful in receiving instruction and in keeping every commandment that is given you." After an affectionate farewell to two-year-old Lucy, Alvin died.[49]

By the following spring, 1824, family routines returned to normal. A new preacher in town taught the need for the different denominations to agree and "worship God with one mind and one heart." Lucy Mack Smith "wished to join them, and [she] tried to persuade [her] husband to do so." Joseph Sr. attended a few times, and the children—except Joseph—followed Lucy. Joseph assured his mother that he could take his Bible "and go out into the woods and learn more in two hours than you could if you were to go to meeting two years." Joseph was growing confidently into his calling. He told his mother that it would not hurt her to join, but prophesied that though the leader of the church preached piously, within one year he would take the last cow of a widowed mother of eight to satisfy a debt. Lucy, who had long since perceived that her son had a gift, was even more impressed when the fellow fulfilled Joseph's prophecy.[50]

Such religion could not satisfy Joseph. Though many came preaching various doctrines, he remained apart, waiting for more instruction by a messenger sent from the presence of God. According to Lucy, Moroni finally told Joseph he could obtain the plates on September 22, 1824, if he would keep them in his hands, take them straight home, and immediately secure them there in a trunk with a good lock and key. The whole family, most of all Joseph, anxiously anticipated that he would return home with them.[51]

He went to the hill on the appointed day, pried up the stone that covered the plates, and looked down on them. He reached down and lifted the plates from their stone box when, according to his mother, "the thought flashed across his mind that there might be something more in the box," something he could profit from after all. Excited, Joseph laid the plates down to cover the box, planning to come back later for the rest. When he turned back to pick up the plates, they were gone, "but where he knew not nor did he know by what means it had been taken away." Alarmed, Joseph knelt and prayed. The angel appeared "and told him that he had not done as he was commanded," that he was still tempted "to secure some imaginary treasure," that he was still too easily overcome by the powers of darkness, not yet vigilant enough, not yet motivated solely by the glory of God.[52]

After the rebuke, Moroni allowed Joseph to raise the stone again and see that the plates were safe in their stone box. Joseph reached for them again but was hurled back. The angel left, and Joseph rose and returned to the house, weeping, disappointed, and fearing that his family would no longer believe him.[53]

Joseph was no sooner in the door than his father asked whether he had obtained the plates. "No, Father," he said. "I could not get them."

"Did you see them?" his father asked.

"Yes," replied Joseph, "I saw them, but could not take them."

"I would have taken them," his father said earnestly, "if I had been in your place."

Subdued, Joseph said, "You do not know what you say. I could not get them, for the angel of the Lord would not let me."[54]

Joseph then related the whole story, causing his parents to fear that he may never qualify to get the plates. "We therefore," Lucy remembered, "doubled our dilligence in prayer and supplication to God, in order that he might be more fully instructed in his duty, and be preserved from all the wiles and machinations of him 'who lieth in wait to deceive.'"[55] Though it was emotionally painful, Joseph's 1824 attempt to obtain the plates was yet another learning opportunity that helped train him into a steward of the Book of Mormon plates, and into a seer who could translate the sacred writings inscribed on them.

There are no detailed records of what happened the next September, in 1825. There is evidence, however, that the temptation for Joseph to use his gift for material gain intensified rather than diminished. With Alvin's death, the burden of finishing the frame home and meeting the annual mortgage payment fell increasingly to Hyrum and, when he married, to Joseph. They scoured the countryside for odd jobs. In October of 1825, Josiah Stowell, a farmer from southeastern New York, enticed Joseph and his father to come work for him. Stowell had, according to Joseph, "heard something of a silver mine having been opened by Spaniards in Harmony, Susquahanah County, State of Pennsylvania, and had previous to my hiring with him been digging

Joseph Smith Receiving the Plates, by Kenneth Riley. © Intellectual Reserve, Inc.

in order if possible to discover the mine."[56] Stowell had also heard of Joseph's gift. He had learned, as Lucy put it, "that he was in possession of certain means, by which he could discern things, that could not be seen by the natural eye." Stowell "offered high wages" for such skill, appealing to the struggling Smith family.[57]

Now Joseph had a dilemma: Should he sell his reputation as a seer for fourteen dollars a month to help his family make the mortgage payment on the farm they had worked awfully hard to improve? It seemed like a harmless decision, and Joseph decided to follow Stowell to Susquehanna

25

County. But in the winter of 1826, Stowell's nephew, Peter Bridgeman, filed a complaint against Joseph with a justice of the peace in South Bainbridge, New York. Joseph was evidently arrested and tried for disorderly conduct that probably stemmed from using his stone to search for buried treasure. One account of the trial reports that the Smiths were "mortified that the wonderful power which God had so miraculously given . . . should be used only in search of filthy lucre."[58]

The digging stopped after a month, and Joseph Sr. returned home while Joseph Jr. stayed to work for the Knight family of Colesville, New York. According to Joseph Knight Jr., Joseph told the Knights "that he had seen a vision, that a personage had appeared to him and told him where there was a book of ancient date buried." They believed and encouraged Joseph.[59]

While digging for Stowell, Joseph boarded with the family of Isaac Hale in Harmony, where he met their tall, dark-haired daughter, Emma. Encouraged by his parents, Josiah Stowell, and the Knights, Joseph courted Emma and sought her hand. On January 18, 1827, Emma Hale married Joseph Smith in South Bainbridge, New York, in a simple ceremony by a justice of the peace. Emma and Joseph then went directly to Manchester, where they lived with Joseph's parents.[60]

But just as Lucy finished getting the new house ready for their arrival, and while she was thanking the Lord for the "prospect of a quiet and comfortable old age," their contractor came to the door to tell her that he had agreed with the mortgage agent to purchase the home and farm. Friends circulated a petition, protesting the sale. Finally the Smiths persuaded Lemuel Durfee to buy the place and let them continue there. "We were now renters," Lucy remembered, deeply discouraged. Once more their fortunes had failed.[61]

"Soon after this," Lucy wrote, Joseph went to town on an errand for his father. Lucy remembered that "he did not return home until the night was considerably advanced," and she worried because she was "aware that God intended him for a good and important work; consequently we expected that the powers of darkness would strive against him more than any other."[62]

"Joseph, why have you stayed so late," his father asked when he finally arrived. "Father," he answered after a while, "I have had the severest chastisement that I ever had in my life." Joseph's father wished to know who presumed to find fault with his son. "Father," Joseph said, "it was the angel of the Lord. He says I have been negligent that the time has now come when the record should be brought forth and that I must be up and doing that I must set myself about the things which God has commanded me to do but Father give yourself no uneasiness as to this reprimand for I know what course I am to pursue, and all will be well."[63]

That summer Emma wrote home, seeking permission to retrieve her clothes, cows, and furniture. Her father agreed, and Joseph set out with a neighbor for Harmony, Pennsylvania. Through tears Isaac Hale accused Joseph of stealing his daughter, pleaded with him to bring her back, and promised to help Joseph get a start in farming. Evidently Joseph wept too and promised to stop using his gift for money and to move to Harmony with Emma. But even as Joseph rolled along in the wagon toward his parents' home, he knew it would be hard for him. "They will all oppose," he said to a neighbor. "They want me to look in the stone for them to dig [for] money." The neighbor testified that "in fact it was as he predicted. They urged him, day after day, to resume his old practice of looking in the stone. He seemed much perplexed as to the course he should pursue."[64] In that dilemma, Joseph received an ultimatum from Moroni. According to Joseph Knight, during Joseph's September 1826 meeting with the angel, he learned that "if he would Do right according to the will of God he mite obtain [the plates] the 22nt Day of September Next and if not he never would have them."[65]

As the time drew near, Joseph Knight and Josiah Stowell made an ostensible business trip upstate in order to be in Manchester on September 22, 1827. At about midnight, Joseph Smith asked his mother if she had a chest with a lock and key. Suspecting his purposes, she fretted that she had nothing of the sort. Joseph assured her all would be well, but Lucy remained sleepless through the night, remembering what she called the "first failure" to return with the plates. Emma appeared in her riding dress and bonnet, and she and Joseph left in Joseph Knight's wagon. That night Moroni entrusted the plates to Joseph, now age twenty-one.[66] Joseph was still prone to mistakes and some sins even after his probationary period, but clearly he gained the Lord's trust and Moroni's confidence. He had faced difficult temptations, overcoming many and repenting when he fell to others. "He had learned to keep the commandments of God" and had become "not only willing, but able" to be the keeper of the sacred record.[67]

The next morning Lucy made breakfast. When Joseph Sr. requested his son's company, Lucy excused Joseph, who had not yet returned home. Lucy also calmed Joseph Knight when he thought his wagon had been stolen. When Joseph Smith arrived, he assured his mother that all was well but could not resist the chance to prolong the anxiety others felt. After eating breakfast, he called Knight aside, "set his foot on the Bed and his head in his hand and says, 'Well I am Dissopinted.' 'Well,' says I [Knight], I am sorry.'

'Well,' says he [Joseph], 'I am grateley Dissopinted: it is ten times Better then I expected.'"[68] Joseph had finally obtained the plates, and with them, ostensibly, some relief from the struggle.

CONCLUSION

Joseph Smith's teenage journey from 1823 to 1827, from a gifted teenager to the Lord's chosen seer, was marked by the trials of helping provide for his struggling family, as well as the temptations and subsequent reproof and repentance rooted in the Lord's efforts to train him to bring forth his word and in the adversary's attempt to upset that trajectory. Joseph learned humility, penitence, and persistence from his temptations and trials. Moroni chastened him several times, and he responded by striving to repent and improve and become what God knew he could be. Joseph was faced with intense financial pressure within his families—both the family he grew up in and his own new union with Emma—which created a natural desire to provide in the best possible way. Yet he learned to control his passions and desires and to not set his heart on riches.

Joseph's teenage years show him struggling, choosing, and becoming what he was called to be, all in the context of his assignment to bring forth the Book of Mormon. There is no need to avoid or apologize for Joseph's confessed foibles. A nurturing God fashioned them into learning experiences that helped Joseph see "the difference between light and darkness and the operation of a good Spirit and an evil one."[69]

As the summer of 1827 ended, Joseph Smith, still far from perfect, had nevertheless qualified himself to obtain the sacred plates. In short, Joseph had four *years* to "choose . . . this *day*" whom he would serve (see Joshua 24:15; emphasis added). He had faced dilemmas, been sorely tempted, been rebuked by an angel, and now, at last, reached a turning point in his life as the Lord's seer. Elder Dallin H. Oaks described this process. He said that "no prophet is free from human frailty, especially before he is called to devote his life to the Lord's work. Line upon line, young Joseph Smith expanded his faith and understanding and his spiritual gifts matured, until he stood with power and stature as the Prophet of the Restoration."[70]

Steven C. Harper is a professor of Church history and doctrine at Brigham Young University.

Steven C. Harper, "The Probation of a Teenage Seer: Joseph Smith's Early Experiences with Moroni," in *The Coming Forth of the Book of Mormon: A Marvelous Work and a Wonder*, ed. Dennis L. Largey, Andrew H. Hedges, John Hilton III, and Kerry Hull (Provo, UT: Religious Studies Center, Brigham Young University; Salt Lake City: Deseret Book, 2015), 23–42.

NOTES

1. In *The Joseph Smith Papers, Histories*, 1:220–21 (hereafter *JSP*, H1); original spelling and punctuation preserved in all *JSP* references.
2. *JSP*, H1:221n55.
3. William W. Phelps, "Praise to the Man," *Hymns* (Salt Lake City: The Church of Jesus Christ of Latter-day Saints, 1985), no. 27.
4. *JSP*, H1:13–14.
5. Alan Taylor, "The Early Republic's Supernatural Economy: Treasure Seeking in the American Northeast, 1780–1830," *American Quarterly* 38, no. 1 (Spring 1986): 7.
6. See "Appendix 1: Agreement of Josiah Stowell and Others, 1 November 1825," in *JSP, Documents*, 1:345–52. For additional evaluation of the agreement, see Larry C. Porter, "A Study of the Origins of the Church of Jesus Christ of Latter-day Saints in the States of New York and Pennsylvania, 1816–1831" (PhD diss., Brigham Young University, 1971), 48–49.
7. For example, in 1831 a Palmyra newspaper reported, "The MANIA of money digging soon began rapidly to diffuse itself through many parts of this country; men and women without distinction of age or sex became marvellous wise in the occult sciences, many dreamed, and others saw visions disclosing to them deep in the bowels of the earth, rich and shining treasures, and to facilitate those *mighty* mining operations . . . divers devices and implements were invented, and although the SPIRIT was always able to retain his precious charge, these discomfited as well as deluded beings would on a succeeding night return to their toil, not in the least doubting that success would eventually attend their labors." *Reflector* (Palmyra, NY), February 1, 1831.
8. Taylor, "Supernatural Economy," 8. More evidence for and analysis of this idea are in Mark Ashurst-McGee, "A Pathway to Prophethood: Joseph Smith Junior as Rodsman, Village Seer, and Judeo-Christian Prophet" (master's thesis, Utah State University, 2000).
9. Taylor, "Supernatural Economy," 10.
10. The best study of this subject is Cornelius Van Dam, *The Urim and Thummim: A Means of Revelation in Ancient Israel* (Winona Lake, IN: Eisenbrauns, 1997), 216.
11. See Genesis 30; Exodus 7, 14. For more on the gift of Aaron in latter-day scriptures, see Dennis L. Largey, ed., *Doctrine and Covenants Reference Companion* (Salt Lake City: Deseret, 2012), s.v. "Gift of Aaron."
12. See Peter French, *John Dee: The World of an Elizabethan Magus* (London: Routledge, 1984).
13. All of the evidence for this claim is presented and analyzed carefully in Ashurst-McGee, "Pathway to Prophethood." The largest collection of documents relative to Joseph Smith's treasure seeking includes several controversial statements by neighbors and some acquaintances of the Smith family who believed that Joseph's ability to discern involved a stone or stones. Many of these statements were gathered in

1833 by a man named Doctor Philastus Hurlbut, an excommunicated Latter-day Saint who was antagonistic to Joseph Smith and the Church. The statements he gathered were published by another critic, Eber D. Howe, in *Mormonism Unvailed* (Painesville, OH: E. D. Howe, 1834), one of the earliest books critical of the Church. Scholarly analysts of the statements have made strong arguments for and against their reliability. For example, Richard L. Anderson argued against the reliability of the statements in "Joseph Smith's New York Reputation Reappraised," *BYU Studies* 10, no. 3 (Spring 1970): 283–314. Rodger I. Anderson argued for the general reliability of the statements in *Joseph Smith's New York Reputation Reexamined* (Salt Lake City: Signature Books, 1990). Marvin S. Hill evaluated the strengths and weaknesses of these arguments in his review of Rodger I. Anderson's book in *BYU Studies* 30, no. 4 (Fall 1990): 70–74.

14. See editorial, November 1837, Far West, Missouri, *Elders' Journal* 1 (November 1837): 27–29; editorial, July 1838, Far West, Missouri, *Elders' Journal* 1 (July 1838): 42–44; and testimony reportedly given by Joseph Smith before justice of the peace Albert Neely in March 1826, according to William D. Purple, "Joseph Smith, The Originator of Mormonism," *Chenango Union* (Norwich, NY) 30, no. 33 (May 2, 1877).

15. See testimony reportedly given by Joseph Smith, according to Purple, "Joseph Smith, The Originator of Mormonism": "He [Joseph Smith] said when he was a lad, he heard of a neighboring girl some three miles from him, who could look into a glass and see anything however hidden from others; that he was seized with a strong desire to see her and her glass; that after much effort he induced his parents to let him visit her. He did so, and was permitted to look in the glass, which was placed in a hat to exclude the light. He was greatly surprised to see but one thing, which was a small stone, a great way off. It soon became luminous, and dazzled his eyes, and after a short time it became as intense as the mid-day sun. . . . This singular circumstance occupied his mind for some years, when he left his father's house, and with his youthful zeal traveled west in search of this luminous stone. . . . After traveling some one hundred and fifty miles he found himself at the mouth of the creek. He did not have the glass with him, but he knew its exact location. He borrowed an old ax and a hoe, and repaired to the tree. With some labor and exertion he found the stone, carried it to the creek, washed and wiped it dry, sat down on the bank, placed it in his hat, and discovered that time, place and distance were annihilated; that all intervening obstacles were removed, and that he possessed one of the attributes of Deity, an All-Seeing-Eye. He arose with a thankful heart, carried his tools to their owner, turned his feet towards the rising sun, and sought with weary limbs his long deserted home."

16. See Willard Chase's statement in Howe, *Mormonism Unvailed*, 240–48.

17. Lucy Mack Smith, History, 1845, MS 2049, handwriting of Howard Coray and Martha Jane Knowlton Coray, [95], Church History Library, The Church of Jesus Christ of Latter-day Saints, Salt Lake City (hereafter CHL).

18. Dean C. Jessee, ed., "Joseph Knight's Recollection of Early Mormon History," *BYU Studies* 17, no. 1 (1976): 29–58 (pdf version, byustudies.byu.edu).

19. "History of Brigham Young," *Deseret News*, March 10, 1858, 3. For more about Joseph Smith's use of seer stones, see chapter 4 in the present volume.

20. *JSP, Journal*, 1:88–89 (hereafter *JSP*, J1).

21. *JSP*, H1:220–30.

22. *JSP*, J1:88–89.

23. See *JSP*, H1:13–14.
24. See *JSP*, H1:220–30.
25. See Isaiah 11; and *JSP*, H1:220–30.
26. *JSP*, H1:224.
27. *JSP*, H1:226.
28. *JSP*, H1:220–30.
29. *JSP*, H1:230.
30. Lucy Mack Smith, History, 1845, p. [82]. See *JSP*, H1:69, 74–75.
31. Terryl L. Givens, *By the Hand of Mormon: The American Scripture That Launched a New World Religion* (New York: Oxford University Press, 2003), 13. See *Latter Day Saints' Messenger and Advocate*, April 1835, 157.
32. *JSP*, H1:230–31.
33. Lucy Mack Smith, History, 1844–1845, handwriting of Martha Jane Knowlton Coray and Howard Coray, book 3, p. [11], CHL.
34. *JSP*, H1:230–32.
35. See Lucy Mack Smith, History, 1845, p. [82].
36. Lucy Mack Smith, History, 1845, p. [83].
37. *JSP*, H1:232.
38. *JSP*, H1:232.
39. *JSP*, H1:82; see also p. 76.
40. *JSP*, H1:82–83.
41. *JSP*, H1:14; see also pp. 82–83.
42. Lucy Mack Smith, History, 1844–1845, book 3, pp. [11–12].
43. *JSP*, H1:83; compare Moses 1.
44. *JSP*, H1:14.
45. Lucy Mack Smith, History, 1845, p. [85].
46. *JSP*, H1:232–34.
47. Lucy Mack Smith, History, 1844–1845, book 4, p. [1].
48. Lucy Mack Smith, History, 1844–1845, book 4, p. [1].
49. Lucy Mack Smith, History, 1844–1845, book 4, pp. [3–5].
50. Lucy Mack Smith, History, 1844–1845, book 4, pp. [7–8].
51. See Lucy Mack Smith, History, 1844–1845, book 4, p. [2].
52. Lucy Mack Smith, History, 1844–1845, book 4, p. [2].
53. See Lucy Mack Smith, History, 1845, p. [89]; and Lucy Mack Smith, History, 1844–1845, book 4, p. [3].
54. Lucy Mack Smith, History 1845, p. [89]; see Lucy Mack Smith, History, 1844–1845, book 4, p. [3].
55. Lucy Mack Smith, History 1845, p. [89]; see Lucy Mack Smith, History, 1844–1845, book 4, p. [3].
56. *JSP*, H1:234.
57. Lucy Mack Smith, History, 1845, p. [95].
58. Purple, "Joseph Smith, the Originator of Mormonism." There are five different contradictory accounts of Joseph's appearance before the justice of the peace, published anywhere from five to fifty-seven years after the event. Only the one cited above claims to be the record of an eyewitness, a fellow named William Purple, who wrote that he kept the records for the justice of the peace. This account includes quite a bit of testimony reportedly from Joseph and claims that he was discharged, meaning released without being cleared or condemned.

59. Joseph Knight Jr., as quoted in Larry C. Porter, "The Colesville Branch and the Coming Forth of the Book of Mormon," *BYU Studies* 10, no. 3 (Spring 1970): 369.

60. See *JSP*, H1:236–37.

61. See Lucy Mack Smith, History, 1845, p. [98]; and Lucy Mack Smith, History, 1844–1845, book 4, p. [11].

62. Lucy Mack Smith, History, 1844–1845, book 5, pp. [4–5].

63. Lucy Mack Smith, History, 1844–1845, book 5, p. [5].

64. Peter Ingersoll Statement, December 2, 1833, in Howe, *Mormonism Unvailed*, 232–37, 248–49.

65. Jessee, "Joseph Knight's Recollection," *BYU Studies* 17, no. 1 (Fall 1976): 33.

66. Lucy Mack Smith, History, 1844–1845, book 5, p. [6].

67. Lucy Mack Smith, History, 1845, p. [85].

68. Jessee, "Joseph Knight's Recollection," 33.

69. Lucy Mack Smith, History, 1844–1845, book 3, pp. [11–12].

70. Dallin H. Oaks, "Recent Events Involving Church History and Forged Documents," *Ensign*, October 1987.

Chapter Three

The Lost 116 Pages Story

What We Do Know, What We Don't Know, and What We Might Know

J. B. HAWS

From the outset, one thing we can say that we *do* know about the story of the lost 116 pages is that from the summer of 1828 until now, this episode has loomed large in the narrative history of The Church of Jesus Christ of Latter-day Saints.[1]

It would be difficult to imagine a more agonizing string of events in the life of Joseph Smith than what he experienced in June and July of 1828. Under pressure, he let Martin Harris take the hundred-plus manuscript pages of the Book of Mormon translation that Martin had scribed while Joseph had dictated.[2] The pages represented two months of work. The day after Joseph and his wife, Emma, bid farewell to Martin, Emma gave birth to their first child. The child was either stillborn or died soon after birth. Emma almost died in childbirth. After two weeks, and although Emma was still very much convalescing, Joseph and Emma's mutual anxiety about those manuscript pages prompted him to leave his wife in the care of her parents and make the long trip to Palmyra to find out why he had not heard anything yet from Martin.

Joseph had good reason to be uneasy as he made the trip. He reported that an angel had taken the interpreters from him even *before* he had discovered that the pages had been lost, taken "in consequence of [his] having wearied the Lord in asking for the privilege of letting Martin Harris take the writings."[3] This nagging anxiety so visibly affected Joseph that a fellow stagecoach passenger insisted that he accompany Joseph on the last leg of the trip to Joseph's parents' home in order to ensure that Joseph did not collapse under the weight of his worries.[4]

The sheer frequency with which the story of the pages' loss was retold in interviews and publications has something to say about the impact it made on all involved. So, too, does the emotion with which Martin Harris recounted this story to interviewers, by their account.[5] And as difficult as later setbacks and persecutions would undoubtedly be in the life of Joseph Smith, there is something uniquely piercing in the pain of self-recrimination. "It is I who have tempted the wrath of God. I should have been satisfied with the first answer which I received from the Lord," Lucy Mack Smith recalled her son crying out when he learned the pages were gone.[6]

This story has also been marked as a definitive moment in the prophetic career of Joseph Smith by two biographers who come at that career from completely different angles.[7] Such was the import of the events of the summer of 1828. This we do know.

What we do *not* know, of course, is what happened to those pages—or even if they are still extant.

Other than that, it seems that the most reasonable approach to be taken here is to discuss things that we *might* know, with varying degrees of substantiation and probability. Therefore, this chapter aims to survey current scholarship related to this formative moment in Latter-day Saint history, to draw on research from the Joseph Smith Papers Project and other documentary evidence to give a sense of the "state of the story," and to consider possible readings of early texts of revelations that grew out of what was both a pivotal point in Joseph Smith's life and ministry and a pivotal point in the development and makeup of the Book of Mormon.

In the end, two things stand out: one is the number of related story elements that point to the believability and consistency of Joseph Smith as a narrator and translator; and the other is the way that this story speaks to a key Book of Mormon thesis—"that the tender mercies of the Lord are over all those whom he hath chosen, because of their faith, to make them mighty even unto the power of deliverance" (1 Nephi 1:20).

PROBABILITIES: PAGES AND PLOTS

The consensus of Joseph Smith's early critics and supporters alike was that the 116 manuscript pages did, at one time, exist. That may seem like stating the obvious, but it is nevertheless worth stating. Even those who thought of Joseph Smith as a charlatan took it as a given that Martin Harris really did have a sheaf of handwritten pages from which he read to friends and family—and then subsequently lost. Joseph Smith and Martin Harris, over the course of the spring of 1828, really had produced *something*—and that something was apparently substantial enough, in Martin Harris's eyes, that he felt sure it would quell his family's doubts about the veracity of the work he was supporting. If anything, it was Martin's enthusiasm for the content of the pages that proved to be his undoing in this case. He had solemnly covenanted to show the pages to only a handful of family members; it was his disregard of this oath that was the transgression that precipitated the devastating loss. Later recollections had Martin not only breaking his promise, but also breaking the lock on his wife's bureau to do so, when the pages were apparently locked in that bureau for safekeeping and Martin wanted to get at them to show them to a visitor.[8]

The corroborating evidence of the pages' existence, then, even if that evidence is all in the form of human testimony, is strong on this point. Martin Harris, throughout his life, affirmed the basic details of the story. Joseph Smith also recounted the story in the preface of the first edition of the Book of Mormon—and that preface was written just a year after the pages were lost. The fact that Joseph Smith made this story so public, so early, speaks to the common-knowledge status of the manuscript's disappearance.[9]

Just as telling, perhaps, is the absence of controverting testimony—the absence of claims, for example, that there never *was* a lost manuscript, or the absence of claims that the losing of the pages was a fabricated tale. This is especially significant when considering the principal actor in this drama—Lucy Harris—who had the most to gain, with regard to reputation, by disputing the *existence* of the pages if such were an open question. Lucy Harris was almost immediately implicated as the thief in question—and arguing that the pages never *existed* would have been a ready alibi to clear her name. But nothing in the historical record suggests that Lucy Harris (or anyone else, for that matter) attempted to dispute the pages' existence. It simply seems that such was not an open question.[10] Instead, as shall be seen, some acquaintances remembered her tacit corroboration of the pages' reality.

A more contested question is whether or not there was a plot to manipulate those pages. Joseph Smith said that he did not retranslate the lost manuscript because he had learned by revelation that a scheme existed to discredit him—and his detractors' manipulation of the 116 pages was central to that scheme. A tradition that has emerged in reminiscences, though, is that Lucy Harris burned the 116 pages immediately, leading one historian to conclude that this is "probably" what happened.[11] Hence, in that view, if Lucy Harris really burned the pages immediately, then Joseph Smith's fears (as outlined in the Book of Mormon preface) reflected a simple paranoia rather than well-founded (or divinely revealed) apprehensions about an actual conspiracy. But challenging Joseph Smith's credibility on that point seems much too hasty a conclusion, one that privileges some sources while downplaying others. This is because other early retellings of the 116 pages story suggest that a different report about the fate of the pages (other than their having been destroyed by fire) was still in circulation within only a few years of the pages' disappearance. For example, E. D. Howe, in his 1834 *Mormonism Unvailed*—a book that draws on affidavits collected by Philastus Hurlbut—wrote, "The facts respecting the lost manuscript, we have not been able to ascertain. They sometimes charge the wife of Harris with having burnt it; but this is denied by her."[12] In addition, John Clark, a former Palmyra pastor who had personal interactions with Martin Harris in 1827 and 1828, also assumed (in an 1840 publication) that Lucy did not immediately destroy the manuscript, but instead planned to use the pages against Joseph Smith. Clark said that Lucy Harris "took the opportunity, when [Martin Harris] was out, to seize the manuscript and put it into the hands of one of her neighbors for safe keeping. When the manuscript was discovered to be missing," Clark continued, "suspicion immediately fastened upon Mrs. Harris, she however refused to give any information in relation to the matter, but she simply replied: 'If this be a divine communication, the same being who revealed it to you can easily replace it.'" The crux of the "plan" that "she had formed . . . to expose the deception," according to Clark, was to "keep the manuscript until the book [of Mormon] was published, and then put these one hundred and sixteen pages into the hands of some one who would publish them, and show how they varied from those published in the Book of Mormon"—since she "[took] it for granted" that the retranslated/reproduced portion "could not possibly" be "verbatim."[13]

John Clark may have, as one historian has read him, inferred the idea of a plot to sabotage Joseph Smith from the preface to the first edition of the Book of Mormon.[14] Yet not to be missed is the fact that the Lucy Harris

Martin Harris, by Lewis A Ramsey. Courtesy of Intellectual Reserve, Inc.

plan that Clark describes is substantially different from the one that the preface describes, raising the possibility at least that Clark may have had other sources of information. It is difficult to ascertain precisely what Clark claimed as the basis of his familiarity with the story of the 116 pages. Clark said that he moved from Palmyra "very soon" after his 1828 conversation with Martin Harris but before the Book of Mormon was published in 1830. He also stated that he had "Harris' own account . . . to me" of the Book of Mormon translation process, including the use of a "thick curtain or blanket suspended between" Joseph Smith and Martin Harris during the translation. If what Clark was describing as "Harris' own account" referred to writing the Book of Mormon translation rather than just the so-called "Anthon transcript" of characters from the plates, then this suggests that at least one of Clark's 1828 interviews with Martin Harris might have come after Martin Harris had returned to Palmyra from Harmony after transcribing the 116 pages. If so, it is possible that Clark was still living in Palmyra when news about the loss of the 116 pages might have initially circulated. At the same time, Clark noted in 1840 that he was familiar with both the Book of Mormon preface and the revelation (now Doctrine and Covenants 10) to which the preface referred. In any case, that preface described the conspirators' plan to *alter* the text of the 116 pages so that this altered "original" would read differently from Joseph Smith's second attempt. However, Clark understood Lucy Harris's strategy to be simply holding on to the original and waiting to expose Joseph Smith when he published a second attempt that "could not possibly [be] verbatim." While it is true that Clark's proposal may have been his inference of the likeliest plot, based on his skepticism of Joseph Smith's work, it is also plausible that he remembered a Palmyra tradition that he picked up from conversations with his former neighbors.[15]

Regardless, there are enough examples of individuals who claimed knowledge about the pages' survival to complicate any easy conclusions about the fate of the pages. John Clark wrote in 1840 that Martin Harris "was indignant at his wife beyond measure—he raved most violently, and it is said [he] actually beat Mrs. H[arris] with a rod—but she remained firm, and would not give up the manuscript." William Hine of Colesville, New York, stated in 1885 that Lucy Harris gave the manuscript to one of his neighbors, a Dr. Seymour. Hine then remembered that Dr. Seymour "read most of it [the lost manuscript] to me when my daughter Irene was born; he read them to his patients about the country. It was a description of the mounds about the country and similar to the 'Book of Mormon.'" There are problems with the dates and places in Hine's record, but his principal assertion was that Lucy Harris had stolen the manuscript and "refused" to return it; "after I came to Kirtland," Hine asserted, "in conversation with Martin Harris, he has many times admitted to me that this statement about his wife and the one hundred sixteen pages as above stated, is true." Charles Comstock Richards remembered that he and his father, Latter-day Saint Apostle Franklin D. Richards, met a man in 1880, Dr. J. R. Pratt, who "told my father that he could put his hand on the manuscript which Martin Harris lost, in an hour, if it was needed."[16]

Hine's and Richards's accounts are late reminiscences that should be treated critically as such, yet so are the recollections of those who claimed that Lucy burned the pages. In 1884 Lorenzo Saunders reported that Lucy Harris herself had told him that she had burned the pages. In fact, Saunders also claimed that Lucy Harris "never denied of burning the papers." As mentioned earlier, though, E. D. Howe reported in 1834 that Lucy Harris *did* deny burning the pages, and it is very conceivable that Howe based this denial on information he received from Philastus Hurlbut, who interviewed Lucy Harris in 1833.[17] Importantly, Howe's publication predated Saunders's reminiscence by fifty years. Of course, Lucy Harris's stealing the manuscript—with conspiratorial aims—on one hand, and Lucy Harris's burning of the manuscript on the other, are not mutually exclusive traditions; it is possible that both traditions reflect actual events. That is, it is possible that she (or others) *did* burn the pages *after* the preface of the Book of Mormon disclosed that Joseph Smith would not retranslate what the preface referred to as the "Book of Lehi," thus thwarting any conspiracy.[18]

In the end, it seems that this question of the fate of the pages, and precisely what motivated their disappearance, cannot be answered with enough certainty to make definitive conclusions. But at the very least, it should be said that an attempt to use these reminiscences to dismiss Joseph Smith's fears or associated revelations as baseless does not do justice to the complexity of the evidence, especially the earliest evidence. To believers *and* to skeptics, Joseph Smith's claim that there existed a plan to discredit him did not seem either unreasonable or implausible.[19]

Rather, there are a number of elements in this narrative that suggest the believability of the story that Joseph Smith and his associates repeatedly told. One is the frank, even severe, honesty of Doctrine and Covenants 3, the revelation that came right after the loss of the pages—and likely the first revelation that Joseph Smith committed to paper. Two Latter-day Saint historians have described what they see as an independent "prophetic voice" evident in that revelation. There is an authenticity in the independence of that voice—and almost surprisingly so, in the way that Joseph Smith is chastised. Richard Bushman wrote, "The speaker stands above and outside Joseph, sharply separated emotionally and intellectually. The rebuke of Joseph is as forthright as the denunciation of Martin Harris. There is no effort to conceal or rationalize, no sign of Joseph justifying himself to prospective followers. The words flow directly from the messenger to Joseph and have the single purpose of setting Joseph straight. . . . At twenty-two, Joseph was speaking prophetically."[20]

Also, in this authenticity vein, Jeffrey R. Holland asked some penetrating questions worth reconsidering: "If the loss of those 116 pages . . . was simply the disappearance of some thoughtful, wisdom literature and a few chapters of remarkably deft fiction, as opponents of the Book of Mormon would say, what's the big deal? Why then all that business about Joseph going through the depths of hell, worrying about whether he was going to get the manuscript back and fearing the rebuke of God. He's a quick study; he's a frontier talent. He can just write some more!" Then, after quoting Lucy Mack Smith's account of Joseph's despair and Martin's hopelessness when the pages were lost, Elder Holland said this:

> Well, my goodness, that's an elaborate little side story—which makes absolutely no sense at all unless, of course, there really were plates, and there really was a translation process going on, and there really had been a solemn covenant made with the Lord, and there really was an enemy who did not want that book to "come forth in this generation" (D&C 10:33). . . . Which is only to say what so many have said before: that if Joseph Smith—or anyone else, for that matter—created the Book of Mormon out of whole cloth, that, to me, is a *far* greater miracle than the proposition that he translated it from an ancient record by an endowment of divine power.[21]

POSSIBILITIES: TEXTS AND TRANSLATION

Reasonable and *plausible* also seem good words to apply to two additional thought-questions that arise in connection with the revelations Joseph Smith received, and the translation work that he did, after the loss of the 116 pages.[22] While these are tangential matters, they nevertheless offer some interesting possibilities about what we might learn about Joseph Smith's early prophetic ministry and education. The first such question deals with the contents of the 116 pages. The second question deals with the resolution of the lost pages story—a resolution that came through the translation of the plates of Nephi.[23]

First: Do we know any story line details that were in the 116 pages but are not in the current Book of Mormon text? For a few years in the 1980s, we *thought* we knew more than we do now, thanks, unfortunately, to Mark Hofmann, a forger who sent shock waves through the Latter-day Saint history community before his deceptions were discovered. In 1982 *BYU Studies* and the *Ensign* published the transcript of a purported January 1829 Lucy Mack Smith letter that a collector had purchased from Mark Hofmann. The letter was an incredible find—a window into the development of the movement and the church that Joseph Smith would lead, written as it appeared to be in the year before that church was even organized. In this letter to her sister, Lucy Smith purportedly described Joseph's loss of a portion of the manuscript this way: "On account of negligence the translation of the first part of the record was carried off by some unknown person but God is faithfull and the work is now about to proceed." Ten lines later in the letter, Lucy recounted to her sister some of the particulars of the Book of Mormon narrative, including the information that Lehi "fled from Jerusalem with his family and also his wife's brother's family a few days before Nebuchadnezzar besieged the City and layed it in ashes." Since that Sariah-Ishmael sibling connection is not explicit in the current text of the Book of Mormon, a reasonable inference was that Lucy had learned the detail from the 116 pages—and that's how the letter was presented in Church publications.[24]

But as is well known now, by 1985 the Lucy Mack Smith letter's provenance was called into serious question. It proved to be one of Mark Hofmann's far-reaching forgeries. His tangled web of deceit and murder unraveled before he could track down the two "finds" that he still sought after: the so-called William McLellin collection and the 116 pages. At the very least, Hofmann's reported plan to forge the lost manuscript speaks to the prevalence—and believability—of reports that the 116 pages were *not* destroyed.[25]

Aside from this forged letter, there is, however, evidence for the possibility that another, authentic Lehi-Ishmael detail from the 116 pages did persist in Latter-day Saint tradition.[26] Nineteenth-century Apostle Erastus Snow mentioned in a sermon documented in the *Journal of Discourses* that

> the Prophet Joseph informed us that the record of Lehi, was contained on the 116 pages that were first translated and subsequently stolen, and of which an abridgement is given us in the first Book of Nephi, which is the record of Nephi individually, he himself being of the lineage of Manasseh; but that Ishmael was of the lineage of Ephraim, and that his sons married into Lehi's family, and Lehi's sons married Ishmael's daughters, thus fulfilling the words of Jacob upon Ephraim and Manasseh in the 48th chapter of Genesis, which says: "And let my name be named on them, and the name of my fathers Abraham and Isaac; and let them grow into a multitude in the midst of the land."[27]

The current Book of Mormon text informs us that Lehi's sons married Ishmael's daughters, but there is no mention of Lehi's *daughters* having married

Ishmael's *sons*, as Elder Snow described it—nor of Ishmael's lineage through Ephraim. A careful reading of this Erastus Snow excerpt does not *require* that the 116 pages be the source of the information about Lehi's daughters and Ishmael's sons, but it seems a very likely inference.[28]

In a "things we might know" vein, then, details like these at least fall into the category of intriguing possibilities and are simply further reminders of just how complex and layered the Book of Mormon narrative is.[29] That complexity and richness becomes especially evident as we think about the source plates of the Book of Mormon. It is on that topic that our second question centers:

Could the reference to what seems like only one set of "plates of Nephi" in what is now Doctrine and Covenants 10—the revelation that informed Joseph Smith how to compensate for the loss of the 116 pages—be a subtle evidence of internal self-consistency in the Book of Mormon translation narrative? This question pivots on two hinges: first, the order of Book of Mormon translation and, second, what Joseph Smith would have understood—and when he understood it—by the phrase "plates of Nephi." What is suggested here, by way of response, is that the intricate link between the Book of Mormon translation work and the corresponding revelation in the Doctrine and Covenants (section 10) offers one more signal of Joseph Smith's narrative consistency and credibility in all of this.

There are enough persuasive bits of evidence to make a convincing case that Joseph Smith translated what we now know as 1 Nephi to Words of Mormon *after* he had translated Mosiah through Moroni. In other words, when Oliver Cowdery arrived in Harmony in April 1829, he likely began scribing as Joseph Smith translated Mosiah, where Joseph and Martin (and Emma and other possible fill-in scribes) had left off. One such piece of evidence that supports this is the appearance of the handwriting of John Whitmer as a scribe in the original Book of Mormon manuscript in the section from 1 Nephi to the Words of Mormon. It seems likely, then, that this section of the Book of Mormon was translated last because Joseph and Emma and Oliver did not arrive at the Whitmer farm until the first part of June 1829, after Joseph and Oliver had already been working on the translation consistently for two months. Another corroborating indicator is that the estimated pace of translation would have put Joseph and Oliver at 3 Nephi in mid-May 1829, right where Oliver said they were when they inquired about baptism, if they had started in April at the beginning of Mosiah. This translation order seems like something that we can assert with a high degree of confidence.[30]

The order of translation is relevant to the story here because when Joseph Smith received the revelation that is now Doctrine and Covenants 10—the spring (probably April or May) 1829 revelation that instructed Joseph on what to do to resolve the lost manuscript dilemma—he had not yet translated that portion now commonly known as the "small plates of Nephi" (1 Nephi–Words of Mormon).[31] Because of that, it seems most likely that Joseph Smith would not yet have thought in terms of "small and large plates of Nephi"—more on that later. At stake, then, is how Joseph would have understood the Lord's words, and the Lord's intent, on that topic. Here is the earliest extant version of that revelation (now Doctrine and Covenants 10:38–42):

> And now, verily I say unto you, that an account of those things that you have written, which have gone out of your hands, are engraven upon the plates of Nephi; yea, and you remember, it was said in those writings, that a more particular account was given of these things upon the plates of Nephi. And now, because the account which is engraven upon the plates of Nephi, is more particular concerning the things, which in my wisdom I would bring to the knowledge of the people in this account: therefore, you shall translate the engravings which are on the plates of Nephi, down even till you come to the reign of king Benjamin, or until you come to that which you have translated, which you have retained; and behold, you shall publish it as the record of Nephi, and thus will I confound those who have altered my words.[32]

The passage just quoted seems to refer to only one set of plates: *the* plates of Nephi. However, today's readers of the Book of Mormon are accustomed to thinking in terms of two sets of "plates of Nephi"—a *large* set and a *small* set. Because of that common contemporary reading, it is not unexpected that a recent and important commentary on Doctrine and Covenants 10 suggested this about the passage just quoted: "The two references to 'the plates of Nephi' in this paragraph [the paragraph is now Doctrine and Covenants 10:38–39] actually point to two different sets of plates."[33] But what if the repeated "plates of Nephi" phrases in Doctrine and Covenants 10:38–45 really do refer to only *one* set of "plates of Nephi," as they seem to do at first glance—and that is the set we know now as the "small plates"? This is the alternative (and perhaps more straightforward) reading suggested here. This reading would give the phrase more consistency because it fits the well-supported "small-plates-last" model of translation. Most important, in line with the theme here about narrative consistency and believability, this reading fits with what Joseph Smith likely would have known (and not known) about the composition of the gold plates *before* translating what is now 1 Nephi through Words of Mormon—remembering that he received Doctrine and Covenants 10 *before* translating 1 Nephi through Words of Mormon. This reading of Doctrine and Covenants 10:38–45 therefore avoids a possible anachronism and adds credence to Joseph Smith's account about the resolution of the lost 116 pages episode.

From everything we can glean about the plates that Joseph Smith possessed, only one section could accurately be called "the plates of Nephi," and that is the "small plates" section. All the other plates that Joseph translated from, based on internal descriptions from the Book of Mormon, consisted of Mormon's and Moroni's abridgments and writings on plates of their own making. Therefore, contemporary students of the Book of Mormon understand the lost manuscript (what Joseph Smith in the preface to the first edition of the Book of Mormon called the "Book of Lehi") as comprising a significant portion of Mormon's *abridgment* of what we now know as "the large plates of Nephi" rather than a translation of the large plates of Nephi themselves. But it is doubtful that Joseph Smith and his scribes would have even thought yet in those terms. For one thing, the descriptors *large* and *small* do not come from Nephi or Mormon, but from Jacob's writings that were included on the small plates (see Jacob 1:1; 3:13)—and Joseph had not yet translated the small plates at the time he received the revelation that is now Doctrine and Covenants 10.

How might Joseph have conceived of the source document for the 116 pages? In the preface to the first edition of the Book of Mormon, he described the contents of the 116 pages as "the Book of Lehi, which was an account abridged from the plates of Lehi"—*not* the plates of Nephi.[34] This characterization suggests a couple of key points. First, it is not unreasonable to infer that Joseph drew his understanding of this from Mormon's own characterization of, or introduction to, the opening portion of his abridgment. That is, since Lehi's story opened the record, it would have been natural for Mormon to designate that portion as the book or plates of Lehi; this fits, for example, the way Mormon introduced and grouped together books like Alma or Helaman, even though those books include abridged records of other custodial authors after Alma or Helaman.[35] And Nephi himself wrote that he began his record (what we now call the "large plates") by documenting the account of his father, Lehi (see 1 Nephi 19:1). Second, up to this point in the Book of Mormon translation process—that is, up to the receipt of Doctrine and Covenants 10—Joseph and Martin had never translated directly from Nephi's writings (or Jacob's or Enos's) or from Nephi's plates, but rather from Mormon's abridgment of those writings—unless Mormon had included quoted passages or excerpts on his own plates from Nephi or Jacob or Enos, as he did with writings and sermons of, say, King Benjamin or Alma. But even those passages would not have come from what we know as "the small plates of Nephi," since before Benjamin's day, the "large plates of Nephi" were apparently kept by a different line of authors than were the small plates (see Jarom 3:14; Omni 1:25)—and Mormon reported that he did not even search out the small plates until he had *finished* abridging the account "down to the reign of this King Benjamin" (Words of Mormon 1:3).[36]

Therefore, if all of the references to the "plates of Nephi" in the revelation that is now section 10 of the Doctrine and Covenants refer to what modern Book of Mormon readers think of as the *small* plates of Nephi, the revelation reads very coherently. Here is a possible reading of the earliest extant copy of the revelation—chapter IX of the Book of Commandments—from that perspective, with suggested parenthetical interpretations: "And now, verily I say unto you, that an account of those things that you have written, which have gone out of your hands [the 116 pages], are engraven upon the plates of Nephi [small plates of Nephi]"—in other words, 'The same basic story elements that you have already covered in translating the Book of Lehi ("an account of those things that you have written") are *also* narrated ("engraven") on the small plates of Nephi.' The revelation continues:

> Yea, and you remember, it was said in those writings [the now-lost writings, or Mormon's abridgment of the Book of Lehi] that a more particular account was given of these things upon the plates of Nephi [the small plates]. And now, because the account which is engraven upon the plates of Nephi [the small plates] is more particular concerning these things, which in my wisdom I would bring to the knowledge of the people in this [more particular] account: therefore, you shall translate the engravings which are on the plates of Nephi [the small plates], down even till you come to the reign of king Benjamin.

(The wording here is another indication that when Joseph recommenced translating after the loss of the 116 pages, he "apparently picked up where he and Harris had stopped, in the book of Mosiah," and then he translated the books of the "small plates" last, based on the instructions in this revelation.)[37]

As if to underscore the differences between the Book of Lehi and the plates of Nephi, the revelation makes this point: "Behold they [those who stole the Book of Lehi manuscript] have only got a part, or an abridgment of the *account* [notice: *not* plates] of Nephi. Behold there are many things engraven on the plates of Nephi [the small plates of Nephi] which do throw great views upon my gospel."[38]

This suggested reading matters because the complexity of the relationship between the two sets of plates of Nephi likely became clear to Joseph Smith only *after* translating the small plates. Hence, it might very well have been anachronistic for a revelation in the spring of 1829 (Doctrine and Covenants 10) to refer to anything other than *one* set of the "plates of Nephi," since Joseph would not yet have been thinking in terms of having more than one record of Nephi, because Mormon included in his compilation only one set of records that appropriately bore the title "the plates of Nephi": the *small* plates. The phrasing of Doctrine and Covenants 10 thus fits with what Joseph Smith would have likely learned "line upon line" as he translated the plates, such that it also fits with a principle outlined in 2 Nephi and elsewhere: the Lord "speaketh unto men according to their language, unto their understanding" (2 Nephi 31:3; see Doctrine and Covenants 1:24).[39]

In summary, the evidence for the order of translation, the dating of Doctrine and Covenants 10, and especially the "plates" phraseology of that revelation—all taken together—make for another example, subtle but noteworthy, of narrative consistency and authenticity in the way Joseph Smith and his associates related the "lost manuscript" chapter of the larger Book of Mormon translation story.

What is more significant, though, for modern readers of the Book of Mormon is the way Doctrine and Covenants 10 characterizes the addition of the small plates material: "Behold, there are many things engraven upon the plates of Nephi which do throw greater views upon my gospel" (v. 45). It is this "greater views" aspect—this indication of providential foresight— that adds to the wonder of the inclusion of the small plates of Nephi, not only in our day but in Mormon's. Elder Boyd K. Packer has even proposed that Mormon's searching out and then reading of the small plates of Nephi, with their "things of [the] soul" (2 Nephi 4:15) orientation, "greatly influenced . . . the rest of his [Mormon's] abridgment."[40]

CONCLUSION: MISUNDERSTANDINGS AND MIRACLES

In any event, thinking through the complex composition of the plates also defuses a criticism of Joseph Smith leveled by E. D. Howe, a criticism based wholly on a misunderstanding of the 116 pages episode. That misunderstanding, perhaps unexpectedly, offers an appropriate note on which to conclude this story. In his *Mormonism Unvailed*, Howe misread the Book of Mormon preface when it drew from the language of the revelation that is now Doctrine and Covenants 10. Howe did not realize that the translation of the "plates of Nephi" was to be a new, though parallel, account of the same time frame covered by the lost "Book of Lehi." Howe charged that the revelation's instruction to Joseph to "translate from the plates of Nephi until thou come to that which ye have translated, which ye have retained, and . . . publish it as the record of Nephi" was simply giving the Book of *Lehi* a new title: "the record of Nephi." Thus, Howe accused, "the Lord, in order to counteract the works of the Devil, is represented by Smith as palming off on the world an acknowledged falsehood,—the records of Lehi must be published as the records of Nephi." Unfortunately, Howe incorrectly read the preface as nothing more than the Lord giving permission for some creative misdirection. What is also unfortunate is that Howe therefore missed what Latter-day Saints see as the miracle of God's foreknowledge in all of this. Howe wrote, "Again, an important record which had been made by a miracle, kept for ages by a miracle, dug from the ground by a miracle, and translated by a miracle, was *stolen* by some one, so that even a miracle could not restore it, and thus were the designs of the Lord counteracted by 'Satan putting it into their hearts to tempt the Lord.'"[41]

Latter-day Saints come to the precisely opposite conclusion. They see in the resolution of this lost manuscript episode—after all of the soul-searching and heart-wrenching emotions it brought to Joseph Smith and Martin Harris—a miracle thousands of years in the making, beginning with Nephi's creation of a second record and continuing with Mormon's addition of that record to his abridgment (and both Nephi and Mormon acknowledged that they acted on inspiration they did not fully understand [see Words of Mormon 1:7; 1 Nephi 9:2, 5]). Latter-day Saints see, in all of this, evidence that the Lord allows humans their agency, but neither human agency exercised in opposition to his will nor the "cunning of the devil" can frustrate the works of God (Doctrine and Covenants 10:43). They see in the 116 pages story a reassurance that "all things" really can "work together for good to them that love God" (Romans 8:28). For them, and for that reason, it is a story worth frequent retelling.

J. B. Haws is an associate professor of Church history and doctrine at Brigham Young University.

J. B. Haws, "The Lost 116 Pages Story: What We Do Know," in *The Coming Forth of the Book of Mormon: A Marvelous Work and a Wonder*, ed. Dennis L. Largey, Andrew H. Hedges, John Hilton III, and Kerry Hull (Provo, UT: Religious Studies Center, Brigham Young University; Salt Lake City: Deseret Book, 2015), 81–102.

NOTES

1. The story is also summarized well in Grant Underwood, "The Book of Lehi," in *Joseph: Exploring the Life and Ministry of the Prophet*, ed. Susan Easton Black and Andrew C. Skinner (Salt Lake City: Deseret Book, 2005), 76–84; and in the historical introduction to Revelation, July 1828 [D&C 3], in *The Joseph Smith Papers, Documents*, 1:6–7 (hereafter *JSP*, D1). In the years since this article was originally published (2015), Don Bradley published an important book-length treatment of this episode and related matters: *The Lost 116 Pages: Reconstructing the Book of Mormon's Missing Stories* (Draper, UT: Greg Kofford Books, 2019). Part 1 (chapters 1–5) deals primarily with the same historical details treated here.

2. A groundbreaking and important book also discusses this episode; see chapter 5 of Michael Hubbard MacKay and Gerrit J. Dirkmaat, *From Darkness unto Light: Joseph Smith's Translation and Publication of the Book of Mormon* (Provo, UT: Religious Studies Center, Brigham Young University; Salt Lake City: Deseret Book, 2015). One new claim the book makes—a claim about the scribing of the 116 pages—has bearing here. *From Darkness unto Light* proposes that "Emma had likely written the *majority* of the 'book of Lehi' before Harris ever arrived" (90; emphasis added). However, and without diminishing Emma's important work as a Book of Mormon scribe (even, perhaps, as the earliest scribe), other evidence suggests that this innovative new claim about Emma's primary role in writing the *majority* of the 116 pages calls for further consideration. The bases for the claim seem problematic. The principal source for the claim is a reminiscent statement by Simon Smith. *From Darkness unto Light* quotes Smith's statement that Martin Harris told him [Smith] that Martin wrote "about one third of the first part of the translation of the plates as [Joseph] interpreted them by the Urim and Thummim" (91). This secondhand report comes from an 1884 letter to the editor of the RLDS Church's *Saints' Herald*, in which Simon Smith is reporting his interview with Martin Harris in 1875. See Simon Smith's published letter in "Correspondence," *Saints' Herald*, May 24, 1884, 324. Significantly, this late reminiscence does not mention Emma at all, as scribe or otherwise; and in any case, Martin Harris's comment, if remembered accurately, could be read as his estimation that the lost manuscript that he scribed was equivalent in length/proportional to about one-third of the eventual Book of Mormon manuscript. That reading seems even more likely, given the way Simon Smith reported the *same* conversation with Martin Harris in writing to the same periodical, but three years earlier (see Bradley, *Lost 116 Pages*, 94–95). In 1881 Smith related the pertinent part of the interview this way: "He [Martin Harris] said also that he acted as scribe for him, when your father [Joseph Smith Jr.; the published letter was addressed to Joseph Smith III] was translating from the plates by the Urim and Thummim, for nearly one third of what is published" ("Correspondence," *Saints' Herald*, February 1, 1881, 43.) Simon Smith also reported in his 1884 account that Martin Harris told him, "I was Joseph's scribe, and wrote for him a *great deal*" (Simon Smith, "Correspondence," May 24, 1884, 324; emphasis

added). *From Darkness unto Light* also quotes from Joseph Knight Sr. to imply that Emma was the earliest principal scribe in the Book of Mormon project: "Now when he [Joseph Smith] Began to translate he was poor and was put to it for provisions and had not one to write for him But his wife and his wifes Brother would sometime write a little for him through the winter" (85). Emma (and her brother) certainly could have been scribes in early translation efforts before Martin Harris's return to Harmony in April 1828. But a closer examination of what follows this statement in Joseph Knight's history complicates that assumption—and complicates any assertion that this source would support Emma's scribing the *majority* of the 116 pages. The "through the winter" time marker seems especially important, since the next line in Joseph Knight's account deals with *Oliver Cowdery's* arrival "the Next Spring," in April 1829—the year following Martin Harris's scribal work. Hence Joseph Knight's reminiscence seems to be pointing to Emma's work as scribe in the winter before Oliver Cowdery's arrival—that is, the winter of *1829* (which postdated the loss of the 116 pages), *not* the winter of 1828. To be sure, Joseph Knight's chronology of things is confused in this recollection. After relating that Oliver Cowdery "Came Down [to Harmony, Pennsylvania] and was soon Convinced of the truth of the work," Knight wrote, "The next Spring Came Martin Harris Down to pennsylvany to write for him and he wrote 116 pages of the first part of the Book of Mormon." While these questions of timing and narrative order make the Joseph Knight source a problematic one for establishing scribal order, what seems especially relevant in the full Joseph Knight account is that he specifically assigned the writing of the 116 pages to Martin Harris. See Dean Jessee, "Joseph Knight's Recollection of Early Mormon History," *BYU Studies* 17, no. 1 (1976): 35. Perhaps most significant in all of this is that locating Emma as a scribe in the interim *between* Martin Harris's work and Oliver Cowdery's arrival (the period "through the winter," in Joseph Knight's memory) also seems to fit with how Joseph Smith himself remembered this early translation work. In Joseph's earliest history, in 1832, *after* recounting the 116 pages story and in the context of discussing *Oliver Cowdery's* arrival, he stated "my wife had writen *some* for me to translate and also my Brothr Samuel H Smith." Joseph Smith, History, circa Summer 1832, in *JSP, Histories*, 1:16; emphasis added (hereafter *JSP*, H1). In Joseph Smith's 1838/1839 history, he said that Martin Harris "returned again unto my house about the twelfth of April Eighteen hundred and twenty eight, and commenced writing for me while I translated from the plates, which we continued untill the fourteenth of June following, by which time he [Martin] had written one hundred and sixteen <pages> of manuscript on foolscap paper." Joseph Smith, History Drafts, 1838–circa 1841 [Draft 2], in *JSP*, H1:244. Thus Joseph Smith's histories seem to support the customary assertion that Martin Harris was the primary scribe for the 116 pages portion of the translation. It should also be noted that *From Darkness unto Light*, 100n33, acknowledges other evidence in support of this customary assertion. See also Bradley, *Lost 116 Pages*, 37–38, 101–3, for an argument that Emma and others were the earliest scribes, but that Martin Harris still scribed the majority of the lost manuscript pages.

3. In *JSP*, H1:246.

4. See Lucy Mack Smith's account of this in Lavina Fielding Anderson, ed., *Lucy's Book: A Critical Edition of Lucy Mack Smith's Family Memoir* (Salt Lake City: Signature Books, 2001), 415–17.

5. See, for example, W. W. Blair's report of an 1860 interview with Martin Harris that was included in an 1880 RLDS printing of Lucy Mack Smith's *Biographical Sketches*

of Joseph Smith the Prophet, and His Progenitors for Many Generations: "He seemed to be still conscience-smitten for permitting them to be stolen"; in Anderson, *Lucy's Book*, 422n179; also in Dan Vogel, ed., *Early Mormon Documents*, 5 vols. (Salt Lake City: Signature Books, 1996–2003), 2:311 (hereafter *EMD*). See also "Interviews with William Pilkington, 1874–1875," *EMD*, 2:350–67.

6. Anderson, *Lucy's Book*, 418.

7. See Richard Lyman Bushman, *Joseph Smith: Rough Stone Rolling* (New York: Alfred A. Knopf, 2005), 69: "Eighteen twenty-eight was a turning point in Joseph Smith's development. It was the year when he found his prophetic voice." Compare Fawn Brodie, *No Man Knows My History: The Life of Joseph Smith, the Mormon Prophet*, 2nd ed. (New York: Alfred A. Knopf, 1979), who saw in the 116 pages episode a point of no return in Joseph Smith's pious fraud: "A retreat from the fantasy he had created was impossible. . . . Although he may not have sensed their significance, these, Joseph's first revelations [after the loss of the 116 pages], marked a turning-point in his life. For they changed the Book of Mormon from what might have been merely an ingenious speculation into a genuinely religious book."

8. See Lucy Mack Smith's account of this in Anderson, *Lucy's Book*, 420–22. W. W. Blair remembered from his 1860 interview with Martin Harris that Martin claimed to have locked the manuscript in his bureau, which he then locked in the parlor, and to have put both keys in his pocket before going to bed—"after which he never saw them [the pages]." In Anderson, *Lucy's Book*, 422n179; also Vogel, *EMD*, 2:311.

9. Joseph Smith also briefly included the story of the 116 pages in his 1832 history; see *JSP*, H1:15–16. For a careful analysis of the timing of the writing of the Book of Mormon's preface, based on the typesetting of the first Book of Mormon signature, see Vogel, *EMD*, 3:480; see also *JSP*, D1:93n360. It is worth noting that it is in the preface to the Book of Mormon that Joseph first "specified the number of pages lost." The printing process, as the editors of *JSP*, D1 suggest, might thus also offer a clue to the source of the number 116: "This page count may be an approximation based on the page numbering found on the printer's manuscript of the Book of Mormon. The top of page 117 in that copy marks the beginning of the book of Mosiah, which corresponds to the end of the period covered in the pages lost by Harris." It is possible, though, that the numbering reflected what had been retained of the original pagination, since the editors of D1 note, "The process of preparing the printer's manuscript and providing portions to the typesetter suggests that the printer's manuscript may not have comprised 116 pages by the time JS wrote the preface." Historical introduction to Preface to the Book of Mormon, circa August 1829, in *JSP*, D1:92–93. Compare Dan Vogel's analysis of the page numbering in Vogel, *EMD*, 3:480–81. For Don Bradley's argument that the lost manuscript was substantially longer than 116 pages, see *Lost 116 Pages*, 84–103.

10. John Clark, a former Palmyra pastor who had personal interactions with Martin Harris in 1827 and 1828, reported that, from very early on, Lucy Harris was the chief suspect in this drama—yet Clark's account (published in 1840) only had Lucy "[refusing] to give any information in relation to the matter." As Clark portrayed it, Lucy did not deny anything; yet Clark, and others, still assumed Lucy Harris was the guilty party. See "Martin Harris Interviews with John A. Clark, 1827 & 1828," in Vogel, *EMD*, 2:269. In the affidavit Lucy Harris gave to Philastus Hurlbut in 1833, she spoke strongly against Joseph Smith's work and her husband's involve-ment—"the delusion of Mormonism," she called it—yet she did not mention the well-publicized 116 pages story. In Vogel, *EMD*, 2:36.

11. See Vogel, *EMD*, 2:270n26; also 3:480–81. See also Linda Sillitoe and Allen Roberts, *Salamander: The Story of the Mormon Forgery Murders*, 2nd ed. (Salt Lake City: Signature Books, 1989), 154–55, where they report that investigators in the Mark Hofmann forgery case met a descendant of Martin Harris who told investigators that her family tradition was that Lucy Harris burned the pages.

12. E. D. Howe, *Mormonism Unvailed* (Painesville, OH: E. D. Howe, 1834), 22. The preface to the first edition of the Book of Mormon is reprinted in "Preface to Book of Mormon, circa August 1829," in *JSP*, D1:93–94.

13. Vogel, *EMD*, 2:269–70.

14. For Dan Vogel's opinion that John Clark's account is based on an "inference taken from the Book of Mormon's preface, rather than any of the principals in the affair," see Vogel, *EMD*, 2:270n26.

15. Vogel, *EMD*, 2:268–69; see Dan Vogel's analysis of John Clark's movements based on census records, in Vogel, *EMD*, 2:260. For a helpful analysis of statements by those who remembered a curtain/sheet hung between Joseph Smith and his scribe, and for an analysis of how that might affect questions of timing in the narrative of translation, see MacKay and Dirkmaat, *From Darkness unto Light*, 91, 100nn34–36.

16. John Clark, in Vogel, *EMD*, 2:270; William Hine, circa March 1885, in Vogel, *EMD*, 4:185–86; Charles Comstock Smith's account is reported in Vogel, *EMD*, 3:481. Recently, author Brant Gardner has also speculated that the "verbatim" issue might have been at the heart of the Lord's instruction not to retranslate the Book of Lehi, but Gardner comes at it from a different perspective, one based on what has been called a "loose" translation model: "Why didn't Joseph simply retranslate it? Ultimately, we have no answer other than the one Joseph gave, but there is another possibility. On some level, Joseph may have understood that he could not translate the same document twice in the same way, not because he lacked divine inspiration, but because the very nature of that inspiration produced a translation that was only a functional equivalent of the inspired meaning." Brant Gardner, *The Gift and Power: Translating the Book of Mormon* (Salt Lake City: Greg Kofford Books, 2011), 285. At the same time, a number of Joseph Smith's associates remembered a Book of Mormon translation process in which the verbiage revealed to Joseph Smith—and least in some instances—was more tightly controlled. See the extensive accounts compiled in John W. Welch, "The Miraculous Translation of the Book of Mormon," in *Opening the Heavens: Accounts of Divine Manifestations, 1820–1844*, ed. John W. Welch (Provo, UT: Brigham Young University Press; Salt Lake City: Deseret Book, 2005), 77–213.

17. Lorenzo Saunders interview, November 12, 1884, in Vogel, *EMD*, 2:149. On E. D. Howe and Philastus Hurlbut, see Dan Vogel's analysis in Vogel, *EMD*, 3:480. There is no mention in Lucy Harris's written affidavit of the 116 pages story, but that does not preclude the possibility that she and Hurlbut discussed the well-known story. See Vogel, *EMD*, 2:36.

18. This could be reflected in William Pilkington's accounts of his interviews with Martin Harris that show Martin considering both traditions concerning the fate of the pages. Pilkington remembered, in a 1834 affidavit, that Martin Harris "believed his Wife burned it up," and then one paragraph later Pilkington reported that "[Harris's] Wife took the manuscript and he never saw it any more. So you see Willie, it was stolen from me." In "Interviews with William Pilkington, 1874–1875," in Vogel, *EMD*, 2:354. It is worth noting that in an autobiography Pilkington composed four years later, he recounted only the theft thesis. Pilkington said, "She [Lucy Harris] took the manuscript from him and she was perusing them when someone

jerked them from her, and then another got it, and Martin told me it disappeared, and he never saw it any more." In "Interviews with William Pilkington," 2:361–62. Lorenzo Saunders did not suggest the timing for the burning of the pages in his reminiscence, but James Reeves did in his 1872 account. Reeves suggested that Lucy Harris had burned the pages even before Martin Harris realized they were gone. However, Reeves's account is problematic (as are most of these late reminiscences) because it pictures Martin Harris "during the long winter evenings . . . [sitting] by the great open fire-place and [studying] his new text stopping now and then to pour a little inspiration into the ear of Aunt Dolly, who usually answered by telling him to 'shut up.'" Martin Harris, of course, had the pages during the summer of 1828. See "James H. Reeves Account, 1872," in Vogel, *EMD*, 2:342.

19. See Bradley, *Lost 116 Pages*, 64–81, for a consideration of other possible conspirators in the theft, including Martin Harris's son-in-law, Flanders Dyke, as well as other Palmyra-area treasure seekers who felt they had been wronged by Joseph Smith.

20. Bushman, *Rough Stone Rolling*, 69. See also Philip L. Barlow, *Mormons and the Bible: The Place of the Latter-day Saints in American Religion*, updated ed. (New York and Oxford: Oxford University Press, 2013), 22–25.

21. Jeffrey R. Holland, "A Standard unto My People," Eighteenth Annual Church Educational System Religious Educators Symposium, August 9, 1994, 5–6.

22. One possibility is that the mechanics of translation changed after the loss of the Book of Lehi manuscript. When Joseph resumed the translation, a curtain no longer was used to separate him from his scribe; instead, the plates stayed on the table, covered by a cloth. And witnesses remembered him using a single seer stone more than the interpreters. See Bushman, *Rough Stone Rolling*, 71–72, for a summary of these recollections.

23. See Richard E. Bennett, "Joseph Smith and the First Principles of the Gospel, 1820–1829," in *Joseph Smith, the Prophet and Seer*, ed. Richard Neitzel Holzapfel and Kent P. Jackson (Provo, UT: Religious Studies Center, Brigham Young University; Salt Lake City: Deseret Book, 2010), 23–50, for insightful commentary on the lessons Joseph Smith learned during and after the 116 pages episode.

24. See Dean C. Jessee, "Lucy Mack Smith's 1829 Letter to Mary Smith Pierce," *BYU Studies* 22, no. 4 (Fall 1982): 461; see also "1829 Lucy Mack Smith Letter Displayed," *Ensign*, October 1982, 70–73, which appeared under this descriptive heading: "Discusses information apparently from 'lost 116 pages'—including Ishmael as Sariah's brother."

25. See Richard E. Turley Jr., *Victims: The LDS Church and the Mark Hofmann Case* (Urbana and Chicago: University of Illinois Press, 1992), 58–67, 271, 318; and Sillitoe and Roberts, *Story of the Mormon Forgery Murders*, 154–55, 534.

26. It is not unlikely that the Erastus Snow quotation discussed in this paragraph served as the inspiration for the information Mark Hofmann included in his forged Lucy Mack Smith letter.

27. Erastus Snow, in *Journal of Discourses* (London: Latter-day Saints' Book Depot, 1883), 23:184.

28. See also Bradley, *Lost 116 Pages*, 157–59, for three other significant nineteenth-century sources (Franklin D. Richards, Orson Pratt, and Charles B. Thompson) who spoke to additional information about Ishmael as a descendant of Ephraim (and Zoram as a descendant of Ephraim, as well)—and that information's likely connection to the lost manuscript.

29. Don Bradley has proposed that there may be lingering textual echoes of Book of Lehi content in the current Book of Mormon as well. These include things like the identity

of Aminadi, an ancestor of Amulek, whose appearance in the Book of Mormon is so brief as to imply that Mormon, as narrator, assumed readers would already know about Aminadi; or the story of how the Jaredite interpreters came into the hands of Nephite seers, something not spelled out in the current text of the Book of Mormon but hinted at in the recollections of Fayette Lapham, who recounted a conversation on that topic with Joseph Smith Sr. See Don Bradley, "Piercing the Veil: Temple Worship in the Lost 116 Pages," paper presented at the 2012 FairMormon Conference, http://www.fairmormon.org/perspectives/fair-conferences/2012-fair-conference/2012-piercing-the-veil-temple-worship-in-the-lost-116-pages. For a fuller account, see Part 2, "The Missing Stories," in Bradley's book *Lost 116 Pages*.

30. For a helpful summary of this, see the historical introduction to Book of Mormon Manuscript Excerpt, circa June 1829 [1 Nephi 2:2b–3:18a], in *JSP*, D1:59–60. See also the translation order and dating analysis in Richard L. Bushman, *Joseph Smith and the Beginnings of Mormonism* (Urbana and Chicago: University of Illinois Press, 1984), 223n67.

31. For the dating of the revelation that is now Doctrine and Covenants 10—and the possibility that it is a composite revelation that was ultimately composed in April or May 1829—see the historical introduction to Revelation, Spring 1829, in *JSP*, D1:38–39.

32. The revelation (the 1833 Book of Commandments version quoted here) is reproduced in Revelation, Spring 1829, in *JSP*, D1:40–42 [D&C 10].

33. The quotation comes from *JSP*, D1:42n93. The reading proposed here is an alternative reading from that suggested in the D1 footnote.

34. Historical introduction to Preface to the Book of Mormon, circa August 1829, in *JSP*, D1:93; emphasis added.

35. See Bradley, *Lost 116 Pages*, 85–88, for Bradley's view that while the "Book of Lehi" was an appropriate "serviceable description for quickly explaining [in the preface to the Book of Mormon] what had occurred" in the loss of the manuscript, "Joseph's use of the term appears to err on the side of simplifying for readers the complexity of the book they were about to encounter," since the lost manuscript covered the time from Lehi to King Benjamin; hence Bradley's conclusion that the "Book of Lehi" likely would have been subdivided by Mormon into smaller "books of many other record keepers across the dozen generations it covered."

36. For a helpful discussion (and accompanying chart) of the custodians of Nephi's two sets of plates, see David Rolph Seely, "Plates of Nephi," in *Book of Mormon Reference Companion*, ed. Dennis L. Largey (Salt Lake City: Deseret Book, 2003), 645–47.

37. *JSP*, H1:38.

38. Revelation, Spring 1829, in *JSP*, D1:40–41 [D&C 10]. The passages quoted here correspond with Doctrine and Covenants 10:38–44. While the pages that contained most of what is now Doctrine and Covenants 10, in an earlier manuscript form, are missing from the "Book of Commandments and Revelations" ("Revelation Book 1" in the JSP designation), the manuscript page with the last part of the revelation (beginning with what corresponds now with Doctrine and Covenants 10:42) is extant in the manuscript Revelation Book 1. See *JSP, Revelations and Translations*, facsimile edition, 13. It is worth noting that without knowing the contents of the 116 lost pages, it is impossible to know to what extent Mormon might have included information about Nephi's creation of a second set of plates. This part of the revelation (Doctrine and Covenants 10) suggests that the Book of Lehi at least alluded to the small plates of Nephi: "It was said in those writings

that a more particular account was given of these things upon the plates of Nephi." Some have read this phrase—"more particular account was given of these things upon the plates of Nephi"—as a description to the large plates of Nephi; however, the revelation's subsequent phrasing and use of the word *particular*—"the account which is engraven upon the plates of Nephi is more particular concerning these things, which in my wisdom I would bring to the knowledge of the people in *this* account [emphasis added]: therefore, you shall translate the engravings which are on the plates of Nephi"—seems to associate the "more particular account" with "this account" which Joseph Smith would "bring to the knowledge of the people," or, in other words, the small plates of Nephi. Thus it is also possible that this mention of the "more particular account" mentioned in the writings of Mormon's abridgment might allude to the impetus behind Mormon's searching out the small plates of Nephi in the first place. In any event, it is telling that the allusion is only to "*the* plates of Nephi" rather than to a specific *set* of Nephi's plates.

39. Even without knowing the precise timing of the receipt of the revelation that is now Doctrine and Covenants 10, it is important to note that Joseph and Oliver would have encountered at least one, and possibly more, references to "plates of Nephi" early in their translation work and likely before the revelation (Doctrine and Covenants 10) was received in full. The phrase "plates of Nephi" appears in Mosiah 1:6, 16; 28:11; Alma 37:2; 44:24—all of which would have likely been translated in April or early May 1829. Given that these are all simply references to the "plates of Nephi," nothing in those verses would have suggested the existence of a second set of "plates of Nephi" to Joseph and Oliver. It is also worth noting that without knowing the contents of the 116 lost pages, it is impossible to know to what extent Mormon might have included, in that early part of his abridgment, information about Nephi's creation of a second set of plates. Doctrine and Covenants 10:39–40 can be read to suggest that the "Book of Lehi" portion of the record at least alluded to the small plates of Nephi and its contents: "It was said in those writings that a more particular account was given of these things upon the plates of Nephi." Some have read this phrase—"more particular account was given of these things upon the plates of Nephi"—as a reference to the large plates of Nephi; however, the revelation's subsequent phrasing and use of the word *particular*—"the account which is engraven upon the plates of Nephi is more particular concerning these things, which in my wisdom I would bring to the knowledge of the people in *this* account [emphasis added]: therefore, you shall translate the engravings which are on the plates of Nephi"—seem to associate the "more particular account" with "this account" that Joseph Smith would "bring to the knowledge of the people," or in other words, the small-plates-of-Nephi account that "you shall translate." It is worth considering that this mention of a "more particular account" that Joseph had apparently already encountered in the writings of Mormon's abridgment (the "Book of Lehi" abridgment) might allude to the impetus behind Mormon's searching out the small plates of Nephi in the first place. In any event, it is telling that the allusion is only to "*the* plates of Nephi" rather than to a specific *set* of Nephi's plates. Thus, the key point is that the phrasing of Doctrine and Covenants 10 seemed tailored to Joseph Smith's (likely) limited understanding at the time—and that reading seems to hold whether one sees "plates of Nephi" in Doctrine and Covenants 10 as referring to one or two sets of plates. Compare Bradley, *Lost 116 Pages*, 85–88, 107–10.

40. Boyd K. Packer, *Let Not Your Heart Be Troubled* (Salt Lake City: Bookcraft, 1991), 276.

41. Howe, *Mormonism Unvailed*, 22–23.

Chapter Four

Firsthand Witness Accounts of the Translation Process

MICHAEL HUBBARD MACKAY
AND GERRIT J. DIRKMAAT

For decades, most Latter-day Saints have had little reason to examine the miraculous translation of the Book of Mormon beyond its most basic details. In recent years, however, references to the translation on national television and the internet have piqued the curiosity of many, and a much broader interest in the translation process has been the result, despite the fact that scholars have been addressing many of these questions for decades.[1] In 2014 the Church released a five-page statement on its website about the translation, one reflecting an understanding of the translation outlined in the introduction to *The Joseph Smith Papers, Documents, Volume 1*. This volume analyzed the documentary record surrounding the translation process and explained what witnesses said about the translation.[2] These two publications mark a concerted effort by the Church to help members understand the details of the translation process.

This chapter will help satisfy the rising interest in the translation of the Book of Mormon by analyzing what witnesses and close associates of Joseph Smith said about the manner in which Joseph Smith translated the gold plates.[3] Both believers and nonbelievers asked Joseph and his associates to explain the process numerous times, and Joseph Smith and his scribes left records of their responses.[4] We have gathered and evaluated these historical documents to help clarify how Joseph Smith and those close to him experienced the translation process. By analyzing the statements of those who witnessed the translation (primarily his scribes), we address what they believe happened. Because they watched Joseph translate, their witness was primarily based on what they saw or what Joseph explained to them about the process. The scribes explained a process that involved physical objects such as seer stones, a hat to block ambient light, and gold plates.

One caveat: Latter-day Saints have always believed that the Book of Mormon came into the world as the result of a series of miraculous events, starting with the appearance of the angel Moroni and proceeding through the completion of a translation of an ancient record. As with any miracle, it is difficult to reconstruct or even understand what happened without having experienced the event firsthand. This limits our ability to understand the translation beyond what witnesses saw and described. As valuable as witness statements are, they do not offer a perfect window into the consciousness of Joseph Smith. We will focus primarily on the historical record and avoid theoretical models or approaches that attempt to identify Joseph's cognition or state of mind during the translation. What Joseph was thinking or experiencing as he translated the book is essentially beyond the realm of historical inquiry. Unless he spoke about it, one can only guess or speculate.

JOSEPH'S WITNESS (BY THE GIFT AND POWER OF GOD)

Joseph Smith declared that he translated the Book of Mormon from an ancient language (reformed Egyptian) into English, but he spoke only one language. His parents provided him with only a limited education, and though he did have a bright mind, he did not have the education necessary to translate one language into another. He later explained that he was taught to read and write, but that these skills "const[it]uted my whole literary acquirements."[5] His wife, Emma, and others emphasized this point to make the production of the Book of Mormon appear even more astounding than it already was. Emma wrote that he "could neither write nor dictate a coherent and well-worded letter, let alone dictat[e] a book like the Book of Mormon."[6] Joseph maintained that he did not possess the ability to write the Book of Mormon on his own. He occasionally referenced his gift to translate throughout his life. In each account he consistently gave God credit for the translation and never claimed that he produced the Book of Mormon from his own efforts or through independent volition.[7]

Unfortunately, Joseph left very little indication about how he translated. In the preface to the 1830 edition to the Book of Mormon, he wrote, "I would inform you that I translated, by the gift and power of God."[8] His friends and family provided further details about the process, but Joseph's public statements consistently described the translation in vague terms associated with the power of God. Yet there were parallels to Joseph's gift in the Book of Mormon. Ammon, for example, described King Mosiah as a person who also had the gift to translate. Ammon declared that "a gift which is greater can no man have, except he should possess the power of God, which no man can; yet a man may have great power given him from God" (Mosiah 8:16). Joseph's and Ammon's statements say little about how God's power enabled them to translate ancient records, but both of them emphasized their callings as seers and prophets.

Some historical accounts claim Joseph explained the process further, but it is also clear that at times Joseph insisted on saying less. For example, in Orange, Ohio, during a conference in the fall of 1831, Joseph explained to the whole conference, "It was not intended to tell the world all the particulars of the coming forth of the book of Mormon."[9] Yet at another conference in Norton, Ohio, in 1834, Joseph apparently "gave a relation of obtaining and translating the Book of Mormon."[10] Nonetheless, Joseph continued to declare ambiguously that by "the gift and Power of God" he translated the Book of Mormon—a statement that by itself leaves readers to wonder about the mechanics of the translation itself. This vagueness has allowed many people to speculate about whether or not any of the produced text was the consequence of Joseph's own thought process and cognition or volition.

Even before Joseph wrote the preface to the Book of Mormon, his July 1828 revelation (Doctrine and Covenants 3:9) provided some insight into how he was able to translate it. In the wording of the earliest manuscript, the revelation explains, "God had given thee sight <and power> to Translate." This suggests that Joseph's gift was his ability to *see* things that others could not. Thus he was a seer. The concept of sight could possibly be a metaphor for a broader interpretation, but there is a parallel in the Book of Mormon that may help make sense of Joseph's revelation. The Book of Mormon explained that King Mosiah was a seer and that he could translate because "he has wherewith that he can *look*, and translate all records that are of ancient date; and it is a gift from God" (Mosiah 8:13). This parallel is even more germane to how Joseph translated because it appears that they both may have used the same device to translate ancient records.

PRIMARY SCRIBES

The basic idea found within most of the historical accounts is that Joseph saw the translation of the Book of Mormon on seer stone interpreters, from which he dictated the text to a scribe who recorded the words. Nevertheless, the procedure appears to have differed slightly from scribe to scribe, as the accounts left by each person include unique elements. Joseph's scribes are extremely important witnesses because they watched the process for hours at a time, and though they apparently never witnessed the words appear on the seer stones, they conversed with Joseph about the translation for months during 1828 and 1829. They offer accounts of the process that are deeply personal and provide experiences that are second only to the experience of Joseph Smith. Therefore, it will be particularly helpful to observe the process through the eyes of Emma Smith, Martin Harris, and Oliver Cowdery—Joseph Smith's three primary scribes.

In December 1827, Joseph and Emma moved to a fourteen-acre farm in Harmony, Pennsylvania, where Joseph began translating the plates. Joseph's history states that in February 1828 he began peering into the interpreters, where he saw the words of the translation. Between that month and the spring of 1828, Joseph Smith may have dictated to Emma as much as two-thirds of a manuscript known as the Book of Lehi.[11]

During a private interview with her son Joseph Smith III in 1879, Emma responded to questions about the translation after a lifetime of thought and contemplation. Just months before her death, Emma told her son that she "frequently wrote day after day" at a small table in their house in Harmony. Joseph could not have concealed anything from Emma, as she sat "at the table close by him"—close enough to see exactly how the translation occurred. Believing that her husband could not have produced the text of the Book of Mormon on his own, Emma was as astonished by the translation as anyone. "Though I was an active participant in the scenes that transpired, and was present during the translation of the plates," she told one interviewer, as mentioned above, "it is marvelous to me, 'a marvel and a wonder,' as much so as to anyone else."[12]

By mid-April 1828, Martin Harris began recording the translation. He was much more outspoken about the translation of the Book of Mormon. Like Emma, Harris sat at the table near Joseph and wrote down the words as Joseph dictated. He likewise mentioned the plates lying on the table, wrapped in or covered with a small tablecloth. He left at least twenty-five statements about his involvement, declaring that "he was favored to write direct from the mouth of the Prophet Joseph Smith." Knowing that Joseph could not translate the ancient characters on the plates, he marveled at the complexity of the text and at how fluidly Joseph dictated the Book of Mormon to him.[13]

Oliver Cowdery began serving as Joseph Smith's scribe on April 7, 1829, in Harmony, Pennsylvania. From April until the end of May, the translation advanced at Joseph Smith's house in Harmony, and the remainder was finished in Fayette, New York, at Peter Whitmer Sr.'s house by the end of June. During that period, Cowdery recorded most of the original manuscript of the Book of Mormon, with some assistance from two unidentified scribes (probably John Whitmer and possibly Christian Whitmer) who helped in June. Unlike Martin Harris and David Whitmer, who lived much longer and spoke often in their later years about their perception of the translation process, Oliver Cowdery died comparatively young, at age forty-three, so he left only a few statements.[14]

THE SEER STONES

The scribes mentioned at least two types of seer stones: the spectacles, or interpreters, and one or more additional seer stones that Joseph had found.[15]

SPECTACLES, OR INTERPRETERS

Joseph explained that Moroni, "the same heavenly messenger" that delivered the plates, also gave him a device that held two stones, which Joseph referred to as "spectacles," and a breastplate to hold the spectacles.[16] (For more about this story, see chapter 2 herein.) Joseph's description of the stones as "spectacles" led to a misunderstanding of the way the stones actually functioned, according to witnesses.[17] The spectacles were simply two seer stones bound together like glasses without the earpieces, though they were not intended to sit on the bridge of a person's nose or wrap around the user's ears. The spectacles were larger than typical glasses.[18] Though most glasses are about six inches from one side to the other, Harris explained that the spectacles were about "eight inches" long.[19]

In the fall of 1830, Cowdery described the interpreters as "two transparent stones in the form of spectacles thro which the translator looked on the engraving & afterwards put his face into a hat & the interpretation then flowed into his mind."[20] In 1831 Cowdery testified under oath that Joseph Smith "found with the plates, from which he translated the book, two transparent stones, resembling glass, set in silver bows" and "that by looking at these, he was able to read in English, the reformed Egyptian characters, which were engraven on the plates."[21] One of Cowdery's earliest converts in Ohio wrote, "In the last part of October, 1830, four men appeared here . . . with a book, which they said contained what was engraven on gold plates found . . . about three years ago by a man named Joseph Smith Jr. who had translated it by looking into a stone or two stones, when put into a dark place, which stones he said were found in the box with the plates."[22] He explained that Cowdery had said, "While [Joseph] looked through the stone spectacles another sat by and wrote what he told them."[23] These statements can be compared with a newspaper article, not associated with Oliver Cowdery but published just a few weeks after the translation work was finished in June 1829. In this article Jonathan Hadley, one of the printers Joseph Smith approached in Palmyra to print the Book of Mormon, claimed that the "very illiterate" Joseph told him the plates were found with a "huge pair of Spectacles" and that "by placing the Spectacles in a hat, and looking into it, Smith could (he said so, at least,) interpret these characters."[24]

Whether this report refers to Joseph's use of the Urim and Thummim in 1829 or to what was done in 1828 before Oliver's time is not certain, but it could refer to both. Drawing similarities between these stones and two stones that constituted the biblical Urim and Thummim, Joseph and others eventually called the Book of Mormon stones Urim and Thummim.[25] Though Oliver Cowdery later used the Book of Mormon term *interpreters*, it is not found in many other accounts, and the term *spectacles* was later used interchangeably with Urim and Thummim.[26] William W. Phelps's article in the January 1833 issue of *The Evening and the Morning Star* exemplifies the use and confusion of these interchangeable terms. It claimed that the Book of Mormon "was translated by the gift and power of God, by an unlearned man, through the aid of a pair of Interpreters, or spectacles—(known, perhaps, in ancient days as Teraphim, or Urim and Thummim)."[27]

OTHER SEER STONES

Martin Harris saw Joseph Smith use the Urim and Thummim, but he also saw Joseph use a single stone. Harris explained that Joseph Smith "possessed a seer stone, by which he was enabled to translate as well as from the Urim and Thummim, and for convenience he then used the seer stone,"[28] which is understandable because the spectacles may have been somewhat awkward to use, making the long hours of translation more difficult.[29]

Harris claimed that he knew how Joseph was translating. He explained that by the "aid of the seer stone, sentences would appear and were read by the Prophet and written by [Martin], and when finished he would say, 'Written,' and if correctly written, that sentence would disappear and another appear in its place, but if not written correctly it remained until corrected." Harris was apparently an active participant in the translation, and his audible exchanges with Joseph made it apparent to him that words were appearing on the seer stone or stones in the hat. Harris believed that this process eliminated the possibility of any volition on the part of Joseph Smith. Joseph did not determine what was included in the text of the Book of Mormon; the translation apparently came directly from that which appeared on the seer stones.[30]

Emma Smith began transcribing again for Joseph Smith in the fall of 1828 and early 1829, but it is unknown what she wrote down for Joseph at this time. Emma wrote to Emma Pilgrim in 1870 that Joseph first "translated by the use of the Urim and Thummim [i.e., spectacles or interpreters], and that was the part that Martin Harris lost [the Book of Lehi], after that he [Joseph Smith] used a small stone, not exactly black, but rather a dark color."[31] Historical documents do not allow us to conclude whether Emma was speaking from actual knowledge or from supposition when she suggested that Joseph Smith carried out the remainder of the translation with this brown stone. She was not a scribe during the period from April to June 1829, but she was in the same house when the translation was taking place.

Because of Emma's statement about the brown stone, some historians have concluded that Joseph Smith used a single seer stone exclusively during this period of the Book of Mormon translation, but Joseph likely used another seer stone, or set of stones used as one device, at that time as well. For example, interviews with Cowdery or speeches by him,[32] as well as one very early account close to the time when Oliver worked as Joseph's scribe, mention the interpreters or Urim and Thummim, which suggests their importance during the time Oliver scribed for Joseph.

USE OF A HAT TO BLOCK AMBIENT LIGHT

Significantly, the use of a hat appears in important witness statements relating to translation in Harmony (Emma Smith, Martin Harris),[33] as well as in Fayette (David Whitmer, Elizabeth Whitmer Cowdery).[34] In fact, before the printing of the Book of Mormon had even begun, in the earliest known account of the translation of the plates, the spectacles were described as being used in conjunction with a hat. The mention of the hat Joseph used often causes modern interpreters to relate the translation to magic. Yet the hat itself is as insignificant to the process as the table Oliver Cowdery used to write on during the translation. It was simply a tool that Joseph apparently used to block out all extraneous light.

According to several accounts, when Joseph used his hat he began the process by placing the stone in the hat in order to read the words that would appear on the stone. Joseph then dictated the words he saw to his scribe. Joseph Knight Sr., who provided financial support for Joseph Smith during the translation, recounted, "Now the way he translated was he put the urim and thummim into his hat and Darkned his Eyes" so that he could see the words a sentence at a time.[35] David Whitmer, one of the Three Witnesses of the Book of Mormon, gave many interviews about the translation between 1878 and 1888. Though he never claimed to have actually seen the words on the stone himself, his statements often spoke of the words appearing on something resembling parchment.[36] His statements typically testified with words to the effect that "Joseph Smith would put the seer stone into a hat, and put his face in the hat, drawing it closely around his face to exclude the light; and in the darkness the spiritual light would shine. Thus the Book of Mormon was translated by the gift and power of God, and not by any power of man."[37]

This process echoes the Book of Mormon account of a stone that "shall shine forth in darkness unto light" (Alma 37:23).[38] In addition, the placing of the seer stone and his face in the hat significantly suggests that Joseph was not reading from notes or a book.[39] In whatever way it happened, David Whitmer and some other commentators believed that the characters and the translation came into Joseph's fields of vision and understanding and he was able to convey those emerging words to his scribes. This validates Joseph's lack of volition in the process and emphasizes Joseph's statements about the translation that it was by the "gift and power of God" that he translated the Book of Mormon. Emma explained that Joseph sat across from her "with his face buried in his hat, with the stone in it, and dictating hour after hour with nothing between us." Addressing criticisms that Joseph read from a prepared script or the Bible, Joseph III carefully inquired about her experience. Emma declared, "He had neither manuscript nor book to read from." In Emma's understanding, Joseph could not have read from anything that was not inside the hat, which was too small to encompass a large manuscript or a sizable Bible. "If he had had anything of the kind [books or manuscripts]," Emma declared, "He could not have concealed it from me."

The Three Witnesses, engraving by H. B. Hall & Sons, 1883. Courtesy of Church History Library.

The seer stone in the hat was central to the translation; it was small enough to fit easily inside the hat, and according to Emma, the words appeared on the stone. Additionally, she explained that the plates "often lay on the table without any attempt at concealment, wrapped in a small linen table cloth."[40]

Witnesses testify that Joseph relied on divine assistance in carrying out the translation. As with the Liahona described in the Book of Mormon (see 1 Nephi 16:26–28), all these sacred objects required righteousness and diligence on Joseph's part in order to provide connectivity with divine inspiration. David Whitmer said that the seer stones worked only when Joseph was "humble and possessed the right feeling towards everyone."[41] Whitmer remembered a time in June 1829 when Joseph had a "stormy quarrel" with Emma. Still upset about their disagreement, Joseph went upstairs to resume the translation, only to find that "he could not translate a single syllable." The miraculous nature of the translation required Joseph Smith to be right before God and man; when this was not the case, his divine gift was temporarily withdrawn. Whitmer said Joseph went "out into the orchard and made supplication to Lord [and] was gone about an hour." He returned to the house, asked Emma for forgiveness, and returned to translating with Oliver Cowdery. The words again began to appear on the stone.[42]

CONTROVERSY REGARDING SEER STONES

Despite their significance to the translation process, the seer stones have become a topic of mystery and even controversy. The most public and successful early attempt to denigrate Joseph Smith's use of the seer stones came with the publication of a book compiled by Eber D. Howe in 1834 called *Mormonism Unvailed.*

Motivated by the conversion of his sister and wife to the restored gospel and funded by a society in Kirtland, Ohio, that opposed the Church, Howe sent Doctor Philastus Hurlbut to New York in 1833 to gather evidence against Joseph Smith and the Book of Mormon. Howe attempted to prove to the public at large that Solomon Spaulding wrote a manuscript that Joseph Smith plagiarized in order to create the Book of Mormon. Howe claimed that, with Sidney Rigdon's help, Joseph plagiarized and appropriated Spaulding's text and manufactured the Book of Mormon.[43] In the process, he deliberately associated Smith's seer stone instrument with the culture of treasure seeking in New York. Instead of viewing the devices as instruments prepared by God for Joseph Smith, he associated them with mystical practices of using "peep stones" to find buried treasure. Howe's false claims stoked public sentiment against the Church and has continued to do so for almost two centuries by encouraging people to understand Joseph Smith's translation of the Book of Mormon as part of his agrarian folk practices. Though the more educated classes often derided folk practices, the agrarian lower and middle classes, most of whom were presumably Christians, openly embraced them. In fact, these practices were often described through natural processes or "scientifically," but Howe attempted to reassociate Smith's seer stones as tools used for money digging.[44]

Folk practices like using a divining rod to find water can potentially represent the antithesis of our modern scientific worldview. Yet in Joseph's lifetime, using stones to see lost or hidden objects was relatively normal, in much the same way that many people today believe that essential oils offer health benefits despite the skeptical response of the scientific community. Joseph occasionally joined with other local youth in attempts to use stones to find valuable objects. E. D. Howe and others negatively portrayed Joseph as a money digger because he knew about Joseph's treasure-seeking adventures with his friends.[45]

Modern historians have seen Joseph's money digging either as part of his religious radicalism or as a developmental period for his religious calling as a prophet. Either way, it has been difficult for historians to detach Joseph Smith's use of a seer stone from 1822 to 1826 from his use of seer stones after 1827 (when he began translating the Book of Mormon). Some historians have attempted to make his early experiences as a treasure digger insignificant, while others have described the same experiences as foundational for Smith's religious experiences as a translator.[46] These polarized views are supported by our knowledge of the culture at the time and by dozens of accounts taken from *Mormonism Unvailed* and other Church-critical sources produced decades later. Rectifying the differences of opinion will likely never happen, and firm conclusions about Joseph's interest in treasure digging may be possible only with the discovery of new documents.[47]

PURPOSE OF THE GOLD PLATES

With Joseph looking into the hat at the seer stones, what need was there for him to even have the plates in his possession? While most of the Book of Mormon translation accounts say little in this regard, the plates may well have served several purposes. Their mere existence may have instilled Joseph with confidence that the words that appeared on the stones were from an ancient record. In the face of persistent pestering, carrying and possessing the plates would have sustained his confidence that the translation process was authentic. His mission was to "translate the engravings which are on the plates" (Doctrine and Covenants 10:41), and he spent some time scrutinizing and transcribing some of the characters on them. Yet the translation usually occurred while the plates lay covered on the table (although some accounts suggest that the plates were sometimes kept in a nearby box under the bed or even hidden in the Whitmers' barn during translation).[48] In addition, the plates encouraged belief in the minds of needed supporters, such as Emma, the Whitmer family, and the Three and the Eight Witnesses, each of whom spoke of having various experiences touching, hefting, feeling, and seeing the plates. The text of the Book of Mormon is abnormally self-aware of the plates; it focuses again and again on the provenance of the gold plates and the sources from which Mormon and Moroni compiled them. It essentially tracks the gold plates and their source material from person to person until the plates end up in the hands of Joseph Smith. The Book of Mormon even prophesies of Joseph's possession and translation of the record. Therefore, the physical plates fulfill thousands of years of preparation, and the witnesses provide authentication of the historicity of the plates. The plates were therefore indispensable for validating the ancient nature of the Book of Mormon.

CONCLUSION

Pulling together the accounts from witnesses and our understanding of the sacred instruments used for translation, we can now understand three components of Joseph Smith's translation process. He explained that he translated (1) by the gift and power of God (like Mosiah) and (2) by way of an instrument (the seer stones), which (3) functioned through "sight" (as Doctrine and Covenants 3:12 indicates). Some of Joseph's close associates also elaborated on what he revealed—most spoke of Joseph's use of the term *Urim and Thummim* (either the spectacles or the seer stone),[49] while a few refer to his use of a single stone[50] placed into a hat used to shield his eyes from extraneous light. Given the different experiences of each of Joseph's scribes discussed above, it seems possible that he was not particular about using a single, consistent procedure. He seems to have alternated between one stone and two. In addition, as Joseph looked into his hat at the seer stones, he left the gold plates covered on the table or locked in a box.

Finally, though an examination of the translation process relying on witness statements alone could be criticized as limited, it provides a historical foundation for others to expand on. Research that utilizes literary theory, historical-cognition studies, textual criticism, and psychological approaches will continue to produce interesting and thought-provoking theories and analyses, but the bedrock of such studies should be a well-documented religious experience given in the words of those who experienced it.[51]

Michael Hubbard MacKay and Gerrit J. Dirkmaat are associate professors of Church history and doctrine at Brigham Young University.

Michael Hubbard MacKay and Gerrit J. Dirkmaat, "Firsthand Witness Accounts of the Translation Process," in *The Coming Forth of the Book of Mormon: A Marvelous Work and a Wonder*, ed. Dennis L. Largey, Andrew H. Hedges, John Hilton III, and Kerry Hull (Provo, UT: Religious Studies Center, Brigham Young University; Salt Lake City: Deseret Book, 2015), 61–79.

NOTES

1. For examples of apologetic scholarship that openly discusses the translation process, see the following works: Richard Lloyd Anderson, *Investigating the Book of Mormon Witnesses* (Salt Lake City: Deseret Book, 1981), 108; Hyrum Andrus, *Joseph Smith: The Man and the Seer* (American Fork, UT: Covenant Communications, 2005), 160–62; Leonard J. Arrington and Davis Bitton, *The Mormon Experience: A History of the Latter-day Saints* (New York: Vintage Books/Random House, 1979), 10–12; Milton V. Backman Jr., *Eyewitness Accounts of the Restoration* (Salt Lake City: Deseret Book, 1986), 84; LeGrand L. Baker, *Joseph and Moroni: The 7 Principles Moroni Taught Joseph Smith* (West Valley, UT: Eborn Books, 2007), 44; Susan Easton Black and Andrew Skinner, *Joseph: Exploring the Life and Ministry of the Prophet* (Salt Lake City: Deseret Book, 2005), 62–63, 266, 270; Steven C. Harper, *Joseph the Seer* (Provo, UT: Harper Publishing, 2005), 49, 62–63; Larry C. Porter and Susan Easton Black, *The Prophet Joseph: Essays on the Life and Mission of Joseph Smith* (Salt Lake City: Deseret Book, 1988), 13–14; John W. Welch, *Opening the Heavens: Accounts of Divine Manifestations, 1820–1844* (Provo, UT: Brigham Young University Press, 2005), 87; John W. Welch, *The Worlds of Joseph Smith: A Bicentennial Conference at the Library of Congress* (Provo, UT: Brigham Young University Press, 2006), 14–15.
2. See "Book of Mormon Translation," Gospel Topics Essays, churchofjesuschrist.org; and *The Joseph Smith Papers, Documents*, 1:xxviii–xxxii (hereafter *JSP*, D1).
3. See Neal A. Maxwell, "By the Gift and Power of God," *Ensign*, January 1997, 26–41; and Russell M. Nelson, "A Treasured Testament," *Ensign*, July 1993, 61.
4. The following are a few publications that try to address the extant sources: John W. Welch, "The Miraculous Translation of the Book of Mormon," in *Opening the Heavens*, 82–98; and Royal Skousen, "Translating the Book of Mormon: Evidence from the Original Manuscript," in *Book of Mormon Authorship Revisited: The Evidence for Ancient Origins*, ed. Noel B. Reynolds (Provo, UT: FARMS, 1997), 61–93. A hierarchy of sources is described in *JSP*, D1:xxviii–xxxii. For a speculative piece

about the translation, see Brant A. Gardner, *The Gift and Power: Translating the Book of Mormon* (Salt Lake City: Greg Kofford Books, 2011).

5. Joseph Smith, History, ca. summer 1832, in *JSP, Histories*, 1:11 (hereafter *JSP*, H1).

6. Joseph Smith III, "Last Testimony of Sister Emma," *Saints' Herald*, October 1, 1879, 289–90. Emma declared that "the Book of Mormon is of divine authenticity—I have not the slightest doubt of it. I am satisfied that no man could have dictated the writing of the manuscripts unless he was inspired; for, when acting as his scribe, your father would dictate to me hour after hour; and when returning after meals, or after interruptions, he would at once begin where he had left off, without either seeing the manuscript of having any portion of it read to him. This was the usual for him to do. It would have been improbable that a learned man could do this; and, for one so ignorant and unlearned as he was, it was simply impossible." William Smith, Joseph's youngest brother, assessed Joseph's writing abilities by claiming that to say Joseph was illiterate was an exaggeration because he "wrote [with] a plain intelegable hand." William Smith, "Notes Written on 'Chambers' Life of Joseph Smith," ca. 1875, Church History Library, The Church of Jesus Christ of Latter-day Saints, Salt Lake City (hereafter CHL).

7. As early as 1834, E. D. Howe in *Mormonism Unvailed* claimed that the text was taken from a manuscript by Solomon Spaulding and through the efforts of Sidney Rigdon. See Matthew P. Roper, "Myth, Memory, and 'Manuscript Found,'" *FARMS Review of Books* 21, no. 2 (2009): 179–223. Other, more nuanced theories have emerged over the years, most of which included Joseph Smith having at least partial volition as he dictated the text. For examples, see Gardner, *The Gift and Power*, part 2; Brigham H. Roberts, *New Witnesses for God*, vol. 2 (Salt Lake City: Deseret Book, 1909); and Skousen, "Translating the Book of Mormon," 61–93.

8. Book of Mormon (Palmyra, NY: Grandin, 1830), iv. The statement specifically refers to the way Joseph Smith translated the book of Lehi in the spring of 1828; Joseph used the same phrase, "gift and power of God," in later years when referring to the translation as a whole.

9. General Conference, Minutes, October 25, 1831, in *JSP*, D2:78–86. Perhaps his most detailed account came in an 1843 letter written to his friend James Arlington Bennet. The characters inscribed on the gold plates, Joseph said, represented a language that "was lost to the world." Reflecting back on the translation, he said, "I stood alone, an unlearned youth, to combat the worldly wisdom and multiplied ignorance of eighteen centuries, with a new revelation." Even here, however, he does not describe the process beyond saying, "by the power of God I translated the Book of Mormon from hieroglyphics." Joseph Smith to James Arlington Bennet, November 13, 1843, Joseph Smith Collection, CHL.

10. See Minute Book 1, 43–47, Joseph Smith Collection, CHL. It was recorded at that meeting that Joseph "gave a relation of obtaining and translating the Book of Mormon."

11. *Saints' Herald*, May 24, 1884, 324. Anthony Metcalf claimed that Harris told him that he "wrote a great deal of the Book of Mormon . . . as Joseph Smith translated or spelled the words out in English." Anthony Metcalf, *Ten Years before the Mast* (Malad City, ID: n.p., 1888), 70–71. In Joseph Smith's 1839 history he writes that Martin Harris "had written one hundred and sixteen <pages> of manuscript on foolscap paper." But there is some doubt about this account since he edited the text to read, "we continued, until the 14th of June; having written. 216—pages of manuscript, on foolscap paper." In *JSP*, H1:244–45.

12. Edmund C. Briggs, "A Visit to Nauvoo in 1856," *Journal of History* (October 1916), 454; and Skousen, "Translating the Book of Mormon," 75–84.

13. Edward Stevenson, "One of the Three Witnesses: Incidents in the Life of Martin Harris," *Millennial Star* 44, nos. 5–6 (January 30 and February 6, 1882): 78–79, 86–87. See Welch, *Opening the Heavens*, 132–41.

14. See Welch, "Miraculous Translation," 141–44; statements recorded by Ashbel Kitchell (1830), Josiah Jones (1841), Reuben Miller (1848), George Q. Cannon (1881), Edward Stevenson (1886), William Frampton (1901), Samuel W. Richards (1907), and Jacob F. Gates (1912).

15. Joseph Smith, History, ca. summer 1832, 5. Joseph Smith seems to have used "spectacles" and "interpreters" interchangeably during the early years. Nancy Towle, an itinerant Methodist preacher, recounted Joseph Smith telling her about "a pair of 'interpreters,' (as he called them,) that resembled spectacles, by looking into which, he could *read* a writing engraven upon the plates, though to himself, in a tongue unknown." Nancy Towle, *Vicissitudes Illustrated in the Experience of Nancy Towle, in Europe and America* (Charleston: James L. Burges, 1832), 138–39.

16. Smith, History, vol. A-1, in *JSP*, H1:7–8.

17. See "Golden Bible," *Palmyra Freeman*, August 11, 1829. See also Diedrich Willers to Reverend Brethren, June 18, 1830, in Welch, "Miraculous Translation," 173.

18. Martin Harris told Charles Anthon that the spectacles were "too large for the breadth of the human face." Charles Anthon to E. D. Howe, February 17, 1834, in *Mormonism Unvailed*, 270–71. One of Joseph Smith's neighbors, Parley Chase, who would not have seen them, improbably exaggerated the size by stating that "the glasses were as big as a breakfast plate." Parley Chase, April 3, 1879, in W. Wyl, *Joseph Smith the Prophet, His Family and His Friends* (Salt Lake City: 1886), 276. A late source more moderately claimed that Joseph had described them as "having very large round glasses, larger than a silver dollar." See Henry G. Tinsley, "Origin of Mormonism," *San Francisco Chronicle*, May 14, 1893, 12.

19. Joel Tiffany, "Mormonism," *Tiffany's Monthly*, June 1859, 165–66. Speculating about this point, we can surmise that the size of the spectacles may have made it difficult for Joseph to focus on the text that appeared on its two stones and possibly forced him to focus on just one of its stones at a time to read the text.

20. Christian Goodwillie, "Shaker Richard McNemar: The Earliest Book of Mormon Reviewer," *Journal of Mormon History* 37, no. 2 (Spring 2001): 143.

21. A. W. Benton, "Mormonites," *Evangelical Magazine and Gospel Advocate* 2 (April 19, 1831).

22. Josiah Jones, "History of the Mormonites," *The Evangelist* 9 (June 1, 1841): 134–35.

23. Jones, "History of the Mormonites," 134–35.

24. "Gold Bible," *Palmyra Freeman*, August 11, 1829.

25. See *JSP*, D1:xxx, xxxiii; and Cornelis van Dam, *The Urim and Thummim: A Means of Revelation in Ancient Israel* (Winona Lake, IN: Eisenbrauns, 1997). Wilford Woodruff apparently saw one of Joseph's seer stones. See Wilford Woodruff Journal, December 27, 1841, CHL; and Richard Van Wagoner and Steven C. Walker, "Joseph Smith: 'The Gift of Seeing,'" *Dialogue: A Journal of Mormon Thought* 15 (Summer 1982): 58–59. See also Mark Ashurst-McGee, "A Pathway to Prophethood: Joseph Smith Junior as Rodsman, Village Seer, and Judeo-Christian Prophet" (master's thesis, Utah State University, 2000), 230–32, 247–48.

26. See Exodus 28:30; Leviticus 8:8; Numbers 27:21; Deuteronomy 33:8; 1 Samuel 14:41–42; 28:6. On the biblical Urim and Thummim, see van Dam, *Urim and*

Thummim. The "Urim and Thummim" mentioned in the Bible is apparently not the same object connected with the Book of Mormon in the book of Ether. In Doctrine and Covenants 17:1, the instrument is described as "the Urium and Thummim, which were given to the brother of Jared upon the mount."

27. "The Book of Mormon," *Evening and the Morning Star*, January 1833, [2]. W. W. Phelps was editor of the paper.

28. Martin Harris, reported by Edward Stevenson to the editor, *Deseret Evening News*, December 13, 1881, 4. The interview occurred in 1870.

29. Each of the following sources describes the seer stones as large and even cumbersome: Tiffany, "Mormonism," 165–66; Deseret Evening News, December 13, 1881, 4; W. Wyl, *Joseph Smith the Prophet*, 276n; and Henry G. Tinsley, "Origin of Mormonism," *San Francisco Chronicle*, May 14, 1893, 12.

30. Stevenson, "One of the Three Witnesses," 78–79, 86–87. Regarding the spelling out of names or difficult English words, Joseph may have done this more often when Harris was the scribe than when Cowdery was the scribe. Although there is evidence in the original manuscript that Joseph sometimes spelled out proper names, the idea that he could not proceed without every word being spelled correctly is contradicted by a number of misspellings in the original manuscript, such as *obediant, immagionations, treasurey, fateagued,* and *miricles* (by Cowdery), *inheretence, tortereth, covanants,* and *passified* (by scribe 2), and *treashury, diligent, desirus,* and several others (by scribe 3), as shown in Skousen, "Translating the Book of Mormon," 65–66, 75–82. Many of these misspellings, written in the rush of dictation, were corrected by Cowdery when he copied the entire text over to make the printer's manuscript from which most of the Book of Mormon was typeset.

31. Emma S. Pilgrim to Emma Bidamon, March 27, 1870, Community of Christ Library-Archives.

32. When Cowdery returned to the Church in 1848, he declared that he "wrote with my own pen the intire book of mormon (Save a few pages) as it fell from the Lips of the prophet." Cowdery further explained, "As he translated it by the gift and power of god, By means of the urum and thummim, or as it is called by that book holy Interperters. I beheld with my eyes. And handled with my hands the gold plates from which it was translated. I also beheld the Interperters." Focusing on his experiences while they translated, he emphatically stated, "That book [the Book of Mormon] is true." Reuben Miller, journal, October 21, 1848, CHL.

33. See Smith III, "Last Testimony of Sister Emma," 289–90; "The Three Witnesses to the Book of Mormon," *Millennial Star* 48 (June 21, 1886): 389–90; and R. W. Alderman reminiscence, in *Naked Truths about Mormonism* (Oakland, CA), January 1888, 3. In addition, Isaac Hale, Joseph Knight, and W. R. Hine also attested to use of the hat in translation that took place in Harmony. "Modern Superstition," *Visitor, or Monthly Instructor* (1841): 154–55; Joseph Knight Sr., History, in Dean Jessee, "Joseph Knight's Recollection of Early Mormon History," *BYU Studies* 17 (Autumn 1976): 353–6; and W. R. Hine statement, in *Naked Truths about Mormonism*, 2.

34. J. L. Traughber Jr., "Testimony of David Whitmer," *Saints' Herald*, November 15, 1879, 341; Eri B. Mullin, Letter to the editor, *Saints' Herald*, March 1, 1880, 76; *Kansas City Daily Journal,* June 5, 1881; George Q. Cannon interview, February 27, 1884, CHL; Zenas H. Gurley, "Questions Asked of David Whitmer," Gurley Collection, CHL; "The Book of Mormon," *Chicago Tribune,* December 17, 1885, 3; *Richmond (Missouri) Democrat,* January 26, 1888; Nathan A. Tanner Jr. to Nathan A. Tanner, February 17, 1909, CHL; and William E. McLellin to "My

Dear Friends," February 1870, Community of Christ Library-Archives. In addition, William Smith also attested to use of the hat in translation that took place in Fayette. William Smith, *William Smith on Mormonism* (Lamoni, IA: Herald Steam Book, 1883), 80; "The Old Soldier's Testimony," *Saints' Herald*, October 4, 1884, 644; and "Statement of J. W. Peterson Concerning William Smith," May 1, 1921, Community of Christ Library-Archives.

35. Joseph Knight Sr., History, 35. Joseph Knight continues: "Then he [Joseph Smith] would take a sentance and it would apper in Brite Roman Letters. Then he would tell the writer and he would write it. Then that would go away the next sentence would Come and so on. But if it was not Spelt rite it would not go away till it was rite, so we see it was marvelous. Thus was the hol [whole] translated." Knight's belief that misspellings caused the sentence to remain on the stone until it was corrected, allowing Joseph Smith to move on with translation, has been refuted by the lack of such corrections in the original manuscript except in the case of a few proper names. Skousen, "Translating the Book of Mormon," 66–82.

36. *David Whitmer Interviews: A Restoration Witness*, ed. Lyndon W. Cook (Provo, UT: Grandin Book, 1991). For example, in 1887 he said: "A piece of something resembling parchment would appear, and on that appeared the writing. One character at a time would appear, and under it was the interpretation in English. Brother Joseph would read off the English to Oliver Cowdery, who was his principal scribe, and when it was written down and repeated to Brother Joseph to see if it was correct, then it would disappear, and another character with the interpretation would appear."

37. David Whitmer, *An Address to All Believers* (Richmond, Mo: David Whitmer, 1887). David Whitmer repeated this description many times. While many of the details about the use of the seer stone in the hat are similar to Emma Smith's statements, the accounts of both Knight and Whitmer differ to some degree. According to Royal Skousen, leading scholar of the text of the Book of Mormon, the original manuscript supports the idea that Joseph saw and dictated multiple words or phrases, one cluster at a time, and that unusual names seem to have been sometimes spelled out and corrected if necessary, as David Whitmer indicated. The English text would not disappear from Joseph's view until he confirmed that what he heard from the scribe was correct. See Briggs, "Visit to Nauvoo in 1856," 454; and Royal Skousen, "How Joseph Smith Translated the Book of Mormon: Evidence from the Original Manuscript," *Journal of Book of Mormon Studies* 7, no. 1 (1998): 5.

38. David Whitmer explained that the hat would "exclude the external light. Then, a spiritual light would shine forth, and parchment would appear before Joseph." William Smith said that the hat, by blocking out the light, relieved Joseph's eyes from "strain." See Welch, "Miraculous Translation," 146, 156, 165.

39. Thus Emma Smith, who mentioned the stone in the hat, could testify with assurance: "He [Joseph] had neither manuscript nor book to read from." Smith III, "Last Testimony of Sister Emma," 289.

40. Smith III, "Last Testimony of Sister Emma," 289–90.

41. Whitmer, *Address to All Believers*, 36.

42. Whitmer, *Address to All Believers*, 30; David Whitmer, interviews with William H. Kelly and G. A. Blakesless, January 15, 1882; and *Omaha Herald*, October 17, 1886, in Cook, *David Whitmer Interviews*, 86, 199.

43. See *JSP*, D3:116–20.

44. See Keith Thomas, *Religion and the Decline of Magic: Studies in Popular Beliefs in Sixteenth and Seventeenth-Century England* (New York: Oxford University Press, 1971),

186, 215–18, 230, 242, 258, 410, 439, 635–36; David H. Hall, *Worlds of Wonder, Days of Judgment: Popular Religious Belief in Early New England* (Cambridge, MA: Harvard University Press, 1989); Jon Butler, *Awash in a Sea of Faith: Christianizing the American People* (Cambridge, MA: Harvard University Press, 1990), 225–88; Stephen A. Marini, *Radical Sects of Revolutionary New England* (Cambridge, MA: Harvard University Press, 1982); and Ann Taves, *Fits, Trances, and Visions: Experiencing Religion and Explaining Experience from Wesley to James* (Princeton, NJ: Princeton University Press, 1999), part 1.

45. See Richard Lyman Bushman, *Joseph Smith and the Beginnings of Mormonism* (Urbana: University of Illinois Press, 1984), 64–76; Ronald W. Walker, "The Persisting Idea of American Treasure Hunting," *BYU Studies* 24, no. 4 (1984): 429–59; and Richard Lloyd Anderson, "The Mature Joseph Smith and Treasure Searching," *BYU Studies* 24, no. 4 (1984): 489–560.

46. See Ashurst-McGee, "Pathway to Prophethood," 157–82; D. Michael Quinn, *Early Mormonism and the Magic World View*, rev. ed. (Salt Lake City: Signature Books, 1998), 30–65; Ronald W. Walker, "Joseph Smith: The Palmyra Seer," *BYU Studies* 24, no. 4 (Fall 1984): 461–72; and Alan Taylor, "The Early Republic's Supernatural Economy: Treasure Seeking in the American Northeast, 1780–1830," *American Quarterly* 38 (Spring 1986): 6–33.

47. For more, see the following document and its historical introduction: *JSP*, D1:345–52.

48. For accounts of the plates being "in the box," see Clark, *Gleanings by the Way*, 228, in Welch, "Miraculous Translation," 134; for accounts of the plates being "on the table," see Smith III, "Last Testimony of Sister Emma," 51, in Welch, "Miraculous Translation," 130.

49. See Joseph Smith, History A-1, in *JSP*, H1:222; "Mormonism—No. II," *Tiffany's Monthly*, May 1859, 163, 165–66; Josiah Jones, "History of the Mormonites," *Evangelist* 9 (June 1, 1841): 132–34; *New Hampshire Gazette*, October 25, 1831; and John Corrill, *A Brief History of the Church of Christ of Latter Day Saints* (St. Louis: By the author, 1839), 7, 12.

50. It is possible that Joseph Smith detached one of the stones from the metal rims of the interpreters. In addition to the three accounts of Martin Harris and two accounts of David Whitmer that speak of him using first the Urim and Thummim and then a single stone, only the report by J. L. Traughber Jr. of a David Whitmer interview insisted that Joseph never used anything but the seer stone. According to Traughber, David Whitmer said that, in his presence, Joseph always used "a dark colored, opaque stone, called a 'seer-stone,'" and never the Urim and Thummim." Traughber Jr., "Testimony of David Whitmer," 341; in Welch, "Miraculous Translation," 145–46. David Whitmer, however, was speaking only of what he saw during the last stage of the translation in June 1829 in Fayette, for he never saw how the translation was conducted elsewhere. Furthermore, David objected that he was misquoted by Traughber. He clarified that he did not say that he "saw Joseph Smith translate" or that he was in the "immediate presence of the translator," but rather was simply "at the place and saw how the translation was conducted." David Whitmer to the editor, *Kansas City Journal*, June 19, 1881.

51. For a more complete discussion of this topic, see Michael Hubbard MacKay and Gerrit J. Dirkmaat, *From Darkness unto Light: Joseph Smith's Translation and Publication of the Book of Mormon* (Provo, UT: Religious Studies Center, Brigham Young University; Salt Lake City: Deseret Book, 2015).

Chapter Five

A Multiplicity of Witnesses

Women and the Translation Process

AMY EASTON-FLAKE AND RACHEL COPE

Four women in early Church history—Mary Whitmer, Lucy Mack Smith, Lucy Harris, and Emma Smith—played significant roles in the coming forth of the Book of Mormon and offered their own witnesses of the plates' reality. While their names and narratives are well known, scholars and members of the Church have largely overlooked their powerful and important contributions to the work of translation, since they were not a part of the official Three or Eight Witnesses. This article addresses this gap in scholarship and historical memory by looking at a variety of sources (both those that are frequently cited and those that have been largely neglected) that recount these women's experiences with the plates. It considers the various ways in which they came to know of the plates' temporality and divinity and shows the multiplicity of witnesses that emerge when we privilege ways of knowing and seeing beyond the visual. Evaluating these women's memories of and interactions with the plates helps us to understand better the translation process and the truly communal effort it required.

MARY MUSSELMAN WHITMER

Mary Whitmer[1] has been referred to as the twelfth witness because her experience with the plates parallels most closely that of the official Three and Eight Witnesses.[2] She is the only known woman to have physically seen the plates, and her experience with them and her role in the translation process aptly illustrate the familial and communal effort that enabled the translation of the Book of Mormon.

In June 1829, Mary and Peter Whitmer opened their home to Joseph Smith, his wife Emma, and Oliver Cowdery so they could complete the translation when persecution in Harmony became intense.[3] Here the translation process progressed rapidly as Joseph and Oliver devoted themselves fully to the work. The Whitmers' willingness to shoulder their temporal concerns for a time enabled Joseph and Oliver's single-minded focus; as the family matriarch, Mary, in particular, bore the brunt of this burden. As her son David reports, "My father and mother had a large family of their own, the addition to it therefore of Joseph, his wife Emma and Oliver very greatly increased the toil and anxiety of my mother. And although she had never complained she had sometimes felt that her labor was too much, or at least she was perhaps beginning to feel so."[4]

Life on an early nineteenth-century New York farm was laborious for anyone, but particularly taxing demands were placed on the farmer's wife, who, according to an 1862 US Department of Agriculture study, "works harder, endures more, than any other on the place."[5] A farmer's wife oversaw the running of the household and was typically responsible for milking, butter churning, gathering eggs, and caring for livestock; planting, weeding, and harvesting the kitchen garden; shearing sheep, turning wool into yarn, and sewing garments; cooking, cleaning, laundering; and the list continues.[6] Much of the additional work of cooking, cleaning, and caring for the visitors invariably fell on Mary, and those burdens must have taxed an already-overworked woman. Encapsulated in David's statement, then, is a reminder of the labor and goods that Mary, along with others, had provided so that Joseph, a poor farmer dependent on the work of his own hands, might give his time and energy to the translation process. If not for the generosity of such people as the Whitmers, Martin and Lucy Harris, and Joseph Knight and his family, Joseph would not have had the resources to translate the plates. Consequently, their labor should be seen as crucial to the work of translation.

That God recognized and valued their sacrifice to aid the work of translation is perhaps most clearly suggested when Mary Whitmer was shown the plates. Her grandson John C. Whitmer summarized her experience as follows:

> One evening, when (after having done her usual day's work in the house) she went to the barn to milk the cows, she met a stranger carrying something on his back that looked like a knapsack. At first she was a little afraid of him, but when he spoke to her in a kind, friendly tone, and began to explain to her the nature of the work which was going on in her house, she was filled with inexpressible joy and satisfaction. He then untied his knapsack and showed her a bundle of plates, which in size and appearance corresponded with the description subsequently given by the witnesses to the Book of Mormon. This strange person turned the leaves of the book of plates over, leaf after leaf, and also showed her the engravings upon them; after which he told her to be patient and faithful in bearing her burden a little longer, promising that if she would do so, she should be blessed; and her reward would be sure, if she proved faithful to the end. The personage then suddenly vanished with the plates, and where he went, she could not tell.[7]

Her son David additionally reported the words the angel spoke to Mary: "You have been very faithful and diligent in your labors, but you are tired because of the increase of your toil, it is proper therefore that you should receive a witness that your faith may be strengthened."[8] In the angel's words, we seem to see God's recognition of Mary and her labor; he acknowledged what Mary was contributing to his work, he appreciated her efforts, and he blessed her for her faithfulness and bolstered her commitment. For Mary, as for the later witnesses, the witnessing experience she had was faith building. At the time, as her grandson reported, it "enabled [her] to perform her household duties with comparative ease, and [to feel] no more inclination to murmur because her lot was hard."[9]

When Mary was shown the plates, she became the first known person to see them besides Joseph Smith. Within the month, all of the male members of her family, except for her husband, would join her in witnessing the physical reality of the plates; indeed, seven of the eleven official witnesses of the Book of Mormon were Whitmers by blood or marriage.[10] The entire Whitmer family enabled the translation work by providing for Joseph's, Emma's, and Oliver's temporal needs, and in turn many of them were privileged to become witnesses of the physical reality of the plates and the divinity of the translation process. Richard Lloyd Anderson has referred to the

Whitmers as "a family that nourished the Church," and, as Mary's story demonstrates, this is certainly the case.[11] They provided the space for the organization of the Church and for the reception of many of the revelations during the New York period, they served missions, and they joined the Saints first in Kirtland and later in Missouri, where Mary's sons and sons-in-law served in many leadership positions. Sadly, in 1838, during a time of great hardship and apostasy, all of the living Whitmers left the Church following a falling-out with Joseph Smith. Nevertheless, Mary, like all of her family and the other witnesses for the gold plates, never altered or denied her testimony of their reality, their divine origin, and the message contained in the book translated from them.[12] For the remainder of her life, she would continue to testify of the book—a book made possible through the collective efforts of Mary and the entire Whitmer family, as well as the Knight, Harris, and Smith families.

LUCY MACK SMITH

As a memoirist and as a participant in the events surrounding the translation and publication of the Book of Mormon, Lucy Mack Smith introduces various ways of witnessing beyond the visual, including record keeping, sensory experiences, and spiritual impressions.[13] In her account, Lucy also broadens the traditional definition of *witness* to include the entire community of people who contributed to the coming forth of this text. As she sees it, her family and friends—female and male—played important roles within the context of a shared story.

During the winter of 1844–1845, just months following the deaths of her sons Joseph, Hyrum, and Samuel, sixty-nine-year-old Lucy dictated her memoir to Martha Jane Knowlton Coray, who hoped to preserve an important story. Lucy's memoir, recorded by a woman for a woman, includes the experiences and perspectives of many female witnesses. The memoir's purpose is captured in the original copyright description, which reads as follows: "The History of Lucy Smith, Wife of Joseph Smith, the first patriarch of [the church of] Jesus Christ of Latter Day Saints, who was the father of Joseph Smith, Prophet, Seer, and Revelator; containing an account of the many persecutions, trials and afflictions which I and my family have endured in bringing forth the Book of Mormon and establishing the church of Jesus Christ of Latter Day Saints."[14] From Lucy's perspective, Joseph alone did not bring forth the Book of Mormon and establish the Church; rather, it was a family affair.

Lucy's memoir, which Leonard Arrington suggests "tells more about Mormon origins than any other single source," documents events surrounding the translation and publication of the Book of Mormon from the perspective of "an observer closely connected to the primary participants" in the Church's early history.[15] However, because the narrative framework of this text is so familiar to Church members, readers often overlook the texture that Lucy's account may add to our understanding of Church history. A closer and more careful read reveals a rich and complex narrative about dedicated, devoted, and flawed believers who willingly made sacrifices to enable the publication of this sacred text. The translation of the Book of Mormon, Lucy's narrative indicates, both required and created a community effort.[16]

The need for communal effort is evidenced from the beginning of Lucy's memoir, which recounts her family's religious heritage. She highlights, for example, the role of spiritual seeking in the lives of her progenitors, and she describes and interprets powerful dreams—both her own and those of her husband—that seem to have foreshadowed the Restoration.[17] She also discusses at length her own commitment to discovering the true gospel and demonstrates how this quest influenced her children.[18] In sharing these stories, Lucy implicitly suggests that generations of the Smith and Mack families both were preparing themselves and were prepared by the Lord for the "marvelous work" they would perform.[19]

Although Joseph's calling to translate the Book of Mormon and to restore the gospel of Jesus Christ plays a central role in Lucy's memoir, she stresses her family's involvement in these events. Lucy notes that after Joseph learned about the gold plates from the angel Moroni, he often gathered his family together and shared his experiences with them. In so doing, she implicitly suggests that he made them active participants in the Restoration. For example, she recalls "all seated round in a circle father Mother sons and Daughters listening in breathless anxiety to the <religious> teachings of a boy 16 <19> yars of age who had never read the Bible through by course in his life."[20] Nonetheless, she continues, "Joseph would give us some of the most ammusing recitals which could be im magined he would de[s]cribe the ancient inhabitants of this continent their dress thier maner of traveling the animals which they rode The cities that were built by them the structure of their buildings with eve ry particular of their mode of warfare their religious worship as particularly as though he had Spent his life with them."[21] Remembering these powerful moments of instruction, William Smith simply explained, "The whole family were melted to tears, and believed all he said."[22] Although the Smiths lacked tangible evidence of the plates at this time, they experienced spiritual confirmation, and thus they anxiously awaited the day when Joseph would receive the important record he had described.[23] Together, the family became witnesses to the Book of Mormon, even before Joseph's acquisition of the plates.

After Joseph had obtained the plates, different forms of witnessing—more sensory in nature—opened up. While they did not physically see the plates, Lucy and other family members saw their outline through the cloth that covered them and even handled them on occasion, thus enabling them to become witnesses of the tangible nature of the object they encountered.[24] Shortly after Joseph and Emma had attained the plates, for example, Lucy handled the Urim and Thummim "with no covering but a silk handkerchief" while advising her son about getting a chest made in order to protect them.[25] Later, Lucy would see the box that held the plates, as well as the outline of the plates through their covering.[26] Lucy's daughter Katharine Smith also witnessed the plate's tangibility when she had the opportunity to "heft" the "package" containing the plates that her elder brother had brought home.[27] She "found them very heavy like gold and also rippled her fingers up the edge of the plates and felt that they were separate metal plates and heard the tinkle of sound that they made."[28] Owing to her recollection of the physical and audible encounters she had with the plates, Herbert S. Salisbury referred to Katherine as "one of the choice, small circle given to bear first-hand witness to the truthfulness of the Prophet's assertions regarding posses-sion of the gold plates."[29] Indeed, the range of experiences that people such as Lucy and Katharine Smith had with the plates broadens the definition of witnessing to include the senses of touch and sound as well as sight.

In addition to explaining people's tangible experiences with the plates, Lucy's history demonstrates that, as the family matriarch, she was involved with and aware of the various events surrounding the coming forth of the Book of Mormon. She is, for example, the only person who knew when Joseph and Emma went to receive the plates.[30] Of this event, she recalled:

> I spent the night in prayer and at reasonable time for rising I went to preparing breakfast my heart fluttering at every footfall for I now expected Joseph & Emma every moment and was in dread of a second disappointment in his obtaining the plates. When the male part of the family sat down to breakfast Mr. Smith [Joseph Smith Sr.] enquired for Joseph for no one but myself knew where he was.[31]

By preserving this story, Lucy reveals that both women and men in the family were intimately involved with the events surrounding the acquisition of the plates. As the translation process ensued, Lucy continued to be among the first and few to know about each aspect of the work. For instance, she, along with her husband and Mary Whitmer, were the first to learn that Oliver Cowdery, Martin Harris, and David Whitmer had been shown the plates by the angel Moroni.[32] And, as soon as the translation was completed, a messenger was sent from Fayette, New York, to share the good news with Lucy.[33] In citing such stories, Lucy's memoir makes it clear that she served as a witness of an important work and felt the importance of preserving details only she knew.

Lucy also contributed to the translation process by making temporal sacrifices that enabled the important spiritual work her family had been called to do—"whilst we worked with our hands we endeavored to remmember the service of & the welfare of our souls," she recalled.[34] Indeed, she and her family sacrificed time, money, and goods in order to enable Joseph to work on this important project.[35] Like Mary Whitmer, Lucy allowed various people associated with the translation, including Joseph and Emma, Joseph Knight, and Lucy Harris and her daughter, to stay in her home; she, along with her daughters, inevitably had to assume additional housekeeping responsibilities on a regular basis.[36] Besides taking on extra household chores, Lucy helped protect the gold plates and prepare for the eventual publication of a new book of scripture. For example, she helped find hiding places for the plates' protection, remained astutely aware of their safety or lack thereof, and met with Martin and Lucy Harris to request financial assistance for the project.[37] In addition to engaging in temporal labors, Lucy willingly defended the translation work and spoke of the plates' reality. On one occasion, a group of men from a local church asked Lucy if they could see the gold plates. To them she declared, "We have not <got >any ny <no> gold bible and neither have we ever had any thing of the kind but we have a translation of some gold plates which was sent to the world to bring the plainess of the Gospel to the children of men and also to give a history of the people that used to inhabit this country."[38] When the men questioned her witness, Lucy continued, "even you should stick my body full of faggots and burn me at the stake I would declare that Jose[p]h has that record and that I know it to be true as long as God gave me breath."[39]

In many other cases, tangible aspects of Lucy's interaction with the Book of Mormon also took on a spiritual form. On one occasion, she agreed to help protect the manuscript pages of the Book of Mormon from the threat of a mob. After placing the manuscript in a trunk, she put it under her bed. While Peter Whitmer guarded her home, Lucy, now lying on the bed, began a reflective train of thought that captured her testimony about the work her family had engaged in. She recalled:

> this identicle work had not only been the object which we as a family had pursued so eagerly but that Prophets of ancient days and angels even the Gr[e]at God had <had> his eye upon it. and said I to myself Shall I fear what man can do will not the angels watch over the precious relict of the worthy dead and the hope of the living and I am I indeed the mother of a prophet of the God of Heaven—the honored instrument in performing so great work—I felt th I was in the purview of angels and my bounded at the thought of the grat condescension of the A[l]mighty—thus I spent the night surrounded by enemies and yet in an extacy of happiness and truly I can say that my soul did magnify and my spirit rejoiced in God my savior.[40]

Here Lucy shows how various aspects of witnessing combine: while protecting tangible manuscript pages, she bore a powerful spiritual witness—in the context of her memoir—about a sacred and divinely inspired work that multiple people had sacrificed for in order to make possible. Because Lucy never saw the plates, we do not refer to her as a Book of Mormon witness; yet, as her memoir demonstrates, she was intimately involved in every event tied to the coming forth of the Book of Mormon.

LUCY HARRIS

Within the pages of her memoir, Lucy Mack Smith introduces her readers to Lucy Harris. Although Lucy Harris is typically remembered for her antagonism toward the Book of Mormon, in part because she claimed to have never actually believed in the gold plates following the manuscript's publication, it is important to recognize that Lucy Smith's history reveals another side of this complex figure.[41] Even though Lucy Mack Smith clearly disliked her neighbor, she still acknowledged Lucy Harris's initial interest in and support of the translation project. She also recalled that Harris had received a powerful spiritual witness of the plates, followed by an audible and tangible witness of them. As a result of these experiences, Smith intimated, Harris had willingly donated a significant amount of money in order to help enable the translation of the Book of Mormon.[42]

Shortly after Joseph and Emma had obtained the plates from the Hill Cumorah, Joseph asked his mother if she would speak with a wealthy acquaintance, Martin Harris, about financing the project. She agreed to do so but decided to first visit with his wife, Lucy, "in order to satisfy" Lucy Harris's curiosity.[43] According to Smith's account, Lucy Harris was intrigued by the story Lucy Mack Smith shared with her and expressed an immediate interest in the plates, offering to donate a considerable sum of money from her own "private purse" for Joseph's translation efforts.[44] She then informed her visitor that she would come to the Smith home one evening in the following week so she could speak with Joseph. When Lucy Harris and her daughter paid a visit to the Smith home, she understandably hoped to see the plates before committing to provide financial support for the project. Although she pleaded with Joseph to let her see the gold plates, he insisted that he could not show them to her, explaining that the angel who had entrusted them into his care told him that he could show them only to those called as witnesses by God. Dissatisfied with this response, Harris declared, "Now Joseph . . . I will tell [you] what I will do If I can get a witness that you do speak the truth I will beleive it."[45] Harris, who was staying at the Smith home overnight, retired to bed following her conversation with Joseph.

The following morning, Lucy Harris shared "a very remarkable dream" she had had that night with the Smith family—a common occurrence in the early nineteenth century.[46] In this dream, she reported, a personage appeared to her and chastised her for importuning "the servant of the Lord."[47] The angel then showed her the plates. As a result of the powerful witness she received through this visionary dream, Lucy was able to describe the record in vivid detail, and she subsequently insisted on giving Joseph twenty-eight dollars (money she had received from her mother prior to her mother's death) to help with the project.[48] Fascinated by the witness Harris had borne and appreciative of her generosity, Joseph allowed her and her daughter to handle the wooden box containing the plates. Martin Harris remembered that his "daughter said, they were about as much as she could lift . . . my wife said they were very heavy."[49] The experience of actually hefting the plates added a tangible and audible witness to the spiritual witness Harris had already received, according to Smith's record.

Although Lucy Harris eventually became antagonistic to the work, in part because she never had the opportunity to see the plates despite her early support for the project, Lucy Smith implies that she continued to believe in their physical reality. On one occasion, for example, Lucy Harris traveled to the Joseph Smith Jr. home in Harmony, Pennsylvania, and insisted she would not leave until she saw the plates. She then ransacked "every nook & corner of the house chest cupboard trunk &c" to no avail.[50] The following day, Lucy searched the grounds surrounding the Smith home until early in the afternoon. She later reported that, upon discovering a location in which she thought the plates might be buried, a "tremendous great black snake stuck up its head before me and commenced hissing at me."[51] Feeling both frightened and frustrated, Lucy discontinued her search at that time. Nonetheless, she continued to believe in the plates' existence and longed for evidence of the work Martin and Joseph were engaged in. Lucy's later opportunity to see the first 116 manuscript pages of the Book of Mormon appeased her for a time. Although she is often blamed for the disappearance of this manuscript, it is important to remember that she was intrigued by this visible witness and allowed Martin to protect the manuscript in her bureau.[52] When Martin later discovered that the translated pages were missing, Lucy "solemnly averred" that she had not taken them.[53] Even when Lucy Harris felt skeptical about the translation project, Smith's account suggests that she continued to believe in the plates' existence. Her early witnessing experiences seem to have convinced her that Joseph indeed had the physical object he claimed to have in his possession.

As remembered by Lucy Mack Smith, Lucy Harris's experiences demonstrate some of the varied ways in which multiple people witnessed the plates and aided Joseph throughout the translation process. Lucy Mack Smith reminds us that women and men—in this case, Lucy and Martin Harris— both offered to provide financial backing for the publication of the Book of Mormon—a manifestation, or witness, in and of itself, of their belief in and commitment to a vast and collective undertaking.[54] The fact that Lucy and Martin had doubts and struggles does not negate their early witnessing experiences, nor should it overshadow the sacrifices they made.

EMMA HALE SMITH

As the person who was with Joseph from the beginning to the end of the translation process and who provided him with immeasurable assistance in various ways, Emma Smith was arguably more intimately involved in the coming forth of the Book of Mormon than any other person besides Joseph. Therefore, by viewing the translation process through her witness, we not only learn of the integral role she played in the work of translation and her own commitment to the coming forth of the Book of Mormon, but we also gain new knowledge about the translation process itself and about the plates' physicality. When the experience is seen through her eyes, as well as those of the other women, the work of translation becomes a familial and communal project, with many people contributing to the success of the endeavor.

Emma's involvement with the ancient Nephite record began when she accompanied Joseph to the Hill Cumorah to receive the long-anticipated plates. Early in his communication with the angel Moroni, Joseph was commanded to bring the right person with him to the hill. He believed that person to be Emma;[55] and thus at midnight on September 22, 1827, the two of them left the Smith home and, with the aid of Joseph Knight's horse and wagon, went to retrieve the plates.[56] After arriving at the Hill Cumorah, Joseph left Emma in the wagon and went alone to retrieve the plates. When he returned a few hours later, he carried a bundle wrapped in his coat. Joseph then left Emma again so he could deposit the plates in a hollowed-out birch log in the woods. For the next three years, Joseph and Emma's lives revolved around the protection and translation of the plates.

Persecution in Palmyra began immediately and required the entire Smith family to aid in the protection of the plates. Needing money to purchase a box to hold the plates, Joseph left a day or two after retrieving them for a well-digging job in Macedon, just west of Palmyra. In his absence, Joseph's father learned of a group of men who, with the aid of a conjurer, planned to find and steal the plates, which had been hidden in the woods. When Joseph Sr. reported what he had overheard to Emma, she directly mounted a horse and rode to warn Joseph. Together, they returned to Palmyra and Joseph retrieved the plates from their hiding place.[57] Three times he was assaulted on his way home. The persecution continued in the days that followed; once mobs came to the Smith home and ransacked their cooper shop in search of the plates.[58] Joseph and Emma soon determined that they must leave Palmyra. Word was sent to Emma's brother, Alva Hale, asking him to come to Palmyra and take them back to Harmony.[59] Once settled in a home located on Emma's parents' property,[60] Joseph and Emma began the work of translation. Although the Hales were antagonistic toward the work, they—like the Smiths—were vital to the translation process because of the space and protection they provided for Joseph and Emma.

Emma served as Joseph's first scribe, and some sources suggest that her work in this capacity may have been more significant and extensive than is commonly recognized. According to Joseph Knight, Emma assisted in "[drawing] of the Caricters" that Martin took to Charles Anthon.[61] She also possibly recorded the majority of Joseph's translation for the lost 116 pages, since Martin Harris remembered that he wrote "about one third of the first part of the translation of the plates as [Joseph] interpreted them by the Urim and Thummim."[62] While it is unknown precisely how long or how much Emma scribed for Joseph, Martin's statement raises the possibility that she recorded two-thirds of the lost 116 pages, which would make her Joseph's most prolific scribe besides Oliver Cowdery. Emma's own reminiscences of the translation work also indicate that her time scribing was extensive: "I frequently wrote day after day, often sitting at the table close by him . . . and [he] and dictating hours after hour with nothing between us."[63]

Emma Smith's witness of this time also provides invaluable insight into the translation process, particularly as she scribed for Joseph both before and after the first 116 manuscript pages had been lost. From her we learn of "[Joseph] sitting with his face buried in his hat, with the stone in it; . . . he had neither manuscript nor book to read from."[64] She also informs us that when Joseph first began translating, he used the Urim and Thummim, but later "he used a small stone, not exactly, black, but was rather a dark color."[65] Each of these details alter common perceptions of how Joseph translated. More specifically of the process, she reports,

> When my husband was translating the Book of Mormon, I wrote a part of it, as he dictated each sentence, word for word, and when he came to proper names he could not pronounce, or long words, he spelled them out, and while I was writing them, if I made any mistake in spelling, he could stop me and correct my spelling, although it was impossible for him to see how I was writing them down at the time. Even the word *Sarah* he could not pronounce at first, but had to spell it, and I would pronounce it for him. When he stopped for any purpose at any time he would, when he commenced again, begin where he left off without any hesitation, and one time while he was translating he stopped suddenly, pale as a sheet, and said, "Emma, did Jerusalem have walls around it?" When I answered, Yes," he replied "Oh! I was afraid I had been deceived." He had such a limited knowledge of history at that time that he did not even know that Jerusalem was surrounded by walls.[66]

Scholars have used such information to argue for a tightly controlled translation process.[67] More important, though, Emma's witness also testifies repeatedly of the divinity of the work as Joseph corrected her spelling without seeing what she wrote, commenced where he left off "without seeing the manuscript or having any portion of it read to him,"[68] and discovered things he did not know about, such as the walls around Jerusalem, as he translated.

Emma's experience as Joseph's scribe contributed to her lasting spiritual witness of the plates' divinity. Nearly fifty years later, she told her son:

> My belief is that the Book of Mormon is of divine authenticity. I have not the slightest doubt of it. I am satisfied that no man could have dictated the writing of the manuscript unless he were inspired. . . . Joseph Smith could neither write nor dictate a coherent and well-worded letter, let alone dictating a book like the Book of Mormon. And, though I was an active participant in the scenes that transpired, and was present during the translation of the plates, and had cognizance of things as they transpired, it is marvelous to me, "a marvel and a wonder," as much so as to any one else.[69]

From the person who knew Joseph best, we learn of his capabilities at the time of translation and how far beyond those capabilities the Book of Mormon extended. The discrepancy between the two reaffirmed for Emma the divinity of the work—a spiritual witness that she would share repeatedly for the rest of her life.

Emma contributed to the work of translation not only through her scribal efforts but also through the support and care she provided Joseph as his wife. Emma was not able to be the full-time scribe that Joseph needed because, as Lucy Smith and Joseph Knight both report, most of her time was spent caring for their home and their temporal needs.[70] Maintaining a home was a full-time occupation in early nineteenth-century America, and Emma, without any hired help, fulfilled this necessary role for Joseph and herself, as well as at times for Martin Harris and Oliver Cowdery. Only with Emma caring for the home in Harmony, Joseph's brother Samuel tending the farm, and Joseph Knight providing food and paper could Joseph and Oliver devote themselves exclusively to the work of translation.[71] Notably, in her role as housekeeper Emma remained a close observer of the translation process as "Oliver Cowdery and [Joseph Smith] wrote in the room where [she] was at work."[72]

Emma, as an eyewitness of the translation process from the moment Joseph received the plates until the time when the Book of Mormon was published, also offered a temporal witness of the plates' physicality. In her role as housekeeper, "she would lift and move [the plates] when she swept and dusted the room and furniture."[73] At times the plates "lay under [their] bed for a few months."[74] Other times they sat in a sack or "wrapped in a small linen tablecloth"[75] on a "small table in their living room in their cabin."[76] Her witness of the plates' physicality takes on an added dimension when she describes "tracing their outline and shape."[77] She reports that the plates "seemed to be pliable like thick paper, and would rustle with a metallic sound when the edges were moved by the thumb, as one does sometimes thumb the edges of a book."[78] Here Emma offers both auditory and tactile witnessing; nevertheless, many have questioned her lack of a visual witness. Interestingly, though, she herself did not seem to; as she told her son, "I did not attempt to handle the plates, other than I have told you, nor uncover them to look at them. I was satisfied that it was the work of God, and therefore did not feel it to be necessary to do so."[79] Emma's complete assurance of the reality of the plates despite her never seeing them is a powerful statement about the validity of other ways of knowing and seeing beyond the visual.

The events surrounding the lost 116 pages illustrate well how the translation process was, in many respects, a truly joint effort for Joseph and Emma and how Emma, too, was deeply invested in the project. The day after Martin left with the 116 pages, Emma gave birth to her first son, who either was stillborn or lived for only a couple of hours.[80] Because Emma had undergone a long and extremely difficult labor, her life was in danger for more than a couple of weeks. As her health improved, Joseph became increasingly anxious about the manuscript, "but he did not mention the subject to Emma for fear of agitating her mind to[o] much for the health of her body."[81] However, as Lucy Mack Smith reports, Emma—also concerned about the manuscript—told her husband, "I feel so uneasy . . . that I cannot ~~and~~ rest and shall not be at ~~rest~~ ease untill I know something about what Mr Harris is doing with it do you not think it would be advisable for you to go and enquire into the reason of his not writing or sending any word back to you since he left us."[82] Emma's concern for the manuscript and insistence that Joseph leave her to inquire after it in the face of her own precarious health situation—and devastation over the loss of her first child—says much about her own commitment to the work.

Although many scholars have attributed Emma's professed concern for the plates to worry about Joseph's increasing despondency about the state of the manuscript,[83] consideration must also be given to Emma's own labor in scribing part of the 116 pages and the countless sacrifices she had made to assist in the translation work, as well as Lucy's statement about Emma's personal agitation over the manuscript. Additionally, Joseph's response to Martin when he learns Martin has lost the manuscript speaks to Emma's deep involvement in the project. "Then must I . . . return to my wife with such a tale as this I dare not do it least I should kill her at once."[84] Given Emma's fragile health, Joseph's words may not have been hyperbolic but rather may demonstrate his actual concern that her health may not have been able to withstand the additional loss of all that they had been working for together. A statement that Emma made at the end of her life that "[she] was an active participant in the scenes that transpired, and was present during the translation of the plates, and had cognizance of things as they transpired" is certainly accurate.[85] And through her witness we gain new knowledge of the translation process and the power in witnesses beyond the visual.

CONCLUSION

Each of these women—Mary Whitmer, Lucy Mack Smith, Lucy Harris, and Emma Smith—aided the work of translation and offered their own witnesses of the plates' reality. By recognizing their contributions, we not only place women back into the narrative in which they were integral actors, but we also expand the scope of ways in which to witness and what it means to be a witness. Touch, sound, spiritual impressions, and visions may in fact produce, as these women illustrate, a more lasting and powerful experience than sight. In turn, through the witnesses of these women, we may see how the translation of the Book of Mormon both required and created community effort; males and females, people young and old, and both family and friends all worked together on this important project. Almost two centuries later, the miracle of this great work may resonate more and build greater faith when we recognize how God used dedicated women and men to bring forth his great work of translation and restoration.

Amy Easton-Flake is an associate professor of ancient scripture at Brigham Young University.

Rachel Cope is an associate professor of Church history and doctrine at Brigham Young University.

Amy Easton-Flake and Rachel Cope, "A Multiplicity of Witnesses: Women and the Translation Process," in *The Coming Forth of the Book of Mormon: A Marvelous Work and a Wonder*, ed. Dennis L. Largey, Andrew H. Hedges, John Hilton III, and Kerry Hull (Provo, UT: Religious Studies Center, Brigham Young University; Salt Lake City: Deseret Book, 2015), 133–53.

NOTES

1. Mary Whitmer was born Mary Musselman in Germany on August 27, 1778. She immigrated to Pennsylvania and married Peter Whitmer, who was also of German descent. They moved to Fayette, New York, in 1809. Information taken from Mary Musselman Whitmer entry in the biographical directory in *The Joseph Smith Papers, Histories*, 1:638 (hereafter *JSP*, H1). For more information, see Andrew Jenson, *Latter-day Saint Biographical Encyclopedia: A Compilation of Biographical Sketches of Prominent Men and Women in the Church of Jesus Christ of Latter-day Saints* (Salt Lake City, UT: Andrew Jenson History Co., 1901), 1:283.

2. See Daniel Peterson, "Defending the Faith: Mary Whitmer, 12th Witness to the Book of Mormon," *Deseret News*, July 18, 2013.

3. See Lucy Mack Smith, History, 1844–1845, handwriting of Martha Jane Knowlton Coray and Howard Coray, 240 pages, with miscellaneous inserted pages, book 8, pp. [8–10], Church History Library, The Church of Jesus Christ of Latter-day Saints, Salt Lake City. In citing book and page numbers, we follow the references available as part of the full text on The Joseph Smith Paper's website (http://josephsmith papers.org/). See also interview of Joseph F. Smith and Orson Pratt with David Whitmer, as reported in *The Latter-day Saints' Millennial Star* 40, December 9, 1878, 772. For more information, see Richard Lloyd Anderson, *Investigating the Book of Mormon Witnesses* (Salt Lake City, UT: Deseret Book, 1981), 67.

4. David Whitmer, "Report of Elders Orson Pratt and Joseph F. Smith," *Deseret Evening News*, November 27, 1878, 1; as cited in Dan Vogel, comp., *Early Mormon Documents* (Salt Lake City: Signature Books, 2003), 5:51–52.

5. As cited in Catherine Clinton and Christine A. Lunardini, eds., *The Columbia Guide to American Women in the Nineteenth Century* (New York: Columbia University Press, 2000), 35.

6. For more information, see Sally Ann McMurry, *Families and Farmhouses in Nineteenth-Century America: Vernacular Design and Social Change* (Cary, NC: Oxford University Press, 1988), 59–61; Clinton and Lunardini, *Columbia Guide to American Women*, 35–36; and Nancy Grey Osterud, *Bonds of Community: The Lives of Farm Women in Nineteenth-Century New York* (Ithaca, NY: Cornell University Press, 1991), 156–58.

7. Statement of John C. Whitmer, quoted in Andrew Jenson, *Historical Record* 7, nos. 8–10 (October 1888): 621.

8. Whitmer, "Report of Elders Orson Pratt and Joseph F. Smith," 1.

9. Statement of John C. Whitmer, quoted in Andrew Jenson, *Historical Record* 7, nos. 8–10 (October 1888), 621.

10. Mary Whitmer raised seven children to adulthood. All five of her sons became witnesses for the gold plates, along with her sons-in-law Hiram Page, who married Catherine in 1825, and Oliver Cowdery, who married Elizabeth in 1832.

11. Richard Lloyd Anderson, "The Whitmers: A Family That Nourished the Church," *Ensign*, August 1979, 35. See Keith Perkins, "True to the Book of Mormon—The Whitmers," *Ensign*, February 1989, 34–42.

12. For more information on the Whitmers' role in the Church, later apostasy, and continual witness of the gold plates, see Anderson, "The Whitmers," 35; and Keith Perkins, "True to the Book of Mormon," 34–42.

13. See, generally, Lucy Mack Smith, History.

14. Copyright for Lucy Mack Smith, "The History of Lucy Smith," July 18, 1845, Robert Harris, Copyright Registry Records for Works Concerning the Mormons to 1870, Church History Library.
15. Leonard J. Arrington, letter to the advisory editor of Arno Press, Edwin S. Gaustad, February 5, 1969; quoted in Jan Shipps, *The Story of a New Religious Tradition* (Urbana: University of Illinois, 1987), 91–92.
16. See, generally, Lucy Mack Smith, History, 1844–1845.
17. See Lucy Mack Smith, History, book 6, p. [5]; Miscellany, [9].
18. See Lucy Mack Smith, History, 1844–1845, book 2, pp. [4–5]; book 9, pp. [5–6].
19. Asael Smith believed and declared that God intended to raise a branch of his family to be of great benefit to humankind. See Richard Lloyd Anderson, *Joseph Smith's New England Heritage: Influences of Grandfathers Solomon Mack and Asael Smith*, 2nd ed. (Salt Lake City: Deseret Book; Provo, UT: Brigham Young University Press, 2003), 147–49, 286; and Joseph Smith, Revelation, February 1829 [D&C 4], in *JSP, Revelations and Translations*, 1:[1], http://josephsmithpapers.org/.
20. Lucy Mack Smith, History, 1844–1845, book 3, p. [12]; book 4, p. [1].
21. Lucy Mack Smith, History, 1844–1845, book 4, pp. [1–2].
22. William Smith, *William Smith on Mormonism* (Lamoni, IA: Herald Steam Book and Job Office, 1883), 9; quoted in Vogel, *Early Mormon Documents*, 1:620.
23. See Smith, *William Smith on Mormonism*, 10.
24. See Smith, *William Smith on Mormonism*, 11–12.
25. See Lucy Mack Smith, History, book 5, p. [7].
26. Lucy Mack Smith, History, 1844–1845, book 5, p. [7].
27. Quoted in Vogel, *Early Mormon Documents*, 1:524.
28. Quoted in Vogel, *Early Mormon Documents*, 1:525.
29. Herbert S. Salisbury, "Things the Prophet's Sister Told Me," July 30, 1944 (San Rafael, CA), original typescript signed by the author, Church History Library. See "The Prophet's Sister Testifies She Lifted the B[ook] of M[ormon] Plates," *Messenger* [Berkeley, CA], October 1954, 1, 6, Community of Christ Library and Archives, Independence, MO; quoted in Vogel, *Early Mormon Documents* 1:649.
30. See Lucy Mack Smith, History, 1844–1845, book 5, p. [6].
31. Lucy Mack Smith, History, 1844–1845, book 5, p. [6].
32. See Lucy Mack Smith, History, 1844–1845, book 8, p. [11].
33. See Lucy Mack Smith, History, 1844–1845, book 8, p. [10].
34. Lucy Mack Smith, History, 1844–1845, book 3, p. [10].
35. See Lucy Mack Smith, History, 1844–1845, book 5, pp. [6, 8, 12].
36. See Lucy Mack Smith, History, 1844–1845, book 5, p. [6]; book 5, p. [4].
37. See Lucy Mack Smith, History, 1844–1845, book 6, pp. [2–3]; book 5, p. [6].
38. Lucy Mack Smith, History, 1844–1845, book 9, pp. [7–8].
39. Lucy Mack Smith, History, 1844–1845, book 9, pp. [7–8].
40. Lucy Mack Smith, History, 1844–1845, book 9, p. [7].
41. See E. D. Howe, *Mormonism Unvailed* (Painesville, OH: Printed and Published by the author, 1834), 254–57, 216–21. Although Lucy Harris may not be claimed as a definitive witness because she refuted the truth of the Church in an affidavit, her behavior is not uncommon and may even be expected in one who becomes antagonistic toward the Church and suffers either indirectly or directly because of Church connections, as she attests she did via Martin. Consequently, Lucy Smith's account of Lucy Harris should be viewed as a credible recollection of events, particularly

since Lucy Smith does not appear to like Harris or have any reason for saying Harris had these experiences if she did not.

42. See Lucy Mack Smith, History, 1844–1845, book 6, pp. [5–6].

43. Lucy Mack Smith, History, 1844–1845, book 6, p. [4]. Compare with Joel Tiffany, interview with Martin Harris, in "Mormonism-No. II," *Tiffany's Monthly*, August 1859, 168–70.

44. Lucy Mack Smith, History, 1844–1845, book 6, pp. [3–5].

45. Lucy Mack Smith, History, 1844–1845, book 6, pp. [5–6].

46. Lucy Mack Smith, History, 1844–1845, book 6, pp. [5–6]. See Mechal Sobel, *Teach Me Dreams: The Search for Self in the Revolutionary Era* (Princeton: Princeton University Press, 2002); and Phyllis Mack, "Agency and the Unconscious: The Methodist Culture of Dreaming," in *Heart Religion in the British Enlightenment: Gender and Emotion in Early Methodism* (New York: Cambridge University Press, 2008), 219–60. Oliver Cowdery had a similar experience before becoming one of the Book of Mormon scribes. The Lord "appeared unto a young man by the name of Oliver Cowdery and showed unto him the plates in a vision, and also the truth of the work, and what the Lord was about to do through me, his unworthy servant. Therefore, he was desirous to come and write for me to translate." *Personal Writings of Joseph Smith*, ed. Dean C. Jessee, rev. ed. (Salt Lake City: Deseret Book; Provo, UT: Brigham Young University Press, 2002), 14, 20; spelling and punctuation modernized.

47. Lucy Mack Smith, History, 1844–1845, book 6, pp. [5–6].

48. See Lucy Mack Smith, History, 1844–1845, book 6, pp. [5–6].

49. Tiffany, interview with Martin Harris, 168.

50. See Lucy Mack Smith, History, 1844–1845, book 6, pp. [8–10].

51. Lucy Mack Smith, History, 1844–1845, book 6, p. [9].

52. As described in Lucy Mack Smith, History, 1844–1845, book 7, pp. [7–8].

53. Lucy Mack Smith, History, 1844–1845, book 7, pp. [7–8].

54. Although Lucy Harris initially offered financial assistance, she later refused to sign the three-thousand-dollar mortgage agreement that was to be used to satisfy the printer, E. B. Grandin.

55. According to Joseph Knight, Joseph was first told by the angel Moroni that he must bring his oldest brother, Alvin, with him. After Alvin's death, Joseph was subsequently shown that he was to bring Emma Hale. See Joseph Knight Sr., "Joseph Knight's Recollection of Early Mormon History," ed. Dean C. Jessee, *BYU Studies* 17, no. 1 (Autumn 1976): 31.

56. Lucy Mack Smith, History, 1844–1845, book 5, p. [6]. Joseph Knight refers in his recollections to a horse and carriage rather than to the horse and wagon that Lucy referenced in her memoir. See "Knight's Recollection," 32.

57. See Lucy Mack Smith, History, 1844–1845, book 5, pp. [9–10].

58. See Lucy Mack Smith, History, 1844–1845, book 5, pp. [11–12]; book 6, pp. [1–3]; and Richard Lyman Bushman, *Joseph Smith: Rough Stone Rolling* (New York: Alfred A. Knopf, 2005), 60–61.

59. See Lucy Mack Smith, History, 1844–1845, book 6, p. [6].

60. Joseph had agreed to purchase the home and thirteen acres from Isaac Hale for two hundred dollars. He made the last payment in August 1830. See Bushman, *Rough Stone Rolling*, 63.

61. "Knight's Recollection," 34.

62. Simon Smith, letters to the editor, April 30, 1884, *Saints' Herald*, 24 May 1884, 324. Sources originally cited and assertion originally made that Emma wrote the translation for the majority of the lost 116 pages in Michael Hubbard MacKay and Gerrit J. Dirkmaat, *From Darkness unto Light: Joseph Smith's Translation and Publication of the Book of Mormon* (Salt Lake City: Religious Studies Center, Brigham Young University; Salt Lake City: Deseret Book, 2015), 90–91. Possibly contradicting this point, Anthony Metcalf claimed that Harris told him that he "wrote a great deal of the Book of Mormon . . . as Joseph Smith translated or spelled the words out in English." See Anthony Metcalf, *Ten Years before the Mast* (Malad City, ID: n.p., 1888), 70–71. The assertion that Emma wrote two-thirds of the lost 116 pages is also in conflict with Joseph's own statement the "he [Martin Harris] had written one hundred and sixteen <pages> of manuscript on foolscap paper" (*JSP*, H1:244). However, this statement by Joseph about the 116 pages does not account for Joseph's other statement in which he wrote that "my wife had written some for me to translate and also my Brothr Samuel H. Smith" (*JSP*, H1:16).

63. Emma Smith Bidamon, interview with Joseph Smith III, February 1879, Miscellany, Community of Christ Library Archives; reproduced in Vogel, *Early Mormon Documents*, 1:539 (hereafter Bidamon interview).

64. Bidamon interview, 1:539.

65. Emma Smith Bidamon to Emma Pilgrim, 27 March 1870, in Emma Smith Papers, Community of Christ Library Archives. Published in *The Return*, 15 July 1895, 2; reproduced in Vogel, *Early Mormon Documents*, 1:532.

66. From Edmund C. Briggs, "A Visit to Nauvoo in 1856," *Journal of History* 9 (January 1916): 454; reproduced in Vogel, *Early Mormon Documents*, 1:530–31.

67. Royal Skousen, "How Joseph Translated the Book of Mormon: Evidence from the Original Manuscript," *Journal of Book of Mormon Studies* 7, no. 1 (1998): 25.

68. Bidamon interview, 1:538.

69. Bidamon interview, 1:538.

70. See Lucy Mack Smith, History, 1844–1845, book 8, p. [4]; and "Knight's Recollection," 35.

71. For more information on Samuel Smith's role, see Lucy Mack Smith, History, 1844–1845, book 8, pp. [1–4]; Linda King Newell and Valeen Tippets Avery, *Mormon Enigma: Emma Hale Smith*, 2nd ed. (Champaign: University of Illinois Press, 1994), 28–29; and Kyle R. Walker, *United by Faith: The Joseph Sr. and Lucy Mack Smith Family* (American Fork, UT: Covenant Communications, 2005), 207–9. For more information on Joseph Knight providing food and supplies, see "Knight's Recollection," 36.

72. Bidamon interview, 1:539.

73. Joseph Smith III to Mrs. E. Horton, March 7, 1900, Miscellany, Community of Christ Library Archives. See Bidamon, interview, 1:546–47.

74. Nels Madson, "Visit to Mrs. Emma Smith Bidamon," 1877 signed statement, Church History Library, in Vogel, *Early Mormon Documents*, 1:546.

75. Bidamon interview, 1:539.

76. Bidamon interview, 1:539.

77. Bidamon interview, 1:539.

78. Bidamon interview, 1:539.

79. Bidamon interview, 1:540.

80. For more information, see Newell and Avery, *Mormon Enigma: Emma Hale Smith*, 2nd ed. (Champaign, IL: University of Illinois Press, 1994), 27.

81. Lucy Mack Smith, History, 1844–1845, book 7, p. [2].
82. Lucy Mack Smith, History, 1844–1845, book 7, p. [2].
83. See Newell and Avery, *Mormon Enigma*, 28; Gracia N. Jones, *Emma and Joseph: Their Divine Mission* (American Fork, UT: Covenant Communications, 1999), 27; and Bushman, *Rough Stone Rolling*, 67.
84. Lucy Mack Smith, History, 1844–1845, book 7, p. [6].
85. Emma Smith Bidamon interview, February 1879, reproduced in Vogel, *Early Mormon Documents*, 1:540.

Chapter Six

Hefted and Handled
Tangible Interactions with Book of Mormon Objects

ANTHONY SWEAT

In his 1839 history, Joseph Smith said that he found the Book of Mormon plates "under a ~~stound~~ stone of considerable size." The plates were "deposited in a stone box" along with "the Urim and Thummin and the Breastplate as stated by the messenger."[1] These plates would be unearthed by Joseph Smith on September 22, 1827, and be carried from Manchester, New York, to Harmony, Pennsylvania, where Joseph would begin to translate the plates in the winter of 1828 and produce the sacred text called the Book of Mormon. Although Joseph begins his narrative of the Book of Mormon's origin by telling us of actual physical relics, some dismiss the physical reality and factual historicity of the Book of Mormon record by consigning the text to the status of an extraordinary work of mystical mythology.[2] They claim the Book of Mormon could be inspired truth—a supernatural, magical work of revealed religious fiction—yet still not be factual, historical truth. However, this position overlooks Joseph Smith's foundation story of the physical origins of the Book of Mormon: actual relics hefted and handled, touched and transported, from one place to another and by one person to another. Joseph Smith did not describe the coming forth of the Book of Mormon the way he described many of his revelations found in the Doctrine and Covenants: as inspired words of the Lord that came to his mind and that he then dictated to a scribe.[3] No, Joseph said the Book of Mormon came forth from a nearby hill, by removing dirt, using a lever to lift a large stone, and removing actual engraved plates and sacred interpreters for the translation of its inscriptions. The Book of Mormon text didn't just pass through Joseph's trance-induced revelatory mind; its palpable relics passed through a working frock, hollowed log, cooper's shop, linen napkin, wooden chest, fireplace hearth, and barrel of beans. As historian Terryl Givens has insightfully deduced, "This continual, extensive, and prolonged engagement with a tangible, visible, grounding artifact is not compatible with a theory that makes him an inspired writer reworking the stuff of his own dreams into a product worthy of the name scripture. . . . The story of the gold plates could not be fanciful mythology and the Book of Mormon still be scripture."[4]

It is logically inconsistent to claim that Joseph Smith disingenuously contrived the explicit origin story of the Book of Mormon and then expected its readers to implicitly accept the very story and teachings that the book contains. How can one accept Joseph Smith's revelation of truth if the story that produced it was a complete fabrication? Either the physical origin story of the Book of Mormon as told by Joseph Smith is true, or it is not. The truthfulness of its text is inextricably linked to its inception report.

The purpose of this article is to examine multiple historical accounts of persons who interacted with actual, physical, tangible objects related to the coming forth of the Book of Mormon—persons who could substantiate the reality of these origin objects. Taken collectively, these material experiences with Book of Mormon relics provide compelling evidence to the truthfulness of Joseph Smith's account of the Book of Mormon's ancient origins. Building on prior research by Andrew Hedges[5] and research by Michael MacKay and Gerrit Dirkmaat,[6] this paper will describe multiple independent accounts from perhaps the most material time period of the book's coming forth: the protection period from when the plates were unearthed in September of 1827 in Manchester, New York, to when they began to be translated in early winter of 1828 in Harmony, Pennsylvania.

TAKEN FROM A STONE BOX

After four years of anxious personal preparation following Joseph Smith's First Vision, the time had come for Joseph to unearth and retrieve the Nephite record. Around midnight on the evening of September 21, 1827, Joseph asked his mother, Lucy, "if [she] had a chest with a lock and key"[7] to store the plates in once he retrieved them, but she did not have anything to offer him. Lucy noticed that Joseph's wife, Emma, was in her riding apparel, and although Joseph didn't mention it specifically, Lucy deduced that he was taking Emma and leaving to get the plates. Without obtaining consent,[8] Joseph took Joseph Knight's horse and wagon, and he and Emma left for the Hill Cumorah. Leaving Emma at the bottom of the hill to wait, Joseph went to retrieve the plates from their ancient burial place.

Often overlooked, the stone box from which the plates were retrieved is one of the first physical evidences of Joseph's origin story of the Book of Mormon plates and text. Joseph described the box in which the plates and interpreters were interred: "The box in which they lay was formed by laying stones together in some kind of cement, in the bottom of the box were laid two stones crossways of the box, and on these stones lay the plates and the other things with them."[9] Meeting the angel Moroni at the site of the stone box, and after having received a sacred charge from the angel that Joseph was now responsible for the plates' care, Joseph removed the plates from their tomb. Because he had not yet prepared a secure place for the plates at home, he initially stored the plates in a hollowed-out birch log on the hill.[10] A few days later, after having obtained a wooden chest from his brother Hyrum in which to secure the plates, Joseph returned to the Hill Cumorah and took the plates home.

Ironically, while much of Joseph's later persecution may have arisen out of others doubting the existence and possession of golden plates, originally the difficulty was due to the exact opposite: certain persons were convinced he had actually retrieved the record.[11] Part of their certainty was due to their interaction with the place where the plates were buried. Willard Chase and Samuel Lawrence, two local friends of Joseph's and associates in some of his previous treasure-seeking ventures, were particularly attuned to Joseph's retrieval of the plates. According to an account by Willard Chase, before Joseph obtained the record, he had taken Samuel Lawrence to the Hill Cumorah and shown him the spot where the Book of Mormon plates were concealed in the stone box. Lawrence asked Joseph "if he had ever discovered anything with the plates of gold; he said no; he then asked him to look in his stone, to see if there was anything with them. He looked, and said there was nothing; he told him to look again, and see if there was not a large pair of specks with the plates; he looked and soon saw a pair of spectacles, the same with which Joseph says he translated the Book of Mormon."[12] Although portions of Chase's account must be read skeptically, Joseph Knight Sr. shared a similar story in his reminiscence, saying Samuel

Lawrence "had Bin to the hill and knew about the things in the hill and he was trying to obtain them."[13]

Lawrence and other local treasure hunters, such as Willard Chase, are likely some of those who, because they had seen the place from which the plates came forth, later convinced an inquiring man named David Whitmer that Joseph had obtained the plates from the hill. David Whitmer would later remember:

> I had conversations with several young men who said that Joseph Smith had certainly golden plates, and that before he attained them he had promised to share with them, but had not done so, and they were very much incensed with him. Said I, 'how do you know that Joe Smith has the plates?' They replied: '*we saw the plates [place] in the hill that he took them out of just as he described it to us before he obtained them.*' These parties were so positive in their statements that I began to believe there must be some foundation for the stories then in circulation all over that part of the country.[14]

In another interview Whitmer told a reporter that "the community in which he [Whitmer] lived . . . was alive with excitement in regard to Smith's finding a great treasure, and they informed him that they knew that Smith had the plates, *as they had seen the place that he had taken them from, on the hill Cumorah.*"[15]

Shortly after Joseph had obtained the plates, Martin Harris and two others also went to the Hill Cumorah to "hunt for some more [stone] boxes." While this is a later reminiscence and he doesn't state with certainty whether or not this was the very box the Book of Mormon plates were removed from, Harris claimed that "indeed we found a stone box" that he and the other two persons were excited about. After unsuccessfully trying to remove the box from the hill, they took a crowbar and "broke one corner off the box." Harris concluded, "Sometime that box will be found, and you will see the corner broken off, then you will know I have told you the truth. Again Brethren as sure as you are standing here and see me just that sure did I see the angel with the golden plates."[16]

The stone box from the Hill Cumorah was also apparently left exposed for the display of residents and visitors to Palmyra for decades. In 1893 Elder Edward Stevenson wrote that during a trip to Palmyra "early on a summer's morning in the year 1870," he had been shown where the stone box once was by a local resident who lived near the Hill Cumorah. Stevenson said, "Questioning him closely he [the local] stated that he had seen some good sized flat stones that had rolled down and lay near the bottom of the hill. This had occurred after the contents of the box had been removed and these stones were doubtless the ones that formerly composed the box. I felt a strong desire to see these ancient relics and told him I would be much pleased to have him inform me where they were to be found. He stated that they had long since been taken away."[17] Testimonies and affidavits of local Palmyra residents such as this man, Martin Harris, Samuel Lawrence, and others corroborate Joseph Smith's testimony of the Book of Mormon relics being found and removed from a stone box he unearthed on the Hill Cumorah.

RESPONSIBLE FOR A RELIC

Returning to the evening of Joseph's retrieval of the plates from the Hill Cumorah, Joseph recounted that the angel Moroni gave him a strict charge regarding their care. Joseph recorded, "The same heavenly messenger delivered them up to me with this charge that I should be responsible for them. That if I should let them go carelessly or through any neglect of mine I should be cut off, but that if I would use all my endeavours to preserve them untill he (the messenger) ~~called~~ should call for them, they should be protected."[18] Because he had nowhere to protect the plates at home, Joseph left them hidden in a Cumorah birch tree "3 miles"[19] from the Smith home and went west to Macedon to take a job digging a well in order to earn money to have a wooden chest made in which to secure the plates.

While Joseph was gone, word apparently spread that he had obtained the record. Samuel Lawrence, Willard Chase, and others had gathered a group of about a dozen men (including a conjurer from sixty to seventy miles away)[20] to find the place where Joseph had secreted the plates. Joseph Smith Sr. learned of their plans and alerted Emma, and she rode on a stray horse to Macedon to alert Joseph that the plates were in danger. Joseph miraculously knew of Emma's coming and went out and met her on the road. Upon hearing the plates may be in danger, Joseph consulted the "Urim and Thummim, and saw that the Record was as yet safe; nevertheless, he concluded to return with his wife."[21] Upon arriving in Palmyra, Joseph went to the Hill Cumorah to retrieve the record, still dressed in his linen working frock. Joseph retrieved the plates from the hollowed log, wrapped them in his frock, and began on his way home through the woods with the record. He was attacked three times on his way home, dislocating his thumb fighting off one of the attackers. Arriving at his parents' home, according to Joseph's sister Katherine, Joseph "came in nearly exhausted, carrying the package of gold plates . . . clasped to his side with his left hand and arm, and his right hand was badly bruised."[22] Family friend Josiah Stowell, who was visiting the Smiths, reported that Joseph then handed him the plates, wrapped in his linen frock, through an open window.[23] Similarly, Martin Harris recounted that upon arriving home, Joseph "handed the plates in at the window," although according to his recollection, the plates "were received from him by his mother [Lucy Smith]."[24]

JOSIAH STOWELL, THE FIRST UNINTENTIONAL WITNESS

Josiah Stowell claimed he was the "first person that took the Plates out of [Joseph Smith's] hands the morning [he] brought them in."[25] Thus Josiah Stowell would have been the first witness to validate Joseph's claims of obtaining tangible plates. However, although Stowell's experience hefting the plates as they were passed to him—feeling of their weight, mass, and shape—constitutes a witness in itself, Josiah Stowell also claimed that he *saw* (albeit unintentionally) the exposed plates as they were passed to him by Joseph. Historians Michael MacKay and Gerrit Dirkmaat summarize what happened:

> In the summer of 1830, after Joseph Smith was charged with disorderly conduct, Stowell was called by the defense and sworn in as a witness. He testified under oath that he saw the plates the day Joseph first brought them home. As Joseph passed them through the window, Stowell caught a glimpse of the plates as a portion of the linen was pulled back. Stowell gave the court the dimensions of the plates and explained that they consisted of gold leaves with characters written on each sheet. The printed transcript of the trial read: "witness saw a corner of it; it resembled a stone of a greenish caste." Because Stowell also mentioned in his statement that the record was made of plates of gold, it is difficult to know what he meant by this description. He may have seen the band that sealed two-thirds of the plates together, which may have been made of copper that had oxidized over the years and turned green. Alternatively, he may have seen the breastplate, which could have also been made of copper and appeared green from oxidation. In any case, the point Stowell made to the court was that the plates were real and that he had seen and felt them.[26]

Stowell thus becomes the first unintentional witness, having an experience somewhat like that which the formal Eight Witnesses later had as they were allowed to heft and see the plates.

TANGIBLE AS OILCLOTHS

Others soon reported having tangible experiences with the plates or other relics Joseph had recovered from the Hill Cumorah. Some few days after Joseph brought the plates home, his mother said that her son called her down from her upstairs work on some oilcloths. Lucy reported, "I finally concluded to go down, and see what he wanted, upon which he handed me the breast-plate spoken of in his history. It was wrapped in a thin muslin handkerchief, so thin that I could see the glistening metal, and ascertain its proportions without any difficulty." Lucy proceeded to describe the breastplate:

> It was concave on one side, and convex on the other, and extended from the neck downwards, as far as the centre of the stomach of a man of extraordinary size. It had four straps of the same material, for the purpose of fastening it to the breast, two of which ran back to go over the shoulders, and the other two were designed to fasten to the hips. They were just the width of two of my fingers, (for I measured them,) and they had holes in the end of them, to be convenient in fastening. After I had examined it, Joseph placed it in the chest with the Urim and Thummim.[27]

Lucy also reported that she saw the Urim and Thummim, or Nephite interpreters. According to her, on the evening Joseph obtained the plates he handed her the spectacles wrapped only in a thin silk handkerchief through which she could see and discern their shape. "I've got a key [the Nephite interpreters]," Joseph told his mother when he came back that evening, and she "took the article of which he spoke into [her] hands."[28] Having examined the object, she later described the seer stones as two "three-cornered" stones set in "silver bows," connected with each other like "old fashioned spectacles." Lucy's experiences and accounts are yet another powerful witness to the tangible reality of Joseph's Book of Mormon origin story. Handling, feeling, measuring, and describing the breastplate and interpreters were not supernatural experiences, explained away by spiritual phenomena, but were as real and tactile as the very oilcloths Lucy had painted only moments before she handled these relics.

COOPER'S SHOP, HEARTHSTONES, AND BEANS

Joseph was warned by the angel Moroni when he took charge of the plates that people would seek to take them from him and that he would need to use all his efforts to preserve them. The Prophet's history relates:

> I soon found out the reason why I had received such strict charges to keep them safe and why it was that the messenger had said that when I had done what was required at my hand, he would call for them, for no sooner was it known that I had them than the most strenious exertions were used to get them from me. Every stratagem that could be invented was resorted to for that purpose. The persecution became more bitter and severe than before, and multitudes were on the alert continualy to get them from me if possible but by the wisdom of God they remained safe in my hands.[29]

Joseph's exertions to keep the plates safe are another example of the palpable reality of the objects obtained from the Hill Cumorah. Not long after bringing the plates home, Joseph was alerted through the Urim and Thummim of a company of men who were coming to find the plates. Joseph and others[30] pulled up the hearthstones from the family fireplace and dug a hole of sufficient size to bury the plates in. They then replaced the hearthstones to conceal what they had done, finishing just before the group of men arrived. According to Joseph Knight Sr., shortly after this Samuel Lawrence and "a grate Rodsman" came to Joseph Smith Sr.'s home and tried to bargain with Joseph Smith "to go shares" with them on the plates. When Joseph refused, the rodsman (whom Brigham Young later described as a wicked man having "possessed as much talent as any man that walked on the American soil")[31] "took out his Rods and hild [held] them up and they pointed Dow[n] to the harth whare they ware hid." The rodsman proclaimed, "It is under that harth."[32] No record exists about what transpired next, but although the rodsman had correctly identified where they were concealed, Joseph obviously succeeded in keeping the plates safe from his hands.

On another occasion, Joseph was apprised of another attempt by a mob to come and take the plates. He took the record from the wooden box, wrapped the plates in some clothes, and hid them in some flax in the second-story loft of the cooper's shop across the road from his parents' home. In order to divert the mob, Joseph nailed shut the box that had housed the plates and buried it in the floorboards of the ground level of the shop. That evening, the mob (following instructions given by Sally Chase after looking through her green seer stone) came and searched around the entire Smith property, and at Chase's instructions searched the cooper's shop. The next morning, Lucy Mack Smith later recalled, "we found the floor of the cooper's shop torn up, and the box which was laid under it shivered in pieces,"[33] but the plates were safe in the loft.

Another concealment of and tangible interaction with the plates came a few months later, when, to escape the harassment they were experiencing at Joseph Smith Sr.'s home in Manchester, Joseph and Emma Smith took up Emma's father's offer to live with him on his farm in Harmony, Pennsylvania. Joseph and Emma would make the move to Harmony in December of 1827. Their plans to relocate became known to a growing mob, who threatened Joseph that "he should never leave until he had shown the plates."[34] Fearful of being accosted by the mob and having his family's property searched until the plates were found, Joseph nailed the plates up in a wooden box and hid them in a barrel of beans, filling it a third of the way, depositing the plates, and then covering them over by filling up the rest of the barrel. Interestingly, Martin Harris, along with Joseph's brother-in-law Alva Hale, may have had a tangible interaction with the plates here, since Alva had come from Harmony to drive Joseph and Emma in his wagon. Although it is uncertain that Alva hefted or handled the box containing the plates, Harris claimed he personally helped Joseph move the box into the barrel of beans.[35] Those who helped Joseph secrete the plates and protect them—removing hearth stones and covering a wrapped relic, as well as loading it into a barrel of beans—provide additional accounts and proofs of a tangible record that had actually, not mystically, been entrusted to Joseph Smith to protect and eventually translate.

HEFTING THE PLATES

Some years before Joseph obtained the Book of Mormon plates, Joseph Smith Sr. had mentioned confidentially to Martin Harris that his son was seeking to obtain from God plates buried in the hill.[36] Although open to the idea, upon hearing that Joseph Smith had obtained a treasure from the Hill Cumorah, Martin Harris initially suggested that perhaps he merely had discovered an "old brass kettle,"[37] but not a divine record. After obtaining the plates, Joseph sent his mother to the Harrises to elicit Martin's support in the translation. A few days later, Martin's wife, Lucy, came to the Smiths' home and questioned Joseph about the record, requesting to see the plates, for which, if Joseph consented, she would lend him financial support. Joseph declined, telling Mrs. Harris that he couldn't show them to her, to which she responded, "Now, Joseph, are you not telling me a lie? Can you look full in my eye, and say before God, that you have in reality found a Record, as you pretend?"[38] Joseph later provided for Lucy Harris and her daughter a similar physical witness of the plates he offered to others: he let them lift the wooden box that contained the plates. Martin Harris recalled that his "daughter said, they were about as much as she could lift. . . . My wife said they were very heavy."[39]

Shortly after his wife's experience,[40] Martin Harris also received a tangible witness of the gold plates, hefting the box containing the plates at the Smith home. A few days after his wife's visit, Martin arrived at the Smith home and questioned various members of the family independently to verify the story of the plates. Later in the day, after Joseph had given Martin his account of finding the plates, Joseph allowed Martin the same experience he had given Martin's wife and daughter a few days earlier, giving him the box with the plates inside. Martin recalled, "While at Mr. Smith's I hefted the plates, and I knew from the heft that they were lead or gold, and I knew that Joseph had not credit enough to buy so much lead. I left Mr. Smith's about eleven o'clock and went home. I retired to my bedroom and prayed God to show me concerning these things, and I covenanted that if it was his work and he would show me so, I would put forth my best ability to bring it before the world. He then showed me that it was his work."[41] Harris stated in an 1859 interview that another man, apparently Alvah Beman, or "Old Mr. Beman" (who helped Joseph hide the plates and provided a box for them), also had the privilege of hefting the plates in the box, relating to Martin Harris that "he heard them jink, but he was not permitted to see them."[42] In that same interview, Harris stated that he "hefted the plates many times, and should think they weighed forty or fifty pounds."[43]

THUMBING AND FEELING THE PLATES

The Harrises and Mr. Beman were not the only ones to have tangible interaction with the plates. Many members of Joseph Smith's immediate family recall also having physical contact and other sensory experiences with the Book of Mormon record. Joseph Smith's little sister Katherine reported that on the day Joseph brought the plates home he handed them to her.[44] On another occasion she said that when cleaning in the Smith home, she "saw a package on the table containing the gold plates," which she picked up to judge the weight, finding them "heavy like gold." However, Katherine's experience moved beyond those who hefted the plates in the box. She said that through the package of cloth she "rippled her fingers up the edge of the plates and felt that they were separate metal plates and heard the tinkle of sound that they made."[45] Her witness of tangible plates moved from simply lifting to the senses of physical touch and sound.

Additionally, Joseph's little brother William, who was a teenager at the time, also recounted having palpable interaction with the Book of Mormon plates. William later wrote that he "hefted the plates as they lay on the table wrapped in an old frock or jacket in which Joseph had brought them home." William's experience was almost identical to that of his sister Katherine. He reported that he too had a tactile and auditory witness of the plates, recounting that he "had thumbed them through the cloth and ascertained that they were thin sheets of some kind of metal."[46]

Other than Joseph Smith, the person who had the most interaction with the tangible reality of the plates was the Prophet's wife, Emma Smith. She later recalled that after Joseph obtained the record, the plates "lay in a box under our bed for months but I never felt at liberty to look at them."[47] In a later interview with her son Joseph III, Emma recounted that when she and Joseph arrived in Harmony, Pennsylvania, she had given Joseph a small linen tablecloth to wrap the plates in. Emma explained that "the plates often lay on the table without any attempt at concealment," wrapped in this cloth.[48] She also recalled, "I once felt of the plates, as they thus lay on the table, tracing their outline and shape. They seemed to be pliable like thick paper, and would rustle with a metalic sound when the edges were moved by the thumb, as one does sometimes thumb the edges of a book."[49] Although some of Emma's answers on other topics in this interview are contrary to the historical record,[50] Emma's description of her tactile and auditory experience with the plates is remarkably consistent with William's and Katherine's descriptions.

Emma also moved the plates around in her Harmony home, as her son Joseph III remembered: "My mother told me that she . . . would lift and move [the plates] when she swept and dusted the room and furniture."[51] Although it would seem Emma naturally desired to view the plates (see Doctrine and Covenants 25:4), her experiences were more than sufficient for her witness of their reality. She told her son: "I knew that he [Joseph] had them, and was not specially curious about them. . . . I did not attempt to handle the plates, other than I have told you, nor uncover them to look at them. I was satisfied that it was the work of God, and therefore did not feel it to be necessary to do so."[52]

Another tactile experience with the plates is described in the testimony of Joseph's father-in-law, Isaac Hale. Joseph and Isaac had a strained relationship owing to Mr. Hale's disapproval of both Joseph's money-digging past and his marriage to Emma.[53] Upon returning to Harmony after eloping with Emma, according to Isaac Hale, Joseph had sworn to him that he had given up his treasure-searching past and that he intended "to work hard for a living."[54] A year into their marriage Joseph and Emma left Palmyra, New York, to live in a small home located on the Hale property in Harmony, Pennsylvania. Upon their arrival, Isaac Hale heard that Joseph had brought "a wonderful book of Plates down with them." Suspicious of Joseph because of his past claims, Isaac doubted the reality of Joseph's obtaining the Book of Mormon plates and confronted him about it. Joseph, under the sacred command given him of God through the angel Moroni to show the plates to nobody except whom God should command, but presumably wanting to allay his new father-in-law's suspicions and convince him that he indeed had an ancient record, offered to let Isaac Hale lift the wooden box containing the plates, just as he had let Lucy Harris, Martin Harris, and Alva Beaman do. Isaac Hale recounted, "I was allowed to feel the weight of the box, and they gave me to understand, that the book of plates was then in the box—into which, however, I was not allowed to look."[55]

Although this experience did not satisfy Isaac Hale as it had others,[56] it is nonetheless yet another example of someone who had a physical interaction with the tangible golden plates. Taking the collective experiences together of the many who did heft, handle, touch, feel, and ripple the plates and hear their metallic rustle during the protection period—along with the eleven formal witnesses who later saw the open plates—one is led to logically deduce, as did one scholar, that *at minimum* "what emerges as alone indisputable is the fact that Joseph Smith [did] possess a set of metal plates."[57]

CONCLUSION

While none of the individual accounts related herein affirms single-handedly the certitude of Joseph's having obtained a sacred record (let alone of translating it correctly), the multiple independently recorded experiences suggest with convincing evidence the existence of the tangible Book of Mormon plates and relics. Descriptions and witnesses of stone boxes from the Hill Cumorah, multiple persons who hefted the plates as they lay inside assorted wooden containers, and those who felt, traced, and outlined the shape of the plates and breastplate or Urim and Thummim through various cloth coverings—never mind the visible and tangible witness of the plates that would come from the eleven formal eyewitnesses of the Book of Mormon—indicate indisputable physicality with respect to the sacred record's origin.

Moreover, Joseph Smith never explained the Book of Mormon as a purely spiritual production of an imaginary people given to teach divine truths. Rather, he repeatedly and consistently declared that the Book of Mormon was an inspired translation done through the "gift, and power of God"[58] of a literal ancient record taken from a stone box from a nearby hill—actual plates created and recorded and preserved by historical prophets and physically entrusted to his care, plates that he really did hide, conceal, and protect and that others really did have tangible experiences with.[59] The Lord has revealed that the translation of that record is true (see Doctrine and Covenants 17:6). The experiences, records, and accounts of various persons who interacted tangibly with the relics of the Book of Mormon during the protection period from September 1827 to the early winter of 1828, taken collectively, confirm that the origin story of the Book of Mormon record is equally true.

Anthony Sweat is an associate teaching professor of Church history and doctrine at BYU.

Anthony Sweat, "Hefted and Handled: Tangible Interactions with Book of Mormon Objects," in *The Coming Forth of the Book of Mormon: A Marvelous Work and a Wonder*, ed. Dennis L. Largey, Andrew H. Hedges, John Hilton III, and Kerry Hull (Provo, UT: Religious Studies Center, Brigham Young University; Salt Lake City: Deseret Book, 2015), 43–59.

NOTES

1. In *The Joseph Smith Papers, Histories*, 1:232 (hereafter *JSP*, H1).
2. See Terryl L. Givens, "'Devices of the Devil': The Book of Mormon as Cultural Product or Sacred Fiction," in *By the Hand of Mormon: The American Scripture That Launched a New World Religion* (New York: Oxford University Press, 2002), 155–84. See also, for example, sociologist Rodney Stark's comparison of Joseph Smith's unique production of modern scripture to Shakespeare's creation of literature and Mozart's musical compositions: "Suppose that someone with the literary gifts of William Shakespeare underwent a series of mental events he or she interpreted as contact with the supernatural. Would it not be likely that the revelations produced in this way would be messages of depth, beauty, and originality? . . . The case of Joseph Smith is remarkably similar." Rodney Stark, *The Rise of Mormonism*, ed. Reid L. Nielson (New York: Columbia University Press, 2005), 40, 42.
3. As William E. McLellin, who served as a scribe for one of Joseph's revelations, described it: "The scribe seats himself at a desk or table, with pen, ink and paper.

The subject of enquiry being understood, the Prophet and Revelator enquires of God. He spiritually sees, hears and feels, and then speaks as he is moved upon by the Holy Ghost, the 'thus saith the Lord,' sentence after sentence." In *The Joseph Smith Papers, Documents*, 1:xxxiii (hereafter *JSP*, D1).

4. Givens, *By the Hand of Mormon*, 178.

5. See Andrew H. Hedges, "'All My Endeavors to Preserve Them': Protecting the Plates in Palmyra, 22 September–December 1827," *Journal of Book of Mormon Studies* 8, no. 2 (1999): 14–23. This work has been foundational to the present study.

6. See Michael Hubbard MacKay and Gerrit J. Dirkmaat, *From Darkness unto Light: Joseph Smith's Translation and Publication of the Book of Mormon* (Provo, UT: Religious Studies Center, Brigham Young University; Salt Lake City: Deseret Book, 2015). This work has been vital to the present study. I am particularly indebted to Michael MacKay for his generous help in providing me with source material from his research for many of the historical accounts related herein.

7. Lucy Smith, *Biographical Sketches of Joseph Smith the Prophet and His Progenitors for Many Generations* (Liverpool: S. W. Richards, 1853), 100.

8. Joseph Knight had apparently not given Joseph permission to take his wagon, for when Knight awoke the next morning and found his horse and wagon missing, he was alarmed that it had been stolen, concluding "that a rogue had stolen them," according to Lucy Smith in her *Biographical Sketches of Joseph Smith*, 101. See also Joseph Knight's Recollection that in the morning "my Horse and Carriage was gone," in Dean C. Jessee, "Joseph Knight's Recollection of Early Mormon History," *BYU Studies* 17, no. 1 (1976): 33.

9. In *JSP*, H1:232.

10. Lucy Smith wrote that "he had deposited [the plates] in a cavity in a birch log 3 miles distant and he too covered it with the bark of the same." Lucy Mack Smith, History, 1844–1845, book 5, p. [11]; book 6, p. [2], Church History Library, The Church of Jesus Christ of Latter-day Saints, Salt Lake City; and Joseph Smith, History, vol. A-1, in *JSP*, H1:8. On Martin Harris's statement that the plates were originally concealed in a hollowed-out tree, see Joel Tiffany, "Mormonism," *Tiffany's Monthly*, August 1859, 165.

11. See Hedges, "'All My Endeavors to Preserve Them,'" 14–23. Hedges summarizes multiple efforts of persons such as Samuel Lawrence, Willard Chase, and Sally Chase to take the plates because "Lawrence and perhaps others had learned of the plates' existence through 'revelation' from illegitimate sources" (p. 19).

12. Testimony of Willard Chase, Manchester, NY, 1833, as cited in Eber D. Howe, *History of Mormonism, or, A Faithful Account of That Singular Imposition and Delusion* (Painesville, OH: 1840), 243.

13. Jessee, "Joseph Knight's Recollection," 32.

14. *Kansas City Daily Journal*, June 5, 1881; reprinted in the *Deseret Evening News*, June 11, 1881; emphasis added.

15. "The Last Man," *Chicago Times*, October 17, 1881, as cited in George Reynolds, *The Myth of the "Manuscript Found"* (Salt Lake City: Juvenile Instructor Office, 1883), 82; emphasis added.

16. Ole A. Jensen, "Testimony of Martin Harris," MS 5569, folder 1, Church History Library.

17. Edward Stevenson, *Reminiscences of Joseph, the Prophet, and the Coming Forth of the Book of Mormon* (Salt Lake City: n.p., 1893), 10, 13.

18. Joseph Smith, History, vol. A-1, 9.

19. Lucy Smith states that Joseph "went to bring the record which he had deposited in a cavity in a birch log 3 miles distant." Lucy Smith, History, book 5, p. [11].

20. Lucy Smith, *Biographical Sketches of Joseph Smith*, 102.

21. Lucy Smith, *Biographical Sketches of Joseph Smith*, 104. Lucy mentioned here that Joseph kept the Urim and Thummim "constantly about his person."

22. Herbert S. Salisbury, "Things the Prophet's Sister Told Me," July 2, 1945, Secure Stacks manuscript, MS 4122 2, folder 1, Church History Library.

23. Martha Campbell to Joseph Smith, December 19, 1843, Church History Library. Because both Lucy Smith and Josiah Stowell were present when Joseph handed the plates in at the window, perhaps they both helped or carried them simultaneously.

24. Tiffany, "Mormonism," 166.

25. Martha Campbell to Joseph Smith, December 19, 1843.

26. MacKay and Dirkmaat, *From Darkness unto Light*, 13.

27. Lucy Smith, *Biographical Sketches of Joseph Smith*, 107.

28. Lucy Smith, *Biographical Sketches of Joseph Smith*, 101.

29. Joseph Smith, History, vol. A-1, 9.

30. See Lucy Smith, *Biographical Sketches*, 108; and Jessee, "Joseph Knight's Recollection," 33–34.

31. Brigham Young, in *Journal of Discourses*, 2:180.

32. Jessee, "Joseph Knight's Recollection," 34. There are conflicting accounts and confusion about who this great rodsman was. Joseph Knight Sr. identified him as "Beeman," perhaps confusing Alvah Beaman, who had helped Joseph hide the plates under the fireplace, as the rodsman.

33. Lucy Smith, *Biographical Sketches of Joseph Smith*, 109.

34. Martin Harris, as quoted in Tiffany, "Mormonism," 170.

35. See Joseph Smith, History, vol. A-1, 5; and Tiffany, "Mormonism," 170.

36. See Hedges, "'All My Endeavors to Preserve Them,'" 18.

37. Tiffany, "Mormonism," 167.

38. Lucy Smith, *Biographical Sketches of Joseph Smith*, 111.

39. Tiffany, "Mormonism," 168.

40. It should be noted that Lucy Harris later denied having ever believed in the reality of the Book of Mormon record. She said the religion of Mormonism "was false" and called it a "delusion." E. D. Howe, *Mormonism Unvailed* (Painesville, OH: E. D. Howe, 1834), 256.

41. Tiffany, "Mormonism," 169–70.

42. Tiffany, "Mormonism," 167.

43. Tiffany, "Mormonism," 166.

44. See Mary Salisbury Hancock, "The Three Sisters of Joseph Smith," *Saints' Herald*, January 11, 1954, 12.

45. "The Prophet's Sister Testifies She Lifted the B of M Plates," *The Messenger* (Berkeley, CA), October 1954, 1, 6. See also Dan Vogel, comp., *Early Mormon Documents* (Salt Lake City: Signature Books, 1996), 1:649.

46. Martha Campbell to Joseph Smith, December 19, 1843.

47. Nels Madsen and Parley P. Pratt, interview of Emma Smith Bidamon, 1877, Secure Stacks manuscript, MS 852, Church History Library, Salt Lake City.

48. "Last Testimony of Sister Emma," *Saints' Herald*, October 1, 1879, 290.

49. "Last Testimony of Sister Emma," 290.

50. For example, when asked in this same interview, "Did he [Joseph Smith] not have other wives than yourself?" Emma responded, "He had no other wife but me; nor

did he to my knowledge ever have." This response is inconsistent with the historical record. See Brian C. Hales, "Emma and Hyrum Accept Plural Marriage," in *Joseph Smith's Polygamy* (Salt Lake City: Greg Kofford Books, 2013), 2:33–61.

51. Joseph Smith III to Mrs. E. Horton, March 7, 1900, Community of Christ Library–Archives, as cited in Vogel, *Early Mormon Documents*, 1:546–47.

52. "Last Testimony of Sister Emma," 290.

53. Isaac described Joseph at this time as a "careless young man" and "insolent to his father" and that he "followed a business [treasure searching through seer stones] I could not approve." Isaac Hale Statement, 1834, in Vogel, *Early Mormon Documents*, 4:284–85.

54. Isaac Hale Statement, 4:285.

55. Isaac Hale Statement, 4:286. See also Howe, *Mormonism Unvailed*, 257–58.

56. Isaac Hale said of the experience that he was "dissatisfied, and informed him [Joseph] that if there was any thing in my house of that description [the plates], which I could not be allowed to see, he must take it away; if he did not, I was determined to see it. After that, the Plates were said to be hid in the woods." Isaac Hale Statement, 4:286.

57. Givens, *By the Hand of Mormon*, 40. Although it is possible that Joseph Smith could have fabricated a set of metal plates as a prop to support his story, Martin Harris stated that he knew Joseph lacked sufficient money or credit to do so: "I knew that Joseph had not credit enough to buy so much lead" to fabricate the plates himself. Tiffany, "Mormonism," 169–70.

58. Joseph Smith, "Church History," in *JSP*, H1:495.

59. Read this detailed, physical description of the plates as an example: "I was also told [by the angel Moroni] where there was deposited some plates on which were engraven an abridgement of the records of the ancient prophets that had existed on this continent. . . . These record were engraven on plates which had the appearance of gold, each plate was six inches wide and eight inches long and not quite so thick as common tin. They were filled with engravings, in Egyptian characters and bound together in a volume, as the leaves of a book with three rings running through the whole. The volume was something near six inches in thickness, a part of which was sealed. . . . Through the medium of the Urim and Thummim I translated the record by the gift, and power of God." Joseph Smith, "Church History," in *JSP*, H1:495.

Chapter Seven

The Restoration of the Priesthoods

RONALD O. BARNEY

Joseph Smith was "about the age of twelve years" when concerns about God and Jesus and his standing before them first stirred his soul.[1] He had grown up in a home with parents who disagreed on the matter of religion. Being drawn to the Presbyterian faith, rooted in Calvinism, his mother, Lucy Mack Smith, held beliefs shaped by the religious doctrine that had dominated the British colonies before the American Revolution. Joseph's father's views about God's earthly work, characterized as Universalism, were considered by local ministers as a perverted form of religion. Though Joseph leaned toward the teachings of the Methodists, a denomination considerably different from the Calvinists that had grown significantly after the Revolution, he likely did not attend church regularly, meaning he was not overly familiar with pulpits and pews. And while he had been taught to read and believe in the Bible as a boy, he had not been saturated with religion as were other young people around him. Not surprisingly, as he grew older he grew more confused about God and his work on earth, as well as his own spiritual welfare. But because he acted on his yearnings for greater knowledge, what followed in his life led to significant religious events, preparing the world for the Savior's Second Coming.

THE NECESSITY OF ANGELIC DELIVERY OF PRIESTHOOD POWERS

After Joseph's initial experiences with God and Jesus in 1820, the appearance of Moroni to him in 1823 and thereafter, resulting in his acquisition of gold plates, inaugurated the young man's prophetic future. While he translated the Book of Mormon, the matter of God's earthly authority became a concern to the young prophet and his scribe, Oliver Cowdery. They had come across a discussion dealing with baptism and the remission of sins and wondered about the authority to perform the baptismal ordinance. As they prayed in the woods for answers, an angel visited them and restored the authority to perform valid baptisms. At the time this authority was called the "lesser" priesthood and was later defined as the Aaronic Priesthood.[2]

Some may wonder why Moroni, as part of his role in the restoration of the gospel, did not transmit his own godly authority during his many visitations to Joseph preceding the delivery of the plates. Elder Orson Pratt, one of the Church's early Twelve Apostles, addressed this question:

> A revelation and restoration to the earth of the *everlasting gospel* through the angel Moroni would be of no benefit to the nations, unless someone should be ordained with authority to preach it and administer its ordinances. . . . Did Moroni ordain Mr. [Joseph] Smith to the [priesthood and] apostleship, and command him to administer ordinances? No, he did not. But why not confer authority by ordination, as well as reveal the everlasting gospel? Because in all probability he had not the right to do so. All angels have not the same authority.[3]

Apparently, Moroni was not given the authority to restore the lost priesthoods.

THE GRADUAL UNFOLDING OF THE RESTORED GOSPEL

If Joseph Smith had made up the stories of his experiences with Deity and with other heavenly beings, as some have claimed, he could have simplified his assertions by reporting that not only did Moroni give him the golden plates, but he also authorized him to do everything else required by God to restore and organize a church in the latter days. It would have been as believable as any other explanation. As it turned out, because of his instincts of protecting his sacred experiences, Joseph revealed over time the sometimes complicated, step-by-step process involved in the restoration of the gospel, which included the specific restoration of God's authority to the earth.

The comprehension of priesthood authority developed in the same manner that we all gain understanding. Elder Neal A. Maxwell noted that the divine procedure of giving "unto the faithful line upon line, precept upon precept" created a "gradual unfolding" that characterized "the history of God's work."[4] Elder Boyd K. Packer clarified further that the entirety of the restoration of the gospel, including the priesthood, must be considered in this light. He stated: "Some suppose that the organization was handed to the Prophet Joseph Smith like a set of plans and specifications for a building, with all of the details known at the beginning. But it did not come that way. Rather, it came a piece at a time as the Brethren were ready and as they inquired of God."[5] Even the concept of authority, as it was initially understood and later more broadly known as priesthood, crystalized over time in the mind of Joseph Smith through revelation and visitations by angelic beings. The surviving historical record confirms this understanding. It also sheds light on the delivery from heavenly messengers of the priesthood of God that at the beginning gave Joseph Smith power to perform authentic baptisms and organize a church, followed later by other prophetic powers.

THE "LESSER" OR AARONIC PRIESTHOOD

In 1829 Joseph Smith and his wife of two years, Emma Hale Smith, lived in a small frame home in a village in northeastern Pennsylvania known as Harmony (today called Oakland). The Smith home, located near Emma's parents' home adjacent to the Susquehanna River, became a particularly important site in the unfolding process of restoring the fulness of the gospel.[6] But Joseph and Emma were not alone in their efforts. Oliver Cowdery became acquainted with Joseph Smith's family by 1829 while he was living near Palmyra, New York. He heard about Joseph's work, and after receiving a visitation from Jesus Christ declaring the work in which Joseph was involved to be true,[7] Oliver moved from New York to Harmony in April 1829 and became Joseph Smith's scribe. While they worked together in the middle of May 1829 translating the plates—Joseph dictating and Oliver transcribing—they arrived at the point in the story where Jesus appeared to the Nephites. Coincident to translating the book of 3 Nephi, Oliver realized that in the current religious climate "it was easily to be seen, that amid the great strife and noise concerning religion, none had authority from God to administer the ordinances of the gospel."

Oliver recorded that after "writing the account given of the Savior's ministry" to those who lived "upon this continent," he and Joseph determined to pray to God about the matter. The result was that he and Joseph were visited by an angel:

> On a sudden, as from the midst of eternity, the voice of the Redeemer spake peace to us, while the vail was parted and the angel of God came down clothed with glory, and delivered the anxiously looked for message. . . . What joy! what wonder! what amazement! . . . our eyes beheld—our ears heard. As in the "blaze of day;" yes, more—above the glitter of the May Sun beam, which then shed its brilliancy over the face of nature! Then his voice, though mild, pierced to the center, and his words, "I am thy fellow servant," dispelled every fear. We listened—we gazed—we admired! 'Twas the voice of the angel from glory—'twas a message from the Most High! and as we heard we rejoiced, while his love enkindled upon our souls, and we were rapt in the vision of the Almighty! Where was room for doubt? No where: uncertainty had fled, doubt had sunk, no more to rise, while fiction and deception had fled forever!

The angel's visitation, besides confirming to Joseph and Oliver their recognition that they were now part of something much larger than themselves, involved the actual bestowal of divine authority. Oliver continued: "We received under his hand the holy priesthood as he said, 'upon you my fellow servants, in the name of Messiah, I confer this priesthood and this authority, which shall remain upon earth that the sons of Levi may yet offer an offering unto the Lord in righteousness!'. . . The assurance that we were in the presence of an angel; the certainty that we heard the voice of Jesus, and the truth unsullied as it flowed from a pure personage, dictated by the will of God, is to me, past description."[8]

Now with authorization to do so, Joseph Smith "by the direction of the angel" baptized his friend Oliver, "the first received into this church, in this day."[9] Joseph, in his own account of the visitation, prepared in 1838–1839, said that following Oliver's baptism, "afterwards he baptized me."[10] When the baptisms were performed, Joseph continued, "I laid my hands upon his head and ordained him to the Aaronick priesthood, and afterward he laid his hands on me and ordained me to the same priesthood, for so we were commanded."[11]

The Restoration of the Aaronic Priesthood, by Del Parson. © Intellectual Reserve, Inc.

THE "GREATER" OR MELCHIZEDEK PRIESTHOOD

To the young men, the reception of heavenly power to perform the gateway ordinance of baptism at the time became of paramount importance. In

113

Joseph Smith's portrayal of the event, which he noted occurred on May 15, 1829, the same angel, whom he identified as John the Baptist, promised that if Joseph Smith and Oliver Cowdery "continued faithful," besides the "priesthood of Aaron," they "should also have the Melchesidec Priesthood" given to them.[12] While both Oliver and Joseph created a brief narrative of their experience with John the Baptist, there is a lack of certainty as to whether it was their intent to recount the reception of the higher or greater priesthood from Peter, James, and John, as they both did regarding the lesser priesthood. At any rate, such a portrayal was never prepared for publication.

Nonetheless, in October 1835 Joseph affirmed the experiences he and Oliver had with the angel bestowing on them the "lesser priesthood" and with the ancient Apostles Peter, James, and John bestowing the greater priesthood. In a blessing he gave to Oliver, recorded on paper but never meant for public and institutional purposes, Joseph stated that they obtained "by the hand of the angel . . . the lesser priesthood," which was then amplified when they received the greater priesthood "under the hands of th<ose> who had been held in reserve for a long season, even those who rescived it under the hand of the Messiah."[13]

Oliver Cowdery also later declared several times that he, with Joseph, had indeed received a divine manifestation in which they were given the greater priesthood of Melchizedek. In 1846 Oliver wrote to one of his close friends, his brother-in-law Phineas Young, and related his experience with the angels: "Had you stood in the presence of John, with our departed Joseph, to receive the Lesser Priesthood—and in the presence of Peter, to receive the Greater . . . you would feel what you have never felt."[14] Oliver, who had been out of sorts with the Church since 1838 and who could have denied the heavenly visitations, undermining more effectively than any other single person the truth claims of Joseph Smith, instead verified his and Joseph's experience with heavenly beings.

In October 1848 Oliver, in a remarkable setting, provided additional verification of his encounter. The Saints had temporarily relocated westward of the Missouri River en route to Utah after being driven from Nauvoo, Illinois, and were holding a regular conference. But as it turned out, the meeting became no regular gathering. Oliver Cowdery, still out of the Church, apparently visited the conference unannounced, intent on reuniting with his former friends. Invited to speak before the audience, Oliver, besides emphasizing his witness of the authenticity of the Book of Mormon, declared to attendees: "I was present with Joseph when an holy angle from god came down from heaven and confered, or restored the Aronic priesthood. And said at the same time that it should remain upon the earth while the earth stands. I was also present with Joseph when the Melchizedek priesthood was confered by the holy angles of god."[15] He was accepted by the Saints and was rebaptized shortly thereafter.[16]

In Joseph Smith's account of the visitation of the ancient apostles, he stated that once he and Oliver Cowdery had been ordained by Jesus's Apostles, they "for some time [had] made this [restoration of authority] a subject of humble prayer." They were surely uncertain about the grand scope of what they had experienced. Later, gathered at the home of Peter Whitmer Sr., where the Church would later be organized, "the Word of the Lord came unto us, in the Chamber [of the Whitmer home] commanding us, that I should ordain Oliver Cowdery to be an Elder in the Church of Jesus Christ, and that he also should ordain me to the same office, and that after having been thus ordained, we should proceed to ordain others to the same office."[17] The authority necessary to empower the Church to perform valid baptisms and to administer in the other functions of the priesthood, including organizing a church itself, had been given by heavenly messengers to Joseph Smith and Oliver Cowdery.[18]

But this was not the final delivery of divine power to Joseph and Oliver. Again, had Joseph contrived God's preoccupation with him, he could have bundled the entirety of God's authority in the person of Moroni. But not only did he define the separate functions and purposes of the "lesser" and "greater" priesthoods, he further described other specific priesthood powers he had been given as conveyed by the ancient prophets of God.[19]

PRIESTHOOD RESTORATION IN THE KIRTLAND HOUSE OF THE LORD

The "lesser" and "greater" priesthoods had empowered the Prophet Joseph and his associates since 1829. Much had been done to expand the growing church, particularly the gathering of the elect through missionary efforts.[20] After outside pressure and the surge of Church membership in Ohio's Western Reserve, Joseph and the Church relocated from New York to Ohio. There other powers of authority were bestowed on Joseph and Oliver. In Kirtland, Ohio, Joseph received a revelation that a "house of God" should be built, a sanctuary where God could further reveal important information.[21] After three years of sacrifice and difficulty, the temple was completed and awaited dedication in the spring of 1836. The dedicatory services for the temple at the end of March and early part of April included another of the important components of priesthood restoration to the early Church, though it has not generally been connected with priesthood restoration like the lesser and greater priesthoods. There were, as witnessed by numerous attendees, remarkable spiritual events that accompanied the solemn assembly and the temple's dedication at the end of March. But it was on April 3, when Joseph Smith and Oliver Cowdery were in the western pulpits of the lower court of the house of the Lord, that the most noted occurrence of the dedicatory period took place. Some have argued that the event paralleled the great New Testament vision on the Mount of Transfiguration where Jesus participated in the transfer of prophetic authority to his Apostles Peter, James, and John.[22]

The significant event of April 3, 1836, was described in Joseph's own journal, likely shortly after the event occurred, penned by his scribe at the time, Oliver Cowdery's brother Warren. According to the prophet's rehearsal, after Jesus appeared to Joseph and Oliver to accept the labors of the Saints in constructing the house of the Lord, a singular moment in itself, the account states that Joseph and Oliver acquired something that perhaps they did not expect: significant divine authority from heavenly messengers that opened more doors as part of the restoration of all things. "The heavens were again opened unto us; and Moses appeared before us. . . . After this, Elias appeared. . . . After this vision had closed, another great and glorious vision burst upon us; for Elijah the prophet, who was taken to heaven without tasting death, stood before us."[23] Thus, after Jesus appeared, Joseph and Oliver were successively visited by Moses, Elias, and Elijah, all administering their particular priesthood powers held during their biblical ministries.

This great episode was part of the larger restoration plan, as described by Joseph to the Saints, where "in the ushering in of the dispensation of the fulness of times" it was required "that a whole and complete and perfect union, and welding together of dispensations, and keys, and powers, and glories should take place." This restoration included revelations and bestowal of authority held by ancient prophets "from the days of Adam even to the present time." But, he told the Saints, "not only this, but those things which never have been revealed from the foundation of the world, but have been kept hid from the wise and prudent, shall be revealed unto babes and sucklings in this, the dispensation of the fulness of times." It was required, according to the prophet, that each of the prophetic figures gave to him "their dispensation, their rights, *their keys*, their honors, their majesty and glory, and *the power of their priesthood*; giving line upon line, precept upon precept; here a little, and there a little."[24] The dramatic panorama of priesthood restoration may appear complicated, but the "dispensation" given to Joseph Smith required all of the power and authority held by the ancient prophets. Joseph Smith testified to the Saints that these priesthood keys had been restored.[25]

DISCLOSURE OF PRIESTHOOD RESTORATION ACCOUNTS

There is one last factor to consider in understanding priesthood restoration. The inquirer may ask, "If priesthood restoration was of such consequence to the early Church, then why didn't Joseph Smith and Oliver Cowdery run to the local newspapers after their visitations to have published what had happened to them?" There are several explanations for the lack of documentation, only two of which will be given here. The first is that given by Joseph himself just after recording his own 1838–1839 account: "we were forced to keep secret the circumstances of our having been baptized, and having received this priesthood; owing to the spirit of persecution which had already manifested itself in the neighborhood."[26] Because both men desired to protect their divine experiences from public attention and ridicule, the accounts revealing the events of priesthood restoration were initially kept in confidence.

This was consistent with the behavior of other prophetic figures who preceded them. During the course of translating the Book of Mormon, for example, Joseph repeated this significant passage to Oliver: "It is given unto many to know the mysteries of God; nevertheless they are laid under a strict command that they shall not impart only according to the portion of his word which he doth grant unto the children of men."[27] In other words, those who receive revelation from God are "under a strict command" to keep it to themselves and share it only as appropriate. While receiving the revelation known as the Book of Moses, Joseph was twice counseled to be discreet: "show them not unto any except them that believe" and "see thou show them unto no man, until I command you, except to them that believe."[28] Clearly there was a sensibility emphasized here that could not have escaped Joseph, which imposed restraint in revealing the revelations of God before it was appropriate.

Not only did Joseph understand this principle, he tried to teach this precept to Church leaders, helping them to understand that keeping sacred experiences sacred was expected of all to whom the Lord revealed sacred matters. In November 1835 Joseph taught the newly called Quorum of the

Twelve about the anticipated outpouring of spiritual gifts as they prepared for the solemn assembly associated with the dedication of the Kirtland Temple. Regarding their ministries, his scribe recorded him stating: "We must be clean every whit. Let us be faithful and silent brethren, and if God gives you a manifestation, keep it to yourself."[29] Thus it is not surprising that Joseph Smith and Oliver Cowdery kept their sacred experiences to themselves until it was required and appropriate that they explain the essential restoration of the priesthood.[30]

With the powers and priesthood that God gave to his ancient prophets now possessed by Joseph Smith and Oliver Cowdery, they could, under the direction of God, perform valid baptisms, give the gift of the Holy Ghost, and organize a church. Joseph F. Smith said in 1894 of Joseph Smith:

> We must not forget the fact that he was the man out of the millions of human beings that inhabited this earth at the time—the only man, that was called of God, by the voice of God Himself, to open up the dispensation of the Gospel to the world for the last time; and this is the great thing to bear in mind, that he was called of God to introduce the Gospel to the world, to restore the holy priesthood to the children of men, to organize the Church of Jesus Christ of Latter-day Saints in the world, and to restore all the ordinances of the Gospel, for the salvation not only of the living, but also of the dead. . . .
>
> He also communed with the Father and the Son and spoke with angels, and they visited him, and conferred blessings and gifts and keys of power upon him that were never before bestowed upon any human being other than the Son of God himself. No man yet that ever lived upon the earth had all the keys of the Gospel and of the dispensations bestowed upon him as were bestowed upon the Prophet Joseph Smith.[31]

The restoration of the priesthood played a central role in the restoration of the gospel through Joseph Smith. But it was not simply a delivery of the "lesser" and "greater" priesthoods to the Prophet and Oliver Cowdery in 1829. It was far more complex and impressive in scope than is generally recognized. The larger understanding of this perspective leads to a greater appreciation of Joseph Smith's significant role in the unfolding of the Lord's work in the "dispensation of the fulness of times."[32]

Ronald O. Barney is a retired historian and archivist for the history department of The Church of Jesus Christ of Latter-day Saints. He is also a former associate editor of The Joseph Smith Papers.

Ronald O. Barney, "The Restoration of the Priesthoods," in *A Reason for Faith: Navigating LDS Doctrine and Church History*, ed. Laura H. Hales (Provo, UT: Religious Studies Center, Brigham Young University; Salt Lake City: Deseret Book, 2016), 59–68.

NOTES

1. In *The Joseph Smith Papers, Histories*, 1:11 (hereafter *JSP*, H1).
2. See Joseph Smith, History Drafts, 1838-circa 1841, Draft 2, in *JSP*, H1:294.
3. Orson Pratt, *Divine Authority, or the Question, Was Joseph Smith Sent of God?* (Liverpool: R. James, 1851), 4. See Orson Pratt, "The Question Answered, Was Joseph Smith Sent of God?," *Frontier Guardian*, February 7, 1849.
4. Neal A. Maxwell, "Out of Obscurity," *Ensign*, November 1984, 8–11.
5. Boyd K. Packer, "The Twelve Apostles," *Ensign*, November 1996, 6.
6. See Mark Lyman Staker, "Where Was the Aaronic Priesthood Restored? Identifying the Location of John the Baptist's Appearance, May 15, 1829," *Mormon Historical Studies* 12, no. 2 (Fall 2011): 143–59.
7. See *JSP*, H1:16.
8. Oliver Cowdery to W. W. Phelps, September 7, 1834, Norton, Ohio, *Latter Day Saints' Messenger and Advocate* 1, no. 1 (October 1834): 15–16.
9. Cowdery to Phelps, September 7, 1834.
10. In *JSP*, H1:294.
11. In *JSP*, H1:294.
12. In *JSP*, H1:326.
13. Joseph Smith blessing to Oliver Cowdery, October 2, 1835, Patriarchal Blessing Book, Book 1, p. 12, Church History Library, The Church of Jesus Christ of Latter-day Saints, Salt Lake City (hereafter CHL); see *JSP, Documents*, 5:513–14. Another extremely important entry in the Patriarchal Blessing Book prepared by Oliver Cowdery in September 1835, one also never meant for public distribution, is a personal narrative of his and Joseph's experience with the angel delivering the lesser priesthood. He wrote that they "diligently sought for the right of the fathers, and the authority of the holy priesthood, and the power to admin[ister] in the same." Consequently they were "drawn out in mighty prayer to know how we might obtain the blessings of baptism and of the Holy Spirit, according to the order of God." In their amazement while in "the heavenly vision the angel came down and bestowed upon us this priesthood." That is, the "angel John" appeared to them and ordained them "unto the lesser or Aaronic priesthood . . . in the town of Harmony, Susquehannah County, Pennsylvania, on Fryday, the 15th day of May, 1829." Oliver Cowdery narrative, Patriarchal Blessing Book, Book 1, pp. 8–9.
14. Oliver Cowdery to Phineas Young, March 23, 1846, Tiffin, Ohio, CHL.
15. Reuben Miller, Journal, October 21, 1848, CHL. See George A. Smith to Orson Pratt, October 31 postscript to October 20, 1848, letter, Carbonca, Council Bluffs, Iowa, *Latter Day Saints' Millennial Star* 11, no. 1 (January 1, 1849): 14.

16. Oliver Cowdery is also reported to have written to Samuel W. Richards in January 1849, again affirming his experiences with Joseph and the heavenly messengers who bestowed on them the priesthoods. See John W. Welch, ed., *Opening the Heavens: Accounts of Divine Manifestations, 1820–1844* (Provo, UT: Brigham Young University Press; Salt Lake City: Deseret Book, 2005), 245, 261n31.

17. In *JSP*, H1:326.

18. See the broad overview of restoration of the priesthoods in the Church's first generation in Ronald O. Barney, *Joseph Smith: History, Methods, and Memory* (Salt Lake City: University of Utah Press, 2020), 161–222.

19. It must be recognized that clarity about the two priesthoods, their authorities, and exact purposes as is known today was during Joseph Smith's lifetime never well understood by Church members. As previously suggested, it took a number of years for the implications of what Joseph and Oliver had received to be comprehended, articulated, and then instituted among Church leaders and members. See Barney, *Joseph Smith*, 183–85.

20. See Doctrine and Covenants 29:7; 33:6–12 (1981 edition).

21. Doctrine and Covenants 88:119.

22. See Matthew 17.

23. Joseph Smith, Journal, April 3, 1836, in *JSP, Journals*, 1:219–22.

24. "Letter from Joseph Smith," *Times and Seasons* 3, no. 23 (October 1, 1842): 935–36; emphasis added. This letter became part of the 1876 edition of the Doctrine and Covenants as section 128 and was canonized in an 1880 general conference of the Church. The cited language can be found in verses 18, 20–21.

25. The Prophet also identified several others of those who delivered to him their authorities in this context. See Doctrine and Covenants 128:21.

26. In *JSP*, H1:294.

27. Alma 12:9.

28. Moses 1:42; 4:32.

29. Joseph Smith, Journal, November 12, 1835, in *JSP*, J1:98; punctuation and capitalization standardized.

30. See the explanation of how Joseph Smith's personality and experiences influenced the manner in which he disclosed what had happened to him in Barney, *Joseph Smith*, 271–91.

31. Joseph F. Smith, "Recollections of the Prophet," in *Collected Discourses*, ed. Brian H. Stuy, 5 vols. (Burbank and Woodland Hills, CA: B. H. S. Publishing, 1987–1992), 5:27–29.

32. See Doctrine and Covenants 121:31.

Selected RSC Publications on Church History in New England, New York, and Pennsylvania, 1805–1830

GENERAL READING

Holzapfel, Richard Neitzel, and Kent P. Jackson, eds. *Joseph Smith, the Prophet and Seer* (2010).

MacKay, Michael Hubbard, and William G. Hartley, eds. *The Rise of the Latter-day Saints: The Journals and Histories of Newel Knight* (2019).

Marsh, W. Jeffrey, ed. *Joseph Smith and the Doctrinal Restoration* (2005).

Ostler, Craig James, Michael Hubbard MacKay, and Barbara Morgan Gardner, eds. *Foundations of the Restoration: Fulfillment of the Covenant Purposes* (2016).

JOSEPH SMITH'S CHILDHOOD AND YOUTH

Cannon, Donald Q., and Arnold K. Garr, eds. *Regional Studies in Latter-day Saint Church History: The New England States* (2004).

Welch, Nathan R. "Joseph Smith's Childhood Illness." *Religious Educator* 10, no. 3 (2009): 131–36.

FIRST VISION

Bennett, Richard E. *1820: Dawning of the Restoration* (2020).

Dodge, Samuel Alonzo, and Steven C. Harper, eds. *Exploring the First Vision* (2012).

Haws, J. B. "Reconciling Joseph Smith—History 1:10 and 1:18–19." *Religious Educator* 14, no. 2 (2013): 97–105.

Holzapfel, Richard Neitzel, Donald L. Enders, Robert F. Parrot, and Larry C. Porter. "Return to the Sacred Grove." *Religious Educator* 11, no. 2 (2010): 147–57.

TRANSLATION OF THE BOOK OF MORMON

Baugh, Alexander L., ed. *Days Never to Be Forgotten: Oliver Cowdery* (2009).

Bennett, Richard E. "Joseph Smith and the First Principles of the Gospel." *Religious Educator* 11, no. 2 (2010): 11–29.

Harper, Steven C. "Evaluating the Book of Mormon Witnesses." *Religious Educator* 11, no. 2 (2010): 37–49.

———. "Joseph Smith and Hearty Repentance." *Religious Educator* 12, no. 2 (2011): 69–81.

Largey, Dennis L., Andrew H. Hedges, John Hilton III, and Kerry Hull, eds. *The Coming Forth of the Book of Mormon: A Marvelous Work and a Wonder* (2015).

MacKay, Michael Hubbard, and Gerrit J. Dirkmaat. *From Darkness unto Light: Joseph Smith's Translation and Publication of the Book of Mormon* (2015).

MacKay, Michael Hubbard, and Nicolas J. Frederick. *Joseph Smith's Seer Stones* (2016).

ORGANIZATION OF THE CHURCH

MacKay, Michael Hubbard. *Sacred Space: Exploring the Birthplace of Mormonism* (2016).

Olsen, Steven L. "Doctrine and Covenants 21: History as Witness." *Religious Educator* 11, no. 3 (2010): 23–27.

Part Two

Church History in Ohio and Missouri

1831–1838

Chapter Eight

Why the Ohio?

Lessons from the Command to Gather to Kirtland

SCOTT C. ESPLIN

"When you face adversity," observed Elder Richard G. Scott (1928–2015), "you can be led to ask many questions. Some serve a useful purpose; others do not. To ask, Why does this have to happen to me? Why do I have to suffer this, now? What have I done to cause this? will lead you into blind alleys. It really does no good to ask questions that reflect opposition to the will of God."[1] This futility in asking "why" was taught by the Lord to his Saints early in the Restoration. The command for the Saints to move from New York to Ohio, found in sections 37 and 38 of the Doctrine and Covenants, presented a significant "why" moment for the early members. These Saints dealt with challenges common to Church members today, including sacrificing material possessions or friends and family in following the Lord's command. Though the Lord addressed some of their concerns in these revelations, other questions regarding the move remained unanswered, helping them learn to trust the omniscience of God and rely on his promised blessings. The revelations themselves, together with the response by Church membership, highlight principles of how to properly act when the "whys" of life are unclear. Lessons from the historical context of these sections can help us deal with similar periods of perplexity in our own lives.

"GO TO THE OHIO" (DOCTRINE AND COVENANTS 37:1)—SETTING UP THE "WHY"

The fledgling Church faced increasing opposition in New York throughout the summer and fall of 1830. Church leaders including Joseph Smith and Oliver Cowdery sought safety in partial seclusion as mobs and legal proceedings hampered their ability to minister to the members. Meanwhile, the work of the Lord expanded. Obedient to a call to serve, Oliver Cowdery, Peter Whitmer Jr., Parley P. Pratt, and Ziba Peterson journeyed westward to Missouri on a mission to the Lamanites. Along the way, they experienced great success in the Ohio community of Kirtland. Following a month-long preaching tour during which the elders baptized nearly 130 converts, Church membership in northern Ohio rivaled that in New York.

Before continuing their mission to the West, Oliver Cowdery and his companions "sent word to Joseph that they wanted . . . some Elder sent to preside over the branch at Kirtland."[2] The Prophet sent John Whitmer, who arrived in mid-January 1831. Upon his arrival, he found a congregation of about three hundred, more than double that previously reported.[3] Reacting to this growth, John Whitmer wrote a letter to Joseph stating "that the church much needed his presence and he would be glad of his assistance in setting in order the affairs of the branch where he presided."[4]

Responding to the need for leadership in Kirtland, the Lord told Joseph Smith and Sidney Rigdon, "Behold, I say unto you that it is not expedient in me that ye should translate any more until ye shall go to the Ohio" (Doctrine and Covenants 37:1). Addressing reasons they should move, the Lord continued, "And this because of the enemy and for your sakes" (v. 1). Furthermore, the Lord expanded the directive to include all Church members: "And again, a commandment I give unto the church, that it is expedient in me that they should assemble together at the Ohio" (v. 3). Reiterating the agency of members in following the command, the Lord concluded, "Behold, here is wisdom, and let every man choose for himself" (v. 4).

These commands must have sparked a series of questions in the minds of the Prophet and his associates. Why would the Lord choose Ohio, with only the newly converted Saints in Kirtland, as the headquarters of the Church? Why was the command to relocate given in the dead of winter? How would the designation of Ohio as the first gathering place in this dispensation aid the work of the Restoration?

Like the Church itself, the state of Ohio was also undergoing an era of rapid growth. During the first three decades of the nineteenth century,

Ohio experienced a tenfold increase in population, growing from seventy-two thousand residents in 1800 to over eight hundred thousand by 1826.[5] During the 1830s, the decade in which the Church was headquartered there, the state's population increased by almost six hundred thousand, and by 1840 Ohio was the third most populous state in the nation behind only New York and Pennsylvania.[6] Kirtland itself kept pace with the growth of the state. In the decade before the Church arrived, the population of the town more than doubled.

Rapid growth in the area, coupled with the availability of land and the opportunity to expand, produced a region ripe for establishing a Church headquarters. Ohio served as an ideal location because it was centrally located within the young nation and thus mission fields across the United States and even north to Canada were easily accessible by river, canal, lake, or land. Furthermore, it was a step closer to Zion, an area of growing interest to Joseph Smith and the Church. From his home in Kirtland, the Prophet made repeated trips to Independence, Missouri, guiding members in their attempts to establish the New Jerusalem. Finally, Ohio represented a place where the Church and its leaders could get a fresh start, protected from the increasing opposition they faced in New York.

View of Kirtland, Ohio. Photograph by George Edward Anderson, 1907. Courtesy of Church History Library.

"ALL THINGS ARE PRESENT BEFORE [HIS] EYES" (DOCTRINE AND COVENANTS 38:2)— RESPONDING TO THE CALL TO GATHER

Understandably, the response of Church members to the command to move must have been electrifying. Concerning a conference of the Church held in early January 1831, Church historian John Whitmer reported, "The solemnities of eternity rested on the congregation, and having previously received a revelation to go to Ohio, [the Saints] desired to know somewhat more concerning this matter." In response, "the Seer enquired of the Lord in the presence of the whole congregation, and thus came the word of the Lord"— Doctrine and Covenants section 38.[7]

The wording of section 38 highlights the "why" questions that must have been circulating throughout Church membership regarding the move. Possibly because the Saints questioned the wisdom of leaving their homes in New York, the section begins with the Lord reiterating his omniscience, declaring that he "knoweth all things, for all things are present before [his] eyes" (v. 2). Furthermore, the Lord promised to be in their midst, with the blessing that "the day soon cometh that ye shall see me, and know that I am" (v. 8). Regarding the dangers threatening the Saints in New York, the Lord encouraged them to "go ye out from among the wicked" (v. 42), warning that "the enemy in the secret chambers seeketh your lives" (v. 28). Finally, addressing the particulars of the move and encouraging haste, he emphasized, "And they that have farms that cannot be sold, let them be left or rented as seemeth them good" (v. 37).

The initial response to this command was mixed. Though the Lord outlined that members should trust both his omniscience and his aid, John Whitmer's history recalls, "After the Lord had manifested the above words [section 38] through Joseph the Seer, there were some divisions among the congregation, some would not receive the above as the word of the Lord: But [held] that Joseph had invented it himself to deceive the people that in the end he might get gain. Now this was because, their hearts were not right in the sight of the Lord, for they wanted to serve God and man; but our Savior has declared that it was impossible to do so."[8]

News of the command to gather and of Joseph's anticipated transfer to Ohio quickly spread outside the Church. As early as mid-January, newspapers in the Kirtland area began revealing details of the move. On January 18, 1831, the Painesville *Telegraph* announced the coming of John Whitmer to the area. Though slightly inaccurate in its assessment of Church doctrine, the account preserves some detail regarding the anticipated arrival of Joseph Smith:

> A young gentleman by the name of *Whitmer* arrived here last week from Manchester, N.Y., the seat of wonders, with a new batch of revelations from God, as he pretended, which have just been communicated to Joseph Smith. As far as we have been able to learn their contents, they are a more particular description of the creation of the world, and a history of Adam and his family, and othe[r] sketches of the anti-deluvian world, which Moses neglected to record. But the more important part of the mission was to inform the brethren that the boundaries of the promised land, or the New Jerusalem, had just been made known to Smith from God—the township of Kirtland, a few miles west of this, is the eastern line and the Pacific Ocean the western line; if the north and south lines have been described, we have not learned them. Orders were also brought to the brethren to sell no more land, but rather buy more. Joseph Smith and all his forces are to be on here soon to take possession of the promised land.[9]

In Ohio, local residents both in and out of the faith braced themselves for the Church's arrival.

"LET YOUR PREACHING BE THE WARNING VOICE" (DOCTRINE AND COVENANTS 38:41)— PREPARING TO LEAVE

Back in New York, area newspapers began covering the Saints' preparations for the exodus. In Palmyra, the *Reflector* published a letter to the editor, written from Waterloo, New York, on January 26, 1831:

> Elder S. Rigdon left this village on Monday morning last in the stage, for the "Holy Land," where all the "Gold Bible" converts, have recently received a *written* commandment from God, through Jo Smith, junior, to repair with all convenient speed after selling off the property. This command was at first resisted by such as had property, (the brethren from the neighboring counties being all assembled by special summons,) but after a night of fasting, prayer and trial, they all consented to obey the holy messenger.—Rigdon has for some time past been arranging matters with Smith for the final departure of the *faithful* for the "far west." The man of many CREEDS, (Rigdon) appears to possess colloquial powers to a considerable degree, and before leaving this vicinity left us his *blessing*. He delivered a discourse at the Court

House immediately preceding his departure, wherein he depicted in strong language, the want of "charity and brotherly love" among the prevailing sects and denominations of professing christians, and sorry I am to admit, that he had too much truth on his side with regard to this particular. After denouncing dreadful vengeance on the whole state of New York, and this village in particular, and recommending to all such as wished to flee from "the wrath to come," to follow him beyond the "western waters," he took his leave.[10]

As is evident from the above account, Church leaders including Joseph Smith and Sidney Rigdon obeyed the Lord's command that "ye shall not go until ye have preached my gospel in those parts, and have strengthened up the church whithersoever it is found, and more especially in Colesville" (Doctrine and Covenants 37:2). Though some may question whether Sidney's preaching had been "the warning voice, every man to his neighbor, in mildness and meekness" (38:41), none can question Sidney's and Joseph's efforts to comply with the Lord's words. As recorded by John Whitmer, "Joseph and Sidney went to Colesville to do the will of the Lord in that part of the land: and to strengthen the disciples in that part of the vineyard, and preach the gosple to a hardened and a wicked people."[11] Describing the response, Whitmer continued, "When Sidney and the Revelator arrivd there, they held prayer meetings, among the disciples, and they also held public meetings but it was all in vain, they threatend to kill them. Therefore, they knew that they were not fit for the Kingdom of God, and well nigh ripe for destruction. The Spirit of the Lord fell upon Sidney, and he spoke with boldness, and he preached the gospel in its purity; but they laughed him to scorn."[12] This may have been part of the Lord's omniscient warning to the Church that "the enemy" was "combined" (38:12) in New York.

"THEY THAT HAVE FARMS" (DOCTRINE AND COVENANTS 38:37)—SACRIFICING POSSESSIONS, FAMILY, AND FRIENDS

After Church leaders raised the warning voice in the area, disposing of property became the primary activity. An informant from Waterloo wrote in Palmyra's local newspaper, "The *Prophet*, Spouse, and whole 'holy family' (as they style themselves,) will follow Rigdon, so soon as their deluded or hypothetical followers, shall be able to dispose of what little real property they possess in this region: one farm (Whitmers) was sold a few days ago for

$2,300. Their first place of destination is understood to be a few miles west of Painesville, Ohio."[13] Indeed, the informant seems to be relatively correct regarding the sale of Peter Whitmer's one-hundred-acre farm in Fayette. Land records from the area indicate that it was sold to Charles Stuart of Waterloo on April 1, 1831, for $2,200. Ironically, in what may indicate the sacrifice Church members made by disposing of property at a discount, the same farm was sold by Stuart just six weeks later for a $300 profit.[14] Faithful Saints like the Whitmers learned the painful lesson that obedience to divine command sometimes requires temporal sacrifice in exchange for spiritual blessings.

Indeed, disposing of property in New York during the late winter and early spring became a chief concern for some members. Because of the directive to leave property if it couldn't be sold (see Doctrine and Covenants 38:37), "Joseph Smith's land, 13 acres and eighty perches, was either 'left or rented' until June 28, 1833, when the property was sold to a brother-in-law, Joseph McKune, Jr."[15] Having already left for Ohio, Joseph Knight Sr. employed attorney William M. Waterman to represent him in his land sale. An ad placed in the *Broome Republican* on May 5, 1831, announced: "FOR SALE, THE farm lately occupied by Joseph Knight, situate in the town of Colesville, near the Colesville Bridge—bounded on one side by the Susquehanna River, and containing about one hundred and forty two acres. On said Farm are two Dwelling Houses, a good Barn, and a fine Orchard. The terms of sale will be liberal—Apply to Wm. M. Waterman."[16] Of the difficulties in selling, Newel Knight remembered "great sacrifices of our property."[17]

Having made arrangements to leave their farm, Joseph and Emma were among the first to comply with the divine command to gather in Ohio. Though Emma was pregnant with twins, the couple, together with at least Edward Partridge, Sidney Ridgon, and Joseph and Polly Knight, left New York in late January, arriving in Kirtland in early February 1831.[18] Again, unfriendly newspaper accounts chronicled their journey. In Palmyra on March 9, 1831, the *Reflector* announced, "We also learn from the State of Ohio, that the work moves on apace. Joe Smith with his *better half*, had arrived in that country,—the prophet well clad, while the *female* exhibited a gold watch—a profusion of rings, &c.—demonstrating the fact, that even *Mormonism* is a 'living business.'"[19] This negative assessment of the Prophet and his family characterizes one of the challenges faced by modern members seeking to obey a directive of the Lord. Obeying the Lord not only requires personal sacrifice, sometimes of property and possessions, but also opens one to ridicule and scorn.

"THE ENEMY IS COMBINED" (DOCTRINE AND COVENANTS 38:12)—PREVENTING PHYSICAL THREATS TO THE PEOPLE

Derision for following the Lord's command can turn to danger; knowing this, the Prophet remained concerned about the welfare of those following him from New York to Ohio. Aware of the Lord's warning that the Saints were to go to Ohio "because of the enemy" (Doctrine and Covenants 37:1), Joseph continued to warn the Saints to be careful. On March 3, 1831, Joseph wrote to his brother Hyrum, who presided over the Saints in Colesville: "My Dearly Beloved Brother Hyrum I have had much Concirn about you but I always remember you in my prayers Calling upon god to keep you Safe in spite of men or devils I think you had better Come into this Country immediately for the Lord has Commanded us that we Should Call the Elders of this Chursh to gether unto this plase as soon as possable."[20] Appending an additional note of concern to the letter, the Prophet warned, "David Jackways has threatened to take father with a supreme writ in the spring you had beter Come to fayette and take father along with you Come in a one horse wagon if you Can do not Come threw Bufalo for they will lie in wait for you God protect you I am Joseph."[21]

Fortunately, the specific threat concerning Joseph Smith Sr. and Hyrum Smith never materialized. However, members leaving New York encountered opposition, especially in Buffalo. When a group of Saints led by Lucy Mack Smith arrived in the town, the Colesville Saints who had preceded them warned them not to mention that they were members of the Church of Christ, "for if you do you will not get a boat nor a house."[22] Specifically, Thomas Marsh warned her, "Now Mother smith if you do sing and have prayers and acknowedge that you are Mormons here in this place as you have done all along you will be Mobbed before morning."[23] Nothing materialized with the mobs, in spite of Lucy's determination to "sing and attend to prayers before sunset mob or no mob."[24] However, one wonders if these perceived threats in Buffalo were not based, at least in some part, on fact. The Prophet himself certainly felt that some danger lay in wait for him and his family there.

"LET EVERY MAN CHOOSE FOR HIMSELF" (DOCTRINE AND COVENANTS 37:4) — HONORING AGENCY IN THE COMMAND

While the physical threat of opposition represented one form of resistance, an appeal to loyalty and friendship was another difficulty the Saints faced as they relocated. Like other moves in the prophetic history of mankind, the move from New York to Ohio provided an opportunity for members to prove their faith. Generally, Church members were obedient to the command to relocate. However, as the Lord indicated in his initial instruction, "every man" was free to "choose for himself" regarding his obedience (Doctrine and Covenants 37:4). As Church membership was "clean, but not all" (38:10), the call to obey a prophet provided an opportunity for the righteous to "go . . . out from among the wicked" (38:42).

Those who were well-respected citizens in their communities especially faced familial and social pressure to remain. Of Martin Harris's leaving Palmyra with the rest of the "Mormon Emigration," a local newspaper declared:

> Several families, numbering about fifty souls, took up their line of march from this town last week for the "promised land," among whom is Martin Harris, one of the original believers in the "Book of Mormon." Mr. Harris was among the early settlers of this town, and has ever borne the character of an honorable and upright man, and an obliging and benevolent neighbor. He had secured to himself by honest industry a respectable fortune—and he has left a large circle of acquaintances and friends to pity his delusion.[25]

One local newspaper account described the dilemma faced by some early members in choosing to follow the Lord's call. New York's *Lockport Balance* emphasized, "In and about the town of Kirtland, Geauga County . . . the deluded followers of the false prophet are repairing. . . . Families, in some instances, have been divided, and in others, mothers have been obliged to follow their deluded husbands, or adopt the disagreeable alternative, of parting with them, and their children."[26] Additional statements seem to support the claim that the call to move divided families. Joseph Hervy recalled watching the various parties leave and later remarked, "My memory is that some twenty or thirty women, girls, men and boys, on foot and in two old-fashioned western emigrant wagons comprised the emigrating party. I well remember hearing it talked that women left their husbands and families to go with Smith."27

Apparently the call to gather divided even those hoping to begin families. More than seventy years after the move, Harriet E. Shay, eyewitness to the departure, shared the following:

> I distinctly remember seeing the followers of Joseph Smith, Jr., of Mormon fame, go by my fathers, George Clappers, house on the east side of the Susquehanna River in the Town of Afton County of Chenango, N.Y. between Afton, formerly South Bainbridge and Ninevah, on what is now known as the Lewis Poole Farm.
>
> To the best of my recollection there were eight (8) or ten (10) wagons. They were covered like western emigrant wagons, and were drawn by oxen.
>
> One reason I remember so distinctly of the wagons going by is from the fact that my Uncle Cornelius Atherton was engaged to be married to Betsy Peck daughter of Hezekiah Peck, who with his wife and son, Reed Peck went with the Mormons at that time. Hezekiah Peck forbade the marriage of Betsy and Uncle Cornelius unless he would join the Mormons and go with them; this Uncle Cornelius would not do.
>
> That day was made impression to me as I witnessed the sorrow of Uncle Cornelius who was at our house when the wagon train went by.
>
> I also remember an incident which occurred about the same time which later became more familiar to me as I became acquainted with the parties. Stephen Pratt was engaged to be married to a Peck girl, a relative of Hezekiah Peck, I think her name was Anna. Just before the followers of Smith started they ran away and were married, therefore, they did not go with the Mormons.28

In Palmyra, the *Reflector* similarly dramatized the choice to obey, likewise highlighting those unwilling to make the sacrifice,

> Our Waterloo correspondent informs us, that two of the most responsible *Mormonites*, as it respects property, in that vicinity, have *demurred* to the divine command, through Jo Smith, requiring them to sell their property and put it into the common *fund*, and repair with all convenient speed to the New Jerusalem, lately located by Cowdery somewhere in the western region. A requisition of *twelve hundred* dollars, in cash, it is said, was made upon one of these gentlemen, (Mr. B.)—"the Lord having need of it." This request was promptly refused by the gentleman, who, at the same time informed the prophet that he would

rather risque his soul as it was (having been dipt) than trust his money or property in the hands of such agents as were applying for it.[29]

As one paper played up refusals to obey, another ridiculed the faithful compliance with divine command. In Painesville, Ohio, the *Telegraph* remarked:

> About two hundred men, women and children, of the deluded followers of Jo Smith's Bible speculation have arrived on our coast during the last week, from the State of New York, & are about seating themselves down upon the "promised land" in this county. It is surely a melancholy comment upon human nature to see so many people at this enlightened age of the world, truckling along at the care of a miserable impostor, submitting themselves, both soul and body, to his spiritual and temporal mandates, without a murmur, or presuming to question that it is all a command direct from Heaven,—Such an abject slavery of the mind may endure for a season; but in due time, like the chains of Popery, the links which bind them will be rent asunder, and reason resume again her empire.[30]

Indeed, the call to gather became a test of faithfulness for the early Saints. Summarizing the results of the gathering during the summer of 1831, John Whitmer observed, "About these days the disciples arrived from State of New York. To this place Kirtland state of Ohio. They had some difficulty because of some that did not continue faithful; who denied the truth and turned into fables. . . . Therefore a part of the Revelation given at Fayette New York was fulfilled. The churches of the State of New York had moved to Ohio, with their Wives and their children, and all their Substance some purchased farms others rented, and thus they situated themselves as convenient as they could."[31] In total, the majority of Church membership in New York, estimated at approximately two hundred people, immigrated to Ohio between January and June of 1831.[32]

"I AM IN YOUR MIDST" (DOCTRINE AND COVENANTS 38:7)—FINDING PEACE THROUGH GOD'S GUIDING HAND DURING TIMES OF UNCERTAINTY

While the revelations surrounding the commanded move to Ohio offered glimpses of the reasons the Saints should go, the Lord also made specific promises to those who would faithfully comply with the command. The Lord reassured those doubting the divine directive that he was "in [their] midst" and that, though they couldn't see him, "the day soon cometh that [they] shall see [him], and know that [he is]" (Doctrine and Covenants 38:7–8). Evidence of God's guiding hand became a theme of the move.

Lucy Mack Smith's account of the journey emphasizes the Lord's miraculous aid. She credits the Lord with protecting them on the journey, aiding them in locating housing along the way, and, most dramatically, parting an ice jam that blocked Buffalo harbor, allowing their boat to narrowly navigate the opening. Stymied in their progress, Lucy remembered declaring to the company, "And now brethren and sisters if you will all of you raise your desires to Heaven that the Ice may give way before us and we be set at liberty to go on our way as sure as the Lord lives it shall be done." Describing the miracle, she continued:

> At that moment a noise was heard like bursting thunder and the captain cried out every man to his post and the ice parted leaving barely a pathway for the boat and that was so narrow that as it passed through the buckets were torn from the water wheel this with the noise of the ice the confusion of the spectaters the word of command from the capt. and the hoarse answering of the sailors was truely dreadful— and our boat and one other had just time enough to get through and the . . . ice closed again.[33]

Newel Knight similarly recorded the hand of the Lord on his journey. Traveling with family and friends, he described a miraculous healing:

> My aunt, Electa Peck fell and broke her shoulder in a most shocking manner. A Surgeon was called who did all he could to relieve her sufferings which was verry great. My aunt dreamed that I returned and laid my hands upon her and prayed for her and she was made whole and pursued on her journey with the Company. This dream she related to the Surgeon who replied if you are able to travel in many weeks it will be a mericl, & he would be a mormon too. I arrived at the place where the Company had stoped, late in the night. On learning of the accident which had happened to my aunt I went to see her. Immediately on seing me entering the room She said: O Brother Newel if you will lay your hands upon me I shall be well and able to go on the journey with you. I s[t]eped up to the bed and in the name of the Lord Jesus Christ, rebuked the pain with which she was suffering and Commanded her to be made whole. And it was done, for the next morning She arose, dressed her self, and pursued the journey with us.[34]

While some like these Saints saw an immediate fulfillment of the Lord's promises in the journey, several of the other promises made to the Saints in section 38 were fulfilled later in Ohio. This seems characteristic of the Lord, who fulfills promises "in his own time, and in his own way, and according to his own will" (Doctrine and Covenants 88:68). In fact, the day did come in which the Saints who had faithfully moved saw the Lord and knew that he was (see 38:8). These revelations include his appearances to the School of the Prophets and later those associated with the dedication of the Kirtland Temple (see 110:1–10; 137:1–3). Additional literal fulfillment of Doctrine and Covenants section 38 includes the giving of the law (see 38:32; 42), members being "endowed with power from on high" (38:32; 110:9), and the gospel going forth from Ohio "among all nations" (38:33; 110:10–11). As the first gathering site, Ohio also became the place where the law of consecration could be revealed, giving every man the chance to "esteem his brother as himself" (38:25) and to "be one" (38:27). Ironically, the section outlining the blessings and promises associated with the move to Ohio also included an apparent warning regarding Kirtland's fall: "And if ye seek the riches which it is the will of the Father to give unto you, ye shall be the richest of all people, for ye shall have the riches of eternity; . . . but beware of pride, lest ye become as the Nephites of old" (38:39). Indeed, the Lord, through his prophet, addressed those asking "why" by giving promises and warnings to the faithful.

CONCLUSION: DEALING WITH THE "WHYS" OF LIFE TODAY

In our lives, we are frequently confronted with "why" scenarios. Why do we have to do certain things? Why doesn't life work out as planned? Why do good people suffer? The lessons the Lord emphasized during the commanded move to Ohio teach principles related to such questions. Moving forward with faith during periods of uncertainty is an essential element of our mortal existence.

Importantly, the Lord's revelations addressing "why" contain parallels for our lives. As with these early members, our personal times of "why" sometimes go unanswered. God offers promises, based on obedience, but he may or may not explain why he gives us a particular commandment. Regarding this phenomenon, President Dallin H. Oaks observed, "If you read the scriptures with the question in mind, 'Why did the Lord command this or why did he command that,' you find that in less than one in a hundred commands was any reason given. It's not the pattern of the Lord to give reasons. We can put reason to revelation. We can put reasons to commandments. When we do we're on our own."[35]

Early Church members were given a glimpse of the reasons why they were to move, but for the most part, they were expected to act with the faith that the Lord "knoweth all things, for all things are present before [his] eyes" (Doctrine and Covenants 38:2). As he did in earlier times, God knows all things today and promises to be with us if we are obedient to his commands. Faithful obedience, as the Saints demonstrated in the move to Ohio, sometimes includes sacrificing material comforts, facing familial and social pressure, and trusting God's omniscience. It requires moving forward when we may not see God's hand, with faith that we someday will (see vv. 7–8). Not knowing all the "whys" of life may, therefore, be by divine design. Ultimately, "reasons" are not the "whys" for obedience. Rather, as President Oaks summarized, "revelations are what we sustain as the will of the Lord and that's where safety lies."[36]

Using the move to Ohio as an example, the Doctrine and Covenants teaches us to trust the Lord's directives even when the specific reasons for commandments are unclear. Summarizing this principle, Elder Robert D. Hales (1932–2017) remarked, "I have come to understand how useless it is to dwell on the *whys, what ifs,* and *if onlys* for which there likely will be given no answers in mortality. To receive the Lord's comfort, we must exercise faith. The questions Why me? Why our family? Why now? are usually unanswerable questions. These questions detract from our spirituality and can destroy our faith. We need to spend our time and energy building our faith by turning to the Lord and asking for strength to overcome the pains and trials of this world and to endure to the end for greater understanding."[37] The move from New York to Ohio built the faith of the early Saints. Studying their experience and applying it in our lives can do the same for us.

Scott C. Esplin is a professor of Church history and doctrine at Brigham Young University.

Scott C. Esplin, "Why the Ohio? Why Anything in My Life? Lessons from the Command to Gather," *Religious Educator* 10, no. 3 (2009): 175–88.

NOTES

1. Richard G. Scott, "Trust in the Lord," *Ensign*, November 1995, 17.
2. Lucy Mack Smith, History, 1844–1845, book 10, pp. [1, 11], in *The Joseph Smith Papers*, http://www.josephsmithpapers.org/.
3. See Milton V. Backman Jr., *The Heavens Resound: A History of the Latter-day Saints in Ohio, 1830–1838* (Salt Lake City: Deseret Book, 1983), 42.
4. Lucy Mack Smith, History, 1844–1845, book 10, pp. [1, 12]. There is some discrepancy regarding the dating of John Whitmer's letter. Lucy Mack Smith's history reports Joseph's receiving the letter inviting him to come to Kirtland in December 1830. Because of this letter, Lucy later stated that Joseph "inquired of the Lord and received [Doctrine and Covenants 37]." However, the January 18 edition of the Painesville *Telegraph*, a local Ohio newspaper, indicated that Elder Whitmer arrived in Ohio during the middle of January. If the newspaper is accurate, one option is that he wrote the letter to Joseph before arriving in Ohio. Another option is that this letter was, indeed, written in mid-January, after John's arrival in Kirtland. If this is the case, the revelation it sparked, requiring Joseph to leave for Ohio immediately, may be different from the one recorded in section 37. The receipt of section 37 on December 30, 1830, may also have been influenced by the arrival of Sidney Rigdon and Edward Partridge in New York. The pair were introduced to the Church in Ohio and subsequently traveled to meet Joseph Smith in early December. See Revelation, 30 December 1830 [D&C 37], p. 49, http://www.josephsmithpapers.org/.
5. See Backman, *Heavens Resound*, 21.
6. See Backman, *Heavens Resound*, 21.
7. John Whitmer, History, 1831–circa 1847, p. 6, http://josephsmithpapers.org/; original spelling preserved.
8. Whitmer, History, 1831–circa 1847, p. 9.
9. "Mormonism," *Telegraph* (Painesville, OH), January 18, 1831.
10. *Reflector* (Palmyra, NY), February 1, 1831.
11. Whitmer, History, 1831–circa 1847, p. 9.
12. Whitmer, History, 1831–circa 1847, p. 10.
13. *Reflector*, February 1, 1831, 95.
14. See Larry C. Porter, *A Study of the Origins of The Church of Jesus Christ of Latter-day Saints in the States of New York and Pennsylvania* (Provo, UT: BYU Studies, 2000), 150, appendix F.
15. Porter, *Study of the Origins of The Church*, 118.
16. Cited in Porter, *Study of the Origins of The Church*, 120.
17. Newel Knight, in *The Rise of the Latter-day Saints: The Journals and Histories of Newel Knight*, ed. Michael Hubbard MacKay and William G. Hartley (Provo, UT: Religious Studies Center, Brigham Young University; Salt Lake City: Deseret Book, 2019), 32.
18. See Porter, *Study of the Origins of The Church*, 128nn47, 49.
19. "Mormonism," *Reflector*, March 9, 1831, 116.
20. Letter to Hyrum Smith, 3–4 March 1831, p. [2], http://www.josephsmithpapers.org/.
21. Letter to Hyrum Smith, 3–4 March 1831, p. [3]. It is unclear what danger Joseph sensed for his father and brother in Buffalo. According to Dean Jessee, David Jackways is "probably David Strong Jackway or Jackways, whose father, William Jackway, . . . came to Palmyra, New York, in 1787. William Jackway owned a 500-acre farm, and he and his son David were hatters by trade. A David Jackways, in his fifties, is

listed in the 1840 Palmyra, New York census." *The Personal Writings of Joseph Smith*, ed. Dean C. Jessee (Salt Lake City: Deseret Book, 1984), 669n8. Apparently Joseph sensed a danger from this person.

22. Lucy Mack Smith, History, 1844–1845, book 10, p. [1]; book 11, p. [6].
23. Lucy Mack Smith, History, 1844–1845, book 10, p. [1]; book 11, p. [7].
24. Lucy Mack Smith, History, 1844–1845, book 10, p. [1]; book 11, p. [7].
25. *Wayne Sentinel* (Palmyra, NY), May 27, 1831.
26. *Lockport (NY) Balance*, May 31, 1831; cited in the *Daily National Intelligencer*, July 6, 1831.
27. Cited in Porter, *Study of the Origins of The Church*, 122.
28. Cited in Porter, *Study of the Origins of The Church*, 121.
29. *Reflector*, March 9, 1831, 116.
30. "Mormon Emigration," *Telegraph*, May 17, 1831.
31. Whitmer, History, 1831–circa 1847, pp. 27, 29.
32. See Backman, *Heavens Resound*, 49.
33. Lucy Mack Smith, History, 1844–1845, book 10, p. [1]; book 12, p. [2].
34. Newel Knight, in MacKay and Hartley, *Rise of the Latter-day Saints*, 32–33.
35. "Apostles Talk about Reasons for Lifting Ban," *Provo Daily Herald*, June 5, 1988, 21.
36. "Apostles Talk about Reasons for Lifting Ban," 21.
37. Robert D. Hales, "Healing Soul and Body," *Ensign*, November 1998, 14.

Chapter Nine

"That They Might Come to Understanding"
Revelation as Process

STEVEN C. HARPER

On a spring Sabbath in 1843, a gathering of Latter-day Saints opened their worship service with a hymn. Wilford Woodruff prayed, and "then Joseph the Seer arose & said It is not wisdom that we should have all knowledge at once presented before us but that we should have a little[. T]hen we can comprehend it."[1] Joseph had learned early in his prophetic ministry about the power of transcendent revelatory events, like his First Vision or his visits from Moroni. But he also learned that such events were part of the process by which revelation distilled over time. Like compound interest on investments, light and knowledge accumulate as revelatory events combine with insight from experience and thought.

In November 1831, as Joseph was preparing to publish his revelation texts, he sought and received a preface for them. In a revelatory event, he dictated the text that is now Doctrine and Covenants section 1. It sets forth the Lord's reason for revealing himself in process to Joseph as he did. "These commandments are of me," the Lord said, speaking of the revelation texts, "and were given unto my servants in their weakness, after the manner of their language, *that they might come to understanding*" (Doctrine and Covenants 1:24; emphasis added). This passage is key in appreciating revelation as a process of communication between a divine being and mortal ones, a process that is not complete once the revelation text has been written or published or read, but rather once it has been internalized and acted upon. Revelation, in this sense, is best understood as a process that leads to understanding rather than an event in which knowledge is fully disclosed in an instant.

Elder David A. Bednar invited us to understand two patterns of the spirit of revelation. One is like turning on a light switch and dispelling darkness in an instant; this is what I mean by a revelatory event, like the First Vision or the reception of section 1. The other is like watching night turn into morning as the rising sun gradually and subtly replaces darkness.[2] This is what I mean by the process of revelation, which yields accumulated insight born of ongoing inspiration. Significantly, it was late in Joseph's life, not on his return from the Sacred Grove, when he articulated the idea that our wise Heavenly Father does not give us all knowledge at once, but in a process that we can understand. It was also late in his life that Joseph wrote reflectively about his remarkable, revelatory life. He reviewed his experiences with a veritable "who's who" of heavenly messengers—Moroni, Michael, Peter, James, John, Gabriel, and Raphael—"all declaring their dispensation . . . giving line upon line, precept upon precept; here a little, and there a little" (Doctrine and Covenants 128:21). Joseph was remembering revelatory events in his past, but he had experienced enough to reflectively recognize that such events were part of the revelatory process.

"Revelation," according to Elder Bednar, "is communication from God to His children on the earth."[3] So a basic understanding of communication theory may help us understand the nature of revelation. In any communication there is an encoder that sends the signal, the decoder that receives it, and the noise between them that hinders perfect transmission and reception. In terms of communication, noise is not always audible. Sound can interrupt revelation, but other kinds of noise hinder communication too. One type, semantic noise, happens when the encoder sends signals that the decoder lacks the power to decipher. Imagine Joseph receiving revelation in Spanish or computer programming code; that would be an example of semantic noise. Another type, psychological noise, happens when a decoder's assumptions, prejudices, preconceived notions, or emotions prevent an accurate interpretation of the signal.

Revelation is communication in which God is a flawless, divine encoder but mortals are the decoders. Various kinds of "noise" prevent perfect understanding. There is no evidence that Joseph Smith thought in technical terms of communication theory, but he understood these ideas well. He did not assume as we might that his revelation texts were faxed from heaven. He understood that the Lord could certainly send signals seamlessly, but he knew better than anyone else that he lacked the power to receive the messages immaculately or to recommunicate them perfectly. He considered it "an awful responsibility to write in the name of the Lord," as he put it, largely because he felt confined by what he called the "total darkness of paper pen and Ink and a crooked broken scattered and imperfect Language."[4]

Religion scholar David Carpenter described revelation as "a *process* mediated through language."[5] The very language whose communicative inadequacies Joseph lamented was the means by which God condescended to Joseph's level and condescends to ours. Remember the Lord's rationale in section 1: he gave the revelations "unto my servants in their weakness, after the manner of their language, [so] that they might come to understanding" (Doctrine and Covenants 1:24). Joseph rightfully regarded his language as a deeply flawed medium for communication. Even so, the Lord consciously revealed the sections of the Doctrine and Covenants in Joseph's corrupt tongue, not in the Lord's own "diction, dialect, or native language."[6] He revealed in the language Joseph could come to understand so that we too could come, by a process, to understand (see v. 24). A divine encoder chose to communicate with his servants in their weakness in order to maximize their ability to comprehend. The communicative limits of Joseph's revelation texts are inherent not in the Lord who gave them but in the imperfect language spoken by his weak servants, who had to decode the divine messages with various kinds of noise inhibiting them. Brigham Young did not believe, as he put it, "that there is a single revelation, among the many God has given to the Church, that is perfect in its fulness. The revelations of God contain correct doctrine and principle, so far as they go; but it is impossible for the poor, weak, low, grovelling, sinful inhabitants of the earth to receive a revelation from the Almighty in all its perfections. He has to speak to us in a manner to meet the extent of our capacities."[7] No wonder Joseph felt the weight of his calling and longed for a pure language.

Joseph also longed for friends who would sustain him and the imperfect texts he made of the revelations he received. In November 1831, he convened a council at the Johnson home in Hiram, Ohio, and said that "the Lord has bestowed a great blessing upon us in giving commandments and revelations." Joseph laid the manuscript revelations before his associates and asked for their help in getting them published. He testified that the contents of such a book should "be prized by this Conference to be worth to the Church the riches of the whole Earth." During the discussion Oliver

Cowdery asked "how many copies of the Book of commandments it was the will of the Lord should be published in the first edition of that work."[8] The council eventually voted for ten thousand. It was in these council meetings, which went on for more than a week, that the Lord revealed the preface for the book, Doctrine and Covenants section 1. In it he essentially said that though he was a divine being, he communicated to mortals in their language so that they could come to understand (see v. 24).

Joseph's history tells us that the council engaged in a discussion "concerning revelations and language."[9] The discussion may well have raised the same issues discussed here about the kind of writing that can be considered scripture. Those in the room must have recognized that they were being asked to support a nearly twenty-six-year-old poorly educated farmer who was planning to publish ten thousand copies of revelations that were unequivocally declared to be the words of Jesus Christ, revelations that called their neighbors idolatrous, referred to Missourians as their enemies, commanded them all to repent, and foretold calamities upon those who continued in wickedness. Moreover, the revelation texts were not always properly punctuated, the spelling was not standardized, and the grammar was inconsistent.

Though lacking confidence in his own language, or perhaps even because of his limitations, Joseph was sure that his revelation texts were divine, if imperfect, productions. He promised the brethren present that they could know for themselves as well. Just a few days earlier, Joseph had prophesied that if the Saints could "all come together with one heart and one mind in perfect faith the vail [sic] might as well be rent to day as next week or any other time."[10] Seeking confirmation of the revelations, the brethren tried to rend the veil like the brother of Jared in the Book of Mormon had done. They failed. Joseph asked the Lord why, and he received the answer in Doctrine and Covenants section 67.

In that text the Lord assured the Church leaders that he had heard their prayers and knew all the desires in their hearts. "There were fears in your hearts," he told them, and "this is the reason that ye did not receive" (v. 3). He then testified of the truthfulness of the Book of Commandments and Revelations lying before them. They had been watching Joseph, listening to him talk, observing his imperfections, and wishing secretly, or perhaps even assuming, that they could do a better job than he; the Lord offered them the opportunity. He told them to have the wisest man in the council (or any of them who cared to) duplicate the simplest revelation in the manuscript revelation book before them. The Lord told the elders that if they succeeded in composing a pseudo-revelation text equal to the least of Joseph's, then they could justifiably say that they did not know the revelations were true. But if they failed, the Lord said he would hold them guilty unless they testified to the veracity of the revelations. The Lord's words led the men to recognize that whatever imperfections the revelation texts showed—communicated as they were in "their language" (1:24), not God's—they conformed to divine laws, were full of holy principles, and were just, virtuous, and good. They could conclude on those criteria that even communicated with a "crooked broken scattered and imperfect Language," such revelations came from God.[11]

Joseph's history and other sources tell us how the brethren acted out the instructions in section 67 and became willing to testify before the world that the revelations were true, but not flawless literary productions. William McLellin, who had acted as scribe the preceding week as Joseph dictated section 66, now "endeavored to write a commandment like unto one of the least of the Lord's, but failed."[12] Joseph had asked the men present "what testimony they were willing to attach to these commandments which should shortly be sent to the world. A number of the brethren arose and said that they were willing to testify to the world that they knew that they were of the Lord," and Joseph revealed a statement for them to sign as witnesses.[13] The resulting "Testimony of the witnesses to the Book of the Lords commandments which he gave to his church through Joseph Smith Jr" reads, "We the undersigners feel willing to bear testimony to all the world of mankind to every creature upon all the face of all the Earth <&> upon the Islands of the Sea that god hath bor born record to our souls through the Holy Ghost shed forth upon us that these commandments are given by inspiration of God & are profitable for all men & are verily true we give this testimony unto the world the Lord being my <our> helper." William McLellin signed this statement, along with four others. Then other elders signed the statement in Missouri when the book arrived there for printing.[14]

The discussion about revelations and language concluded as "the brethren arose in turn and bore witness to the truth of the Book of Commandments. After which br. Joseph Smith jr arose & expressed his feelings and gratitude."[15] With a clear sense that the revelation texts were both human and divine, the November 1831 conference resolved that Joseph "correct those errors or mistakes which he may discover by the holy Spirit."[16] Joseph, and to some extent others (including Oliver Cowdery, Sidney Rigdon, and the printer William Phelps), thus edited his revelation texts repeatedly based on the same premise that informed their original receipt, namely that Joseph

Smith represented the voice of God as he condescended to communicate in Joseph's broken language.[17] Joseph only admonished his associates that they "be careful not to alter the sense" of the revelation manuscripts.[18]

Editing the revelation texts was no simple matter, even without textual variants and other complexities. For example, Joseph Smith dictated a revelation on December 6, 1832, as Sidney Rigdon wrote it (Doctrine and Covenants 86). Frederick Williams then transcribed the text. Orson Hyde copied this transcription. John Whitmer then recorded Hyde's copy in the Book of Commandments and Revelations, from which it was finally edited for publication. Few of Joseph's revelations made their textual journeys so arduously, but not one of them is an urtext, meaning a pristine original. By a process imbued both with God's power and with faltering human mediation, Joseph somehow received the words of these texts and transmitted them to his scribe, who committed them to paper, then into manuscript books, and finally into published volumes of scripture. Not only were there both intentional and erroneous changes made at every step, but also, as a mortal decoder imprisoned by a broken language, Joseph originally received the revelations imperfectly. "He never considered the wording infallible," and he continued to revise and amend his revelation texts throughout his life to reflect his latest understanding and to increase their ability to communicate the mind of God.[19]

Revising, amending, and expanding earlier revelation texts is the prerogative of prophets, and Joseph Smith considered such revisions one of his major responsibilities. He revised the Bible, making hundreds of changes in the process that were designed not to restore lost or ancient text (as some of his revisions were) but rather to improve communication for a modern English-speaking audience. He edited the Book of Mormon after it was published in 1830, adding a clarifying clause to 1 Nephi 20:1 and revising numerous Hebraisms to communicate better with English readers, for example.

Similarly, Joseph edited his own revelation texts. He added information on priesthood offices or quorums to revelations that were originally received before such knowledge had been revealed to him. The current version of section 20 includes information about priesthood offices that was not known when that text was originally written on April 10, 1830. Section 42 now says that the bishop and his counselors should administer the law of consecration, but the Church's lone bishop did not yet have counselors when that text was originally written. Section 68, originally revealed in 1831, said that bishops should be chosen by a council of high priests; it now puts that responsibility in the hands of the First Presidency, which was organized in 1832.

In addition to incorporating more material as it became clear to him, Joseph and other "stewards over the revelations" (Doctrine and Covenants 70:3) edited his revelation texts in order to make them communicate more clearly. The revelation in section 20, for example, originally said that one duty of an apostle was "to administer the flesh and blood of Christ," meaning the sacrament. Before publishing it in the Doctrine and Covenants, Joseph amended this clause to its current reading, namely, "to administer bread and wine—the emblems of the flesh and blood of Christ" (v. 40). Section 7 is another text whose original wording may have been clear to Joseph but whose meaning would be ambiguous to us at best if Joseph had not clarified it. Given to answer the question of whether the Apostle John lived or died, the text originally had John asking the Lord, "Give unto me power that I may bring souls unto thee." Joseph amended it for publication in the Doctrine and Covenants so that it clarifies what John asked for and received: "Give unto me power over death, that I may live and bring souls unto thee" (v. 2).

Joseph not only added newly revealed or clarifying text but also deleted some passages from his revelation texts that were no longer relevant, as in section 51's original instruction to Bishop Edward Partridge to obtain a deed for Leman Copley's land if Copley was willing, which he was not. Joseph apparently amended the law of consecration to reconcile its wording with changing legal dynamics. Moreover, he, Sidney Rigdon, and others made hundreds of simple changes for clarity of communication. For instance, they added surnames to given names mentioned in the texts so that readers who were not intimate with the situation and the subject of the revelation could make more sense of it. Oliver Cowdery reported to the Saints on the progress of this process, saying that the revelation texts "are now correct," adding, "if not in every word, at least in principle."[20]

Critics prey on the ignorance and assumptions of some Saints by writing about this process with clever titles like *Doctored Covenants*.[21] Why all the changes? they ask, but they are not on a quest for answers as much as they are trying to insinuate that the Church tries to keep its members ignorant of its sinister manipulations of scripture. Joseph, his associates, and their successors did not alter the revelation texts conspiratorially. Joseph revised his revelation texts with the sustaining vote of Church leaders and openly before the Saints. Noting that some critics present the many editorial changes made to the revelations as evidence that they are not true, President

Boyd K. Packer observed, "They cite these changes, of which there are many examples, as though they themselves were announcing revelation, as though they were the only ones that knew of them. Of course there have been changes and corrections. Anyone who has done even limited research knows that. When properly reviewed, such corrections become a testimony for, not against, the truth of the books."[22]

William McLellin originally had that understanding, but he lost it. A week before he tried unsuccessfully to compose a pseudorevelation text, McLellin wrote the original dictation manuscript of section 66 as Joseph rendered the Lord's communication in the best words he had at his disposal. McLellin later testified that in this revelation the Lord answered every one of his intimate questions, which were unknown to Joseph. McLellin subsequently reported to his relatives that he had spent about three weeks with Joseph, "and from my acquaintance then and until now I can truely say I believe him to be a man of God. A Prophet, a Seer and Revelater to the church of christ." Later in the same letter, McLellin related, "We believe that Joseph Smith is a true Prophet or Seer of the Lord and that he has power and does receive revelations from God, and that these revelations when received are of divine Authority in the church of Christ."[23]

William McLellin knew as well as anyone that Joseph received revelations, that they were both divine and human products, and that Joseph had been appointed by the Church to prepare them for publication, including revising "by the holy Spirit."[24] But in 1871, McLellin asserted that Joseph Smith had lost power to act for God in 1834 after Joseph and others edited the revelation texts for publication. "Now if the Lord gave those revelations," McLellin reasoned, "he said what he meant, and meant what he said."[25] Though he was present—a participant who knew better and who testified repeatedly with good evidence that Joseph's revelations were true—William McLellin later assumed, as many Latter-day Saints do, that Joseph "simply repeated word-for-word to his scribe what he heard God say to him." Grant Underwood, a careful analyst of Joseph's revelation texts, wrote that "Joseph seems to have had a healthy awareness of the inadequacy of finite, human language, including his own, to perfectly communicate an infinite, divine revelation."[26] McLellin, however, concluded that Joseph could receive revelation flawlessly and communicate it perfectly and that everyone would understand the full import and meaning of his revelations in an instant, in a single event, as if by turning on a light switch.

Those who, like William McLellin, argue for perfect scriptures (which, notice, is not a scriptural doctrine) assume that divine communication is complete and perfect, that mortals can decode the divine without corruption. They do not recognize that it takes revelation to understand a revelation. Consider some examples. Six times in the Doctrine and Covenants the Lord says, "I come quickly" (33:18; 35:27; 39:24; 41:4; 49:28; 68:35). What does he mean? Does the adverb *quickly* mean "speedily" or does it mean "soon"? Both possibilities existed in Joseph's language.[27] All six instances of that prophecy had been revealed by 1832. Because it has been so long since then, at least by our sense of time, should we conclude that the Lord meant not that he comes soon but that when he comes, it will be speedy? Or should we consider that our interpretation of *soon* is not the intended one? Of course, we need not conclude that it is either soon or speedy. It may be both. But if so, how should *soon* be understood?

Some passages of Joseph's revelations could not be understood well at the time they were received, not even by Joseph. The Lord, for example, told the earliest Saints who were called to settle Jackson County, Missouri, that Zion would be built there, but not yet. Rather, it would "follow after much tribulation" (Doctrine and Covenants 58:2–4). How much, they could not have imagined, as the Lord explained: "Ye cannot behold with your natural eyes, for the present time, the design of your God concerning those things which shall come hereafter" (v. 3). Again the Lord prophesied "much tribulation" in anticipation of Zion, but the depth, breadth, and length of that tribulation would be finally understood only in the process of time and experience.

After the bewildered Saints were driven from Jackson County, the Lord reminded Joseph of this tribulation clause, which had much more meaning in that context (see Doctrine and Covenants 103:12). Then the Lord told Joseph that Zion in Missouri would "come by power," and he called for an army to march to Missouri to reclaim the Saints' land (v. 15). Every man who subsequently marched thought that he would provide the military power the Lord must have meant. But when they arrived, the Lord taught them more as part of his process of revelation. He taught them that Zion would not yet be redeemed, that the Saints must "wait for a little season" (105:9). He taught that the power he intended was an endowment waiting for them in the temple back in Kirtland, Ohio, and that they should return there. Why had the Lord not spared them the trouble? Perhaps the Lord let them make the journey because they became sanctified in the process and were better positioned to understand the Lord's purposes after their tribulation than they were before. Joseph wrote, after several months of unjust imprisonment at Liberty, Missouri, "It seems to me that my heart will always be more tender after this than ever it was before." He recognized that experiences "give us that knowledge to understand the minds of the Ancients," like Abraham. "For my part," Joseph wrote, "I think I never could have felt as I now do if I had not suffered the wrongs that I have suffered."[28] Even though Joseph had been in the presence of God and Christ and had entertained ministering angels and learned from them the mysteries of godliness, he still needed time and experience in order to process the revelations he had received and internalize their implications. Joseph processed much revelation in that stinking dungeon cell, where he learned that what had seemed like purposeless, interminable suffering to him was a small moment of exalting experience to God. He wrote, as a result of his revelations and reflections, that "the things of God Are of deep import, and time and expeariance and carful and pondurous and solom though[ts] can only find them out."[29]

In addition to time, experience, careful pondering, and solemn thought, the Holy Ghost is vital to the process of revelation. When elders were bewildered by strange, counterfeit spiritual gifts in the spring of 1831, the Lord invited them to come and reason with him, "that ye may understand" (Doctrine and Covenants 50:10). The Lord asked the elders questions that caused them to think carefully and solemnly about their recent experiences and to compare their experiences with the Holy Spirit with the manifestations they had observed but not understood. Having done such careful thinking, they were ready to understand that unless the Spirit of God mediated communication, that communication was not coming from God. "Why is it that ye cannot understand and know," the Lord asked the elders, "that he that receiveth the word by the Spirit of truth receiveth it as it is preached by the Spirit of truth?" Only communication mediated by the Holy Ghost enables the encoder ("he that preacheth") and the decoder ("he that receiveth") to "understand one another." Communication by the power of the Holy Ghost is edifying. It builds and grows and illuminates line upon line until understanding is full and complete and "perfect" (vv. 22–25; see 93:26–28). Without the Holy Ghost, communication can be a dark, confusing process. The Holy Ghost is the perfect mediator of otherwise imperfect communication; revelation is communication that is mediated by the power of the Holy Ghost. Reading a revelation text by the power of the Holy Ghost and thinking about it carefully over time and in light of experience will enable us to "come to understanding" (1:24).

In this way of thinking about revelation as a process by which we come to understand, the question is not whether the Lord said what he meant and meant what he said. The question, rather, is whether we have understood what he meant and acted obediently on what he said. The question is not whether words were accurately written "with ink" or "on tablets of stone," but whether they were written "with the Spirit of the living God . . . on tablets of human hearts" (2 Corinthians 3:3 New Revised Standard Version).

It seems likely that the Lord will continue to reveal to us in our language so that we might come to understand by experience and careful thought in light of the Holy Ghost. Such language is not stagnant. Unless enlivened by the Holy Ghost, ink on a page arranged into words will not communicate with us all that the Lord intends, even if it was originally perfect. Prophets will continue to guide us as we continue to receive revelation actively in an ongoing quest for light and knowledge. They may amend the scriptures "by the holy Spirit," as Joseph did, when they discern ways to communicate with today's global congregation more clearly.[30]

The prophets have made changes to the scriptures throughout history, including in this dispensation. I remember how as a missionary I ignorantly tried to refute charges that there had been hundreds of textual changes made to the Book of Mormon. Today, thanks to the work of devoted, faithful Latter-day Saint scholars, it is clear that there have been thousands of such changes, including many by Joseph Smith and others by prophets since.[31] Similarly, the publication of a critical edition of Joseph Smith's New Translation of the Bible shows that he made thousands of changes to the biblical text as well.[32] We can choose to recoil in ignorance and disbelief from such facts, or we can rejoice that we live in a time of wonderful discovery of our scriptural texts.

Perhaps we can learn from history how to approach this moment of enlightenment. European scholars in the early modern period (1500–1800) began to study the Bible critically, using historical, textual, and linguistic analyses to assess the composition of biblical texts. They discovered that the oldest source materials for the Bible show the influence of several writers of what we casually call the books of Moses, all written from different periods and perspectives. It became obvious that the biblical texts had been revised and redacted again and again. As evidence and arguments mounted that biblical texts had been composed in a more complicated process than many believers had assumed, some concluded that mortal influence on scripture making precluded the possibility that the Bible was divinely inspired. Other people entrenched behind fundamentalism, the idea set forth by a group of American Protestants in the late nineteenth and early twentieth centuries that the Bible is inerrant. These two camps created a false dilemma, unnecessarily concluding that the scriptures must be either divine or human texts.

Latter-day Saints are now faced with a similar situation regarding Restoration scripture. In 2009 the Church Historian's Press published *The Joseph Smith Papers: Manuscript Revelation Books*, a massive eight-pound volume that includes painstaking transcriptions and high-resolution images of the earliest extant manuscripts of Joseph Smith's revelation texts. As with the oldest biblical manuscripts, these texts are full of evidence that the revelations were revised and redacted. Studying them leads to "a richer, more nuanced view, one that sees Joseph as more than a mere human fax machine through whom God communicated revelation texts composed in heaven."[33] This is not a problem for believers who think of revelation as a process of communication between God and mortals whereby we come to understand the revelations. It is not a problem for Saints who believe the eighth and ninth articles of faith and the title page of the Book of Mormon. The definition of scripture set forth in the Doctrine and Covenants does not envision a pristine, unchangeable set of marks on a page but rather describes scripture as "the mind of the Lord" communicated "by the Holy Ghost" through fallible servants in their imperfect languages (68:3–4; see 1:24). However, the reality of these revelation texts and the process of revelation they evidence can be a problem for those who make fundamentalist assumptions about scripture—assumptions that are not doctrinal, scriptural, or consistent with the teachings of Joseph Smith.

The doctrine of The Church of Jesus Christ of Latter-day Saints is that God has revealed himself in the past, does so now, and will yet, but that the records of such revelations are not the revelations themselves; they are but representations captured in our language so that we might come to understand them if we consider the words carefully and solemnly, in light of experience and the Holy Spirit. We make no claim that any scripture is inerrant or infallible. In fact, the title page of the Book of Mormon asserts that even that most correct book is a combination of "the things of God" and "the mistakes of men." Such was Joseph Smith's understanding of scripture, including the scriptures based on his revelation texts. Joseph knew better than anyone else that the words he dictated were both human and divine, the voice of God clothed in the words of his own limited, early American English vocabulary. He regarded himself as a revelator whose understanding accumulated over time. Joseph recognized as a result of the revelatory process that the texts of his revelations were not set in stone. Rather, he felt responsible to revise and redact them to reflect his latest understanding. He was always open, in other words, to receive more revelation. He knew, too, especially as he reflected with the aid of much experience, that a loving God sometimes turns on the lights in an instant, but even then it takes time for our eyes to adjust, and then it requires experience for us to make sense of what we see.

Steven C. Harper is a professor of Church history and doctrine at Brigham Young University.

Steven C. Harper, "'That They Might Come to Understanding': Revelation as Process," in *You Shall Have My Word: Exploring the Text of the Doctrine and Covenants*, ed. Scott C. Esplin, Richard O. Cowan, and Rachel Cope (Provo, UT: Religious Studies Center, Brigham Young University; Salt Lake City: Deseret Book, 2012), 19–33.

NOTES

1. Wilford Woodruff Journal, May 14, 1843, Yelrome, Hancock County, Illinois, in *The Words of Joseph Smith: The Contemporary Accounts of the Nauvoo Discourses of the Prophet Joseph*, ed. Andrew F. Ehat and Lyndon W. Cook (Provo, UT: Religious Studies Center, Brigham Young University, 1980), 200–202.
2. David A. Bednar, "The Spirit of Revelation," *Ensign*, May 2011, 87.
3. Bednar, "Spirit of Revelation," 87.
4. Manuscript History, Book A–1, 161–62, Church History Library, The Church of Jesus Christ of Latter-day Saints, Salt Lake City, handwriting of Willard Richards. Joseph Smith to William W. Phelps, November 27, 1832, in *The Personal Writings of Joseph Smith*, ed. Dean C. Jessee, rev. ed. (Salt Lake City: Deseret Book; Provo, UT: Brigham Young University Press, 2002), 284–87.
5. David Carpenter, "Revelation in Comparative Perspective: Lessons for Inter-religious Dialogue," *Journal of Ecumenical Studies* 29, no. 2 (Spring 1992): 185–86; emphasis in original.
6. Richard Lyman Bushman, *Joseph Smith: Rough Stone Rolling* (New York: Alfred A. Knopf, 2005), 174.
7. Brigham Young, in *Journal of Discourses* (London: Latter-day Saints' Book Depot, 1855), 2:314.
8. Minute Book 2, p. 18, http://josephsmithpapers.org/.
9. Joseph Smith, History, 1838–1856, volume A-1 [23 December 1805–30 August 1834], p. 161, http://josephsmithpapers.org/. See also Jan Shipps and John W. Welch, eds., *The Journals of William E. McLellin, 1831–1836* (Urbana: University of Illinois Press; Provo, UT: BYU Studies, 1994), 251.
10. Minute Book 2, p. 11.
11. See Joseph Smith to William W. Phelps, November 27, 1832, in Jessee, *Personal Writings of Joseph Smith*, 284–87; and Letter to William W. Phelps, 27 November 1832, p. 1, http://josephsmithpapers.org/.
12. Smith, History, 1838–1856, volume A-1, p. 162.

13. Minute Book 2, p. 16.
14. In *The Joseph Smith Papers, Revelations and Translations*, 1:214–15.
15. See Far West Record, November 1–2, 1831.
16. Minutes, 8 November 1831, p. 16, http://josephsmithpapers.org/.
17. Joseph's journal entry for December 1, 1832, for instance, says that he "wrote and corrected revelations &c." *The Joseph Smith Papers, Journals*, 1:10.
18. Joseph Smith to William W. Phelps, July 31, 1832, in Jessee, *Personal Writings of Joseph Smith*, 284–87.
19. Bushman, *Rough Stone Rolling*, 174.
20. Oliver Cowdery, *The Evening and Morning Star* (1835; repr., Burlington, WI: n.p., 1992), 16. Grant Underwood elaborates more examples of revisions in "Revelation, Text, and Revision: Insight from the Book of Commandments and Revelations," *BYU Studies* 48, no. 3 (2009): 77.
21. Greg Anderson, *Doctored Covenants* (Salt Lake City: Modern Microfilm, 1963).
22. Boyd K. Packer, in Conference Report, April 1974, 137.
23. *The Journals of William E. McLellin: 1831–1836*, ed. John W. Welch and Jan Shipps (Provo, UT: BYU Studies), 79–84.
24. Minutes, 8 November 1831, p. 16, http://josephsmithpapers.org/.
25. Stan Larson and Samuel J. Passey, eds., *The William E. McLellin Papers, 1854–1880* (Salt Lake City: Signature Books, 2007), 474–75; *Joseph Smith Papers, Revelations and Translations, Manuscript Revelation Books*, xxix.
26. Underwood, "Revelation, Text, and Revision,"78.
27. See Noah Webster, *An American Dictionary of the English Language* (New York: S. Converse, 1828; reprinted in facsimile by the Foundation for American Christian Education, San Francisco, 1967), s.v. "quickly."
28. Joseph Smith to Presendia Huntington Buell, March 15, 1839, Liberty, Missouri, in Jessee, *Personal Writings of Joseph Smith*, 386–87.
29. Joseph Smith, Hyrum Smith, Lyman Wight, Caleb Baldwin, and Alexander McRae, Letter to the Church and Edward Partridge, 20 March 1839, p. 12, http://josephsmithpapers.org/; and Jessee, *Personal Writings of Joseph Smith*, 388–407.
30. Minute Book 2, p. 16.
31. For example, see "The Book of Mormon Critical Text Project," *Journal of Book of Mormon Studies* 7, no. 1 (1998): 30.
32. See Scott H. Faulring, Kent P. Jackson, and Robert J. Matthews, eds., *Joseph Smith's New Translation of the Bible: Original Manuscripts* (Provo, UT: Religious Studies Center, Brigham Young University, 2004), passim.
33. Underwood, "Revelation, Text, and Revision," 78.

Chapter Ten

"A Covenant and a Deed Which Cannot Be Broken"

The Continuing Saga of Consecration

CASEY PAUL GRIFFITHS

Among modern Latter-day Saints there is a tendency to use past-tense or future-tense language when speaking of the law of consecration, as if consecration is either something that Church members *used* to live or something the Saints *will come* to live in the future. Not only is this an inaccurate reading of the early revelations of the Restoration, but it also directly ignores standard practice in the Church today. Consecration was introduced by the Lord as "a covenant and a deed which cannot be broken" to fulfill his command to "remember the poor" (Doctrine and Covenants 42:30).[1] This study serves to provide a broad overview of the practice of consecration within the Church, from 1831 to the present. While it is impossible to fully explore consecration in all its forms in a work as brief as this one, historical examples from every period of Church history show a consistent series of attempts by the leaders of the Church to understand the principles of consecration and adapt them to their own circumstances. The few examples mentioned here demonstrate that, while the means and methods of the *practice* of consecration underwent alterations throughout the history of the Church, the *doctrines* and *principles* of consecration have never been rescinded. The attempts to implement the principles form a golden thread of charity running throughout the entire history of the Church and even into the present day.[2]

CHURCH PRACTICE AND PRINCIPLES

One of the misunderstandings about the law of consecration surrounds the operation introduced by the Lord in an early revelation given to the Prophet Joseph Smith (Doctrine and Covenants 42).[3] Part of the tendency to refer to the law of consecration as a practice of the past grows out of a belief that this revelation, given in 1831, represents the only way consecration can be fully carried out. This view ignores the continual alterations made to the methodology of consecration found throughout the revelations of Joseph Smith. Consecration is perhaps best thought of as a set of guiding principles and doctrines introduced throughout the Doctrine and Covenants, and not a strict set of rules. The practice of consecration, like many Church practices, has been continually altered to fit the needs of the changing Church. The way consecration was practiced in 1831 Kirtland, 1838 Missouri, or 1870s Utah does not necessarily represent the best way for it to operate in the global Church of the twenty-first century. President Boyd K. Packer explained, "Changes in organization or procedures are a testimony that revelation is ongoing. . . . The doctrines will remain fixed, eternal; the organizations, programs, and procedures will be altered by Him whose church this is."[4] The first step toward understanding consecration is to identify the key doctrines and principles found in the revelations of Joseph Smith.

PRINCIPLES OF CONSECRATION

The most basic approach to understanding consecration is to examine the meaning of the word itself and how it was used in the time frame of the early Restoration. An 1828 dictionary defined *consecration* as "the act or ceremony of separating from a common to a sacred use." The entry further adds "consecration does not make a person or a thing *holy*, but declares it to be *sacred*, that is, devoted to God or to divine service."[5] This is a broad definition of the term but is perhaps the most useful in order to comprehend the wide range of practical applications of the law of consecration. Throughout the history of the Latter-day Saints the terms *law of consecration* and *United Order* both refer to attempts to devote the temporal and spiritual resources of the Church to assist the poor and needy. In practice these attempts took many forms. While the law of consecration for the early

Saints in Kirtland or Nauvoo was markedly different from today's practice, Saints in all ages make the covenant to offer their resources to the sacred use of God's kingdom.

A cursory reading of the revelations of Joseph Smith provides insight to the importance of consecration. Speaking conservatively, at least twenty-four revelations in the Doctrine and Covenants deal directly with consecration and different methods of implementing it.[6] The earliest mention of an organized form of caring for the poor is found in a January 1831 revelation in which the Lord commands the Saints that certain men should be appointed among them to "look to the poor and the needy, and administer to their relief that they shall not suffer" (Doctrine and Covenants 38:35).[7] A few weeks later, after Joseph Smith arrived in Kirtland, Ohio, a revelation was given labeled in its earliest forms as "The Laws of the Church of Christ."[8] This revelation gave the first specific instructions about how to provide for the poor and needy.

The portion of the revelation detailing consecration begins, "Behold thou shalt consecrate *all* thy properties that which thou hast unto me with a covenant and deed which cannot be broken and they shall be laid before the Bishop of my church."[9] Inclusion of the word *all* leads the reader to believe that every single item of property possessed by an individual must be submitted to the priesthood leaders. The Prophet and his associates clarified this in later editions of the revelation, most significantly in the 1835 edition of the Doctrine and Covenants, which changed the passage to instruct the Saints to "consecrate *of* thy properties."[10] Consecration of properties denotes a sacrifice of resources to benefit the poor but leads away from a completely communal interpretation of the law that would require all property to be given to the Church.

This is further bolstered by the next instruction given in the revelation, when the Lord provides instructions for the priesthood leaders charged with administering the law. They must provide a stewardship, allowing participants to be stewards over their "own property, or that which he has received by consecration, as much as is sufficient for himself and family" (Doctrine and Covenants 42:32).[11] Additional revelations confirmed that while unity was a primary goal of the law, equality was a relative term. Following the Lord's counsel in the earliest copies of the revelation, stewardships were provided not just according to the needs and wants of an individual or family. When the revelation was first published in the 1835 edition of the Doctrine and Covenants, the Prophet was inspired to add the phrase "according to his circumstances" (51:3).[12] Provisions were also added to clarify that Saints who chose to no longer participate in the law retained their stewardships but could not reclaim what they had consecrated (see 42:37; 51:5).[13] Private ownership of property and voluntary participation served as key principles of the law from the start. Joseph Smith and other Church leaders wrote in an 1833 letter, "Every man must be his own judge how much he should receive and how much he should suffer to remain in the hands of the Bishop. . . . The matter of consecration must be done by mutual consent of both parties."[14]

Another key component of the law consisted of the use of surpluses to provide for "a storehouse, to administer to the poor and the needy" and also for purchasing land, "building houses of worship" and "building up of the New Jerusalem" (42:34–35).[15] Other revelations instruct that the storehouse be directed under the hands of a bishop or church agents "appointed by the voice of the church" (51:12–13).[16] The storehouse was "common property of the whole church," with every person improving their "talents"—a word denoting both the New Testament currency and the gifts and abilities given by the Lord (82:18).[17] An undergirding motivation for the law was the need for the Saints to sacrifice in order to build a faithful community with the New Jerusalem on their spiritual horizon.[18]

Finally, the Lord commanded the Saints to avoid pride, be modest in dress, and be clean (42:40–41). The revelation also commanded the Saints to eschew idleness, warning "he that is idle shall not eat the bread nor wear the garments of the laborer" (42:42).[19] (By no means do these statements represent a comprehensive treatment of all of the Lord's commandments to early Saints concerning consecration. Our aim here is simply to provide a summary of the key principles of the law.) Throughout the history of the Church, these principles remained consistent. Since 1831, successive generations of Church leadership have applied them in a wide variety of circumstances. This is logical given the varied circumstances the Saints have found themselves in, from times when the entire membership of the Church consisted of a small handful of people to today, when millions of Saints live in diverse circumstances around the globe. In an effort to illustrate the different applications of the law of consecration, we will now embark on a brief overview of the history of consecration in the Church from its founding to the present day.

CONSECRATION IN THE EARLY RESTORATION, 1831–1844

One of the key evidences that the law of consecration was not intended to strictly follow the mode of operation explained in Doctrine and Covenants

42 is found in the versatile ways Joseph Smith directed the practice of the law. In some ways, consecration began in the Church as a grassroots effort. When Joseph Smith arrived in Kirtland, Ohio, he already found members trying to implement a form of communal living on their own. One outside observer from the time noted, "Isaac Morley had contended that in order to restore the ancient order of things in the Church of Christ, it was necessary that there should be a community of goods among the brethren; and accordingly a number of them removed to his house and farm, and built houses and worked and lived together, and composed what is here called the 'Big Family,' which at this time consisted of 50 or 60, old and young."[20]

The new converts in Kirtland began the effort out of a sincere desire to adhere to the scriptures, but a lack of specific direction caused problems to emerge immediately. Church historian John Whitmer later recorded, "The disciples had all things in common, and were going to destruction very fast as to temporal things. . . . Therefore they would take each other's clothes and other property and use it without leave, which brought on confusion."[21] When Joseph Smith arrived in Kirtland in February 1831, a number of members clamored to know the Lord's will concerning the practice of communal living. In response to these requests, the Lord provided the revelations that revealed the foundational principles of consecration (Doctrine and Covenants 42; 51).

The first attempt to practice the principles of the law in Kirtland was short-lived. The initial signs of trouble appeared in June 1831, when Leman Copley, a recent convert, rescinded on an offer to allow Church members arriving from Colesville, New York, to settle on his land. In a revelation the Lord informed the Colesville Saints that "the covenant which they made unto me has been broken, even so it has become void and of none effect" (Doctrine and Covenants 54:4). The Lord condemned Copley for breaking his oath but assured blessings for those who "kept the covenant and observed the commandment, for they shall obtain mercy" (vv. 5–6).[22]

The episode involving Leman Copley and the Colesville Saints serves as a dramatic example of some of the challenges facing consecration, but it was not the end of attempts at consecration among the early members of the Church. Through Joseph Smith's presidency the Lord offered a number of different ways to adapt the principles of consecration to meet the needs of the young Church. In a revelation given in November 1831, the Lord commanded Joseph Smith and five others to create an organization to manage the publication of Church materials, including the scriptures and other supplies. Funds raised through the work of this firm could be used to provide for the temporal needs of its members, with the Lord directing that the surplus "be given into my storehouse and the benefits thereof shall be consecrated unto the inhabitants of Zion and unto their generations" (Doctrine and Covenants 70:7–8).[23] In the minutes of this organization it was referred to as the Literary Firm.[24] In March 1832 another revelation directed Church leadership to organize several Church-owned businesses, such as Newel K. Whitney's store in Kirtland, Ohio, and A. Sidney Gilbert's store in Independence, Missouri, to serve as a "storehouse for the poor" (78:3). These businesses, along with the Literary Firm and other Church interests, were brought together in a new organization referred to by its members as the United Firm (78:8).[25] This organization, at times referred to by the code name "United Order," has been referred to as the Church's "first master plan of business and finance."[26] The United Firm continued to play a key role in the financial affairs of the Church until 1834, when it was divided into two separate orders, one in Ohio and the other in Missouri, partly because of the persecution faced by Church members in Missouri, but also because of the transgressions and covetousness of the Saints (see 104:51, 78–86).[27]

The United Firm was only one of several examples where the principles of consecration were applied in different ways to meet the needs of the Church. In August 1833 Joseph Smith received a revelation directing the organization of a committee to oversee the construction of the house of the Lord, later known as the Kirtland Temple, along with a "house for the presidency" and a "house for the printing of the translation of my scriptures" (Doctrine and Covenants 88:119; 94:3,10).[28] When the Lord dissolved the United Firm, he commanded Church leaders to create two treasuries. The first was designated as "exclusive of the sacred things, for the purpose of printing these sacred things," a reference to the scriptures (104:60–66). At the same time the Lord set up "another treasury" for the purpose of "improving upon the properties which I have appointed unto you" (vv. 67–68).[29] These moves demonstrated the importance of disseminating revelations as widely as possible.

Throughout most of the 1830s, the Saints made various attempts to practice the law of consecration. One of the most important revelations in its development was given in Far West, Missouri, in July 1839. The revelation came in answer to the Prophet's question, "O! Lord, show unto thy servants how much thou requirest of the properties of thy people for a Tithing?" The reply came: "I require all their surplus property to be put into the hands of the bishop of my church in Zion, for the building of mine house, and for the laying of the foundation of Zion and for the priesthood, and for the debts of the Presidency of my Church. And this shall be the beginning of the tithing of my people. And after that, those who have thus been tithed, shall pay one tenth of all their interest annually; and this shall be a standing law unto them forever" (Doctrine and Covenants 119:1–4).[30] From the text it is clear that the law of tithing was not intended to replace the law of consecration. All the principles of consecration remained intact, with the added command for the Saints to contribute an additional tithe of ten percent.[31]

A mistaken impression has arisen within the Church that the law of tithing, given in 1838, replaced the law of consecration. In many ways the law of tithing required a greater sacrifice than the law of consecration: consecration required members to give their surplus *after* their needs were satisfied; tithing required ten percent *before* any of their needs were met.[32] However, the requirement to give up a surplus did not end. After section 119 was given, Brigham Young asked Joseph Smith, "Who shall be the judge of what is surplus property?" to which the Prophet responded, "Let them be the judge for themselves."[33]

The extreme trials of 1838–40 as the Prophet Joseph and other Church leaders languished in Liberty Jail and the Saints sought refuge in Illinois caused a further suspension in the Saints' attempts to live the law of consecration. Recognizing the suffering of the Saints, the Prophet continued to urge them to comply with the principles of the law, writing, "For a man to consecrate his property . . . is nothing more nor less than to feed the hungry, clothe the naked, visit the widow and the fatherless, the sick and the afflicted, and do all he can to administer to their relief in their afflictions, and for him and his house to serve the Lord."[34]

Amid the difficulties surrounding the move to Illinois and the creation of the city of Nauvoo out of the malarial swamps on the banks of the Mississippi River, Joseph Smith steered a conservative course, freeing the people from their obligation to comply with all facets of the law. Elias Smith recorded a discourse given by the Prophet in 1840: "He said that the law of consecration could not be kept here and that it was the will of the Lord we should desist from trying to keep it . . . and that he assumed the whole responsibility of not keeping it until proposed by himself."[35]

Historians have at times referred to the Nauvoo era as a fallow period for consecration, but more recently documentary evidence has emerged demonstrating attempts to implement a more regimented practice of the doctrine during this time. A meeting recorded in Wilford Woodruff's journal from June 18, 1842, notes that "Joseph commanded the Twelve to organize the Church more according to the Law of God," a likely reference to a renewed attempt to implement consecration.[36] Only a few days later Brigham Young preached a sermon on "the law of consecration, and union of action in building up the city and providing labor for the city and providing labor and food for the poor."[37] Recently historians Mitchell K. Schaefer and Sherilyn Farnes identified and published twenty affidavits of consecration dating from June 1842, the same period as when Joseph made this request of the Twelve.[38] Lewis Ziegler, a Latter-day Saint from the period, wrote in his affidavit, "I for my part feel willing to lay what little is Committed to what is my trust at the Apostle[s'] feet . . . asking the hand of my heavenly Father to strengthen their hands abundantly."[39]

These attempts to renew earlier practices of consecration do not appear to have been fruitful, but the doctrine of consecration remained at the core of the Saints' relationship with the Lord. As evidence of this, a covenant to commit to live the law of consecration was included in the sacred rites of the temple when they were revealed to Joseph Smith during his ministry in Nauvoo.[40]

THE UNITED ORDER IN THE WEST, 1846–1885

The emergency conditions surrounding the exodus from Nauvoo and the eventual migration of the main body of the Church to the Salt Lake Valley made it difficult to set a uniform system for the practice of consecration. Nevertheless, the principles of the law remained a vital part of the beliefs of the Saints. In October 1845, Brigham Young proposed a covenant "that we take all the saints with us to the extent of our ability, that is, our influence and property."[41] The Lord reiterated the need for consecration in a revelation given at Winter Quarters, declaring, "Let each company bear an equal proportion, according to the dividend of their property, in taking the poor, the widows, the fatherless" and that "every man use all his influence and property to remove this people to the place where the Lord shall locate a stake of Zion" (Doctrine and Covenants 136:8, 10). As the settlements of the Saints spread throughout the Intermountain West, cooperation in irrigation and agricultural projects became essential for their survival. As the Saints became more settled, Brigham Young made attempts to launch a more formal program of consecration in the 1850s, though the conflict with the federal government of the United States in 1857 brought a practical end to most of these efforts.[42]

A more spirited effort to bring practice to the principles of consecration began in 1874 and lasted until roughly 1885.[43] Failure to live the law of consecration had long lingered in the minds of Church leaders, and Brigham Young spearheaded an effort to return the Saints to the ideals of consecration. According to reports of a meeting held in April 1874, "President Young showed very clearly that it [the united order] was not a personal speculation; that himself with the rest would put in all he possessed for the accomplishment of the work he was engaged in. . . . The intention was to elevate the poor, and make them as comfortable and happy as well as the rich. He wanted no poor in our midst, nor would there be any when the Order got fully established."[44] Spurred on by the encouragement of Church leaders, new united orders sprang up throughout the Intermountain West. In initiating these efforts, Church leaders did not follow the exact same procedures given in the Doctrine and Covenants. Instead they taught the principles of the law and allowed the leaders in each individual settlement to work out procedures for the implementation of consecration. Thus, the systems of consecration varied from place to place, with consecration working slightly differently in St. George than it did in Kanab, Orderville, or any of the locations where the Saints organized their efforts. The entire Churchwide effort was loosely labeled "the United Order" or the "Order of Enoch," though it differed in many respects from the united order of Joseph Smith's day.[45]

INTERLUDE: THE TRANSITIONAL PERIOD AND THE LAW OF TITHING, 1885–1935

Success varied in each of these efforts, but most ended when the Church became embroiled in the battle with the government of the United States over plural marriage. The battle financially exhausted the Church, making any new attempts to practice the law of consecration out of the question.[46] In the wake of fiscal devastation left by the anti-polygamy crusades, Church leaders worked to place the Church back on a stable footing. As part of this effort, leaders emphasized the law of tithing as the most practical means of accomplishing their goals. It is during this period that the belief that the law of tithing had replaced consecration became more prevalent. For instance, in April 1900 Joseph F. Smith, then a counselor in the First Presidency taught, "The Lord revealed to his people in the incipiency of His work a law [consecration] which was more perfect than the law of tithing. It comprehended larger things, greater power and a more speedy accomplishment of the purposes of the Lord. But the people were unprepared to live by it, and the Lord, out of mercy to the people, suspended the more perfect law, and gave the law of tithing."[47]

While there was no revelation officially suspending the law of consecration, President Smith was correct in stating that during this period, when the Church was transitioning from its relative isolation in the West and moving closer to the mainstream of society, the practices of consecration received less emphasis and the more clear-cut guidelines of tithing, a subset of the entire law, were given emphasis. At the same time, the Church did not abandon its charge to assist the poor and needy. During this period bishops were still given instruction to use fast offerings and Relief Society contributions to care for the poor. Church handbooks from the period instructed local leaders to send their surplus to Church headquarters to assist more needy wards and branches, though it was rare at the time for Church units to use less than their members contributed.[48]

These offerings allowed leaders to care for the immediate needs of the poor, but a larger, overarching structure to implement consecration did not exist. Furthermore, a general perception lingered that consecration was a future goal. In 1931 Elder Orson F. Whitney taught, "The Lord withdrew the Law of Consecration and gave his people a lesser law, one easier to live, but pointing forward, like the other to something grand and glorious in the future."[49] While Elder Whitney's comments imply a distant promise of future consecration, they came on the eve of the most successful and long-lasting implementation of consecration practices within the Church.

THE CHURCH WELFARE PROGRAM, 1935–PRESENT

Ironically, the most enduring practical implementation of the law of consecration was born out of one of the worst economic catastrophes in history. In the depths of the Great Depression, Harold B. Lee, the president of the Pioneer Stake in Salt Lake City, launched an innovative series of programs designed to provide work and support for the struggling members of the stake. A storehouse where food and commodities could be gathered and distributed to the needy was built. Lee and his counselors purchased warehouses, a farm, and other enterprises, and the men of the stake were given opportunities to work for what they would receive from the storehouse. The particulars of the plan were new to the Church, but President Lee was quick to point out that the principles behind it were not. In an article explaining the plan, Lee wrote, "The Church security plan is not something new to the Church; neither does it contemplate a new organization in the Church to carry out its purposes; but rather it is an expression of a philosophy that is as old as the Church itself, incorporated into a program of stimulation and cooperation to meet the demands of Church members in the solution of present day economic problems."[50]

While Harold B. Lee and other stake presidents worked from the ground up to care for the poor, leaders in the top echelons of Church government also began to reexamine consecration. J. Reuben Clark, a newly called counselor in the First Presidency, began to make an extensive study of the revelations in the Doctrine and Covenants pertaining to consecration.[51] As President Clark and other Church leaders observed the success of these programs, a plan began to develop to apply the principles of consecration on a wider level. On April 18, 1936, the First Presidency met with Harold B. Lee, who later wrote, "President [Heber J.] Grant said he wanted to take a 'leaf out of the Pioneer Stake's book in caring for the people of the Church. . . . He said that nothing was more important for the Church to do than to take care of its needy people and that so far as he was concerned, everything else must be sacrificed [so that] proper relief [could be] extended to our people."[52] Harold B. Lee was named as the managing director of the new program, and at the October general conference the following fall, the First Presidency announced the launch of the Church welfare plan. At a meeting for stake presidents, the First Presidency declared, "The real long term objective of the Welfare Plan is the building of character in the members of the Church, givers and receivers, rescuing all that is finest down deep inside of them, and bring to flower and fruitage the latent richness of the spirit, which after all is the mission and purpose and reason for being of this Church."[53]

During the infancy of the Church welfare program, Church leaders downplayed the similarities between the new program and the early efforts of Church members. Speaking of the Church welfare system and the law of consecration, President J. Reuben Clark noted, "We have all said that the Welfare Plan is not the United Order and was not intended to be." He then added, "However, I should like to suggest to you that perhaps, after all, when the Welfare Plan gets thoroughly into operation—it is not so yet—we shall not be so very far from carrying out the great fundamentals of the United Order."[54]

CONSECRATION IN OUR TIME AND BEYOND

Is the Church welfare system the same thing as the United Order? Church members do not follow the exact methodology first mentioned in the revelations of Joseph Smith, but the principles of consecration have endured. Consecration, stewardships, storehouses, and nearly every component of the early revelations eventually found their way into the structure of the Church welfare systems. In 1943 J. Reuben Clark presented a plan to the Quorum of the Twelve in which he noted, "I took it upon myself to make a study of the financial operations of the Church from the beginning down through and until after the death of the Prophet [Joseph Smith]."[55] At a ten-year anniversary of the Welfare Plan, President Clark reflected, "The Lord has always been mindful of the poor and of the unfortunate, and He has always charged His Church and its members to see to it that none of their brethren and their sisters suffer."[56]

Church leaders of this founding generation never became comfortable identifying their work to create the Church welfare plan as the same thing as the law of consecration, but the ensuing generations began to recognize the fulfillment of the principles of the law in the new plan. In a 1966 general conference address, Elder Marion G. Romney of the Quorum of the Twelve (who later became President of the Quorum of the Twelve) exhorted priesthood holders to "live strictly by the principles of the United Order insofar as they are embodied in present church practices, such as the fast offering, tithing, and the welfare activities. He then added, "Through these practices we could as individuals, if we were of a mind to do so, implement in our own lives all the basic principles of the United Order."[57] In 1975 Elder Romney said, "The procedural method for teaching Church Welfare has now changed, but the objectives of the program remain the same. *Its principles are eternal.* It is the gospel in its perfection—the united order, toward which we move."[58]

As time progressed, Church leaders became more comfortable in seeing the Church welfare program as another iteration of consecration. In an address given in 2011, President Henry B. Eyring stated that the Lord's "way of helping has at times been called living the law of consecration. In another period His way was called the united order. In our time it is called the Church welfare program." Providing a summary of the evolution of the law, President Eyring added, "The names and details of the operation are changed to fit the needs and conditions of people. But always the Lord's way to help those in temporal need requires people who out of love have consecrated themselves and what they have to God and to His work."[59]

There is nothing past tense about the law of consecration. It remains a vital part of the work of the Lord's kingdom on the Earth. The doctrines of consecration are eternal and will always have a place in the Church. The eternal components of the law—love for God, love for neighbor, agency, stewardship, and accountability—are a vital part of the gospel of Jesus Christ. The temporal applications of the law, deeds, economic practices, and building and publishing projects are subject to frequent change. Until the return of the Savior, we shall have the poor with us always (see Matthew 26:11), and as long as the poor are with us, we also have a charge to provide care and solace to them. The law of consecration is not an ideal, or a commandment; it is a covenant entered into by every worthy member of the Church. President Eyring taught, "He has invited and commanded us to participate in His work to lift up those in need. We make a covenant to do that in the waters of baptism and in the holy temples of God. We renew the covenant on Sundays when we partake of the sacrament."[60] Though often misunderstood, overlooked, or forgotten, the covenant of consecration will always be a foundational part of the Restoration and the operation of the Lord's true Church.

Casey Paul Griffiths is an associate teaching professor of Church history and doctrine at Brigham Young University.

Casey Paul Griffiths, "'A Covenant and a Deed Which Cannot Be Broken': The Continuing Saga of Consecration," in *Foundations of the Restoration: Fulfillment of the Covenant Purposes*, ed. Craig James Ostler, Michael Hubbard MacKay, and Barbara Morgan Gardner (Provo, UT: Religious Studies Center, Brigham Young University; Salt Lake City: Deseret Book, 2016), 121–37.

NOTES

1. The admonition to "remember the poor" and to consecrate properties "for their [the poor's] support" was first added in the 1835 edition of the Doctrine and Covenants. See *The Joseph Smith Papers, Documents*, 1:251 (hereafter *JSP*, D1); see also *The Parallel Doctrine and Covenants: The 1832–33, 1833, and 1835 editions of Joseph Smith's Revelations* (Salt Lake City: Signature Books, 2009), 68.

2. I am indebted to many authors who have argued this point before me, chiefly Lyndon W. Cook in *Joseph Smith and the Law of Consecration* (Provo, UT: Grandin Book, 1985), viii; Craig Ostler, "The Laws of Consecration, Stewardship, and Tithing," in *Sperry Symposium Classics: The Doctrine and Covenants*, ed. Craig K.

Manscill (Salt Lake City: Deseret Book, 2004); and Steven C. Harper, "'All Things Are the Lord's': The Law of Consecration in the Doctrine and Covenants," in *The Doctrine and Covenants: Revelations in Context* (Salt Lake City: Deseret Book, 2008).

3. See Revelation, 9 February 1831 [D&C 42:1–72], in *JSP*, D1:245–56.

4. Boyd K. Packer, "Revelation in a Changing World," *Ensign*, November 1989.

5. Noah Webster, *An American Dictionary of the English Language* (1828), online edition, http://webstersdictionary1828.com/Dictionary/consecration.

6. See Craig James Ostler, "Consecration," in *Doctrine and Covenants Reference Companion*, ed. Dennis L. Largey (Salt Lake City: Deseret Book, 2012), 106. The sections focusing primarily on consecration are Doctrine and Covenants 38, 42, 44, 48, 51, 54, 56, 58, 70, 72, 78, 82–85, 92, 96–97, 104–6, 119–120, and 136.

7. Revelation, 2 January 1831 [D&C 38], in *JSP*, D1:233.

8. Revelation, 9 February 1831, in *JSP*, D1:245–56.

9. In *JSP*, D1:251; spelling and capitalization modernized and emphasis added.

10. See Doctrine and Covenants 42:30; and *JSP, Revelations and Translations*, 2:105, 218, 433 (hereafter *JSP*, R2). The change in wording first appeared in *The Evening and Morning Star*, July 1832. It has remained consistent in every published version of the revelation down to the present day (2020).

11. Revelation, 9 February 1831, in *JSP*, D1: 251–52.

12. Revelation, 20 May 1831 [D&C 51], in *JSP*, D1:314–16; and Book of Commandments, in *JSP*, R2:127.

13. See Doctrine and Covenants (1835), section XXIII, 156, in *JSP*, R2:460; and revelation, 9 February 1831, in *JSP*, D1:252.

14. Letter to Church Leaders in Jackson County, Missouri, 25 June 1833, in *JSP*, D3:153.

15. Revelation, 9 February 1831, in *JSP*, D1:252.

16. Revelation, 20 May 1831, in *JSP*, D1:316.

17. Revelation, 26 April 1832 [D&C 82], in *JSP*, D2:236.

18. See Ostler, "Consecration," 158.

19. See Revelation, 9 February 1831, in *JSP*, D1:252.

20. Josiah Jones, "History of the Mormonites," *The Evangelist* 9 (1 June 1831): 132, quoted in Mark Lyman Staker, *Hearken, O Ye People: The Historical Setting for Joseph Smith's Ohio Revelations* (Salt Lake City: Greg Kofford Books, 2009), 45.

21. In *JSP, Histories*, 2:22–23 (hereafter *JSP*, H2).

22. Revelation, 10 June 1831 [D&C 54], in *JSP*, D1:335–36.

23. Revelation, 12 November 1831 [D&C 70], in *JSP*, D2:140.

24. Minutes, 30 April 1832, in *JSP*, D2:238, spelling corrected.

25. Minutes, circa 1 May 1832, in *JSP*, D2:244.

26. Staker, *Hearken, O Ye People*, 231; and Max H Parkin, "Joseph Smith and the United Firm: The Growth and Decline of the Church's First Master Plan of Business and Finance, Ohio and Missouri, 1832–1834," *BYU Studies* 46, no. 3 (2007): 56–60.

27. See Revelation, 23 April 1834 [D&C 104], *The Joseph Smith Papers*, http://josephsmithpapers.org/.

28. Revelation, 2 August 1833-B [D&C 94], in *JSP*, D3:206.

29. Revelation, 23 April 1834 [D&C 104], in Book of Commandments Book C, pp. [19–43], http://josephsmithpapers.org/.

30. Revelation, 8 July 1838-C [D&C 119], in Joseph Smith, Journal, March–September 1838, 56, http://josephsmithpapers.org/.

31. See Ostler, "Consecration," 172.

32. See Joseph Fielding McConkie and Craig J. Ostler, *Revelations of the Restoration* (Salt Lake City: Deseret Book, 2000), 936.

33. *The Complete Discourses of Brigham Young*, ed. Richard S. Van Wagoner (Salt Lake City: Smith-Pettit Foundation, 2009), 970.

34. Joseph Smith, Letter to the Church in Caldwell County, Missouri, 16 December 1838, http://josephsmithpapers.org/.

35. Discourse, 6 March 1840, as Reported by Elias Smith, http://josephsmithpapers .org/. Another witness recorded the Prophet saying, "Thus saith the Lord you need not observe the Law of Consecration until our case was decided in congress." Discourse, 6 March 1840, as Reported by John Smith, http://josephsmithpapers.org/.

36. *The Words of Joseph Smith*, comp. Andrew F. Ehat and Lyndon W. Cook (Provo, UT: Religious Studies Center, Brigham Young University, 1980), 124–25.

37. *Complete Discourses of Brigham Young*, 1:20.

38. See Mitchell K. Shaefer and Sherilyn Farnes, "Myself . . . I Consecrate to the God of Heaven," *BYU Studies* 50, no. 3 (2011): 101.

39. Shaefer and Farnes, "Myself . . . I Consecrate," 132, original spelling and punctuation preserved. Shaefer and Farnes note that this affidavit of consecration is the only known documentation of Lewis Ziegler.

40. See Cook, *Joseph Smith and the Law of Consecration*, 90.

41. *Complete Discourses of Brigham Young*, 102; see Leonard J. Arrington, Feramorz Y. Fox, and Dean L. May, *Building the City of God: Community and Cooperation among the Mormons* (Salt Lake City: Deseret Book, 1976), 42.

42. See Arrington, Fox, and May, *Building the City of God*, 48, 63, 77–78.

43. See Edward J. Allen, *The Second United Order Among the Mormons* (New York: AMS Press, 1967), 10.

44. Quoted in *Deseret News*, April 22, 1874, from the *Beaver (Utah) Enterprise*.

45. See Arrington, Fox, and May, *Building the City of God*, which provides a detailed analysis of consecration systems in Brigham City, St. George, Richfield, Kanab, Orderville, Utah Valley, Cache Valley, Bear Lake Valley, and in other Latter-day Saint settlements in Arizona, Nevada, and Mexico.

46. See Arrington, Fox, and May, *Building the City of God*, 311–37.

47. Joseph F. Smith, in Conference Report, April 1900, 47.

48. See Bruce D. Blumell, "Welfare before Welfare: Twentieth-Century LDS Church Charity before the Great Depression," *Journal of Mormon History* 6 (1979): 92.

49. Orson F. Whitney, in Conference Report, April 1931, 63.

50. Harold B. Lee, "Church Security, Retrospect, Introspect, Prospect," *Improvement Era*, April 1937, 204.

51. Two unpublished documents in Clark's papers, "Notes on Church Finances," produced in June 1942, and "Study of the United Order," from March 1943, demonstrate Clark's serious intent to reform Church finances in line with the revelation in the Doctrine and Covenants. J. Reuben Clark Jr. papers, MSS 303, box 188, L. Tom Perry Special Collections, Harold B. Lee Library, Brigham Young University, Provo, Utah.

52. Glen L. Rudd, *Pure Religion: The Story of Church Welfare Since 1930* (Salt Lake City: The Church of Jesus Christ of Latter-day Saints, 1995), 39–40; and Garth Mangum and Bruce Blumell, *The Mormons' War on Poverty* (Salt Lake City: University of Utah Press, 1993), 130–32.

53. Rudd, *Pure Religion*, 45.

54. J. Reuben Clark Jr., in Conference Report, October 1942, 58.

55. J. Reuben Clark, "General Principles Underlying Church Finances," J. Reuben Clark Jr. papers, MSS 303, box 188.

56. J. Reuben Clark Jr. address, ca. 1946, J. Reuben Clark Jr. papers, MSS 303, box 158, 1.

57. Marion G. Romney, "Socialism and the United Order," *Improvement Era*, June 1966, 537.

58. Quoted in Arrington, Fox, and May, *Building the City of God*, 361; emphasis added.

59. Henry B. Eyring, "Opportunities to Do Good," *Ensign*, May 2011.

60. Eyring, "Opportunities to Do Good."

Chapter Eleven

"Her Borders Must Be Enlarged"

Evolving Conceptions of Zion

TAUNALYN F. RUTHERFORD

The establishment of Zion in preparation for Christ's Second Coming has always been a vital part of the "ongoing process" of the Restoration of the gospel.[1] It was central to the work of Joseph Smith and has continued to be so with each of his successors from Brigham Young to Russell M. Nelson; however, conceptions of Zion and its establishment have passed through an "ongoing process" of change as well. When the Lord revealed that he had "consecrated the land of Kirtland . . . for a stake to Zion," he also declared, "For Zion must increase in beauty, and in holiness; her borders must be enlarged; her stakes must be strengthened" (Doctrine and Covenants 82:13–14). It is clear that through revelation Joseph foresaw the "enlarged" borders of Zion beyond Missouri. We can see in the foundations laid by Joseph Smith a pattern for a global church—an ever-enlarging Zion. Scholars point to secular influences that have caused changes in Latter-day Saint understandings of Zion and changes in policies of gathering, and it is important to be aware of and understand such explanations. However, it is crucial in a study of the ongoing Restoration to see the hand of the Lord as well as his foreknowledge of modern events as having brought to fruition modern conceptions of Zion. Early revelations can seem to be at odds with the modern globalization of the Church unless viewed through the lens of the Lord's foreknowledge. As the title suggests, this chapter will show how the Lord revealed and prepared a way for a much larger Zion than what some early Saints initially conceived.

FOUNDATIONAL CONCEPTS OF ZION ESTABLISHED THROUGH JOSEPH SMITH: ZION AND THE BOOK OF MORMON

The coming forth of the Book of Mormon was a significant part of the establishment of foundational concepts of Zion in the Restoration. According to Joseph's account, during Moroni's first appearance to him, Moroni quoted Joel's prophecy of events of the "great and the terrible day of the Lord" and that "in *mount Zion* and in Jerusalem shall be deliverance."[2] The Book of Mormon contains numerous references to Zion in addition to the many times that Isaiah quotations mention Zion. For instance, the angel tells Nephi, "Blessed are they who shall seek to bring forth my Zion at that day [when the Lord brings forth the plain and precious gospel], for they shall have the gift and the power of the Holy Ghost" (1 Nephi 13:37). Nephi writes, "All who fight against Zion shall be destroyed" (1 Nephi 22:14).[3] Jacob adds his witness: "He that fighteth against Zion shall perish" (2 Nephi 10:13).[4] Abinadi testifies of a coming Zion, as does the Savior himself in his teachings to the Nephites (see Mosiah 15:29; 3 Nephi 16:18; 21:1). Finally, at a crowning moment in the Book of Mormon, a Zion society was established after the ministry of Christ to the Nephites (see 4 Nephi), and Moroni's final words admonish, "put on thy beautiful garments, O daughter of Zion; and strengthen thy stakes and enlarge thy borders forever, that thou mayest no more be confounded" (Moroni 10:31).

The Book of Mormon is evidence that in the very early stages of the Restoration the concept of Zion was significant. As Joseph and his followers began to read and internalize the message of the Book of Mormon, Ether's prophecy of a New Jerusalem on "this land" (Ether 13:2–12) became a particular interest, as was the prophecy by the Savior to the Nephites of a gathering of his people to Zion in America (see 3 Nephi 20:10–21:29). This interest brought about an enquiry of "Six Elders of the Church and three members" who seemed to believe "that the Book of Mormon prophecy about Zion would soon be fulfilled."[5] The Lord responded by calling the elders "to bring to pass the gathering of [his] elect" and specified that they would "be gathered in unto one place upon the face of this land" in preparation for his return (Doctrine and Covenants 29:7–12). Revelations had come previously through Joseph Smith calling followers to "seek to bring forth and establish the cause of Zion."[6] This revelation marked an important conceptual change from Zion as simply a cause to a specific, central gathering place for Zion.

THE LOCATION OF ZION

I acknowledge the complexity of Joseph Smith's understanding and revelations concerning Zion. It was simultaneously a cause and a geographical location or center to which those who choose Zion and flee Babylon can gather and a condition or internal state of righteousness. A pivotal process of revelation that expanded latter-day understandings of Zion was Joseph Smith's translation of the Bible, particularly the narrative of Enoch, which from a mere 5 verses in Genesis extended to 110 verses in the Book of Moses.[7] A definition of Zion is proclaimed in the narrative of Enoch: "And the Lord called his people Zion because they were of one heart and one mind, and dwelt in righteousness, and there was no poor among them" (Moses 7:18). The quest for just such a Zion became central to all that the Prophet did. The concept of consecration was also an important aspect of the project of Zion. It is impossible to fully separate the cause of Zion, the internal conditions of Zion, and the location of Zion as a gathering place; however, because of the constraints of this chapter, I will focus primarily on the changing conceptions of Zion as a geographical location and the accompanying doctrine of gathering.

As noted earlier, a September 1830 revelation had spoken of the gathering of the Lord's elect "unto one place upon the face of this land" (Doctrine and Covenants 29:8). In a follow-up to this revelation the Lord called Oliver Cowdery to preach to the "Lamanites" and promised that the location of the "city Zion" would "be given hereafter." A clue was also added: the location of Zion would "be on the borders by the Lamanites" (28:8–9).[8] That Joseph's concept of Zion encompassed more than just the much-anticipated geographic location for the city is evidenced in a letter he wrote to members in Colesville from Fayette, New York, dated December 2, 1830, in which he reports, "Zion is prospering here."[9] The anticipation of the location of the city of Zion, the New Jerusalem increased in March 1831 as revelations encouraged the Saints to prepare to "gather out of the eastern lands" and "gather up" their riches to be prepared to "purchase an inheritance" in Zion, the location of which had still not been revealed (45:64–66; 48:3–6). In July of 1831 the Lord declared Missouri as the land "for the gathering of the

Dedicating the temple lot in Independence, Missouri, by Harold T. Kilbourn. © Intellectual Reserve, Inc.

saints" and as "the place for the city of Zion" (57:1–2). Furthermore, the Lord declared "the place which is now called Independence" as "the center place" and specified "a spot for the temple" that was "lying westward, upon a lot which is not far from the courthouse" (v. 3).

STAKES OF ZION

While Joseph Smith's revelations established Independence, Missouri, as the center place and the location of the future city of Zion, the concept of gathering to Zion in the revelations was always more expansive. For instance, as early as November 1831 Joseph received a revelation in which the voice of the Lord declared, "Send forth the elders of my church unto the nations which are afar off." These elders were to cry, "Go ye forth unto the land of Zion, that the borders of my people may be enlarged, and that her stakes may be strengthened and that Zion may go forth unto the regions round about" (Doctrine and Covenants 133:8–9). By April 1832, the concept of a stake had been further solidified when Kirtland was designated as the first "stake to Zion" (82:13). The reason for the consecration of the stake in Kirtland was given by the Lord: "For Zion must increase in beauty, and in holiness; her borders must be enlarged; her stakes must be strengthened; yea, verily I say unto you, Zion must arise and put on her beautiful garments" (v. 14). Independence and later other surrounding cities where the Saints were driven to settle in Missouri were seen as Zion, the center place for the metaphorical tent, and outlying areas became stakes of this central Zion. The importance of stakes in the conception of the expansion of Zion and of gathering was thus established early in the foundations that Joseph Smith restored. Isaiah's metaphor of Zion's stakes, cords, tents, and borders was quoted in the Book of Mormon and in the revelations that came in the process of establishing the Church. In 1836 Joseph pleaded in the dedicatory prayer of the Kirtland Temple that the Lord would "appoint unto Zion other stakes besides this one which thou hast appointed, that the gathering of thy people may roll on in great power and majesty" (109:59).

THE REDEMPTION OF ZION BY POWER

The Prophet's initial dream of Zion in Missouri "abruptly turned to nightmare"[10] in 1833 when in the midst of violence the Saints in Independence were driven from their Zion and the designation of Independence as the center place became problematic. Some of the greatest ambiguity for Joseph and these early Saints came because of the elusive nature of building Zion in Jackson County, Missouri. For instance, the Lord cautioned Joseph, "Zion shall be redeemed, although she is chastened for a little season" (Doctrine and Covenants 100:13). Yet, for Joseph, this "little season" spanned his lifetime. In a state of perplexity Joseph wrote, "I know that Zion, in the own due time of the Lord will be redeemed, but how many will be the days of her purification, tribulation, and affliction, the Lord has kept hid from my eyes; and when I enquire concerning this subject the voice of the Lord is, Be still, and know that I am God!"[11] As we witness the struggles and disappointments of Joseph Smith associated with the tenuous nature of building Zion, we can gain strength for our own efforts. In December 1833 a revelation promised, "Zion shall not be moved out of her place, notwithstanding her children are scattered." Then the Lord specified that "there is none other place appointed than that which I have appointed; neither shall there be any other place appointed than that which I have appointed, for the work of the gathering of my saints" (101:17–20). President Harold B. Lee interpreted this verse in 1973, explaining, "In the early years of the Church specific places to which the Saints were to be gathered together were given, and the Lord directed that these gathering places should not be changed."[12] In other words, "none other place than that which I have appointed" referred not only to Jackson County but to all subsequent gathering places designated by the Lord through his prophet. Church history reflects this interpretation as latter-day prophets established gathering places in other areas in Missouri, then Illinois, Winter Quarters, and eventually the valley of the Great Salt Lake and the surrounding territory.

Independence, Missouri, was not forgotten, however, and the uncertainty of this elusive Zion deepened with the seemingly failed attempt to redeem Zion with an army. In what has been called a "purposefully ambiguous" revelation that led to the establishment of an army called Zion's Camp, the Lord states, "the redemption of Zion must needs come by power," but without any clear articulation of what kind of power.[13] The efforts of redeeming Zion through temporal power in the case of Zion's Camp required tremendous faith, perhaps even "Abrahamic" faith and a willingness to sacrifice lives.[14] The Lord allowed Joseph and the members of Zion's Camp to pass through a trying and seemingly unsuccessful mission to redeem Zion by physical force. After the Zion's Camp sacrifice was made, and in the midst of the resulting uncertainty and trial of faith, the Lord was more specific, stating that "the power to redeem Zion would come not from a confrontation in Missouri but from an endowment in the house of the Lord back in Kirtland."[15]

The Lord's redemption of Zion by power flowing from covenants and endowments in the temple is the consistent thread running through revelations of Zion and all policies given in all times. Nephi saw this redemption of Zion in the latter days as "the power of the Lamb of God . . . descended . . . upon the covenant people of the Lord, who were scattered upon all the face of the earth; and they were armed with righteousness and with the power of God in great glory" (1 Nephi 14:14). The language used in the dedicatory prayer of the Kirtland Temple echoes this prophecy as Joseph pleaded, "We ask thee, Holy Father, that thy servants may go forth from this house armed with thy power" (Doctrine and Covenants 109:22). The necessity of temples and temple covenants and the power that would flow through them is intricately linked with the cause of Zion at a very early stage of the Restoration. The relationship of the power to redeem and establish Zion with temple covenants and the strengthening of stakes resonates in Moroni's final plea to his latter-day readers: "Put on thy beautiful garments, O daughter of Zion: and strengthen thy stakes and enlarge thy borders" (Moroni 10:31).

Joseph's project of Zion building extended to include the enlarged borders of new cities appointed as gathering places for the Saints who came increasingly from outside the United States. When the Saints left Missouri and settled in Nauvoo, Joseph's conception of Zion enlarged and he is recorded as declaring that "Zion referred to all of North and South America and anywhere Saints gathered."[16] One example of Joseph's enlarged conception of Zion is a March 1841 revelation giving "the will of the Lord concerning the saints in the Territory of Iowa." They were told to "gather themselves together unto the places which I shall appoint unto them by my servant Joseph, and build up cities." Furthermore, "all those that come from the east, and the west and the north and the south" were to "take up their inheritance" in an appointed city "and in all the stakes which" the Lord had appointed (Doctrine and Covenants 125:1–4).

ZION IN THE WEST

Brigham Young biographer John Turner suggests that in 1844 Joseph's "final" conception of Zion as all of North and South America, as well as his counsel to elders that churches should be built where converts received the gospel, was Joseph hinting about "an end to the doctrine of gathering."[17] Turner sees Brigham Young as turning this vision another direction and seeing Joseph Smith's words as "a prediction of a glorious and expansive future for the church."[18] Joseph may have been foreseeing the end of the gathering as it had been administered during the early years of the Restoration but certainly not the end of the doctrine of gathering. Brigham Young's vision of gathering and establishing Zion was specific to his period of the ongoing Restoration. Changes in conceptions, articulations, and administration do not equal changes in foundational doctrines.

Turner suggests, "Whereas Smith built cities of Zion, Young more literally established God's kingdom upon the earth. He spoke of the construction of many temples and encouraged the planned dispersal of Mormon emigrants throughout the region." Turner also argues that Brigham Young established "a new model of gathering" in the Great Basin.[19] It enriches our understanding of Church history to envision Brigham Young's "new model of gathering." However, we can be mindful of the ways Brigham Young's administration of the "gathering"—and that of any other Latter-day prophet for that matter—resonates with foundational doctrines of Zion built by Joseph Smith. As another scholar explains, "From its earliest day, Mormonism's message of restoration of Primitive Christianity went hand-in-glove with a policy of gathering its converts to central locations: initially Ohio, then Missouri, then Illinois, and finally the Great Basin."[20] Although the central geographical gathering location has varied, the principles have remained unchanged. A revelation given through Brigham Young at Winter Quarters proclaimed "the Word and Will of the Lord concerning the Camp of Israel in their journeying to the West." The revelation encouraged Saints to use all their "influence and property to remove this people to the place where the Lord shall locate a stake of Zion" (Doctrine and Covenants 136:1, 10). The revelation also echoed a familiar theme promising that "Zion shall be redeemed in mine own due time" (136:18). Brigham Young continued to appoint other places "for the work of the gathering" as the early revelation had specified (101:20). He continued to build temples and stakes, and his success in settling a major portion of the western United States attests to his project of enlarging the borders of Zion.

In 1881 John Taylor spoke of how he was "endeavoring to build up the Zion of our God" by traveling around "all through the Territory, visiting almost all the settlements." He stressed that Zion was "not confined to our prominent cities, but includes all the cities of the Saints."[21] During the presidency of John Taylor, Orson Pratt spoke on how the Lord would "stretch forth the curtains of Zion; He will lengthen her cords and strengthen her Stakes and will multiply them not only throughout this mountain Territory, but throughout the united States."[22] Then, in an attempt to reconcile the place of the "City of Zion when it is built in Jackson County," Pratt clarified that the city of Zion will not be called a stake since "the Lord never called it a Stake in any revelation." Rather, "it is to be the headquarters, it is to be the place where the Son of Man will come and dwell . . . ; it will be the great central city, and the outward branches will be called Stakes wherever they shall be organized as such."[23]

Historical events have played a role in changing conceptions of Zion. An important example of this occurred in 1887 when the antipolygamy-driven

Edmunds-Tucker Act was passed and, among other detrimental financial implications for the Church, dissolved the Perpetual Emigrating Fund. This reality occurred in tandem with the closing of the frontier era, since "by the end of the nineteenth century virtually all habitable locations within the Mormon domain that were suitable for agriculture had been occupied."[24] Thus, during the concluding years of the nineteenth century, Church leaders saw the need to reenvision the policies surrounding the building of Zion and began to deemphasize gathering to the Great Basin. In 1911 an official letter from the First Presidency "urged converts to stay where they were and live according to the ideals of Zion in their own homelands." Scholars have interpreted this to have caused a transformation of "Zion in the hearts and minds of the Latter-day Saints from a literal place to an ideal."[25] Harold B. Lee articulated the way in which this 1911 policy reflected the doctrine of gathering outlined in Doctrine and Covenants 101:20–21. As mentioned previously, President Lee emphasized that gathering places were to be appointed by the Lord. He also emphasized that when the Lord "directed that these gathering places should not be changed," the Lord "gave one qualification: 'Until the day cometh when there is found no more room for them; and then I have other places which I will appoint unto them, and they shall be called stakes, for the curtains or the strength of Zion.'"[26] This qualification was thus present in the foundations of the Restoration and not solely a modification growing out of modernization.

MODERN CONCEPTIONS OF ZION

Gathering to an appointed place "ended in the early 1950s, when President David O. McKay issued a call for Saints to 'gather' together in their homelands and backed this call up through the creation of stakes, meetinghouses, and temples worldwide."[27] According to biographers, McKay brought the "rise of Modern Mormonism."[28] An illustrative anecdote from McKay's biography tells of an interview by *New York Times* reporter Alden Whitman, who asked McKay, "What do you regard as the most outstanding accomplishment of your ministry as President of the Church?" to which McKay replied, "The making of the Church a world-wide organization."[29] One of the ways he did this was through his expansion of Zion to include international temples and stakes. Scholars argue that McKay's focus on international temples and stake building was in part an effort to "stem the tide of foreign immigration to Utah."[30] While this may be one aspect of the policy, the vision of enlarging the borders of Zion was undoubtedly a central motivation. The temples built during the McKay administration in Europe and New Zealand proved crucial to expanding the reach of Zion. It was unique to build temples before the firm establishment of stakes in these countries, but it was a "calculated risk" that proved to "anchor church members in their native countries, thus curtailing emigration to the United States and allowing the creation of overseas stakes."[31] Scholars have argued that McKay abandoned the doctrine of gathering[32] and that "coincident with the decision to urge people to stay in their native lands was a redefinition of the concept of Zion."[33] Furthermore, policy changes and expansion of international temples and stakes are often cast as a drastic change in the doctrines surrounding Zion, that although Zion "had earlier referred to a geographical location, now it was recast as a state of being."[34] To conflate policy changes with changing of doctrine is problematic and overlooks the ways Zion has always been both a state of being in the foundational scriptural literature as well having connections to geographical place. As this chapter has shown, from the foundations of the Restoration, Zion was conceptualized to include the building of units that are called stakes, which simultaneously support the "tent of Zion" and function as new center places of gathering. The doctrine of gathering is constant, but the conceptions of *how* to gather logistically change and even expand.

A helpful metaphor to understand the internationalization of latter-day Zion suggests that religions are like tents with fluid boundaries and thus "yield themselves to be discreetly and deliberately dismantled, relocated and reassembled. Religions are not finished products; they constantly hand themselves over to their adherents."[35] I find this especially helpful to build on Isaiah's use of the metaphorical tent of Zion with curtains, cords, and borders and the way the structure of the modern Church has evolved to allow for a metaphorical one-tent structure to stretch over vast distances, oceans, and borders. While never letting go of the ideal of the "one heart and one mind" single tent of Zion, Church leaders clearly saw the need for simplified "tents" (meaning both structural aspects of missions, districts, and branches as well as a more simplified focus on the essential aspects of the gospel of Jesus Christ and a jettisoning of cultural trappings) that could be dismantled, transported, and reassembled anywhere in the world. Then the independent but "correlated" tent-like units become fully incorporated into the larger tent as stakes that anchor and strengthen Zion. Furthermore, when a stake of Zion is organized, it is "handed over to its adherents" in that the local leadership becomes responsible and independent in administering the programs of the Church and a new "center" of Zion is created.

The process of building from small groups of members, which grow into branches that eventually become part of districts, which work persistently to become a stake, is an arduous task. Leaders of the Church before the global expansion that took place in the last half of the twentieth century understood that the "cause of Zion" as it had evolved in the Great Basin was not easily transportable internationally. Priesthood correlation can be seen as part of the process of dismantling that the Church has undertaken in order to make the Church organization transportable. Matthew Bowman charts this correlation effort, noting its initial growth from 1945 to 1978. By the mid-nineteenth century, auxiliary programs of the Church were almost completely autonomous: writing their own curriculum, publishing journals independently, and overseeing their own finances. This resulted in "fragmentation, overlap and dysfunction," according to Bowman.[36] Thus, during the McKay administration, a correlation committee was organized to "correlate the courses of study given by the quorums and auxiliaries of the Church," which eventually extended their reach to correlate and centralize authority over budgets, periodicals, and other programs and bring them under the control of committees headed by members of the Quorum of the Twelve.[37] Harold B. Lee, who spoke often of enlarging the borders of Zion through strengthening her stakes, was the chairman of the Correlation Committee.[38] Critics of correlation view it as a complication or added scaffolding, but as Bowman explains, "correlation made it possible for Mormonism to become a global religion," as it simplified and streamlined what was a before a "patchwork quilt of curriculum," allowing it to be exportable overseas.[39]

One example of the dismantling of provincial, difficult-to-transport elements of Mormonism was the revelation in 1978 granting priesthood authority to every worthy male member of the Church. The Gospel Topics essay "Race and the Priesthood" explains, "As the Church grew worldwide, its overarching mission to 'go ye therefore and teach all nations' seemed increasingly incompatible with the priesthood and temple restrictions."[40] The wording of the revelation, now canonized as Official Declaration 2 ("The Lord has now made known his will for the blessing of all his children throughout the earth"),[41] indicates not only the extension of priesthood authority but the fact that "the Church's scope and ambitions were broadening" and "the goal of becoming a truly global church suddenly seemed within reach."[42] During general conference in October of 1978, President Spencer W. Kimball put an emphasis on the word *must* as he quoted, "The Lord declared: 'For Zion *must* increase in beauty, and in holiness; her borders *must* be enlarged; her stakes *must* be strengthened; yea, verily I say unto you Zion *must* arise and put on her beautiful garments.'"[43] Then President Kimball reiterated the revised gathering policy by saying: "We are building up the strength of Zion—her cords or stakes—throughout the world. Therefore we counsel our people to remain in their native lands and gather out the elect of God and teach them the ways of the Lord."[44]

Seeing how international Church growth played an important part in the 1978 revelation can aid in the "dismantling" process that continues today as Latter-day Saints overcome cultural barriers like racism to truly be of one mind and one heart. According to President Dallin H. Oaks, dismantling on an institutional level occurred immediately as "the Church reacted swiftly to the revelation on the priesthood" and performed ordinations and gave temple recommends to worthy members previously denied these blessings. Additionally, "the reasons that had been given to try to explain the prior restrictions on members of African ancestry—even those voiced by revered Church leaders—were promptly and publicly disavowed." Dismantling, however, happens both institutionally as well as on an individual basis. As President Oaks lamented, "Changes in the hearts and practices of individual members did not come suddenly and universally," and "some, in their personal lives, continued the attitudes of racism that have been painful to so many throughout the world, including the past 40 years."[45] Understanding the relationship of the 1978 revelation to the principle of establishing Zion can strengthen members in stakes worldwide.

The establishment of international stakes during the last half of the twentieth century accompanied changes in the conception of the gathering and building of Zion. Rather than gathering to a centralized Zion, members were told to remain in their native lands where stakes of Zion would be driven into foreign soil, thus strengthening Saints in "distant" locations. President Harold B. Lee gave the landmark talk, quoted previously, on the need to "strengthen the stakes of zion" in 1973 and proclaimed, "The borders of Zion, where the righteous and pure in heart may dwell, must now begin to be enlarged. The stakes of Zion must be strengthened." In the address, President Lee referred extensively to a talk given by Elder Bruce R. McConkie of the Quorum of the Twelve at the Mexico City Area Conference in August 1973. Elder McConkie expounded on the themes of Zion, the gathering, and the stakes of Zion and repeated a similar message to a congregation of members in 1977 in Lima, Peru. The 1977 talk was reprinted in the Church's official periodical, the *Ensign*, at the request of then-Church President Spencer W. Kimball. In the talk, Elder McConkie divides the "gathering of Israel and the establishment of Zion in the latter days" into three phases or periods.

Phase one began with the establishment of the Church in 1830. It included Joseph Smith's First Vision and the appearance of Moses in the Kirtland Temple in 1836 to restore the keys of the gathering of Israel. That phase ends, according to McConkie, with the "secure establishment of the Church in the United States and Canada, a period of about 125 years." Phase two began with "the creation of stakes of Zion in overseas areas beginning in the 1950s" and will end when Christ returns. Phase three spans the Millennium, "from our Lord's second coming until the kingdom is perfected and the knowledge of God covers the earth" to the end of that thousand-year period.[46]

To explain the change in conceptions of gathering and establishing Zion, McConkie argued that gathering facilitates the community build-ing needed to strengthen the covenant people and the receipt of temple blessings. During phase one it was necessary to gather to "the tops of the mountains of North America," where there were "congregations strong enough for the Saints to strengthen each other" and where there were temples "where the fullness of the ordinances of exaltation are performed."[47] McConkie proclaimed, "We are living in a new day. The Church of Jesus Christ of Latter-day Saints is fast becoming a worldwide church," and the evidence of this "new day" is the building of temples and stakes "at the ends of the earth." He emphasized that "the gathering place for Peruvians is in the stakes of Zion in Peru, or in the places which soon will become stakes. The gathering place for Chileans is in Chile; for Bolivians it is in Bolivia; for Koreans it is in Korea; and so it goes through all the length and breadth of the earth."[48]

Elder McConkie's message is indicative of the manner in which modern prophets and general Church leaders have continued to further envision the establishment of Zion. President Ezra Taft Benson taught in his "timeless sermon" on pride, "My dear brethren and sisters, we must prepare to redeem Zion. It was essentially the sin of pride that kept us from establishing Zion in the days of the Prophet Joseph Smith. It was the same sin of pride that brought consecration to an end among the Nephites. (See 4 Ne. 1:24–25.) Pride is the great stumbling block to Zion. I repeat: Pride *is* the great stumbling block to Zion."[49] Elder Neal A. Maxwell's teachings on the challenges of building Zion in the midst of Babylon have been widely quoted. For instance, Elder D. Todd Christofferson reiter-ated Elder Maxwell's quotable phrase about the need for Latter-day Saints to "establish our residence in Zion and give up the summer cottage in Babylon" in a conference address entitled "Come to Zion."[50] Elder Christofferson reminded members of the first attempt to establish Zion in Missouri and the reasons the Lord gave for their not obtaining it (see Doctrine and Covenants 101:6; 105:3–4). Then he cautioned, "Rather than judge these early Saints too harshly, however, we should look to ourselves to see if we are doing any better." Elder Christofferson declared, "Zion is Zion because of the character, attributes, and faithfulness of her citizens." Then he added, "If we would establish Zion in our homes, branches, wards and stakes, we must rise to this standard." Elder Christofferson listed three things required for building Zion. "It will be necessary (1) to become unified in one heart and one mind; (2) to become, individually and collectively, a holy people; and (3) to care for the poor and needy with such effectiveness that we eliminate poverty among us. We cannot wait until Zion comes for these things to happen—Zion will come only as they happen."[51] When Church leaders in the twenty-first century teach about establishing Zion, they are not solely referring to an ideal but are speaking to members in the entire world who are carrying on the work of building actual stakes of Zion. President Gordon B. Hinckley spoke about the establishment of Zion, yet even more importantly he expanded its global existence through the instigation of building smaller temples in more of the world and beginning programs like the Perpetual Education Fund.

President Russell M. Nelson has likewise emphasized the establishment of Zion through inspiring members to be a part of the gathering of scattered Israel on both sides of the veil. In a worldwide youth devotional, President Nelson called the gathering "the most important thing taking place on the earth today" and invited the youth to "stand with the youth from all around the world and experience the thrill of being a member of the Lord's youth battalion in 'Zion's army' by singing the closing hymn, 'Hope of Israel.'" He has extended the invitation to participate in the gathering to the entire Church membership.[52]

President Nelson is also expanding the borders of Zion through announcing the building of temples near stakes of Zion across the earth. In some cases, as in the announcement of a temple in Shanghai and in Dubai, temples are being built to reach members in branches and districts without waiting for the stake structure to be fully in place. As President Nelson explained, "In God's goodness and generosity, He is bringing the blessings of the temple closer to His children *everywhere*."[53]

The Church of Jesus Christ of Latter-day Saints is expanding into a global church and is beginning to fully realize the Lord's prophetic admonition: "For Zion must increase in beauty, and in holiness; her borders must be enlarged; her stakes must be strengthened" (Doctrine and Covenants 82:14). Efforts to enlarge the borders of Zion and strengthen her stakes bring beauty that comes from the diversity of members and holiness as the blessings of the temple and the power to redeem Zion flow into the lives of more of the Lord's children all over the earth. Latter-day Saints in the "borders" of Zion have a strong love for and devotion to the Savior and his restored gospel. Members worldwide are invited to envision themselves in the ongoing Restoration of the gospel and envision their role in the work of establishing Zion. The study of the establishment of Zion in Missouri or any other point in the history of the restored gospel should ultimately lead to a discussion of how the revelations and foundations laid by Joseph Smith prophesy of the eventual internationalization of Zion. As Joseph Smith proclaimed, "The building up of Zion . . . is a theme upon which prophets, priests and kings have dwelt with peculiar delight; they have looked forward with joyful anticipation to the day in which we live," but "it is left for us to see, participate in and help to roll forward the Latter-day glory."[54]

Taunalyn F. Rutherford is an adjunct professor of Church history and doctrine at Brigham Young University.

Taunalyn Rutherford, "'Her Borders Must Be Enlarged': Evolving Conceptions of Zion," in *Foundations of the Restoration: Fulfillment of the Covenant Purposes*, ed. Craig James Ostler, Michael Hubbard MacKay, and Barbara Morgan Gardner (Provo, UT: Religious Studies Center, Brigham Young University; Salt Lake City: Deseret Book, 2016), 139–155.

NOTES

1. See Dieter F. Uchtdorf, "Are You Sleeping through the Restoration?," *Ensign*, May 2014, 59. See also Jeffrey R. Holland, "Miracles of the Restoration," *Ensign*, November 1994. Since the first publication of this essay, the concept of an "ongoing Restoration" has been further emphasized. The doctrine "that the promised Restoration goes forward through continuing revelation" was always implicit but was made more explicit in statements by President Russell M. Nelson ("The Restoration of the Fulness of the Gospel of Jesus Christ: A Bicentennial Proclamation to the World," April 5, 2020, churchofjesuschrist.org). In Chile in October 2018 he said, "We are witnesses to a process of restoration. If you think the Church has been fully

restored, you are just seeing the beginning. There's much more to come. Wait until next year—and then the next year. Eat your vitamin pills. Get your rest. It's going to be exciting!" ("Latter-day Saint Prophet, Wife and Apostle Share Insights of Global Ministry," October 30, 2018, https://newsroom.churchofjesuschrist.org/). In Brazil he said, "I want our members to know that the Restoration is a continuing process" ("'We have a lot to do,' says President Nelson as Latin America Ministry Tour ends in Brazil," September 2, 2019, https://thechurchnews.com/). During the April 2020 general conference, in addition to the quotation from the Restoration proclamation above, there were seven other references to the doctrine (see the talks by Douglas D. Holmes, Henry B. Eyring, Gerrit W. Gong, Jean B. Bingham, and Quentin L. Cook in *Ensign*, May 2020).

2. Joel 2: 28–32; emphasis added; Joseph Smith—History 1:40.

3. See also 2 Nephi 26:30–31; 27:3; 28:21.

4. See also 2 Nephi 6:13.

5. See heading by John Whitmer to Revelation, September 1830-A in Revelation Book 1, in *The Joseph Smith Papers*, historical introduction for Revelation, September 1830-A [D&C 29], http://josephsmithpapers.org/.

6. Doctrine and Covenants 6:6; 11:6; 12:6; 14:6; 21:7.

7. See Richard Lyman Bushman, *Joseph Smith: Rough Stone Rolling* (New York: Alfred A. Knopf, 2005), 138.

8. See also Covenant of Oliver Cowdery and others, 17 October 1830, http://josephsmithpapers.org/. According to the historical introduction to the document, "the signed covenant indicates that Cowdery, Whitmer, Pratt, and Peterson were to not only preach the gospel among the Lamanites but also 'rear up a pillar as a witness where the Temple of God shall be built' in the New Jerusalem."

9. See Letter to the Church in Colesville, 2 December 1830, http://josephsmithpapers .org/.

10. Terryl Givens and Fiona Givens, *The Crucible of Doubt: Reflections on the Quest for Faith* (Salt Lake City: Deseret Book, 2014), 124.

11. Joseph Smith, Kirtland, Ohio, to Edward Partridge, William W. Phelps, John Whitmer, Algernon Sidney Gilbert, John Corrill, Isaac Morley and all Saints, Independence, Missouri, 10 December 1833, Joseph Smith Letterbook 1, http://josephsmithpapers.org/.

12. Harold B. Lee, "Strengthen the Stakes of Zion," *Ensign*, July 1973, 4.

13. See Steve Harper, *Making Sense of the Doctrine and Covenants: A Guided Tour through Modern Revelations* (Salt Lake City: Deseret Book, 2008), 381; and Doctrine and Covenants 103:15.

14. See Doctrine and Covenants 101:4.

15. Harper, *Making Sense of the Doctrine and Covenants*, 381; see Doctrine and Covenants 105:11, 18, 33.

16. See "Zion (place)," http://josephsmithpapers.org/place/zion-place. See also Martha Jane Knowlton, Notebook, July 19, 1840, ca. 1850, Church History Library, The Church of Jesus Christ of Latter-day Saints, Salt Lake City; Joseph Smith, "Church History," *Times and Seasons*, March 1, 1842, 710; *The Words of Joseph Smith: The Contemporary Accounts of the Nauvoo Discourses of the Prophet Joseph Smith*, ed. Andrew F. Ehat and Lyndon W. Cook (Provo, UT: Religious Studies Center, Brigham Young University, 1980), 362–85; and Wilford Woodruff Journal, April 8, 1844, in Ehat and Cook, *Words of Joseph Smith*.

17. John G. Turner, *Brigham Young: Pioneer Prophet* (Cambridge, MA: Harvard University Press, 2012), 106.
18. Turner, *Brigham Young*, 106.
19. Turner, *Brigham Young*, 181.
20. Gregory A. Prince and Wm. Robert Wright, *David O. McKay and the Rise of Modern Mormonism* (Salt Lake City: University of Utah Press, 2005), 363.
21. John Taylor, "The Building Up of Zion," in *Journal of Discourses*, 22:312 (October 19, 1881).
22. Orson Pratt, "The Divine Authority of the Holy Priesthood, Etc.," in *Journal of Discourses*, 22:27 (October 10, 1880).
23. Pratt, "Divine Authority of the Holy Priesthood, Etc.," 22:27.
24. Prince and Wright, *David O. McKay*, 363.
25. Seth L. Bryant, Henri Gooren, Rich Phillips, and David G. Stewart Jr., "Conversion and Retention in Mormonism," *The Oxford Handbook of Religious Conversion*, ed. Lewis R. Rambo and Charles E. Farhadian (New York: Oxford University Press, 2014), 763.
26. Harold B. Lee, "Strengthen the Stakes of Zion," *Ensign*, July 1973, 4. See Doctrine and Covenants 101:20–21.
27. Fred E. Woods, "Gathering to Zion 1840–1890," in *Mapping Mormonism: An Atlas of Latter-day Saint History*, ed. Brandon Plewe, S. Kent Brown, Donald Q. Cannon, and Richard H. Jackson (Provo, UT: BYU Press, 2012), 104.
28. See generally Prince and Wright, *David O. McKay*.
29. Prince and Wright, *David O. McKay*, 358.
30. Prince and Wright, *David O. McKay*, 256.
31. Prince and Wright, *David O. McKay*, 261.
32. Prince and Wright, *David O. McKay*, 372.
33. Prince and Wright, *David O. McKay*, 366.
34. Prince and Wright, *David O. McKay*, 366.
35. Sathianathan Clarke, "Section Three: Transformations of Caste and Tribe," in *Religious Conversion in India: Modes, Motivations, and Meanings*, ed. Rowena Robinson and Sathianathan Clarke (New Delhi: Oxford University Press, 2003), 217; emphasis added.
36. Matthew Bowman, *The Mormon People: The Making of an American Faith* (New York: Random House, 2012), 194.
37. Bowman, *Mormon People*, 194.
38. See Harold B. Lee, "Strengthen the Stakes of Zion," *Ensign*, May 1973, 4; Harold B. Lee, "Make Our Lord and Master Your Friend," in Conference Report, October 1968, 59; Harold B. Lee, "The Work in Great Britain," in Conference Report, April, 1960, 106. All of these conference addresses focus on the question of "Where is Zion?" and how the "Lord has place the responsibility of directing the work of gathering in the hands of his divinely appointed leaders" and the importance of stakes of Zion all over the world.
39. Bowman, *Mormon People*, 191.
40. "Race and the Priesthood," Gospel Topics, https://lds.org/topics/race-and-the-priesthood.
41. See Official Declaration 2.
42. Bowman, *Mormon People*, 215.
43. Spencer W. Kimball, "Fruit of Our Welfare Services Labors," *Ensign*, November 1978, 76.

44. Kimball, "The Fruit of Our Welfare Services Labors," 76.

45. Dallin H. Oaks, "President Oaks' full remarks from the LDS Church's 'Be One' celebration," June 1, 2018, https://thechurchnews.com/.

46. Bruce R. McConkie, "Come: Let Israel Build Zion," *Ensign*, *May* 1977, 65.

47. McConkie, "Come: Let Israel Build Zion," 117.

48. McConkie, "Come: Let Israel Build Zion," 117–18.

49. Ezra Taft Benson, "Beware of Pride" (April 1989 general conference). See Dieter F. Uchtdorf, "Pride and the Priesthood" (October 2010 general conference), in which he adds his "voice as another witness" to President Benson's "timeless sermon."

50. See Neal A. Maxwell, "A Wonderful Flood of Light" (Brigham Young University devotional, March 1989), quoted in D. Todd Christofferson, "Come to Zion," *Ensign*, November 2008, 39.

51. Christofferson, "Come to Zion," 38.

52. Russell M. Nelson, "Hope of Israel," Worldwide Youth Devotional, June 3, 2018, https://churchofjesuschrist.org/. See his related messages: "Sisters' Participation in the Gathering of Israel," https://churchofjesuschrist.org/; "The Gathering of Scattered Israel," *Ensign*, November 2006; and "Remnants Gathered, Covenants Fulfilled," in *Sperry Symposium Classics: The Old Testament*, ed. Paul Y. Hoskisson (Provo, UT: Religious Studies Center, Brigham Young University; Salt Lake City: Deseret Book, 2005), 1–17.

53. Russell M. Nelson, "Go Forward in Faith," *Ensign*, May 2020, 114–16; emphasis in original.

54. Joseph Smith, quoted in David A. Bednar, "Let This House Be Built unto My Name," *Ensign*, May 2020, 84–87.

Chapter Twelve

Redemption's Grand Design for Both the Living and the Dead

JENNIFER C. LANE

Redemption is a golden thread running through the tapestry of scripture. If we follow it back, we find its origins in the ancient world. Today we often use the terms *save* and *redeem* interchangeably, and understandably so, because they both testify of Christ's role as Savior and Redeemer. But when we look more closely at the terms themselves and their Old Testament background, we find that redemption is a subset of salvation. Salvation can imply help and deliverance through any means. Redemption, however, is a particular kind of salvation.[1] It specifically means deliverance from bondage through the payment of a ransom price.[2] Redemption emphasizes both captivity and payment—that a person would remain in bondage or captivity without the intervention of a redeemer to provide a ransom. In the ancient Near East, people became slaves or were in bondage by selling themselves because of debt or by becoming prisoners of war. It was a widespread practice to be redeemed from captivity through the payment of a ransom price.

This ancient meaning of *redemption* becomes even more illuminating from a gospel perspective with the unique practice of redemption in Israel. While the ancient Israelites shared the general Semitic root term for "redeem" (*pādāh*) with their neighbors, they had another term for "redeem" (*gāʾal*) that was unique to them. In Israelite practice, the *gōʾēl*, or "kinsman-redeemer," was a family member, specifically the oldest male member in an extended family.[3] This background enlivens the description of the Lord as the Redeemer of Israel. Because of the covenants we make, he becomes our collective Father, seeking to rescue us and buy us out of bondage.

In the Old Testament world, covenants with the Lord were not sterile business formalities but adoptions.[4] Entering into a covenant was not making a contract; it was becoming part of a family and often involved receiving a new name.[5] This practice can be seen both in individuals receiving new names and also in taking on the Lord's name and becoming his: "O Israel, fear not: for I have redeemed thee, I have called thee by thy name; thou art mine" (Isaiah 43:1).

The golden thread of redemption is woven throughout the Doctrine and Covenants, and seen in this light, the deeper significance of *Redeemer* and *redemption* comes to life. First, the Saints are clearly understood as covenant Israel, the Lord's adopted people. The Lord speaks to them as he did to his ancient covenant people: "I am the Lord your God, even the God of your fathers, the God of Abraham and of Isaac and of Jacob. I am he who led the children of Israel out of the land of Egypt; and my arm is stretched out in the last days, to save my people Israel" (Doctrine and Covenants 136:21–22). The understanding that the Lord redeemed the children of Israel *because of* the covenants is a central gospel theme (see Exodus 6:2–8; Deuteronomy 7:8; 1 Nephi 17:40).[6]

In addition, the concept of the "redemption of Zion" found repeatedly in the Doctrine and Covenants is tied to the understanding of the Lord as the Redeemer of Israel, who restores things to their proper state. Both land that had been lost as well as people who were in captivity were restored by this kinsman-redeemer.

REDEMPTION OF THE LAND: REDEMPTION OF ZION

One prominent theme of redemption in the Doctrine and Covenants is the redemption of Zion. The loss and recovery of the "promised land" is both a biblical and latter-day concern. As the Saints were driven from Jackson County, Missouri, and as we go through our own times of extreme hardship and discouragement, it was, and is, important for the Saints to remember that the Lord is bound to act as our Redeemer just as he redeemed the children of Israel because of the covenant relationship that had been established.

In Deuteronomy the Lord's redemption of Israel is directly tied to the covenants made by the patriarchs: "The Lord did not set his love upon you, nor choose you, because ye were more in number than any people; for ye were the fewest of all people: but because the Lord loved you, and *because he would keep the oath which he had sworn unto your fathers, hath the Lord brought you out with a mighty hand, and redeemed you out of the house of bondmen*, from the hand of Pharaoh king of Egypt" (Deuteronomy 7:7–8; emphasis added). In Leviticus this covenant memory had a specific tie to the promise of land: "Then will I remember my covenant with Jacob, and also my covenant with Isaac, and also my covenant with Abraham will I remember; and I will remember the land" (Leviticus 26:42).

In the Doctrine and Covenants we first see the Redeemer's responsibility for the restoration of land discussed in sections 100–105. The redemption of Zion is initially used to mean that Jackson County, Missouri, will be returned to the Saints. This idea of the land being returned to its proper state is one of the functions of the kinsman-redeemer in the Old Testament and among the Israelites. In these sections the Saints are gradually told that the Lord will redeem Zion, but it will be in his time and will require the Saints to receive an endowment from on high. In these revelations the physical sense of the kinsman-redeemer redeeming the land and restoring it to its proper owners is gradually developed into a long-term vision of the redemption of Zion as the Lord sanctifying and preparing his people. This spiritual vision of the redemption of Zion will also include a return of the land, but it is no longer the central feature of the message. The Lord still promises to redeem because of his covenant relationship with his people, but the developing vision of what is involved in redemption becomes more profound and personal.

The development of this doctrine begins during the troubles in October 1833 when the Saints are told, "Zion shall be redeemed, although she is chastened for a little season" (Doctrine and Covenants 100:13). How long this "little season" would be or what the chastening would include are not specified. In December of the same year, after the Saints were driven from their homes, the Lord explained that he would not forget his covenant promises. He promised that he would act to "redeem my vineyard; for it is mine" (101:56). The Lord gave this parable of the nobleman and the vineyard with olive trees "that you may know my will concerning the redemption of Zion" (v. 43).

In this parable the Jackson County Saints are told that they have a responsibility to do their part to reclaim the land. The servants are to be gathered and to go "straightway unto the land of my vineyard, and redeem my vineyard; for it is mine" (Doctrine and Covenants 101:56). This command foreshadows the role of Zion's Camp, initially understood by the participants to be about the physical redemption of the land. The Saints were told that their responsibility to participate in the redemption of the land also included legal petitions: "It is my will that they should continue to importune for redress, and redemption, by the hands of those who are placed as rulers and are in authority over you" (v. 76).

It is clear that the redemption of Zion is contingent not on the Lord's willingness to fulfill his covenant role but on the obedience of Israel to its covenants. The Lord explains, "There is even now already in store sufficient, yea, even an abundance, to redeem Zion, and establish her waste places, no more to be thrown down, *were* the churches, who call themselves after my name, *willing* to hearken to my voice" (Doctrine and Covenants 101:75; emphasis added). This potential for redemption was not realized at this time because the covenant people who "call themselves after [the Lord's] name," as part of the new family relationship of the covenant, were not "willing to hearken to [his] voice."

The relationship of covenant faithfulness and redeeming the land is emphasized in section 103. In February 1834 the Lord tells his people "how to act in the discharge of your duties concerning the salvation and redemption of your brethren, who have been scattered on the land of Zion" (v. 1). He explains that the blessings of redemption he offered would come after tribulations and would result in "your redemption, and the redemption of your brethren, even their restoration to the land of Zion, to be established, no more to be thrown down" (v. 13). Again he stresses that his redemption is contingent on their covenant faithfulness: "Nevertheless, if they pollute their inheritances they shall be thrown down; for I will not spare them if they pollute their inheritances" (v. 14).

The Lord's voice as the Redeemer of Israel to his modern covenant people is that of assurance that redemption is in his hands. By referring to his acts as the Redeemer of Israel in biblical times, the Lord reinforces that his people need not fear they will be abandoned if they are faithful to their covenant relationships: "Behold, I say unto you, the redemption of Zion must needs come by power; therefore, I will raise up unto my people a man, who shall lead them like as Moses led the children of Israel. For ye are the children of Israel, and of the seed of Abraham, and ye must needs be led out of bondage by power, and with a stretched-out arm. And as your fathers were led at the first, even so shall the redemption of Zion be" (Doctrine and Covenants 103:15–18). The direct parallels to the redemption of the covenant people in ancient times could not be more clear.

The spiritual dimension of redemption in the Lord's latter-day work can be seen in the context of the winter of 1833–34. Here, in sections 103 and 105, this pattern can be found in the Lord's specific directions for the gathering of Zion's Camp, which was to march to Jackson County. Those who participated, as was mentioned earlier, envisioned their actions as leading to the short-term physical redemption of the land. In section 103 Sidney Rigdon was told to "lift up his voice in the congregations in the eastern countries, in preparing the churches to keep the commandments which I have given unto them concerning the restoration and redemption of Zion" (103:29). Some of the Saints in the East, but not as many as were hoped for, gathered for this effort for the redemption of Zion.

Once Zion's Camp finally arrived in Missouri, they were taught that the redemption of Zion was not going to be what they had expected. Section 105 gives this further insight into the Lord's plans. First, the Lord expressed displeasure with the Saints collectively and explained that their own choices were keeping them from seeing the redemption of Zion: "Verily I say unto you who have assembled yourselves together that you may learn my will concerning the redemption of mine afflicted people—Behold, I say unto you, were it not for the transgressions of my people, speaking concerning the church and not individuals, they might have been redeemed even now" (vv. 1–2). He specifically explains that their lack of obedience, unity, and consecration prevent the redemption of Zion.

This is one of the most significant revelatory moments in early Church history because the Lord explains here that redemption is not simply to return to a place of God but to a state of being like God. Zion could not be redeemed by people who were not themselves redeemed from the natural man. The redemption of Zion required the redemption of people: "Zion cannot be built up unless it is by the principles of the law of the celestial kingdom; otherwise I cannot receive her unto myself" (Doctrine and Covenants 105:5). Zion is a people as much as a place. This principle had recently been reinforced in section 97, given in August 1833, where the Lord clearly explained, "This is Zion—THE PURE IN HEART" (v. 21). We are in bondage to our sins and weaknesses until we allow the Lord to redeem us through our faith, repentance, and covenant faithfulness. In Christ's atoning sacrifice, his ransom payment has been offered, but we experience redemption only when we choose to make and keep covenants. As we choose redemption, his sanctifying power brings us out of bondage to the natural man and makes us Zion, the pure in heart.[7]

Given this more expansive, spiritual vision of the redemption of Zion, it is clear why the process of sanctifying the Church is ongoing. Section 105 also clarifies the role of the temple and temple covenants in allowing that redemption from our fallen state to take place:

> Therefore, in consequence of the transgressions of my people, it is expedient in me that mine elders should wait for a little season for the redemption of Zion—
>
> That they themselves may be prepared, and that my people may be taught more perfectly, and have experience, and know more perfectly concerning their duty, and the things which I require at their hands.
>
> And this cannot be brought to pass until mine elders are endowed with power from on high.
>
> For behold, I have prepared a great endowment and blessing to be poured out upon them, inasmuch as they are faithful and continue in humility before me.
>
> Therefore it is expedient in me that mine elders should wait for a little season, for the redemption of Zion. (Doctrine and Covenants 105:9–13)

This section clearly connects our spiritual redemption as individuals and as a people with the endowment of "power from on high." As we become the Lord's covenant people even more and take his name upon us more fully, we experience a greater degree of redemption.

This is precisely the message of the parable given in section 101, and the Lord returns to the imagery here in section 105. He explains that his command to gather "the strength of my house" for "the redemption of my people" was not accomplished as it should have been because so many Church members were not obedient to the call to sacrifice and unite with Zion's Camp: "the strength of mine house have not hearkened unto my words" (vv. 16–17). However, despite the opportunity for collective redemption that was forfeited, the Lord recognizes those faithful members who did obey: "But inasmuch as there are those who have hearkened unto my words, I have prepared a blessing and an endowment for them, if they continue faithful" (v. 18). These blessings were richly poured out as the Quorum of the Twelve Apostles and the Seventy were soon selected from those who were choosing spiritual redemption through their faithfulness and obedience. From among these leaders, those who stayed faithful went on to receive their endowments in the Nauvoo Temple.

Section 105 emphasizes again how this revelation serves to shift an understanding of redemption from the focus on redeeming the land. In verse 34 the Lord commands: "And let those commandments which I have given concerning Zion and her law be executed and fulfilled, after her redemption." This has been taken to mean the temporary suspension of requirements for the Church to collectively live the law of consecration the way it was earlier explained. The Lord's desire for us to live the law of consecration as explained in the Doctrine and Covenants is clearly ongoing, but until we as a people are redeemed from our selfishness and jealousy through deeper conversion and sanctification, a specific institutional implementation of something like the law of consecration and stewardship or of a "United Order" serves little use.

The promise of the physical redemption of the land is real, and requests for its fulfillment can be seen in the dedicatory prayer of the Kirtland Temple, in which Joseph pleads that the Lord will "redeem that which thou didst appoint a Zion unto thy people" (Doctrine and Covenants 109:51). There is also a prayer for the redemption of Jerusalem and the Jews (see vv. 62–63). These prayers can, perhaps, be seen as both temporal and spiritual in compass. It is clear that the discussion of redemption can be found in many other contexts in the Doctrine and Covenants, and this shared physical and spiritual dimension is an ongoing theme.

REDEMPTION OF THE BODY AND SPIRIT

Returning to the world of the ancient Near East, kinsman-redeemers in ancient Israel were responsible not only to redeem land but also to buy people out of bondage. As noted earlier, people in this ancient world could find themselves in bondage as slaves either because they were prisoners of war or because they had sold themselves, or been sold, to pay off a debt. The kinsman-redeemer would then repay that debt or ransom money and restore the one in bondage to his or her previous state. This social practice was then used by the prophets to explain the relationship between the covenant family of Israel and their adoptive Father and Redeemer, the Lord. Because of his covenant relationship with the house of Israel, Jehovah had become the *gō'ēl*, or Redeemer of Israel. Isaiah expresses this, saying: "Doubtless thou art our father, though Abraham be ignorant of us, and Israel [Jacob] acknowledge us not: thou, O Lord, art our father, our redeemer; thy name is from everlasting" (Isaiah 63:16). Because of their covenant relationship,

Israel could rely on the Lord to act as their Kinsman-Redeemer, even when blood relations failed.

The imagery of physical and spiritual death as forms of bondage from which we are redeemed through the payment of Christ's atoning sacrifice is the central message of the gospel (see 3 Nephi 27:13–21; 2 Nephi 9:5–27). The Apostle Paul taught that "ye are not your own; . . . ye are bought with a price" (1 Corinthians 6:19–20). The Book of Mormon prophets repeatedly emphasize that we have been redeemed from the captivity of the devil, "the bands of death," and "the chains of hell" through the redemption of the Savior (see 1 Nephi 14:4–7; 2 Nephi 1:18; 2:27; Alma 5:7–10; 12:11; 13:30; 40:13; 3 Nephi 18:15). This emphasis on both bondage and payment is an essential point that makes the doctrine of redemption a particularly important witness to human captivity owing to the Fall and the role of Christ's atoning sacrifice to pay the price of our deliverance. If we were to see the terms *salvation* and *redemption* as simply interchangeable, we would miss this vital spiritual truth.

Both the physical and spiritual aspects of Christ's redemption addressed in other books of scripture can be found in revelations contained in the Doctrine and Covenants. Resurrection is explained as redemption of the body, and we also see how through covenant relationships Christ can act as our Redeemer from spiritual death. This spiritual redemption can be seen in regard to both the living and the dead. The Doctrine and Covenants's unique message is that the redemption of Christ can be extended to those in the spirit world through their repentance and forming covenant relationships with Christ. This additional insight into redemption is essential in understanding the work of temples and family history in the latter days.

Resurrection as redemption of the body. The redemption of all who have lived from the bondage of physical death is a key component of the good news of the gospel. Paul testified that "for as in Adam all die, even so in Christ shall all be made alive" (1 Corinthians 15:22). Moroni taught that "because of the redemption of man, which came by Jesus Christ, they are brought back into the presence of the Lord; yea, *this is wherein all men are redeemed*, because the death of Christ bringeth to pass the resurrection, which bringeth to pass a redemption from an endless sleep" (Mormon 9:13). Unlike spiritual redemption, this universal aspect of Christ's redemption does not require any personal covenant relationship with Christ. People do not have to choose to be redeemed physically.[8]

While the doctrine of the resurrection of the body is also found in the Bible, the further witness found in the Doctrine and Covenants and the

Book of Mormon is particularly important in our modern day because people are increasingly inclined not to believe in physical resurrection and not to see death as bondage. The Doctrine and Covenants reaffirms the doctrine of resurrection as physical redemption and further explains how it relates to our true nature and God's nature. In section 45, clarifying the revelation Christ gave to his disciples on the Mount of Olives, the Savior tells them they had "looked upon the long absence of [their] spirits from [their] bodies to be a bondage" (v. 17). Christ then promises that "day of redemption shall come" (v. 17). This same understanding of the separation of body and spirit as bondage can be found in section 93, where we learn about God's nature and our own: "The elements are eternal, and spirit and element, inseparably connected, receive a fulness of joy; and when separated, man cannot receive a fulness of joy" (vv. 33–34). The Restoration teaching of an embodied God helps us to appreciate the importance of physical redemption in allowing us to receive the joy that he experiences.

This emphasis on the bondage of physical death is particularly important in the vision of the spirit world in section 138. Here the faithful covenant Saints who lived before Christ's birth "were assembled awaiting the advent of the Son of God into the spirit world, to declare their redemption from the bands of death" (v. 16), and we find the same clear doctrine about the need for body and spirit to be united as was revealed in section 93. The Redeemer brings things to their proper state: "Their sleeping dust was to be restored unto its perfect frame, bone to his bone, and the sinews and the flesh upon them, the spirit and the body to be united never again to be divided, that they might receive a fulness of joy" (138:17). The separation of our spirits and bodies is a bondage that prevents us from enjoying the kind of life that God enjoys.

Yet it is not simply redemption from the bondage of physical death that will bring us this fullness of joy. In speaking to his disciples on the Mount of Olives, the Savior explains what full redemption will mean: "If ye have slept in peace blessed are you; for as you now behold me and know that I am, even so shall ye come unto me and your souls shall live, and your redemption shall be perfected" (Doctrine and Covenants 45:46). Having our souls live and our redemption perfected will require both physical and spiritual redemption. We will need to come unto Christ both as we stand before him at Judgment Day and also as we are perfected through our covenant relationship with him.

The Doctrine and Covenants clarifies that "the day of redemption" will be different for people depending on the extent they allowed Christ to redeem them spiritually. As Moroni explained, resurrection is redemption from the bondage of physical death, but it also brings us to the presence of God for judgment: "They shall come forth, both small and great, and all shall stand before his bar, being redeemed and loosed from this eternal band of death, which death is a temporal death. And then cometh the judgment of the Holy One upon them; and then cometh the time that he that is filthy shall be filthy still; and he that is righteous shall be righteous still; he that is happy shall be happy still; and he that is unhappy shall be unhappy still" (Mormon 9:13–14). We become what we have chosen to become. The Doctrine and Covenants clarifies that our resurrected bodies will literally embody the choices that we have made in this life in response to Christ's offer of spiritual redemption (see Doctrine and Covenants 88:21–31). Those who have chosen to be redeemed through making and keeping covenants will be free from all that keeps them away from being with and like God. Those who have refused to receive the redemption offered them through covenant relationships with the Redeemer will be left "to enjoy that which they are willing to receive" (v. 32).

Covenants, sanctification, and spiritual redemption. In teaching the people of Zarahemla, Alma explained that without Christ's redemption people are "encircled about by the bands of death, and the chains of hell, and an everlasting destruction . . . await[s] them" (Alma 5:7). This metaphor of captivity is central to the ancient meaning of redemption. We are in bondage, and through the payment of a price we can be loosed from our chains and restored to our original status. The Doctrine and Covenants not only teaches about the redemption from the bands of death but also serves as an additional witness of how Christ's Atonement becomes the payment to loose us from the chains of hell.

In these explanations, covenants and repentance allow us to choose spiritual redemption. Christ's redemption price is universal: "He suffereth the pains of all men, yea, the pains of every living creature, both men, women, and children, who belong to the family of Adam" (2 Nephi 9:21). He has already paid this price, but the application of it is individual. We decide the degree to which we receive Christ's gift. The revelations in the Doctrine and Covenants clarify that it is through our repentance and covenant faithfulness that he can act to redeem us from our spiritual bondage.

The Doctrine and Covenants emphasizes the universal offer of spiritual redemption through Christ; it witnesses that this message was taught in all dispensations. Adam and his family were kept from physical death "until I, the Lord God, should send forth angels to declare unto them repentance and redemption, through faith on the name of mine Only Begotten Son" (Doctrine and Covenants 29:42). The gift of full redemption, being "raised in immortality unto eternal life," was designed to be given to "even as many as would believe" (v. 43). The choice of faith, repentance, baptism, and the gift of the Holy Ghost allows spiritual redemption to become active. Those who are not redeemed are not abandoned by the Redeemer, but they simply "cannot be redeemed from their spiritual fall, because they repent not" (v. 44). When we understand spiritual redemption as the conversion and sanctification that come from faith in Christ, we understand that he cannot redeem us *in* our sins, but only *from* them (see Helaman 5:10).

The Doctrine and Covenants's accompanying message emphasizing the breadth of redemption clarifies that all those who are not capable of choosing spiritual redemption through Christ are not damned by their inability. The principle that "little children are redeemed from the foundation of the world through mine Only Begotten" (Doctrine and Covenants 29:46) helps us understand the great mercy of God in redeeming those who cannot choose to make and keep covenants, such as little children before the age of accountability and those with mental impairments. The Atonement of Christ allows all of us to be redeemed, but most of us are able and required to choose to make Christ our spiritual Father and Redeemer through covenant.

This message that we are free to choose Christ's redemption is a stark contrast to the notion of total depravity, in which the Fall makes it impossible for people to choose good of their own accord. The Doctrine and Covenants confirms the important teaching of the Book of Mormon that it is actually the Atonement of Christ that redeems us from the bondage that we would have been in and makes it possible for us to choose between captivity and liberty (see 2 Nephi 2:26–27). In section 93 the Lord reaffirms this broad-ranging vision of redemption, declaring that "every spirit of man was innocent in the beginning; and God having redeemed man from the fall, men became again, in their infant state, innocent before God" (v. 38). This redemption from the first death along with the physical redemption from the bonds of death are universal gifts that make right that which was lost in the Fall—our immortality and freedom from spiritual death—a loss brought about by Adam's transgression.

In the Pearl of Great Price, the Lord teaches Adam: "I have forgiven thee thy transgression in the Garden of Eden. Hence came the saying abroad among the people, that the Son of God hath atoned for original guilt, wherein the sins of the parents cannot be answered upon the heads of the children, for they are whole from the foundation of the world" (Moses

6:53–54). Given this freedom to choose, made possible by Christ's redemption, we are then accountable for our choices: "Thus saith the Lord; for I am God, and have sent mine Only Begotten Son into the world for the redemption of the world, and have decreed that he that receiveth him shall be saved, and he that receiveth him not shall be damned" (Doctrine and Covenants 49:5).

For Christ's covenant people, the knowledge of how to receive spiritual redemption is a priceless gift to enjoy and to share. The mission of the Church to perfect the Saints, proclaim the gospel, redeem the dead, and care for the poor and needy is all a mission of redemption. As members, we are redeemed as we deepen our conversion and sanctification through faith and repentance. Through missionary work, we invite others to enter covenant relationships with Christ so they too may experience the spiritual redemption of forgiveness and sanctification. This prayer that others may enjoy redemption is echoed in the dedicatory prayer of the Kirtland Temple. Joseph pleads with the Lord that "all the scattered remnants of Israel, who have been driven to the ends of the earth, come to a knowledge of the truth, believe in the Messiah, and be redeemed from oppression, and rejoice before thee" (Doctrine and Covenants 109:67).

We see in this prayer how Joseph's covenant faithfulness gives him confidence to call on his Redeemer: "O Lord, remember thy servant, Joseph Smith, Jun., and all his afflictions and persecutions—how he has covenanted with Jehovah, and vowed to thee, O Mighty God of Jacob—and the commandments which thou hast given unto him, and that he hath sincerely striven to do thy will" (v. 68). He prays that the Lord will convert those in opposition to the truth: "Have mercy upon all their immediate connections, that their prejudices may be broken up and swept away as with a flood; that they may be converted and redeemed with Israel, and know that thou art God" (v. 70). Joseph Smith is asking in confidence that the Lord will remember his faithful covenant people with redemption. Like him, we can also know that the Lord is faithful to his covenant relationship with us. We can have faith in the faithfulness of our Redeemer (see Hebrews 11:11–19). Because of the covenants that we have made, we are Christ's spiritual children and are called by his name (see Mosiah 5:7–12), and the Lord has promised that he will redeem his people (see, for example, 2 Samuel 7:22–24).

This promise of redemption seen throughout the Old Testament and other books of scripture is reaffirmed in the Doctrine of Covenants. The Lord answered a question posed by Elias Higbee in section 113 about whom Isaiah was referring to when he said, "Put on thy strength, O Zion" (v. 7).

The Lord responded with a message that should give heart and courage to all who seek to make and keep covenants with him: "He [Isaiah] had reference to those whom God should call in the last days, who should hold the power of priesthood to bring again Zion, and the redemption of Israel; and to put on her strength is to put on the authority of the priesthood, which she, Zion, has a right to by lineage; also to return to that power which she had lost" (v. 8). The redemption of Israel is ongoing as people choose to "come unto Christ, who is the Holy One of Israel, and partake of his salvation, and the power of his redemption" (Omni 1:26).

THE DAY OF REDEMPTION AND THE REDEMPTION OF THE DEAD

The Doctrine and Covenants provides a radically new perspective on the reach of Christ's redemption. While Christianity has long given assent to the idea of the resurrection of the body, the good news of this universal redemption from physical death has at times been clouded by worries that only few would actually enjoy God's presence in the next life. It has sometimes been feared that many, if not most, would be resurrected to suffer eternally. Those who had not heard of Christ and received baptism were presumed to be lost. Many who were basically good were not good enough and thus in danger of hellfire. The message of the Restoration contained in the Doctrine and Covenants is a joyful answer with an expansive vision of redemption.

We are taught in sections 76 and 88 that almost all will be redeemed by Christ from the hell of being separated from God and be able to enjoy the presence of God in some degree. We are also taught that these gradations of redemption are not due to any lack of power or desire on the part of the Redeemer, but only on the desire of individuals to be redeemed. The spiritual blessings of full redemption, being restored to the presence of God the Father in eternal life, will not be limited by a person's earthly opportunities. The power of Christ to rescue people from spiritual bondage is not limited by when or where they were born. The covenants needed to allow Christ to be our spiritual Redeemer are available to all through the work of the temples.

Resurrection as the day of redemption. The gradations of redemption and resurrection become clear in the Doctrine and Covenants's teachings on the degrees of glory. The sweeping vision in section 76 extends redemption to more than those in "heaven" because to some extent he redeems all who will be in any of the degrees of glory. However, the fullness of the redemption that Christ offers is available only to those who enter into covenant relationships with him and are faithful to those covenants. Section 88 clarifies how the redemption of resurrection is for all, but how it literally differs in degrees of light and glory depends on how we respond to Christ's offer of spiritual redemption.

The foundation of the doctrine taught in section 88 is the explanation that Christ is our hope of redemption, "that through the redemption which is made for you is brought to pass the resurrection from the dead" (v. 14). This is tied to the basic principle that "the spirit and the body are the soul of man" (v. 15) and a corresponding explanation that Christ as the Redeemer restores things to their proper order: "And the resurrection from the dead is the redemption of the soul. And the redemption of the soul is through him that quickeneth all things" (vv. 16–17). It is essential to remember that without the redemption of resurrection all would be eternally lost and in bondage to Satan, never to be restored to the presence of God (see 2 Nephi 9:6–9). It is sobering and humbling to remember that "the redemption of the soul is through him that quickeneth all things" (Doctrine and Covenants 88:17). Christ's ransom price was sufficient to compensate for the eternal suffering and banishment of all God's children. Because of Christ's redemption, all will be brought back into God's presence for judgment, and all but the sons of perdition will be able to remain in the light of one of the members of the Godhead in a kingdom of glory.

In the Doctrine and Covenants's description of resurrection as the "day of redemption," we see several important and interrelated points. Not all will be resurrected at the same time, and not all will be resurrected to dwell in the same degree of God's glory. Here is found the interwoven strands of human agency and the power of redemption. While the ransom price of Christ's Atonement was paid for the souls of all, body and spirit, not all will choose to receive and apply that payment. This is most tragically so with those sons of perdition who have received all and then completely reject and fight against that relationship.[9] Speaking of these, Christ explains that they are "the only ones on whom the second death shall have any power; yea, verily, the only ones who shall not be redeemed in the due time of the Lord, after the sufferings of his wrath. For all the rest shall be brought forth by the resurrection of the dead, through the triumph and the glory of the Lamb, who was slain" (Doctrine and Covenants 76:37–39). This might be mistakenly understood as saying that the sons of perdition are not resurrected, but we do know that "the death of Christ shall loose the bands of this temporal death, that all shall be raised from this temporal death" (Alma 11:42). All will be resurrected and brought to stand before Christ at Judgment Day. However, in this very small group of individuals, physical immortality is coupled with the second death, meaning that they have chosen banishment from any degree of light and life that comes from God.

The positive corollary of this sorrowful vision is Christ's glorious proclamation that he "shall redeem all things, except that which he hath not put into his power" (Doctrine and Covenants 77:12). This means that the day of resurrection will be a day of redemption for all others, essentially all that have ever lived. As mentioned earlier, the "day of redemption" will be staggered, beginning with the righteous. We also learn that those who will be raised to telestial glory "shall not be redeemed from the devil until the last resurrection, until the Lord, even Christ the Lamb, shall have finished his work" (76:85). They will be redeemed from hell at the end of the Millennium and will be able to enjoy the presence of the Holy Ghost in the telestial kingdom, but they will not receive the fullness of redemption because they were not willing to receive the message of Christ's redemption and the gospel covenants offered them through the messengers in the spirit world (see 138:30–34).

Section 88 also gives an outline of the sequence of the "day of redemption," and in it we see degrees of spiritual redemption from captivity to darkness and spiritual death. The last group mentioned are the sons of perdition, "who shall remain filthy still" (v. 102). They are preceded by those "found under condemnation" who "live not again until the thousand years are ended" (vv. 100–101). The Resurrection begins with the covenant Saints from previous and current dispensations (see vv. 97–98). Then, after the resurrection of those who have already prepared to receive celestial glory, "cometh the redemption of those who are Christ's at his coming; who have received their part in that prison which is prepared for them, that they might receive the gospel, and be judged according to men in the flesh" (v. 99). Some may have taken this statement along with Doctrine and Covenants 76:71–74 to mean that those who do not receive the gospel during mortality will not be resurrected to celestial glory and eternal life.[10] But we must remember that the Second Coming of Christ will take place at the beginning of the Millennium, and in some ways the work for the dead will still just be starting. The "first fruits" (88:98) of those who are Christ's covenant people will be able to receive their full redemption of a glorious resurrection at the time of his arrival. The resurrection and judgment of those who have not yet had a chance to become his covenant people must be delayed until they are ready.

The redemption of the dead. The Doctrine and Covenants's all-embracing vision of redemption can be seen in the Lord's explanation that after his Second Coming the Millennium will be the time when "the heathen nations be redeemed, and they that knew no law shall have part in the first resurrection; and it shall be tolerable for them" (45:54). The vexing problem of "what of those who have not heard?" is answered in the additional revelation of the Restoration. Christ is the Redeemer of Israel. Both ancient and modern Saints have taken him to be their spiritual Father and have become his spiritual children through covenant. Because of this covenant relationship, the spiritual redemption of conversion and sanctification can bring us out of bondage to sin and our fallen natures.

The percentage of people who have had access to the message of redemption and also the priesthood authority to make covenant relationships is, however, miniscule. Yet the plan of redemption was not designed for a tiny fraction of God's children. Well does the language of section 128 break into effusive praise at God's merciful and expansive plan to offer the power of Christ's redemption to all who have ever lived: "Brethren, shall we not go on in so great a cause? Go forward and not backward. Courage, brethren; and on, on to the victory! Let your hearts rejoice, and be exceedingly glad. Let the earth break forth into singing. Let the dead speak forth anthems of eternal praise to the King Immanuel, who hath ordained, before the world was, that which would enable us to redeem them out of their prison; for the prisoners shall go free" (v. 22). Vicarious covenants made available in the holy temples will allow everyone who has ever lived the opportunity to receive the fullness of Christ's redeeming power.

The full scope of this wondrous love and mercy is revealed in section 138. President Joseph F. Smith was "reflecting upon the great atoning sacrifice that was made by the Son of God, for the redemption of the world; and the great and wonderful love made manifest by the Father and the Son in the coming of the Redeemer into the world; that through his atonement, and by obedience to the principles of the gospel, mankind might be saved" (vv. 2–4). President Smith knew the great ransom price that had been paid for the redemption of the world. He also knew that it was only by making and keeping covenants, "obedience to the principles of the gospel," that people could receive spiritual redemption in their lives.

The vision recorded in section 138 clarifies the universal message of scripture, the golden thread of redemption, and extends it to all who have ever lived. In the spirit world, Christ taught the Saints "the everlasting gospel, the doctrine of the resurrection and the redemption of mankind from the fall, and from individual sins on conditions of repentance" (v. 19). These Saints had already made and kept their covenants, and they "rejoiced in their redemption, and bowed the knee and acknowledged the Son of God as their Redeemer and Deliverer from death and the chains of hell" (v. 23).

The vision did not end with this joyous encounter, but with a commission for those Saints in the spirit world and for us in mortality to share the blessings of redemption that we enjoy. They were to "carry the message of redemption unto all the dead" (v. 37). This message is shared with all, no matter how they have lived their lives: "Thus was the gospel preached to those who had died in their sins, without a knowledge of the truth, or in transgression, having rejected the prophets" (v. 32). By teaching the faithful covenant Saints directly in paradise and then organizing them to share this message with those in spirit prison, the Lord "made known among the dead, both small and great, the unrighteous as well as the faithful, that redemption had been wrought through the sacrifice of the Son of God upon the cross" (v. 35). Through this teaching and the accompanying temple work, Christ's redemption is made available to all. The Saints in the spirit world teach "faith in God, repentance from sin, vicarious baptism for the remission of sins, the gift of the Holy Ghost by the laying on of hands, and all other principles of the gospel that were necessary for them to know in order to qualify themselves that they might be judged according to men in the flesh, but live according to God in the spirit" (vv. 33–34). The Redeemer paid the ransom price for all and stands ready to redeem all who will choose him as their Redeemer.

This work of redemption, while "wrought through the sacrifice of the Son of God upon the cross" (Doctrine and Covenants 138:35), requires that we choose to make and keep covenant relationships to allow Christ to act as our Redeemer. Those in the spirit world can exercise faith in the message of Christ's redemption and begin to repent from their sins, but that is not enough: "They without us cannot be made perfect" (128:15). As spirits they can be taught about baptism, the gift of the Holy Ghost, and temple covenants, but they cannot perform these ordinances. It is requisite that we who have become the Lord's family, his covenant people, extend these redemptive blessings to others. So much is this vicarious work a part of our own process of spiritual redemption that the Lord taught that "they without us cannot be made perfect—neither can we without our dead be made perfect" (v. 15). This teaching has even further implications in the binding together of family ties that becomes part of exaltation as the fullness of redemption. Not only are we restored to God's presence through

Christ's merciful redemption, but his redeeming power binds us together as husbands and wives, parents and children, throughout the generations (see 138:47–48). So this perfecting dimension of temple work includes being made whole as families forever but also becoming whole and spiritually refined now in mortality. The very act of temple service has a sanctifying and spiritually redeeming power.

As we become his covenant people, Christ gives us his name. This is an essential feature of a covenant in the ancient world and reflects the new nature and relationship that covenant creates. The ancient themes of a name conveying one's nature and of a covenant as the creation of family relationships are both well illustrated in Mosiah 5:7–8: "Because of the covenant which ye have made ye shall be called the children of Christ. . . . There is no other name given whereby salvation cometh; therefore, I would that ye should take upon you the name of Christ." We are Christ's covenant family. He is our spiritual Father, and he is inviting us to take his name and his nature upon us. As we accept that invitation through our repentance and conversion, we receive his redemption. Only to the extent that we leave behind the natural man and become Saints through the Atonement of Christ is the redemption working in our lives (see 3:19).

As we recognize the ancient role of a name as part of the covenant, Joseph Smith's dedicatory prayer of the Kirtland Temple becomes more meaningful. He prays for blessings "over thy people upon whom thy name shall be put in this house" (Doctrine and Covenants 109:26). Section 109 clearly connects the giving of the Lord's name to the temple: "And we ask thee, Holy Father, that thy servants may go forth from this house armed with thy power, and *that thy name may be upon them*, and thy glory be round about them, and thine angels have charge over them" (v. 22; emphasis added). We learn here that part of being armed with God's power is connected with receiving his name more fully in the ordinances of the temple.[11] By arming us with that power and then asking us to dedicate ourselves to the redemption of all around us—members, nonmembers, and those who are dead—Christ is asking us to fully take his name upon us, to become as he is.

The Doctrine and Covenants's revelations about the redemption of the dead clarify how these ancient concepts of covenant, name, and redemption have direct meaning in living the gospel today. We can see from this understanding of Christ as the covenant Redeemer of Israel that our work in the temples allows us to become "Saviors on Mount Zion" not because we have redeemed the dead ourselves (Christ is their Redeemer) but because we are becoming like him in vicariously working for the redemption of others (see

Obadiah 1:17, 21). The sacrifice, mercy, and love manifest in the transcendent redemption wrought on our behalf calls us to lives of greater sacrifice and mercy to others. As we respond to his redeeming love with mercy toward others, we become redeemed. As we become instruments in his hands, we more fully take on Christ's name and nature as a kinsman-redeemer.

CONCLUSION: THE LORD WILL REDEEM HIS PEOPLE

The collective redemption of the covenant people can be seen in their singing the song of redeeming love as a people. We see this response to redemption in Alma 5: "And again I ask, were the bands of death broken, and the chains of hell which encircled them about, were they loosed? I say unto you, Yea, they were loosed, and their souls did expand, and they did sing redeeming love. And I say unto you that they are saved" (v. 9). The Doctrine and Covenants stands as a second witness to the Book of Mormon teaching about redeemed souls singing the song of redeeming love.

The Doctrine and Covenants explains that this joyous response to the experience of spiritual redemption will be found in the promises connected with the Millennium. We can see how the process of sanctification preceded this time when "my people shall be redeemed and shall reign with me on earth" (43:29) because his elect shall, in the Lord's words, "abide the day of my coming; for they shall be purified, even as I am pure" (35:21). With the return of the Savior and the resurrection of the just, the Saints will experience both spiritual and physical redemption.

Understanding the ancient relationship of covenant and redemption allows us to more fully appreciate the content of this millennial hymn. We are told that at this day

> All shall know me, who remain, even from the least unto the greatest, and shall be filled with the knowledge of the Lord, and shall see eye to eye, and shall lift up their voice, and with the voice together sing this new song, saying:
>
> The Lord hath brought again Zion;
> The Lord hath redeemed his people, Israel,
> According to the election of grace,
> Which was brought to pass by the faith
> And covenant of their fathers.
> The Lord hath redeemed his people;

And Satan is bound and time is no longer.
The Lord hath gathered all things in one.
The Lord hath brought down Zion from above.
The Lord hath brought up Zion from beneath.
(Doctrine and Covenants 84:98–100)

The promised redemption and sanctification of Zion will be fully accomplished because the Lord remembers "the faith and covenant of their fathers."

The Doctrine and Covenants testifies of Christ's role as our Redeemer and of our place in the Father's grand design for the redemption of his children. As the Redeemer of Israel, the Lord Jehovah spoke through his prophets in ancient days. With a more profound understanding of the ancient context of the biblical imagery used in modern scripture, we can more fully hear the Lord's voice in the Doctrine and Covenants. Once we grasp the doctrine of redemption, our appreciation of this golden thread enriches our vision of the latter-day work. Without knowing its ancient meaning, the expression "redeeming the dead" misses some of the power and depth it could convey. Connected to the ancient biblical meaning, the message of the redemption of the dead, which is so central to the Restoration and the work of our dispensation, comes to life. Christ has paid an infinite price to redeem all of Heavenly Father's children. The Restoration allows us to receive that gift and to offer it to all who have ever lived. With this understanding, we more deeply appreciate the privilege of making covenants and vicariously performing this work for our ancestors. These covenants make us part of the family of Christ and allow him to act on our behalf as the Kinsman-Redeemer of Israel.

Jennifer C. Lane is a professor of religious education at Brigham Young University–Hawaii.

Jennifer C. Lane, "Redemption's Grand Design for Both the Living and the Dead," in *The Doctrine and Covenants, Revelations in Context*, ed. Andrew H. Hedges, J. Spencer Fluhman, and Alonzo L. Gaskill (Provo, UT: Religious Studies Center; Salt Lake City: Deseret Book, 2008), 188–211.

NOTES

1. In the following section, I summarize my previous research on the Lord as the Redeemer of Israel. For a more in-depth discussion of these issues and a summary of the scholarship on renaming, covenants as family relationships, the role of the kinsman-redeemer, and Jehovah as the Redeemer of Israel in the Old Testament,

see Jennifer C. Lane, "The Lord Will Redeem His People: Adoptive Covenant and Redemption in the Old Testament," in *Sperry Symposium Classics: The Old Testament*, ed. Paul Y. Hoskisson (Provo, UT: Religious Studies Center, Brigham Young University; Salt Lake City: Deseret Book, 2005), 298–310. I have written elsewhere about adoptive covenant and redemption in the New Testament, the Book of Mormon, and the Book of Abraham.

2. A brief overview of redemption in the Old Testament is provided by Helmer Ringgren, "*Ga'al*," in *Theological Dictionary of the Old Testament* (Grand Rapids, MI: Eerdmans, 1975), 2:354; Jeremiah Unterman, "Redemption (OT)," in *The Anchor Bible Dictionary*, ed. David Noel Freedman (New York: Doubleday, 1992), 5:650–54; and J. Murray, "Redeemer; Redemption," in *The International Standard Bible Encyclopedia*, ed. Geoffrey W. Bromiley (Grand Rapids, MI: Eerdmans, 1979), 4:61–63.

3. While we may be most familiar with the *gō'ēl*'s responsibilities as seen in the book of Ruth, the kinsman-redeemer was also responsible to buy back sold property; buy back a man who had sold himself to a foreigner as a slave; avenge blood and kill a relative's murderer; receive atonement money; and, figuratively, to be a helper in a lawsuit (see Ringgren, "Ga'al," 351–52). An excellent discussion of the role of the kinsman-redeemer can be found in Robert L. Hubbard, "The Go'el in Ancient Israel: Theological Reflections on an Israelite Institution," *Bulletin for Biblical Research* 1 (1991): 3–19.

4. On creating family relationships in covenants, see, for example, Dennis J. McCarthy, *Treaty and Covenant: A Study in the Ancient Oriental Documents and in the Old Testament* (Rome: Biblical Institute Press, 1978), 266. He comments: "To see a great chief and eat in his place is to join his family, . . . the whole group related by blood or not which stood under the authority and protection of the father. One is united to him as a client to his patron who protects him and whom he serves. . . . *Covenant is something one makes by a rite, not something one is born to or forced into, and it can be described in family terms.* God is patron and father, Israel servant and son" (McCarthy, *Treaty and Covenant*, 266; emphasis added).

5. The Hebrew word *šēm*, pronounced *shem*, usually translated "name," can also be rendered "remembrance" or "memorial," indicating that the name acts as a reminder to its bearers and others. The name shows both the true nature of its bearer and indicates his relationship to others. Central background on the role of names and renaming in showing new family relationships can be found in G. F. Hawthorne, "Name," *International Standard Bible Encyclopedia* (Grand Rapids, MI: Eerdmans, 1979), 3:481–83; and Bruce H. Porter and Stephen D. Ricks, "Names in Antiquity: Old, New, and Hidden," in *By Study and Also by Faith*, ed. John M. Lundquist and Stephen D. Ricks (Salt Lake City: Deseret Book, 1990), 1:501–22.

6. While this concept is particularly clear and relevant in light of the additional truths of the Restoration, the biblical connections between covenant and redemption have been noticed by only a few scholars. See my discussion in "The Redemption of Abraham," in *The Book of Abraham: Astronomy, Papyrus, and Covenant*, ed. John Gee and Brian M. Hauglid (Provo, UT: Institute for the Study and Preservation of Ancient Religious Texts, 2005), 3:167–68.

7. I discuss the theme of sanctification as redemption in more depth in "Choosing Redemption," in *Living the Book of Mormon: Abiding by Its Precepts*, ed. Charles Swift and Gaye Strathearn (Provo, UT: Religious Studies Center; Salt Lake City: Deseret Book, 2007), 163–75.

8. They do not even need to want to be redeemed. Redemption from physical death requires no choice on our part, perhaps because our being in its bondage was not our choice. We are all in bondage to death because of the Fall, and we have all been redeemed through Christ's death and Resurrection (see 1 Corinthians 15:21–23).

9. Joseph Smith, Discourse, 7 April 1844, as Reported by *Times and Seasons*, p. 616, *The Joseph Smith Papers*, http://josephsmithpapers.org/.

10. A careful reading of Doctrine and Covenants 76:71–74 reveals that this passage does not include a discussion about the timing when people in the terrestrial kingdom received the *gospel of Christ*, but when they received the "testimony of Jesus." Their willingness to receive the "testimony of Jesus" but not the full gospel of Jesus Christ is what characterizes those in the terrestrial kingdom, not *when* they received what they were willing to receive. All those in the celestial kingdom receive both the "testimony of Jesus" and the gospel (including the ordinances of baptism and the laying on of hands for the gift of the Holy Ghost; see 76:51–52). All those in the telestial kingdom receive neither the testimony of Jesus nor the gospel of Christ (see v. 82). See Stephen Robinson and H. Dean Garrett, *A Commentary on the Doctrine and Covenants* (Salt Lake City: Deseret Book, 2001), 2:303–4, 314–19.

11. See David A. Bednar, "Honorably Hold a Name and Standing," *Ensign*, May 2009, 97–98; and Dallin H. Oaks, "Taking upon Us the Name of Jesus Christ," *Ensign*, May 1985, 81.

Chapter Thirteen

Joseph Smith and the Kirtland Temple, 1836

STEVEN C. HARPER

The story of the Kirtland Temple began in Joseph Smith's bedroom. "When I was about 17 years," Joseph said, "I had another vision of angels; in the night season, after I had retired to bed; I had not been asleep, but was meditating on my past life and experience. I was well aware I had not kept the commandments, and I repented heartily for all my sins and transgressions, and humbled myself before him, whose eye surveys all things at a glance. All at once the room was illuminated above the brightness of the sun; An angel appeared before me."

"I am a Messenger sent from God," he told Joseph, introducing himself as Moroni. He said that God had vital work for Joseph to do. There was a sacred book written on golden plates and buried in a nearby hillside. "He explained many of the prophecies to me," Joseph said, including "Malachi 4th chapter." Moroni appeared three times that night and twice the next day, emphasizing and expounding the same message. There was something vital in that prophecy—something Joseph needed to know.[1]

When Joseph wrote his history beginning in 1838, he captured the words Moroni spoke, noting the "little variation from the way it reads in our Bibles." Moroni "quoted the fifth verse [of Malachi 4] thus, 'Behold I will reveal unto you the Priesthood by the hand of Elijah the prophet before the coming of the great and dreadful day of the Lord.' He also quoted the next verse differently. 'And he shall plant in the hearts of the children the promises made to their fathers, and the hearts of the children shall turn to their fathers, if it were not so the whole earth would be utterly wasted at his coming.'"[2]

The angel's words obviously made a deep impression on the teenage seer. Whether he understood all the words that night is not clear, but they remained in his mind and heart until he witnessed their fulfillment and comprehended them well. Malachi foretold that Elijah, the Old Testament prophet, would return to the earth on a mission to turn the hearts of the first Israelites (with whom God made covenants) to the hearts of their descendants (to whom Malachi wrote). The prophecy was vague. All a Bible reader could tell is that the Lord would send Elijah sometime before the Second Coming—but to do what? Moroni made the prophecy directly relevant to Joseph, specifying that Elijah would reveal priesthood that would plant the same promises God made to the patriarchs deep in the hearts of their covenant-keeping descendants.

Young Joseph had only sought forgiveness of personal sins, but here was an angel telling him that he had a role in fulfilling ancient prophecy, adding that "if it were not so, the whole earth would be utterly wasted" (Doctrine and Covenants 2:3). Nearly thirteen years passed before Elijah fulfilled the prophecy by bringing Joseph the priesthood keys needed to seal families. Meanwhile, Moroni prepared Joseph to receive and use those keys. Joseph's role was to use them—and enable others to use them—to give every willing soul, living and dead, full access to the Atonement of Jesus Christ. He was to assist the Savior in offering eternal life. Elder Russell M. Nelson taught that "eternal life, made possible by the Atonement, is the supreme purpose of Creation. To phrase that statement in its negative form, if families were not sealed in holy temples, the whole earth would be utterly wasted."[3] So, in one sense, Moroni enlisted the seventeen-year-old seer to save the world.

THE TEMPLE REVELATION

Joseph subsequently translated the Book of Mormon, received the holy priesthood, restored the Church of Jesus Christ, and obeyed a revealed command to gather all who were willing to Ohio. There, in December 1832, he assembled nine high priests in his translating room and taught them that "to receive revelation and the blessing of Heaven, it was necessary to have our minds on God and exercise faith and become of one heart and one mind."

Kirtland Temple. Photo by George Edward Anderson, ca. early 1900s. Courtesy of Church History Library.

He asked them each to pray in turn that the Lord would "reveal His will to us concerning the upbuilding of Zion and for the benefit of the saints and for the duty . . . of the elders." Each man "bowed down before the Lord, after which each one arose and spoke in his turn his feelings and determination to keep the commandments of God."[4]

The revelation known as Doctrine and Covenants section 88 began to flow, and by nine o'clock that night it had not ended. The brethren retired but returned the next morning and received more revelation.[5] Samuel Smith,

Joseph's younger brother and one of those present, wrote briefly about the experience. He did not like to write, and what he chose to put down tells us what he thought was important about the revelation. Like Joseph, he focused on what the Lord told him to do:

> Some of the elders assembled together & the word of the Lord was given through Joseph & the Lord declared that those Elders who were the first labourers in this last vineyard should assemble themselves together that they should call a solemn assembly & evry man call upon the name of the Lord & continue in Prayre that they should Sanctify themselves & wash their hands and feet for a testimony that their garments were clean from the Blood of all men & the Lord commanded we the first Elders to Establish a School & appoint a teacher among them & get learning by study & by faith.[6]

Section 88 is a thoroughly temple-oriented revelation. Beginning with a promise of eternal life through Jesus Christ to the faithful, the revelation describes the purposeful creation of the earth and then tells how to obey divine law to advance by degrees of light or glory through a perfect resurrection and into the presence of God.[7]

Section 88 is expansive. It maps the universe. Its concepts stretch the mind, inviting inquiry and awe. "Truth shineth," it says, introducing a string of related if not synonymous concepts that include *truth, light, power, life, spirit,* and even *law* (see vv. 7–15). The concepts in section 88 pervade other temple texts. Methodist scholar Margaret Barker wrote that in such texts "light and life . . . are linked and set in opposition to darkness and death. The presence of God is light; coming into the presence of God transforms whatever is dead and gives it life."[8]

The word *therefore* in verse 117 marks the beginning of the Lord's final point in the initial two-day revelation (see vv. 117–26). This concluding segment reviews the revelation's instructions in what one might call the "therefore, what?" It is a temple-preparation text. The "therefore, what?" of the whole revelation is "therefore, sanctify yourselves that your minds become single to God, and the days will come that you shall see him" (v. 68).

In response to section 88's command for the Saints to build a house of God, call a solemn assembly in it, and present themselves there sanctified in order to enter the Lord's presence, the Saints were obedient. They built the Kirtland Temple, the first in this last dispensation, and entered, both symbolically and literally, into the presence of the Lord.

PREPARING TO ENTER THE LORD'S PRESENCE

But the process was not easy or cheap; ultimate blessings never are. Joseph struggled to help the Saints understand what section 88 called the "great and last promise" (v. 69). It was a promise of entering the Lord's presence based on the conditions that they would build a temple, convene a solemn assembly in it, and sanctify their lives in the process. A few days after section 88 was completed, Joseph sent a copy of it with a rebuke to Church leaders in Missouri. Hard feelings continued to fester there, and the Missouri Saints had not acted on section 84's earlier command to build a temple in Zion. "I send you the . . . Lord's message of peace to us," Joseph wrote,

> for though our Brethren in Zion, indulge in feelings towards us, which are not according to the requirements of the new covenant yet we have the satisfaction of knowing that the Lord approves of us & has accepted us, & established his name in kirtland for the salvation of the nations, for the Lord will have a place from whence his word will go forth in these last days in purity, for if Zion, will not purify herself so as to be approved of in all things in his sight he will seek another people for his work will go on untill Isreal is gathered & they who will not hear his voice must expect to feel his wrath.[9]

Joseph drew on section 84 to remind the Missouri Saints that, like the children of Israel, they were in danger of losing their temple blessings. "Seek to purify yourselves, & also all the inhabitants of Zion," he wrote, "lest the Lords anger be kindled to fierceness, repent, repent, is the voice of God, to Zion, & yet strange as it may appear, yet it is true mankind will presist in self Justification until all their eniquity is exposed & their character past being redeemed, & that which is treasured up in their hearts be exposed to the gaze of mankind, I say to you (& what I say to you, I say to all) hear the <warning> voice of God lest Zion fall, & the Lord swear in his wrath the inhabitants of Zion shall not enter into my rest."[10]

Joseph assured the Saints in Zion that "the Brethren in Kirtland pray for you unceasingly, for knowing the terrors of the Lord, they greatly fear for you." Referring to the copy of section 88 he had sent, Joseph suggested that the Lord, frustrated with disobedience in Zion, had also commanded the Saints in Kirtland to build a temple. "You will see," Joseph wrote, "that the Lord commanded us in Kirtland to build an house of God, & establish a school for the Prophets, this is the word of the Lord to us, & we must yea the Lord helping us we will obey, as on conditions of our obedience, he has promised <us> great things, yea <even> a visit from the heavens to honor us with his own presence."[11]

Joseph had learned from section 84 that the only way into the presence of God was through the temple. Nothing, therefore, should be more important. Yet, like Moses, he worried that Latter-day Saints would harden their hearts and provoke the Lord's wrath (see Doctrine and Covenants 84:24). "We greatly fear before the Lord lest we should fail of this great honor which our master proposes to confer on us," Joseph said. "We are seeking for humility & great faith lest we be ashamed in his presence." He concluded his letter to the Missouri Saints by saying that "if the fountain of our tears are not dried up we will <still> weep for Zion, this from your brother who trembles greatly for Zion, and for the wrath of heaven which awaits her if she repent not."[12]

Joseph worked hard to get the Saints to see the importance of the momentous revelation and to understand the temple and ultimate blessings. Like Moses, he wanted to usher his sometimes shortsighted people into the presence of the Lord (see Doctrine and Covenants 84). The temple revelations preoccupied Joseph's attention. He wanted their promised blessings, and he worked to explain them to the Saints. Joseph was driven by section 88's command to build a temple and by the promise that the Lord would honor them with his presence (see v. 68). He urged the Saints forward, at enormous sacrifice, to build the house of the Lord in Kirtland. Joseph established schools and convened priesthood meetings to train and motivate the brethren because the promise that the Savior would "visit from the heavens" was predicated not only on building the temple but on his command to "sanctify yourselves" (v. 68).

The Saints in Kirtland began building the house of the Lord in the summer of 1833 and, after some interruptions and a rebuke (see section 95), they dedicated it in 1836. Joseph, meanwhile, instructed the Saints to purify and prepare themselves for an outpouring of the Lord's power—an endowment. In November 1835 he met with the newly called Apostles. He confessed his own shortcomings and then taught them section 88, or, as he called it, "how to prepare your selves for the great things that God is about to bring to pass."[13]

Joseph told them he had assumed the Church was fully organized, but then the Lord had taught him more, including "the ordinance of the washing of feet" mentioned in section 88:139. "This we have not done as yet," Joseph taught the Apostles, "but it is necessary now as much as it was in the days of the Saviour, and we must have a place prepared, that we may attend to this ordinance, aside from the world." He continued to emphasize the need for the temple:

> We must have all things prepared and call our solem assembly as the Lord has commanded us [see Doctrine and Covenants 88:70], that we may be able to accomplish his great work: and it mu[s]t be done in Gods own way, the house of the Lord must be prepared, and the solem assembly called and organized in it according to the order of the house of God and in it we must attend to the ordinance of washing of feet; it was never intended for any but official members, it is calculated to unite our hearts, that we may be one in feeling and sentiment and that our faith may be strong, so that satan cannot over throw us, nor have any power over us,—the endowment you are so anxious about you cannot comprehend now, nor could Gabriel explain it to the understanding of your dark minds, but strive to be prepared in your hearts, be faithful in all things that when we meet in the solem assembly that is such as God shall name out of all the official members, will meet, and we must be clean evry whit.[14]

Echoing section 88:123–26, Joseph urged the brethren:

> Do not watch for iniquity in each other if you do you will not get an endowment for God will not bestow it on such; but if we are faithful and live by every word that procedes forth from the mouth of God I will venture to prophesy that we shall get a blessing that will be worth remembering if we should live as long as John the Revelator, our blessings will be such as we have not realized before, nor in this generation. The order of the house of God has and ever will be the same, even after Christ comes, and after the termination of the thousand years it will be the same, and we shall finally roll into the celestial Kingdom of God and enjoy it forever [see Doctrine and Covenants 88:96–117]:—you need an endowment brethren in order that you may be prepared and able to over come all things.[15]

Joseph helped them understand the relationship between the power with which God intended to endow them and their calling to preach the gospel (see Doctrine and Covenants 88:80–82). Then he concluded his teaching by reaffirming what section 88 twice calls the "great and last promise": "I feel disposed to speak a few words more to you, my brethren, concerning the endowment, all who are prepared and are sufficiently pure to abide the presence of the Lord, will see him in the solemn assembly" (vv. 69, 75).[16] William Phelps wrote to his wife in Missouri about what he was learning from Joseph. "Our meeting[s] will grow more and more solemn, and will continue till the great solemn assembly when the house is finished! We are preparing to make ourselves clean, by first cleansing our hearts, forsaking our sins, forgiving every body; putting on clean decent clothes, by anointing our heads and by keeping all the commandments. As we come nearer to God we see our imperfections and nothingness plainer and plainer."[17] Oliver Cowdery gave even more detail about one of these temple preparation meetings, noting how the Latter-day Saints followed Old Testament patterns in washing and anointing priests for temple service. Oliver wrote that he met with Joseph and others at the Prophet's house. "And after pure water was prepared, called upon the Lord and proceeded to wash each other's bodies, and bathe the same with whiskey, perfumed with cinnamon. This we did that we might be clean before the Lord for the Sabbath, confessing our sins and covenanting to be faithful to God. While performing this washing with solemnity, our minds were filled with many reflections upon the propriety of the same, and how the priests anciently used to wash always before ministering before the Lord."[18]

REDEMPTION OF THE DEAD

When the house of the Lord (as the early Saints called the Kirtland Temple) was nearing completion, Joseph convened the preparation meetings in the rooms of its third-floor garret on the evening of January 21, 1836. There, in the westernmost room, Joseph met with his secretary, other members of the First Presidency, his father (the Church's patriarch), and the bishoprics from Missouri and Ohio. The brethren came to the meeting freshly bathed, symbolizing their efforts to repent and present themselves sanctified before the Lord. The First Presidency consecrated oil, then anointed and blessed Father Smith, who in turn anointed and blessed Joseph. Then the heavens opened. Oliver Cowdery wrote that "the glorious scene is too great to be described. . . . I only say, that the heavens were opened to many, and great and marvelous things were shown." Bishop Edward Partridge affirmed that some of the brethren "saw visions & others were blessed with the outpouring of the Holy Ghost."[19] Joseph was the only one present who described in detail some of what he experienced.

Doctrine and Covenants section 137 derives from Joseph's journal, where he described his vision of the future celestial kingdom. There he saw his oldest brother, Alvin, who had died painfully in 1823, shortly after Moroni appeared to Joseph and taught him of the Book of Mormon plates.

Nearly twenty years later, Joseph dictated an entry in the Book of the Law of the Lord, the blessing and record book he kept near the end of his life. "I remember well the pangs of sorrow that swelled my youthful bosom and almost burst my tender heart, when he died," Joseph said of Alvin. "He was the oldest, and the noblest of my fathers family. He was one of the noblest of the sons of men."[20] Even so, at Alvin's funeral his mother's minister, Reverend Benjamin Stockton, "intimated very strongly that he had gone to hell, for Alvin was not a Church member." Joseph's father "did not like it."[21] Father Smith recognized what theologians call the "soteriological problem," meaning a dilemma between doctrines of salvation.[22] The problem seems to arise from three truths, any two of which can work together but not all three:

1. God desires the salvation of his children.
2. Salvation comes only through one's acceptance of Christ's Atonement.
3. Many, many of God's children have lived and died without an opportunity to accept Christ's Atonement.

The Book of Mormon clarified that unaccountable infants would not be damned, but it said nothing of accountable adults who died before accepting the gospel. Joseph received the priesthood, restored the Church, worked to establish Zion, and built the house of the Lord. But for all Joseph knew, Reverend Stockton had been right. Not until the temple was nearly finished did the Lord refute the reverend's doctrine. Then he did so beautifully in the vision recorded for us in Doctrine and Covenants section 137. The point of that revelation is to resolve the soteriological problem, which it does in verses 7–10. But before revealing the answer, the Lord showed Joseph a vision that begged the question. Joseph envisioned the flaming gate to the celestial world, the golden streets, and the Father and the Son on their blazing throne. He saw Adam and Abraham. And he saw Alvin and his parents there too. He "marveled" at Alvin's appearance since he had not been baptized before his death (v. 6).

The Lord spoke the answer not just for Alvin but for "all who have died without a knowledge of this gospel, who would have received it if they had been permitted to tarry" (v. 7). They will inherit celestial glory. Indeed, anyone who dies without knowing the gospel but who would have received it otherwise will receive it. The emphatic point is that death is not a deadline that determines salvation, "for I, the Lord, will judge all men according to their works, according to the desire of their hearts" (v. 9). Desire—not the timing of one's death—is the determinant of salvation through Christ.

Some of the greatest theological minds have wrestled with the soteriological problem. Early Christians believed that the Lord had planned a "rescue for the dead," as one scholar called it.[23] Put simply, early Christians baptized each other for their kindred dead, as the Apostle Paul noted at 1 Corinthians 15:29 and Hugh Nibley demonstrated.[24] Later Christian philosophers recognized the problem and believed that Christ would somehow save all the righteous, but already they had lost the significance of truths Peter and Paul taught, leaving no certain answer to the question, "Shall those be wholly deprived of the kingdom of heaven who died before Christ's coming?"[25] Then later, largely influenced by Augustine, Christianity apostatized generally from the doctrine of redemption for the dead, giving rise to the soteriological problem.

By the eighteenth century, the Puritan theologian Jonathan Edwards longed to find a solution. One contemporary Evangelical scholar finds in Edwards the seeds of a "dispositional soteriology," or a doctrine of salvation that only requires one's disposition to be redeemed by God through Christ. It does not require one to knowingly accept the Savior.[26] But such a solution negates agency and Bible passages to the contrary. The question persists—what about those who never heard? The revealed answer is not to subtract from the three known truths but to add one that makes them all compatible and whole rather than problematic. That truth is found in verses 8–9 of section 137: all who have died or will die without knowledge of the gospel who would otherwise have received it will receive it according to their desires and thus inherit the celestial kingdom. "Thank God for Joseph Smith!" wrote Latter-day Saint philosopher David L. Paulsen, who knows full well the problem and therefore appreciates the profound solution. His gratitude for Joseph is "not merely for being God's conduit in resolving one more thorny problem of evil, but for being the instrument through whom God restored the knowledge and priesthood powers that make the redemption of the dead possible."[27]

Later, in Nauvoo, Joseph revealed the ordinance of baptism for the dead that enables all humankind to make and keep gospel covenants (see sections 127–28). Joseph taught the doctrine to his father on his deathbed. In contrast to his reaction to Reverend Stockton's sermon, Father Smith was "delighted to hear" the truth and asked Joseph to attend to the ordinance. Joseph and Hyrum fulfilled their father's dying wish. "I see Alvin," Father

Smith said just a few minutes before his passing.[28] Prophetically, section 137 solved a persistent problem faced by Joseph's family and many, many others.

THE TEMPLE DEDICATION

Meanwhile, in March 1836 the Saints put finishing touches on the house of the Lord in Kirtland and prepared to assemble in it solemnly as section 88 had commanded them more than three years earlier (see Doctrine and Covenants 88:70, 117). Joseph spent the day before the solemn assembly making final arrangements with his counselors and secretaries.[29] Oliver Cowdery's diary tells us that he assisted Joseph "in writing a prayer for the dedication of the house."[30] The next morning the house of the Lord filled to capacity with nearly a thousand Saints. An overflow meeting convened next door. The solemn assembly began at nine with scripture readings, choir singing, prayer, a sermon, and the sustaining of Joseph Smith as prophet and seer. In the afternoon session the sustaining continued, with each quorum and the general body of the Church sustaining, in turn, the leaders of the Church.[31] Another hymn followed, "after which," Joseph's journal says, "I offered to God the . . . dedication prayer."[32]

That prayer is preserved for us in Doctrine and Covenants section 109. It is an inspired prayer. It begins with thanks to God, then makes requests of him in the name of Jesus Christ. It is based heavily on section 88's temple instructions as well as other temple-related scriptural texts. It "sums up the Church's concerns in 1836, bringing before God each major project."[33] It is a temple prayer.

What does one pray for in such settings? Joseph began by asking God to accept the temple on the terms that he had given in section 88 and that the Saints had tried to fulfill in order to obtain the promised blessing of entering the Lord's presence (see 88:68; 109:4–12). Joseph prayed that all who worshipped in the temple would be endowed with God's power and that they would be taught by God "that they may grow up in thee, and receive a fulness of the Holy Ghost, and be organized according to thy laws, and be prepared to obtain every needful thing" (109:15). Joseph prayed, in other words, a temple prayer that the Saints would become like their Heavenly Father by degrees of glory as they obeyed his laws and prepared to enter his presence. He prayed for what section 88 taught him to pray for.

Joseph prayed that the Saints, "armed" or endowed with priesthood power from the temple, could go to "the ends of the earth" with the "exceedingly great and glorious tidings" of the gospel to fulfill prophecies

(109:22–23). He asked Heavenly Father to protect the Saints from their enemies (see vv. 24–33). He asked for mercy upon the Saints and to seal the anointing ordinances that many of the priesthood brethren had received in the weeks leading up to the solemn assembly. He asked for the gifts of the Spirit to be poured out as on the biblical day of Pentecost (see Acts 2:2–3). He asked the Lord to protect and empower the missionaries and postpone judgment until they had gathered the righteous. He prayed that God's will would be done "and not ours" (Doctrine and Covenants 109:44).

Joseph prayed that the Saints would be delivered from the prophesied calamities. He asked Heavenly Father to remember the Saints who had been oppressed and driven from Jackson County, Missouri, and he prayed for their deliverance. He asked how long their afflictions would continue until avenged (see 109:49). He asked for mercy "upon the wicked mob, who have driven thy people, that they may cease to spoil, that they may repent of their sins if repentance is to be found" (v. 50). Joseph prayed for Zion.

Joseph prayed for mercy on all nations and political leaders so that the principles of individual agency captured in the United States Constitution would be established forever. He prayed for "all the poor, the needy, and afflicted ones of the earth" (v. 55). He prayed for an end to prejudices so that the missionaries "may gather out the righteous to build a holy city to thy name, as thou hast commanded them" (v. 58). He asked for more stakes to facilitate the gathering and growth of Zion. He asked for mercy for the scattered remnants of Jacob and for the Jews. Indeed, he prayed for "all the scattered remnants of Israel, who have been driven to the ends of the earth, [to] come to a knowledge of the truth, believe in the Messiah, and be redeemed from oppression" (v. 67).

Joseph prayed for himself, reminding the Lord of his sincere effort to keep his covenants. He asked for mercy upon his family, praying that Emma and the children "may be exalted in thy presence" (v. 69). This is the first usage of *exalted* in Joseph's revelations to refer to the fulness of salvation through temple blessings.[34] Joseph prayed for his in-laws to be converted. He prayed for the others in the First Presidency and their families. He prayed for all the Saints and their families and their sick and afflicted. He prayed, again, for "all the poor and meek of the earth" and for the glorious kingdom of God to fill the earth as prophesied (see vv. 68–74).

Joseph prayed that the Saints would rise in the First Resurrection with pure garments, "robes of righteousness," and "crowns of glory upon our heads" to "reap eternal joy" (v. 76). Thrice repeating his petition, Joseph asked the Lord to "hear us" and accept the prayers and petitions and offerings of the Saints in building a house to his name (v. 78). He prayed for grace to enable the Saints to join the choirs surrounding God's throne in the heavenly temple "singing Hosanna to God and the Lamb" (v. 79). Joseph concluded the prayer, "And let these, thine anointed ones, be clothed with salvation, and thy saints shout aloud for joy. Amen, and Amen" (v. 80).

Joseph's prayer dedicated the first house of the Lord in the last dispensation and set the pattern for all subsequent solemn assemblies held for the same holy purposes. It teaches the Saints how to pray, including what to pray for, and to ask according to the will of God. It teaches the doctrine and evokes the imagery of the temple, perhaps most poignantly in the idea that temple worshippers can "grow up" by degrees of glory until they become like their Heavenly Father (compare section 93). This is what it means to be exalted in God's presence. The temple revelations call this "fulness," including having a fulness of joy. The prayer continues the expansive work of the temple revelations in sections 76, 84, 88, and 93 and points us forward to the culminating revelation on exaltation: section 132:1–20. Joseph's temple prayer invites mortals, who occupy a polluted telestial planet where they cannot think of more than one thing at a time and generally only in finite terms, to receive power that will enable them to journey to the real world where God lives "enthroned, with glory, honor, power, majesty, might, dominion, truth, justice, judgment, mercy, and an infinity of fulness, from everlasting to everlasting" (109:77).[35]

KEYS

A week after he dedicated the house of the Lord in Kirtland, Joseph attended meetings there, including an afternoon sacrament meeting. For Christians it was Easter Sunday, while Jews were celebrating the Passover season.[36] After sacrament, Joseph and Oliver Cowdery retreated behind the heavy curtains used to divide the room. They bowed in what Joseph's journal describes as "solemn, but silent prayer to the Most High," noting that "after rising from prayer [a] vision was opened to both of them."[37]

The Lord unveiled the minds of his seers, who envisioned and heard the Lord standing before them. Three times, in a voice like rushing water, he declared, "I am," evoking Old Testament revelations in which he repeatedly identified himself saying, "I am the Lord your God" (see Exodus 20; Leviticus 19). This is a play on the related words of the Hebrew verb for *to be* and the name transliterated in English as *Jehovah*. It is the Lord Jesus Christ declaring that he is the God who told Moses to tell the Israelites that "I AM hath sent me unto you" (Exodus 3:14). It is Jesus of Nazareth testifying that he is the God of Israel, the promised Messiah, and proclaiming it in this dispensation in a building that still exists.

In a powerful juxtaposition of present and past verb tenses, the Savior declared himself the crucified Christ who conquered death: "I am he who liveth. I am he who was slain; I am your advocate with the Father" (Doctrine and Covenants 110:4). He forgave Joseph and Oliver, pronounced them clean, and commanded them and those who had built the temple to rejoice. He accepted the temple and made conditional promises to manifest himself to his people there, prophesying that tens of thousands would rejoice in the endowment poured out on his servants in the house of the Lord as its fame spread to foreign lands.

The Lord disappeared, and Moses appeared and committed keys for gathering Israel from all the earth, the permission to lead the lost tribes of Israel from their scattered locations. Next Elias appeared and dispensed the gospel of Abraham, saying that "in us and our seed all generations after us should be blessed" (110:12). Another glorious vision followed as Elijah, who went to heaven without tasting death, appeared and said that it was time to fulfill Malachi's prophecy that Elijah would turn the hearts of the fathers to their children and vice versa before the dreadful day of the Lord. The vision closed with a heavenly announcement that Joseph now held the keys of the last dispensation. He had received the priesthood several years earlier. What he had now was permission to put it to work in new ways— including sealing families, officiating in temple ordinances, and sending missionaries globally.

The glorious vision, recorded for us in Doctrine and Covenants section 110, fulfilled the Lord's conditional promise to the Saints in section 38 that if they would move to Ohio and build him a holy house, he would endow them with power in it (see sections 38, 88, 95). It fulfilled section 88's great and last promise that the sanctified would come into the presence of the Lord.[38] Finally, the vision fulfilled Malachi's multilayered prophecy. Through Malachi the Lord prophesied, "I will send you Elijah the prophet before the coming of the great and dreadful day of the Lord" (Malachi 4:5). Moroni reiterated that prophecy to Joseph Smith in 1823 (see Doctrine and Covenants 2). Elijah fulfilled it less than thirteen years later. Jews had long awaited Elijah's prophesied return and still invite him into their homes during the Passover Seder. During the very season that some Jews were celebrating the sacred meal with the hope that Elijah would return, he came to the house of the Lord.[39]

Moses's appearance is just as significant. "His appearance in company with Elijah offers another striking parallel between Mormon teachings and Jewish tradition, according to which Moses and Elijah would arrive together at the 'end of time.'"[40] Joseph and Oliver's vision reenacts the endowment received in the biblical account of the Mount of Transfiguration (see Matthew 17:1–9).

Few texts weld dispensations as thoroughly as this revelation. Given on Easter and during the Passover season, the revelation links Israel's Old Testament deliverance with Christ's New Testament resurrection and affirms that Joseph Smith and the temple-building Latter-day Saints are the heirs of God's promises to the Israelite patriarchs. Christ is the Passover lamb who "was slain" and then resurrected and now appears to Joseph in Kirtland to approve of the latter-day work and commission the Prophet to fulfill the work of Moses (the gathering of Israel), Elias (the gospel of Abraham), and Elijah (the sealing of families).

Joseph put these priesthood keys to use against great opposition. Not long after receiving the keys from Moses to gather Israel, Joseph found Heber C. Kimball in the temple and whispered in his ear a mission call to Great Britain. Joseph had previously sent missionaries on short local or regional missions. Heber and his companions began the ongoing process of gathering Israel from the ends of the earth. Though oppressed by what seems like a concerted opposition that included financial collapse, widespread apostasy, an executive order driving the Saints from Missouri, and then unjust imprisonment in Liberty, Missouri, Joseph began to teach and administer the ordinances of the temple. In sum, the endowment of priesthood keys he had received authorized him to begin performing temple ordinances.

The vision recorded in section 110 communicated temple knowledge and power. It came in the temple behind a veil, was recorded but not preached, and was acted on but not publicly explained.[41] After the revelation, Joseph used the keys to gather, endow, and seal in anticipation of the Savior's Second Coming. Section 110 marks the restoration of temple-related power and knowledge that Moses possessed and "plainly taught" but that had been forfeited by the children of Israel (see Doctrine and Covenants 84:19–25).

"SO GREAT A CAUSE"

Imagine for a moment being Joseph Smith. Imagine that you are a seventeen-year-old seer. You know that God lives and Jesus is the very Christ, that they love you and have promised to provide you further knowledge in due time. But you don't have any idea about temples, salvation for the dead, or the prophecies of Isaiah, Joel, and Malachi. You do not have the first hint that Malachi's prophecy of Elijah's return will intimately involve you. You're worried about simple, sincere things: your own teenage sins, the religious divisions in your family, and your uncertain future. You pray for personal forgiveness, and an angel greets you with a staggering learning curve and a call to assist in saving the world.

Now you are twenty-seven years old. You have just received one of the most sublime revelations on record, including a command to build a house for the Lord and assemble your followers in it, solemn and sanctified (see Doctrine and Covenants 88). You have your own weaknesses and sins to wrestle with in addition to the shortcomings of a sincere but fallen body of Latter-day Saints. You do everything in your power to explain the imperative need they have for the power that flows only through the temple and the Savior's promise to reveal himself if you will build him a house and sanctify your lives. Try as you might, the Saints are slow to grasp the magnitude of what you alone seem to sense. You keep trying. You quarry rock. You get the Saints to see as you see, to sacrifice as you sacrifice, and to be sanctified as you are sanctified through service. You rebuke them. You receive rebukes. You wash, anoint, and bless them. You wash their feet. You have an indomitable will. You raise the house of the Lord upward until it is finished. And then you call the solemn assembly as you were commanded. You do exactly as you were commanded to do, and then you report on your mission. You kneel in solemn prayer and anticipate the promised blessings. You expect the Lord to unveil himself, to appear in his holy house. And he does. He forgives your sins. Perhaps you remember your seventeen-year-old prayer for just such a blessing.

You are thirty years old. Moses, Elias, and Elijah have committed into your hands the keys of the last dispensation. You now have all the power and permission you need to gather Israel, endow them with power, and seal them together before the Lord's imminent coming. All hell seems to break loose. Intense opposition stalks you. The "envy and wrath of man" are your lot all the days of your life (Doctrine and Covenants 127:2). Your best efforts to deliver your people financially result in bankruptcy. You receive a revelation warning you and your faithful friends to flee Kirtland and the house of the Lord. You arrive in Missouri only to have an extermination order issued against you. You are captured, charged with treason, and imprisoned on a capital offense in a state where there is no due process of law for Latter-day Saints. You are imprisoned in a tiny, stinking, depressing cellar, powerless to support your refugee wife and children. If God had not called you to the work, you would back out. "But I cannot back out," you say, for "I have no doubt of the truth."[42] And so you work and watch and fight and pray with all your might and zeal.[43] Eventually, the Lord delivers you from your enemies so you can exercise the keys of the holy priesthood. You reunite with your family and call for the Apostles.

Five years to the day before you will be killed, you begin the process of endowing the Apostles with power.[44] You teach, endow, and ordain them as quickly as you can. Three months before your death, you finish. "I roll the burthen and responsibility of leading this church off from my shoulders on to yours," you tell the Apostles. "Now, round up your shoulders and stand under it like men; for the Lord is going to let me rest a while."[45] You are thirty-eight years old. The commission you received at age seventeen from an angel sent from the presence of God specifically to you is now fulfilled. Your work on earth is done. You are no longer safe. You publicly declare, "I dont blame you for not believing my history had I not experienced it [I] could not believe it myself."[46] It has been remarkable—not because you were flawless or immortal, but because you were not. You were an imperfect, sincere seventeen-year-old seeking the salvation of your soul. Little did you know that your own salvation would be so wrapped up in God's vast, eternal plan for the salvation of the human family. But as you began to grasp the glad tidings, as you began to piece together line by line and precept by precept, with the help of ministering angels, how the keys, powers, and privileges of the holy priesthood would be restored to everyone who wants them, you rejoiced and resolved to push the work forward. "Forward and not backward," you said to the Saints. "Courage, brethren; and on, on to the victory! Let your hearts rejoice, and be exceedingly glad. Let the earth break forth into anthems of eternal praise to the King Immanuel, who hath ordained, before the world was, that which would enable us to redeem them out of their prison; for the prisoners shall go free" (Doctrine and Covenants 128:22).

Indeed, they shall. Because of what occurred in the house of the Lord in Kirtland, the prisoners shall go free. Oh, how well Joseph knew what it meant for the prisoners to be free! His heart rejoiced and was exceedingly glad. I fervently pray that Joseph's rhetorical question will ever ring in our ears—"Shall we not go on in so great a cause?" (Doctrine and Covenants 128:22). We are the heirs of Joseph's legacy. Let us spend our lives gathering, endowing, and sealing the living and the dead. Let us present ourselves sanctified in the house of the Lord against great opposition. Let us "as Latter-day Saints, offer unto the Lord an offering in righteousness; and let us present in his holy temple . . . the records of our dead, which shall be worthy of all acceptation" (Doctrine and Covenants 128:24).

Steven C. Harper is a professor of Church history and doctrine at Brigham Young University.

Steven C. Harper, "Joseph Smith and the Kirtland Temple, 1836," in *Joseph Smith, the Prophet and Seer*, ed. Richard Neitzel Holzapfel and Kent P. Jackson (Provo, UT: Religious Studies Center, Brigham Young University; Salt Lake City: Deseret Book, 2010), 233–60.

NOTES

1. *The Papers of Joseph Smith*, ed. Dean C. Jessee (Salt Lake City: Deseret Book, 1989–92), 1:127; and Joseph Smith, History, 1834–1836, p. 121, *The Joseph Smith Papers*, http://josephsmithpapers.org/.
2. Jessee, *Papers of Joseph Smith*, 1:278; Joseph Smith, History, 1838–1856, volume A-1 [23 December 1805–30 August 1834], pp. 5–6, http://josephsmithpapers.org/.
3. Russell M. Nelson, in Conference Report, October 1996, 97.
4. Kirtland Minute Book, December 27, 1832, Church History Library, The Church of Jesus Christ of Latter-day Saints, Salt Lake City (hereafter CHL); and Minute Book 1, pp. 3–4, http://josephsmithpapers.org/.
5. Kirtland Minute Book, December 27, 1832; Kirtland Revelation Book, 47–48, 166, CHL; and Minute Book 1, p. 4, http://josephsmithpapers.org/.
6. Samuel Harrison Smith Diary, February 1832–May 1833, MS 4213, p. 29, CHL.
7. See Richard Lyman Bushman, *Joseph Smith: Rough Stone Rolling* (New York: Alfred A. Knopf, 2005), 206.
8. Margaret Barker, *On Heaven as It Is in Earth: Temple Symbolism in the New Testament* (Edinburgh: T&T Clark, 1995), 13.
9. Joseph Smith, Kirtland, Ohio, to William W. Phelps, Independence, Missouri, January 11, 1833, in Joseph Smith Letterbook 1, 18–20, in hand of Frederick G. Williams, Joseph Smith Collection, CHL.
10. Joseph Smith to William W. Phelps, January 11, 1833, 18–20. Compare with Doctrine and Covenants 84:23–25.
11. Joseph Smith to William W. Phelps, January 11, 1833, 18–20.
12. Joseph Smith to William W. Phelps, January 11, 1833, 18–20.
13. Joseph Smith, Discourse, Kirtland, Ohio, November 12, 1835, Joseph Smith Journal, in Jessee, *Papers of Joseph Smith*, 2:76; see pp. 75–78.

14. Joseph Smith, Discourse, November 12, 1835, 2:76–77.
15. Joseph Smith, Discourse, November 12, 1835, 2:77.
16. See Smith, History, 1834–1836, p. 128; fulfillments of this prophecy are documented in Steven C. Harper, "'A Pentecost and Endowment Indeed': Six Eyewitness Accounts of the Kirtland Temple Experience," in *Opening the Heavens: Accounts of Divine Manifestations, 1820–1844*, ed. John W. Welch and Erick B. Carlson (Provo, UT: Brigham Young University Press; and Salt Lake City: Deseret Book, 2005), 327–71.
17. William W. Phelps to Sally Waterman Phelps, January 1836, L. Tom Perry Special Collections, Harold B. Lee Library, Brigham Young University, Provo, UT.
18. Leonard J. Arrington, "Oliver Cowdery's Kirtland, Ohio, 'Sketch Book,'" *BYU Studies* 12, no. 4 (1972): 4–5 (pdf version, byustudies.byu.edu).
19. Harper, "'A Pentecost and Endowment Indeed,'" 338, 344; see Joseph's description on p. 354.
20. Jessee, *Papers of Joseph Smith*, 2:440.
21. According to Joseph's brother William Smith, cited in *Deseret News*, January 20, 1894, cited in Bushman, *Rough Stone Rolling*, 110.
22. David L. Paulsen, "Joseph Smith and the Problem of Evil," *BYU Studies* 39, no. 1 (2000): 61.
23. See Jeffrey A. Trumbower, *Rescue for the Dead: The Posthumous Salvation of Non-Christians in Early Christianity* (New York: Oxford University Press, 2001).
24. See Hugh Nibley, *Mormonism and Early Christianity* (Salt Lake City: Deseret Book; Provo, UT: FARMS, 1987), 148–49.
25. Nibley, *Mormonism and Early Christianity*, 103.
26. See Gerald R. McDermott, *Jonathan Edwards Confronts the Gods* (New York: Oxford University Press, 2000).
27. Paulsen, "Joseph Smith and the Problem of Evil," 62.
28. Lucy Mack Smith, History, 1845, pp. 296, 301, http://josephsmithpapers.org/; Richard E. Turley Jr., "The Latter-day Saint Doctrine of Baptism for the Dead," BYU family history fireside, Joseph Smith Building, November 9, 2001, copy in author's possession. Nauvoo baptismal records show that Alvin was baptized at the instance of his brother Hyrum (Nauvoo Temple, Baptisms for the Dead, 1840–45, Book A, 145, 149, CHL).
29. See Jessee, *Papers of Joseph Smith*, 2:191.
30. Arrington, "Oliver Cowdery's Kirtland, Ohio, 'Sketch Book,'" 9.
31. Harper, "'A Pentecost and Endowment Indeed,'" 327–71.
32. Jessee, *Papers of Joseph Smith*, 2:195.
33. Bushman, *Rough Stone Rolling*, 317.
34. See Doctrine and Covenants section 49:10, 23 for earlier usages in a different context.
35. Hugh Nibley, "A House of Glory," FARMS Preliminary Report (Provo, UT: FARMS, 1993).
36. See John P. Pratt, "The Restoration of Priesthood Keys on Easter 1836, Part 2: Symbolism of Passover and of Elijah's Return," *Ensign*, July 1985, 55.
37. Jessee, *Papers of Joseph Smith*, 2:209.
38. See Joseph Smith to William W. Phelps, January 11, 1833, 18–20.
39. See Stephen D. Ricks, "The Appearance of Elijah and Moses in the Kirtland Temple and the Jewish Passover," *BYU Studies* 23, no. 4 (1983): 483–86.
40. Ricks, "Appearance of Elijah and Moses," 485.

41. See Bushman, *Rough Stone Rolling*, 320–21.
42. Joseph Smith, Discourse, April 6, 1843, Nauvoo, Illinois, Joseph Smith, Papers, Journals, CHL; also in Faulring, *An American Prophet's Record: The Diaries and Journals of Joseph Smith* (Salt Lake City: Signature Books, 1989), 347–50; *The Words of Joseph Smith: The Contemporary Accounts of the Nauvoo Discourses of the Prophet Joseph*, ed. Andrew F. Ehat and Lyndon W. Cook (Salt Lake City: Bookcraft, 1980), 177–80; and Joseph Smith, Discourse, 6 April 1843–B, as Reported by Willard Richards, p. [72], http://josephsmithpapers.org/.
43. See Will L. Thompson, "Put Your Shoulder to the Wheel," *Hymns* (Salt Lake City: The Church of Jesus Christ of Latter-day Saints), no. 252.
44. See Journal of Wilford Woodruff, June 27, 1839, CHL.
45. Orson Hyde, certificate about the Twelve, circa March 1845, CHL.
46. Joseph Smith, Discourse, April 7, 1844, Nauvoo, Illinois, Joseph Smith, Papers, Journals, CHL; also in Ehat and Cook, *Words of Joseph Smith*, 340–43; Faulring, *An American Prophet's Record*, 465–76; and Joseph Smith, Discourse, 7 April 1844, as Reported by Willard Richards, p. [71], http://josephsmithpapers.org/.

Chapter Fourteen

Hyrum Smith's Liberty Jail Letters

KENNETH L. ALFORD AND CRAIG K. MANSCILL

The story of Liberty Jail has frequently and appropriately been told from the perspective of Joseph Smith. Joseph sent nine letters while in jail in the ironically named town of Liberty, Missouri (see table 1).[1] Three of those letters were sent to Emma, his beloved wife. The first letter, written on the day he arrived at Liberty Jail (December 1, 1838), was brief. Addressing it to his "Dear companion," he wrote to "take this oppertunity to inform you that we arrived in Liberty and commited to Joal [jail] this Evening but we are all in good spirits."[2] In his last letter, written on April 4, shortly before his incarceration ended, he expressed his love for Emma and offered her encouragement and advice.[3]

The day after Joseph dictated his March 20 letter[4]—arguably one of the two most famous and oft-quoted letters he ever wrote—he penned his second letter to Emma that served as a cover and introduction for the much longer letter dictated the previous day. Addressing Emma as "Affectionate Wife," he explained, "I have sent an Epistle to the church directed to you because I wanted you to have the first reading of it and then I want Father and Mother to have a coppy of it keep the original yourself as I dectated the matter myself." At the end of his three-page cover letter, Joseph touchingly asked his wife, "My Dear Emma do you think that my being cast into prison by the mob renders me less worthy of your friendsship," and then he provided the answer he hoped to receive: "No I do not think so."[5] Joseph's two letters to Bishop Edward Partridge and the Church—from which Doctrine and Covenants sections 121, 122, and 123 would later be drawn—are the focus of this essay. The first letter was written on March 20; the second was written sometime around March 22. (We will generally refer to them in this essay as the Partridge letters.)

Joseph's brother Hyrum was incarcerated in Liberty Jail with Joseph, but his experience has largely been downplayed or ignored. Hyrum also wrote several letters while in Liberty Jail, and his letters provide valuable information about conditions and events during the imprisonment, give context to events that were occurring in the Church at large, and add insights into the struggles his family endured during the Missouri persecutions and then as refugees in Illinois. A close study of Hyrum's letters provides insights into the development, writing, and doctrines espoused in Doctrine and Covenants 121, 122, and 123.

JOSEPH'S LIBERTY JAIL LETTERS	DATE
To Emma Hale Smith (wife) (informing his wife that they had arrived at the jail)	1 December 1838
To the Saints in Caldwell County (guidance and instructions)	16 December 1838
Letter to Heber C. Kimball and Brigham Young (directing them to manage the affairs of the Church)	16 January 1839
To Presendia Huntington Buell (friend) (thanking her for friendship and interest in their welfare)	15 March 1839
To the Church and Edward Partridge (includes the text of Doctrine and Covenants 121:1–33)	20 March 1839
To Emma Hale Smith (responding to a letter from her)	21 March 1839
To Isaac Galland (businessman) (expressed a desire to purchase land from him)	22 March 1839
To Edward Partridge and the Church (includes the text of 121:34–46; 122; and 123)	circa 22 March 1839
To Emma Hale Smith (expressed his love and gave her advice and encouragement)	4 April 1839

Table 1. Joseph Smith's Liberty Jail letters

PRELUDE TO LIBERTY JAIL

Joseph Smith, Sidney Rigdon, Parley P. Pratt, and other leaders were betrayed at Far West into the hands of Major General Samuel D. Lucas and the Missouri militia on October 31, 1838.[6] Hyrum Smith and Amasa Lyman were captured later that day while attempting to flee to Iowa.[7] In Richmond, Missouri, on November 29, 1838, Austin A. King, a Fifth Judicial Circuit judge, signed the court order charging six prisoners with "treason against the state of Missouri."[8] The six men were Joseph Smith, who would turn thirty-four years old in three weeks; Sidney Rigdon, forty-five; Hyrum Smith, thirty-eight; Alexander McRae, thirty-one, the youngest member of the group; Lyman Wight, forty-two; and Caleb Baldwin, forty-seven, who was the oldest.

Hyrum later testified that he heard the judge say "that there was no law for us, nor for the Mormons, in the state of Missouri; that he had sworn to see them exterminated, and to see the Governor's order executed to the very letter, and that he would do so."[9] The detainees were bound over to Sheriff Samuel Hadley for transport to Liberty Jail. Before being taken to jail, they were handcuffed and chained together. During the course of his work, the blacksmith informed the prisoners that "the judge [had] stated his intention to keep us in jail until all the Mormons were driven out of the state."[10] With the exception of Sidney Rigdon, who was freed on February 5, 1839, the detainees would be incarcerated the entire winter—from December 1, 1838, until April 6, 1839—in the unheated jail.[11]

Isolated from Church headquarters, the jailed Church leadership was rendered unable to lead the Church out of Missouri. Communication with the outside world was limited to letters and visitors. As Liberty is forty miles from Far West, it was possible for family, friends, and Church leaders to call on the prisoners. All the men except Hyrum received visits from their wives during December.[12] They were visited in January over twenty times, with all of the wives visiting at least once. During one of those visits, Hyrum blessed his newborn son, Joseph Fielding Smith.[13] Jail visitors decreased during February and March as an increasing number of Church and family members fled Missouri for the safety of Illinois.

Hyrum later commented, "We endeavored to find out for what cause [we were to be thrust into jail], but all that we could learn was [that it was] because we were Mormons."[14] Life in the jail was difficult. Hyrum reported that "poison was administered to us three or four times, the effect it had upon our systems was, that it vomitted us almost to death, and then we would lay in a torpid stupid state, not even caring or wishing for life." He also said, "We were also subjected to the necessity of eating human flesh for the space of 5 days or go without food, except a little coffee or a little corn bread—the latter I chose in preference to the former. We none of us partook of the flesh except Lyman Wight."[15]

BISHOP PARTRIDGE'S MARCH 5 LETTER

On March 5 Bishop Edward Partridge wrote a letter from Quincy, Illinois, to provide details of the Church in Illinois for the "Beloved Brethren" in Liberty Jail. Partridge explained that he wrote because of "an opportunity to send direct to you by br[other] Rogers."[16] In addition to Partridge's letter, David Rogers also carried a March 6 letter from Don Carlos and William Smith, two of Joseph and Hyrum's brothers, and a March 7 letter from Emma, Joseph's wife.[17] Rogers left Quincy on March 10, 1839, and delivered the letters on March 19.[18]

LIBERTY JAIL CORRESPONDENCE

In the difficult conditions of Liberty Jail, the prisoners faced several challenges when it came to writing and receiving letters. The first problem, as Hyrum mentioned in his March 19 letter to his wife Mary, was that they were often in need of paper and ink. The second was difficulty receiving letters. And third was the challenge of finding trustworthy people to deliver their letters. As an increasing number of Church members fled Missouri, letters became the only viable means of communication with family members and Church leaders now in Illinois.

We are currently aware of seven letters Hyrum Smith wrote from Liberty Jail (see table 2).[19] Six of them are dated and were penned during March and April 1839. At least four of the letters, and possibly five, were written before Joseph dictated the Partridge letters of instruction, portions of which would be canonized as Doctrine and Covenants 121–123. Hyrum's first two letters, both dated March 16, were written to his wife Mary Fielding Smith and Hannah Grinnals. Hannah was a longtime, trusted friend who lived with Hyrum and Mary for almost twenty years. She first appears in the historical record in 1837 giving aid to Hyrum's family when his daughter Sarah was born and his first wife, Jerusha, died while he was away on Church business. Hannah likewise assisted Mary with Joseph F. Smith's birth on November 13, 1838, almost two weeks after Hyrum was arrested.[20] When Hyrum wrote to Hannah from Liberty Jail, he thanked her for "friends[h]ip you have manifested towords my family I feel grateful to you for your Kindness." He included words of encouragement and counsel to his daughter Lovina and to Clarinda, who was likely Hannah's daughter, as well as general counsel to his other children ("little John little Hiram little Jerusha & little Sarah") that they "must be good little children till farther [*sic*] comes home." He also confided to Hannah, "I want you should stay with the family and nev[e]r leave them My home shall be your home for I shall have a home though I have none now . . . my house shall be your home."[21]

HYRUM'S LIBERTY JAIL LETTERS	DATE
To Mary Fielding Smith (wife) (shared details of an attempted jailbreak)	16 March 1839
To Hannah Grinnals (family friend) (words of encouragement and friendship)	16 March 1839
To Mary Fielding Smith (discussed what it was like to be imprisoned)	19 March 1839
To Mary Fielding Smith (gently chided Mary for not writing to him more often)	20 March 1839
To Mary Fielding Smith (primarily paraphrasing of a Robert Burns poem)	23 March 1839
To Mary Fielding Smith (a discussion of family matters and a fellow prisoner)	5 April 1839 (based on a Liberty, Missouri, postmark; the letter itself is undated)
To Mary Fielding Smith (compared his situation in jail to Joseph in Egypt)	Undated

Table 2. Hyrum Smith's Liberty Jail letters

Hyrum's five remaining letters were written to Mary. While we can date four of those letters (March 19, 20, 23 and April 5), the fifth remains undated because the first page is missing.[22] Hyrum addressed the undated letter to Mary at Quincy, Illinois, which provides some clue as to the approximate date it was written. Joseph's and Hyrum's families left Far West on February 7. We are uncertain when they reached Illinois, but we know they settled in Quincy, Illinois, before March 5, 1839. In his March 5 letter to the Liberty Jail inmates, Bishop Edward Partridge informed Joseph and Hyrum that "Brother Joseph's wife lives at Judge [John] Cleveland[']s, I have not seen her but I sent her word of this opportunity to send to you. Br[other] Hyrum's wife lives not far from me." Bishop Partridge added, "I have been to see her a number of times, her health was very poor," implying Mary Fielding Smith had arrived in Quincy well before March 5.[23]

In a March 6 letter to Hyrum and Joseph written from Quincy, their younger brother Don Carlos explained, "Father's family have all arrived in this state except you two. . . . Emma and Children are well, they live three miles from here, and have a tolerable good place. Hyrum's children and mother Grinolds[24] are living at present with father; they are all well, Mary [Fielding Smith] has not got her health yet, but I think it increases slowly. She lives in the house with old Father Dixon, likewise Br[other] [Robert B.] Thompson and family; they are probably a half mile from Father's."[25] Given the short time Joseph and Hyrum remained incarcerated after the Partridge letters were written in March (they left the jail, never to return, on April 6), there is a greater possibility that the undated letter from Hyrum to Mary was written before Joseph's March 20 letter of counsel and instruction rather than on some later date.

JOSEPH'S MARCH 1839 PARTRIDGE LETTERS

In two long letters totaling twenty-six pages, Joseph wrote "To the church of the Latterday saints at Quincy Illinois and scattered abroad and to Bishop [Edward] Partridge in particular."[26] The first letter, written on March 20, 1839, was signed by the five men who remained in Liberty Jail—Joseph Smith, Hyrum Smith, Lyman Wight, Caleb Baldwin, and Alexander McRae.[27] Those seventeen pages include text that would eventually be canonized as Doctrine and Covenants 121:1–33.

The second letter, dated in *The Joseph Smith Papers* as "circa 22 March 1839," is an additional nine handwritten pages. Those pages begin with the heading "Continued to the church of Latter-day-saints" and are signed by the same five detainees. One of the purposes of the additional pages was "to offer further reflections to Bishop [Edward] Partridge and to the church of Jesus Christ of Latter day saints whom we love with a fervent love."[28] It is from the second letter that Doctrine and Covenants sections 121 (vv. 34–46), 122, and 123 were later excerpted and added to the Doctrine and Covenants.

The letters were recorded "by Alexander McRae and Caleb Baldwin, who acted as scribes for Joseph Smith."[29] Historian Stephen C. Harper has concluded that "frequent misplaced and misspelled words show the rush in which the dictation was scribbled down."[30] Inspection of the original pages shows that Joseph made a few corrections to the text.

Lyman Wight's journal states that "Brother Ripley [almost certainly Alanson Ripley, a participant in Zion's Camp who served on a committee that assisted poor members of the Church in moving from Missouri] came in and took our package of letters for Quincy" on March 22—providing sufficient time and opportunity for the second of the Partridge letters to have been dictated and signed on either March 21 or 22.[31]

HYRUM'S RELATIONSHIP WITH DOCTRINE AND COVENANTS 121–123

The two Partridge letters dictated by Joseph Smith contain "some of the most sublime revelations ever received by any prophet in any dispensation."[32] It is reasonable to consider that many of the thoughts, feelings, doctrines, counsel, and teachings found throughout those two letters—in both the canonized and noncanonized sections—had been germinating for many weeks before being recorded. With so little to occupy their time in jail, Joseph and his fellow prisoners had many days to reflect on the content expressed in that letter. That would be especially true for conversations Joseph had with his beloved brother Hyrum. The overlapping content in Joseph's and Hyrum's letters demonstrates that they included some of that conversation in their letters. Hyrum's letters also demonstrate that some of the ideas in sections 121–123 took shape orally before they were committed to paper.

Excerpts from Hyrum's letters are included in tables 3–7. Text in the left-hand columns is from Hyrum's Liberty Jail diary and letters. The right-hand columns list similarly themed excerpts from sections 121, 122, and 123. We will leave it to the reader to draw conclusions as to whether the presumed interchange of ideas between brothers can be seen within Hyrum's letters and diary entries.

Hyrum Smith kept a contemporary diary while incarcerated in Liberty Jail. The three excerpts below (in table 3) from Hyrum's diary under the dates of March 15 and 18 share sentiments similar to verses found in Doctrine and Covenants 122 and 123.

HYRUM'S DIARY	CANONIZED PORTIONS OF JOSEPH'S LETTER
"I was with several others Committed to Jail for my religion" (15 March 1839)	"And if thou shouldst be cast into the pit" (Doctrine and Covenants 122:7)
"the same acqisations was had a gainst the son of god" (15 March 1839)	"The Son of Man hath descended below them all." (122:8)
"Kept in close Confine ment and our familees we're Driven out of the state they also were Robed of all theyr [*smudged*] goods and substance for theyr suport all most maked [naked] and Destitute as they were when they were born in to the world all this by a hellish mob let loose by the athoreties of the state to practise their wicked Designs upon an inosent people and for no other cause than to put Down their <our> Religion" (18 March 1839)	"It is an imperative duty that we owe to God, to angels, with whom we shall be brought to stand, and also to ourselves, to our wives and children, who have been made to bow down with grief, sorrow, and care, under the most damning hand of murder, tyranny, and oppression, supported and urged on and upheld by the influence of that spirit which hath so strongly riveted the creeds of the fathers, who have inherited lies, upon the hearts of the children, and filled the world with confusion, and has been growing stronger and stronger, and is now the very mainspring of all corruption, and the whole earth groans under the weight of its iniquity." (123:7)

Table 3. Excerpts from Hyrum Smith's diary, March 1839

Hyrum's March 16 letter to Mary Fielding Smith. In this letter, addressed to "Mary, my dear Companion," Hyrum shared details regarding an attempted jailbreak. As he explained:

> Some friend put some auguers [augers] in to the window & an iron bar we made a hole in through the logs in the lower room & through the stone wall all but the out side stone which was suffitiently large to pass out when it was pushed out but we were hind[e]red for want of handles to the auguers the logs were so hard that the handles would split & we had to make new ones with our fire wood we had to bore the hole for the shank with my penknife which delayed time in Spite of <all> we could do the day of Examination came on before in the after noon. that Evening we was ready to make our Essape [escape] & we were discovered & prevented of making our Essape there apeared to be no hard feelings on the part of the Sheriff & Jailor but the old Baptists

& prisbiterians & Me[t]hodests were very mutch Excited they turned out in tens as volenteers to gard the Jail till the Jail was mended.[33]

Hyrum closed this letter with the following plea: "O god in the name of thy son preserve the life & health of my bosom companeon & may she be prsious [precious] in thy sight & all the little children & that is pertaining to my family & hasten the time when we shall meet in Each others Embrass [Embrace]." The following statements in this letter sound like text included in Doctrine and Covenants 121–123:

HYRUM'S CORRESPONDENCE	CANONIZED PORTIONS OF JOSEPH'S LETTER
"O god how long shall we suffer these things will not though [thou] deliver us & make us free Still thy will be done O lord."	"O God, where art thou? . . . How long shall thy hand be stayed . . . ? Yea, O Lord, how long shall they suffer these wrongs and unlawful oppressions . . . ?" (Doctrine and Covenants 121:1–3)
"O lord god wilt though [thou] hear the pra[y]er of your servant"	"let thine ear be inclined" (121:4)
"May the lord bless you & give you stren[g]th to Endure all these things"	"And then, if thou endure it well, God shall exalt thee on high." (121:8)

Table 4. Excerpts from Hyrum Smith's March 16, 1839, letter to Mary Fielding Smith

Hyrum's March 19 letter to Mary Fielding Smith. From this letter we learn that Hyrum was ill—"q[u]ite out of hea[l]th to day have Kept my bed all day"—the day before Joseph dictated his March 20 letter. He expressed his disappointment "that I did not hear from you & the family by your own pen" and let her know that "brother Pa[r]tr[i]dge says he imformed you of the oppertunity of sending [a letter] by brother Rodgers." He conceded that "I do not Know but your was sick so that you could not write." Hyrum shared that he was "verry anxious to hear from you," and he worried about his family. "I have been informed," he wrote, "that you are sepperated from the family . . . on this side of the river & you on the other . . . my feelings & anxiety is sutch that my sleep has departed from me." And then Hyrum confided that his jail experience was wearing on him: "My faith understanding & Judgement is not suffitient to over come these feelings of sorrow a word from you might possibly be sattisfactory or in degree relieve my feelings of anxiety that sleep may return." He also provided a glimpse into the physical toll life in jail exacted. "Excuse my poor writing my nerves are some what affected & <my hands> are this Evening q[u]ite swolen & fingers are stiff & painfull with the rheum[a]tism."[34] Two statements from this letter sound similar to the canonized portions of Joseph's March 20 letter:

HYRUM'S CORRESPONDENCE	CANONIZED PORTIONS OF JOSEPH'S LETTER
"God has said that he would deliver us from the power of our Enemeis in his own due time we try to be as patient as possible"	"My son, peace be unto thy soul; thine adversity and thine afflictions shall be but a small moment; and then, if thou endure it well, God shall exalt thee on high; thou shalt triumph over all thy foes." (Doctrine and Covenants 121:7–8)
"the bonds of true friendship & love"	"Thy friends do stand by thee, and they shall hail thee again with warm hearts and friendly hands." (121:9)

Table 5. Excerpts from Hyrum Smith's March 19, 1839, letter to Mary Fielding Smith

Hyrum's March 20 letter to Mary Fielding Smith. Hyrum informed Mary that David Rogers visited that morning and that Alanson Ripley was also there and "is a going to start back to [*faded*] this after noon." Ripley did not depart, though, until March 22. Toward the end of this letter, Hyrum again gently chided Mary for not writing: "I thought if you could not write you could send a friendly word. . . . I do not wish to harrow up your feelings if they are inocent but I thought it strange that you did not send one word to me when I thought you Knew I was so anxious to hear from you. . . . If you have no feelings for me as a husband you could sent or caused to be sent some information concerning the little babe or those little children that lies near my hart."[35] Unlike the other letters to Mary, this letter has no signature or address.[36] As this letter is dated the same day as Joseph's letter, it is no surprise that several concepts from the latter found their way into the former.

HYRUM'S CORRESPONDENCE	CANONIZED PORTIONS OF JOSEPH'S LETTER
"if you have not forsaken me"	"O God, where art thou? And where is the pavilion that covereth thy hiding place?" (Doctrine and Covenants 121:1)
"our Enemies must be left without Excuse those that seek our hurt will see their folly sooner or later"	"Let thine anger be kindled against our enemies; and, in the fury of thine heart, with thy sword avenge us of our wrongs." (121:5)
"our sufferings will only cal[l] to mind the sufferings of the aintients [ancients]"	"Remember thy suffering saints, O our God. . . . Thou art not yet as Job." (121:6, 10)
"we must be patient in tribulation"	"If thou art called to pass through tribulation . . ." (122:5)

Table 6. Excerpts from Hyrum Smith's March 20, 1839, letter to Mary Fielding Smith

Hyrum's undated (presumably pre-March 20) letter to Mary Fielding Smith. This letter is addressed (on the final page) to "Mrs Mary Smith, Q[u]incy Adams Co Ilinois." In the extant pages, Hyrum compares their situation to Joseph in Egypt, who "was sold by his bretheren notwithstanding he was cast in to prison for many years yet the power of wisdom was there all though men thought to disgrace him but they fail'd." He shared his opinion with Mary that "bonds and imprisenments and persecutions are no dis grace to the Saints it is that is common in all ages of the world since the days of adam for he was persecuted by his own posterity in the days of Seth with sutch violence he had to flee out of his own count[r]y to an other land." He closed this letter by asking Mary to "pray for me my companion I will pray for <you> unceasingly as mutch as I can." After signing his name, he asked Mary to "Excuse all imperfections."[37]

HYRUM'S CORRESPONDENCE	CANONIZED PORTIONS OF JOSEPH'S LETTER
"that the wicked ungodly oppresser shall come to a speedy distruction and have no Excuse in the Day of Judgement"	"Let thine anger be kindled against our enemies; and, in the fury of thine heart, with thy sword avenge us of our wrongs." (Doctrine and Covenants 121:5)
"he was patient in tribulation and harkened to that redeeming power that saves"	"And then, if thou endure it well, God shall exalt thee on high; thou shalt triumph over all thy foes." (121:8)
"wisdom shows us that these things are for our salvation spiritualy and temporaly"	
"all these things are to make us wise and inteligent that we may be the happy recippient of the hi[gh]est glory"	
"bonds and imprisenments and persecutions are no dis grace to the Saints"	"And those who swear falsely against my servants, that they might bring them into bondage and death . . ." (121:18)
"that what we do not learn by precept we may learn by Experince"	"We have learned by sad experience that it is the nature and disposition of almost all men, as soon as they get a little authority, as they suppose, they will immediately begin to exercise unrighteous dominion." (121:39)
"the scepter of the kingdom shall be in their hands"	"thy scepter an unchanging scepter of righteousness and truth" (121:46)
"if they are cast in to the pit it shall b[*faded*] be with them and deliver them all though th[e]y are left in bonds"	"And if thou shouldst be cast into the pit . . ." (122:7)

Table 7. Excerpts from an undated letter from Hyrum Smith to Mary Fielding Smith

As these letter excerpts demonstrate, Hyrum Smith appears to have been involved in discussions regarding the doctrines and concepts included in the Partridge letters. For a brief time, those letters of instruction served almost as a de facto Church presidency while the Church was deprived of Joseph and Hyrum's presence. It should not come as a surprise that Joseph and Hyrum discussed much of the contents of Joseph's March letters to Edward Partridge; they were sharing the same space and experiencing the same trying conditions, emotions, and family difficulties. Plus, there was a strong and lifelong bond between them.

There are additional similarities to Joseph's March letters to Edward Partridge in Hyrum's subsequent letters and diary entries, but they do not necessarily reflect discussions that could have occurred between Joseph and Hyrum before Joseph dictated the long March letters.

RELEASE FROM LIBERTY JAIL

The five prisoners left Liberty Jail on April 6 and were taken to Daviess County to appear before Judge Birch. For ten days a ribald and irreverent grand jury boasted of abuses they had perpetrated on the Mormons. Hyrum reported that after ten days of the grand jury's drunken antics, "we were indicted for treason, murder, arson, larceny, theft, and stealing."[38] The prisoners requested a change of venue to Marion County but were granted instead a change to Boone County. "They fitted us out with a two horse wagon, and horses, and four men, besides the sheriff, to be our guard," according to Hyrum. "There were five of us [prisoners]. We started from Gallatin the sun about two hours high, P.M., and went as far as Diahman that evening and staid till morning. There we bought two horses of the guard, and paid for one of them in our clothing, which we had with us; and for the other we gave our note." Upon reaching Boone County, "we bought a jug of whiskey; with which we treated the company." The sheriff informed the prisoners that Judge Birch had instructed him "never to carry us to Boon[e] county . . . and said he, I shall take a good drink of grog and go to bed, and you may do as you have a mind to. Three others of the guard drank pretty freely of whiskey, sweetened with honey; they also went to bed, and were soon asleep, and the other guard went along with us, and helped to saddle the horses."[39]

Joseph and Hyrum mounted the horses, and Caleb Baldwin, Lyman Wight, and Alexander McRae started walking to Quincy, Illinois. Joseph and Hyrum reached Quincy on April 22, 1839, where they found their families "in a state of poverty, although in good health."[40] Their extended ordeal had reached an end.

AFTERMATH

Joseph Smith's March 1839 letters to Bishop Partridge and the Church were considered historical documents and were not canonized during Joseph and

Hyrum's lifetime. Both letters were published several times before Doctrine and Covenants 121–123 was canonized, including excerpts printed in the *Times and Seasons*, the *Deseret News*, and the British *Millennial Star*.[41] Sometime before January 15, 1875, Elder Orson Pratt received an assignment from Brigham Young to work on a new edition of the Doctrine and Covenants, "arranging the order in which the revelations are to be inserted." Elder Pratt "divided the various revelations into verses, and arranged them for printing, according to the order of date in which they were revealed."[42] Responsibility regarding which excerpts from the Partridge letters would be canonized was also apparently left to Elder Pratt. The six excerpts (five of which were stitched together to become Doctrine and Covenants 121 and 122, with a final excerpt providing the text for section 123) were included in the 1876 edition of the Doctrine and Covenants. The Pearl of Great Price was sustained as one of the four standard works of the Church during the October 1880 general conference; Doctrine and Covenants 121, 122, and 123 were canonized at the same time.[43]

Kenneth L. Alford is a professor of Church history and doctrine at Brigham Young University.

Craig K. Manscill is an associate professor of Church history and doctrine at Brigham Young University.

Kenneth L. Alford and Craig K. Manscill, "Hyrum Smith's Liberty Jail Letters," in *Foundations of the Restoration: Fulfillment of the Covenant Purposes*, ed. Craig James Ostler, Michael Hubbard MacKay, and Barbara Morgan Gardner (Provo, UT: Religious Studies Center, Brigham Young University; Salt Lake City: Deseret Book, 2016), 189–206.

NOTES

1. For a discussion of Joseph Smith's Liberty Jail letters, see H. Dean Garrett, "Seven Letters from Liberty," in *Regional Studies in Latter-day Saint Church History: Missouri*, ed. Arnold K. Garr and Clark V. Johnson (Provo, UT: Department of Church History and Doctrine, Brigham Young University, 1994), 189–90. Garrett's essay was written before the Joseph Smith Papers Project. See also *The Joseph Smith Papers, Documents*, 6:293–406.
2. Letter to Emma Smith, 1 December 1838, [1], *The Joseph Smith Papers*, http://josephsmithpapers.org/.
3. See Letter to Emma Smith, 4 April 1839, [1], http://josephsmithpapers.org/.

4. See Letter to the Church and Edward Partridge, 20 March 1839, 1, http://josephsmithpapers.org/.
5. Letter to Emma Smith, 21 March 1839, [1], http://josephsmithpapers.org/.
6. It is insightful to note that both Lilburn W. Boggs and Samuel D. Lucas were residents of Jackson County, Missouri, and had figured prominently in the 1833 expulsion of the Saints. In 1833 Boggs was Missouri's lieutenant governor and Lucas was a county court justice and colonel of local militia. See Leland H. Gentry and Todd M. Compton, *Fire and Sword: A History of the Latter-day Saints in Northern Missouri, 1836–39* (Salt Lake City: Greg Kofford Books, 2011), 15.
7. Church Educational System, *Church History in the Fulness of Times Student Manual: Religion 341 through 343* (Salt Lake City: The Church of Jesus Christ of Latter-day Saints, 2003), 205.
8. Judge King had determined the outcome before the hearing. "If a cohort of angels were to come down and declare we were clear, Doniphan said it would all be the same, for he (King) had determined from the begining to cast us into prison." Sidney Rigdon, *Appeal to the American People*, 1840, 67, http://josephsmithpapers.org/.
9. Joseph Smith, History, 1838–1856, volume D-1 [1 August 1842–1 July 1843], p. 1615, http://www.josephsmithpapers.org/.
10. Joseph Smith, History, 1838–1856, volume D-1, p. 1615.
11. See Clark V. Johnson, ed., *Mormon Redress Petitions: Documents of the 1833–1838 Missouri Conflict* (Provo, UT: Religious Studies Center, Brigham Young University, 1992), 680–81. On July 1, 1843, Sidney Rigdon testified before the Municipal Court of Nauvoo that in January 1839 "I was ordered to be discharged from prison, and the rest remanded back. . . . It was some ten days after this before I dared leave the jail. . . . Just at dark, the sheriff and jailer came to the jail with our supper. . . . I whispered to the jailer to blow out all the candles but one, and step away from the door with that one. All this was done. The sheriff then took me by the arm, and an apparent scuffle ensued. . . . We reached the door, which was quickly opened, and we both reached the street. He took me by the hand and bade me farewell, telling me to make my escape, which I did with all possible speed." See Joseph Smith, History, 1838–1856, volume E-1 [1 July 1843–30 April 1844], p. 1651, http://josephsmithpapers.org/.
12. Joseph Smith III and Heman C. Smith, *The History of the Reorganized Church of Jesus Christ of Latter Day Saints, Volume 2, 1836–1844* (Independence, MO: Herald House, 1967), 2:309 (hereafter *History of the Reorganized Church*). Mary Fielding Smith had recently given birth to a son, Joseph F. Smith, on November 13, 1838, and her health remained poor for many weeks.
13. *History of the Reorganized Church*, 2:315.
14. Lucy Mack Smith, History, 1845, 273, http://josephsmithpapers.org/.
15. Hyrum Smith, quoted in Lucy Mack Smith, History, 1845, 273.
16. Letter from Edward Partridge, 5 March 1839, 3, http://josephsmithpapers.org/.
17. See Letter from Don Carlos Smith and William Smith, 6 March 1839, 38, http://josephsmithpapers.org/.
18. Elder David White Rogers, Journal History, March 17, 1839, Church History Library, The Church of Jesus Christ of Latter-day Saints, Salt Lake City, 2–4 (hereafter CHL). The typewritten copy of Rogers's statement that appears in the Journal History is dated February 1, 1839, at Quincy, Illinois. The date is somewhat problematic because most of the statement outlines events that occurred well after February 1, 1839. It seems likely that Rogers began his statement, which details his

efforts with S. Bent and Israel Barlow to find a suitable location for the Saints to settle in Illinois, on February 1 and simply did not redate the completed statement. Rogers recorded: "We left Far West on the 20th. I have visited the brethren in Richmond Jail in the meantime. And on the morrow [March 21] we visited the Prophet Joseph Smith in Liberty Jail." There appears to be a dating error in Rogers's account, though, because both Hyrum and Joseph wrote that they received Bishop Partridge's letter on March 19—not March 21 as Rogers remembered. In a letter to his wife Mary, dated March 19, Hyrum wrote that "we receaved a letter this evening from brother [Edward] Pa[r]tridge by the hand of brother Rodgers it was q[u]ite late when it came to us & we was out of paper except this scrap & the mesinger said he should start very Erley in the morning." Holograph, Hyrum Smith to Mary Fielding Smith, March 19, 1839, MS 2779, CHL. In his March 20 letter (a few lines before the location where the text for Doctrine and Covenants 121:7–25 would later be extracted), Joseph stated that "we received some letters last evening one from Emma one from Don C. Smith and one from Bishop Partridge all breathing a kind and consoling spirit"— showing that Rogers arrived at the jail on March 19. See Letter to the Church and Edward Partridge, 20 March 1839, 1.

19. Table 2 lists Hyrum's personal correspondence. As a member of the First Presidency, Hyrum also signed the January 16, March 20, and circa March 22, 1839, letters listed in table 1. Please note that an earlier version of this essay incorrectly listed eight private letters written by Hyrum Smith in Liberty Jail. The correct number is currently believed to be seven. On close examination, the letter dated April 3 in the 2016 publication was an incomplete and poor-quality copy of the April 5 letter.

20. Lucy Mack Smith referred to Hannah as "Mrs. Grenolds." The spelling *Grinnals* is from the Nauvoo Temple Endowment Register, which records her endowment on December 13, 1845, and gives her date of birth as November 3, 1783. The Hannah Grennell (born November 3, 1796, Killingsworth, Connecticut) found in the Church's patriarchal blessing index may be the same person despite the discrepancy in the year of birth. The blessing, given in Nauvoo on July 4, 1845, records her parents as William Woodstock and Elizabeth with no last name given. The patriarchal blessing indicates that Hannah would receive her companion and children in the resurrection of the just, suggesting that she may have been a widowed mother of more than one child. The 1850 federal census lists a sixty-six-year-old Hannah Grennells, born in Connecticut, as a member of Mary Smith's home. This is consistent with the 1840 federal census (from Hancock County, Illinois), which lists a woman between fifty and sixty years of age living in Hyrum's home. If the girl listed with Hannah in the 1840 census is her daughter Clarinda, then she and Hyrum's daughter Lovina were near the same age. According to historian Don C. Corbett, Hannah "died two years after Mary Smith, who passed away on 21 September 1852 at the age of fifty-eight." If Hannah died in 1854, however, she would have been seventy according to the 1850 federal census. Mary Fielding Smith's obituary appeared in the December 11, 1852, *Deseret News*. If Hannah had a published obituary, it is yet to be located. Considering Hannah's long-term relationship and significant contributions to Hyrum's family, there is an amazing paucity of information about her. See Don Cecil Corbett, *Mary Fielding Smith: Daughter of Britain* (Salt Lake City: Deseret Book, 1970); Pearson H. Corbett, *Hyrum Smith, Patriarch* (Salt

Lake City: Deseret Book, 1976); and Orson F. Whitney, *Life of Heber C. Kimball* (Salt Lake City: Bookcraft, 1978).

21. Hyrum Smith to Sister Grinnals, March 16, 1839, Special Collections, Harold B. Lee Library, Brigham Young University, VMSS 774, series 2, box 1, folders 18–20. All transcriptions of Hyrum's Liberty Jail letters and diaries are from the Hyrum Smith Papers Project directed by Craig K. Manscill and Kenneth L. Alford.

22. The Hyrum Smith to Mary Fielding Smith letters from 1839 reside in the CHL (MS 2779).

23. Letter from Edward Partridge, 5 March 1839, 3. Bishop Partridge also kindly included what he knew about the status and location of the wives and families of Lyman Wight, Caleb Baldwin, and Alexander McRae.

24. One of the many variant spellings of *Grinnals.*

25. Letter from Don Carlos Smith and William Smith, 6 March 1839, 38.

26. The Joseph Smith Papers Project originally assigned a March 20, 1839, date to both Partridge letters—referring to the first letter as "Part-A" and the second as "Part-B." That changed with the publication of *The Joseph Smith Papers, Documents, Volume 6.* The second letter is now dated "circa 22 March" by *The Joseph Smith Papers.* See Letter to the Church and Edward Partridge, 20 March 1839, 1; and Letter to Edward Partridge and the Church, circa 22 March 1839, 1, http://josephsmith papers.org/.

27. See Letter to the Church and Edward Partridge, 20 March 1839, 1. When the six prisoners were remanded to Liberty Jail by Judge Austin A. King for the "said charge of treason," Sidney Rigdon was "to answer in the county of Caldwell." The other five prisoners were "to answer in the county of Daviess." Partly as a result, Sidney Rigdon was released from Liberty Jail on February 5, well before the March 20 letter was written. See *History of the Reorganized Church,* 2:294.

28. Letter to the Church and Edward Partridge, 20 March 1839, 1.

29. Dean C. Jessee and John W. Welch, "Revelations in Context: Joseph Smith's Letter from Liberty Jail, 20 March 1839," *BYU Studies* 39, no. 3 (2000): 125.

30. Steven C. Harper, *Making Sense of the Doctrine and Covenants* (Salt Lake City: Deseret Book, 2008), 448.

31. Ripley had made previous visits to the jail. See *History of the Reorganized Church,* 2:315–23; and Holograph, Hyrum Smith to Mary Fielding Smith, March 16, 1839, MS 2779, CHL.

32. Neal A. Maxwell, "A Choice Seer," *Ensign,* August 1986.

33. Holograph, Hyrum Smith to Mary Fielding Smith, March 16, 1839.

34. Holograph, Hyrum Smith to Mary Fielding Smith, March 19, 1839.

35. Mary Fielding Smith was ill much of the time Hyrum was incarcerated in Missouri, which is likely why she did not reply to Hyrum's letters.

36. Holograph, Hyrum Smith to Mary Fielding Smith, March 20, 1839, MS 2779, CHL.

37. Holograph, Hyrum Smith to Mary Fielding Smith, undated (written from Liberty Jail).

38. Joseph Smith, History, 1838–1856, volume D-1, p. 1617.

39. Joseph Smith, History, 1838–1856, volume D-1, p. 1618.

40. Statement of Hyrum Smith, 1 July 1843, in Joseph Smith, History, 1838–1856, volume D-1, p. 1618.

41. As noted by Jessee and Welch, "Revelations in Context," 131, the March 20 letter was published in the *Times and Seasons* (May and July 1840), the *Deseret News*

(January 26 and February 2, 1854), and the *Millennial Star* (December 1840, October 1844, and January 27 and February 10, 1855).

42. Church Historian's Office, Journal, CR 100 1, 1844–1879, January 15, 1875, CHL. See also Journal History, January 15, 1875, and "New and Revised Edition of the Book of Doctrine and Covenants," Historian's Office, Journal, January 15, 1875, 70, CHL.

43. See Richard E. Turley Jr. and William W. Slaughter, *How We Got the Doctrine and Covenants* (Salt Lake City: Deseret Book, 2012), 98–99.

Selected RSC Publications on Church History in Ohio and Missouri, 1831–1838

GENERAL READING

Dorius, Guy L., Craig K. Manscill, and Craig James Ostler, eds. *Regional Studies in Latter-day Saint Church History: Ohio and Upper Canada* (2006).

MacKay, Michael Hubbard, and William G. Hartley, eds. *The Rise of the Latter-day Saints: The Journals and Histories of Newel Knight* (2019).

Ostler, Craig James, Michael Hubbard MacKay, and Barbara Morgan Gardner, eds. *Foundations of the Restoration: Fulfillment of the Covenant Purposes* (2016).

Van Orden, Bruce A. *We'll Sing and We'll Shout: The Life and Times of W. W. Phelps* (2018).

THE DOCTRINE AND COVENANTS AND MODERN REVELATION

Cope, Rachel, Carter Charles, and Jordan T. Watkins. *How and What You Worship: Christology and Praxis in the Revelations of Joseph Smith* (2020).

Esplin, Scott C., Richard O. Cowan, and Rachel Cope, eds. *You Shall Have My Word: Exploring the Text of the Doctrine and Covenants* (2012).

Hedges, Andrew H., J. Spencer Fluhman, and Alonzo L. Gaskill, eds. *The Doctrine and Covenants: Revelations in Context* (2008).

Ostler, Craig J. "Doctrine and Covenants 93: How and What We Worship." *Religious Educator* 3, no. 2 (2002): 77–85.

TRIALS IN OHIO AND MISSOURI

Esplin, Scott C. "The Fall of Kirtland: The Doctrine and Covenants' Role in Reaffirming Joseph." *Religious Educator* 8, no. 1 (2007): 13–24.

Wessel, Ryan J. "The Textual Context of Doctrine and Covenants 121–23." *Religious Educator* 13, no. 1 (2012): 103–15.

Part Three

Church History in Illinois

1839–1846

Chapter Fifteen

"For Their Salvation Is Necessary and Essential to Our Salvation"

Joseph Smith and the Practice of Baptism and Confirmation for the Dead

ALEXANDER L. BAUGH

The *Elders' Journal* of July 1838, published in Far West, Missouri, included a series of twenty questions related to Mormonism, the answers to which bear the editorial pen of Joseph Smith. Question number sixteen posed the following query: "If the Mormon doctrine is true, what has become of all those who have died since the days of the apostles?" The Prophet answered, "All those who have not had an opportunity of hearing the gospel, *and being administered to by an inspired man in the flesh*, must have it hereafter, before they can be finally judged."[1] Significantly, the answer given by the Prophet marks his first known statement concerning the doctrine of vicarious work for the dead. However, it was not until more than two years later that the principle was put into practice.

On August 10, 1840, Seymour Brunson, a devoted friend of Joseph Smith and a member of the Nauvoo high council, died.[2] Five days later, on August 15, Joseph Smith preached the funeral sermon for Brunson, during which time he elucidated the ordinance of baptism for the dead.[3] Unfortunately, no contemporary account of the Prophet's discourse exists. However, Simon Baker was present at the funeral services and later stated that during the meeting the Prophet read extensively from 1 Corinthians 15, then noted a particular widow in the congregation whose son had died without baptism. After referring to the statement Jesus made to Nicodemus that a man must be born of the water and of the Spirit (see John 3:5), Baker recalled the Prophet saying that the Saints "could now act for their friends who had departed this life, and that the plan of salvation was calculated to save all who were willing to obey the requirements of the law of God."[4]

Baker's account of what Joseph Smith preached on the occasion of Brunson's funeral is consistent with a statement by Joseph Smith in a letter dated December 15, 1840, and addressed to the members of the Twelve, most of whom were serving in Great Britain. In the letter he cites 1 Corinthians 15:29 while noting that he spoke about the verse in his remarks at Brunson's funeral, then briefly expounds on the subject:

> I presume the doctrine of "Baptizm for the dead," has ere this reached your ears, and may have raised some inquiries in your minds, respecting the same. I cannot in this letter give you all the information you may desire on the subject, but aside from my knowledge[e] independent of the Bible, I would say that it was certainly practiced by the ancient churches And. St. Paul endeavors to prove the doctrine of the resurrection from the same, and says "else what shall they do who are baptized for the dead["] &c &c. I first mentioned the doctrine in public, when preaching the funeral sermon of Bro [Seymour] Brunson, and have since then given general instructions to the Church on the subject. The saints have the privilege of being baptized for those of their relatives who are dead, who they feel to believe would have embraced the gospel if they had been privileged with hearing it, and who have received the gospel in the spirit, through the instrumentality of those who may have been commissioned to preach to them while in prison. Without enlarging on the subject, you will undoubtedly see its consistancy and reasonableness, and presents the the Gospel of Christ in probably a more enlarged scale than some have imagined it. But as the performance of this right is more particularly confined to this place, it will not be necessary to enter into particulars, at the same time I allways feel glad to give all the information in my power, but my space will not allow me to do it.[5]

While it is not known precisely when the first proxy baptism or baptisms were performed, the first known documented baptism for the dead took place on Sunday, September 13, 1840. On that occasion Jane Neyman requested that Harvey Olmstead baptize her in behalf of her deceased son,

Cyrus Livingston Neyman. Vienna Jacques witnessed the proxy baptism by riding into the Mississippi River on horseback to hear and observe the ordinance. A short while later, upon learning the words Olmstead used in performing the baptism, Joseph Smith gave his approval.[6]

In the early 1840s, Nauvoo had four landing sites on the Mississippi River—the Upper Stone House Landing, the Kimball Wharf, the Lower Stone House Landing, and the Main Street Dock near Joseph Smith's homestead and later the Nauvoo House. Each of these locations likely would have provided a suitable place for baptisms to be performed, although the ordinance was conducted at any number of locations near the riverbank. Traditionally, the Main Street Landing has been the site generally believed to be where baptisms, both for the living and the dead, were performed most frequently.[7]

Alvin Smith, Joseph Smith's older brother who died in November 1823, may have been one of the first deceased persons to have his proxy baptismal work performed. Lucy Mack Smith recalled that just before her husband's death, Joseph told his father "that it was . . . the privilege of the Saints to be baptized for the dead," whereupon Joseph Sr. requested that "Joseph be baptized for Alvin immediately."[8] Significantly, Joseph Sr. died on September 14, 1840, less than a month after the Prophet first taught the doctrine of baptism for the dead, and only one day after the reported date that Jane Neyman was baptized in behalf of her deceased son. If Joseph and the Smith family were true to their father's request that Alvin's baptism be done "immediately," the likelihood exists that it was performed sometime around mid-September. The record containing the early proxy ordinance information indicates that Hyrum acted as proxy (not Joseph, as Father Smith requested), but does not give any date other than the year 1840.[9] The ordinance was performed for Alvin a second time, again by Hyrum, in 1841 and was probably done after the font was completed, installed, and dedicated in the basement of the temple.[10] A friend and contemporary of the Prophet, Aroet Hale, stated that Joseph Smith instructed the Saints "to have the work done over as quick as the temple was finished, when it could be done more perfect."[11]

DEVELOPMENTAL PROCEDURES, PRACTICES, AND PROVISIONS

The early procedure and practice of baptism for the dead during the Nauvoo years were developmental and not as clearly defined as they are today. In the case of Jane Neyman and her deceased son, for example, a female was baptized in behalf of a male. Second, although a witness was present (Vienna Jacques), the person was not a priesthood holder. Third, no mention is made of a proxy confirmation following the baptism. Fourth, no "official" baptismal record is known to exist. And finally, the ordinance was performed in the Mississippi River, not in a temple font. In consideration of these irregularities, in 1873 Brigham Young provided the following explanation:

> When Joseph received the revelation that we have in our possession concerning the dead, the subject was opened to him, not in full but in part, and he kept on receiving. When he had first received the knowledge by the spirit of revelation how the dead could be officiated for, there are brethren and sisters here, I can see quite a number here who were in Nauvoo, and you recollect that when this doctrine was first revealed, and in hurrying in the administration of baptism for the dead, that sisters were baptized for their male friends, were baptized for their fathers, their grandfathers, their mothers and their grandmothers, &c. I just mention this so that you will come to understanding, that as we knew nothing about this matter at first, the old Saints recollect, there was little by little given, and the subject was made plain, but little was given at once. Consequently, in the first place people were baptized for their friends and no record was kept. Joseph afterwards kept a record, &c. Then women were baptized for men and men for women.[12]

What Brigham Young is saying is that a full understanding of the correct procedures for properly performing the ordinance was not given at first; additional instruction was given as the principle and practice came to be more understood. Yet it appears that the practice of men being baptized for women and women for men continued until April 1845, at which time Brigham Young, in his capacity as the head of the Church by virtue of his being the senior member of the Twelve, prescribed that the proxies be of the same gender as the persons for whom they were being baptized.[13] Another example was the need for proper record keeping. Between September 1840, when the first known proxy baptisms were performed, and September 1842, a general proxy baptism record had not been kept. Recognizing this deficiency, Joseph Smith directed that a recorder be present to properly record the ordinance and that an archival record of all the ordinances be maintained in the temple (see Doctrine and Covenants 127:5–9; 128:2–9).[14]

As indicated, the first proxy baptisms were performed at Nauvoo in the Mississippi River. In the first revelatory instruction concerning baptism for the dead, given on January 19, 1841, five months after the first baptisms for the dead were performed, the Saints were instructed that this practice would be temporary: "For a baptismal font there is not upon the earth, that they, my saints, may be baptized for the dead—for this ordinance belongeth to my house, and cannot be acceptable to me, only in the days of your poverty, wherein ye are not able to build a house unto me" (Doctrine and Covenants 124:29–30; see vv. 31–34). In essence, the revelation allowed a provision for the performance of the ordinance outside the temple until a font could be completed and placed in the temple, or until the temple itself was completed.

The Saints enthusiastically embraced the doctrine and practice. Examining the records of baptisms for the dead performed in 1841, M. Guy Bishop calculated that 6,818 baptisms for the dead were performed.[15] Bishop also notes that in 1841 the most active Latter-day Saint proxy was Nehemiah Brush, who was baptized for more than one hundred deceased relatives and friends. The most baptized woman was Sarah M. Cleveland, who performed the vicarious saving ordinance for forty deceased persons.[16]

Several people recorded their experiences and first impressions of seeing or participating in the new practice. "I saw the Elders baptizing for the dead in the Mississippi River," Robert Horne wrote. "This was something new to me and the beauty of this great principle dawned upon me. I had never heard of such a doctrine then. Orson Pratt was baptizing. Brother Joseph stood on the banks."[17] Aroet Hale remembered Joseph Smith performing more than two hundred baptisms in the Mississippi River. "Then the apostles and other elders went into the river and continued the same ordinance. Hundreds were baptized there."[18] Wilford Woodruff wrote that Joseph Smith "went into the Mississippi River, and so did I, as well as others, and we each baptized a hundred for the dead."[19] Interestingly, while the Prophet was known to have officiated in performing the ordinance, there is no record that he ever participated as a proxy.[20]

BAPTISM FOR THE DEAD PRACTICED OUTSIDE NAUVOO

An often-overlooked part of Doctrine and Covenants section 124 is a provision in the revelation that temporarily allowed the Saints living outside Nauvoo to perform the ordinance. The revelation reads, "And after this time [after the Saints had a sufficient time to complete a place in the temple to perform baptisms], your baptisms for the dead, *by those who are scattered abroad*, are not acceptable unto me, saith the Lord. For it is ordained that in Zion, and in her stakes, and in Jerusalem, those places which I have appointed for refuge, shall be the places for your baptisms for the dead" (Doctrine and Covenants 124:35–36; emphasis added).

Historical sources reveal that baptisms for the dead were indeed performed by Latter-day Saints living in areas other than Nauvoo. On November 9, 1840, a meeting was held at the home of Melvin Wilbur in Quincy in Adams County, Illinois. Somewhere near the Wilbur property, perhaps in the Mississippi River, Ezra T. Benson was baptized for his deceased brother, John Benson.[21] At this same time, members of the Lima/Yelrome Branch, situated just a few miles north of Quincy, were also performing the ordinance. On November 7, 1840, John Murdock, Gardner Snow, Edmund Durfee, Albert Miner, Levi Osgood, Joseph Allen, Lane Durfee, Lydia B. English, and Sarah Weston "performed baptisms for their dead friends." One week later, on November 14, the ordinance was attended to again by six branch members.[22] The fact that there is evidence showing Latter-day Saints performing baptisms for the dead in these outlying areas suggests that Mormons in other settlement communities, such as Montrose, Nashville, Ramus, LaHarpe, and Plymouth, may have also engaged in the practice.

Significantly, baptism for the dead was also briefly practiced in Kirtland, Ohio. In fact, it was probably due to problems associated with the leadership of the Church in Kirtland that the practice of baptism for the dead outside the temple was cut short. During the Church's October 1840 general conference held in Nauvoo, Almon W. Babbitt was appointed to preside as stake president over approximately three to four hundred Latter-day Saints still residing in Kirtland.[23] At the time of the conference, it had only been six weeks since Joseph Smith first publically revealed the doctrine of baptism for the dead, and during one of the sessions the Prophet delivered another major discourse on the subject.[24] Clearly, Babbitt knew of the doctrine before leaving Nauvoo and then taught the principle to the Ohio Saints after his arrival. On May 23, 1841, during a conference in Kirtland at which he presided, Babbitt entertained the subject. The minutes of the conference include the following report: "Elder Babbitt delivered a discourse on baptism for the dead, from 1 Peter 4:6, to a very large audience, setting forth that doctrine as compatible with the mercy of God, and grand council of heaven." W. W. Phelps, the conference clerk, followed Babbitt and "continued the same subject from 1 Corinthians 15:22, bringing scripture upon scripture to prove the consistency of this doctrine."[25] The conference minutes end with the following entry: "About 25 baptisms took place, the most of which were for the dead."[26] During the years the Church was in Ohio, a small dam was situated across a portion of the east branch of the Chagrin River in the Kirtland Flats area; the baptisms likely took place there.

Evidence that Latter-day Saints indeed practiced baptism for the dead in Kirtland in the early 1840s is also supported by Alfred Holbrook, a nonmember who lived in the Kirtland area. In constructing his memoirs, Holbrook remembered the Saints instituting the practice in Kirtland but observed that the doctrine was rather strange to him, noting that "it seemed to me and others that this was running baptism into the ground."[27]

It is not known to what extent baptisms for the dead were performed in Kirtland, but the practice was relatively short-lived. Contrary to the First Presidency's counsel, Babbitt began preaching and promoting Kirtland, rather than Nauvoo, as the main gathering place. News of Babbitt's counter-manding reached Church leaders in Nauvoo and was likely a primary reason why on October 2, 1841, during a general conference of the Church in Nauvoo, Babbitt was disfellowshipped.[28] Then the following day, October 3, the Prophet announced, "There shall be no more baptisms for the dead, until the ordinance can be attended to in the Lord's House. . . . *For thus saith the Lord!*"[29] Four weeks later, on October 31, Hyrum Smith, representing the First Presidency, addressed a letter to the Kirtland Saints encouraging them to leave Ohio and move to Nauvoo so that "the House of the Lord and the baptismal font shall be finished," then added with possible reference to proxy work that "any proceedings of the Saints otherwise than to put forth their hands with their might to do this work, is not according to the will of God."[30] In short, Babbitt's conduct and the lack of confidence exhibited by Church leaders in his leadership contributed to the cessation of the practice of baptism for the dead outside the temple both in and around Nauvoo as well as Kirtland.[31]

However, a second and perhaps an even more important contributing factor that led Joseph Smith to disallow river baptisms in behalf of the dead had to do with the confirmation ordinance. Today, the ordinance of baptism, whether for the living or in behalf of the dead, is always accompanied by a second ordinance—confirmation (i.e., confirming an individual a member of the Church and conferring the gift of the Holy Ghost). The one, baptism, must be followed by the other, confirmation. However, there is evidence that during the period when baptisms for the dead were permitted outside the temple, the ordinance was not accompanied by proxy confirmation. It was not until November 1841, when the first baptisms for the dead were done in the temple font, that the first confirmations for the dead were also performed.[32] Such an explanation clarifies why many baptisms for the dead performed outside the temple were redone after the temple font was put into use.

The allowance and practice of performing proxy baptisms outside the temple was relatively short-lived, lasting approximately thirteen and a half months (August 15, 1840, to October 3, 1841). With the announcement that such a practice must cease, the Latter-day Saints in Nauvoo moved quickly to comply with Joseph Smith's directive.

NAUVOO TEMPLE FONT

At the time of Joseph Smith's October 1841 announcement suspending the practice of proxy baptism outside the temple, Elijah Fordham, a master craftsman, had already been engaged for several months in constructing and carving a large, oval-shaped wooden font to be used as a temporary baptistry until a more permanent stone structure could be made. Within a month after the Prophet's declaration, Fordham completed his work and the basin-like structure was put into place in the temple's basement. A description of the font is given in the Prophet's Manuscript History:

> The baptismal Font is situated in the centre of the basement room under the main hall of the temple, it is constructed of pine timber and put together of staves tongued and grooved, oval shaped 16 feet long, east and West and 12 feet wide; 7 feet High from the foundation, the Basin 4 feet deep, the moulding of the cap and base are formed of beautiful carved work in antique style. The sides are finished with pannel work. A flight of Stairs on the North and South sides leading up and down into the bason Guarded by side railing. The font stands upon 12 oxen 4 on each side, and 2 at each end, their heads shoulders and fore legs projecting out from under the font they are carved out of pine plank, glued together and copied after the most beautiful five year old steer that could be found in the country and they are an excellent striking likeness of the original, the Horns, were Geometrically formed after the most perfect horns that could be procured, the oxen and ornamental mouldings of the Font were carved by Elder Elijah Fordham from the city of New York which occupied eight months of time. The font was enclosed by a temporary frame building sided up with split oak clap boards with a roof of the same material, and was so low that the timbers of the first storey were laid above it, the water was supplied from a well 30 feet deep in the east end of the basement.
>
> This font was built for the Baptisms for the dead until the Temple should be finished when a more durable one will supply its place.[33]

Although temple construction was still in the beginning stages, the placement of a font within the building proper was enough to satisfy the Prophet Joseph Smith's strict directive that the ordinance must "be attended to in the Lord's house." As evidence of Joseph Smith's approval, on November 8, 1841, he officially dedicated the baptismal font. William Clayton, the Prophet's secretary, wrote, "On the 8th day of November 1841 the font was dedicated by president Joseph Smith at 5 o clock in the evening." Further, "After [the] dedication brother Reuben McBride was the first person baptized under the direction of the president. He was baptized by President B. Young."[34] At the time, Reuben McBride resided in Kirtland, Ohio, but was in Nauvoo on Church business.[35] Knowing that McBride would shortly return to Ohio (probably within a matter of a few days) and thereafter no longer be able to have the opportunity to perform proxy ordinances, Joseph Smith granted him the privilege of being the first person to be baptized for the dead in the new baptistry.[36]

A portion of a significant and interesting letter, written by Reuben McBride from Fillmore, Utah, in 1886 to his sister, Martha McBride (Knight, Kimball),[37] sheds additional light concerning the first proxy temple baptisms:

> Dear Sister Martha: I Received your kind and welcome letter Some time ago, but circumstances has been Such that hindered me till now the Subject you wrote uppon is one of the greatest importance the first Work that I done for our Dead Relitives was done in Nauvoo I think in the fall of [18]42 but you know for you was there.[38] Bro. Joseph Smith made a bee[39] and had the Font in the Temple filled with water from the Wells.[40] He Said he, wished me to be Baptised in the Font before I went back to Ohio. we met. Joseph, Spoke and the Font Dedicated and he Joseph Said Blessed is the first, man Baptised in this Font. Brigham Young Baptised me. I was Baptised Six times. Joseph took off his mantle and Wrapt it around me took me in his Carrage and, drove to your House He talked all the way goeing to your House.[41]

Some confusion exists regarding precisely when the first proxy baptisms in the Nauvoo Temple were actually performed. For example, Wilford Woodruff recorded the following entry in his journal under the date of November 21, 1841:

> 21st Sunday I met in Council with the Twelve at Elder B. Youngs. Then attended the general Assembly near the Temple. Heard a discours by Elder Taylor followed by President Hyram Smith. I then met the

Twelve at B. Youngs untill 4 o-clock at which time we repaired to the Baptismal Font in the Temple for the purpose of Baptizing for the dead, for the remision of Sins & for healing. It was truly an interesting seene. It was the first FONT erected for this glorious purpose in this last dispensation. It was dedicated By President Joseph Smith & the Twelve for Baptizing for the Dead &c & *this was the first time the font had been prepared for the reception of candidates.*

On the sabbath a large Congregation assembled. Elders B Young and H C Kimball & J Taylor went forward & Baptized about 40 persons. Elder W Richards, G. A. Smith & myself assisted in confirming them.[42]

Significantly, an entry in the Manuscript History under the date of November 21, 1841, supports President Woodruff's claims: "The Twelve met in Council at President [Brigham] Young's; and at 4 o'clock repaired to the Baptismal font in the basement of the Temple. Elders Brigham Young Heber C. Kimball, and John Taylor, baptized about 40 persons; for the dead. Elders Willard Richards, Wilford Woodruff, and Geo. A. Smith confirming[.] *These were the first baptisms for the dead in the font.*"[43]

How can Wilford Woodruff's journal entry and the statement in the Manuscript History of the Church, both of which indicate that the first proxy baptisms performed in the Nauvoo Temple were performed on November 21, 1841, be reconciled with William Clayton's statement and Reuben McBride's letter, both cited above, that the first proxy baptisms were actually done nearly two weeks earlier, on November 8, 1841? Quite simply, the service on November 8 was a *private*, informal function and therefore was attended by only a few people—the Prophet, Brigham Young, William Clayton, Reuben McBride, and perhaps a few others. The font was in place, and since McBride was in Nauvoo and about to return to Kirtland, Joseph Smith used the occasion to dedicate the font and let McBride have the opportunity to be baptized. No record of McBride's proxy work appears in the Nauvoo Temple baptism registry, suggesting that this occasion was an informal and perhaps even somewhat spontaneous ceremony.[44] The baptismal service held nearly two weeks later on November 21, however, was the first *public* or *general* ceremony involving a number of Latter-day Saint leaders and members. Woodruff did not leave record of the dedication of the font and of McBride's proxy baptisms because Woodruff was simply unaware of the earlier meeting and service and therefore assumed that the November 21 date was the first baptismal service of its kind. The omission or error in the Prophet's Manuscript History resulted from Church historians who, years later, failed to properly incorporate into the Prophet's history Clayton's record of McBride's November 8, 1841, proxy baptisms and instead referred to Woodruff's November 21 entry as the date the first proxy baptisms occurred.[45]

Baptisms for the dead continued to be performed in the Nauvoo Temple's wooden font until late 1845 or early 1846, when it was replaced with a stone font.[46]

EXCEPTIONS

Although the Saints were instructed not to perform proxy baptisms outside the temple after the October 1841 conference, a few recorded instances have been found that show exceptions to the policy. Charlotte Haven, a nonmember who lived in Nauvoo in 1842 to 1843, wrote a letter to her family in the East in which she described a baptismal service she observed being performed in behalf of the dead. The letter is dated May 2, 1843:

> Last Sunday morning . . . was a balmy spring day, so we took a bee-line for the river, down the street north of our house. Arriving there we rested a while on a log, watching the thin sheets of ice as they slowly came down and floated by. Then we followed the bank toward town, and rounding a little point covered with willows and cottonwoods, we spied quite a crowd of people, and soon perceived there was a baptism. Two elders stood knee-deep in the ice cold water, and immersed one another as fast as they could come down the bank. We soon observed that some of them went in and were plunged several times. We were told that they were baptized for the dead who had not had an opportunity of adopting the doctrines of the Latter Day Saints. So these poor mortals in ice-cold water were releasing their ancestors and relatives from purgatory! We drew a little nearer and heard several names repeated by the elders as the victims were douched, and you can imagine our surprise when the name George Washington was called. So after these fifty years he is out of purgatory and on his way to the "celestial" heaven! It was enough and we continued our walk homeward.[47]

Wilford Woodruff recorded an instance when he and others performed baptisms for the dead outside the temple after Joseph Smith's October 1841 injunction banning the practice. On August 26, 1844, he recorded in his journal that he and his wife Phebe "went to the River in company with Mrs. Woodruff to be baptized for some our dead friends." He continued, "I was baptized for five of my friends under hands of G. A. Smith & confirmed under the hands of Elder Richards." He then notes the names for whom he was baptized, each of whom was a relative. Phebe was also baptized for five deceased persons, members of her family.[48] Even though the temple's wooden font was in place in November 1841, and the stone font in use in late 1845, ongoing temple construction may have prohibited use of the baptistry at times, which necessitated that proxy baptisms be performed elsewhere.

During the Nauvoo period, Joseph Smith frequently addressed the Saints regarding the importance of providing the sacred saving ordinances, particularly baptism and confirmation, in behalf of the dead.[49] Perhaps his most prodigious teachings on the subject appeared in a September 6, 1842, letter to the Saints in which he emphasized the imperative that those who have received the restored gospel in mortality have a sacred responsibility to perform the saving ordinances in behalf of the dead. "Let me assure you," he wrote, "that these principles in relation to the dead and the living . . . cannot be lightly passed over. . . . For their salvation is necessary and essential to *our* salvation . . . [because] they without us cannot be made perfect—neither can we [meaning the living] without our dead be made perfect" (Doctrine and Covenants 128:15; emphasis added).

POST-NAUVOO BAPTISMS AND CONFIRMATIONS FOR THE DEAD

Following the Nauvoo exodus, with the exception of a few documented instances, baptism and confirmation for the dead were not practiced again until 1867. The first of these known to have occurred took place on April 4, 1848. While in Iowa, just before his return trip to the Salt Lake Valley, Wilford Woodruff performed nine baptisms for deceased persons in the Missouri River, followed by four confirmations.[50] On August 21, 1855, Margaret E. Moffatt was baptized and confirmed by Ezra Taft Benson for Lyrena Evans Moffatt in City Creek in Salt Lake City. Two years later, on October 23, 1857, Nancy Kent was baptized for Nabby Howe and Fanny Smith was baptized for Nabby Young, with John and Joseph Young offici-ating.[51] These two baptisms took place in the baptismal font affixed to the Endowment House in Salt Lake City.[52]

Beginning in 1867, Church leaders once again allowed members to perform baptisms for the dead in the Endowment House font. This practice continued for a period of nine years (1867–76) until the completion and dedication of the St. George Temple in 1877. One example of this is the case of Martin Harris, one of the Three Witnesses to the Book of Mormon. On

August 29, 1870, Harris, who had been living in Kirtland, Ohio, arrived in Utah. During the first week of September he met with several Church leaders, who instructed him concerning some of the doctrines that had been revealed since his disaffection from the Church in late 1837, including the principle of baptism for the dead. Following his own rebaptism by Edward Stevenson and reconfirmation by Orson Pratt, "he returned into the font and was baptized for several of his dead friends—fathers, grandfathers, etc., . . . [and] his sister also was baptized for the female relatives, and they were confirmed for and in behalf of those whom they were baptized for, . . . Jos. F. Smith being mouth."[53]

With the completion of the St. George Temple in 1877, all the ordinances performed in behalf of the dead—baptism, confirmation, washing and anointing, priesthood ordination, endowment, and sealing—could be administered in a temple. Thereafter, the practice of performing temple ordinances, including baptism and confirmation for the dead outside the temple, came to a permanent end.

CONCLUSION

The doctrines and principles associated with the Latter-day Saint practice of baptism in behalf of the dead provide a reasonable and logical answer to the age-old question held by Christians regarding what will become of those who die without a sufficient knowledge of Jesus Christ and his gospel. The answer is simple and straightforward: because the saving ordinances can be performed in behalf of the dead, they too can qualify to be heirs of the kingdom of God. It is one of the most profound and significant principles instituted and taught by the Prophet Joseph Smith. Furthermore, the introduction of proxy baptism for the dead (including confirmation) in Nauvoo also inaugurated the beginning of modern-day temple work by The Church of Jesus Christ of Latter-day Saints.[54] For those who have embraced the restored gospel, the doctrines and practices associated with the redemption of the dead, taught nowhere else by any other Christian church or society, represent yet another witness of Joseph Smith's divine prophetic calling.

Alexander L. Baugh is a professor of Church history and doctrine at Brigham Young University.

Alexander L. Baugh, "'For Their Salvation Is Necessary and Essential to Our Salvation': Joseph Smith and the Practice of Baptism and Confirmation for the Dead," in *An Eye of Faith: Essays in Honor of Richard O. Cowan*, ed. Kenneth L. Alford and

Richard E. Bennett (Provo, UT: Religious Studies Center, Brigham Young University; Salt Lake City: Deseret Book, 2015), 113–37.

NOTES

1. *Elders' Journal of The Church of the Latter Day Saints* 1, no. 3 (July 1838): 43; emphasis added.
2. See *Times and Seasons* 1, no. 11 (September 1840): 176; see also Joseph Smith Manuscript History, August 19, 1840, vol. C–1, 1089, Church History Library, The Church of Jesus Christ of Latter-day Saints, Salt Lake City (hereafter Manuscript History); and Journal History of the Church of Jesus Christ of Latter-day Saints, August 10, 1840, Church History Library (hereafter Journal History). Seymour Brunson was baptized in Ohio in January 1831. He played an active role as captain in the Caldwell County militia during the 1838 Mormon conflict in Missouri. At the time of his death, he was a devoted friend of Joseph Smith and a member of the Nauvoo high council. See "A Short Sketch of Seymour Brunson, Sr.," *Nauvoo Journal* 4, no. 1 (Spring 1992): 3–5.
3. The date of August 15, 1840, is usually given as the date for Seymour Brunson's funeral. See Journal History, August 15, 1840. Significantly, no mention of the funeral service is mentioned in the Manuscript History.
4. Simon Baker, statement, in Journal History, August 15, 1840; also cited in *The Words of Joseph Smith*, comp. Andrew F. Ehat and Lyndon W. Cook (Provo, UT: Religious Studies Center, Brigham Young University, 1980), 49n1.
5. Joseph Smith to the Quorum of the Twelve, December 15, 1840, in *The Joseph Smith Papers, Documents*, 7:469–70 (original spelling and punctuation preserved); also in Manuscript History, C–1, 1118.
6. See Jane Neyman and Vienna Jacques, statement, November 29, 1854, in Journal History, August 15, 1840. The Journal History gives the name spelling *Neymon*. A discrepancy exists regarding the actual date when the first baptism for the dead was performed. A note in the Nauvoo Baptisms for the Dead, Book A, indicates the baptism took place on Sunday, September 12, 1840. See Nauvoo Baptisms for the Dead, Book A, attached note, microfilm no. 183,376, Family History Library, Salt Lake City, Utah, microfilm copy, Harold B. Lee Library, Brigham Young University, Provo, Utah. However, this is an error since September 12, 1840, was a Saturday, not a Sunday. Therefore it can be concluded that the correct date was Sunday, September 13, 1840.
7. See LaMar C. Berrett, Keith W. Perkins, and Donald Q. Cannon, *Sacred Places, Ohio and Illinois: A Comprehensive Guide to Early LDS Historical Sites* (Salt Lake City: Deseret Book, 2002), 104–5, 115–17, 133–34, 195–96.
8. Lucy Mack Smith, *Lucy's Book: A Critical Edition of Lucy Mack Smith's Family Memoir*, ed. Lavina Fielding Anderson (Salt Lake City: Signature Books, 2001), 714.
9. See Nauvoo Baptisms for the Dead, Book A, 145.
10. See Nauvoo Baptisms for the Dead, Book A, 149.
11. Aroet Lucious Hale, "Diary of Aroet Lucious Hale, 1828–1849," typescript, 8, L. Tom Perry Special Collections, Harold B. Lee Library; spelling and capitalization corrected. Although the document is titled as a diary, it is actually an autobiography.
12. Brigham Young, in *Journal of Discourses*, 26 vols. (London: Latter-day Saints' Book Depot, 1874), 16:165–66.

13. Brigham Young, "Speech," April 6, 1845, *Times and Seasons* 6, no. 12 (July 1, 1845): 954. Wilford Woodruff later recalled: "When that [baptism for the dead] was first revealed . . . a man would be baptized for both male and female [but] afterward we obtained more light upon the subject and President Young taught the people that men should attend to those ordinances for the male portion of their dead friends and females for females." Journal History, April 9, 1857.

14. The main reason given by Joseph Smith of the need for a proper record of proxy ordinances centered in his teachings that whatsoever is recorded on earth is recorded in heaven, and whatsoever is not recorded on earth is not recorded in heaven. See Doctrine and Covenants 128:8. Another reason for the need of a general Church record of proxy ordinances was to try to ensure that a deceased person's proxy work would not be repeated.

15. See M. Guy Bishop, "'What Has Become of Our Fathers?': Baptism for the Dead at Nauvoo," *Dialogue: A Journal of Mormon Thought* 23, no. 2 (Summer 1990): 88–89. Since instructions regarding accurate record keeping were not in place at that time, the 6,818 figure would have been larger.

16. See Bishop, "'What Has Become of Our Fathers?,'" 90.

17. "Reminiscences of the Church in Nauvoo," *Millennial Star* 55, no. 36 (September 4, 1893): 585.

18. Hale, "Diary," 8.

19. Wilford Woodruff, "The Law of Adoption," April 8, 1894, general conference address in Brian H. Stuy, ed., *Collected Discourses*, 5 vols. (Burbank, CA, and Woodland Hills, UT: B. H. S. Publishing, 1987–92), 4:71.

20. See Bishop, "'What Has Become of Our Fathers?,'" 92.

21. See Nauvoo Baptisms for the Dead, Book A, attached note. See also "A Record of the Branch in Quincy," November 9 and November 15, 1840, Church History Library; Richard E. Bennett, "'Quincy—The Home of Our Adoption': A Study of the Mormons in Quincy, Illinois, 1838–40," *Mormon Historical Studies* 2, no. 1 (Spring 2001): 115; also in Susan Easton Black and Richard E. Bennett, *A City of Refuge: Quincy, Illinois* (Salt Lake City: Millennial Press, 2000), 101; and Bishop, "'What Has Become of Our Fathers?,'" 87–88.

22. "Early Branches (Lima, Adams, Illinois to Mendon Monroe, New York)," *Nauvoo Journal* 3, no. 2 (April 1991): 43; spelling corrected.

23. See Manuscript History, October 3, 1840, vol. C–1, 1103.

24. See Manuscript History, October 4, 1840, vol. C–1, 1104.

25. "Minutes of a Conference, held in Kirtland, Ohio, May 22nd 1841," *Times and Seasons* 2, no. 17 (July 1, 1841): 459; also in Lyndon W. Cook and Milton V. Backman Jr., eds., *Kirtland Elders' Quorum Record, 1836–1841* (Provo, UT: Grandin Book, 1985), 58.

26. "Minutes of a Conference," 460; also in Cook and Backman, *Kirtland Elders' Quorum Record*, 59.

27. Alfred Holbrook, *Reminiscences of the Happy Life of a Teacher* (Cincinnati: Elm Street Printing Company, 1885), 223. Holbrook claims that the Mormon practice of baptism for the dead was introduced and took place in Kirtland while Joseph Smith and Sidney Rigdon were residing there (i.e., before 1838). This is an obvious error, since the practice did not begin until May 1841, more than three years after the Prophet and Rigdon left northeastern Ohio. However, the fact that Holbrook had any knowledge of it whatsoever indicates that he was at least aware that it was practiced by the Saints there.

28. See Manuscript History, October 2, 1841, vol. C–1, 1228.

29. Manuscript History, October 3, 1841, vol. C–1, 1230. Warren Foote was present on this occasion and reported the following: "A large congregation assembled this forenoon. Joseph Smith preached on the subject of baptism for the dead. Among a great many other things, he said that the Saints could be baptized for any of their dead relatives, or friends, who had not been murderers. Such could not be baptized for. The Lord had other ways of dealing with murderers." Warren Foote, "Autobiography of Warren Foote," 57, typescript, Perry Special Collections.

30. Manuscript History, October 31, 1841, vol. C–1, 1243.

31. For a brief discussion of Kirtland under Babbitt's leadership, see Davis Bitton, "The Waning of Mormon Kirtland," *BYU Studies* 12, no. 4 (Summer 1972): 456–57. Biographical information on Babbitt's life and church involvement is found in Andrew Jenson, *Latter-day Saint Biographical Encyclopedia*, 4 vols. (Salt Lake City: Andrew Jenson History Company, 1901), 1:284–86; and A. Gary Anderson, "Almon W. Babbitt and the Golden Calf," in *Regional Studies in Latter-day Saint Church History: Illinois*, ed. H. Dean Garrett (Provo, UT: Department of Church History and Doctrine, Brigham Young University, 1995), 35–54. For a discussion of the baptisms for the dead performed in Kirtland, Ohio, see Alexander L. Baugh, "'For This Ordinance Belongeth to My House': The Practice of Baptism for the Dead Outside the Nauvoo Temple," *Mormon Historical Studies* 3, no. 1 (Spring 2002): 47–58.

32. A November 21, 1841, journal entry by Wilford Woodruff indicates that he, along with Willard Richards and George A. Smith, officiated in the proxy confirmations for some forty deceased persons in the Nauvoo Temple baptistry. This marked the first known instance that the ordinance of confirmation for the dead was performed. See *Wilford Woodruff's Journal, 1833–1898, Typescript*, ed. Scott G. Kenney, 9 vols. (Midvale, UT: Signature Books, 1983–84), 2:138–39.

33. Manuscript History, November 8, 1841, C–1, addenda 44; original spelling preserved.

34. William Clayton, *The Nauvoo Diaries and Writings of William Clayton, Private Secretary of the Prophet Joseph Smith: Part 1, The Nauvoo Temple History Journal*, ed. Fred C. Collier (Salt Lake City: Collier's Publishing, 1990), 11; also cited in James B. Allen, *No Toil or Labor Fear: The Story of William Clayton* (Provo, UT: Brigham Young University Press, 2002), 420. It is important to note that the entry in the Manuscript History under this date has sometimes been interpreted to suggest that Brigham Young dedicated the font. The entry reads: "At five o'clock P.M. I attended the dedication of the Baptismal Font in the Lord's house. President Brigham Young was Spokesman." Manuscript History, November 8, 1841, C–1, addenda, 44. However, Clayton's entry makes it clear that Joseph Smith dedicated the font; Brigham Young acted as the "spokesman" who baptized Reuben McBride.

35. In May 1841, Reuben McBride was sustained and ordained, along with Hiram Winters, as a counselor in the Kirtland bishopric to Thomas Burdick. See *Times and Seasons* 2, no. 17 (July 1, 1841): 458. Four months later, at the October 1841 general conference, a motion was passed giving McBride power of attorney and authorizing him to transact all Church-related business in Kirtland, replacing Oliver Granger, who had died. See *Times and Seasons* 2, no. 24 (October 15, 1841): 579. Upon learning of his new legal responsibilities, McBride apparently traveled from Kirtland to Nauvoo to receive instruction and to be provided with the necessary paperwork. A certificate granting McBride power of attorney was signed on October 28, 1841. See *Millennial Star* 18, no. 47 (November 22, 1856): 741–42.

36. Reuben McBride was baptized on March 4, 1834, in New York and soon after his conversion moved to Kirtland, Ohio. When the main body of the Saints left Ohio

in 1838, McBride remained in Kirtland, and in 1841 Joseph Smith authorized him to take charge of the temple and other Church properties. He came to Utah in 1850 and eventually settled in Fillmore, Millard County, Utah. He died on February 26, 1891. See Jenson, *Latter-day Saint Biographical Encyclopedia*, 4:690.

37. Martha McBride Knight Kimball, born March 17, 1805, in Chester, Orange County, New York. She married Vinson Knight, who died in Nauvoo on July 31, 1842. She was married for time to Heber C. Kimball on January 26, 1846, and was sealed to Joseph Smith at the same time. She died on November 20, 1901, in Hooper, Weber County, Utah. See Susan Easton Black, comp., *Membership of The Church of Jesus Christ of Latter-day Saints, 1830–1848*, 50 vols. (Provo, UT: Religious Studies Center, 1989), 29:925–26.

38. Although McBride states that the first proxy baptisms performed in the Nauvoo Temple were done in the fall of 1842 (he being the first), as indicated in the main text, the correct date is 1841. His statement that his sister Martha was "there" could be interpreted to mean that she was present at the time McBride was baptized in the Nauvoo Temple font. However, later in the letter he indicates that following the baptism Joseph Smith drove him to Martha's house, which suggests she was not present. It appears that McBride was merely stating that Martha was living in Nauvoo at the time the first temple proxy baptisms were performed (namely, 1841).

39. The "bee" McBride refers to is probably a bucket brigade or a bucket line. He notes that Joseph Smith made a "bee," meaning that he organized a group of people to form a line and had them pass buckets or pails of water from the well (or wells) to the font in order to fill it.

40. In the Nauvoo Temple archaeological investigations conducted in the 1960s, two wells were discovered in the temple basement area—one situated underneath the west vestibule (identified as Well A) and another situated approximately twenty feet east of the baptismal font (identified as Well B). The east well was the primary water supply for the font. See Virginia S. Huntington and J. C. Huntington, *Rediscovery of the Nauvoo Temple: Report on the Archeological Excavations* (Salt Lake City: Nauvoo Restoration, 1971), 29–32.

41. Reuben McBride to Martha McBride Knight Kimball, November 1, 1886, MS 25144, Church History Library. The original letter is part of the Marion Adaline Belnap Kerr Family Papers. McBride's capitalization, spelling, and punctuation have been retained. The important elements of the letter are that (1) Joseph Smith told Reuben McBride that Joseph wanted him to have the privilege of being the first person baptized in the Nauvoo Temple—the two men met and subsequently went to the temple so the ordinance could be performed; (2) the Prophet spoke and offered a dedicatory prayer; (3) Brigham Young was present and baptized McBride in behalf of six of McBride's deceased relatives; and (4) following the ceremony, Joseph Smith drove McBride to the home of his sister.

42. See *Wilford Woodruff's Journal*, 2:138–39; emphasis added.

43. Manuscript History, November 21, 1841, vol. C–1, addenda 44–45; emphasis added.

44. Reuben McBride's mother, Abigale Mead McBride, and his two brothers, John and Samuel McBride, performed proxy baptisms in Nauvoo, but there is no record of Reuben's proxy work. See Susan Easton Black and Harvey Bischoff Black, *Annotated Record of Baptisms for the Dead, 1840–1845: Nauvoo, Hancock County, Illinois*, 7 vols. (Provo, UT: Center for Family History and Genealogy, Brigham Young University, 2002), 4:2354–60, 2362–65.

45. For a discussion on the first baptisms performed in the Nauvoo Temple, see Alexander L. Baugh, "'Blessed Is the First Man Baptised in This Font': Reuben McBride, First Proxy to Be Baptized for the Dead in the Nauvoo Temple," *Mormon Historical Studies* 3 no. 2 (Fall 2002): 253–61.

46. The *Times and Seasons* reported in January 1846 that "the Font, standing upon the twelve stone oxen, is about ready." *Times and Seasons* 6, no. 21 (January 20, 1846): 1096. However, Virginia S. and J. C. Harrington, in their report of the archaeological investigations of the Nauvoo Temple property, give evidence showing the stone font was probably being used in late 1845. See Virginia S. and J. C. Harrington, *Rediscovery of the Nauvoo Temple: Report on Archaeological Excavations* (Salt Lake City: Deseret News Press, 1971), 33. Author Don F. Colvin wrote that the wooden font was removed in July 1845 and that the stone font was in place by late August or early September. See Don F. Colvin, *Nauvoo Temple: A Story of Faith* (American Fork, UT: Covenant Communications, 2002), 184–85.

47. Charlotte Haven, "A Girl's Letters from Nauvoo," *Overland Monthly and Out West Magazine* 16, no. 96 (December 1890): 629–30.

48. *Wilford Woodruff's Journal*, 2:455. On this occasion, both Wilford and Phebe were rebaptized for relatives for whom they had previously been baptized on May 29 and August 25, 1842. See *Wilford Woodruff's Journal*, 2:177, 204.

49. Between August 1840 and September 1842, Joseph Smith addressed the Saints on the subject of baptism for the dead on at least seven occasions. See Ehat and Cook, *Words of Joseph Smith*, 37 (August 15, 1840), 38 (October 4, 1840), 71 (May 9, 1841), 77–79 (October 3, 1841), 109–10 (March 27, 1842), 111 (April 7, 1842), and 131 (August 31, 1842). In 1843–44 Joseph Smith addressed the subject on four occasions. See Ehat and Cook, *Words of Joseph Smith*, 210–11, 213 (June 11, 1843), 333 (March 10, 1844), 362–64 (April 8, 1844), and 368, 370–72 (May 12, 1844).

50. See *Wilford Woodruff's Journal*, 3:336.

51. Endowment House Baptisms for the Dead, 1867, 1–2, microfilm no. 183,382, Family History Library, copy in Harold B. Lee Library. The baptism and confirmation information of Lyrena Evans Moffatt, Nabby Howe, and Nabby Young are the first three that appear in the 1867 register.

52. The Endowment House was dedicated on May 5, 1855. The font was dedicated on October 2, 1856. See Richard O. Cowan, *Temples to Dot the Earth* (Salt Lake City: Bookcraft, 1994), 69. See also A. William Lund, "The Endowment House," *Improvement Era* 39, no. 4 (April 1936): 213.

53. *Deseret Evening News*, September 5, 1870; also in Edward Stevenson, "One of the Three Witnesses: Incidents in the Life of Martin Harris," *Millennial Star* 44, no. 6 (February 6, 1882): 87. Concerning the proxy baptisms done in the Endowment House, Brigham Young said in 1873: "We can, at the present time, go into the Endowment House and be baptized for the dead, receive our washings and anointing, etc., for there we have a font that has been erected, dedicated expressly for baptizing people for the remission of sins, for their health and for their dead friends." Brigham Young, in *Journal of Discourses*, 16:186.

54. Besides baptism and confirmation, the ordinances of washing and anointing, priesthood ordination (for men), the endowment, and marriage sealing (for both the living and the dead) were also prescribed.

Chapter Sixteen

Thoughts on Reclaiming the History of Relief Society

RACHEL COPE

In 1881 Emmeline B. Wells made an astute observation: "History tells us very little about women; judging from its pages, one would suppose that their lives were insignificant and their opinions worthless. . . . Volumes of unwritten history yet remain, the sequel to the lives of brave and heroic men. But although the historians of the past have been neglectful of woman, and it is the exception if she be mentioned at all; yet the future will deal more generously with womankind, and the historian of the present age will find it very embarrassing to ignore woman in the records of the nineteenth century."[1]

In addition to being an early proponent of women's history, Wells was also a convert to the Church, a polygamous wife, a prolific writer, an advocate of female suffrage, editor of the *Woman's Exponent* (the suffrage magazine), and Relief Society General President.[2] Her life goal, as she once noted in her diary, was to "do all in [her] power to help elevate the condition of [her] own people, especially women."[3]

For Wells, elevating women involved a process of remembering, documenting, preserving, recording, sharing, and teaching. In her mind, personal identity and the establishment of community were an outgrowth of historical consciousness. She thus wanted Latter-day Saint women to value their history so they could recognize their potential, broaden their minds, and make contributions in social, political, and spiritual contexts.

Upon assuming the role of Relief Society General President at the beginning of the twentieth century, Wells became deeply concerned by women's lack of historical memory, particularly in relation to Relief Society and its purpose—a concern that had also been expressed by Eliza R. Snow when called by Brigham Young to reintroduce the Relief Society organization in 1868. In 2010 Julie B. Beck, then serving as the fifteenth Relief Society General President, echoed the sentiments of Snow and Wells. She explained that after pondering about, praying about, fasting about, and discussing ways to help Latter-day Saint women face their challenges and reach their potential, it became clear to her that "the sisters of the Church should know and learn from the history of Relief Society."[4] Latter-day Saint women have forgotten "who we are" and "what we are to do," Beck explained.[5]

As a member of the Relief Society organization, as a historian of women and religion, and as a religious educator, I have been struck by these over-the-pulpit calls to remember women's history. I am intrigued by the recognition that history is central to understanding Latter-day Saint womanhood—that women's identity and purpose as a part of the saving work of the Church spring from a connection to the past. At the same time, I recognize the historical forgetfulness that the call to remember implies. Since the history of Relief Society has been documented and shared at key points in time (three examples of which will be considered in this essay), why hasn't the story been passed down continuously from one generation to another? Indeed, why have different generations of Relief Society General Presidents had to reclaim the history of Relief Society? And, finally, how might we change this pattern of remembering and forgetting and remembering and forgetting?

In order to consider some of the questions just posed, I will provide a brief sketch of the preserving and forgetting of Relief Society history and conclude with a few suggestions about how we might maintain historical consciousness in the future, an important goal if we hope to help our students—male and female—envision their place in the work of salvation.

RELIEF SOCIETY

In 1839 Church members settled along the Upper Mississippi River Valley. There they established the city of Nauvoo, Illinois. During the earliest stages of settlement, they began building a temple—a sacred space dedicated to the performance of salvific ordinances. Throughout the temple's construction period, Church members donated various resources and men served as volunteer laborers one day in ten.[6]

In 1842 Sarah Granger Kimball and Margaret Cooke discussed how women, as well as men, might contribute to the construction of the Nauvoo Temple. Both agreed that they could provide shirts for volunteer laborers. As a result of this conversation, Kimball contemplated forming a female benevolent society (a common practice at the time) that would enable Latter-day Saint women to engage in acts of service throughout their community.[7] In March 1842 a small group of women convened in Kimball's home to discuss the possibility of creating the society she had envisioned. Enthusiastic responses to the idea resulted in a collective decision to organize a benevolent society.

At the request of the other women in attendance at the meeting, Eliza R. Snow drafted a constitution for their fledgling organization. She subsequently shared it with Joseph Smith. Delighted by the idea of a women's society, the Prophet Joseph encouraged the prospect, while also suggesting that the women of the Church could expand the scope of their society by incorporating spiritual as well as temporal work into its mission.[8]

On March 17, 1842, twenty women met with Joseph Smith, John Taylor, and Willard Richards to officially establish their new society. In this meeting, the Prophet explained that he would organize the women of the Church under the pattern and direction of the priesthood; in essence, he was suggesting that their society could transcend traditional benevolent organizations through its placement within a soteriological framework.[9] In addition to engaging in acts of service and charity, the Prophet Joseph explained that Latter-day Saint women should also commit themselves to the work of salvation. Of this discussion, Elizabeth Ann Smith Whitney recalled, "President Joseph Smith had great faith in the sisters' labors, and ever sought to encourage them in the performance of their duties which pertained to these Societies, which he said were not only for benevolent purposes and spiritual improvement, but were actually to save souls."[10]

The women attending the March 17 meeting elected Emma Smith as president of the society and agreed to name it the Female Relief Society of Nauvoo. The Prophet Joseph Smith's references to organizing women under the pattern and direction of the priesthood and committing them to the work of salvation suggested that women were as essential as men to the work of God and that both sexes had access to the spiritual power, blessings, and gifts of the priesthood.[11]

From its inception, then, Relief Society encouraged women to place themselves within a larger cosmological history; it defined their purpose here and in the hereafter. Relief Society also provided a space in which women could give and receive religious instruction. Emma Smith, for example, heeded the revelatory counsel, now canonized as Doctrine and Covenants 25, to "expound scriptures" and "exhort the church."[12] Furthermore, Joseph Smith—who had previously focused on instructing and training men—met with and taught members of the Relief Society about their role in the plan of salvation and prepared them for the covenants they would eventually make within the walls of the temple. Up to that point, women's involvement with the temple had been focused on providing furnishings, handiwork, and clothing for the laborers. The Prophet's interest in organizing a society for women became an invitation to them to participate in temple worship. In the context of Relief Society meetings they also learned about the priesthood and about spiritual gifts. They came to recognize that the temple gave them access to the saving ordinances of the gospel and allowed them to perform baptisms for the dead in behalf of their deceased loved ones. For women, as Carol Cornwall Madsen so aptly noted, this "opened up a new concept of spiritual participation relating to the 'privileges, blessings and gifts of the priesthood' which not only enhanced their position in the church but offered limitless potential in the hereafter."[13]

ELIZA R. SNOW

As secretary of the Female Relief Society of Nauvoo, Eliza R. Snow—who had experience as a recorder, transcriber, and published poet—kept a meticulous record of the society's early meetings, which she titled "A Book of Records. Containing the proceedings of The Female Relief Society of Nauvoo." By creating this book, Snow explicitly became a historian of Relief Society. As scholars have since noted, her "precision indicates her belief that she was constructing a significant, enduring record."[14]

Snow kept the minutes of Relief Society meetings that were held in 1842 and in early 1843. Aware of their particular import, she recorded the sermons that Joseph Smith gave to members of the Relief Society—the only extant accounts of his teachings as specifically addressed to women.[15] Although Snow moved twenty-five miles south of Nauvoo in early 1843, thus precluding her from regular attendance at subsequent Relief Society meetings, she left the record she had been keeping in Nauvoo so other women could detail the proceedings she missed. Phoebe M. Wheeler, Hannah Ells, and an unidentified scribe took notes in Snow's place.[16]

In 1844 Relief Society meetings were suspended owing to controversies associated with plural marriage. Shortly thereafter, Joseph Smith was murdered, and two years following his death, Church members began their migration west. During this tumultuous period, Snow reclaimed the Relief Society record and took it with her as she left Nauvoo for the Rocky Mountains. She recognized the importance of the document she had created and was committed to preserving it.

Shortly after settling in the Rocky Mountains, a small group of Latter-day Saint women established societies "of females for the purpose of making clothing for Indian women and children."[17] Because other groups of women soon followed their example, a resurgence of Relief Society occurred in many wards. During the reformation that swept over the faith in the mid-1850s, a strong spiritual component was infused into the charitable labors that members of the Relief Society engaged in. This period of renewal "reaffirmed the sisters' sense of united purpose and continuity with their Nauvoo roots."[18]

As a result of the Utah War and the Civil War, the revival of Relief Society eventually waned, and the organization essentially disappeared for a second time.[19] On December 6, 1867, however, Brigham Young called on each bishop to organize a Relief Society group within his ward, hoping this would help improve the temporal affairs of the Saints. Noting the tenuous nature of the society's reorganization, the prophet Brigham then asked Eliza R. Snow to facilitate the renewal of Relief Society.[20]

In her efforts to reestablish Relief Society, Snow engaged in a thorough study of the book of records she had kept in Nauvoo. She believed that reorganization required historical awareness—she had to understand the purpose of Relief Society in order to help other women grasp its significance. Snow thus "carried [the record] and cited it when she addressed Relief Society women in Utah."[21] She relied on the minutes she had kept to shape women's memory of Relief Society origins so they could "reclaim the vitality and spirit" of this sacred organization.[22] In particular, Snow stressed the salvific scope of Joseph Smith's teachings, underscoring the idea that Relief Society was more than a benevolent society or a relief organization. She taught that it was a way for women to engage in the work of salvation and a means to reach their rightful place in God's kingdom. As one of the earliest historians of Latter-day Saint women, she created, preserved, and encouraged a familiarity with the past, hoping to "invest Mormon women with a sense of the spiritual power that Joseph opened to them."[23]

EMMELINE B. WELLS

Although Emmeline B. Wells was a teenager when the Relief Society was organized in Nauvoo, she was familiar with and intrigued by its history. Like Snow, she had a strong sense of historical consciousness and hoped to preserve and disseminate the history of Relief Society specifically and the history of Latter-day Saint women generally. In 1872, therefore, Wells made a verbatim copy of the Relief Society minutes and then used them to expand the work Snow had initiated.[24]

As an author and an editor, Wells found creative ways to increase women's exposure to their history; she hoped that this awareness would legitimize and extend their participation in the Church as well as in broader society. In order to accomplish this goal, she authored and published over fifty articles in the *Woman's Exponent* that highlighted, analyzed, and interpreted central themes detailed in the Nauvoo Relief Society minutes.[25] Her efforts made the information recorded in these important documents readily accessible to women for the first time.

In addition to sharing the history of Relief Society through the written word in the *Woman's Exponent*, Wells served as the fifth general president of the organization—the last president to have been acquainted with Joseph Smith and to have personal connections to Relief Society origins. During her tenure as president, therefore, Wells hoped to "transmit the memory and meaning of Relief Society beginnings to a second generation of Mormon women."[26] She believed that those who remembered their history would come to recognize the power and influence they could have in various spheres; in her mind, women had the capacity to make a difference within and without the home.[27]

Although Snow and Wells acted as early historians of Latter-day Saint women, few present-day Church members are aware of their efforts to preserve such an important dimension of Church history. Snow created and preserved the words of the Prophet and sought to make his teachings to women familiar and, by extension, life changing.[28] Wells built on and expanded the scope of Snow's work, making Relief Society history accessible over the pulpit and in print. Both found ways to infuse the Relief Society organization with meaning and purpose, to highlight its role within the scope of salvific work, and to carry its memory to present and future generations of women.

Wells's death in 1921, however, "broke the connecting chain of memory" to Relief Society origins.[29] Because the historical witnesses of the organization of the Relief Society no longer lived, forgetfulness eventually ensued—an all-too-common pattern in women's history. Indeed, even though women have been documenting their experiences at least since medieval times, historian Gerda Lerner has explained how every generation of women seems to be unaware that women from the preceding generation had already "amassed collections of 'women worthies.'"[30] Owing to this lack of a historiographical precedent, each generation of women is left to reinvent the wheel.[31] Sadly, many twentieth-century Latter-day Saint women fell into this same category of historical forgetfulness.[32] Since remembered history has typically centered on male leaders (this is true within and without the Church), far too few were familiar with the documents Eliza R. Snow preserved and the articles Wells published. And thus the vital messages they contained—particularly the need for women to engage in the work of salvation—were largely forgotten. Recently, however, another Relief Society General President has recognized the need for women to recover their history.[33]

JULIE B. BECK

From 2007 to 2012, Julie B. Beck served as the fifteenth General President of the Relief Society. Throughout her tenure, many of the talks she gave seemed to be laced with a historical undertone: over and over again, she highlighted the purpose and significance of the Relief Society organization.[34]

In the 2010 general meeting, Beck's historical consciousness became increasingly clear. Prompted to rectify the problem of forgetfulness, she announced that a historical account about Relief Society was being written and would eventually be distributed to members of the Church.[35] The purpose of this work, she explained, was to restore a sense of identity and purpose, to initiate positive change, and to unite women together in the work of salvation.[36] As if echoing the thoughtful sentiments of Gerda Lerner, she reminded a vast and diverse audience of women—united by a common faith—that "not having a history truly matters."[37]

Like Snow and Wells, Beck stressed the salvific purpose of Relief Society.[38] By turning to the records of the past, she was able to reclaim the words and the vision of the Prophet Joseph Smith in relation to this fundamental organization. She understood that modern women needed the reminder that Relief Society is more than a social club or an organization that performs temporal acts of service—it is a spiritual organization that has been given the charge to save souls.[39] Relief Society is, as Beck later explained in a BYU devotional, akin to priesthood quorums—both were designed to "help us become who our Heavenly Father needs us to become."[40]

CONCLUSION

Although Julie B. Beck recently reclaimed the history of Relief Society, we cannot assume that historical forgetfulness will not follow in succeeding generations. (Surely Eliza R. Snow and Emmeline B. Wells assumed, or at least hoped, that their efforts to preserve Relief Society history would impact every generation of Latter-day Saint women.) Remembering is active. It requires thoughtfulness, awareness, and creativity. It encourages us to think about old topics in new ways and to open our minds to a more expansive and complex narrative.

As religious educators, we are responsible to invite all of our students to engage in the work of salvation. And the possibilities for that engagement are ever increasing: our students are serving missions at younger ages, and more of those students are women. Consequently, women are also receiving their endowments at younger ages. They are being given greater leadership responsibilities as missionaries—their stewardships are increasing.[41] Indeed, they are being given, more than ever before, opportunities to fulfill the mission of Relief Society, as taught by Joseph Smith.

To aid with the ever-increasing work of salvation, and to avoid previous patterns of historical forgetfulness, each of us needs to make a greater effort to "know and learn from the history of Relief Society" and to teach its importance to our students, male and female.[42] What if, for example, we incorporated Joseph Smith's teachings from the Relief Society minutes into some of our lessons? We could also draw on stories from the scriptures and from Church history that are about women as well as men. We could read and quote from talks given by female leaders, thus helping our students recognize the importance of the work they do and the counsel they provide, as well as the significance and import of the auxiliaries they represent.[43]

If we teach younger generations of students to consider the importance of Relief Society history—to value God's salvific work as engaged in by women—then remembering will inevitably follow. If it becomes a part of who they are and how they understand the gospel, they will preserve it, they will teach it, they will make it the norm. "As we move the Lord's work forward," Sister Beck suggested, "the history of Relief Society will continue to be written by faithful sisters [and faithful brothers] throughout the world."[44] And forgetfulness can become a thing of the past.

Rachel Cope is an associate professor of Church history and doctrine at Brigham Young University.

Rachel Cope, "Thoughts on Reclaiming the History of Relief Society," *Religious Educator* 15, no. 3 (2014): 91–101.

NOTES

1. Emmeline B. Wells, "Self-Made Women," *Woman's Exponent*, March 1, 1881, 148.
2. See Carol Cornwall Madsen, *An Advocate for Women: The Public Life of Emmeline B. Wells, 1870–1920* (Provo, UT: Brigham Young University Press, 2005). See also Carol Cornwall Madsen, "Emmeline B. Wells: Romantic Rebel," in *Supporting Saints: Life Stories of Nineteenth-Century Mormons*, ed. Donald Q. Cannon and David J. Whittaker (Provo, UT: Religious Studies Center, Brigham Young University, 1985), 305–41.
3. Emmeline B. Wells, diary, January 4, 1878, L. Tom Perry Special Collections, Harold B. Lee Library, Brigham Young University, Provo, Utah (hereafter Perry Special Collections).
4. Julie B. Beck, "'Daughters in My Kingdom': The History and Work of Relief Society," *Ensign*, November 2010, 114.
5. Beck, "'Daughters in My Kingdom,'" 114.
6. See Glen M. Leonard, *Nauvoo: A Place of Peace, a People of Promise* (Salt Lake City: Deseret Book, 2002), 237.
7. See Lori Ginzberg, *Women and the Work of Benevolence: Morality, Politics, and Class in the Nineteenth-Century United States* (New Haven, CT: Yale University Press, 1990).
8. See Nauvoo Relief Society Minute Book, March 31, 1842, https://www.josephsmith papers.org/paper-summary/nauvoo-relief-society-minute-book/19. See also Jill Mulvay Derr, Janath Russell Cannon, and Maureen Ursenbach Beecher, *Women of Covenant: The Story of Relief Society* (Salt Lake City: Deseret Book, 1992), 79; Jill Mulvay Derr and Carol Cornwall Madsen, "Preserving the Record and Memory of the Female Relief Society of Nauvoo," *Journal of Mormon History* 35, no. 3 (2009): 88–117; and Jill Mulvay Derr and Carol Cornwall Madsen, "'Something Better' for the Sisters: Joseph Smith and the Female Relief Society of Nauvoo," in *Joseph Smith*

and the Doctrinal Restoration (Provo, UT: Religious Studies Center, Brigham Young University; Salt Lake City: Deseret Book, 2005), 123–43.

9. See Nauvoo Relief Society Minute Book, March 31, 1842.

10. Carol Cornwall Madsen, *In Their Own Words: Women and the Story of Nauvoo* (Salt Lake City: Deseret Book, 1994), 200–201.

11. This principle has been confirmed by modern-day Apostle M. Russell Ballard, who said, "In our Heavenly Father's great priesthood-endowed plan, men have the unique responsibility to administer the priesthood, but they are not the priesthood. . . . In the eternal perspective, both the procreative power and the priesthood power are shared by husband and wife." M. Russell Ballard, "This Is My Work and Glory," *Ensign*, May 2013, 19. See also Dallin H. Oaks, "The Keys and Authority of the Priesthood," *Ensign*, May 2014, 49–52.

12. Doctrine and Covenants 25:7.

13. Carol Cornwall Madsen, "Mormon Women and the Temple: Toward a New Understanding," in *Mormon Women in Historical and Cultural Perspective*, ed. Maureen Ursenbach Beecher and Lavina Fielding Anderson (Chicago: University of Illinois Press, 1987), 83–84.

14. Madsen, "Mormon Women and the Temple," 92.

15. See Madsen, "Mormon Women and the Temple," 94.

16. See Derr and Madsen, "Preserving the Record," 94.

17. "Record of the Female Relief Society Organized on the 9th of Feby in the City of the Great Salt Lake 1854," holograph, Louisa R. Taylor Papers, Perry Special Collections.

18. See "Relief Society in the Early Days," *Woman's Exponent*, July 1, 1895, 21; Susa Young Gates, "Relief Society Beginnings in Utah," *Relief Society Magazine* 9, April 1922; "Record of the Relief Society from First Organization to Conference Apr. 5, 1892, Book II," cataloged as Relief Society Record, 1880–1892; Eliza R. Snow, "Relief Society," *Deseret Evening News*, April 18, 1868, 2; and Derr, Cannon, and Beecher, *Women of Covenant*, 79.

19. See Derr, Cannon, and Beecher, *Women of Covenant*, 59–82.

20. See Derr, Cannon, and Beecher, *Women of Covenant*, 83–126.

21. Derr and Madsen, "Preserving the Record," 90.

22. Derr and Madsen, "Preserving the Record," 104.

23. Derr and Madsen, "Preserving the Record," 105.

24. Holograph copy in Emmeline Wells Papers, Perry Special Collections.

25. See, for example, "Sermons and Writings of the Prophet Joseph, His Teachings to the Relief Society," *Woman's Exponent*, August 15, 1884, 44, 52; "The Relief Society: Extracts from the Records," *Woman's Exponent*, November 1905, 36–38; and "The Relief Society (Copied from the Original Records), Eliza R. Snow, Secretary," *Woman's Exponent*, February 1911, 49.

26. Derr and Madsen, "Preserving the Record," 90.

27. See, for example, Emmeline B. Wells, diary, January 4, 1878, and May 23, 1908, Perry Special Collections; "A Noble Woman," *Deseret Evening News*, March 5, 1910, 4; Blanche Beachwood [Emmeline B. Wells's penname], "Real Women," *Woman's Exponent*, June 1, 1874, 118; and Blanche Beachwood, "Real Women," *Woman's Exponent*, April 1, 1976, 118. See also Carol Cornwall Madsen, *An Advocate for Women: The Public Life of Emmeline B. Wells, 1870–1920* (Provo, UT: Brigham Young University Press, 2005); and Carol Cornwall Madsen, "Telling the Untold Story: Emmeline B. Wells as Historian," in *Telling the Story of Mormon History,*

Proceedings of the 2002 Symposium of the Joseph Fielding Smith Institute for Latter-day Saint History at Brigham Young University, ed. William G. Hartley (Provo, UT: Joseph Fielding Smith Institute for Latter-day Saint History, Brigham Young University, 2004).

28. The content of the Relief Society minutes is readily available through the Joseph Smith Papers Project (including scans of the original and a transcription) at http://josephsmithpapers.org/paper-summary/nauvoo-relief-society-minute-book/1 and is also available as a recent Deseret Book publication: Sheri L. Dew and Virginia H. Pearce, *The Beginning of Better Days: Divine Instruction to Women from the Prophet Joseph Smith* (Salt Lake City: Desert Book, 2012).

29. Derr and Madsen, "Preserving the Record," 113.

30. Gerda Lerner, *Creation of Feminist Consciousness: From the Middle Ages to Eighteen-seventy* (New York: Oxford University Press, 1994), 210.

31. See Lerner, *Creation of Feminist Consciousness*, 166.

32. Latter-day Saint women's history has become a thriving academic field with the rise of women's history in the 1970s; however, it remains comparatively unfamiliar to lay readers.

33. This statement is not intended to suggest that other Relief Society General Presidents have not acknowledged the history of Relief Society, nor is it meant to imply that the organization of Relief Society has not been discussed and celebrated throughout the Church. The statement is, however, making note of a recent example of a Relief Society General President who made a concerted effort—akin to Snow and Wells—to reclaim a forgotten history.

34. See the following by Julie B. Beck: "Fulfilling the Purpose of Relief Society," October 2008 general conference; "Relief Society: A Sacred Work," October 2009 general conference; "'Daughters in My Kingdom,'" October 2010 general conference; "What I Hope My Granddaughters (and Grandsons) Will Understand about Relief Society," October 2011 general conference; "The Vision of Prophets regarding Relief Society: Faith, Family, Relief," April 2012 general conference; and "Why We Are Organized into Quorums and Relief Societies," *Religious Educator* 14, no. 1 (2013):19–33.

35. See Susan W. Tanner, *Daughters in My Kingdom* (Salt Lake City: Intellectual Reserve, 2011).

36. See Beck, "'Daughters in My Kingdom.'"

37. Gerda Lerner, *Why History Matters: Life and Thought* (New York: Oxford University Press, 1988), 208.

38. See Derr, Cannon, and Beecher, *Women of Covenant*, 79; Derr and Madsen, "Preserving the Record," 88–117; Derr and Madsen, "'Something Better' for the Sisters," 123–43; Nauvoo Relief Society Minute Book, March 30, 1842; and Dew and Pearce, *The Beginning of Better Days*.

39. See Beck, "'Daughters in My Kingdom.'"

40. Julie B. Beck, "Why We Are Organized into Quorums and Relief Societies," BYU devotional, January 17, 2012, https://speeches.byu.edu/, 29.

41. In addition, the roles and leadership responsibilities of mission presidents' wives are increasing, and the scope of international leadership is expanding with the recent announcement that international board members are being called to serve with the Young Women organization. See "Mormon Women Leaders Announce International Board Members," https://newsroom.churchofjesuschrist.org/article/mormon-auxiliary-leaders-announce-international-board-members.

42. Beck, "'Daughters in My Kingdom,'" 114.
43. For more ideas, see Neylan McBaine, *Women at Church: Magnifying LDS Women's Local Impact* (Sandy, UT: Greg Kofford Books, 2014).
44. Beck, "'Daughters in My Kingdom,'" 115.

Chapter Seventeen

"Line upon Line"

Joseph Smith's Growing Understanding of the Eternal Family

R. DEVAN JENSEN, MICHAEL A. GOODMAN, AND
BARBARA MORGAN GARDNER

"The past is a foreign country: they do things differently there." So begins L. P. Hartley's novel *The Go-Between*. This statement reminds religious educators to study history as it unfolded and to avoid presentism, or "an attitude toward the past dominated by present-day attitudes and experiences."[1] Latter-day Saint doctrines did not spring up fully formed as we have them today. The historical record shows that Joseph Smith did not begin with a full understanding of the doctrines of eternal families and sealing ordinances as we teach them today. In fact, the Prophet Joseph Smith dictated a revelation on August 6, 1833, that the Lord "will give unto the faithful line upon line, precept upon precept" (Doctrine and Covenants 98:12). Joseph Smith was searching for answers to complex questions such as how life continues after death, how family and friends can secure salvation in the afterlife (especially without receiving the ordinances of salvation on earth), and what role our ancestors play in our own salvation. We conclude that although Joseph Smith recorded many revelations and visitations by heavenly messengers, he reasoned through the process of how to implement doctrines pertaining to the eternal family, particularly the sealing ordinances. As with other parts of the Restoration, Joseph Smith continued to develop deeper understandings of Malachi's prophecies, Elijah's mission, temple ordinances, and sealings.

Using the scriptures and historical insights from the Joseph Smith Papers Project as well as other primary and secondary sources, we concisely explain and document (1) how such foundational doctrines on the eternal family emerged over time; (2) how the doctrines developed in the context of tragedy that motivated deep and searching questions about death, salvation, and the eternal nature of families; and (3) how the practice of sealing family members for eternity emerged, including practices of plural marriage and familial adoptions that have since been discontinued. We demonstrate how early statements of doctrines continue to adapt and become more refined to meet the needs of individual families and the overall Church. Though separate aspects of this history have been treated in greater detail by others, this article seeks to summarize and synthesize a wide range of material to help religious educators access these important sources.[2]

MALACHI'S PROPHECIES, ELIJAH'S MISSION

In Manchester, New York, seventeen-year-old Joseph Smith Jr. told his father that on September 21, 1823, while he was praying "to Almighty God for forgiveness of all [his] sins and follies" the angel Moroni visited and taught him.[3] The heavenly messenger appeared five times within a twenty-four-hour period, repeating four times a significant selection of biblical prophecies to prepare the teenager mentally, emotionally, and spiritually for his future work. Joseph Smith was recording these experiences between 1839 and 1844, at a time when he had had significant experiences with events in the Kirtland Temple and likely the Nauvoo Temple that gave shape and meaning to his early spiritual manifestations. These early revelatory experiences included Malachi's promises about the temple, Elijah's turning the hearts of the children to their fathers, and priesthood authority. Joseph Smith said that Moroni "first quoted part of the third chapter of Malachi" (Joseph Smith—History 1:36).[4] Although we do not know how much of Malachi 3 was quoted, the chapter begins with a prophecy that the Lord would "suddenly come to his temple" (promised again in Doctrine and Covenants 36:8, recorded in December 1830).[5] Malachi 3 also refers to a messenger preparing the way of the Lord[6] and a prophecy that "the sons of Levi" would again make "an offering in righteousness" (Malachi 3:1, 3). We have no indication that Joseph understood what that offering was to be at that time. By 1842 Joseph would link this prophecy with presenting in the temple a worthy record of our dead (Doctrine and Covenants 128:17, 24).

Moroni quoted Malachi 4:5–6 with an important difference: the Lord would "reveal . . . the *Priesthood,* by the hand of Elijah the prophet" and would also "plant in the hearts of the children the *promises* made to the fathers, and the hearts of the children shall turn[7] to their fathers" (Joseph Smith—History 1:38–39; emphasis altered; see also Doctrine and Covenants 2:1–2; and Joseph Smith—History 1:36). It is likely that Joseph initially understood "the promises made to the fathers" as referring to the covenant fathers of Israel. A revelation received in the fall of 1830 refers to Elijah's promise of "turning the hearts of the fathers, . . . and also, with Joseph and Jacob, and Isaac, and Abraham, your fathers, *by whom the promises remain*" (Doctrine and Covenants 27:9–10; emphasis added). How would this understanding transform into a uniting of parents with their children in the afterlife? Though Joseph does not leave any explicit explanation of that transformation, the historical record provides some evidence that the deaths of family and friends and the hope of future resurrection and reunion became major catalysts for seeking revelation clarifying relationships in the next life.

QUESTIONS ABOUT DEATH AND SALVATION

Such doctrinal understandings developed during times of tragedies that motivated Joseph Smith's deep and searching questions about death, salvation, and the eternal nature of families. Historian Samuel Brown described a nineteenth-century American culture of "holy death," noting that "the Smith family knew premature death well. Joseph's mother, Lucy Mack Smith . . . , lost seven of her eleven children, while in the next generation Joseph Jr. lost six of his eleven."[8] Just two months after Moroni's first visit, on November 19, 1823, Joseph's oldest brother, Alvin, died at age twenty-five. At the funeral services held in the local Presbyterian church, Reverend Stockton "intimated very strongly" that Alvin had "gone to hell" because he was "not a church member," reported Alvin's brother William, who added, "He [Alvin] was a good boy, and my father did not like it."[9] Reverend Stockton's assertion deeply troubled the Smiths, some of whom had Universalist beliefs.[10] Joseph Sr., Lucy Mack Smith, and Joseph Jr. all pondered the status of Alvin as an unbaptized believer,[11] and those questions of Alvin's unresolved status would find resolution in Joseph Jr.'s 1836 vision of his brother's salvation, to be discussed later. This is a clear example of how Joseph's theological understanding developed in the context of personal tragedy and his desire to understand how Christ's redemptive work paved the way for loved ones' salvation beyond the general understanding of his own day.

As Joseph Smith continued to learn line upon line, he gained a greater understanding of the importance of people being sealed or welded together both into God's eternal family as well as within their own individual families. Joseph wed Emma Hale in South Bainbridge, New York, on January 18, 1827. There is no evidence that at the time of their marriage Joseph knew that marriage was supposed to last through eternity, and he likely accepted the predominant Christian understanding that marriage was for this life only and did not continue in heaven. Joseph and Emma moved to Harmony, Pennsylvania, where Joseph continued to translate the Book of Mormon and where Martin Harris insisted on borrowing the manuscript pages. On June 15, 1828, Joseph and Emma's first child was born and died the same day. For two weeks after the baby's death, Joseph nursed Emma back to full strength. Despite her frail health and the tragic loss of their son, Emma urged Joseph to travel to Palmyra to find out why Martin Harris had neither returned the manuscript pages he had taken nor sent them any letter in months. When Joseph traveled to Palmyra and learned that Martin Harris had lost the pages, Joseph exclaimed, "I have lost my soul!"[12] But his thoughts quickly turned to Emma in her physically and emotionally weakened state: "Then must I," said Joseph, "return with such a tale as this? I dare not do it."[13] In agony, Joseph Smith recorded in 1832 that he "cried unto the Lord that he would provide for me to accomplish the work whereunto he had commanded me" and that the "Lord appeared unto a young man by the name of Oliver Cowd[e]ry and shewed unto him the plates in a vision and also the truth of the work and what the Lord was about to do through me his unworthy Servant therefore he was desiorous [sic] to come and write for me."[14]

As he translated the Book of Mormon, Joseph dictated three poignant passages pertaining to the salvation of little children that the Smiths would have pondered. First was the account of King Benjamin's parting words to his people, where he quoted the words of an angel that "the infant perisheth not that dieth in his infancy" and would be "blameless before God" (Mosiah 3:18, 21). Next, the book of Mosiah offers Abinadi's eloquent testimony in the court of King Noah that "little children" would receive "eternal life" (Mosiah 15:25). Third, Mormon's letter to his son Moroni affirmed that "little children are alive in Christ, even from the foundation of the world; if not so, God is a partial God, and also a changeable God, and a respecter to persons; for how many little children have died without baptism! Wherefore, if little children could not be saved without baptism, these must have gone to an endless hell" (Moroni 8:12–13).[15] Though we have no written evidence that Joseph connected these passages to his own baby's death, it would seem strange if the passages didn't stir thoughts and feelings in the recently bereaved father and mother. These Book of Mormon doctrines of salvation for unbaptized infants challenged the sectarian stance of most organized churches and later became key doctrinal teachings regarding the family.[16]

EARLY TEMPLE WORSHIP, PRIESTHOOD KEYS IN KIRTLAND

In January 1831 Church members were commanded to gather at "the Ohio," where a house of the Lord would be built and they would be washed, anointed, and endowed with power from on high (see Doctrine and Covenants 38:32). Though very basic compared with the Nauvoo endowment or the modern endowment, the Kirtland endowment was a first step in Joseph's implementation of the temple ordinances that were precursors to the modern-day sealing ordinance. After moving to the Isaac Morley farm in Kirtland, Joseph offered a memorable discourse on October 25, inviting the Saints to develop perfect love so their names might be written in "the Lamb's book of life," or sealed up to eternal life.[17]

Then tragedy struck the Smith family again. Emma gave birth to unnamed twins on April 30, 1831, in Kirtland. They lived only about three hours. It just so happened that John and Julia Murdock, two of Joseph's friends and fellow members of the Church, gave birth to twins the following day, but Julia died in childbirth. The Smiths adopted the Murdock twins, which proved to be a temporary source of comfort to the mourning parents. A watershed doctrinal moment followed in February 1832 when Joseph Smith and Sidney Rigdon learned that heaven consisted of many kingdoms.[18] They further learned that salvation came through the Atonement of Jesus Christ by way of ordinances such as baptism and the laying on of hands for the gift of the Holy Ghost (see Doctrine and Covenants 76:51–52). In that same revelation we see harbingers of future temple promises that those who are sealed by the Holy Spirit of promise will become kings and priests (and presumably queens and priestesses), receiving a fullness of the Father's glory (see vv. 52–56). The Son of God even made it possible for "the spirits of men kept in prison" to receive the gospel message so "they might be judged according to men in the flesh" (v. 73). This revelation opened the door for later clarifications that proxy baptisms could be performed for our dead in order to hold them to the same standards as the living. Though Joseph never explicitly connected Doctrine and Covenants 76 to Doctrine and Covenants 128 and baptism for the dead, the doctrines contained in section 76 are a prerequisite to the development of the doctrine of the eternal family.

Tragedy continued to influence Joseph's establishment of ways to seal friends and family to God, if not yet to each other, in heaven. On March 24, 1832, Joseph and Emma Smith were caring for their twins, who were sick with the measles, at the John and Elsa Johnson farm in Hiram, Ohio, when a mob of about twenty-five men dragged Joseph into the cold air and tarred and feathered him.[19] Joseph Murdock Smith, one of the adopted twins, died six days later, likely from a combination of both measles and exposure. Emma particularly grieved for the child.[20] Joseph poured his emotions into church service. He traveled to Zion (Missouri) to fulfill a commandment given on March 1, 1832.[21] While there, he visited his friends from the Colesville Branch who had relocated there, sealing them up to eternal life, according to Joseph Knight.[22] Historian Jonathan Stapley wrote, "'Sealing' as a ritual act dates to the first years of the Restoration, when elders with the High Priesthood sealed up church members and congregations into eternal life."[23] In essence, Joseph was performing a "group sealing" with the promise of eternal life.

Four years later, as part of worship services in the Kirtland Temple in January 1836, the general Church presidency gave Joseph Sr. a priesthood blessing, and Joseph Jr. then saw a vision of Alvin in heaven with his parents. One of the remarkable aspects of this vision is that Joseph Sr. and Lucy were still alive at the time of the blessing. It appears that the revelations Joseph had received earlier, promising that little children who died without the chance to be baptized would have eternal life, was expanded as a result of this vision. Joseph "marveled" that the unbaptized Alvin could be saved in the celestial kingdom. He recorded that "all who have died without a knowledge of this gospel, who would have received it if they had been permitted to tarry, shall be heirs of the celestial kingdom of God" and that "all children who die before they arrive at the years of accountability are saved in the celestial kingdom of heaven" (Doctrine and Covenants 137:7, 10). Not only could little children who died without baptism be saved, but so could all who died without the opportunity of hearing the gospel and receiving the ordinances thereof. Again, we see the connection between the death of family and friends and the continuing development of Joseph's understanding of our role in saving and sealing our loved ones unto eternal life.

But how, specifically, were Alvin and innocent children to be saved in the celestial kingdom? On April 3, 1836, a week after the dedication of the Kirtland Temple, Joseph, Oliver, and other members gathered in the temple. It was Easter Sunday and also Passover season—a time when Jews expected Elijah to return to earth.[24] Joseph later recorded that after closing the canvas curtains or veils, he and Oliver saw a vision of the resurrected Lord Jesus Christ coming to his temple.[25] They received priesthood keys from Moses, Elias, and Elijah[26] "to turn the hearts of the Fathers to the children and the children to the fathers."[27] Though we lack specific documentation that Joseph linked Elijah's visitation to the concept of sealings at that time, Joseph later stated that Elijah restored the keys "of the fulness of the Melchizedek Priesthood," including authority to perform ceremonies to "seal" for eternity both marriages and relationships for the living and the dead. It is unclear whether Joseph at that time understood how those keys could bind together families, and he did not exercise that authority for about another four years.[28] Still, the bestowal of authority was a further prerequisite to Joseph's ability in later years to understand the sealing powers in connection to family relationships. As the years passed, he would gain further understanding of those keys. In a Sunday address early in 1844, Joseph Smith explained that the word *turn* [in Malachi 4] should be translated as *bind* or *seal*,[29] meaning the sealing of families as eternal units (see Doctrine and Covenants 110:13–15). Joseph emphasized that the "welding" or "sealing" of God's children are accomplished in two distinct and perhaps related ways: through entrance into God's family by virtue of baptism or baptism for the dead, and then through sealings of couples, families, and deceased friends, as discussed below.

BAPTISMS FOR THE DEAD IN NAUVOO

A few years later, the Saints began working to transform the disease-ridden swampland of Commerce into the city of Nauvoo the Beautiful. Because of the conditions under which the Saints labored, many died from malaria and other diseases. These deaths further prompted questions about how to secure salvation for the dead. The story of Joseph's friend Seymour Brunson is striking. "Although still robust at age forty," wrote Ryan Tobler, "Seymour Brunson went out one evening to drive away some stray cattle and caught cold, which led to something more serious, and then to his untimely death." Tobler noted that "to the Saints, the death of a hardy soul like Brunson was unsettling; it was one of those occasions, as the Mormon Prophet Joseph

Smith later put it, through which 'we have again the warning voice sounded in our midst which shows the uncertainty of human life.'"[30] As part of Joseph's funeral sermon on August 15, 1840, he introduced an electrifying new doctrine: vicarious baptism for the dead.[31] After quoting 1 Corinthians 15, Joseph informed the Saints that they "could now act for their friends who had departed this life, and that the plan of salvation was calculated to save all who were willing to obey the requirements of the law of God."[32] A woman at the funeral, Jane Neyman (also spelled Nymon), asked to be baptized in behalf of her deceased son Cyrus. Vienna Jaques rode on horseback into the river to witness the first recorded proxy baptism in modern times.[33] Even though Joseph told Church members they could "act for their friends," most began proxy baptisms for family members. According to Susan Easton Black, 97 percent of those first proxy baptisms were performed for family members.[34]

This practice would soon have personal application for the Smiths as further tragedy continued to provide the context for Joseph's further expansion of the doctrines necessary to understand the role of family in securing salvation. When Joseph Smith Sr. returned home on September 13, 1840, he was so sick that he began vomiting blood. Lucy Mack Smith called her children to his deathbed. Lucy's history shows the importance the Smiths placed on ensuring Alvin's salvation. She recorded the moment when Joseph Jr. "informed his father, that it was then the priviledge of the saints to be baptized for the dead. . . . Mr. Smith was delighted to hear [this], and requested that Joseph should be baptized for Alvin immediately."[35] After blessing each of his children, Joseph Sr. died on September 14. Hyrum soon served as proxy so that Alvin could be baptized vicariously and receive salvation.[36] Though we see the family's quest to ensure Alvin's salvation by way of vicarious ordinances, we do not yet sense an understanding of the possibility to seal families together nor the necessity of such sealings. Yet baptism and baptism for the dead are precursors that enable the salvation of loved ones by adopting them into the family of God; Joseph would come to understand this as a necessary step in family sealings. Hence, baptism for the dead was a preliminary step in the process, and one that would involve a sealing, not necessarily to fellow family members, but rather a binding authority to make it efficacious in heaven. Referring to vicarious work for the dead, the Prophet Joseph said, "This doctrine presents in a clear light, the wisdom and mercy of God, in preparing an ordinance for the salvation of the dead, being baptized by proxy, their names recorded in heaven, and they judged according to the deeds done in the body. . . . Those saints who

The Nauvoo Temple, daguerreotype, ca. 1850. Courtesy of Church History Library.

neglect it, in behalf of their deceased relatives, do it at the peril of their own salvation."[37] Hence he clarified that our salvation is inextricably entwined with that of our ancestors.

In an epistle to the Saints on September 6, 1842, Joseph emphasized the importance of performing vicarious baptisms through "the sealing and binding power." He warned that "the earth will be smitten with a curse unless there is a welding link of some kind or other between the fathers and the children, upon some subject or other—and behold what is that subject? It is the baptism for the dead. For we without them cannot be made perfect; neither can they without us be made perfect." Though not fleshed out in detail, this declaration indicates some connectivity not only between the person baptized and God but between "the fathers and the children." This further connects the concept of baptism, sealing, and familial ties in the next life. He praised the visitation of heavenly messengers with "their keys, their honors, their majesty and glory, and the power of their priesthood; giving line upon line, precept upon precept; here a little, and there a little." Joseph then celebrated the Lord's great work of salvation, saying, "Let the dead speak forth anthems of eternal praise to the King Immanuel, who hath ordained, before the world was, that which would enable us to redeem them out of their prison; for the prisoners shall go free." He concluded with a call to action: "Let us, therefore, as a church and a people, and as Latter-day Saints, offer unto the Lord an offering in righteousness; and let us present in his holy temple, when it is finished, a book containing the records of our dead, which shall be worthy of all acceptation" (Doctrine and Covenants 128:14, 18, 21–22, 24).

Joseph Smith preached on August 13, 1843, on the topic of Malachi's prophecies at a funeral sermon for probate judge Elias Higbee. Of this sermon William Clayton recorded, "When speaking of the passage 'I will send Elijah the prophet &c' he [Joseph Smith] said it should read and he shall turn the hearts of the children to the <u>covenant</u> made with their fathers . . . meaning the everlasting covenant thereby making their calling & election sure." Joseph added, "When a seal is put upon the father and mother it secures their posterity so that they cannot be lost but will be saved by virtue of the covenant of their father."[38] Smith clarified two weeks later that "seal[ing] the hearts of the fathers to the children and the children to the fathers" would take place through temple rituals of "anointing & sealing."[39]

Joseph Smith expanded this theme in his last public sermon: "The greatest responsibility in this world that God has laid upon us, is to seek after our dead. The Apostle says, 'they without us cannot be made perfect'; for it is necessary that the sealing power should be in our hands to seal our children and our dead. . . . It is necessary that those who are gone before, and those who come after us should have salvation in common with us, and thus hath God made it obligatory upon man. Hence God said 'I will send Elijah the prophet before the coming of the great and dreadful day of the Lord; and he shall turn the hearts of the fathers to the children, and the hearts of the children to their fathers, lest I come and smite the earth with a curse."[40] Joseph Smith urged the Saints in "building their temples[,] erecting their Baptismal fonts & going forth & receiving all the ordinances, Baptisms, Confirmations, washings anointings ordinations, & sealing powers upon our heads in behalf of all our Progenitors who are <u>dead</u> & redeem them that they may come forth in the first resurrection & be exhalted to thrones of glory with us, & herein is the chain that binds the hearts of the fathers to the Children, & the Children to the Fathers which fulfills the mission of Elijah."[41] Though not explaining exactly what it meant to be "exhalted to thrones of glory *with us*," Joseph continued to develop the doctrinal foundation that would ultimately lead to our current understanding of familial ties in the hereafter. Joseph concluded that God could bind the human family together in an eternal chain through the ordinances of salvation performed by children in behalf of their progenitors.

MARRIAGES FOR TIME AND ETERNITY

In addition to proxy temple work in behalf of the Saints' kindred dead, Joseph Smith developed the doctrinal foundation to unite families by performing marriages for both time and eternity. The way these practices unfolded was complicated legally, emotionally, and theologically. By looking at how sealings were practiced in Joseph's day, we can see a process unfolding that brings us to the understanding we have today. He initially married couples until death and then later began sealing couples for eternity. Part of Joseph's early work included plural marriages in ways that Church leaders and members no longer practice.

Joseph's initial understanding and practice of marriage largely mirrored his Protestant cultural upbringings—namely, monogamy, the only legal form of marriage in the United States.[42] On May 7, 1831, Joseph gave his first recorded revelation on the subject of marriage to help Leman Copley, a former Shaker, who believed that marriage was inferior to celibacy: "I say unto you, that whoso forbiddeth to marry is not ordained of God, for marriage is ordained of God unto man. Wherefore, it is lawful that he should have one wife, and they twain shall be one flesh, and all this that the earth might answer the end of its creation; and that it might be filled with the measure of man, according to his creation before the world was made" (Doctrine and Covenants 49:15–17). Though some sects of the day did not share this understanding, it was not strange for fellow Christians to declare that marriage was ordained of God, that it united a man and a woman, and that it matched the designs of God for his children.

Joseph officiated at Lydia Goldthwaite Bailey and Newel Knight's wedding on November 24, 1835. Some have wondered if the Prophet was authorized to perform the marriage because Sidney Rigdon had been denied state sanction to perform such marriages.[43] However, Ohio's 1824 marriage law stated that "a religious society . . . could perform marriages without a license so long as the ceremony was done 'agreeable to the rules and regulations of their respective churches.'"[44] Joseph Smith clearly believed he had the legal and religious authority to perform the wedding. His wording at the ceremony largely matched the instructions given in the 1835 version of the Doctrine and Covenants.

> First, the officiator was instructed to make such comments "as he shall be directed by the holy Spirit" and ascertain whether there were legal impediments to the marriage. If none, he addressed the couple: "You both mutually agree to be each other's companion, husband and wife, observing the legal rights belonging to this condition; that is, keeping yourselves wholly for each other, and from all others, during your lives." Once the bride and groom answered in the affirmative, the officiator was to "pronounce them 'husband and wife' in the name of the Lord Jesus Christ, and by virtue of the laws of the country." Then he would conclude: "May God add his blessings and keep you to fulfill your covenants from henceforth and forever. Amen."[45]

Joseph did make a curious claim. After saying that marriage was an institution of heaven, he stated "that it was necessary it should be solemnized by the authority of the everlasting Priesthood."[46] This wasn't an attempt to say civil marriages wouldn't be recognized in the Church but rather that, in its proper order, marriage should be officiated by the authority of the priesthood—a precursor to the concept that eternal marriages would require priesthood keys and authority to solemnize them. By 1837 Joseph had officiated at nineteen weddings, largely following the pattern he used in the Bailey-Knight wedding.[47]

It appears that Joseph began to preach about the possibility of eternal marriage to his close friends at least by 1835. In Kirtland he seems to have begun teaching this doctrine to a select few. In May 1835 William W. Phelps and his son Waterman were called to Kirtland, where they made their home with Joseph Smith and helped a committee compile the Doctrine and Covenants. Phelps wrote a letter to his wife, Sally, explaining that they could be married for eternity: "A new idea, Sally, if you and I continue faithful to the end, we are certain to be one in the Lord throughout eternity; this is one of the most glorious consolations we can have in the flesh."[48] We presume that William Phelps got this idea from Joseph because others more explicitly claimed to have received this doctrine through Joseph before he taught the revealed truths that would later become Doctrine and Covenants 131 and 132. Four years after W. W. Phelps made his claim, Parley P. Pratt learned of the doctrine of the eternal family in Philadelphia from Joseph Smith:

> It was at this time [1839] that I received from him the first idea of eternal family organization, and the eternal union of the sexes. . . .
>
> It was from him that I learned that the wife of my bosom might be secured to me for time and all eternity; and that the refined sympathies and affections which endeared us to each other emanated from the fountain of divine eternal love. It was from him that I learned that we might cultivate these affections, and grow and increase in the same to all eternity; while the result of our endless union would be an offspring as numerous as the stars of heaven, or the sands of the sea shore.[49]

Though this statement was recorded in Parley P. Pratt's autobiography and thus was written several years after 1839, it is one of the earliest stated evidences that Joseph was actively teaching eternal marriage before 1840. At that point, Joseph does not seem to have indicated the necessity of husband-wife sealings, only the possibility of such sealings. From the documentary evidence, we cannot tell if that distinction became clear to Joseph much before he taught it explicitly at Ramus, Illinois.

On May 16, 1843, Joseph was enjoying an evening with Benjamin and Melissa Johnson, friends living in Ramus, when he invited them to be married "according to the law of the Lord." Benjamin thought Joseph was joking and refused unless his wife should court him again. Joseph explained that he was in earnest and sealed them "by the Holy Spirit of Promise."[50] Joseph explained that such persons will inherit "eternal glory, for [they are] sealed up by the power of the Priesthood, unto eternal life, having taken the step which is necessary for that purpose." He added, "Except a man and his wife enter into an everlasting covenant and be married for eternity, while in this probation; by the power and authority of the Holy Priesthood; they will cease to increase when they die, that is, that they will not have any children after the resurrection; but those who are married by the power and author-ity of the Priesthood in this life, and continue without committing the sin against the Holy Ghost, will continue to increase and have children in the celestial glory."[51] William Clayton recorded these teachings on this occasion in his journal, and they became the basis of Doctrine and Covenants 131. Clayton recorded Joseph's teaching that "in the celestial glory there are three heavens or degrees; and in order to obtain the highest, a man must enter this order of the priesthood" (Doctrine and Covenants 131:1–2).

This is perhaps the earliest recorded statement from the Prophet to the effect that the eternal sealings of husband and wife were not only possible but also salvific. Not only could spouses be sealed together for eternity as earlier statements make clear, such as those reviewed above from W. W. Phelps and Parley P. Pratt, but without such sealings, the eternal progress of the individual spouses would be limited and exaltation would be impossible. On May 28, 1843, the Prophet Joseph was sealed to Emma Smith for eternity in the room above their store at a meeting of the anointed quorum (a select group of leaders who had been endowed before the completion of the Nauvoo Temple).[52]

PLURAL MARRIAGE AND DYNASTIC SEALINGS

One challenge in understanding Joseph's teachings on marriage and family in eternity is that he and others often referred to both monogamous and plural marriages of eternal duration by the term *celestial marriage*. As a result, some have conflated the terms. Though not synonymous, it would be a mistake to think that the concepts of eternal marriage and plural marriage were unrelated.

Joseph Smith's translation of the Old Testament had introduced him to the concept of plural marriage, and people who knew him well said that he received a revelation in 1831 to begin practicing it.[53] Joseph initially hesitated, likely because it differed from traditional marriage norms and perhaps because he was familiar with the Book of Mormon's warning against its practice without divine sanction (see Genesis 16; compare Jacob 2:30). Joseph reported that a few years later an angel appeared with a drawn sword and told him to practice plural marriage.[54] The angel told him to keep the practice private until the Lord made it publicly known.[55] In the mid-1830s, Joseph proposed marriage to Fanny Alger, a young woman who lived with the Smiths.[56] With approval from her parents,[57] her uncle Levi Hancock performed the marriage.[58] Careful estimates suggest that Joseph Smith eventually was sealed to between thirty and forty women.[59] By the Nauvoo period at least, Church leaders "distinguished between sealings for time and eternity and sealings for eternity only. Sealings for time and eternity included commitments and relationships during this life, generally including the possibility of sexual relations. Eternity-only sealings indicated relationships in the next life alone."[60] In such sealings, romance was subordinated to being sealed in an eternal chain. Historian Kathleen Flake argues that "priestly order" dominated such relationships and that "it was a love subordinated to religious devotion and ordered by religious, not romantic, ideals."[61]

By looking at firsthand accounts of various participants, we begin to see how those early members viewed plural marriage as a process of creating a "dynastic" chain[62]—with individual sealings functioning like links to bind all the children of God to each other. Lucy Walker recorded a remarkable invitation in 1842 to enter into "celestial marriage" (a term at times used synonymously with plural marriage) in order to "prove an everlasting blessing to my father's house" and "form a chain that could never be broken."[63] Like other women, she resisted being sealed until she personally received a clear and powerful manifestation of divine sanction. She considered herself sealed to Joseph Smith for eternity,[64] without which she would be "single & alone" for eternity, being "outside of the heavenly structure."[65] A Gospel Topics essay offers a possible reason for such dynastic sealings: "These sealings may have provided a way to create an eternal bond or link between Joseph's family and other families within the Church. These ties extended both *vertically*, from parent to child, and *horizontally*, from one family to another."[66]

When the Prophet and scribes recorded what is now Doctrine and Covenants section 132 on July 12, 1843, they documented the necessity of eternal marriage for exaltation. This section contained information on both eternal marriage and plural marriage. Joseph prayed to know how God justified Abraham, Isaac, Jacob, Moses, David, and Solomon in having many wives.[67] Joseph further recorded that any marriages performed by secular authority "are not of force when they are dead" and stated that individuals not sealed by priesthood authority "cannot be enlarged, but remain separately and singly, without exaltation" (vv. 15, 17). This concept matched well with the same idea contained in the Bible (see Matthew 22:30)—that some marriages would not continue into the eternities. Joseph taught that priesthood authority could "seal" a man and woman as husband and wife so that after death they could "pass by the angels and the gods . . . to their exaltation and glory in all things, . . . which glory shall be a fulness and a continuation of the seeds forever" (Doctrine and Covenants 132:19; compare vv. 34–35).

When Joseph introduced the practice of plural marriage in the Church, it was limited to a select group of participants, and the practice was not made public. As noted in a Gospel Topics essay, "This principle was among the most challenging aspects of the Restoration—for Joseph personally and for other Church members. Plural marriage tested faith and provoked controversy and opposition. Few Latter-day Saints initially welcomed the restoration of a biblical practice entirely foreign to their sensibilities. But many later testified of powerful spiritual experiences that helped them overcome their hesitation and gave them courage to accept this practice."[68] The practice was discontinued under President Wilford Woodruff, as we discuss in a later section.

PROXY SEALINGS FOR ETERNITY

In 1843 the Prophet Joseph Smith began to extend the blessings of eternal marriage to beloved friends who were deceased. Robert Thompson, Joseph's personal secretary and coeditor of the *Times and Seasons*, had died of malaria at age thirty, leaving behind his wife, Mercy, and three-year-old daughter. One night in the spring of 1843, Mercy dreamed of her beloved Robert and heard her marriage vows being repeated. She was staying in the home of her sister Mary, who was married to Hyrum Smith. That same night Hyrum returned home and reported "a very remarkable Dream" of his deceased wife, Jerusha, and two deceased children. He found a note left from Joseph Smith asking him to visit his house. Joseph told Hyrum and Mary that "marriages contracted for time only lasted for time and were no more one until a new contract was made, for All Eternity."[69]

On May 29, the morning after Joseph and Emma were sealed, Brigham and Mary Ann Young, Willard and Jennetta Richards, Hyrum and Mary Fielding Smith, and Mercy Thompson gathered above the store to be sealed. Hyrum wondered what would happen to his first wife, Jerusha, who had died six years previous. Joseph said, "You can have her sealed to you upon the same principle as you can be baptized for the dead," adding that both wives could be sealed for eternity. Mary served as proxy for Jerusha and chose to be sealed as well, saying, "I love you and I do not want to be separated from you."[70]

Joseph told Mary's sister, Mercy, that she could be sealed to Robert with her brother-in-law Hyrum acting as proxy for the deceased. Mercy was thrilled, and she wrote, "Some may think I could envy Queen Victoria in some of her glory," she recorded. "Not while my name stands first on this list in this Dispensation of women sealed to a Dead Husband through divine revelation."[71] Thus began the practice of living proxies being sealed for deceased persons, a major development in ordinance work.

Months later, after Joseph related a visitation from the deceased Robert Thompson, Mercy chose to be married for time as a plural wife to Hyrum Smith on August 11, though she retained her last name and chose to be reunited with Robert in the Resurrection.[72]

ADOPTION

By the end of his life, Joseph understood the necessity both of binding all of God's children together in a great chain and also for husbands and wives to be eternally married to qualify for exaltation. Yet the precise way this was to happen was not fully understood in the Church. Such ordinances in Joseph Smith's day were much more fluid and spontaneous than our present sealings. As Todd Compton notes, "Marriage, sealing, and adoption, in fact, were nearly interchangeable concepts."[73] For example, on October 16, 1843, the Prophet sealed Dr. John M. Bernhisel to his sisters, aunts, cousins, and friends.[74] After the death of Joseph Smith, Dr. Bernhisel also chose to be sealed to Joseph in a patrilineal way through a practice called adoption that Brigham Young initiated.[75] On February 16, 1847, Brigham Young taught members to be sealed in a chain of priesthood authority extending back to the Father. Or, as Jonathan Stapley asserts, "The first generation of Saints were to be the nucleus from which the network of heaven—the links in the chain of the priesthood—was to extend."[76] At the time, Brigham Young taught that members should be sealed only to believers and not to family members who had not yet accepted the gospel, saying, "Were we to wait to redeem our dead relatives before we Could link the Chain of the Priesthood we would never accomplish it."[77] Many members chose to be sealed to Joseph Smith, Brigham Young, or other leaders in the hopes that "this action would secure the salvation of their families in a worthy priesthood lineage if their own progenitors did not accept the gospel in the next life."[78]

Though these practices would seem foreign in our day, Joseph and the rest of the Church leadership were learning how exactly to implement the revelations Joseph had received. Doctrine and Covenants 131 was clear on the need for husbands and wives to be sealed; however, how to seal all of God's children together into a "great chain" was less clear. The words of the

Prophet indicated a need for all of God's children to be sealed together. But one question centered on whether everyone needed to be sealed to someone who was already in the covenant. Many leaders believed so. This led to the practice of sealing hundreds of early members to leaders such as Joseph or Brigham or Wilford, similar to what John Bernhisel did. In fact, it was Church policy for the first several decades after Joseph's death that a person could not be sealed to his or her parents unless they were in the covenant.[79] As historian Gordon Irving wrote:

> Church policy directed that children of faithful members of the Church not "born in the covenant" be *sealed* to their natural parents, whether any or all of those involved were living or not. If natural parents had not been baptized Mormons during life or had apostatized from the Church, their children were to be *adopted* to someone else. The sealing of a person to a dead non-Mormon was seen as being risky since the departed parent might not accept the gospel in the spirit world. Such uncertainty about one's position in the next life was unacceptable, especially to converts whose parents had been strongly opposed to Mormonism during life.
>
> The same ruling applied in part to sealings of husbands and wives. If both were dead, the sealing could be performed whether the two had been members of the Church in life or not. But if the widow of a non-Mormon came to Utah, as so many did, she was to be sealed to some good brother in the church rather than to her late husband.[80]

This policy led to complex hierarchies depending on the order in which one was sealed to a Church leader, sometimes leading to tension between members as they claimed seniority and privileges based on the sequence of sealing and seniority of the leader. "Within a year of finishing the temple work in Nauvoo, Brigham Young told his fellow travelers, 'This Principle [adoption] I am aware is not clearly understood by many of the Elders in this Church at the present time as it will Hereafter be: And I confess that I have had [only] a smattering of those things[;] but when it is necessary I will attain to more knowledge on the subject & consequently will be enabled to teach & practice more.'"[81]

In 1845, while clarifying that baptism for the dead should be performed by proxies of the same gender, President Young said, "The Lord has led this people all the while in this way, by giving them here a little and there a little, thus he increases their wisdom, and he that receives a little and is thankful for that shall receive more." He concluded, "Joseph in his lifetime did not receive every thing connected with the doctrine of redemption, but he has left the key with those who understand how to obtain and teach to this great people all that is necessary for their salvation and exaltation in the celestial kingdom of our God."[82]

President Young continued to see the importance of adoptions and sealings even as he grappled to understand how to implement them. His manuscript history reports a dream involving Joseph Smith in mid-February 1847. Of all the things Brigham Young wanted clarified, he asked about "the doctrine of adoption and sealing doctrine." He said, "The Brethren have a great anxiety to understand the law of adoption, or sealing principles; and if you have a word of council for me, I should be glad to receive it." In the dream, Joseph Smith said: "Tell the Brethren if they will follow the Spirit of the Lord they will go right. Be sure to tell the people to keep the Spirit of the Lord; and if they will, they will find themselves just as they were organized by our Father in Heaven before they came into the world. Our Father in Heaven organized the human family, but they are all disorganized in great confusion." President Young then saw "how it must be joined together [into a] perfect chain from Father Adam to his latest posterity."[83]

CHANGES UNDER PRESIDENT WOODRUFF

Church leaders taught that marriage and posterity were the highest blessings of eternity; to provide those blessings to deceased family members, President Brigham Young instructed Wilford Woodruff to seal "unmarried female ancestors as wives to living descendants."[84] Consequently, President Woodruff was sealed to about three hundred single women from his father's and mother's households. This practice continued alongside plural marriage for the living, which grew increasingly difficult because of federal prosecution such as the Morrill Anti-Bigamy Act (1862), the Edmunds Act (1882), and the Edmunds–Tucker Act (1887) that disincorporated the Church and imposed fines on members practicing plural marriage.

After years of federal pressure and prayers for divine guidance, President Woodruff's "manifesto" announced a revelation in 1890 discontinuing the practice of plural marriage (see Official Declaration 1). Many members struggled to accept the transition from a cherished doctrine; in the process, excommunications, additional manifestos, and apostate offshoot churches resulted.

In the April 1894 general conference, President Woodruff announced a revelation discontinuing adoption to prominent Church leaders. Instead, family members were to be sealed:

> You have acted up to all the light and knowledge that you have had; but you have now something more to do than what you have done. We have not fully carried out those principles in fulfillment of the revelations of God to us, in sealing the hearts of the fathers to the children and the children to the fathers. I have not felt satisfied, neither did President Taylor, neither has any man since the Prophet Joseph who has attended to the ordinance of adoption in the temples of our God. We have felt that there was more to be revealed upon this subject than we had received. . . . Let every man be adopted to his father. . . . That is the will of God; and then you will do exactly what God said when He declared He would send Elijah the prophet in the last days. . . . We want the Latter-day Saints from this time to trace their genealogies as far as they can, and to be sealed to their fathers and mothers. Have children sealed to their parents, and run this chain through as far as you can get it.[85]

Thus, he established the current practice of sealing children to parents, running the chain back through the generations. The Genealogical Society was organized that same year to help the Saints do this. A recent Gospel Topics essay summarizes our current understanding of this doctrine: "Today such eternal bonds are achieved through the temple marriages of individuals who are also sealed to their own birth families, in this way linking families together."[86]

CONCLUSION

Over many decades, Joseph Smith and his prophetic successors learned—and taught—line upon line about Malachi's prophecy, Elijah's mission, temple worship, and sealings. This article traced how Joseph Smith developed doctrines on the eternal family in the midst of tragedies that motivated deep and searching questions. Those questions often revolved around the question of salvation for those who had passed away and the nature of our relationships with our deceased family members. The prophetic process of studying things out in one's mind and asking for revelatory clarification (see Doctrine and Covenants 9:8–9) is clearly demonstrated in Joseph Smith's "line upon line" developmental understanding of the nature of familial relationships in eternity. By the time of Joseph's death, he had shared the necessity for a man and a woman to be sealed for eternity to obtain exaltation and for the human family to be sealed together as children of God—bound through a covenantal chain. This article also demonstrated how the authority to seal husbands and wives for eternity was used to perform plural marriage for the living and adoptions to priesthood leaders—practices discontinued in the 1890s. Since then, prophets have continued to refine the doctrine of the eternal family line upon line.[87]

R. Devan Jensen is executive editor at the Religious Studies Center at Brigham Young University.

Michael A. Goodman is an associate professor of Church history and doctrine at Brigham Young University.

Barbara Morgan Gardner is an associate professor of Church history and doctrine at Brigham Young University.

R. Devan Jensen, Michael A. Goodman, and Barbara Morgan Gardner, "'Line upon Line': Joseph Smith's Growing Understanding of the Eternal Family," *Religious Educator* 20, no. 1 (2019): 34–59.

NOTES

Special thanks to Richard E. Bennett, Richard O. Cowan, Gerrit Dirkmaat, and Tyler A. Balli for formative review and research help.

1. *Merriam-Webster's Collegiate Dictionary*, 11th ed., s.v. "presentism."
2. Primary documents include the Book of Mormon, the Doctrine and Covenants, Joseph Smith's other revelations and sermons, and Lucy Mack Smith's history as documented by the Joseph Smith Papers Project (online and print volumes). Other primary documents include Scott G. Kenney, ed., *Wilford Woodruff's Journal, 1833–1898, Typescript*, 9 vols. (Midvale, UT: Signature Books, 1983–84), and later accounts of plural marriage by Joseph Smith's contemporaries. Plural marriage broke with societal norms and was thus rarely documented during Joseph Smith's lifetime. Major secondary sources include Samuel Morris Brown, *In Heaven as It Is on Earth: Joseph Smith and the Early Mormon Conquest of Death* (New York: Oxford, 2012); Samuel Brown, "Early Mormon Adoption Theology and the Mechanics of Salvation," *Journal of Mormon History* 37, no. 2 (Summer 2011): 1–52; Richard Lyman Bushman, *Joseph Smith: Rough Stone Rolling* (New York: Alfred A. Knopf, 2005); Todd Compton, *In Sacred Loneliness: The Plural Wives of Joseph Smith* (Salt Lake City: Signature Books, 1997); Amy Easton-Flake, "Infant Salvation: Book of Mormon Theology in a Nineteenth-Century Context," in *Abinadi: He Came Among Them in Disguise*, ed. Shon D. Hopkin (Provo, UT: Religious Studies Center, Brigham Young University; Salt Lake City: Deseret Book, 2018), 233–62; Kathleen Flake, "The Development of Early Mormon Marriage Rites," *Journal of Mormon History* 41, no. 1 (2015): 77–102; Kathleen Flake, *The Emotional and Priestly Logic of Plural Marriage*, Leonard J. Arrington Mormon History Lecture Series, no. 15 (Logan: Utah State University Press, 2010); Brian C. Hales, *Joseph Smith's Polygamy*, 3 vols. (Salt Lake City: Greg Kofford Books, 2013); Gordon Irving, "The Law

of Adoption: One Phase in the Development of Mormon Concept of Salvation, 1830–1900," *BYU Studies* 14 (Spring 1974): 291–314; Jonathan Stapley, "Adoptive Sealing Ritual in Mormonism," *Journal of Mormon History* 37, no. 2 (Summer 2011): 53–102; Jonathan Stapley, *The Power of Godliness: Mormon Liturgy and Cosmology* (New York: Oxford University Press, 2018); and Ryan G. Tobler, "'Saviors on Mount Zion': Mormon Sacramentalism, Mortality, and the Baptism for the Dead," *Journal of Mormon History* 39, no. 4 (2013): 182–238. Other important secondary sources, including the Gospel Topics essays, provide useful context and explanation.

3. Joseph Smith, History, 1838–1856, vol. A-1 [11 June 1839–24 August 1843], http://josephsmithpapers.org/.

4. Joseph Smith, History, 1838–1856, vol. A-1.

5. Revelation, 9 December 1830 [D&C 36], http://josephsmithpapers.org/. Later, the Book of Mormon translation quoted Malachi 3 in its entirety, underscoring its importance.

6. Like many other Old Testament prophecies, multiple applications are possible. One is "John the Baptist, who prepared the way for the Savior's first appearance (see Matt. 11:10) and who also was the first angelic messenger to bestow priesthood keys and authority in our dispensation, preparing the way for the Savior's Second Coming (see D&C 13)." Another is to "a latter-day messenger who was called to prepare the way so that 'the Lord, whom ye seek, shall suddenly come to his temple' (Mal. 3:1)." This might refer to Joseph Smith himself. W. Jeffrey Marsh, "Training from the Old Testament: Moroni's Lessons for a Prophet," *Ensign*, August 1998, 12.

7. Noah Webster, *An American Dictionary of the English Language* (1828), notes the etymology of *turn* as "Latin *turnus*; *torniare*, to turn; *tornare*, to return; *torneare*, *tornire*, to turn, to fence round," http://webstersdictionary1828.com/Dictionary /turn.

8. Brown, *In Heaven as It Is on Earth*, 19. Brown seems to be using *premature death* to mean death that came earlier than expected.

9. "The Testimony of William Smith," *Millennial Star*, February 26, 1894, 133; see also Lucy Mack Smith, *Joseph Smith and His Progenitors* (Independence, MO: Herald Publishing House, 1969), 101.

10. See Casey Paul Griffiths, "Universalism and the Revelations of Joseph Smith," in *The Doctrine and Covenants, Revelations in Context*, ed. Andrew H. Hedges, J. Spencer Fluhman, and Alonzo L. Gaskill (Provo, UT: Religious Studies Center; Salt Lake City: Deseret Book, 2008), 168–87.

11. See Brown, *In Heaven as It Is on Earth*, 50.

12. Lucy Mack Smith, History, 1845, 131, http://josephsmithpapers.org/.

13. Lucy Mack Smith, History, 1845, 131.

14. Joseph Smith, History, circa Summer 1832, http://josephsmithpapers.org/.

15. For the timing of the translation, see Michael Hubbard MacKay and Gerrit J. Dirkmaat, *From Darkness unto Light: Joseph Smith's Translation and Publication of the Book of Mormon* (Provo, UT: Religious Studies Center; Salt Lake City: Deseret Book, 2015), 124.

16. The Book of Mormon passages are discussed in historical context in Easton-Flake, "Infant Salvation," 233–62.

17. "Isaac Morley Farm, Kirtland, Ohio," https://history.lds.org/article/historic-sites/ohio /isaac-morley-farm-kirtland.

18. For context, see J. B. Haws, "Joseph Smith, Emanuel Swedenborg, and Section 76: Importance of the Bible in Latter-day Revelation," in *Revelations in Context*, 142–67; and Robert J. Woodford, "Joseph Smith and 'The Vision,'" in *Joseph Smith, the Prophet and Seer*, ed. Richard Neitzel Holzapfel and Kent P. Jackson (Provo, UT: Religious Studies Center; Salt Lake City: Deseret Book, 2010), 101–26.

19. See Joseph Smith, History, 1838–56, volume A-1, 205–7; see also Mark L. Staker, *Hearken, O Ye People: The Historical Setting of Joseph Smith's Ohio Revelations* (Salt Lake City: Greg Kofford Books, 2009), 349–52.

20. See Linda King Newell and Valeen Tippetts Avery, *Mormon Enigma: Emma Hale Smith* (Urbana: University of Illinois Press, 1994), 43.

21. See *The Joseph Smith Papers, Documents*, 2:198.

22. See Dean C. Jessee, "Joseph Knight's Recollection of Early Mormon History," *BYU Studies* 17, no. 1 (Autumn 1976): 7.

23. Stapley, *Power of Godliness*, 36–37.

24. See Stephen D. Ricks, "The Appearance of Elijah and Moses in the Kirtland Temple and the Jewish Passover," *BYU Studies Quarterly* 23, no. 4 (1983): 1–4.

25. See Trever R. Anderson, "Doctrine and Covenants Section 110: From Vision to Canonization" (master's thesis, Brigham Young University, 2010), 3–4.

26. For context, see Kenneth L. Alford, "I Will Send You Elijah the Prophet," in *You Shall Have My Word: Exploring the Text of the Doctrine and Covenants*, ed. Scott C. Esplin, Richard O. Cowan, and Rachel Cope (Provo, UT: Religious Studies Center; Salt Lake City: Deseret Book, 2012), 34–49.

27. Joseph Smith, Journal, 1835–1836, http://josephsmithpapers.org/.

28. See Joseph Smith, History, vol. A-1, 5–6; Robert B. Thompson, sermon notes, October 5, 1840, Joseph Smith Collection, Church History Library, The Church of Jesus Christ of Latter-day Saints, Salt Lake City (hereafter CHL); Martha Jane Knowlton Coray, Notebook, ca. 1850, August 13, 1843, CHL; Joseph Smith, Journal, August 27, 1842, Joseph Smith Collection, CHL; and Woodruff, Journal, March 10, 1844, as cited in *The Joseph Smith Papers, Journals*, 1:222n478.

29. Joseph Smith, in *Wilford Woodruff's Journal*, 2:341. In Doctrine and Covenants 128:18, Smith used the phrase "welding link of some kind or other between the fathers and the children."

30. Tobler, "'Saviors on Mount Zion,'" 184.

31. Baptism "began simply, as a reinterpretation of the Protestant image of a believer's adoption to Christ." Brown, In *Heaven as It Is on Earth*, 208. For example, in 1837 Elder Parley P. Pratt explained: "Both Jew and Gentile were included in sin and unbelief; and none could be citizens without the law of adoption. All that believed on the name of the King had power to be adopted, but there was but one invariable rule or plan by which they were adopted; and all that undertook to claim citizenship, in any other way whatever, were counted thieves and robbers, and could never obtain the seal of adoption. This rule was laid down in the Savior's teaching to Nicodemus, namely: 'Except a man be born of water (that is, baptized in water), and of the Spirit (that is, baptized with the Spirit), he cannot enter into the kingdom of God.'" Parley P. Pratt, *A Voice of Warning* (New York: Sandford, 1837), 34.

32. Simon Baker, as cited in *The Words of Joseph Smith*, ed. Andrew F. Ehat and Lyndon W. Cook (Provo, UT: Religious Studies Center, 1980), 49.

33. Jane Neymon and Vienna Jaques, Statement, November 29, 1854, Historian's Office, JS History Documents, ca. 1839–1880, CHL. See also Alexander L. Baugh, "'For This Ordinance Belongeth to My House': The Practice of Baptism for the

Dead Outside the Nauvoo Temple," *Mormon Historical Studies* 3, no. 1 (Spring 2002): 48.

34. See Susan Easton Black, "'A Voice of Gladness for the Living and the Dead' (D&C 128:19)," *Religious Educator* 3, no. 2 (2002): 143–44.

35. Lucy Mack Smith, History, 1845, 345.

36. See M. Guy Bishop, "'What Has Happened to Our Fathers?': Baptism for the Dead at Nauvoo," *Dialogue: A Journal of Mormon Thought* 23, no. 2 (Summer 1990): 85–97.

37. Joseph Smith, History, 1838–1856, vol. C-1 [24 February 1845–3 July 1845], http://josephsmithpapers.org/.

38. Joseph Smith, Discourse, Nauvoo, Hancock Co., IL, August 13, 1843; in William Clayton, Journal, 13 August 1843, pp. [86]–[87], CHL; also found at http://josephsmithpapers.org/.

39. Ehat and Cook, *Words of Joseph Smith*, 244, August 27, 1843.

40. Joseph Smith, History, 1838–1856, volume E-1 [1 July 1843–30 April 1844], http://josephsmithpapers.org/.

41. Joseph Smith, Discourse, Nauvoo, Hancock Co., IL, January 21, 1844, in Wilford Woodruff, Journal, p. [182], CHL; also found at http://josephsmithpapers.org/.

42. For a detailed study of early Latter-day Saint marriage practices, see Kathleen Flake, "The Development of Early Mormon Marriage Rites," *Journal of Mormon History* 41, no. 1 (2015): 77–102.

43. See M. Scott Bradshaw, "Joseph Smith's Performance of Marriages in Ohio," *BYU Studies* 39, no. 4 (2000): 23–24.

44. Ohio's "Act Regulating Marriages" (1824), as quoted in William G. Hartley, "Newel and Lydia Bailey Knight's Kirtland Love Story and Historic Wedding," *BYU Studies* 39 no. 4 (2000): 18.

45. Flake, "Development of Early Mormon Marriage Rites, 1831–1853," 80n7.

46. M. Guy Bishop, "Eternal Marriage in Early Mormon Marital Beliefs," *The Historian* 53, no. 1 (Autumn 1990): 77–87.

47. Bradford, "Joseph Smith's Performance of Marriages in Ohio," 23–69.

48. W. W. Phelps to Sally Phelps, May 26, 1835, in Journal History of the Church, CHL.

49. Parley P. Pratt, *Autobiography of Parley P. Pratt*, ed. Parley P. Pratt Jr. (Salt Lake City: Deseret Book, 1985), 259–60.

50. Benjamin F. Johnson, *My Life's Review: The Autobiography of Benjamin F. Johnson*, ed. Lyndon W. Cook and Kevin V. Harker (Provo, UT: Grandin Book, 1997), 85–86.

51. History, 1838–1856, volume D-1 [1 August 1842–1 July 1843], http//josephsmith papers.org/.

52. Joseph Smith, Journal, 28 May 1843, *in The Joseph Smith Papers, Journals*, 3:25; see also 25n88; see also "Anointed Quorum ('Holy Order')," Church History Topics, https://lds.org/languages/eng/content/history/topics/anointed-quorum.

53. See Andrew Jenson, "Plural Marriage," *Historical Record*, May 1887, 232–33; and "Report of Elders Orson Pratt and Joseph F. Smith," *Millennial Star*, 16 December 1878, 788. For context, see Danel W. Bachman, "New Light on an Old Hypothesis: The Ohio Origins of the Revelation on Eternal Marriage," *Journal of Mormon History* 5 (1978): 19–32.

54. For context, see historical introduction to letter from Thomas B. Marsh, 15 February 1838, in *The Joseph Smith Papers, Documents*, 6:12. See also Brian C. Hales,

"Encouraging Joseph Smith to Practice Plural Marriage: The Accounts of the Angel with a Drawn Sword," *Mormon Historical Studies* 11, no. 2 (Fall 2010): 69–70.

55. See Lorenzo Snow, Affidavit, August 26, 1869; Joseph F. Smith, Affidavits about Celestial Marriage, CHL. Because plural marriage was such a controversial practice, much of the material was not recorded until years later.

56. See "Fanny Alger," Church History Topics, https://www.lds.org/languages/eng /content/history/topics/fanny-alger.

57. For further details, see Compton, *In Sacred Loneliness*, 32–33.

58. See Mosiah Hancock, Narrative, in Levi Hancock, Autobiography, circa 1896, 63, CHL.

59. See Hales, *Joseph Smith's Polygamy*, 2:272–73.

60. "Plural Marriage in Kirtland and Nauvoo," https://lds.org/topics/plural-marriage -in-kirtland-and-nauvoo.

61. Flake, *Emotional and Priestly Logic of Plural Marriage*, 15.

62. Bushman, *Joseph Smith: Rough Stone Rolling*, 491; and Compton, *In Sacred Loneliness*, 12, 347, 497; see also Brown, "Early Mormon Adoption Theology," 32–35; Stapley, "Adoptive Sealing Ritual in Mormonism," 53–102; and Brown, *In Heaven as It Is on Earth*, ch. 8.

63. Lucy Walker, as quoted in Compton, *In Sacred Loneliness*, 463.

64. Compton, *In Sacred Loneliness*, 465.

65. Stapley, *Power of Godliness*, 37.

66. "Plural Marriage in Kirtland and Nauvoo."

67. See Revelation, 12 July 1843 [D&C 132], http://josephsmithpapers.org/.

68. "Joseph Smith and Plural Marriage," https://lds.org/study/history/topics/joseph -smith-and-plural-marriage.

69. Mercy Rachel Fielding Thompson, Reminiscence, in *In Their Own Words: Women and the Story of Nauvoo*, ed. Carol Cornwall Madsen (Salt Lake City: Deseret Book, 1994), 195; spelling modernized.

70. Joseph Smith, History, 1838–1856, volume E-1 [1 July 1843–30 April 1844], http://josephsmithpapers.org/.

71. Thompson, Reminiscence, 195.

72. See Jed Woodworth, "Mercy Thompson and the Revelation on Marriage," in *Revelations in Context*, 285.

73. Todd Compton, "A Trajectory of Plurality: An Overview of Joseph Smith's Thirty-three Plural Wives," *Dialogue: A Journal of Mormon Thought* 29, no. 2 (Summer 1996): 14.

74. Specifically, Joseph Smith's office journal records Dr. Bernhisel's sealing on October 16, 1843, to "Maria Bernhisel, sister; Brother Samuel's wife, Catherine Kremer; Mary Shatto, (Aunt); Madalena Lupferd, (distant relative); Catherine Bernhisel, Aunt; Hannah Bower, Aunt; Elizabeth Sheively, Aunt; Hannah Bower, cousin; Maria Lawrence, (intimate friend); Sarah Crosby, intimate friend, [deceased] . . . ; Mary Ann Bloom, cousin." See Brown, "Early Mormon Adoption Theology," 4.

75. See Brown, *In Heaven as It Is on Earth*, 203.

76. Stapley, *Power of Godliness*, 41.

77. Brigham Young, as cited in Kenney, *Wilford Woodruff's Journal*, 3:134–37.

78. James B. Allen, Jessie L. Embry, and Kahlile B. Mehr, *Hearts Turned to the Fathers: A History of the Genealogical Society of Utah, 1894–1994* (Provo, UT: BYU Studies, 1995), 42.

79. Stapley, "Adoptive Sealing Ritual in Mormonism," 53–54.

80. Irving, "Law of Adoption," 306.
81. Kenney, *Wilford Woodruff's Journal*, 3:134.
82. Brigham Young, "Speech," *Times and Seasons*, 1 July 1845, 955.
83. Manuscript History of Brigham Young, 1847–1850, February 23, 1847, 35; see also "Pres. B. Young's Dream Feb. 17, 1847," Brigham Young Office Files, CR 1234/1, box 75 (reel 87), folder 34, CHL.
84. Stapley, *Power of Godliness*, 42.
85. Wilford Woodruff, April 8, 1894, in Brian H. Stuy, ed., *Collected Discourses*, 5 vols. (Sandy, UT: B. H. S. Publishing, 1987), 4:72.
86. "Plural Marriage in Kirtland and Nauvoo."
87. Such refinements included formation of the Genealogical Society of Utah, the Family History Library, the Family History Department, the Granite Mountain Records Vault, and FamilySearch.

Chapter Eighteen

Eternal Marriage and Plural Marriage

ANDREW H. HEDGES

Of all that Joseph Smith taught and did over the course of his prophetic ministry, the doctrines and practices he revealed regarding marriage have arguably been the most controversial. The bold declaration that through the authority of the restored priesthood men and women can be married for time and eternity—indeed, *must* be married for time and eternity if they are to receive the blessings of eternal life—challenged fundamental, mainstream Christian beliefs and doctrines about the nature and importance of marriage in the next life and seemed to fly in the face of the Savior's own teachings on the subject (see Matthew 22:30; Luke 20:34–35). Even more problematic than "eternal marriage" was "plural marriage," or the doctrine that through the authority of that same priesthood one man could be married to more than one woman at the same time. In nineteenth-century America, marriage between one man and one woman was considered a pillar of Western society, and any deviation from the norm threatened to destroy the foundation of civilization itself. Monogamy—or at least fidelity to a single partner at a time—is still considered the norm in much of the world, leading to ongoing questions about Joseph Smith's practice of plural marriage that can be difficult to answer today, even for faithful members of the Church.

This essay reviews Joseph Smith's revelations, teachings, and practices regarding eternal marriage and plural marriage and addresses significant issues that these doctrines and practices—especially those regarding plural marriage—might raise for members of the Church today. Topics include the dating of Doctrine and Covenants 132, the doctrine and practice of eternal marriage during Joseph Smith's lifetime, the justification and possible reasons for plural marriage, the difficulties of understanding how it was first practiced, and questions about Joseph Smith's plural wives (their identification, ages, and marital status when they were sealed to Joseph as well as the nature of their relationships with him). The essay closes with a review of the end of plural marriage in this dispensation and a brief discussion of what the doctrine of plural marriage might mean, and not mean, for Latter-day Saints today.

DOCTRINE AND COVENANTS 132

On July 12, 1843, Joseph Smith dictated a revelation to William Clayton explaining the principles of eternal and plural marriage.[1] According to the revelation itself—now canonized as Doctrine and Covenants 132—its origin lay in Joseph's inquiries of the Lord about how Abraham, Isaac, Jacob, and other Old Testament prophets and leaders were justified "as touching the principle and doctrine of their having many wives and concubines" (v. 1). Other sources indicate that Joseph had learned at least the outlines of the revelation much earlier[2] and that he had been teaching and practicing its principles for some time. July 12, 1843, then, is best understood as the day the revelation was first recorded, and not as the day it was first received.[3]

ETERNAL MARRIAGE

Regarding eternal marriage, the revelation teaches that a husband and wife who have been "sealed" during their lives by someone holding the appropriate priesthood authority will, after being resurrected, "pass by the angels, and the gods, which are set there, to their exaltation and glory in all things, . . . which glory shall be a fulness and a continuation of the seeds forever and ever" (Doctrine and Covenants 132:19). Marriages that have not been contracted under this authority, on the other hand, will not be of force after death, and the men and women involved will "remain separately and singly, without exaltation . . . to all eternity" (see vv. 15–17).

According to William Clayton, Joseph had explained and clarified this doctrine while on a visit to Benjamin and Melissa Johnson in Ramus, Illinois, two months earlier. "He [Joseph] said that except a man and his wife enter into an everlasting covenant and be married for eternity while in this probation by the power and authority of the Holy priesthood," Clayton recorded, "they will cease to increase when they die (i.e. they will not have any children in the resurrection[)], but those who are married by the power & authority of the priesthood in this life & continue without committing the sin against the Holy Ghost will continue to increase & have children in the celestial glory."[4] Joseph and his wife Emma Hale Smith, who had been married by the laws of New York State in January 1827, were evidently sealed for eternity on May 28, 1843, as were several of Joseph's close associates in Nauvoo the following day.[5]

PLURAL MARRIAGE: JUSTIFICATION AND REASONS

Just as he had taught and implemented the doctrine of eternal marriage before recording Doctrine and Covenants 132 in July 1843, Joseph was also teaching and practicing plural marriage by that time. Both the Book of Mormon and section 132 provide reasons for introducing this practice in this dispensation, as well as the doctrine and principles behind its proper implementation. According to section 132, for example, the practice was an integral part of the Lord's plan to "restore all things" in this dispensation (vv. 40, 45). Further, the Book of Mormon prophet Jacob taught that monogamy was God's rule generally but that on occasion, when God would "raise up seed" unto himself, he would command his people to practice some form of plural marriage (Jacob 2:30). Doctrine and Covenants 132, accordingly, teaches that Old Testament patriarchs, prophets, and leaders like Abraham, Jacob, Moses, and David had been commanded of God to take multiple wives and that they were under no condemnation for obeying that commandment (see vv. 35–38). At the same time, the revelation teaches, those who take a plural wife on their own, without God's consent—as David did in the case of Bathsheba—come under severe condemnation (see 2 Samuel 11–12; Doctrine and Covenants 132:38–39). As section 132 and other sources make clear, Joseph Smith, like ancient prophets before him, had received the commandment and authority from God to institute plural marriage among the faithful Saints of his time (see vv. 30–40, 45, 48, 52, 61–62).[6]

Upon its restoration in this dispensation, plural marriage was tightly controlled by Joseph Smith. And after his death, those who entered into these relationships also were required to have the approval of Church leaders, who sought to ensure that the couples were worthy and capable of living in such relationships. As a result, during the time that plural marriage was practiced, many children were born and raised in homes headed by the most faithful and committed Latter-day Saint men and women—an effect that might at least partly explain what the Lord meant when he said that plural marriage was a way to "raise up seed" unto himself. One might even argue that the practice helped lay a stronger foundation of faithful members early in the Church's history than would have been possible otherwise, as it allowed virtually every man and woman the opportunity for marriage, it reduced financial inequality as faithful women from poorer backgrounds were able to marry faithful, capable men of means, it helped unite converts from a variety of countries and cultures by increasing the frequency of ethnic intermarriages, and it fostered a sense of "group identification" and uniqueness among Latter-day Saints.[7] The fact that many plural marriages were also eternal marriages, however, suggests that the reasons for instituting plural marriage, as well as its effects, extended beyond the benefits it provided to nineteenth-century Mormon society.

SOURCES FOR UNDERSTANDING JOSEPH SMITH'S PLURAL MARRIAGES

While a variety of excellent sources exist for understanding how plural marriage worked in early Utah, the same is not true for Joseph Smith's lifetime. As editors for the Joseph Smith Papers point out, "most of the information on the practice during this period comes either from later affidavits and reminiscences or from reports of disaffected members of the church at the time—none of which, for a variety reasons, can be considered entirely reliable historical sources for delineating how plural marriage was understood and practiced by those involved at the time."[8] The accuracy of the first type of record—that is, records generated through memory—is compromised by "the selective and social nature of human memory and its susceptibility to being influenced by more recent events," while the second type—records generated by disaffected members of the Church—is subject to being colored by the resentment, fear, and anger the writer may have felt toward the Church.[9] In addition, many of the sources on plural marriage during the Joseph Smith era of Church history are second- or thirdhand accounts, rather than accounts by the people who were actually involved in the relationship. Those accounts created by people close to the actual participants—family members, for example—are probably more accurate than those created by people who knew the participants less well or not at all, but all such accounts must be used with more caution than those created by the men and women who were actually involved.

JOSEPH SMITH'S PLURAL WIVES

For these reasons, then, historians today know less about early plural marriages—including Joseph Smith's—than some might think. For example, we are unable to say when, precisely, Joseph began practicing plural marriage or to identify with certainty his first plural wife. Some sources suggest that he married Fanny Alger in Kirtland during the mid-1830s, but the evidence is far from conclusive.[10] Better sources exist for possible plural marriages in Nauvoo, beginning with Louisa Beman in April 1841.[11] Similarly, historians are unable to identify with certainty each of the women Joseph married as plural wives, or even how many plural wives Joseph married during his lifetime. Approximately twenty women have left records claiming to have been one of his plural wives, with the amount and quality of corroborating records in each case varying significantly. Family members and close friends of another ten or so women have identified them as plural wives, although no records making that claim generated by these women themselves have been located. More distant sources have identified several other women as his plural wives as well. Given the limitations of these sources (as described above), one might reasonably conclude that approximately thirty women had been married to Joseph Smith as plural wives by the time of his death in June 1844.

JOSEPH SMITH'S RELATIONSHIP WITH HIS PLURAL WIVES

Just as the available sources preclude positive identification of all of Joseph Smith's plural wives, they also do not provide a thorough understanding of the nature of his relationship with those wives. The fact that William Clayton's plural wife Margaret Moon gave birth to a son ten months after her marriage to Clayton indicates that at least some plural marriages contracted during the Nauvoo era included conjugal relations;[12] and decades later, in

1892, two well-documented plural wives of Joseph Smith, Malissa Lott and Emily Partridge, testified under oath that their marriages to Smith included such relations. Later accounts, both first- and secondhand, suggest that the same held for at least some of his other wives as well.[13] At the same time, however, some of Joseph Smith's plural marriages probably did not include marital relations;[14] and "the fact that a number of women were sealed to Joseph Smith after his death, when there was no opportunity for conjugal relationships," suggests that such relations were not necessarily part of the marriage in all cases.[15] To date, no solid evidence has been located indicating that Joseph Smith had any children with any of his plural wives.[16]

"POLYANDROUS" SEALINGS

Several of the women who were evidently sealed to Joseph Smith as plural wives were already married to other men at the time of their sealing to him. Why such sealings were performed is unclear, although several possibilities suggest themselves. Some of these sealings, and perhaps most, may have come about as a result of Smith's well-documented hesitancy to marry specific women as plural wives when he was initially commanded to do so. Several years appear to have elapsed between the time of the commandment and his decision to obey it, during which time the women he had been told to marry—who had been single at the time of the commandment—married other men. Joseph Smith evidently believed that he was still required to marry these women as plural wives in spite of their having married someone else in the interim.[17]

That some of the women were married to men who were not members of the Church may have been another consideration, for according to Doctrine and Covenants 132, only faithful men and women who were sealed to faithful spouses were eligible for exaltation in the kingdom of God (see vv. 7, 13–21).[18] Similarly, that same revelation taught that if a righteous woman was married to a man who had committed adultery, Joseph Smith would "have power, by the power of [God's] Holy Priesthood, to take her and give her unto him that hath not committed adultery but hath been faithful" (vv. 43–44). To what extent these or other considerations were behind these so-called polyandrous sealings is largely unknown, as even fewer reliable sources are extant for these complex relationships than are available for Smith's marriages to unmarried women.[19] No reliable sources have been located indicating that any of these marriages included conjugal relations,[20] although it should be noted that nothing in section 132 or any of Joseph Smith's other revelations "provides any doctrinal reason for why any authorized plural marriage could not have included such relations."[21]

It should be noted, too, that the best available evidence does not support the charge some have made that Joseph Smith was sealed to some men's wives after having sent them on missions. The cases of Marinda Nancy Johnson Hyde, wife of Apostle Orson Hyde, and Sarah Pratt, wife of Apostle Orson Pratt, are frequently invoked as evidence for this charge. Orson Hyde left on a mission in April 1840 and did not return to Nauvoo until December 1842. Thomas Bullock, one of Joseph Smith's clerks, later recorded that Marinda was sealed to Joseph as a plural wife in April 1842, which would have been several months before Hyde's return. Marinda herself, however—who was in a much better position to know the particulars of her sealing to Joseph than Bullock was—dated the event to May 1843, several months after Hyde's return. In Sarah Pratt's case, it was Nauvoo dissident John C. Bennett who initially made the charge that Joseph had made advances toward her while Pratt was on a mission. Testimony from a variety of other sources, however (including witnesses who were not members of the Church), indicate that it was Sarah and Bennett, rather than Sarah and Joseph, who had been involved in a relationship during Pratt's absence.[22]

AGE, CONSENT, AND EMMA

Several of Joseph Smith's plural wives were in their teens when they were sealed to him, with the youngest, Helen Mar Kimball, being fourteen years old at the time. While marriage at such an age was not common in that period, it was legal, and other examples have been found of women marrying in their mid-teens in that era.[23] Joseph also told at least some of his plural wives—and presumably all of them—that they had the right and ability to obtain their own testimony of plural marriage before they entered into such a relationship.[24] Lucy Walker, for example, who was sealed to Joseph as a plural wife on May 1, 1843, reported in a sworn statement in 1902 that "[w]hen the Prophet Joseph Smith first mentioned the principle of plural marriage to me I felt indignant and so expressed myself to him, because my feelings and education were averse to anything of that nature. But he assured me that this doctrine had been revealed to him of the Lord, and that I was entitled to receive a testimony of its divine origin for myself. He counselled me to pray to the Lord, which I did, and thereupon received from him a powerful and irresistible testimony of the truthfulness and divinity of plural marriage, which testimony has abided with me ever since."[25]

Purgatory, by Anthony Sweat. © Anthony Sweat, used with permission.

Similarly, section 132 seems to indicate that a man's first wife must give her consent before he can take a second wife—a requirement evidently known as the "law of Sarah" (vv. 61, 65). Although Joseph's first wife, Emma Hale Smith, "had a difficult time accepting plural marriage," several sources indicate that she "agreed to and even attended at least some" of these marriages, and "several people close to her and Joseph later reported that she told them or others that she knew it was a true doctrine."[26] At the same time, it is clear that on at least some occasions, Emma's opposition to the practice resulted in Joseph's being sealed to other women without her knowledge. This may have been done in accordance with the Lord's instructions as given in Doctrine and Covenants 132:64–65, which teaches that if the man who holds the keys of administering plural marriage teaches his wife about the practice and she rejects it, he is "exempt from the law of Sarah" and is to "receive all things whatsoever . . . the Lord . . . will give unto him." Such may have been the case in March 1843 when Emily and Eliza Partridge were sealed to Joseph as plural wives. That Emma was unaware of the sealings is suggested by the fact that two months later, in May 1843, she told Joseph that she would allow him to be sealed to the two women as plural wives and the ceremonies were then repeated.[27]

JOSEPH SMITH'S DENIALS OF PLURAL MARRIAGE

Joseph did not publicly teach the doctrine of plural marriage during his lifetime, choosing rather to limit its practice to a relatively few trusted associates. Even as he and these others fulfilled the Lord's command to take plural wives, he continued to emphasize the Lord's usual standard that "no man shall have but one wife," and he directed Church leaders to discipline "those who were preaching teaching . . . the doctrin[e] of plurality of wives" without his consent or direction.[28] Joseph and others involved with plural marriage consistently denied the existence of the practice, although the language they employed in doing so was sometimes evasive. Their reasons for the denials are unclear but may include the need to present a message consistent with the public doctrine of monogamy, fear of reprisal, and the fact that rumors about the practice were often so inaccurate that admitting to it would be admitting to something that, in its details, was not true.[29]

UTAH AND THE END OF PLURAL MARRIAGE

By the time of Joseph Smith's death in June 1844, twenty-nine men in addition to himself had married plural wives in Nauvoo. Under the direction of Brigham Young and the Quorum of the Twelve, that number had grown to between 150 and 200 by the time the Saints left the area in early 1846.[30] The number of people participating in plural marriage continued to grow over the ensuing years, with the result that "probably half of those living in Utah Territory in 1857 experienced life in a polygamous family as a husband, wife, or child at some time during their lives."[31] The number of participants began to decline shortly thereafter, however, and by 1870, according to one estimate, only "25 to 30 percent of the population lived in polygamous households."[32] Federal anti-polygamy legislation during the 1860s, 1870s, and 1880s hastened the trend, and in 1890 Church President Wilford Woodruff, acting under inspiration, issued a statement, known as the Manifesto, in which he "declared his intention to abide by U.S. law forbidding plural marriage and to use his influence to convince members of the Church to do likewise."[33] Some Church leaders continued to perform plural marriages on a limited basis between 1890 and 1904, however, especially in Mexico and Canada, but also in the United States. In 1904 Church President Joseph F. Smith issued a second statement, often known as the Second Manifesto, strictly prohibiting new plural marriages from taking place anywhere in the world. That standard has remained in place to the present time, and "today, any person who practices plural marriage cannot become or remain a member of the Church."[34]

PLURAL MARRIAGE IN THE FUTURE

No scriptural support exists for the notion that plural marriage will be restored again in this dispensation or that it is or will be a requirement for exaltation. Jacob 2:30 makes it clear that monogamy is the Lord's general standard, and Doctrine and Covenants 132:19–20 clearly states that "a man" and "a wife"—singular—married by the proper authority can be exalted. Some have understood verses 1–4 in section 132 to say that those who learn about plural marriage must obey it or be damned, but verse 7 makes it clear that the "law" the Lord is discussing in those verses is not plural marriage but rather the requirement that "all covenants, contracts, bonds," and other agreements be "entered into and sealed by the Holy Spirit of promise" if they are to be of any "efficacy, virtue, or force in and after the resurrection from the dead."[35] Statements by Brigham Young and other early Church leaders asserting the necessity of plural marriage must be understood in the context of the times in which they were made and are not considered Church doctrine today. One might find a somewhat analogous situation in the ancient law of circumcision, which was required of a certain people at a certain time to fulfill a specific purpose but is not expected or required of everyone in every dispensation.

From what can be determined from the records, at least some, and possibly most, of those who were involved in plural marriages that included sealing for eternity believed that those sealings would be in effect in the next life.[36] Current Church policy allows a man to be sealed to another wife after a previous wife, to whom he was also sealed, has died, and for a woman who was legally married to more than one man over the course of her life to be sealed by proxy to each of them after all concerned are deceased. Given the current state of our knowledge about the next life, it is unclear precisely how any of these situations—including plural marriage sealings—will be resolved in the next life.[37]

CONCLUSION

Joseph Smith's revelations, teachings, and practices on marriage—especially plural marriage—will likely continue to be a source of questions and controversy for years to come. Hopefully, additional sources will come to light that will help us better understand how and when the Prophet instituted the practice, who was involved, and the marital dynamics that it included. Hopefully, too, we'll gain a better understanding of *why* the Lord restored the practice in the latter days and what might have been accomplished under plural marriage that could not have been accomplished under monogamy. In the meantime, I think there are several conclusions about Joseph Smith's practice of plural marriage in which Latter-day Saints today can place their full faith and confidence. Other important considerations about the study of plural marriage must be kept in mind as we seek additional understanding on the topic.

- First, Joseph Smith practiced and taught plural marriage as a prophet of God and was acting under His direction and authority when he instituted it in this dispensation.

- Second, available historical sources on Joseph Smith's plural marriages are limited in number and poor in quality, leaving many basic questions about the identity of his wives, the nature of their relationships with him, and other considerations incompletely resolved.

- Third, the best available records suggest that women involved in plural marriages received their own testimonies of the doctrine before being sealed to Joseph Smith or other men as plural wives.

- Fourth, given the conditions under which it was practiced in the early days of the Church, plural marriage may have helped lay a stronger foundation of faithful Church members than would have been possible under monogamy.

- Fifth, the 1890 Manifesto, issued under inspiration by President Wilford Woodruff, led to the eventual discontinuance of plural marriage in 1904. Members of The Church of Jesus Christ of Latter-day Saints do not practice plural marriage today.

- And sixth, there is nothing in the scriptures or current teachings of Church leaders suggesting that plural marriage is or will be a requirement for exaltation for Church members living today.

As we are true to our faith and testimony of Joseph Smith's prophetic calling, and similarly true to the highest scholarly standards of historical research and writing, I am confident that the things that appear so darkly through the glass to us today will one day make much more sense and call forth our even greater appreciation for the men and women who faithfully gave their all to fulfill a revelation that so clearly challenged their most fundamental beliefs and moral sensibilities. As they were true to the best in themselves, so we must be true to the best in ourselves if we are to have any hope of fully understanding their world and of making sense of such a complex and difficult topic.

———————

Andrew H. Hedges is a professor of Church history and doctrine at Brigham Young University.

The foregoing essay is a reading used in the BYU Online Foundations of the Restoration course.

NOTES

1. See Joseph Smith, Journal, July 12, 1843, Joseph Smith Collection, Church History Library, The Church of Jesus Christ of Latter-day Saints, Salt Lake City (hereafter cited as CHL). Annotated typescripts of this and other entries from Joseph Smith's Nauvoo journals cited in this essay are available in *The Joseph Smith Papers, Journals* 2 (hereafter *JSP*, J2, etc.).
2. See Orson Pratt, in *Journal of Discourses*, 13:193 (October 7, 1869); and Danel W. Bachman, "New Light on an Old Hypothesis: The Ohio Origins of the Revelation on Eternal Marriage," *Journal of Mormon History* 5 (1978): 19–32.
3. For a brief account of the events surrounding the recording of this revelation, see *JSP*, J3:57n259.

4. William Clayton, Journal, May 16, 1843, CHL, as cited in *JSP*, J3:17. Portions of Joseph's teaching on this day were later canonized as Doctrine and Covenants 131.
5. See Smith, Journal, May 28, 29, 1843, CHL. Willard Richards, who was keeping Joseph Smith's journal at the time, recorded parts of these entries in shorthand. For a transliteration of the shorthand, see *JSP*, J3:25. See also "Reminiscence of Mercy Rachel Fielding Thompson," quoted in Carol Cornwall Madsen, *In Their Own Words: Women and the Story of Nauvoo* (Salt Lake City: Deseret Book, 1994), 194–95.
6. See Brian C. Hales, "Encouraging Joseph Smith to Practice Plural Marriage: The Accounts of the Angel with a Drawn Sword," *Mormon Historical Studies* 11, no. 2 (Fall 2010): 69–70.
7. "Plural Marriage and Families in Early Utah," Gospel Topics, www.churchofjesuschrist.org/.
8. *JSP*, J2:xxv.
9. *JSP*, J2:xxvn51.
10. Principal sources for this possible plural marriage include Mosiah Hancock, Narrative in Levi Hancock, Autobiography, 63, CHL; and Oliver Cowdery to Warren Cowdery, January 21, 1838, Oliver Cowdery, Letterbook, Huntington Library, San Marino, California; Minute Book 2, April 12, 1838, CHL.
11. Principal sources include Joseph Bates Noble, Affidavit, June 6, 1869, Joseph F. Smith Affidavit Books, CHL; Wilford Woodruff, Journal, January 22, 1869, Wilford Woodruff Collection, CHL; and Temple Lot Transcript, part 3, pp. 432, 436, questions 793, 861, CHL.
12. See *JSP*, J2:xxvn52.
13. See Temple Lot Transcript, part 3, pp. 105–6, 371, 384, questions 224–60, 480–84, 751–62, CHL; Benjamin Johnson to George F. Gibbs, 1903, in Dean R. Zimmerman, *I Knew the Prophets* (Bountiful, UT: Horizon, 1976), 41–44; and Lucy Walker Smith Kimball, Affidavit, 1903, in Joseph F. Smith, Affidavits about Plural Marriage, 1869–1915, CHL.
14. Helen Mar Kimball, for example, reported that her marriage to Joseph Smith was "for eternity alone." See "Plural Marriage in Kirtland and Nauvoo," Gospel Topics, www.churchofjesuschrist.org/.
15. *JSP*, J2:xxvn53.
16. In some cases, researchers have been able to employ genetic testing to determine Joseph Smith's alleged paternity of several individuals. The results have been negative in each case. See Ugo A. Perego, Natalie M. Myers, and Scott R. Woodward, "Reconstructing the Y-Chromosome of Joseph Smith: Genealogical Applications," *Journal of Mormon History* 31 (Summer 2005): 70–88; Ugo A. Perego, Jane E. Ekins, and Scott R. Woodward, "Resolving the Paternities of Oliver N. Buell and Mosiah L. Hancock through DNA," *John Whitmer Historical Association Journal* 28 (2008): 128–36; and Ugo A. Perego, "Using Science to Answer Questions from Latter-day Saint History: The Case of Josephine Lyon's Paternity," *BYU Studies Quarterly* 58, no. 4 (2019): 143–50.
17. This scenario seems to at least partly explain Joseph Smith's sealings to Mary Elizabeth Lightner and Marinda Nancy Johnson Hyde, for example. See Mary Elizabeth Lightner to Wilford Woodruff, October 7, 1887, Mary E. Lightner Papers, L. Tom Perry Special Collections, Harold B. Lee Library, Brigham Young University, Provo, Utah; Mary Elizabeth Lightner, Statement, February 8, 1902, Lightner Papers;

Mary Elizabeth Lightner, Remarks, April 14, 1905, Lightner Papers; and Marinda Nancy Johnson Hyde, Undated Statement, CHL.

18. Mary Elizabeth Lightner, for example, reported that she "went forward and was sealed to Joseph for Eternity" after her non–Latter-day Saint husband refused to join the Church. Lightner, Remarks, April 14, 1905.

19. Richard L. Bushman has suggested another possibility for these marriages—that is, that they provided Joseph Smith with a way to bind or seal other families to his for the eternal benefit of both. See Richard Lyman Bushman, *Joseph Smith: Rough Stone Rolling* (New York: Alfred A. Knopf, 2005), 437–46.

20. See "Plural Marriage in Kirtland and Nauvoo," note 30.

21. *JSP*, J2:xxv.

22. For an annotated discussion of the issues surrounding Marinda Hyde and Sarah Pratt, see *JSP*, J2:xxvi, xxx.

23. See "Plural Marriage in Kirtland and Nauvoo"; and J. Spencer Fluhman, "'A Subject That Can Bear Investigation': Anguish, Faith, and Joseph Smith's Youngest Plural Wife," in *No Weapon Shall Prosper: New Light on Sensitive Issues*, ed. Robert L. Millet (Provo, UT: Religious Studies Center, Brigham Young University; Salt Lake City: Deseret Book, 2011), 104–19.

24. See Lightner, Remarks, April 14, 1905; and Lucy Walker Smith Kimball, Affidavit, 1902, in Joseph F. Smith, Affidavits about Plural Marriage, 1869–1915, CHL.

25. Kimball Affidavit, 1902.

26. *JSP*, J3:xix and note 27.

27. See Eliza Maria Partridge Lyman, Affidavit, July 1, 1869, Millard County, Utah Territory, Joseph F. Smith Affidavit Books, CHL; Emily Dow Partridge Young, Affidavit, May 1, 1869, Salt Lake County, Utah Territory, Joseph F. Smith Affidavit Books, CHL; and Emily Dow Partridge Young, Diary and Reminiscences, February 1874—November 1883, typescript, CHL.

28. Joseph Smith, Journal, October 5, 1843, CHL.

29. As the editors of the Joseph Smith Papers note, for example, the term John C. Bennett used for plural marriage, "spiritual wifery," was not used by those practicing plural marriage in Nauvoo. Nor is there any corroborating evidence for Bennett's description of Joseph's plural wives as a "seraglio. . . . divided into three distinct orders or degrees." *JSP*, J2:xixn23.

30. See Kathryn M. Daynes, *More Wives Than One: Transformation of the Mormon Marriage System, 1840–1910* (Urbana: University of Illinois Press, 2001), 32, 35; and Brian C. Hales, *Joseph Smith's Polygamy, Volume 1: History* (Sandy, UT: Greg Kofford Books, 2013), 3.

31. "Plural Marriage and Families in Early Utah."

32. "Plural Marriage and Families in Early Utah."

33. "Plural Marriage and Families in Early Utah."

34. "Plural Marriage and Families in Early Utah."

35. See Marcus B. Nash, "The New and Everlasting Covenant," *Ensign*, December 2015, 40–47.

36. Joseph Smith's plural wife Lucy Walker, for example, who married Heber C. Kimball "for time" after Joseph's death, wrote in 1902 that "during the whole of my married life with him [Kimball] he never failed to regard me as the wife for eternity of his devoted friend, the Prophet Joseph Smith." Kimball, Affidavit, 1902 (underlining in original).

37. "Plural Marriage in Kirtland and Nauvoo."

Chapter Nineteen

Enemies Within

Robert Foster, the Higbees, and the Martyrdom of Joseph Smith

ANDREW H. HEDGES

On June 7, 1844, seven dissenters from The Church of Jesus Christ of Latter-day Saints—William and Wilson Law, Francis M. and Chauncey L. Higbee, Robert and Charles Foster, and Charles Ivins—published the first and only issue of the *Nauvoo Expositor*, a four-page, six-column paper whose purpose was to provide "a full, candid and succinct statement of facts, as they exist in the city of Nauvoo, fearless of whose particular case they apply."[1] Concerned that the paper's accusations and inflammatory rhetoric would result in violence against Nauvoo, the city council three days later ordered Joseph Smith, in his capacity as mayor of the city, to "destroy the Nauvoo Expositor establishment as a nuisance." Joseph passed the order on to Nauvoo city marshal John P. Greene, who reported later that evening "that he had removed the press, type—& printed paper—& fixtures into the street & fired them."[2] The following day, June 11, one of the paper's publishers, Francis Higbee, went before Thomas Morrison, a Hancock County justice of the peace, and accused Joseph and seventeen other men of having committed a riot, "wherein they with force & violence broke into the printing office of the Nauvoo Expositor and unlawfully & with force burned & destroyed the printing press, type & fixtures of the same." Morrison immediately issued a warrant for Joseph's arrest, thus setting into motion the legal process that would lead to the Prophet's murder at Carthage Jail less than three weeks later.[3]

As one of the key events leading to Joseph Smith's death, the destruction of the *Expositor* has received a significant amount of attention from historians over the years.[4] At the same time, relatively little work has been done on the history of the seven men who published the paper, especially the history of their relationship with Joseph in Nauvoo and the reasons behind their defection from the Church. William Law has received the most attention in this regard, although reliance on later sources and reminiscent accounts has colored the story somewhat.[5] For the others, authors have generally been content to provide a brief description of who they were and what their difficulties with the Prophet were but have neglected to carefully trace the development of these problems and the significant points of contact between them. In the cases of Charles Foster, Wilson Law, and Charles Ivins, such brief treatment has been unavoidable, as very few sources detailing their deteriorating relationship with Joseph have been located. More information, however, is available for Robert D. Foster, Francis M. Higbee, and Chauncey L. Higbee, especially as it relates to events preceding the arrival of the *Expositor* press in Nauvoo on May 7, 1844—an event that clearly marks the beginning of a new and united effort on the part of these men to discomfit the Prophet and his supporters. This article, then, details Joseph's relationship with Foster and the two Higbees in Nauvoo up to that point in an effort to provide a more complete account of the events and issues leading to these men's united animosity toward Joseph Smith during the last few years of his life than has been available in the past.

BEGINNINGS

Although their experiences in and with the Church were significantly different, all three men had achieved some degree of prominence in Nauvoo by the time they turned against Joseph Smith. Chauncey and Francis, sons of the Prophet's friend Elias Higbee, had been in the Church the longest, having been baptized in 1832 around the ages of eleven and twelve, respectively. Along with other members of their family, both endured several periods of persecution in Missouri between 1833 and 1839. Both also practiced law in Nauvoo and served as aides-de-camp to Major Generals John C. Bennett and Wilson Law in the Nauvoo Legion.[6] Foster, on the other hand, appears to have joined the Church shortly before accompanying Joseph on part of his trip to Washington, DC, in autumn 1839 and so missed the Missouri troubles. He speculated heavily in lands on the bluff area of Nauvoo and, like the Higbees, practiced law. He was also a successful and well-respected physician, as evidenced by his appearing as an expert witness in the celebrated *Dana v. Brink* malpractice suit[7] and serving as surgeon general of the Legion.[8]

Prominence, however, was no insurance against poor behavior. The first hint that all was not well with the Higbee brothers in Nauvoo is a mild rebuke Joseph delivered on January 28, 1842, to their father, Elias Higbee, a member of the temple committee at the time. "The Lord is not well pleased with you," Joseph told Higbee, "& you must straiten up your loins and do better, & your family also. . . . You must arise & shake yourself & be active & make your children industrious & help build the Temple."[9] Three months later, it became clear that the situation had deteriorated rather than improved, with George Miller formally charging Chauncey Higbee in May with "unchaste and unvirtuous conduct with the widow Miller and others." The Nauvoo high council heard the case on May 21, 1842, at which point three witnesses testified that Higbee had seduced several women by telling them it was no sin "to have free intercourse with women if it was kept secret."[10] Sarah Miller, Margaret Nyman, and Matilda Nyman—three of Higbee's victims—formally recorded their accounts of Higbee's actions three days later, at which point the high council formally excommunicated him from the Church.[11] Making matters worse, Higbee appears to have responded by retaliating against Joseph, leading to his arrest the same day for "slander and defamation" against the Prophet and his wife Emma. Higbee was released on a two-hundred-dollar bond, but he was obviously very upset with Joseph Smith.[12]

Cryptic entries in Joseph's journal, which was being kept by Willard Richards at the time, indicate that something was brewing with Francis Higbee at approximately the same time. On May 13, 1842, Richards wrote that Joseph "had private interview with Pres[iden]t Rigdon . . . concerning certain evil reports put in circulation by F. M.," followed by several illegible words. Draft notes written later for Joseph Smith's history supply "Higbee" after "F. M.," making it clear that the compilers of the history, at least, had reason to believe Francis M. Higbee was behind at least some of the developing issues between Joseph and Sidney Rigdon in 1842.[13] Similarly, Richards noted on June 29, 1842, that Joseph "held a long conversation with Francis Higby," who "found fault with being exposed." According to Richards, Joseph told the young man that "he spoke of him in self defence," after which Higbee "appeard humble & promisd to reform."[14]

Neither entry provides any details about the situation with Higbee at this time, but records generated almost two years later offer some suggestions. Evidently, sometime during the summer of 1841, Higbee had contracted "the Pox"—probably syphilis—from a prostitute who had visited Nauvoo from Warsaw, Illinois. At the same time, Higbee also reportedly told John C. Bennett, who was treating him, that he had seduced a young lady in Nauvoo. Bennett passed the news on to Joseph, who reported that when he tried to inform the girl's parents of the problem, both Bennett and Higbee changed their story and lied about Joseph in some fashion in order to "blind the family."[15] The entries in Joseph's journal about "evil reports" and Higbee's concern over being "exposed," referenced previously, may have been written in this context, at a time when the Prophet had been forced to defend himself and explain what really had happened. If so, it was a move that Higbee clearly did not like, though his own actions had precipitated it.

Following this brief flurry of activity in May and June 1842, Joseph appears to have had very little to do with the Higbees—at least for a time. The same cannot be said, however, of Robert D. Foster, who appears frequently in Joseph's journal between March 1842 and early 1844. Foster's relationship with the Prophet during these years varied considerably; the two men seem to have been friends at some points and opponents at others. On March 10, 1842, for example, Foster was clearly on Joseph's side when he testified before the Nauvoo municipal court that Amos Davis had used "indec[e]nt and abusive Language" against Joseph the previous day.[16] Two months later, in turn, Joseph spoke "at considerable length" in support of the Masonic lodge, forgiving Foster after lodge members found him guilty of abusing Henry G. Sherwood and Samuel Smith.[17] The following day, May 21, 1842, Joseph and the Nauvoo high council similarly ruled in Foster's favor after the latter had been charged with "unchristian conduct" by Nathan T. Knight, and on July 19 Joseph, Foster, and several others went for a long ride together "to look at Timber Land."[18] Early in 1843, however, Richards noted in Joseph's journal that Foster "took an active part in electioneering for the written opposition ticket, & obstructing passage to the polls" during the Nauvoo city elections. Furthermore, Richards wrote that Foster was supporting businessman William H. Rollosson for Nauvoo postmaster rather than Joseph Smith, who had been "recommended for the appointment" in November 1842.[19] The Prophet called Foster out on at least some of these activities at a public meeting on February 21, 1843, and also chastised him for drawing labor and means from building the Nauvoo Temple and Nauvoo House by promoting his own building developments of the area. Foster acknowledged the correctness of Joseph's accusations but also claimed that he had given one thousand dollars to "this house"—meaning, probably, the Nauvoo House—and that he intended to contribute more. Foster also claimed he had been unaware of Joseph's desire to be appointed postmaster.[20]

Three days later, on February 24, 1843, Joseph visited Foster and "had some conversation" about the issues he had raised at the meeting. Although Foster showed "some feeling on the occasion," subsequent journal entries suggest that the two men managed to bury their differences relatively quickly.[21] In the middle of March, Richards noted both men engaging in conversation together and commenting on large circles that were visible around the moon.[22] The rapport seems to have held even when Joseph and Orson Spencer decided against Foster on a charge of debt later in the month,[23] with Foster taking an active role in preventing the Prophet's enemies from transporting him to Missouri after his arrest near Dixon, Illinois, on June 23.[24] In October, Foster also "voluntaryly came forward" and donated five dollars toward the purchase of an eight-dollar book in which Willard Richards and William W. Phelps could continue writing Joseph Smith's history.[25] Joseph, in turn, was comfortable appealing to Foster in his capacity as justice of the peace on December 18 when John Elliot verbally threatened Joseph's life. He also chose to deliver an important speech in front of Foster's "Mammoth Hotel"—one of the building projects he had publicly denounced in his February 21, 1843 speech—to "several thousand people . . . on sealing the hearts of the fathers to the chidrn [children] & the heart of the childrn to the fathers" in January 1844.[26] Richards also noted in Joseph's journal the abuse Foster suffered at the hands of Church opponents in Carthage who objected to his election as school commissioner in August 1843, as well as Foster's efforts to enforce the law—again, in his capacity as justice of the peace—in the face of gathering opposition against the Church.[27] Whatever friction or tension had existed between the Prophet and Foster early in 1843 appears to have been forgotten shortly afterward, with both men evidently taking an active and sympathetic interest in each other's life and welfare over the ensuing months.

OPPOSITION AND CONSPIRACY, JANUARY–MARCH 1844

By January 1844, some eighteen months after he had promised Joseph that he would reform, Francis Higbee was again causing problems for the

Prophet. At the time, the Nauvoo City Council was trying to determine the origins of a rumor that Joseph had identified William Law and William Marks as traitors and that he had secretly instructed the Nauvoo police to somehow put them "out of the way." In spite of clear evidence and testimony from several dozen people that the rumors were unfounded, Law and Marks continued to feel threatened after two days of careful investigation.[28] On January 5—the third day of the inquiry—Francis Higbee took the stand and testified that he, for one, had received an impression "from some source" that Law, Marks, and several others "could not subscribe to all things in the church, and it might make trouble." Without making any clarifications, Higbee then left the meeting without permission, prompting Joseph—who understood what Higbee's testimony might imply—to remark that he, Higbee, "had better stay at home & hold his tongue, lest rumor turn upon him" and that "the young men of the City had better withdraw from him & . . . not consider him the standard."[29] According to William Law, Joseph also told those present that Higbee had been "conniving with Missouri"; that he "only disgraced anyone who associated with him"; that he, Joseph, "had denied him the privilege of his house . . . and would not allow him to associate with his females"; and that he, Joseph, had once been asked "to lay hands on him when he stank from a cause that he did not like to name."[30] While the details behind all but the last of these remarks—a clear reference to the results of Higbee's earlier indiscretion with the prostitute—are lacking from the historical record, Joseph was evidently giving voice to several months of pent-up frustration with Higbee's behavior.

Five days later, on January 10, 1844, Higbee wrote a letter to Joseph about what Higbee called "the inconsiderate, the unwarented, and unheard of Attack" Joseph had made against him before the city council and demanded an immediate investigation into the matter. In a roundabout way, Higbee also tried to deny the events of 1841. "I want you to thoroughly understand," Higbee wrote, "I look upon that species of crime, as the greatest, the most distructive to human happiness, and the most fatal to all earthly enjoyment." Higbee also suggested that Joseph's "attack" on his character was motivated by Higbee's own staunch opposition to plural marriage, the news of which had reached his ears by this time. "Any revelation commanding or in any wise suffering sexual intercourse, under any other form, than that prescribed by the laws of our Country, which has been ratified by special revelation through you, is of <u>HELL</u>," Higbee told the Prophet, "and I bid defiance to any or all such."[31]

Higbee hadn't sent the letter four days later, when he visited Orson Pratt at his home. According to Pratt, Higbee used "slanderous and abusive epithets and language" against Joseph Smith and read his letter to the Apostle. The following day, January 15, Joseph received word that Higbee was planning to sue him for ten thousand dollars—an action that was cut short when Pratt, on the same day, charged Higbee with leaving the city council "without leave" and for slandering Joseph in his home the day before.[32] The municipal court, presided over by Orson Spencer, began hearing the case at 10:00 a.m. on January 16, but it adjourned after some time in order for its members, in their capacity as members of the city council, to pass a number of much-needed ordinances. During the break, the case took an unexpected turn when Joseph and Higbee talked through their issues with one another and reconciled, with Higbee acknowledging the "slanderous letter" he had written and the "many hard things" he had said against Joseph, and Joseph frankly forgiving him. "I went before the council & stated that all difficulties between me and Francis M. Higbee are eternally buried, and I am to be his friend forever," Joseph's journal entry reads for that day, "to which F M Higby replied I will be his friend forever, & his right hand man." Joseph also "explained at length respecting what, in substance, he had said at previous councils on the same subject," while Higbee mentioned "his distraction of mind the past week" and reaffirmed his friendship to Joseph. In token of their having "eternally buried" the past, Joseph's comments about Higbee in the January 5 city council meeting were then "stricken" from the minutes of the meeting with five large Xs.[33]

As it turned out, "forever" was relatively short-lived. On February 26 Higbee served as the defense attorney for Orsamus F. Bostwick, who had been accused by Hyrum Smith of slander. Joseph himself presided over the case in the Nauvoo Mayor's Court. After hearing from witness John Scott that Bostwick had accused Hyrum of having several "spiritual wives,"[34] and that he had also accused various women in Nauvoo of living as prostitutes, Joseph found Bostwick guilty and fined him fifty dollars and the costs of the court. Afterwards, Higbee, as Bostwick's attorney, declared his intention to appeal the decision to the municipal court "& then to the circuit court" in Carthage. "I told him what I thought of him—& for trying to cary such a suit to Carthage," Joseph's journal reads for that day. "It was to stir up the mob—& bring them upon us."[35] Still upset with the two men ten days later, Joseph discussed their "proceedings" in a meeting of "six or eight thousand" Church members on March 7 and asked "the people to speak out, [and] say whether such men should be tolerated and supported in our midst." Feeling that the "conduct of such men" tied the hands of the city officers, Joseph declared his intention "from this time . . . to bring such characters before the committee of the whole" and to "give them in to the hands of the mob" if they persisted in their course.[36]

Joseph's relationship with Robert D. Foster also took a turn for the worse at this March 7 meeting. Shortly after discussing the Bostwick-Higbee problem, Joseph mentioned "another man" who, in an article published in the *New York Weekly Tribune*, had accused Joseph of misusing funds donated for building the temple—"that splendid monument of folly and wickedness," the author wrote.[37] Robert Foster's brother, Charles, asked Joseph if he was suggesting that he was the author of the article, to which Joseph replied in the affirmative. "You shall hear from me," Charles Foster fumed, to which Joseph responded, "I fine you $10.00—for that threat, and distu[r]bi[n]g the me[e]ti[n]g." Robert Foster then jumped into the fray, telling Joseph that Charles hadn't threatened him and that no one present had heard a threat. According to Willard Richards, "hundreds" of those present disagreed. The tiff ended shortly afterward when Joseph threatened to fine Robert Foster if he continued to speak.[38]

While it may appear that Joseph was being unnecessarily harsh with Bostwick, Higbee, and the Fosters at this time, a close look at recent events shows that he had good reason to be concerned with their activities. Opposition to the Church and its members in Hancock County, which had been on the rise ever since their vote had decided the August 1843 election, had reached near fever pitch by March 1844. In January a meeting of Church opponents in the county had even gone so far as to call on Illinois governor Thomas Ford to amend the Nauvoo charter, disarm members of the Church, call out a portion of the militia to arrest Joseph Smith, and repeal some of the city's ordinances. Ford had responded that he lacked the authority to carry into execution such "absurd and preposterous" requests and told both Church members and their opponents in the area "to beware of carrying matters to extremity." Refusing to take sides in the growing conflict, Ford also explained that he was "bound by the laws and the constitution to regard you all as citizens of the state, possessed of equal rights and privileges: and to cherish the rights of one as dearly as the rights of another."[39] Joseph had publicly endorsed Ford's counsel in late February and had pledged to "cultivate peace and friendship with all, mind our own business, and come off with flying colors, respected, because, in respecting others, we respect ourselves."[40] Bostwick's charges, Higbee's threat to appeal Bostwick's conviction to the court in Carthage, and the Fosters' dissent at this time threatened to undermine the goodwill Joseph was trying to build with Ford and with Church opponents in the area, leaving him no other option but to roundly and publicly condemn their activities.

The March 7 meeting moved on to other matters, but the situation with the Fosters and Higbees grew worse over the ensuing days. Sometime around March 15, Robert Foster told Merinus G. Eaton that someone had visited Foster's home in his absence, had attempted to somehow turn his wife against him, had taught her the "spiritual wife doctrine," had tried to seduce her, and then had sat down to a meal with her. When Foster had returned home, the visitor had greeted him politely and then left. "Jealous that something was wrong," Foster then asked his wife what the two had been talking about in his absence. When his wife refused to say, Foster told Eaton he had put a pistol to his wife's head and threatened to shoot her if she didn't speak. When she still refused, Foster gave her a double-barreled pistol and told her to defend herself, upon which his wife fainted "through fear and excitement." When she came to, Foster reported, she told him how the visitor had attempted to turn her against him, and "by preaching the spiritual wife system to her had endeavored to seduce her."[41]

Foster apparently didn't tell Eaton who the visitor was, but Joseph, when he heard about it, felt that he was the one who was implicated. On March 23, Joseph rode with William Clayton and Alexander Neibaur to Foster's home, evidently in an effort to clear Joseph's name. Foster was away, but the three men eventually found his wife, Sarah, at a neighbor's home. According to Clayton, Joseph asked Sarah if he had ever made any indecent proposals to her, taught her "the spiritual wife doctrine," or done or said anything immoral or indecent—all of the things, in essence, that her husband was accusing someone of having done recently. Sarah replied in the negative to each question. "After some further conversation on the subject," Clayton recorded, Joseph and his companions left, with Joseph and Neibaur eventually continuing on to the Prophet's farm outside Nauvoo.[42]

The following day, March 24, 1844, Joseph told a congregation of Saints something else Foster had told Eaton: that William and Wilson Law, Robert Foster, Chauncey Higbee, and another Nauvoo dissenter, Joseph H. Jackson, "had held a caucus, desig[n]ing to destroy all the Smith family in a few weeks."[43] According to Wilford Woodruff, who was present, Joseph also told the gathering that the "foundation" for the conspiracy was a set of lies about Joseph "hatched up" by Chauncey Higbee, including the report that Joseph had "had mens heads cut off in Missouri" and that he had "had a sword run through the hearts of the people" whom he wanted "put out of the way."[44]

Further details about the conspiracy emerged three days later, when Eaton and Abiathar Williams—who, like Eaton, had met with Foster and other dissenters earlier in the month—made separate affidavits concerning what they heard from those involved. According to Eaton, Joseph H. Jackson had said "that he should not be surprised if there should be a real muss and an insurrection in the city in less than two months" and that he expected men from Carthage to join in the fray.[45] By Williams's account, Jackson had also said that "he should not be surprised if in two weeks there should not be one of the Smith family left alive in Nauvoo."[46]

PUSHING THE LEGAL LIMITS, APRIL–MAY 1844

Joseph was not the only person in authority that Foster and the Higbee brothers were opposing at the time. On March 31 Alexander Mills, one of Nauvoo's policemen, told Joseph that one of the Higbees had drawn a pistol on him the previous night. The following day, April 1, both Chauncey and Francis were tried before Daniel H. Wells, justice of the peace, "for assaulting the police," although it is unclear if the case was related to the incident with Mills or some other altercation. Wells acquitted both men of the charge but fined Chauncey Higbee ten dollars "for abusive Language to the Marshal" in a separate trial.[47] This case had originated when Higbee had become angry with Joel S. Miles, a constable in Nauvoo, over the wording of a warrant that had been issued for William H. J. Marr, who was accused of almost beating a black man to death on suspicion that he had robbed a store the night of March 29. Overhearing Higbee's verbal abuse of Miles, Nauvoo city marshal John P. Greene had told him to not "use impertinent language," to which Higbee responded, "God damn you. Who are you? Who cares for you! I am here myself, go your way." On an order from Greene, Nauvoo policeman Andrew Lytle and his brother John then arrested Higbee, who, after receiving the ten-dollar fine, complained of false imprisonment before Robert Foster. Foster, in turn, issued a warrant for the arrest of Greene and the Lytle brothers, who quickly applied to the Nauvoo municipal court for a writ of habeas corpus after they were apprehended. Determining that the charge of false imprisonment had "originated in a malicious and vexatious suit" instigated by Higbee, the court discharged the three men on April 3 "on the merits of the case" and concluded that "Chauncey L. Higbee was a very disorderly person."[48]

Robert Foster's opposition to Nauvoo authorities and the rule of law at this time went deeper than his misguided support for Chauncey Higbee's accusations against the marshal and police. In the case of the beaten black man referenced previously, J. Easton was also arrested for participating in the crime. Greene was planning to take Easton before Wells for trial, but before he could do so, Foster issued a separate warrant for Easton's arrest, tried him, and acquitted him in his own court. Suspecting that Foster's movements were an effort "to thwart the ends of justice, and screen the prisoner from the condemnation he justly deserves," Joseph confronted Foster about his proceedings. Foster claimed that he was unaware that Easton was already under arrest when he had issued his own warrant and held his own trial, but when he called on one of the jurors to corroborate his story, the juror maintained that he felt all along "it was in part a sham trial, and a mere mockery of justice."[49] After recounting the whole affair, the editor of the *Nauvoo Neighbor* also reported that Foster had recently been fined ten dollars for gambling. "We are sorry to find," the editor lamented, "that our lawyers and magistrates should be taking the lead among gamblers and disorderly persons and be numbered among law-breakers, rather than supporting virtue, law, and the dignity of the city."[50]

Just as he had with Francis Higbee earlier, Joseph attempted to openly discuss his differences with Foster and Chauncey Higbee in an apparent effort to bring about some sort of reconciliation. On 16 April, for example, Richards noted that Joseph "had a long talk with Chauncey L. Higbee" and read to him the affidavits Abiathar Williams and Merinus G. Eaton had made, detailing Higbee's accusations against Joseph and his involvement in the conspiracy against the Prophet's life.[51] Richards neglected to note Higbee's response, suggesting that nothing came of the interview. Three days earlier, Joseph had met with similar results when he had attempted to reconcile with Foster. "Have I ever misused you any way?" Joseph asked, to which Foster responded, "I do not feel at liberty to answer this qu[e]stion under existing circumstances." Joseph asked two more times with the same results and then invited, "Tell me where I have done wrong & I will ask your forgiveness." Foster declined the offer, prompting Joseph, who evidently felt he had done all he could to resolve their differences, to charge Foster with "unchristian like conduct in general, for abusing my character privately, for throwing out slanderous insinuations agai[n]st me, for conspiring against my peace & safety, for conspiring against my life, for conspiring against the peace of my family, and for lying."[52] Five days later, on 18 April, several members of the Quorum of the Twelve Apostles, members of the Nauvoo high council, and several other members of the Church—but not Joseph—met in council and excommunicated Foster and several other dissidents from the Church for "unchristianlike conduct."[53]

The disdain Robert Foster and Chauncey Higbee held both for the law and for Joseph Smith manifested itself again on April 26, one week after Foster's excommunication. The excitement began when a fight broke out between brothers Augustine and Orson Spencer after Augustine launched into a tirade against Joseph and Hyrum Smith at Orson's home.[54] Nauvoo city marshal John P. Greene was called to the scene and arrested Augustine for assault, who then resisted Greene's efforts to convey him to the mayor's office—that is, Joseph's office—for trial. Greene called upon Robert Foster, Charles Foster, and Chauncey Higbee, who were nearby, to assist him, but they refused. "They swore they would not," the *Nauvoo Neighbor* reported, "and said they would see the mayor and the city d—d, and then they would not." Greene somehow managed to get Spencer to Joseph's office, where he was fined one hundred dollars, after which Joseph, still acting in his capacity as mayor, ordered that the two Fosters and Higbee be arrested "for refusing to assist the officer when called upon." Greene didn't have far to go to find them; the three men had evidently followed him and Spencer to Joseph's office. All three resisted arrest, prompting Joseph to come to Greene's aid. At this point, according to the *Neighbor*, Charles Foster "immediately drew a double barrelled pistol and presented it to the mayor's breast."[55] According to later testimony, Robert Foster somehow "interfered" and the pistol was wrenched from his brother's hand, but the verbal onslaught was just beginning, with Higbee and Charles Foster saying "they would be God damnd, if they would not shoot the mayor" and that they "would consider [themselves] favord of God—for the privilege of shooting or ridding the world of such a Tyrant." All three men were taken into custody and fined one hundred dollars each.[56]

After fining Foster the one hundred dollars, Joseph then issued a warrant for his arrest "on complaint of Willard Richards," who accused Foster of shaking his fists in his (Richards's) face and saying, "You . . . are another Damned black hearted villain. You tried to seduce my wife on the boat when she was going to New York.—and I can prove it."[57] The case came up for trial before Joseph the next day but was adjourned to Monday, April 29, "after much conversation with the Mayor," Richards recorded, "in which he [Foster] charged Joseph with many crimes . . . and a great variety of vile & false epithets & charges." At one point in the discussion, according to Richards, Foster "agreed to meet Joseph on 2d—monday of may at the stand and have a settlement" of some sort, "and then said he would publish it [in the] Warsaw paper"—probably meaning the *Warsaw Signal*, whose editor, Thomas Sharp, had been waging a crusade against the Church for some time. While it is unclear what the contemplated "settlement" would have looked like, Foster's intention to publish it in the *Signal* did not sit well with the Prophet. "Joseph told him, if he did not agree to be quiet—not attempt to raise a mob . . . he would not meet him," Richards recounted, "[but that] if he would be quiet he [Joseph] [would] publish it in the [Nauvoo] Neighbor." When Foster rejected the proposal, Joseph said he was finished trying to effect a peace with him, declared himself free from Foster's blood, and "deliverd him into the hand of God & shook his garments aga[in]st him."[58]

Foster spent the next day (Sunday, April 28) with Francis Higbee, William and Wilson Law, and several others inviting various families in Nauvoo to join the church they had recently created on the grounds that Joseph was a fallen prophet. Foster and Higbee were members of the new organization's Quorum of the Twelve Apostles, and William Law served as president.[59] Little wonder, then, that when the original case involving Foster's threats toward Richards came up on April 29, Joseph opted to transfer it to city alderman William Marks.[60] No record of Marks's decision has been located.

By the end of the following week, it was clear that Joseph's break with Foster and the Higbees was complete. On May 6, the Council of Fifty met and agreed to deliver the three men over to the "buffetings of Satan"—a somewhat cryptic phrase often employed at the time in connection with excommunication, with the added scriptural implication that the punishment would remain in force irrevocably "until the day of redemption."[61] Following the council meeting, Joseph was arrested on complaint of Francis Higbee—the only one of the three who had not been formally excommunicated by this point and who, as we have seen, had done the most to reconcile with Joseph in the past. In what might be seen as a show of solidarity with the other two men, and despite his earlier agreement with Joseph that their differences were "eternally buried," Higbee was suing Joseph for five thousand dollars in damages for the statements he had made about his character—including the allusion to his venereal disease—in the city council meeting on January 5 "and on divers other days and times with in one year last past."[62] Following his arrest, Joseph petitioned the municipal court for a writ of habeas corpus on the grounds that Higbee was "actuated by no other motive than a desire to persecute and harass" him and to place him "into the hands of his Enemies."[63] At the hearing two days later, Joseph explained at length his comments at the January city council meeting, after which several others who were present corroborated his account. After hearing the testimony, the court, "convinced [that] the suit was instituted through malice, & ought not to be countenanced," ordered that Joseph be discharged from arrest and that Higbee pay the court costs, which amounted to about $36.14.[64] Higbee was excommunicated ten days later, on May 18, 1844, by the Nauvoo high council for "apostatizing."[65]

Fittingly enough, the press on which Francis and Chauncey Higbee, Robert Foster, and other dissenters would publish the *Nauvoo Expositor* arrived at Foster's home on May 7, the day before the municipal court ordered Joseph's release in the Higbee case.[66] While its arrival and the subsequent effort to publish the first issue of the paper didn't prevent Joseph's enemies from continuing to pursue him through other means—both Foster and Francis Higbee, for example, as well as the Law brothers, formally charged Joseph with a variety of crimes over the course of the following month[67]—it did signal an expansion of the tactics the Prophet's enemies were willing to employ to discredit him. The production of the *Expositor* also signaled the first time that Foster's and both Higbees' names were all associated in the same effort against Joseph—Francis Higbee's name, for example, had not been brought up in connection with the conspiracy forming against Joseph in March 1844, while Chauncey Higbee was evidently not involved with the dissenters' new church. All three, though, along with several others, signed on to the project that ultimately led to Joseph's death in Carthage the following month.

CONCLUSION

According to the seven publishers of the *Nauvoo Expositor*, their opposition to Joseph Smith was rooted predominantly in their concern about the combination of church and state in Nauvoo, "the doctrine of *many Gods*" that Joseph had been teaching, and Joseph's practice of plural marriage.[68] A careful look at some of these men's relationship with Joseph in Nauvoo before the arrival of the press on which the paper would be published, however, suggests that a variety of other issues also played a role in their disaffection from the Prophet and the Church. Robert Foster, whose relationship with Joseph in Nauvoo had been generally positive (with one or two minor exceptions), appears to have first turned against Joseph after believing that someone had made improper advances toward his wife in his absence. While the full details of this incident may never be known, Foster's subsequent accusation that Willard Richards had also attempted to seduce his wife while the two were on a boat bound for New York betrays a certain insecurity on his part regarding his wife and raises the distinct possibility—as does his wife's own statements, as recorded by William Clayton—that his animosity toward Joseph on this score was largely unfounded. Foster also appears to have lashed out in various ways against the requirements and officers of the law in Nauvoo during this time, suggesting that at least some of his opposition to Joseph was part of a larger personal crusade against the established order and authorities of the time.

A significant part of the Higbees' animosity toward Joseph seems to have been rooted in Joseph's disavowal of the brothers' well-documented amorous exploits. Chauncey Higbee appears to have made no effort to rejoin the Church following his excommunication on this score in May 1842, and, like Foster, he turned his ire not only against Joseph Smith but against other authorities in Nauvoo as well. Like Foster, Chauncey also appears to have rebuffed Joseph's efforts to reconcile during this period and was reportedly a charter member of the conspiracy formed in March 1844 to destroy the Prophet and his family. Francis Higbee, on the other hand, did accept the olive branch Joseph extended to him after he (Joseph) indiscreetly remarked at a city council meeting about Higbee's contracting "the Pox" in 1841, but he lost the Prophet's trust shortly afterward when he threatened to appeal a potentially inflammatory legal case to the circuit court in Carthage. No doubt aware of his brother Chauncey's ongoing conflicts with Joseph and other Nauvoo authorities, Francis emerged from the background and charged Joseph with defamation of character in May 1844, more than a year after Joseph's remarks to the city council and some three years after his illness.

Whatever the reason for their disaffection from Joseph and the church he led, the members of this particular trio wasted little time in joining forces against the Prophet. By the end of March 1844, at least two of them—Foster and Chauncey Higbee—were identified as members of a conspiracy against Joseph's life. Both men openly mocked Joseph and other Nauvoo authorities on at least two occasions in April, and by the end of the month, both Foster and Francis Higbee were members of William Law's new church. In the end, however, it was the *Nauvoo Expositor* that served as their most powerful weapon against Joseph and that brought each man's increasingly tumultuous relationship with the Prophet to an effective close.

Andrew H. Hedges is a professor of Church history and doctrine at Brigham Young University.

Andrew H. Hedges, "Joseph Smith, Robert Foster, and Chauncey and Francis Higbee," *Religious Educator* 18, no. 1 (2017): 88–111.

NOTES

1. *Nauvoo Expositor*, June 7, 1844.
2. Joseph Smith, journal, June 10, 1844, Joseph Smith Collection, Church History Library, The Church of Jesus Christ of Latter-day Saints, Salt Lake City (hereafter CHL).
3. Thomas Morrison, Warrant for Joseph Smith et al., June 11, 1844, copy, Joseph Smith Collection, CHL,
4. For example, see Dallin H. Oaks, "The Suppression of the *Nauvoo Expositor*," *Utah Law Review* 9 (Winter 1965): 862–903; Robert Bruce Flanders, *Nauvoo: Kingdom on the Mississippi* (Urbana: University of Illinois Press, 1975), 308; Glen M. Leonard, *Nauvoo: A Place of Peace, a People of Promise* (Provo, UT: Brigham Young University Press; Salt Lake City: Deseret Book, 2002), 362–66; and Richard L. Bushman, *Joseph Smith: Rough Stone Rolling* (New York: Alfred A. Knopf, 2005), 539–41.
5. See Lyndon W. Cook, "William Law, Nauvoo Dissenter," *BYU Studies* 22, no.1 (Winter 1982): 47–72; and Lyndon W. Cook, *William Law* (Orem, UT: Grandin Book, 1994). Law's opposition to Joseph appears to have been rooted primarily in his opposition to plural marriage. According to William Clayton, he was also angry at Joseph for not sealing him to his wife, Jane, "in consequence of his being an adulterer." See Cook, *William Law*, 41–42, 46; William Clayton, journal, June 12, 1844, as cited in *The Joseph Smith Papers, Journals*, 3:xxiiin48 (hereafter *JSP*, J3).
6. See *JSP*, J3:414–15.
7. Charles Dana accused Dr. William Brink of causing premature childbirth and physical harm to his wife in October 1842. The case was heard in the Nauvoo mayor's court, with Joseph Smith presiding, on March 2–3, 1843. The case received a significant amount of attention (Willard Richards devoted over forty pages of Joseph Smith's journal to an account of the trial, for example), as several of the expert witnesses for the prosecution—including Foster—were "regular" physicians who had been trained in medical schools, while the defendant, William Brink, was a Thomsonian or "botanic" physician. In essence, the validity and credibility of Thomsonian medicine was on trial in this case. For an annotated account of the trial, see *The Joseph Smith Papers, Journals*, 2:280–94.
8. See *JSP*, J3:406–7; and Smith, journal, March 2–3, 1843.
9. Smith, journal, January 28, 1842 (second of two entries for this date).
10. Nauvoo High Council Minutes, May [21] and 24, 1842, CHL.
11. Smith, journal, May 24. 1842; "Chauncey Higbee," *Nauvoo Neighbor*, May 29, 1844; Nauvoo High Council Minutes, May [21] and 24, 1842. According to these women's testimonies, Higbee had approached Margaret Nyman "some time during the month of March last," Matilda Nyman "during this spring," and Sarah Miller "soon after the special conference this spring," which was held April 6–8, 1842, in Nauvoo. See "Conference Minutes," *Times and Seasons* 3 (15 April 1842): 761–63.
12. Smith, journal, May 24, 1842.

13. Smith, journal, May 13, 1842; and Historian's Office, Joseph Smith History, draft notes, May 13, 1842, CHL.
14. Smith, journal, June 29, 1842.
15. Francis M. Higbee v. Joseph Smith, May 8, 1844, Nauvoo City Records, 1841–1845, CHL. According to the city records, Sidney Rigdon, Hyrum Smith, Orrin Porter Rockwell, Cyrus Wheelock, Joel S. Miles, Henry G. Sherwood, Heber C. Kimball, and Brigham Young corroborated Joseph Smith's version of events.
16. Smith, journal, March 10, 1842.
17. Smith, journal, May 20, 1842. Richards recorded part of this entry in shorthand; for a transliteration of the shorthand, see *JSP*, J2, 61.
18. Smith, journal, May 21 and July 19, 1842; and Nauvoo High Council Minutes, May [21], 1842.
19. Smith, journal, February 11 and 13, 1843, and November 8, 1842.
20. Smith, journal, February 21, 1844.
21. Smith, journal, February 24, 1844.
22. Smith, journal, March 14 and 16, 1843.
23. See Smith, journal, March 29, 1843; and Historian's Office, Joseph Smith History, draft notes, March 29, 1843.
24. In early June 1843, a special term of the Daviess County, Missouri, Circuit Court had indicted Joseph on the charge of treason for his alleged activities in that county in 1838. Having received a requisition from Missouri governor Thomas Reynolds for Joseph's extradition, Illinois governor Thomas Ford issued a warrant for his arrest on June 17. Foster, who evidently left Nauvoo on June 25 with several dozen other men to intercept Joseph and his captors, was later dispatched by Joseph to announce his anticipated return to Nauvoo on June 30 and to see that the Nauvoo band was on hand "to meet him at Hyrums farm" and escort him into the city. See Daviess County Circuit Court Records, vol. A, p. 372; Indictment, June 1843, State of Missouri v. Joseph Smith for Treason (Daviess Co. Cir. Ct. 1843), Western Americana Collection, Beinecke Rare Book and Manuscript Library, Yale University, New Haven, CT; Warrant for Joseph Smith, June 17, 1843, copy, Joseph Smith Collection, CHL; "Missouri vs Joseph Smith," *Times and Seasons* 4 (1 July 1843): 242–43; and Smith, journal, June 25 and 29, 1843.
25. Smith, journal, October 29, 1843.
26. Smith, journal, January 21, 1844.
27. See Smith, journal, August 12, 1843, January 6, 1844; see also "Disagreeable Affair at Carthage," *Nauvoo Neighbor*, January 10, 1844.
28. Smith, journal, January 3 and 4, 1844; and Nauvoo City Council Minutes, January 3 and 5, 1844.
29. Smith, journal, January 5, 1844; Nauvoo City Council Minutes, January 5, 1844.
30. William Law, "Record of Doings at Nauvoo in 1844," January 5, 1844, in Cook, *William Law*, 45–46.
31. Francis M. Higbee to Joseph Smith, January 10, 1844, Joseph Smith Collection, CHL.
32. Orson Pratt, Affidavit, January 15, 1844, Nauvoo City Records, 1841–1845; and Smith, journal, January 15, 1844.
33. Smith, journal, January 16, 1844; Nauvoo Municipal Court Docket, January 16, 1844, CHL; and Nauvoo City Council Minutes, January 5 and 16, 1844, CHL.
34. A term used by dissidents in Nauvoo to refer to plural marriage.

35. Smith, journal, February 26, 1844; and City of Nauvoo vs. O. F. Bostwick, John Scott statement, February 26, 1844, Nauvoo City Records, 1841–1845.

36. Smith, journal, March 7, 1844; and Wilford Woodruff, journal, March 7, 1844, Wilford Woodruff Collection, CHL.

37. "The Mormons and their Prophet—Legislation at Nauvoo—The Temple," *New York Weekly Tribune*, February 3, 1844.

38. Smith, journal, March 7, 1844. Based on available evidence, it is unclear whether Charles Foster was the author of the article or not.

39. Thomas Ford, to the "citizens of Hancock County, Mormons and all," January 29, 1844, in *Warsaw Signal*, February 14, 1844.

40. "Pacific Innuendo," *Nauvoo Neighbor*, February 21, 1844; and "To the Editor of the Neighbor," *Nauvoo Neighbor*, February 21, 1844.

41. M[erinus] G. Eaton, Affidavit, March 27, 1844, in *Nauvoo Neighbor*, April 17, 1844.

42. William Clayton, journal, March 23, 1844, as cited in *JSP*, J3:207n906.

43. Smith, journal, March 24, 1844. Jackson sold land for Joseph Smith in May 1843 and was appointed an aide-de-camp for Joseph Smith in the Nauvoo Legion in January 1844. His reasons for turning against Joseph are obscure, as he later claimed to have gone to Nauvoo "to gain the confidence of the Prophet, that [he] might discover and disclose to the world his real designs and the nature of his operations." *JSP*, J3:418, 157; and Joseph H. Jackson, *The Adventures and Experience of Joseph H. Jackson: Disclosing the Depths of Mormon Villainy Practiced in Nauvoo* (Warsaw, IL, 1846).

44. Woodruff, journal, March 24, 1844, Wilford Woodruff Collection, CHL.

45. M[erinus] G. Eaton, Affidavit, March 27, 1844, in *Nauvoo Neighbor*, April 17, 1844.

46. Abiathar B. Williams, Affidavit, March 27, 1844, in *Nauvoo Neighbor*, April 17, 1844.

47. Smith, journal, March 31 and April 1, 1844. Willard Richards wrote in Joseph's journal that it was Francis Higbee who was fined, but the records cited in the following note indicate that it was Chauncey Higbee rather than Francis.

48. "Robbery and Lynching," *Nauvoo Neighbor*, April 3, 1844; Nauvoo Municipal Court Docket, April 2 and 3, 1844, CHL; John P. Greene et al., Petition, April 3, 1844, Nauvoo City Records, 1841–1845; and Smith, journal, April 2 and 3, 1844.

49. "Robbery and Lynching," *Nauvoo Neighbor*, April 3, 1844; see Smith, journal, April 1, 1844.

50. "Robbery and Lynching," *Nauvoo Neighbor*, April 3, 1844.

51. Smith, journal, April 16, 1844.

52. Smith, journal, April 13, 1844.

53. Smith, journal, April 18, 1844.

54. See Smith, journal, April 26, 1844; and Lucy Mack Smith, *Biographical Sketches of Joseph Smith the Prophet and His Progenitors for Many Generations* (Liverpool: S. W. Richards, 1853), 275–76.

55. "Outrage," *Nauvoo Neighbor*, May 1, 1844.

56. Smith, journal, April 26, 1844; "Outrage," *Nauvoo Neighbor*, May 1, 1844. For *interfered*, Richards wrote *intefed* in Smith's journal. The three men appealed their conviction to the Nauvoo municipal court, which called for the case on June 3, 1844. None of the appellants appeared, however, and the municipal court dismissed

the appeal "for want of prosecution." See Smith, journal, April 26, 1844; and Nauvoo Municipal Court Docket, June 3, 1844.

57. Smith, journal, April 26, 1844.

58. Smith, journal, April 27, 1844.

59. Smith, journal, April 28, 1844. Law's church met weekly each Sunday through May 26 and possibly beyond, although it appears to have faded quickly after that. According to the *Warsaw Signal*, "about three hundred" people attended the May 12 meeting. See Cook, *William Law*, 54; and "The New Church," *Warsaw Signal*, May 15, 1844.

60. Smith, journal, April 29, 1844.

61. Council of Fifty, "Record," May 6, 1844, CHL, in *JSP*, J3:244n1104; and Doctrine and Covenants 78:12. The council also delivered William and Wilson Law to the "buffetings of Satan" at this time.

62. Smith, journal, January 16 and May 6, 1844; Francis Higbee, Declaration, May 1, 1844, Higbee v. Joseph Smith, Hancock County, IL, Circuit Court Legal Documents, L. Tom Perry Special Collections, Harold B. Lee Library, Brigham Young University, Provo, UT.

63. Smith, journal, May 6, 1844; Joseph Smith, Petition, May 6, 1844, in Francis M. Higbee v. Joseph Smith, May 8, 1844, Nauvoo City Records, 1841–1845.

64. Francis M. Higbee v. Joseph Smith, May 8, 1844, Nauvoo City Records, 1841–1845.

65. Nauvoo High Council Minutes, May 18, 1844.

66. Smith, journal, May 7, 1844.

67. Foster later charged Joseph with perjury, leading to an indictment on May 24, 1844. On May 25 Higbee charged him with having "received states prope[r]ty," although no indictment on that charge has been located. William and Wilson Law charged him with adultery and fornication, leading to an indictment on May 23. See Smith, journal, May 25, 1844; Indictment, May 24, 1844, State of Illinois v. Joseph Smith for Perjury, Hancock County Circuit Court, 1844, photocopy, Nineteenth-Century Legal Documents Collection, CHL; Indictment, May 23, 1844, State of Illinois v. Joseph Smith for Adultery, Hancock County Circuit Court, 1844, Hancock County Circuit Court Indictments and Arrest Warrants, CHL.

68. *Nauvoo Expositor*, June 7, 1844.

Selected RSC Publications on Church History in Illinois, 1839–1846

GENERAL READING

Cope, Rachel, Carter Charles, and Jordan T. Watkins, eds. *How and What You Worship: Christology and Praxis in the Revelations of Joseph Smith* (2020).

Ivie, Evan L., and Douglas C. Heiner. "Deaths in Early Nauvoo, Illinois, 1839–46, and in Winter Quarters, Nebraska, 1846–48." *Religious Educator* 10, no. 3 (2009): 163–74.

MacKay, Michael Hubbard, and William G. Hartley, eds. *The Rise of the Latter-day Saints: The Journals and Histories of Newel Knight* (2019).

Van Orden, Bruce A. *We'll Sing and We'll Shout: The Life and Times of W. W. Phelps* (2018).

DOCTRINAL DEVELOPMENTS

Colvin, Don F. *Nauvoo Temple: A Story of Faith* (2002).

Harper, Steven C. "Endowed with Power." *Religious Educator* 5, no. 2 (2004): 83–99.

Hedges Andrew H. "They Pursue Me without Cause": Joseph Smith in Hiding and D&C 127, 128." *Religious Educator* 16, no. 1 (2015): 43–59.

Hedges, Andrew H., Rachel Cope, Gerrit J. Dirkmaat, and Thomas A. Wayment. "Discussing Difficult Topics: Plural Marriage." *Religious Educator* 17, no. 1 (2016): 10–21.

POLITICAL AND ORGANIZATIONAL EXPANSION

Black, Susan Easton. "The University of Nauvoo, 1841–45." *Religious Educator* 10, no. 3 (2009): 189–206.

Grow, Matthew J., and R. Eric Smith, eds. *The Council of Fifty: What the Records Reveal about Mormon History* (2017).

Sainsbury, Derek R. *Storming the Nation: The Unknown Contributions of Joseph Smith's Political Missionaries* (2020).

Wilkinson, Carol, and Cynthia Doxey Green. *The Field Is White: Harvest in the Three Counties of England* (2017).

Part Four

Church History in Salt Lake City and Beyond

1847–present

Chapter Twenty

"This Shall Be Our Covenant"

Brigham Young and Doctrine and Covenants 136

CHAD M. ORTON

Two and one-half years after Brigham Young assumed the primary leadership role for The Church of Jesus Christ of Latter-day Saints, and nearly a year after the first Saints left Nauvoo, Illinois, to begin the journey west, the responsibility of leading the Church had taken a physical toll on him. By January 1847 he had lost so much weight that his clothes no longer fit. The reason was that the Latter-day Saints had literally and figuratively become stuck in the mud. Worn out and needing wisdom on how to extricate the Church and move the work forward, Brigham received the answers he desperately needed when the Lord revealed his "Word and Will," a revelation later canonized as Doctrine and Covenants section 136.

Because this only canonized revelation of Brigham Young begins by addressing "the Camp of Israel in their journeyings to the west" (v. 1), it has been primarily viewed, and often glossed over, as simply a "how to" guide for organizing pioneer companies. While the revelation contains specific organizational concepts (see vv. 3, 5, 7, 15), organizing companies for emigration was only one aspect of its contribution toward advancing the work. More importantly, the revelation helped to refocus Brigham and the Saints on the importance of the covenants they had made and served as a reminder that both personal salvation and the progress of the Church were dependent on harkening to the word of Lord and being on the covenant path.[1]

Received at a pivotal time in the history of the Church, the "Word and Will of the Lord" became a seminal moment for Brigham and provided him an important "before and after" lesson. The "before" was the 1846 journey across Iowa; the "after" was the 1847 travels of the vanguard pioneer company from Winter Quarters to the Salt Lake Valley.[2] Having proved the word of the Lord during the 1847 exodus, he subsequently included the revelation's principles in his teaching as he continued to lead the Saints after they had reached their promised land.[3] Thus, while section 136 had a great effect on Brigham as "American Moses" in gathering the Latter-day Saints, it also had an influence on him in his role as "American Joshua" overseeing Latter-day Saint settlement of the West.

THE BEFORE: IOWA, 1846

When Brigham made the decision for the Saints to begin leaving Nauvoo in February 1846's bitter cold, he fully expected to lead the vanguard company of approximately three hundred men to their new home that year.[4] His goal was to arrive early enough to grow crops that would help sustain the thousands of Latter-day Saints who would subsequently join them before the year was out. Instead of reaching the Rocky Mountains, however, his company struggled to make it across Iowa. Rather than taking four to five weeks to reach the Missouri River as anticipated, that portion of the journey had taken more than four months. The delay in part was the result of heavy rains that caused streams and rivers to rise significantly above normal levels and turned rolling plains into muddy quagmires.

Iowa's mud and swollen rivers would have been less problematic if the advance company had not been joined by more than a thousand others, an unwieldy number that further slowed its progress. Many of these Saints had left Nauvoo ahead of schedule because of fears regarding the Church's enemies, while others were simply eager to get on the road or to travel with Brigham and other members of the Twelve in a time of uncertainty. Having left earlier than planned, a large number were ill-prepared for the journey. Helen Mar Kimball Whitney recalled, "There was such a great desire among the people and such a determination to emigrate with the first company that there [were] hundreds [who] started without the necessary outfit."[5] The situation prompted a frustrated Brigham to declare three months into the journey: "The Saints have crowded on us all the while, and have completely tied our hands by importuning and saying do not leave us behind. Wherever you go we want to go and be with you, and thus our hands and feet have been bound which has caused our delay."[6]

WINTER QUARTERS, 1846–47

When the advance company finally reached the Missouri River in mid-June 1846, their energy and supplies were largely spent. As a result, they were forced to find a place to winter and try again the following year.

In addition to these pioneers, thousands of other Latter-day Saints had left Nauvoo as scheduled, expecting their journey would end that year in the place that God had prepared for them "far away in the West."[7] Instead, they also needed a temporary home. By the fall of 1846, more than seven thousand were in exile near the Missouri River, living in caves, wagons, makeshift hovels, and log cabins, primarily at Winter Quarters, Nebraska, and Kanesville, Iowa. Another three thousand were forced to winter under similar conditions at settlements further back along the trail. At these various locations, many were sick or dying from malnutrition and exposure, and a number were experiencing a crisis of faith.

Not only had the delays and the resulting disappointment of not reaching the promised land taken a physical and emotional toll on Brigham, but to this was added the stress and toil of having to prepare for the upcoming emigration season while at the same time having to see to it that the needs of the Saints were met. Shortly before the "Word and Will" was received, it was reported that Brigham slept "with one eye open and one foot out of bed, and when anything is wanted, he is on hand."[8] Not surprisingly, all of this made Winter Quarters among the most difficult periods of his life. He wrote at the time that he felt "like a father with a great family of children around me" and later recalled that his responsibilities pressed down on him like a "twenty-five ton weight."[9] The task that he had been given was beyond his natural ability, and he needed assistance if he was to accomplish the work.

"WORD AND WILL OF THE LORD" IS RECEIVED

Although the Iowa experience and the stress of Winter Quarters weakened Brigham physically, they helped prepare him to receive the "Word and Will of the Lord" at a time when it would be both welcomed and fully embraced.[10]

On January 14, 1847, after months of contemplation, councils, and prayer, Brigham received the help he anxiously sought to move the work forward.[11] Two days later the revelation was presented to the Saints at Winter Quarters.

While most principles of the revelation had been previously revealed to Joseph Smith or could be found in ancient scripture, the Saints had not always acted as if they were important. Now, however, they found a ready place in Brigham's heart. As Brigham's subsequent actions demonstrated, the message he took away from this revelation was straightforward. Modern Israel, like ancient Israel, had become "lost" in the wilderness because the people had not always harkened to the voice of the Lord. Brigham and the Saints had been doing things their way and hadn't made as much progress as they had hoped. Now it was time to try it the Lord's way.[12]

In addition to providing Brigham the answers he needed to put the Church back on track, the revelation served as a powerful witness to Brigham and the Saints that because they were on the Lord's errand, the Lord did not expect them to carry out his work without his help. In presenting the revelation to the Saints, Brigham emphatically reassured them that the Church continued to be "led by Revelation just as much since the death of Joseph Smith as before."[13]

IMPLEMENTING THE "WORD AND WILL"

As instructed in the revelation (vv. 3, 15), beginning in 1847 Brigham placed a renewed emphasis on organizing emigrating companies with "captains of hundreds, captains of fifties, and captains of tens, with a president and his two counselors at their head."[14] Brigham had attempted to organize the Saints in a similar manner before their leaving Nauvoo, but the organizational structure had not always been viewed as essential. Now in 1847 the way the Saints were organized would become so important that even before Brigham began dictating the revelation he directed "that letters be written to instruct the brethren how to organize companies for emigration."[15]

The revelation's organizational pattern was not new. Moses, at the suggestion of his father-in-law and with the blessing of the Lord, first employed it during the Exodus. Jethro, seeing the toll that the journey was taking upon his son-in-law, encouraged Moses to appoint "rulers of thousands, and rulers of hundreds, rulers of fifties, and rulers of tens," "able men, such as fear God, men of truth, hating covetousness." Jethro envisioned these men serving as the leaders and judges over their respective groups, taking to Moses only the "great matter[s]" they could not resolve. Jethro told Moses that this organizational model would make the journey "easier" on him since these rulers could "bear the burden with" him. Jethro encouraged Moses to take this pattern to the Lord to see if "God command thee so," noting that if he did command it, "then thou shalt be able to endure, and all this people shall also go to their place in peace."[16]

Joseph Smith had used a similar pattern in organizing "Zion's Camp" in 1834, calling the leaders "captains" rather than "rulers."[17] The model was also employed on a limited basis during the Latter-day Saint exodus from Missouri during the winter of 1838–39, although most of those fleeing the state traveled as families or in small groups they organized themselves.

In addition to giving a renewed emphasis to this aspect of company organization, Brigham also implemented two other organizational changes. First, the size of a company would be limited to no more than one hundred wagons. Secondly, members of a specific company were to remain part of that company throughout the journey, except in unusual circumstances. This policy of having membership in one company was a marked departure from the fluidity of company membership that was an aspect of the exodus across Iowa and that would continue to be a common practice among non-Latter-day Saint emigrants.[18] Although the ideal was not always realized, beginning in 1847 the Latter-day Saint exodus became "the most carefully orchestrated, deliberately planned, and abundantly organized hegira in all of American history."[19]

At the same time that he was making preparations for the 1847 emigration, Brigham embraced the Lord's injunction that when "companies are organized let them go to with their might, to prepare for those who are to tarry," by preparing "houses, and fields for raising grain" (vv. 6, 9). In connection with the Twelve, he sent out instructions that all who remained behind needed to be "amply provided for," declaring that "those who are going to remove this spring" had the responsibility to "use all diligence in plowing, planting, sowing and building for those who are to remain."[20]

In addition to designating the land that was to be used for the planting and sowing when conditions that spring would allow, he "counseled the brethren to get timber and season it" in the meantime so that there would be lumber available in 1848 to build wagons for that year's emigration.[21] Because Winter Quarters had been established in what was widely known as "Indian land," he set in motion plans for the creation of a stockade in the event of a conflict.[22] Shortly before the vanguard company left, he also requested "those who were ready to start to assist in removing some families" to better living quarters.[23]

In addition to overseeing the general needs of the Saints, Brigham also focused attention on the families of the members of the vanguard company. He met "with the brethren of the Twelve, the presidents of companies and captains" and outlined "the policy to be pursued by the Pioneers in leaving their families."[24] One aspect of this policy stipulated that no one would be allowed to go west unless each "individual in his family" had "300 lbs of bread stuff" to live on.[25]

THE TWELVE TO TEACH THE LORD'S WILL

Equally important as the instruction on *how* the exodus was to be organized was the Lord's declaration about *who* was to lead the Saints. The "Word and Will of the Lord" proclaimed that the journey, and thus the future of the Church, was "under the direction of the Twelve Apostles" (v. 3).[26] Because the revelation served as a testament that the Twelve were the authorized successors to Joseph Smith until the First Presidency was reorganized, Hosea Stout concluded that it would "put to silence the wild bickering and suggestions of those who are ever in the way. . . . They will now have to come to this standard or come out in open rebellion to the Will of the Lord."[27]

Of the six men specifically commanded in the revelation to organize companies (see vv. 12–14), five were members of the Twelve (Ezra T. Benson, Orson Pratt, Wilford Woodruff, Amasa Lyman, and George A. Smith), while the sixth, Erastus Snow, would fill a vacancy in the Quorum in 1849. None of those men, however, would travel with the companies they organized. Instead, each was a member of the first pioneer company to enter the Salt Lake Valley.[28] By employing the revelation's organizational pattern, Brigham and the Twelve were now freed up to lead out and provide general leadership for the Church since the day-to-day responsibility for each company of Saints now resided with its presidency and captains.

As significant as was the Lord's testimony of the Twelve was his declaration that they had the collective responsibility to "teach this, my will, to the saints" (v. 16). The fact that the Church was organized according to the word of the Lord little mattered if the Saints' behavior also did not collectively reflect the will of the Lord.[29] In this regard the revelation served as a forceful reminder to Brigham that he and other members of the Twelve had a similar charge to that given to Moses—they were to teach the "ordinances and laws" and to show the Saints "the way wherein they must walk, and the work that they must do."[30]

Immediately Brigham went to work to ensure that members of the Twelve fully understood what the Lord expected of both them and the Latter-day Saints. While a number of Saints had willfully ignored counsel during the previous year's journey, there was also a large number who had not been sufficiently taught what was expected of them, a situation that the Twelve were now charged to rectify. Brigham also informed Church members that the Twelve would "communicate with, instruct, and counsel you as they shall be directed by the Holy Spirit, and we call upon you to give heed to their admonitions in all things, which if you do, ye shall find peace and rest, and safety and prosperity."[31]

ESTABLISHING THE TRAIL ALONG THE COVENANT PATH

Central to the revelation was the reminder that modern Israel was a covenant people and that covenants were an essential aspect of the Lord's work. In verse 2 the Lord declared that the Latter-day Saints were to undertake their exodus "with a covenant and promise to keep all the commandments and statues of the Lord our God." In verse 4 the "Word and Will" further stated that "this shall be our covenant—that we will walk in all the ordinances of the Lord."

Before leaving Nauvoo, Brigham had written that the most important thing "for the salvation of the Church" was for the Latter-day Saints to reach their promised land.[32] Following the revelation, his declarations stressed that behavior was more essential to the salvation and destiny of the Church and its members than physical location.[33] He would emphasize to the vanguard company that their responsibility extended beyond just blazing a trail that others would follow in the coming months and years. They also had a duty to see that the trail was established along the Lord's covenant path and in harmony with the revealed word of the Lord.[34]

Besides their baptismal covenants, many Latter-day Saints had made temple covenants in the months leading up to the exodus from Nauvoo. During that time, Brigham oversaw a concerted effort to ensure that as many Saints as possible received their endowments and participated in other sacred ordinances in the Nauvoo Temple before heading into the wilderness.[35] Section 136 served as a reminder that while it was important to make covenants, it was equally as important to strive to keep them.[36]

The "Word and Will of the Lord" also emphatically reminded the Saints that their ultimate success was dependent on God: "I am he who led the children of Israel out of the land of Egypt; and my arm is stretched out in the last days, to save my people Israel" (v. 22). Besides making a direct tie between the exoduses of modern and ancient Israel, the revelation indirectly provided the Latter-day Saints a connection to the journey of Lehi and Nephi, during which the Lord declared: "Inasmuch as ye shall keep my commandments, ye shall prosper, and shall be led to a land of promise. . . . I will prepare the way before you, if it so be that he shall keep my commandments; wherefore, inasmuch as ye shall keep my commandments ye shall be led towards the promised land; and ye shall know that it is by me that ye are led. . . . After ye have arrived in the promised land, ye shall know that I, the Lord, am God; and that I, the Lord, did deliver you."[37]

Although section 136's reference to ordinances, covenants, and obedience brought new hope, it also served as a warning. After the Saints failed to redeem Zion in 1834, the Lord admonished the Saints: "Were it not for the transgressions of my people, speaking concerning the church and not individuals, they might have been redeemed even now. But behold, they have not learned to be obedient to the things which I require at their hands."[38] The lessons of the past were not lost on Brigham in 1847.

With a new understanding came a new attitude and a renewed energy. As God's people, they not only had the responsibility to undertake the journey in a different manner, they also had the privilege. The ultimate success of the Saints settling their promised land was now less dependent on maps, wagons, and supplies than upon aligning their efforts with the word and will of the Lord. If they were to accomplish the task before them, spiritual preparation was more important than physical preparation, and personal behavior more important than personal property.

While Brigham may have had concerns during his travels across Iowa about how the Saints would succeed, he was certain during the journey from Winter Quarters that if the Saints were endeavoring to keep their covenants and live according to the revealed word they could not fail, even if they again encountered circumstances beyond their control. Believing that they could bind the Lord to help them because of their faithfulness, Brigham "warned all who intended to proceed to the mountains that iniquity would not be tolerated in the Camp of Israel." He also declared that he "did not want any to join [the vanguard] company unless they would obey the word and will of the Lord, live in honesty and assist to build up the kingdom of God."[39] Only after the Saints had been taught what was expected of them and agreed to live according to the revealed word were they permitted to add their names to the list of those who could emigrate.

Although a shortage of food had been a major issue during the Saints' journey across Iowa, after the revelation Brigham believed that food and supplies need not be a primary concern if the Saints were striving to fulfill their part of their covenants. Four days after receiving section 136, he publicly proclaimed that he "had not cattle sufficient to go to the mountains" but that he "had no more doubts nor fears of going to the mountains, and felt as much security as if [he] possessed the treasures of the East."[40] He further stated that each member of the vanguard company needed to take only one hundred pounds of food on the journey into the wilderness, declaring that all "who had not faith to start with that amount" could stay at Winter Quarters.[41]

A month into the journey, Brigham responded to the fears of some that the company might not reach their destination in time to plant crops: "Well, suppose we [do] not. We [have] done all we could & travelled as fast as our Teams were able to go." He reassured the company that if they had done their part he would feel "as well satisfied as if we had a thousand acres planted with grain. The Lord would do the rest."[42] Convinced that the Lord was as capable of making it rain manna on the plains of North America as on the plains of Arabia, Brigham's testimony echoed the words of the prophet Isaiah: "I never felt clearer in mind than on this journey. My peace is like a river between my God and myself."[43]

Even the number of men making up the 1847 vanguard company may be evidence of this new attitude. Rather than 300 men, the number was halved to 144.[44] While there is no contemporary account as to why that specific number, a popular but unsupported belief has arisen that it reflected the twelve tribes of Israel.[45]

THE AFTER: WINTER QUARTERS TO THE SALT LAKE VALLEY, 1847

What is certain is that there was a noticeable change among the Saints following the revelation. William Clayton observed: "It truly seemed as though the cloud had burst and we had emerged into a new element, a new atmosphere, and a new society."[46] The experiences at Winter Quarters, coupled with the subsequent journey to the Salt Lake Valley, became a teaching moment for the Twelve in terms of leading the Church, and for the Latter-day Saints generally in giving heed to the will of the Lord. George A. Smith declared that the Saints would look back at their journey as "one of the greatest schools they ever were in," while Wilford Woodruff wrote, "We are now in a place where we are proving ourselves."[47] In addition to proving the faith and obedience of Brigham and the Saints, the journey would become an exercise in proving the word of the Lord.

In spite of the Saints' new commitment, the 1847 exodus was not without its trials. The vanguard company repeatedly found their resolve and faith tried. The initial plan was to leave "one month before grass grows," but no later than March 15. However, spring was late in coming and the early grass grew weeks later than anticipated. Because of the unseasonably cold weather, the company was unable to get underway from its rendezvous location until mid-April.[48] The excitement of finally beginning the journey was soon tempered by the realities of unseasonably cold nights, windswept prairies, challenging river crossings, the loss of stock, and days filled with long, monotonous travel.

While there was an overall reformation in conduct among the members of the vanguard company, at times Brigham, having become passionately committed to the principles of the revelation, found himself frustrated with the behavior of some company members. In late May he read "the Word and Will of the Lord" to the company and "expressed his views and feelings . . . that they were forgetting their mission." He further proclaimed that he would "rather travel with 10 righteous men who would keep the command-ments of God than the whole camp while in a careless manner and forget-ting God."[49] The following day he declared that he wanted the company "to covenant to turn to the Lord with all their hearts. . . . I have said many things to the brethren about the strictness of their walk and conduct when we left the gentiles, and told them that we would have to walk upright or the law would be put in force. . . . If we don't repent and quit our wicked-ness we will have more hindrances than we have had, and worse storms to encounter." Having reproved with sharpness, Brigham then "very tenderly blessed the brethren and prayed that God would enable them to fulfill their covenants."[50]

Ultimately, the 1847 emigration stood in dramatic contrast to the pre-vious year's journey. While Brigham Young's company had traveled around three hundred miles in 1846, in 1847 the vanguard pioneer company traveled approximately one thousand miles in a shorter amount of time. Brigham attributed the difference to the Lord keeping his promise to lead and bless the Saints because of their efforts to align their will with his.

"THE WORD AND WILL": *THE* PRACTICAL APPROACH

After a brief stay in the Salt Lake Valley, Brigham returned to Winter Quarters in the fall of 1847. During the return trip he encountered the companies that Church leaders had organized according to the revelation. Instead of these companies traveling according to the "Word and Will of the Lord" and subsequent decisions of the Twelve, they had essentially become one large company consisting of nearly fifteen hundred people and six hundred wagons.[51] There had been many problems along the way, including company members contending over the best camping spots.

More disconcerting to Brigham was the fact that this large company included two members of the Twelve—Parley P. Pratt and John Taylor. Both of these men had chosen not to travel with the vanguard company and the rest of the Twelve because they had just returned from missions to England and wanted more time before they undertook the westward journey. Although neither had been at Winter Quarters when section 136 was received and began to be implemented, Brigham had seen to it that they were taught about the revelation and informed about the decisions of the Twelve.

However, when Pratt and Taylor were preparing to leave the rendezvous location in mid-June, they concluded they would have to set aside the revelation and the decisions of the Twelve if they were to reach the valley that fall. "Theory is not what we will see now so much as the practical," Pratt declared at the time.[52] For Brigham, the word of the Lord was not theory—it *was* the practical approach. When Brigham discovered what had happened and why, he could not hide his frustration with Pratt and Taylor: "Our companies were perfectly organized. . . . Why should our whole winter's work be set at naught[?] . . . If the Quorum of the Twelve does a thing it is not in the power of two of them to rip it up. . . . I know you have had a hard time and you have brought it on yourself. . . . We've got the machine a moving[;] it is not your business to stick your hands among the cogs and stop the wheel."[53] In essence, Brigham reminded them what he had previously publicly declared: "When God tells a man what to do, he admits of no argument, and I want no arguments."[54] Both Pratt and Taylor accepted the reproof and acknowledged their mistake.[55]

"THE WORD AND WILL": PERSONAL ANCHOR POINTS

Having proven for himself how the Saints were better off heeding the word and will of the Lord, Brigham never forgot the lessons he learned as a result of having received and implemented section 136. His focus on the benefits of covenants and the importance of hearkening to the revealed word of the Lord caused the anxiety he felt at Winter Quarters to fade away. He subsequently found himself "full of peace by day and by night" and sleeping as "soundly as a healthy child in the lap of its mother."[56]

Near the end of his life Brigham emphatically declared: "There is great delight in the law of the Lord to me, for the simple reason—it is pure, holy, just, and true. . . . My religion is to know the will of God and do it."[57] Not only had section 136's general principles become personal anchor points for him, but during the thirty years that he led the Church he faithfully taught the Saints through word and deed the importance of making them, along with other aspects of the revealed word of the Lord, anchor points in their own lives as well.

"BEAR AN EQUAL PROPORTION"

In verses 8 and 10, the "Word and Will of the Lord" declared that the Saints had the responsibility to "bear an equal proportion, according to the dividend of their property, in taking the poor, the widows, the fatherless, and the families of those who have gone into the army [Mormon Battalion], that the cries of the widow and fatherless come not up into the ears of the Lord against this people. . . . Let every man use all his influence and property to remove this people."[58] Before leaving Nauvoo, Brigham had moved at the October 1845 conference "that we take all the saints with us, to the extent of our ability, that is, our influence and property." While 214 Saints signed the "Nauvoo Covenant," it was not a sufficient number to meet the needs of all who wanted to start west.[59] As a result, in the fall of 1846 several hundred Latter-day Saints who had remained behind because of poverty and sickness were driven from Nauvoo by armed mobs, most unprepared for the journey.

Following the revelation, Brigham emphasized the Saints' collective responsibility to assist those who needed help emigrating. As soon as companies were organized for the 1847 emigration, he instructed the captains of ten "to ascertain what property their ten possessed, so that the widows and women whose husbands were in the army might be taken along, so far as there was means to take them."[60] He and other members of the Twelve also instructed the Saints that "the widow and the fatherless must not be forgotten, let as many of them be taken as can." They further noted that they wanted each company "to take as many of the sisters whose husbands . . . are in the army, so that when we meet the Battalion, they will bless us, greet their families with thanksgiving, and immediately go to planting, plowing and sowing, instead of being obliged to walk back some hundreds of miles further, after their long and tedious journey and wasting their flesh, and blood, and bones to no purpose."[61]

Part of Brigham's frustration with Pratt and Taylor centered on the fact that they had not brought with them as many of these members as anticipated, in spite of the Lord's promise that if the Saints would "do this with a pure heart, in all faithfulness, ye shall be blessed; you shall be blessed in your flocks, and in your herds, and in your fields, and in your houses, and in your families" (v. 11). As a result of the decision to ignore this aspect of the revelation, more than thirty Mormon Battalion members, upon arriving at Salt Lake and discovering their families had been left behind, immediately undertook the long journey back to the Missouri River in the fall of 1847.

Once settled in Utah, Brigham through word and deed continued to emphasize the need for the Saints to help the poor and widows. "The Latter-day Saints . . . have got to learn that the interest of their brethren is their own interest, or they never can be saved in the celestial kingdom of God," he declared.[62] On another occasion he proclaimed: "The Lord will bless that people that is full of charity, kindness and good works. When our monthly fast days come round, do we think of the poor? If we do, we should send in our mite, no matter what it is. . . . If God has not sustained us after all that we have passed through, let some one tell how we have been sustained."[63]

In addition to using his own resources to help gather the Saints and support them once they had arrived in Utah, Brigham introduced specific programs such as the Perpetual Emigrating Fund and the use of handcarts and down-and-back companies, thus allowing members to gather who lacked sufficient means to purchase a wagon and team. He also tried to keep the concept of pure religion before the Saints by organizing United Orders and attempting to implement the law of consecration.

"IN MINE OWN DUE TIME"

In the revelation the Lord declared that "Zion shall be redeemed in mine own due time" (v. 18). Because Brigham had been so anxious to reach the Saints' promised land in 1846, he had not fully embraced what Joseph Smith had told him in a dream he had during the whirl of activities leading up to the exodus from Nauvoo: "Brother Brigham don't be in a hurry—this was repeated the second and third time, when it came with a degree of sharpness."[64] To ancient Israel, the Lord had made a similar declaration: "For ye shall not go out with haste, nor go by flight: for the Lord will go before you; and the God of Israel shall be your rearward."[65]

Having learned his lesson during the 1846 and 1847 westward journeys, Brigham counseled those who would be returning to Winter Quarters in the fall of 1847 to "not give way to an over anxious Spirit so that your Spirits arrive at Winter Quarters before the time that your bodies can possibly arrive there."[66] He later encouraged all the Saints to slow down and make certain they were putting the Lord first: "You are in too much of a hurry. You do not go to meeting enough, you do not pray enough, you do not read the Scriptures enough, you do not meditate enough, you are all the time on the wing, and in such a hurry that you do not know what to do first." He concluded that many listening to him likely had not prayed that morning, their reason being that they had too much to do. "Stop! Wait!" he pleaded. "When you get up in the morning, before you suffer yourselves to eat one mouthful of food, . . . bow down before the Lord, ask him to forgive your sins, and protect you through the day, to preserve you from temptation and all evil, to guide your steps aright, that you may do something that day that shall be beneficial to the kingdom of God on the earth. Have you time to do this? Elders, sisters, have you time to pray? This is the counsel I have for the Latter-day Saints to-day. Stop, do not be in a hurry."[67]

"LET HIM THAT IS IGNORANT LEARN WISDOM"

The revelation also warned against pride and the attitude of some members that they really were not dependent on the Lord: "And if any shall seek to build up himself, and seeketh not my counsel, he shall have no power, and his folly shall be made manifest. . . . Let him that is ignorant learn wisdom by humbling himself and calling upon the Lord his God, that his eyes may be opened that he may see, and his ears opened that he may hear; for my Spirit is sent forth into the world to enlighten the humble and contrite, and to the condemnation of the ungodly" (vv. 19, 32–33).

Shortly after Brigham received the "Word and Will of the Lord," Joseph Smith again appeared to him in a dream. In response to Brigham's request for advice, Joseph declared: "Tell the people to be humble and faithful, and be sure to keep the spirit of the Lord and it will lead them right. Be careful and do not turn away the small still voice; it will teach them what to do and where to go; it will yield the fruits of the kingdom. Tell the brethren to keep their hearts open to conviction, so that when the Holy Ghost comes to them, their hearts will be ready to receive it." Joseph further noted that the Saints "can tell the Spirit of the Lord from all other spirits; it will take malice, hatred, strife and all evil from their hearts; and their whole desire will be to do good, bring forth righteousness and build up the kingdom of God. Tell the brethren if they will follow the Spirit of the Lord, they will go right."[68]

Like Joseph Smith, Brigham was uneducated by the standards of the day. Also like Joseph, Brigham readily acknowledged that his accomplishments, including leading the Saints to their promised land, were not the result of his natural talents and abilities as a leader but because he was a devoted follower: "What I know . . . I have received from the heavens, . . . not alone through my natural ability, and I give God the glory and the praise. Men talk about what has been accomplished under my direction, and attribute it to my wisdom and ability; but it is all by the power of God, and by intelligence received from him."[69] On another occasion he stated: "What do you suppose I think when I hear people say, 'O, see what the Mormons have done in the mountains. It is Brigham Young. What a head he has got!' . . . It is the Lord that has done this. It is not any one man or set of men; only as we are led and guided by the spirit."[70]

Near the end of Brigham's life, a visitor to the Beehive House, Brigham's home in Salt Lake City, commented on a painting of the Prophet Joseph hanging on the wall, observing that it "did not show any great amount of strength, intelligence, or culture." In response Brigham acknowledged that Joseph Smith "was not a man of education, but received such enlightenment from the Holy Spirit that he needed nothing more to fit him for his work as a leader." Brigham then added, "And this is my own case also. . . . All that I have acquired is by my own exertions and by the grace of God, who sometimes chooses the weak things of earth to manifest His glory."[71]

Brigham warned the Saints: "If you do not open your hearts so that the Spirit of God can enter your hearts and teach you the right way, I know that you are a ruined people."[72] On another occasion he stated: "I think there is more responsibility on myself than any other one man on this earth pertaining to the salvation of the human family; yet my path is a pleasant path to walk. . . . All I have to do is to live . . . [so as to] keep my spirit, feelings and conscience like a sheet of blank paper, and let the Spirit and power of God write upon it what he pleases. When he writes, I will read; but if I read before he writes, I am very likely to be wrong."[73]

Brigham also decried the fact that there were individuals in the Church who had lofty opinions of themselves, observing on one occasion, "I have seen men who belonged to this kingdom, and who really thought that if they were not associated with it, it could not progress."[74] On another occasion he declared, "Never ask how big we are, or inquire who we are." Instead, he wanted the Saints to ask, "What can I do to build up the kingdom of God upon the earth?"[75]

Because his desire was to build the kingdom, in addition to seeking to know the Lord's will, Brigham was not above doing the small things. He willingly undertook tasks that many leaders left to others. When a ferry was needed during the 1847 journey, he "went to work with all his strength" and assisted in making "a first rate White Pine and white Cotton Wood Raft."[76] The following year on his second journey to Utah, he crossed and recrossed the North Platte River assisting company members safely across.[77]

During the early days in the valley, Brigham spent time physically assisting Saints by chopping wood, building houses, and so on, often at the expense of other duties. On one occasion when Jedediah M. Grant sought out Brigham on a public matter, Grant found him shingling a roof. Frustrated, Grant told him: "Now, Brother Brigham, don't you think it is time you quit pounding nails and spending your time in work like this? We have many carpenters but only one Governor and one President of the Church. The people need you more than they need a good carpenter."[78] Reluctantly Brigham came down from the roof to fulfill the roles that were his alone.

While Brigham would give his ecclesiastical and civic duties their proper attention, he also continued to do the little things. On one occasion a stranger approached Brigham while he was on the steps of his carriage loading luggage for a journey. "Is Governor Young in this carriage?" the man asked. "No, sir," Brigham replied, "but he is on the steps of it."[79] Elizabeth Kane reported that during a journey she and her husband Thomas L. Kane made through Utah with Brigham in 1872 he personally inspected "every wheel, axle, horse and mule, and suit of harness belonging to the party" to make sure they were in good condition.[80]

He also did not take himself too seriously. During a visit to the home of Anson Call, Brigham took one of Call's young daughters on his knee and as he started to tell her how pretty she was the child blurted out, "Your eyes look just like our sow's!" To this Brigham replied: "Take me to the pig pen. I want to see this pig that has eyes just like mine." When the story was later retold, Brigham laughed as much as anyone.[81]

One contemporary critic of Brigham acknowledged that "the whole secret" of his "influence lies in his real sincerity. . . . For the sake of his religion, he has over and over again left his family, confronted the world, endured hunger, come back poor, made wealth and given it to the Church. . . . No holiday friend nor summer prophet, he has shared their trials as well as their prosperity."[82] Because Brigham did not view himself as greater than his calling or above the work that the Saints had been asked to do, it is not surprising that those who knew him best lovingly referred to him as "Brother Brigham."

"KEEP ALL YOUR PLEDGES"

In verses 20, 25–26, the "Word and Will of the Lord" stressed the need for the Saints to adhere to the Judeo-Christian values of dealing honestly with their fellow men: "Keep all your pledges one with another; and covet not that which is thy brother's. . . . If thou borrowest of thy neighbor, thou shalt restore that which thou hast borrowed; and if thou canst not repay then go straightway and tell thy neighbor, lest he condemn thee. If thou shalt find that which thy neighbor has lost, thou shalt make diligent search till thou shalt deliver it to him again." Brigham taught the Saints, "Honest hearts produce honest actions—holy desires produce corresponding outward works."[83] He also declared, "I have no fellowship for a man that will make a promise and not fulfil it."[84]

When Brigham learned in 1866 that a note for a debt he incurred around 1826 while living in Auburn, New York, had been found, he asked his son John W., who was bound for a mission to Europe, to make a side trip to Auburn and cancel the debt: "A man by the name of Richard Steele kept a drug store about forty years ago. . . . He had my note for three dollars ($3.00), which I wished to take up, but he could not find it, and said that I must be mistaken about it. I offered to pay the amount, but he refused to receive it." Brigham told his son that while Steele "may be dead . . . his heir or heirs may be living" and were entitled to the money. In addition to paying the amount owed, Brigham instructed John W. to also pay forty years' interest.[85]

"THOU ART HIS STEWARD"

Section 136 proclaimed: "Thou shalt be diligent in preserving what thou hast, that thou mayest be a wise steward; for it is the free gift of the Lord thy God, and thou art his steward" (v. 27). By word and deed Brigham directed the Saints' attention to their responsibility to both beautify and protect the earth. "Not one particle of all that comprises this vast creation of God is our own," he declared.[86] "How long have we got to live before we find out that we have nothing to consecrate to the Lord—that all belongs to the Father in heaven; that these mountains are His; the valleys, the timber, the water, the soil; in fine, the earth and its fullness."[87]

Because of the interdependence between the temporal and spiritual, Brigham taught that the misuse of the earth's resources was part of the ongoing battle between good and evil: "The enemy and opposer of Jesus[,] . . . Satan, never owned the earth; he never made a particle of it; his labor is not to create, but to destroy; while, on the other hand, the labor of the Son of God is to create, preserve, purify, build up, and exalt all things—the earth and its fullness—to his standard of greatness and perfection; to restore all things to their paradisiacal state and make them glorious. The work of the one is to preserve and sanctify, the work of the other is to waste away, deface and destroy."[88]

In 1847 Brigham reminded the vanguard pioneer company of Joseph Smith's "instructions—given both on Zion's Camp and by revelation—not to kill any of the animals or birds, or any thing created by Almighty God that had life, for the [mere] sake of destroying it."[89] Two weeks later when men began to indiscriminately shoot buffalo, a frustrated Brigham declared that "it was a sin to waste life and flesh."[90] He believed that God had not given mankind the right to selfishly and wastefully exploit the earth or to needlessly destroy his creations. Brigham's belief stood in sharp contrast to what one European visitor observed in other areas of the American West. "Nothing on the face of the broad Earth is sacred to [the frontiersman]," this visitor wrote. "Nature presents herself as his slave," and man treats the world around him in a "shockingly irreverent manner."[91]

During Mark Twain's visit to California in 1861, he spent four hours in a canoe on Lake Tahoe watching a forest fire that he had accidently started. "It was wonderful to see with what fierce speed the tall sheet of flame traveled!" he gushed. After it was safe to return to shore, Twain felt a pang of regret—not for the destruction he had caused, but because his actions had caused him to miss dinner.[92] By contrast, following the 1860 twenty-fourth of July celebration in Big Cottonwood Canyon, an Eastern newspaper reporter was surprised to see that Brigham remained behind "after everyone was gone" and went to each campfire to "see that all fires were extinguished."[93]

A long-term effect of Brigham as a steward of the Lord is City Creek Canyon, one of Salt Lake City's natural treasures. Recognizing that City

Creek was "the primary source of life-sustaining water" for the city, and wanting to show the "community a plan" for taking care of the canyon, he took the extraordinary step in 1850 of petitioning the legislature "to grant unto him the exclusive control" over the canyon to ensure "that the water may be continued pure unto the inhabitants of Great Salt Lake City."[94] He did this because of concerns about people who "lay down their religion at the mouth of the kanyon, saying, 'thou lie there, until I go for my load of wood.'"[95] In 1853, after having built a road into City Creek and implementing a plan for the use of the canyon, Brigham allowed city residents back into the canyon.

Thirteen years after Brigham appropriated City Creek for the purpose of preserving it, Fitz Hugh Ludlow visited Salt Lake City. Like others, he noted the famous open streams that ran along the street. He was taken aback, however, by the fact that the "inhabitants of Salt Lake City" drew a "supply of water for all purposes" from these streams. Ludlow noted: "All the earlier association of an Eastern man connect the gutter with ideas of sewerage; and a day or two must pass before he can accustom himself to the sight of his waiter dipping up from the street the pitcher of drink water for which he has rung, or the pail full which is going into the kitchen to boil his dinner. . . . Dead leaves and sand, the same foreign matters as the wind drifts into any forest spring, are necessarily found in such an open conduit; but no garbage, nothing offensive of any kind, disturbs its purity." Unaware that these streams were being watched over by a faithful steward who had received his errand from the Lord, Ludlow marveled that "the water seems to take care of itself." [96]

"PRAISE THE LORD"

In verse 28 the "Word and Will" declared, "If thou art merry, praise the Lord with singing, with music, with dancing, and with a prayer of praise and thanksgiving." Because many religionists felt that music and dancing were largely inconsistent with a Christ-centered life, Brigham grew up in a household that viewed them as sins. He later informed the Saints: "I had not a chance to dance when I was young, and never heard the enchanting tones of the violin, until I was eleven years of age; and then I thought I was on the high way to hell, if I suffered myself to linger and listen to it."[97] However, before leaving Winter Quarters, Brigham became a proponent of these activities. Within days of receiving section 136, Brigham proposed a social to show "to the world that this people can be made what God designed them. Nothing will infringe more upon the traditions of some men than to dance," he declared, noting that "the Lord said He wanted His saints to praise Him in all things." He further noted that "for some weeks past I could not wake up at any time of the night but I heard the axes at work. Some were building for the destitute and the widow; and now my feelings are, dance all night, if you desire to so do, for there is no harm in it. . . . I enjoin the Bishops that they gather the widow, the poor and the fatherless together and remember them in the festivities of Israel."[98]

While understanding the need for recreation, Brigham also understood the need for moderation and raised a warning voice against members who allowed diversions to consume their lives. To the vanguard company he declared: "There is no harm [that] will arise from merriment or dancing if Brethren, when they have indulged in it, know when to stop. But the Devil takes advantage of it to lead the mind away from the Lord."[99]

While at Winter Quarters, someone established a "dancing school" that Brigham attended.[100] After reaching the Salt Lake Valley, Brigham oversaw the establishment of such a school and pushed for the Saints to build social halls and theaters. At one point he became so concerned about the social needs of the Saints that he sent a circular letter to each bishop offering advice on holding ward socials.[101]

Clarissa Young Spencer concluded, "One of Father's most outstanding qualities as a leader was the manner in which he looked after the temporal and social welfare of his people along with guiding them in their spiritual needs."[102] Another daughter, Susa Young Gates, felt that her father "manifested even more godly inspiration in his carefully regulated social activities and associated pleasure than in his pulpit exercises. He kept the people busy, gave legitimate amusements full sway and encouraged the cultivation of every power, every gift and emotion of the human soul." She noted that "people would have had in those grinding years of toil, too few holidays and far too little of the spirit of holiday-making which is the spirit of fellowship and socialized spiritual communion, but for Brigham Young's wise policy."[103] As with other aspects of the "Word and Will of the Lord," while the implementation and successful oversight were Brigham's, the inspiration was the Lord's.

TRIALS, PERSECUTION, AND THE MARTYRDOM

The revelation also discussed the trials and persecutions the Saints' had endured: "My people must be tried in all things, that they may be prepared to receive the glory that I have for them, even the glory of Zion; and he that will not bear chastisement is not worthy of my kingdom" (v. 31). Brigham subsequently taught that "in everything the Saints may rejoice," including persecution, since it was "necessary to purge them, and prepare the wicked for their doom."[104]

Concerning the scourges the Saints had collectively endured in Ohio, Missouri, and Illinois, Brigham declared: "If we did not exactly deserve it [at the time], there have been times when we did deserve it. . . . It was good for [us] and gave us an experience."[105] On the fifth anniversary of the Saints' arrival in the Salt Lake Valley, he proclaimed: "Be humble, be faithful to your God, true to His Church, benevolent to the strangers that may pass through our territory, and kind to all people; serving the Lord with all your might, trusting in him. . . . [Someday] we will celebrate our perfect and absolute deliverance from the power of the devil; [but] we only celebrate now our deliverance from the good brick houses we have left [at Nauvoo], from our farms and lands, and from the graves of our fathers."[106]

Brigham counseled the Saints to "cast all bitterness" out of their hearts.[107] Regarding the wrongs they had suffered, he reiterated the Lord's injunction that all must forgive, or "there remaineth in [them] the greater sin. . . . Ye ought to say in your hearts—let God judge between me and thee, and reward thee according to thy deeds."[108] In March 1852 Brigham proclaimed: "Suppose every heart should say, if my neighbor does wrong to me, I will not complain, the Lord will take care of him. Let every heart be firm, and every one say, I will never contend any more with a man for property, I will not be cruel to my fellow-creature, but I will do all the good I can, and as little evil as possible. . . . I wish men would look upon that eternity which is before them. . . . It is a source of mortification to me to think that I ever should be guilty of doing wrong, or of neglecting to do good to my fellow men, even if they have abused me."[109] Five years later he wrote in his journal, "I wish to meet *all men* at the judgment Bar of God without any to fear me or accuse me of a wrong action."[110]

In multiple verses (17, 30, 34–36, 40–42) the Lord specifically addressed the enemies of the Church. Verse 17 instructed the Saints to "fear not thine enemies; for they shall not have power to stop my work," while verse 30 stated, "Fear not thine enemies, for they are in mine hands and I will do my pleasure with them." Brigham frequently addressed this idea during the early days in the valley. In 1850 he wrote: "We feel no fear. We are in the hands of our heavenly Father, the God of Abraham and Joseph who guided us to this Land. . . . He is our Father and our Protector. We live in his

Light, are Guided by his Wisdom, Protected by his Shadow, Upheld by his Strength."[111] Later he told the Saints that if they would do "the will of God . . . there is no fear from any quarter."[112] He also counseled, "I want you to bid farewell to every fear, and say God will take care of his kingdom. . . . It is he who has preserved us—not we."[113]

As soldiers with the US Army approached Utah in August 1857 during the so-called Utah War, Brigham reassured the Saints: "Cannot this Kingdom be overthrown? No. They might as well try to obliterate the sun. . . . God is at the helm. . . . Do not be angry with [the army], for they are in the hands of God. Instead of feeling a spirit to punish them, or anything like wrath, you live your religion."[114] The following month as the immediate threat of armed conflict began to diminish, Brigham wrote to Church leaders in southern Utah: "God rules. He has overruled for our deliverance this time once again and he will always do so if we live our religion, be united in our faith and good works. All is well with us."[115]

Initially, Brigham gave vent to strong feelings following the martyrdom. "I have never yet talked as rough in these mountains as I did in the United States when they killed Joseph," he noted.[116] While the emotional wounds brought on by the death of his friend and mentor were deep, the Lord's declaration in the "Word and Will" helped remind him that they need not be long-lasting. "I took him [Joseph] to myself. Many have marveled because of his death; but it was needful that he should seal his testimony with his blood, that he might be honored and the wicked might be condemned" (vv. 38–39).

In 1849 Brigham told the Saints that Joseph "lived just as long as the Lord let him live. But the Lord said, 'Now let my servant seal up his testimony with his blood.'"[117] Later he reminded the Saints, "If it had been the will of the Lord that Joseph and Hyrum should have lived, they would have lived."[118]

While Brigham's critics have long portrayed him as a man bent on avenging past wrongs the Saints had endured, including the martyrdom of Joseph and Hyrum, Brigham did not fixate on those wrongs. "It is very seldom that I refer to past scenes," he noted in 1856. "They occupy but a small portion of my time and attention. Do you wish to know the reason of this? It is because there is an eternity ahead of me, and my eyes are ever open and gazing upon it."[119] On another occasion he proclaimed: "Instead of crying over our sufferings, as some seem inclined to do, I would rather tell a good story, and leave the crying to others."[120]

He declared that "all evil is contrary to our covenants and obligations to God" and taught that to "make the doing of God's will and the keeping of his commandments a constant habit" will cause it to "become perfectly natural and easy for you to walk uprightly before Him."[121] He further taught: "Let us live so that we can say we are the Saints of God; and when the finger of scorn is pointed at us and we are held in derision and the nations talk about us, let us show an example before them that is worthy of imitation, that they cannot but blush before all sensible and intelligent persons when they say, 'There is a people that sin; there is a people that are corrupt.' . . . Let them howl and bark against us as much as they please, but let us live so that they have no reason to say a word."[122]

"BE DILIGENT IN KEEPING ALL MY COMMANDMENTS"

The revelation closed with the Lord's warning that the Saints needed to "be diligent in keeping all my commandments, lest judgments come upon you, and your faith fail[s] you, and your enemies triumph over you. . . . Amen and Amen" (v. 42). As President of the Church, Brigham raised a warning voice along these same lines. "If persons neglect to obey the law of God and to walk humbly before Him darkness will come into their minds and they will be left to believe that which is false and erroneous," he declared. "Their minds will become dim, their eyes will be beclouded and they will be unable to see things as they are."[123] On another occasion he taught: "If the Saints neglect to pray, and violate the day that is set apart for the worship of God, they will lose his Spirit. If a man shall suffer himself to be overcome with anger, and curse and swear, taking the name of the Deity in vain, he cannot retain the Holy Spirit. In short, if a man shall do anything which he knows to be wrong, and repenteth not, he cannot enjoy the Holy Spirit but will walk in darkness and ultimately deny the faith."[124]

Addressing a comment of a person who publicly proclaimed his intention to stay in the Church, Brigham declared: "What in the name of common sense is there to hang on to, if [one] does not hang on to the Church? I do not know of anything. You might as well take a lone straw in the midst of the ocean to save yourselves. . . . There is nothing but the Gospel to hang on to!"[125]

SUMMARY

While section 136 immediately provided Brigham the answers that he needed to lead the Church at a pivotal time in his presidency, the long-term lessons he learned regarding the importance of keeping sacred covenants and obeying the revealed word of the Lord remain relevant today. The revelation serves as a testament that the Lord reveals his secrets—including secrets of ultimate success and true happiness—to "his servants the prophets."[126] It also serves as a reminder that all Latter-day Saints can receive for themselves the "Word and Will of the Lord" to help them with their own circumstances and challenges.

Chad M. Orton is a historic sites curator for the Church History Department of The Church of Jesus Christ of Latter-day Saints.

Chad M. Orton, "'This Shall Be Our Covenant': Brigham Young and D&C 136," *Religious Educator* 19, no. 2 (2018): 119–51.

NOTES

1. Doctrine and Covenants 68:4 defines the word of the Lord as "the power of God unto salvation." While speaking of the gathering of Israel in the latter days, Nephi told his brothers: "And at that day shall the remnant of our seed know that they are of the house of Israel, and that they are the covenant people of the Lord; and . . . they shall come to the knowledge of their Redeemer and the very points of his doctrine, that they may know how to come unto him and be saved" (1 Nephi 15:14).

2. For a more in-depth look at the Latter-day Saint exodus from Nauvoo to Utah and the circumstances surrounding Brigham Young's receiving the "Word and Will of the Lord," see Richard E. Bennett, *We'll Find the Place: The Mormon Exodus, 1846–1848* (Salt Lake City: Deseret Book, 1997).

3. Brigham's actions after receiving section 136 are consistent with what the prophet Alma taught in his discourse on faith: "We will compare the word to a seed. Now, if ye give place, that a seed may be planted in your heart, behold, if it be a true seed, or a good seed, if ye do not cast it out by your unbelief, that ye will resist the Spirit of the Lord, behold, it will begin to swell within your breasts; and when you feel these swelling motions, ye will begin to say within yourselves—It must needs be that this is a good seed, or that the word is good for it beginneth to enlarge my soul; yea, it beginneth to enlighten my understanding, yea, it beginneth to be delicious to me" (Alma 32:28).

4. Brigham moved up the date when the Saints would begin leaving Nauvoo in part because he believed that "God will rule the elements, and the Prince and power of the air will be stayed." Historian's Office, History of the Church, January 24, 1846, Church History Library, The Church of Jesus Christ of Latter-day Saints, Salt Lake City (hereafter CHL).

5. Helen Mar Kimball Whitney, "Our Travels beyond the Mississippi," *Women's Exponent*, December 1, 1883, 102.

6. Historian's Office, History of the Church, May 3, 1846. Eleven weeks after Brigham Young left Nauvoo, his company had traveled only about 145 miles and barely made it halfway across Iowa. Something needed to change if he and other members of the company were to reach the Salt Lake Valley that year. On April 26 Brigham directed the company to begin work on a settlement where members that

were slowing their progress could stop to rest and regain their strength, resupply, and seek out better outfits. For a little over two weeks, men split rails; built houses, fences, and bridges; dug wells; and cleared, plowed, and planted fields. When the company moved out of this new community, which they had named Garden Grove, several hundred Saints remained behind.

A short distance later, in a last-ditch attempt to reach the Rocky Mountains, the company again stopped for two weeks beginning on May 18 to create a second settlement that they called Mount Pisgah. Brigham now ordered other company members to stop until they were better able to undertake the journey. Before the company left Mt. Pisgah, a number of the Saints who had left Nauvoo around the first of May as originally planned caught up with the advance company, a fact that likely added to Brigham's anxiety and frustration. See William G. Hartley and A. Gary Anderson, *Iowa and Nebraska*, vol. 5 of *Sacred Places: A Comprehensive Guide to Early LDS Historical Sites*, ed. Lamar C. Berrett (Salt Lake City: Deseret Book, 2006), 72, 74–75, 83, 86.

While the settlements of Garden Grove and Mount Pisgah were initially viewed as necessary to help speed the journey of the advance company, later that year they would become home to thousands of additional Latter-day Saints who needed a place to winter.

7.   William Clayton, "Come, Come, Ye Saints," *Hymns* (Salt Lake City: The Church of Jesus Christ of Latter-day Saints, 1985), no. 30.

8.   Historian's Office, History of the Church, January 7, 1847.

9.   Brigham Young to Jesse C. Little, February 6, 1847, General Correspondence, Outgoing, Brigham Young Office Files, CHL; and Brigham Young, in *Journal of Discourses* (London: Latter-day Saints' Book Depot, 1854–86), 1:166.

10. In a revelation to the Prophet Joseph Smith, the Lord declared: "And my people must needs be chastened until they learn obedience, if it must needs be, by the things which they suffer" (Doctrine and Covenants 105:6).

11. Like Joseph Smith before him, Brigham Young found the words of James to be true: "If any of you lack wisdom, let him ask of God, that giveth to all men liberally, and upbraideth not; and it shall be given him. But let him ask in faith, nothing wavering" (James 1:5–6).

The fact that Brigham received section 136 in the middle of the westward journey and not before leaving Nauvoo is consistent with the truth taught by Elder Richard G. Scott during the April 2007 General Conference: "I wonder if we can ever really fathom the immense power of prayer until we encounter an overpowering, urgent problem and realize that we are powerless to resolve it. Then we will turn to our Father in humble recognition of our total dependence on Him." Richard G. Scott, "Using the Supernal Gift of Prayer," *Ensign*, May 2007, 8.

When the 2013 Latter-day Saint edition of the scriptures was published, the date for the revelation was accidently deleted from the section introduction. Hosea Stout was present at the council meeting where "the word of the Lord was obtained." He noted in his journal that it was "a source of much joy and gratification to be present on such an occasion and my feeling can be better felt than described." Hosea Stout diary, January 14, 1847, as published in Juanita Brooks, *On the Mormon Frontier: The Diary of Hosea Stout*, 2 vols. (Salt Lake City: University of Utah Press and Utah State Historical Society, 1982), 1:227, 229. For other references to the date of the revelation having been received on January 14, see Historian's Office, History of the Church, January 14, 1847; and Wilford Woodruff journal, January 14, 1847, Wilford Woodruff Collection, CHL.

12. Proverbs 3:5–7 states the concept this way: "Trust in the Lord with all thine heart; and lean not unto thine own understanding. In all thy ways acknowledge him, and he shall direct thy paths. Be not wise in thine own eyes; fear the Lord, and depart from evil."

13. Historian's Office, History of the Church, January 17, 1847.

14. Having adopted the organizational principles outlined in the revelation, Church leaders would adapt them to individual circumstances. While emigrating companies were organized with a presidency, the division into tens, fifties, and hundreds became a guiding principle rather than hard and fast numbers. Actual divisions within a company usually reflected the makeup and needs of that company.

15. Historian's Office, History of the Church, January 14, 1847.

16. Exodus 18:21–23.

17. Following the expulsion of the Latter-day Saints from Jackson County, Missouri, Joseph Smith led an expedition from Kirtland, Ohio, to western Missouri during May and June 1834 in an attempt to regain the land from which they had been expelled. A revelation given to the Prophet Joseph declared that if the Saints would allow the Lord to lead them, they would be able to redeem Zion. In this revelation, the Lord also made reference to Moses and the exodus (see Doctrine and Covenants 103:15–18). A subsequent revelation declared that Zion's Camp was unsuccessful in its stated purpose because the Saints had "not learned to be obedient to the things which I required at their hands, but are full of all manner of evil, and do not impart of their substance, as becometh saints, to the poor and afflicted among them; and are not united according to the union required by the law of the celestial kingdom" (105:3–4). Ultimately, the Prophet Joseph disbanded the expedition rather than attempt to redeem Zion through violence.

18. The organizational concepts revealed in the revelation, along with those that Brigham initiated on his own, remain at the heart of how the Church is organized today. Rather than being organized into emigrating companies, Latter-day Saints are now part of branches, wards, districts, and stakes, each of which has a "presidency," "captains" that have direct responsibility for smaller groups within each unit, and a defined membership established on guiding principles regarding the size of units.

19. Bennett, We'll Find the Place, 73.

20. "Twelve Apostles to the Saints," January 27, 1847, as included in Historian's Office, History of the Church, January 27, 1847.

21. Historian's Office, History of the Church, January 16, 1847.

22. Hosea Stout diary, March 22, 1847, as published in Brooks, On the Mormon Frontier, 1:242.

23. Historian's Office, History of the Church, April 2, 1847; Historian's Office, History of the Church, March 26, 1847.

24. Historian's Office, History of the Church, March 21,1847.

25. Hosea Stout diary, March 15, 1847, as published in Brooks, On the Mormon Frontier, 1:241. Brigham and the Twelve also counseled "those who remain" that they had a responsibility to "do all they can" to assist those who were going to the valley in 1847 since they would be preparing a place for them to settle. Church leaders concluded that this type of cooperation, coupled "with a little time and patience, and a great deal of active industry," would result in "every man and woman" one day being "found in their own order and place amidst the habitations of the righteous."

"Twelve Apostles to the Saints," January 27, 1847, as included in Historian's Office, History of the Church, January 27, 1847.

26. In addition to those who continued to put forth claims that they were Joseph's appointed successor to lead the Church, another potential challenger to the authority of the Twelve in the minds of some was the Council of Fifty. Established in Nauvoo by Joseph Smith shortly before his death to help establish the political Kingdom of God in the Saints' new home in the Rocky Mountains, it had also played a role in planning the westward trek from Nauvoo. The "Word and Will" served as a reminder that this council, although including members of the Twelve, was subservient to priesthood authority. For more information on the Council of Fifty, see Matthew J. Grow and R. Eric Smith, *The Council of Fifty: What the Records Reveal about Mormon History* (Provo, UT: Religious Studies Center, Brigham Young University; Salt Lake City: Deseret Book, 2017). Although it is a common practice today to reorganize the First Presidency soon after the death of a prophet, it was not until December 1847, two and a half years following the martyrdom, that Brigham Young was sustained as President of the Church and the First Presidency was reconstituted.

27. Hosea Stout diary, January 14, 1847, as published in Brooks, *On the Mormon Frontier*, 1:229.

28. In addition to the five men mentioned in the revelation, the vanguard pioneer company included three other members of the Twelve—Brigham Young, Heber C. Kimball, and Willard Richards, who would form the First Presidency when it was reorganized in December 1847. Parley P. Pratt and John Taylor arrived in Winter Quarters shortly before the company left, but chose instead to travel later in the year. Orson Hyde was appointed to remain behind to oversee affairs at Winter Quarters and surrounding settlements until Brigham Young returned. The final member of the Twelve, Lyman Wight, had previously gone to Texas with a small group of followers and would subsequently be excommunicated for apostasy.

29. Brigham had recognized before this time that the Saints' behavior had played a role in their problems but was not certain how best to address the problem. In late December 1846 he had raised the possibility of implementing "a reformation" among the Saints so "that all might exercise themselves in the principles of righteousness," but he had not acted on the idea. Historian's Office, History of the Church, December 20. 1846.

30. Exodus 18:20.

31. Historian's Office, History of the Church, 27 January 1847. In presenting the revelation to the Saints at Ponca, Nebraska, Brigham wrote that the revelation "has become a law unto all saints" and that "union, obedience, and brotherly love, will secure you from future dangers." Historian's Office, History of the Church, January 27, 1847. Previously the Lord had declared: "Behold, I give unto you a commandment, that when ye are assembled together ye shall instruct and edify each other, that ye may know how to act and direct my church, how to act upon the points of my law and commandments, which I have given. And thus ye shall become instructed in the law of my Church and be sanctified by that which ye have received, and ye shall bind yourselves to act in all holiness before me" (Doctrine and Covenants 43:8–9).

32. Brigham Young to William Huntington, June 28, 1846, General Correspondence, Outgoing, Brigham Young Office Files.

33. Brigham was not alone in this view. After hearing the revelation read, Horace Eldredge publicly declared that "its execution would prove our salvation." Historian's Office,

History of the Church, January 16, 1847. In 1855 Brigham expounded further on the importance of obedience: "We are fast becoming a great people, but it is not so much numbers that will make us mighty as it is purity[,] faithfulness and obedience and submission to the requirements and will of the Lord our God. Let us continually seek unto him for wisdom and strength to keep his commandments and perform our duties as good and faithful servants, before him keeping ourselves pure and holy and walking blameless in all of his ordinances." Brigham Young to John Van Cott, June 20, 1855, General Correspondence, Outgoing, Brigham Young Office files.

34. As the vanguard company began its journey, Brigham declared that he wanted the company to "go in such a manner as to claim the blessings of Heaven." Historian's Office, History of the Church, April 15, 1847.

35. For a look at the covenants that Latter-day Saints make, see "Understanding Our Covenants with God," *Ensign*, July 2012, 22–25. Brigham later taught that "all the sacrifice that the Lord asks of his people is strict obedience to our own covenants that we have made with our God, and . . . to serve him with an undivided heart." Brigham Young discourse, June 21, 1874, as published in *Journal of Discourses*, 18:246.

36. The Lord had promised the Saints that through temple ordinances he would "endow those whom I have chosen with power from on high" (Doctrine and Covenants 95:8). At the same time, he warned that the realization of this power was dependent on behavior: "If you keep not my commandments, the love of the Father shall not continue with you, therefore you shall walk in darkness" (95:12). Instead of claiming the promised blessings associated with their covenants, the Saints in essence had been "walking in darkness at noon-day" during their journey (95:6).

37. 1 Nephi 2:20; 17:13–14. Following his journey, Nephi declared: "My God hath been my support; he hath led me through mine afflictions in the wilderness; and he hath preserved me upon the waters of the great deep. . . . O Lord, I have trusted in thee, and I will trust in thee forever. I will not put my trust in the arm of flesh; for I know that cursed is he that putteth his trust in the arm of flesh. Yea, cursed is he that putteth his trust in man or maketh flesh his arm" (2 Nephi 4:20, 34).

38. Doctrine and Covenants 105:2–3.

39. Historian's Office, History of the Church, January 18, 1847.

40. Historian's Office, History of the Church, January 18, 1847. Previously the Lord had declared, "Look to me in every thought; doubt not, fear not" (Doctrine and Covenants 6:36).

41. Historian's Office, History of the Church, March 3, 1847.

42. Norton Jacob journal, May 23, 1847, as published in Ronald O. Barney, *The Mormon Vanguard Brigade: Norton Jacob's Record* (Logan: Utah State University Press, 2005), 145; spelling standardized. It was in the context of covenant keeping and obedience that the Lord declared, "I, the Lord, am bound when ye do what I say; but when ye do not what I say, ye have no promise" (Doctrine and Covenants 82:10).

43. Historian's Office, General Church Minutes, 1839–1877, May 23, 1847, CHL; spelling standardized. Isaiah 48:17–18 states, "Thus said the Lord, thy Redeemer, the Holy One of Israel; I am the Lord thy God which teacheth thee to profit, which leadeth thee by the way that thou shouldest go. O that thou hadst hearkened to my commandments! then had thy peace been as a river, and they righteousness as the waves of the sea." See 1 Nephi 20:17–18.

44. Although it is widely believed that the vanguard company only ever consisted of 143 men (plus 3 women and 2 children), in reality 144 men began the journey. After having traveled to the rendezvous location on the Elkhorn River, Ellis Eames

dropped out of the company on April 18. According to William Clayton, the reason was "poor health, spitting blood, etc." William Clayton diary, April 18, 1847, CHL. Because of the short time he spent with the company, Eames has often not been listed among its members.

45. While Orson F. Whitney was one of the first to note that "twelve times twelve men had been chosen," he also concluded, "Whether designedly or otherwise we know not." Orson F. Whitney, *History of Utah*, 4 vols. (Salt Lake City: George Q. Cannon and Sons, 1892–1904), 1:301.

46. Clayton diary, May 29, 1847.

47. Historian's Office, General Church Minutes, May 23, 1847; Woodruff journal, May 16, 1847.

48. Although some members of the company had left their homes in late March, it was not until mid-April that the company was officially organized before leaving its rendezvous location on April 17 at the Elkhorn River approximately twenty-seven miles west of Winter Quarters.

49. Woodruff journal, May 28, 1847.

50. Clayton diary, May 29, 1847.

51. In addition to how they were traveling, the number in this combined company was likely also a concern to Brigham. Unlike the previous year when the goal was to get everyone to the Salt Lake Valley, the Twelve had decided that only "about one hundred families should follow the Pioneers, including as many of the soldiers families as could be fitted out." Historian's Office, History of the Church, March 21, 1847.

52. Historical Department, Office journal, June 15, 1847, CHL.

53. Historian's Office, General Church Minutes, September 4, 1847; spelling standardized. Wilford Woodruff described this meeting of the Twelve as "one of the most interesting Councils we ever held together on the earth." He noted that Pratt and Taylor were "reproved Sharply for undoing what the majority of the quorum had done in the organizing of the camps for travelling," in which they had "spent the whole winter in organizing & which was Also governed by revelation." Woodruff journal, September 4, 1847.

54. Historian's Office, History of the Church, June 28, 1846.

55. Pratt later made reference to the meeting in his autobiography: "A council was called, in which I was highly censured and chastened by President Young and others. This arose in part from some defect in the organization under my superintendence at the Elk Horn, and in part from other misunderstandings on the road. I was charged with neglecting to observe the order of organization entered into under the superintendence of the President before he left the camps at Winter Quarters; and of variously interfering with previous arrangements. In short, I was severely reproved and chastened. I no doubt deserved this chastisement; and I humbled myself, acknowledged my faults and errors, and asked forgiveness. I was frankly forgiven, and, bidding each other farewell, each company passed on their way. This school of experience made me more humble and careful in future, and I think it was the means of making me a wiser and better man ever after." *The Autobiography of Parley Parker Pratt*, ed. Scot Facer Proctor and Maurine Jensen Proctor, rev. ed. (Salt Lake City: Deseret Book, 2000), 454).

56. Brigham Young, in *Journal of Discourses*, 12:151 and 7:281.

57. Brigham Young, in *Journal of Discourses*, 14:115, 118. In the "Word and Will," the Lord declared that individuals needed to be "faithful in keeping all my words that I have given you from the days of Adam to Abraham, from Abraham to Moses; from

Moses to Jesus and the apostles; and from Jesus and his apostles to Joseph Smith" (v. 37). During the April 1999 general conference, President James E. Faust taught, "When obedience becomes our goal, it is no longer an irritation; instead of a stumbling block, it becomes a building block." "Obedience: The Path to Freedom," *Ensign*, May 1999, 47. In a previous conference, Elder Donald L. Staheli quoted President Ezra Taft Benson as teaching this same principle a little differently: "When obedience ceases to be an irritant and becomes our quest, in that moment God will endow us with power." "Obedience—Life's Greatest Challenge," *Ensign*, May 1998, 82. Staheli's conference address is currently the only known source for that statement.

58. In the Doctrine and Covenants the Lord frequently makes clear the Church's responsibility for the poor, including "Look to the poor and needy, and administer to their relief that they shall not suffer" (38:35); "Thou wilt remember the poor, and consecrate of thy properties for their support" (42:30); and "Remember in all things the poor and the needy, the sick and the afflicted, for he that doeth not these things, the same is not my disciple" (52:40). On June 7, 1846, a week before establishing Winter Quarters, Brigham declared that there were those who had "hedged up their own way by praying continually . . . I am poor, I have done all I could for the church" and as a result "all the devils between this and the nether most part of hell are acting in concert with their prayers." John D. Lee journal, June 7, 1846, CHL.

59. As reported in *Latter-day Saints' Millennial Star* 6, no. 12 (December 1, 1845): 197; and Bennett, *We'll Find the Place*, 28n58.

60. Historian's Office, History of the Church, 24 January 1847.

61. "Twelve Apostles to the Saints," 27 January 1847, as included in Historian's Office, History of the Church, 27 January 1847.

62. Brigham Young, in *Journal of Discourses*, 3:331.

63. Brigham Young, in *Journal of Discourses*, 13:279.

64. Brigham Young diary, August 17, 1845, Brigham Young Office Files.

65. Isaiah 52:12.

66. Brigham Young to Shadrach Roundy and Tunis Rappelye, August 16, 1847, General Correspondence, Outgoing, Brigham Young Office Files.

67. Brigham Young, in *Journal of Discourses*, 15:36.

68. Brigham Young vision, February 17, 1847, Brigham Young Office Files.

69. Brigham Young, in *Journal of Discourses*, 16:46.

70. Brigham Young, in *Journal of Discourses*, 14:81.

71. Mrs. Frank [Miriam] Leslie, *California: A Pleasure Trip from Gotham to the Golden Gate* (New York: G. W. Carlton & Co., 1877), 98.

72. Clayton diary, May 29, 1847.

73. Brigham Young, in *Journal of Discourses*, 14:79.

74. Brigham Young, in *Journal of Discourses*, 11:252.

75. Brigham Young discourse, 8 April 1852, as reported in *Millennial Star* 16 (May 27, 1854): 327.

76. Thomas Bullock journal, June 16, 1847, CHL.

77. John D. Lee, diary, June 15, 1848, as published in *A Mormon Chronicle: The Diaries of John D. Lee, 1848–1876*, ed. Robert Glass Cleland and Juanita Brooks, 2 vols. (Salt Lake City: University of Utah Press, 1983): 1:39.

78. Susa Young Gates and Leah D. Widtsoe, *The Life Story of Brigham Young* (New York: Macmillan, 1930), 212.

79. Brigham Young, in *Journal of Discourses*, 1:104.

80. Elizabeth Wood Kane, *Twelve Mormon Homes Visited on Succession on Journey through Utah to Arizona* (Philadelphia: William Wood, 1874), 5.
81. Leonard J. Arrington, *Brigham Young: American Moses* (New York: Alfred A. Knopf, 1985), 308.
82. John Hyde, *Mormonism: Its Leaders and Designs* (New York: W. P. Fetridge & Co., 1857), 170.
83. Brigham Young, in *Journal of Discourses*, 6:170.
84. Brigham Young discourse, November 13, 1870, in *Journal of Discourses*, 13:301.
85. Brigham Young to John W. Young, February 7, 1866, letterpress copybook, 8:69–70, Brigham Young Office Files.
86. Brigham Young discourse, June 3, 1860, in *Journal of Discourses*, 8:67.
87. Brigham Young discourse, June 3, 1855, in *Journal of Discourses*, 2:308.
88. Brigham Young discourse, July 3, 1864, in *Journal of Discourses*, 10:320.
89. Bullock journal, April 25, 1847.
90. Appleton M. Harmon diary, May 7, 1847, CHL.
91. William A. Baillie–Grohman, *Camps in the Rockies: Being a Narrative of Life on the Frontier, and Sport in the Rocky Mountains, with an Account of the Cattle Ranches of the West* (New York: Charles Scribner & Sons, 1882), 21.
92. Mark Twain, *Roughing It* (Hartford, CT: American Publishing, 1872), 176–77.
93. "Interesting from Utah," *Millennial Star* (November 3, 1860): 702.
94. Dale L. Morgan, *The State of Deseret* (Logan: Utah State University Press, 1987), 160.
95. Brigham Young discourse, October 9, 1852, in *Journal of Discourses*, 1:211.
96. Fitz Hugh Ludlow, *The Heart of the Continent: A Record to Travel Across the Plains and in Oregon, with an Examination of the Mormon Principle* (New York: Hurd and Houghton, 1870): 328–29.
97. Brigham Young discourse, February 6, 1853, in *Journal of Discourses*, 2:94.
98. Historian's Office, History of the Church, February 5, 1847.
99. Jacob journal, May 28, 1847, in Barney, *Mormon Vanguard Brigade*, 150.
100. Historian's Office, History of the Church, February 15, 1847.
101. Brigham Young to Edward Hunter and All the Bishops in the Church, December 30, 1875; photocopy in author's possession.
102. Clarissa Young Spencer and Mable Harmer, *Brigham Young at Home* (Salt Lake City: Deseret Book, 1963), 169.
103. Gates and Widtsoe, *Life Story of Brigham Young*, 266.
104. Brigham Young discourse, August 1,1852, in *Journal of Discourses*, 1:359.
105. Brigham Young discourse, April 8, 1871, in *Journal of Discourses*, 14:97.
106. Brigham Young discourse, July 24, 1852, in *Journal of Discourses*, 1:146.
107. Brigham Young discourse, August 5, 1860, in *Journal of Discourses*, 8:33.
108. Doctrine and Covenants 64:9, 11.
109. Brigham Young discourse, March 4, 1852, in *Journal of Discourses*, 1:32–33.
110. *Diary of Brigham Young, 1857*, ed. Everett L. Cooley (Salt Lake City: Tanner Trust Fund/University of Utah Library, 1980), 62 (August 19, 1857); emphasis in original.
111. Brigham Young to Orson Hyde, July 28, 1850, in *Frontier Guardian*, September 14, 1850.
112. Brigham Young discourse, April 17, 1870, in *Journal of Discourses*, 13:318.
113. James H. Martineau journal, December 30, 1856, in Donald G. Godfrey and Rebecca S. Martineau-McCarty, eds., *An Uncommon Common Pioneer: The Journals of James Henry Martineau, 1828–1918* (Provo, UT: Religious Studies Center, Brigham Young University, 2008): 58–59.

114. Brigham Young discourse, August 30, 1857, in *Journal of Discourses*, 5:168, 170–71.

115. Brigham Young to Isaac C. Haight, September 10, 1857, letterpress copybook 3:827–28, Brigham Young Office Files. This letter was a response to an inquiry from local leaders in Cedar City, Utah, about how they should respond to members of a California-bound emigrant wagon train who had created a minor disturbance while passing through their community. When some community leaders learned that Haight had set in motion a plan to retaliate by giving the train a "brush" along the Santa Clara River, they raised objections. In response, Haight sent a letter to Brigham asking how they should respond. Unfortunately, the same day that the messenger started for Salt Lake, a decision was made independent of the council to change the original plan and attack the train at Mountain Meadows. Upon learning that the train had been attacked, Haight, rather than waiting for Brigham's response, set in motion a plan that resulted in the cold-blooded murder of approximately 120 emigrants. For a detailed study of the Mountain Meadows Massacre, see Ronald W. Walker, Richard E. Turley Jr., and Glen M. Leonard, *Massacre at Mountain Meadows: An American Tragedy* (New York: Oxford University Press, 2008).

116. Brigham Young discourse, July 8, 1855, in *Journal of Discourses*, 2:317.

117. Historian's Office, History of the Church, July 8, 1849.

118. Brigham Young discourse, January 2, 1870, in *Journal of Discourses*, 13:95.

119. Brigham Young discourse, August 31, 1856, in *Journal of Discourses*, 4:42. On another occasion Brigham stated: "At times when I think of addressing you, it occurs to me that strict sermonizing upon topics pertaining to the distant future, or reviewing the history of the past, will doubtless please and highly interest a portion of my hearers; but my judgment and the spirit of intelligence that is in me teach that, by taking such a course, the people could not be instructed pertaining to their every-day duties. For this reason, I do not feel impressed to instruct you on duties to be performed a hundred years hence, but rather to give those instructions pertaining to the present, to our daily walk and conversation, that we may know how to benefit ourselves under the passing time, and present privileges, and be able to lay a foundation for future happiness." Brigham Young discourse, March 23, 1856, in *Journal of Discourses*, 3:272.

120. Brigham Young discourse, October 8, 1868, in *Journal of Discourses*, 12:287.

121. "Brigham Young. Remarkable Interview with the Salt Lake Prophet," *New York Herald*, May 6, 1877; and Brigham Young to Brigham Heber Young, September 30, 1867, letterpress copybook, 10:406–10, Brigham Young Office Files.

122. Brigham Young discourse, January 2, 1870, *Journal of Discourses*, 13:91.

123. Brigham Young discourse, January 2, 1870, in *Journal of Discourses*, 13:91.

124. Brigham Young, "Summary of Instructions," August 1–10, 1865, in *Journal of Discourses*, 11:134.

125. Brigham Young discourse, August 24, 1872, in *Journal of Discourses*, 15:136. On another occasion Brigham declared: "We are in the midst of the ocean. A storm comes on, and, as sailors say, she labors very hard. 'I am not going to stay here,' says one; 'I don't believe this is the "Ship Zion."' 'But we are in the midst of the ocean.' 'I don't care, I am not going to stay here.' Off goes the coat, and he jumps overboard. Will he not be drowned? Yes. So with those who leave this Church. It is the 'Old Ship Zion,' let us stay in it. Is there any wisdom in all doing as we are all told? Yes." Brigham Young discourse, May 15, 1865, in *Journal of Discourses*, 11:107.

126. Amos 3:7.

Chapter Twenty-One

Administration in the "DO"
John Taylor's Administration from Hiding in the Underground

ERIC PERKINS AND MARY JANE WOODGER

On a late summer afternoon in 1886, President John Taylor was sitting in the George Stringfellow parlor with Charles Barrell (one of his bodyguards) when the bulb of a nearby lamp burst, sending broken glass shooting throughout the room. At the time little more was thought of the incident. However, a week later President John Taylor dreamed that there was symbolism in the broken lamp. Another bodyguard, Samuel Bateman, recorded in his journal that the "breaking of the globe was interpreted to him [President Taylor] in a dream that the deputies surprised us and we were scattered and nary two of us were together."[1] Up to that point, despite several close calls, President John Taylor and his entourage had managed to stay together and escape being arrested by federal deputies by using tips and informants. If, as the dream suggested, President Taylor and his group were separated, it might lead to their greatest fear: the prophet's arrest.

Some Latter-day Saints may be surprised to learn that a President of The Church of Jesus Christ of Latter-day Saints lived a clandestine existence because he was in danger of being imprisoned. What precipitated this situation was legislation that made it easy for the government to prosecute polygamists. In March 1882 President Taylor became aware of impending danger owing to legislation. "Upon learning of the passage of the law,"

President George Q. Cannon wrote to Church attorney Franklin S. Richards, "knowing that he [President Taylor] would be selected as a target for attack, . . . he called his family together and submitted to them a proposition that his wives should each return to her private residence . . . and leave him to live in the Gardo House [presidential residence]."[2] Ultimately this plan did not work, and John Taylor was forced into hiding.

In this environment General Authorities were protected by bodyguards and forced into hiding. Samuel W. Taylor, author and grandson of President Taylor, wrote, "Underground headquarters for the church was variously called 'Safe Retreat,' 'Halfway House,' and, most generally, the 'DO.' Undergrounders were 'on the dodge,' thus, 'DO' in the 'cohab code.'"[3] Though it is impossible to pin down who first used this code word, "DO" is commonly found in journals and letters by those associated with General Authorities of the time.

John Taylor's administration was limited by exile. Forced to move from hideout to hideout, he was rarely in a safe-enough position to meet with his counselors in the First Presidency, George Q. Cannon and Joseph F. Smith, or members of the Quorum of the Twelve. Furthermore, his presidency was limited by his inability to be among general Church membership. On the other hand, those Saints who harbored the President during this time (1885–87) found their lives enriched through a close association with their prophet. This chapter offers a glimpse into John Taylor's life while in the DO, including the hardships he experienced trying to lead while in hiding, which included the inability to meet and consult with other General Authorities, his disconnection from the body of the Church, and the abnormal lifestyle of a man on the run as opposed to the regimented schedule of a seasoned Church leader. Especially damaging was the loss of contact with his family.

With the body of the Church outside the United States borders, the practice of plural marriage went public in August 1852 during a special conference called by Brigham Young. In an address by Orson Pratt, plural marriage was officially announced to the three thousand in attendance.[4] For many the announcement did not come as a surprise. It was common knowledge that some of the Saints practiced plural marriage. What was surprising was that Church leadership publicly announced what most already knew.

When the Church was headquartered in Nauvoo, the majority of the Twelve and First Presidency had received an invitation to practice plural marriage from the Prophet Joseph Smith. Sometime after Joseph Smith first taught John Taylor about plural marriage, he explained to Taylor privately,

"Those things that have been spoken of must be fulfilled, and if they are not entered into right away, the keys will be turned." After some thought, Elder Taylor hesitantly replied, "Brother Joseph, I will try and carry these things out."[5] Taylor's selection for his first plural wife was Elizabeth Kaighin, the cousin of his first wife, Leonora Cannon. John and Elizabeth were married in December 1843. Subsequently, he married sixteen women.

At the time of President Taylor's second marriage, the Church was experiencing relative peace in Nauvoo; however, that peace did not last and the Saints were forced to flee in 1846. They arrived in the Great Basin the following year. Aided by isolation during the mid-1800s, the Church enjoyed prosperity living along the Rocky Mountain corridor. The first federal legislation aimed at Church members practicing plural marriage came on July 1, 1862, when Abraham Lincoln signed the Morrill Anti-Bigamy Act. This act was intended to punish any US citizen practicing plural marriage. The act remained in force despite petitions from the Church and Utah Territory's inability to prosecute offenders. Little was done to enforce the law, mostly because the federal government was preoccupied with the Civil War.[6]

Twenty years later, in 1882, Senator George Edmunds stirred up new interest in legal action against polygamy. His amendment to the Morrill Act included the prosecution of those practicing unlawful cohabitation through requiring licenses for marriage. It restricted polygamists' rights to serve in public office, vote, or serve on a jury and granted amnesty for those who denounced the practice.[7] The Edmunds Act was passed by Congress on March 14, 1882, and signed into law by President Chester Arthur the following week. Latter-day Saints felt that these legal actions, aimed directly at them, were made by corrupt legislators and were an infringement upon their rights. Joseph F. Smith's feelings about the United States at the time were typical of most Saints' views. Writing from a place he identified only as "Camp Terra Incognition," he declared, "I have almost come to the conclusion that in the future [the United States] should be styled the land of oppression and the home of the slave. . . . Legislators, executors, and adjudicheiors [sic] of the government are and have been for years corrupt, rotten to the very core, and they yearly grow worse and worse until by and by the whole structure of the government will be shattered to the foundations and riven to atoms."[8]

When enforcement of the Edmunds Law seemed probable, President John Taylor and other Church leaders began considering options against prosecution, which included relocation of the Church body. In a letter sent to stake presidents in Arizona on December 6, 1884, Presidents John Taylor and George Q. Cannon wrote, "A general attack is being made upon our liberties throughout all the Territories where our people reside. . . . There can be no question that there is apparently a concert of action on their [the federal officers'] part to push our people to the wall and to destroy our religious liberty and with it our religion itself."[9] Within a few weeks of drafting this letter in January 1885, Presidents Taylor, Cannon, and Smith, along with various members of the Quorum of the Twelve, traveled south to inspect temporary relocation sites in Arizona, California, and northern Mexico.[10] En route they met Apostles Erastus Snow and Moses Thatcher, who were returning from a similar trip to Mexico. Neither the First Presidency trip nor the Thatcher–Snow trips proved successful. It was deemed impossible, after forty years of growth in the Salt Lake Valley, to coordinate moving the entire Church body. Besides, federal officials were not after all Church members: their main targets were the First Presidency and the Quorum of the Twelve Apostles. On the last leg of the trip, in California, the First Presidency received news that federal deputies in Utah had issued warrants for their arrest. Of the trip Joseph F. Smith reported: "To me it is very funny that a man should be suspected of matrimony with every young lady who may chance to call on his folks. . . . I parted with the brethren. They sped off towards home and I remained alone to return to the Pacific and there embark for distant lands."[11]

President Taylor's counselors—slightly younger and carefully watched by federal officials—ended the exploratory trip early and entered exile, while President Taylor returned to Salt Lake City at the end of January 1885.[12] With exodus out of the question, options were to either accept imprisonment or go into hiding. Subsequently, "a family council was held and [it was decided that] all the wives but one, Margaret, who had the largest family," should move from the presidential residence known as the Gardo House and return to their original residences known as Taylor Row, on 100 West and 45 South in Salt Lake City.[13]

On February 1, President Taylor entered the Salt Lake Tabernacle to deliver his last public address. Deputies stood at the exits, waiting until the end of the conference to make an arrest. It is difficult to understand what kept deputies from going inside and arresting President Taylor.[14] Uncertainty filled the air as President Taylor addressed the congregation:

> It may suit others to violate the law, to trample upon human rights and desecrate the sacred temple of liberty . . . in the name of Justice; but we profess to be governed by higher, by nobler and more exalted

principles . . . ; and if Jesus could afford to endure the attacks of sinners against Himself, we . . . ought to be able to endure a little. . . .

When men begin to tear down the barriers and tamper with the fundamental principles and institutions of our country, they are playing a very dangerous game, and are severing the bonds which hold society together.[15]

President Taylor delivered a warning that must have greatly impacted the congregation. John Mills Whitaker, who would later marry Ida Taylor, one of the President's daughters, recorded, "I was there when President Taylor got up and delivered the last address he ever delivered in public. . . . I can see that old gentleman pull his overcoat up, hold it together, and he said, 'We'll hold it together until this storm passes. And it will pass.'"[16]

After speaking for almost two hours, he closed with a final warning: "You will see trouble, TROUBLE, TROUBLE enough in these United States. And as I have said before I say today: I tell you in the name of God, *woe*! to them that fight against Zion, for God will fight against them."[17] He then exited through the Tabernacle's basement, where his bodyguards, Charles Barrell[18] and Samuel Bateman, were waiting.

From the Salt Lake Tabernacle, President Taylor immediately went into hiding. His first secret residence was the home of Bishop Samuel Bennion in Taylorsville. During the first year, he switched locations eighteen times, often returning to previous hideouts. In over two years of exile, President Taylor and his bodyguards stayed in twenty-two different locations, from Nephi to Kaysville.[19] On more than one occasion, they were forced to flee in the middle of the night. One such incident took place just a month after President Taylor had been in the DO, when the Hansen home in Sugarhouse was discovered by deputies. Bodyguards Samuel Bateman and Charles Wilcken hurried him into the night in search of a new hideout. Not sure of where to go, and going against the sound advice of his bodyguards and good judgment, President Taylor settled into the Gardo House for the rest of the evening. His insistence on going home for one night nearly led to his imprisonment.[20]

After President Taylor entered the Gardo House, his family wasted no time in nursing him. He had a cold, and escaping into the cold night had done little to help it. His wife prepared a pan of hot water to soak his feet and applied various treatments to alleviate his congestion. All seemed calm and safe when suddenly Taylor ran from the room to the third floor to hide in a secret closet built for just such an emergency. He had heard a noise outside, a preselected warning sound that provided him with enough time to hide. Deputies sent the household into a frenzy. Helpless to defend his family or himself, Taylor listened as the women pleaded with deputies to be careful with fragile items during the search. The sound of heavy boots ascending the stairs grew louder as two deputies insisted on searching the room where he was hiding. Luckily for the President, after a quick glance into the room, the deputies believed the excuse given by John W. Taylor, President Taylor's son, that the room was used mainly for storage. They left without discovering the hidden prophet. Deputies searched the house for a few more moments and then left, satisfied that he was not there. Before sunrise the next day, the exiled party was secreted away to west Salt Lake to the farm of David James.[21]

News of this dangerous night spread fast. Of that close call, young William Brown wrote to his parents on March 15 that he was "happy to say that they did not get him [President Taylor]."[22] President Taylor never returned to the presidential residence again.

Any reputable source of warning justified relocation, but traveling during either the day or night was unsafe. Short, quick trips from one residence to another were the best way to stay undetected. Families like the Stringfellows made it possible for President Taylor to evade arrest and find comfort, though "life on the fly" was constantly unnerving for a man who was "perfectly immaculate in his dress," wearing "fine linen shirts and ties."[23]

One of the most visited homes during exile was the John Carlisle home in South Jordan. The Carlisles had met John Taylor when he served a mission to the Isle of Jersey in England. Elizabeth Carlisle said that "he was such a fine, humble man, and when these men were in need of help she was proud to have them stay at her home."[24] Located near the Jordan River at 4060 South and 700 West, the home was well situated for safety and security. There was a double-door barn for quick and easy unloading of hay and other supplies. This barn also was a convenient place for President Taylor to hide when he came hurriedly from the nearby William Hill house. Also, there was a boat that could be used to cross the river in a hurry. Family tradition holds that Elizabeth Carlisle hung quilts along a clothesline in the back yard in order to give those in hiding some space to get some exercise without being discovered.

Just a little farther east of the Carlisle home was the home of William H. Hill. The friendship between the Taylors and the Hills dated back to the 1830s when both families, who were living in Toronto, joined the Church. The Hill home, located between 300 and 500 East and 3900 and 4500 South in what is known today as the Millcreek area (Salt Lake City), had twelve rooms, allowing for the accommodations of family members and several Church leaders at a time. Even before the exile, General Authorities had stayed overnight at the Hill residence during conferences and other meetings rather than travel home at night. On more than one occasion, President Taylor and others were hidden in a cellar under the Hill house or transported to the Carlisle home in a wagon full of hay. President Taylor's respect and concern toward the families who housed him is recorded by a Hill relative who said, "While at the Hill house, he [President Taylor] dedicated the place as one of safety for Brother and Sister Hill and family, and their posterity."[25] Realizing he was not only avoiding his own arrest by evading authorities but also putting those who hid him in jeopardy, he offered blessings and dedications of their homes.

Evidently his blessing on this residence was efficacious for William Hill, who was set apart to serve a mission on November 20, 1886. According to the family, federal authorities arrived at the Hill residence with the intent to arrest Hill just moments before his departure on his mission. Rather than exiting through the front door, he barely escaped through a back window.[26]

Though families like the Carlisles and Hills provided protection for the prophet, the thought of him being cared for by others was a frequent concern for his wives. Being aware of their worry, he often sent reassurance that he was in good hands. For instance, on March 10, 1887, he wrote to his wife Maggie: "We are quite comfortably situated and I am camping out quite well, and although we are supported for the time being I do not forget you and your family in my prayers, that God may preserve you, comfort you, and teach you, lead you in the path of life, and that we may keep our covenants unimpaired, faithfully to the end."[27]

Such letters to his family provided reassurance that separation did not take them out of his thoughts. Always signing his letters "I remain your affectionate husband," he wrote Maggie on September 8, 1886, "I have not forgotten you, nor do I suspect to in time or in eternity."[28]

Though exile limited his ability to fulfill his role as his family's patriarch, it did not diminish his desire. By way of illustration, when John Mills Whitaker proposed marriage to his daughter Ida, President Taylor was extremely upset that Whitaker had not informed him of his intentions, though such a meeting to obtain permission was impossible with the prophet in hiding. President Taylor wrote to Ida, "No man has a right, without the consent of the father, to make such a proposal."[29] When the situation was ironed out, the couple was married on September 22, 1886, though President Taylor was unable to attend any of the festivities.

John Taylor was also very anxious to provide for the temporal needs of his family even though he was in hiding, and he counseled others in the same predicament do likewise. In a letter from exile to Bishop J. H. Richards, he counseled that the families of brethren who were imprisoned or on the run "should be cared for during the absence and confinement of their natural protectors, and not be allowed to suffer for the want of any of the necessities of life."[30] An example of John Taylor's dedication to the physical well-being of his family is found in a letter sent in October 1886: "The children must have had the shoes that you refer to, and I also enclose an order for $10 on ZCMI and an order for $10 for a coat you speak of for Maggie. I also send $10 for yourself and $10 in cash for the purchase of the wrap that you speak of. If you can add $4 to it, it will make up what you wanted, as I do not wish to make such heavy drafts at one time."[31]

By today's standards, the money he sent in this letter would be nine hundred dollars.[32] While shoes and coats were needed, what his family wanted most was to have some physical contact with their father and husband. This desire was mutual. He wrote, "You say you would be pleased to see me and I know you would, but that could not give you more pleasure than it would give me to see and embrace you and our dear children again. I thank the Lord, however, that you and they are so comfortably situated, and if I can do anything to add to your comfort, I shall be happy to do so."[33]

The separation was especially poignant on special occasions. On his seventy-eighth birthday he disclosed to his family, "You speak in regard to my birthday, that while I did not want any ostentatious display, I would like to have the family get together in that day, and if I can find time, will write something for the occasion. . . . In regard to my seeing you I have not been able to, up to this pursuit, make arrangements which were satisfactory. . . . I should be quite as much pleasant to see you as you would to see me."[34]

Neither he nor his family members were ever granted their desire to be together. His family celebrated holidays as if he were present and sometimes would send him gifts through a secretive mail route, such as a beehive decoration to attach to the pocket watch he received for his birthday.[35] Though he was not able to enjoy time with his family, President Taylor found time to do a few things he enjoyed. Much time was spent competing against his bodyguards in checkers and "pitching quoits," a game similar to horseshoes, one of his favorite pastimes while in exile. Bodyguard Samuel Bateman made many journal entries about who won for the day, recording that the President played quoits even when he was not feeling well.[36]

His exile was not synonymous with leisure, however. President Taylor, describing his life in the DO, said to his family, "While you and the family have very little to do outside of your few domestic chores, I am kept busy every day with the duties of my office, just the same as when at home, surrounded without the endearments of family."[37]

John Taylor met exile resolutely. Reflections on his circumstances revealed meaning to his hardships. He was not simply hiding from being imprisoned for laws he did not agree with; rather, he was suffering an almost necessary persecution that would refine him for future glory:

> These experiences, however, are necessary for . . . the role of Saints as it is for others who have walked in the footsteps of Jesus. . . . When men shall revile you and persecute you and say all manner of evil against you for my name's sake, rejoice and be exceedingly glad, for great is your reward in heaven, for so persecuted they the prophets which were before you. . . . It is true. Yes, it was true in the prophets' days, it was true in the days of Jesus, it is true in our day. . . . You may ask, "Do you do this?" Yes. I feel to thank God that I am a Latter-Day Saint and considered worthy to share . . . what the former-day saints had to pass through. And it is only a very little that I and my brethren endure when compared to that what the Saints endured in former times.[38]

Despite this positive attitude, his ability to lead was greatly diminished in hiding. Whereas his preexile administration had established the Primary Association in 1878, celebrated the forgiving of the poor's debt in the Jubilee Year of 1880, ordained six Apostles, and dedicated the Logan Temple in 1884, his postexile administration was unmarked by major organizational developments. The long administrative period of silence was interrupted only by one new directive when President Taylor called for the publication of a new Church hymnal, the first to include both lyrics and musical scores.[39]

Most of the Church's business took place through secret correspondence. Though Joseph F. Smith's administrative duties must have been less than the prophet's, he reported in one day receiving eight pounds of mail during hiding.[40] Issues facing the prophet through a constant stream of letters were varied and daunting. For instance, during two days in November 1886, letter books show President Taylor dealt with the construction of a canal on the Sevier River, a woman wanting to prove her husband's guilt in committing adultery, and a suit against trespassing and damages to Church property in Laie, Hawaii.[41] Much of the correspondence sent to President Taylor's attention included requests for the specific disbursement of Church funds.

One such letter was a request for money to be sent to provide for homesteads for Native Americans.[42] By the summer of 1887, exile was beginning to take its toll on his health but did not slow down his attention to his duties. Family members observed, "What a volume of business Taylor attended to as a dying man!"[43]

During exile John Taylor never personally addressed a Church body. His addresses were read by others at general conferences held in outlying areas rather than at the Tabernacle. Any revelations received by a Church President in hiding presented special challenges. One situation still clouded with controversy is a supposed revelation given to President Taylor on September 27, 1886, that dealt with the new and everlasting covenant. Historian Brian C. Hales tells us that "though unsigned, [the revelation] appears to be in Taylor's handwriting."[44] We have no record that John Taylor discussed its existence or significance with other General Authorities or Church congregations.

Of all uncanonized revelations, this one coming from the secrecy of hiding may be one of the most controversial because many modern polygamists have used its phraseology to support their continued practice of plural marriage. In a fundamentalist tract written decades later, Lorin C. Woolley, who supported plural marriage long after the Manifesto of 1890 by President Wilford Woodruff, claims to have been present as a teenager when the revelation was received. In the ensuing years, "Mormon fundamentalists rallied in opposition to what they perceived as a cover up," notes Hales, who challenges the Fundamentalists' interpretation of the Taylor revelation by "asserting . . . that the wording of the revelation . . . alludes to broader and more numerous gospel principles than plural marriage alone. . . . The divine process that produced the 1886 revelation to John Taylor was continuous revelation. Church members might argue that this revelation did not, and could not, signal an end to additional continuous revelation being received by the 'one' man regarding plural marriage. Nor should any particular revelation be considered to be the 'final word' on the topic it discusses. . . . The greatest significance of the 1886 revelation stems not from what it says, but from the reaction of some Church leaders to its existence."[45]

Almost five decades after the alleged revelation, the First Presidency declared in 1933:

> As to this pretended revelation it should be said that the archives of the Church contain no such revelation; the archives contain no record of any such a revelation, nor any evidence justifying a belief that any such revelation was ever given. . . .

Since this pretended revelation, if ever given, was never presented to and adopted by the Church or by any council of the Church, and since to the contrary, an inspired rule of action, the Manifesto, was (subsequently to the pretended revelation) presented to and adopted by the Church, which inspired rule in its terms, purport, and effect was directly opposite to the interpretation given to the pretended revelation, the said pretended revelation could have no validity and no binding effect and force upon Church members, and action under it would be unauthorized, illegal, and void.[46]

One can see from this example that the difficulties of administering from the DO lingered long after General Authorities came out of exile.

The chase for the prophet did not lessen as time went on and added to his declining health. As late as February 9, 1887, just five months before he passed away, deputies searched the temple, tithing offices, and the Gardo and Lion Houses for some of the Brethren and offered eight hundred dollars for information leading to their capture.[47] In May 1887, George Q. Cannon wrote to John W. Young, "President Taylor's health is not good and I heartily wish that something would be done in his case. It seems most cruel and barbarous proceeding for him to be kept as he is."[48] On July 1, 1887, President George Q. Cannon confided to Elder Wilford Woodruff: "It becomes my painful duty to advise you concerning President Taylor's health." Cannon wrote that he noticed a steady decline in the President's health, though he "constantly asserted that he would recover."[49] By July 1887, Salt Lake resident and entrepreneur Joseph A. West acknowledged in a letter to the prophet the "distressing confinement to which you must be subjected in order to avoid the very vigilant watch of the d[e]puties and to prevent them from discovering your hiding place."[50]

On July 29, Presidents Cannon and Smith announced the death of President Taylor in the *Deseret News*. The counselors thanked Church members for their sympathy for the President of the Church being forced to live out the rest of his life in hiding. They informed the readers that "his constant desire was to do everything in his power to relieve the Latter-day Saints from the oppression under which they suffer." The edition included an editorial written by future Apostle Charles W. Penrose, who insisted that exile was a leading factor of the prophet's declining health and death. Penrose explained that part of the problem lay in the lack of "proper exercise," which caused his limbs to swell. Even more directly, he stated, "President John Taylor has been killed by the cruelty of officials who have . . . misrepresented the Government of the United States." It was then emphatically declared that the Church would continue on as it had when Joseph Smith and Brigham Young passed away, despite the fact that most general Church leaders remained in hiding.[51]

The interpretation of the broken lamp in President's Taylor's dream of September 1886 eventually came true, but not in the way President Taylor first feared. With his death the group that protected him disbanded. His bodyguards continued to avoid capture but eventually found it possible to return to their families. For the families who harbored President Taylor, life returned to normal. President Taylor's counselors lived in exile until President Cannon was arrested and imprisoned for a short time. As the dream's interpretation suggested, those in hiding faced loneliness when they were separated. For those forced to remain in hiding, that loneliness lasted until President Wilford Woodruff received the Manifesto, ending plural marriage and Church administration from the underground.

APPENDIX A

Transcript of John Taylor's hiding places, 1885–87; in John Taylor Family Papers, MS 0050, folder 6, item 411, Special Collections, J. Willard Marriott Library, University of Utah, Salt Lake City; original spelling preserved.

1885		
February 1st	1 Bishop Samuel Bennion	Taylorsville, 48th South, 17th West
February 10th	Bishop's sister-in-law Bennion	Taylorsville, 48th South, 17th West February 15th
Chas Bagley	Big Cottonwood	
February 20th	Peter Hansen	Sugarhouse Ward
March 28th	David James Farm Sam Obray	North Point (over Jordon)
July 11th	2 Bishop Bennion	Taylorsville (took a trip to Nephi)
July 14th	2 John Carlisle	8th West, 30th South
July 15th	Mormie Hintze	East Millcreek
July 17th	2 Peter Hansen	Sugar House Ward
August 13th	George Baylie	East Millcreek
August 19th	James Godfrey	South Cottonwood

Sept 28th	3 John Carlisle	South Cottonwood
October 2nd	2 James Godfrey	South Cottonwood
December 9th	Wm Taylor	Little Cottonwood
December 10th	3 James Godfrey	South Cottonwood
To Parawan, Christmas		

1886

January 10th	4 John Carlisle	Mill Creek
January 20th	Frank Armstrong	11th Ward, Salt Lake City
Feb 8th	Alfred Solomon	19th Ward, Salt Lake City
March 11th	S. J. Sudbury	City Creek Canyon
March 16th	Wm White & sons	16th Ward, Salt Lake City
June 10th	2 Alfred Solomon	19th W, Salt Lake City
June 30th	Henry Day	Draper
July 12th	James Livingston	Stone Quarrie Little Cottonwood
July 14th	4 James Godfrey	South Cottonwood
July 15th	2 Henry Day	Draper
July 18th	1 Bishop Stuart	Draper
July 20th	3 Henry Day	Draper
July 27th	2 Bishop Stuart	Draper
Aug 6th	4 Henry Day	Draper
Aug 6th	John Carlisle	Draper
September 5th	George Stringfillow	Draper
September 5th	2 Wm White & sons	16th Ward, Salt Lake City
September 14th	John W. Woolley	Centerville
October 11th	Orren Randall	Centerville
October 12th	2 John W. Wooley	Centerville
November 3rd	3 Wm White & sons	16th Ward, Salt Lake City
November 9th	3 J. W. Wooley	Centerville
November 22nd	Thomas F. Roueche	Kaysville

Eric Perkins teaches US history at Rolling Hills Middle School in Diamond Springs, California.

Mary Jane Woodger is a professor of Church history and doctrine at Brigham Young University.

Eric Perkins and Mary Jane Woodger, "Administration from the Underground," in *Champion of Liberty: John Taylor*, ed. Mary Jane Woodger (Provo, UT: Religious Studies Center, Brigham Young University, 2009), 347–70.

NOTES

1. Diary of Samuel Bateman, 1886–1909, September 14, 1886, typescript, L. Tom Perry Special Collections, Harold B. Lee Library, Brigham Young University, Provo, Utah.
2. George Q. Cannon to Franklin S. Richards, April 1887, John Taylor Family Papers, 1844–1944, MS 0050, box 1b, folder 33, Special Collections, J. Willard Marriott Library, University of Utah, Salt Lake City.
3. Samuel W. Taylor, *The Last Pioneer: John Taylor, a Mormon Prophet* (Salt Lake City: Signature Books, 1999), 336n1.
4. See David J. Whittaker, "The Bone in the Throat: Orson Pratt and the Public Announcement of Plural Marriage," *Western Historical Quarterly* 18, no. 3 (July 1987): 301–3.
5. John Taylor, in *Journal of Discourses* (London: Latter-day Saints' Book Depot, 1854–86), 24:231.
6. See Richard S. Van Wagoner, *Mormon Polygamy: A History* (Salt Lake City: Signature Books, 1992), 107.
7. See Edmunds-Tucker Act, March 3, 1887, ch. 397, 24 statute 635; see also Van Wagoner, *Mormon Polygamy*, 117.
8. Joseph F. Smith to Mary Taylor Schwartz, December 10, 1884, Joseph Fielding Smith Letters, Joseph F. Smith letters to Mary Taylor Schwartz Smith, 1884–1917, MS 30633, Church History Library, The Church of Jesus Christ of Latter-day Saints, Salt Lake City (hereafter CHL).
9. First Presidency to Stake Presidents, December 6, 1884, John Taylor Family Papers, MS 0050, box 20, folder 3, Special Collections, J. Willard Marriott Library.
10. See Taylor, *Last Pioneer*, 327.
11. Joseph F. Smith to John Henry Smith, January 19, 1885, John Taylor Family Papers, MS 0050, box 7A, folder 19, Special Collections, J. Willard Marriott Library.
12. See Van Wagoner, *Mormon Polygamy*, 122–24.
13. "Unsigned 1885 Letter, Raid of the Gardo House," March 15, 1885, William Brown Papers, 1877–1938, MS 18232, CHL; see also Julia T. Neville interview with Ezra Oakley Taylor, undated, MS 10004, 5, CHL; and Margarite Whitaker Chipman, "The Life of Ida Oakley Taylor Whitaker," Whitaker Family Biographical Sketches, 1982–1987, MS 9737, CHL.
14. Other Church leaders experienced similar events. Apostles Wilford Woodruff and Erastus Snow were able to walk undetected by a group of deputies waiting for them

outside the Church Historian's Office. See Whitaker Family Biographical Sketches, MS 9737, CHL.

15. John Taylor, "Discourse by President John Taylor, delivered in the Tabernacle, Salt Lake City, Sunday, February 1, 1885," Special Collections, J. Willard Marriott Library.

16. John M. Whitaker interview, 1957, AV 1068, 7, CHL.

17. Taylor, *Last Pioneer*, 335.

18. Charles Barrell, who sometimes went by "Birrell" to mislead enemies of the Church, was a natural-born actor. He was capable of disguising his voice and physical appearance and doing whatever else was needed for hiding his true identity. It was said of him, "Many were the dangers and experiences he gladly faced to save lives of others in those trying times." O. K. Neilson, "The Life of Charles Barrell," John Taylor Family Papers, MS 0050, box 8, folder 17, Special Collections, J. Willard Marriott Library.

19. For a complete list of all locations, see appendix A.

20. See Taylor, *Last Pioneer*, 337–38.

21. See Taylor, *Last Pioneer*, 338–39.

22. William Brown to parents, March 15, 1885, William Brown Papers, 1877–1938, MS 18232, CHL.

23. Chipman, "Life of Ida Oakley Taylor Whitaker."

24. Alfred Carlisle interview, April 6, 1978, interviewed by Etta Carlisle, The John Carlisle and William H. Hill Homes, MS 2088, CHL.

25. Carlisle interview.

26. See Carlisle interview.

27. John Taylor to Maggie Taylor, March 10, 1887, Margaret M. Taylor Papers, 1866–94, MS 2185, CHL.

28. John Taylor to Mrs. Margaret "Maggie" Taylor, September 8, 1886, Margaret M. Taylor Papers, MS 2185, CHL.

29. Elaine Chipman Hepworth, "Sketch of John Mills Whitaker," Whitaker Family Biographical Sketches, MS 9737, CHL.

30. John Taylor and George Q. Cannon to Bishop J. H. Richards, St. Joseph Apache Company, Arizona, May 19, 1885, Joseph H. Richards Letters, 1878–1885, MS 15646, CHL.

31. John Taylor to Mrs. Maggie White Taylor, October 11, 1886, Margaret M. Taylor Papers, MS 2185, CHL.

32. MeasuringWorth.com, http://measuringworth.com/ppowerus/.

33. John Taylor to wife, February 2, 1887, Margaret M. Taylor Papers, MS 2185, CHL.

34. John Taylor to Mrs. Maggie White Taylor, October 11, 1886, Margaret M. Taylor Papers, MS 2185, CHL.

35. John Taylor to wife, November 19, 1886, Margaret M. Taylor Papers, MS 2185, CHL.

36. Diary of Samuel Bateman, April 10, 1887.

37. John Taylor to wife, February 2, 1887, MS 2185, CHL.

38. John Taylor to wife, February 2, 1887.

39. See Paul Nolan Hyde and Dennis A. Wright, "John Taylor," in *Presidents of the Church: The Lives and Teachings of the Modern Prophets*, ed. Craig Manscill, Robert C. Freeman, and Dennis A. Wright (Springville, UT: Cedar Fort, 2008), 76–77.

40. See Joseph F. Smith to "My Darling Boy," August 26, 1886, Joseph F. Smith Letters to Mary Taylor Schwartz Smith, 1884–1917, MS 30633, CHL.

41. See John Taylor to James Jack, November 19, 1886, Salt Lake City, John Taylor Family Papers, MS 0050, box 3A, folder 23, 306, Special Collections, J. Willard Marriott Library; John Taylor to Angus Cannon, Salt Lake City, November 19, 1886, item 306a in the same collection; and John Taylor to James Jack, item 308 in the same collections.

42. See President John Taylor to James Jack, Esq., September 25, 1886, and Thomas E. Taylor to John Taylor, March 25, 1886; both in John Taylor Family Papers, MS 0050, box 6, folder 16, Special Collections, J. Willard Marriott Library.

43. Internal correspondence between Samuel and Raymond Taylor, John Taylor Family Papers, MS 0050, Special Collections, J. Willard Marriott Library.

44. Brian C. Hales, *Mormon Polygamy and Mormon Fundamentalism* (Salt Lake City: Greg Kofford Books, 2006), 37.

45. Hales, *Mormon Polygamy and Mormon Fundamentalism*, 41.

46. "Official Statement on Plural Marriage," *Church News*, June 17, 1933.

47. See Joseph F. Smith to My Sweet Companion, March 4, 1887, Joseph F. Smith Letters to Mary Taylor Schwartz Smith, 1884–1917, MS 30633, CHL.

48. George Q. Cannon to John W. Young, May 20, 1887, John Taylor Family Papers, MS 0050, box 3A, folder 23, 308, Special Collections, J. Willard Marriott Library.

49. George Q. Cannon to Wilford Woodruff, July 1, 1887, John Taylor Family Papers, MS 0050, box 3A, folder 5, 169, Special Collections, J. Willard Marriott Library.

50. Joseph A. West to John Taylor, July 4, 1887, MS 0050, John Taylor Family Papers, box 1b, folder 38, Special Collections, J. Willard Marriott Library.

51. George Q. Cannon and Joseph F. Smith, "Announcement of the Death of President John Taylor," *Deseret News Semi-Weekly*, July 29, 1887; and Charles W. Penrose, "Honor to the Departed," *Deseret News Semi-Weekly*, July 29, 1887, MS 0050, box 1B, folder 39, John Taylor Family Papers, Special Collections, J. Willard Marriott Library.

Chapter Twenty-Two

"And I Saw the Hosts of the Dead, Both Small and Great"

Joseph F. Smith, World War I, and His Visions of the Dead

RICHARD E. BENNETT

> As I pondered over these things which are written, the eyes of my understanding were opened, and the Spirit of the Lord rested upon me, and I saw the hosts of the dead, both small and great. (Doctrine and Covenants 138:11)

Joseph F. Smith's discourses on life, death, and war are revered today by Latter-day Saints as profoundly important doctrinal contributions. Sixth President of The Church of Jesus Christ of Latter-day Saints (he served from 1901 to 1918) and nephew of Joseph Smith, the founder of the Church, President Smith proclaimed some of his most comforting and most important discourses on the topics of death and suffering during the waning months of World War I. His final sermon, entitled "Vision of the Redemption of the Dead," and now canonized as revelation by the Church, stands as an authoritative, scriptural declaration of its time.

A thorough study of the historical process that brought this doctrinal statement out of obscurity and into the realm of modern Latter-day Saint scripture begs to be written. However, the purpose of this paper is to place this and his other wartime sermons in their historical context, to suggest their place in the wider tapestry of Christian thought, and to argue for their fuller application as commentary on temple work, war, and several other critical issues of the day. Just as it took Church leaders years to rediscover the full importance of President Smith's vision of the redemption of the dead and its significance as a vital assist to modern temple work, so also Latter-day Saint historians have been slow to view it as a unique commentary of the age. To the views and comments of other religionists of the day who were sharing their own important visions at war's end, Joseph F. Smith's must now be added.[1]

At the "eleventh hour of the eleventh day of the eleventh month," schoolchildren across Canada and throughout much of the British Commonwealth of Nations bow their heads in grateful remembrance for those who died in war. To this day, Remembrance Day, November 11, is a Sabbath-day-like observance, a tolling bell, in honor of those who gave their "last true measure of devotion" to the cause of God, king, and country. Canadians wear scarlet poppies on their lapels and gather respectfully at public war memorials across the land, sing hymns, honor mothers who lost sons in battle, and listen reverently to the following poem, penned in 1915 by the Canadian physician Lieutenant Colonel John McCrae during the frightful Second Battle of Ypres, where men by the tens of thousands were dying in the blooming poppy fields in the Flanders region of Belgium:

> In Flanders fields the poppies blow
> Between the crosses, row on row,
> That mark our place; and in the sky
> The larks, still bravely singing, fly
> Scarce heard amid the guns below.
>
> We are the Dead. Short days ago
> We lived, felt dawn, saw sunset glow,
> Loved and were loved, and now we lie
> In Flanders fields.
>
> Take up our quarrel with the foe:
> To you from failing hands we throw
> The torch; be yours to hold it high.
> If ye break faith with us who die
> We shall not sleep, though poppies grow
> In Flanders fields.[2]

Indeed, "lest we forget," more than nine million men in uniform and countless legions of civilians perished in the battlefields, battleships, and bombed-out byways of World War I. Another twenty-one million were

Joseph F. Smith, photograph by Emil Clausen, 1910. Courtesy of Intellectual Reserve, Inc.

permanently scarred and disfigured. Whatever the causes of that conflict, they have long been overshadowed by the "sickening mists of slaughter" that, like a pestilence, hung over the world for four and a half years. The terrible battles of the Marne, Gallipoli, Verdun, the Somme, Jutland, Passchendaele, Ypres, Vimy Ridge, and many others are killing fields synonymous with unmitigated human slaughter in what some have described as a nineteenth-century war fought with twentieth-century weaponry. This was the conflict, remember, that witnessed the awful stalemate of protracted trench warfare and pitched hand-to-hand combat in the "no-man's lands" of western Europe, the introduction of Germany's lethal submarine attacks, chemical-gas mass killings, and aerial bombings on a frightening scale. Yet the Great War, that "war to end all wars," became but the catalyst and springboard for an even deadlier conflict a generation later. And with its long-prayed-for conclusion on 11 November 1918 came prayers for a lasting peace, hopes for a League of Nations that would guarantee future world peace, and sermons and visions that spoke of new hopes and new dreams for a blighted world.

JOSEPH F. SMITH'S RESPONSES TO WAR

Compared to the other great religions of the time, The Church of Jesus Christ of Latter-day Saints, with a membership then of only a few hundred thousand, most of whom lived in Utah and surrounding states, may seem like a very small voice in a vastly overcrowded cathedral. Though as many as fifteen thousand saw battle, mainly as enlisted men in the United States Army, Latter-day Saints were largely spared the tragedy of killing one another, unlike the gruesome specter of Catholics shooting Catholics and of Lutherans gunning down fellow Lutherans on some forlorn and distant battlefield of Europe. Headquartered far away in the tops of the Rocky Mountains of the American West, the Church remained relatively unscathed from the intimate hell and awful horror of war, much as it had done during America's Civil War fifty years before. Nevertheless, its leaders held definite positions toward the war, some of which modified over time.

With the sudden, unexpected outbreak of the war and in response to Democratic President Woodrow Wilson's request for prayers of peace, Joseph F. Smith, a confirmed Republican, and his counselors in the First Presidency, the highest ecclesiastical body in the Church, called upon the entire membership to support the nation's president and to pray for peace. "We deplore the calamities which have come upon the people in Europe," he declared, "the terrible slaughter of brave men, the awful sufferings of women and children, and all the disasters that are befalling the world in consequence of the impending conflicts, and earnestly hope and pray that they may be brought to a speedy end."[3]

His second counselor, Charles W. Penrose, speaking further on President Smith's behalf, condemned neither side in the war: "We ask Thee, O

Lord, to look in mercy upon those nations. No matter what may have been the cause which has brought about the tumult and the conflict now prevailing, wilt Thou grant, we pray Thee, that it be overruled for good, so that the time shall come when, though thrones may totter and empires fall, liberty and freedom shall come to the oppressed nations of Europe, and indeed throughout the world."[4] This spirit of the entire Church praying for peace lasted throughout the war.[5]

Speaking in the general conference of the Church just one month after the outbreak of war, President Smith expressed, for the first time, his public interpretation of the war and of its causes. Still stunned by news of the enormously high numbers of casualties so soon inflicted, he reiterated his desire for peace, pointed to the "deplorable" spectacle of war, and blamed it not on God but squarely on man's inhumanity to man, on dishonest politics, on broken treaties, and, above all, on the apostate conditions he believed were endemic to modern Christianity. "God did not design or cause this," he preached. "It is deplorable to the heavens that such a condition should exist among men."[6] Choosing not to interpret the conflict in economic, political, or even nationalist tones, he ever saw it, at base, as the result of moral decline, of religious bankruptcy, and of the world's refusal to accept the full gospel of Jesus Christ. "Here we have nations arrayed against nations," he said, "and yet in every one of these nations are so-called Christian peoples professing to worship the same God, professing to possess belief in the same divine Redeemer . . . and yet these nations are divided against the other, and each is praying to his God for wrath upon and victory over his enemies."[7] Loyal in every way to the message of the Book of Mormon and the Restoration of the gospel of Jesus Christ, he saw it this way:

> Would it be possible—could it be possible, for this condition to exist if the people of the world possessed really the true knowledge of the Gospel of Jesus Christ? And if they really possessed the Spirit of the living God—could this condition exist? No; it could not exist, but war would cease, and contention and strife would be at an end. . . . Why does it exist? Because they are not one with God, nor with Christ. They have not entered into the true fold, and the result is they do not possess the spirit of the true Shepherd sufficiently to govern and control their acts in the ways of peace and righteousness.[8]

The only real and lasting antidote to the sin of war, he believed, was the promulgation of the restored gospel of Jesus Christ "as far as we have power to send it forth through the elders of the Church."[9] Though the war was not the work of God, President Smith was nonetheless quick to see in it a fulfilment of divine prophecy, both ancient and modern. "The newspapers are full of the wars and the rumors of wars," he wrote in a private family letter of November 1914, "which seem to be literally poured out upon all nations as foretold by the Prophet [Joseph Smith] in 1832. The reports of the carnage and destruction going on in Europe are sickening and deplorable, and from the latest reports the field of carnage is greatly enlarging instead of diminishing."[10]

A few weeks later, in his annual Christmas greeting to the Church for December 1914, he returned to this same theme. "The sudden 'outpouring' of the spirit of war upon the European nations which startled the whole world and was unexpected at the time of its occurrence, had long been expected by the Latter-day Saints, as it was foretold by the Prophet Joseph Smith on Christmas Day, December 25th, 1832."[11]

Yet no one took pleasure in seeing such foreboding prophecy fulfilled. Nor could prophecies be made tantamount to divine imposition on the affairs of men. At stake was the agency—and the evil—of man. As the cold calamity of war spread across the battlefields of Europe, President Smith continually stressed this point. "God, doubtless, could avert war," he said in December of 1914, "prevent crime, destroy poverty, chase away darkness, overcome error, and make all things bright, beautiful and joyful. But this would involve the destruction of a vital and fundamental attribute of His sons and daughters that they become acquainted with evil as well as good, with darkness as well as light, with error as well as truth and with the results of the infraction of eternal laws."[12] Thus, the war was seen as a schoolmaster, a judgment of man's own doing, a terrible lesson of what inevitably transpires when hate and greed rule the day.

Despite these broken laws and with them the inevitable fulfillment of calamitous prophecy, there can be found, like a stream of clear water running throughout President Smith's teachings, the doctrine of ultimate redemption and resolution:

> Therefore [God] has permitted the evils which have been brought about by the acts of His creatures, but will control their ultimate results for His glory and the progress and exaltation of His sons and daughters, when they have learned obedience by the things they suffer. . . . The foreknowledge of God does not imply His action in bringing about that which He foresees.[13]

Vowing initially not to take sides in the struggle, President Smith found it increasingly challenging, however, to remain neutral. The dreadful sinking of the *Lusitania* in May 1915 struck an ominous chord in America, intent as the country was in staying clear of the conflict. His colleague, James E. Talmage, then a member of the Church's Quorum of the Twelve Apostles, and an Englishman by birth, described the sinking as "one of the most barbarous developments of the European war," charging Germany for staining its hands "with innocent blood never to be washed away."[14]

Despite such wartime atrocities, President Smith clung to the hope that America could somehow remain detached from the war. "I am glad that we have kept out of war so far, and I hope and pray that we may not be under the necessity of sending our sons to war, or experience as a nation the distress, the anguish and sorrow that come from a condition such as exists upon the old continent."[15]

Nevertheless, as America lurched reluctantly toward war, he came to see America's involvement as a necessity. News of the Zeppelin bombing raids over England, and his consequent fear for the safety of his own mission-president son and missionaries then serving in England, particularly bothered him and led him to question ever further Germany's wartime tactics. "It seems to me that the only object of such raids is the wanton and wicked destruction of property and the taking of defenseless lives," he wrote.

> It appears that the spirit of murder, the shedding of blood, not only of combatants but of anyone connected with the enemy's country seems to have taken possession of the people, or at least the ruling powers in Germany. What they gain by it, I do not know. It is hardly possible that they expect to intimidate the people by such actions, and it surely does not diminish the forces of the opposition. By such unnecessary and useless raids in the name of warfare, they are losing the respect of all the nations of the earth.[16]

A staunch patriot, he was soon to admit the obvious: "I have a feeling in my heart that the United States has a glorious destiny to fulfil, and that part of that glorious destiny is to extend liberty to the oppressed, as far as it is possible to all nations, to all people." Gradually, he forged a cautious, nonpacifist view in behalf of the entire Church: "I do not want war; but the Lord has said it shall be poured out upon all nations, and if we escape, it will be 'by the skin of our teeth.' I would rather the oppressors should be killed, or destroyed, than to allow the oppressors to kill the innocent."[17]

If Latter-day Saints must fight—and thousands of them soon enlisted in the cause—their attitude must ever be that of "peace and good will toward all mankind, . . . that they will not forget that they are also soldiers of the Cross, that they are ministers of life and not of death; and when they go forth, they may go forth in the spirit of defending the liberties of mankind rather than for the purpose of destroying the enemy. . . . Let the soldiers that go out from Utah be and remain men of honor."[18] Eager to demonstrate loyalty to an America still suspicious of the Church and of some of its teachings and to support President Wilson's entry into the war, President Smith led active campaigns to enlist Latter-day Saints in the ranks of the military and to involve the Church and its membership in the various Liberty Bond drives of the time, raising hundreds of thousands of dollars in the process.[19]

Significantly, his writings bear an absence of malice or a spirit of vengeance toward the aggressor. Less critical than other younger leaders, such as James E. Talmage, who, although not given to retribution, felt Germany had a debt to pay, President Smith was ever slow to condemn. Said he: "Let the Lord exercise vengeance where vengeance is needed. And let me not judge my fellow men, nor condemn them lest I condemn them wrongly."[20]

Meanwhile, until the war ended, Latter-day Saints joined with others in praying for peace and in taking up arms in the cause of victory over the enemy. America's involvement eventually turned the tide of war, ultimately bringing a defeated Germany and the other Axis powers to Versailles. And though half a world away, news of the pending peace was as jubilantly received in Utah as it was most everywhere else in the free world.[21]

THE ARMISTICE

The Latter-day Saints were, of course, not alone in proclaiming a vision of the war and of peace. A sampling of what others saw as the war wore on may be instructive. Randall Thomas Davidson, Archbishop of Canterbury, by the time the conflict had ended was still trying earnestly to see meaning out of a senseless war, to see divine purpose in man's malignancy, and to bring vision to a groping world. "There, then, with all that the war has brought us of darkened homes and of shattered hopes for those we loved," he said in his war-closing sermon of gratitude preached at Westminster Abbey in London on November 10, 1918,

> with all its hindering and setting back of our common efforts and energies to promote things peaceable and lovely and of good report,

[the war] has, beyond any doubt, been our schoolmaster to bring us to a larger vision of the world as God sees it. It is one of the great things which our sons, our dear sons, have wrought for us by their dauntless sacrifice. . . . Just now, this week, when the whole life—I do not think I am exaggerating—the whole life of the world is being re-conditioned, re-established, re-set for good. This is that crisis-hour. Something has happened, is happening, which can best find description in . . . the living word or message of God to man. It cuts right to the centre of our being.[22]

He closed a later sermon with his particular vision of a new Christian paradigm:

Jesus Christ is the real centre and strength of the best hopes and efforts man can make for the bettering and the brightening of the world. Only we must quietly, determinedly, thoughtfully, take His law and His message as our guide. . . . The task is hardest perhaps when we are dealing with life's largest relationship—the relationship between peoples. Can we carry the Christian creed and rule there? Who shall dare to say we cannot? It needs a yet larger outlook. . . . Surely it is a vision from on high.[23]

Pope Benedict XV, in his first encyclical immediately following the end of the war, rejoiced that "the clash of arms has ceased," allowing "humanity [to] breathe again after so many trials and sorrows." Next only to gratitude, his sentiment was one of profound regret, bordering on apology, that a leading cause of the war had been the "deplorable fact that the ministers of the Word" had not more courageously taught true religion rather than the politics of accommodation from the pulpit. The conscience of Christianity had been scarred by its own advocates. "The blame certainly must be laid on those ministers of the Gospel," he lamented. He went on to chastise the pulpit by calling for a new vision, a new order of valiant, righteous Christian spokesmen who would declare peace and the cross fearlessly. "It must be our earnest endeavor everywhere to bring back the preaching of the Word of God to the norm and ideal to which it must be directed according to the command of Christ Our Lord, and the laws of the Church."[24]

The official American Catholic response may best be seen in the pastoral letters of its bishops. At its base, the war showed a deep "moral evil" in man where "spiritual suffering" and "sin abounded." Despite all of mankind's progress—"the advance of civilization, the diffusion of knowledge, the unlimited freedom of thought, the growing relaxation of moral restraint— . . . we are facing grave peril." Scientific and materialistic progress notwithstanding, a world without moral discipline and faith will lead only to destruction. The only true vision of hope is "the truth and the life of Jesus Christ," and the Catholic Church must uphold the dignity of man, defend the rights of the people, relieve distress, consecrate sacrifice, and bind all classes together in the love of the Savior.[25]

James Cardinal Gibbons of Baltimore, the leading American Catholic spokesman, in calling upon Americans to "thank God for the victory of the allies and to ask him for grace to 'walk in the ways of wisdom, obedience and humility,'" ordered his priests to substitute the prayer of thanksgiving in the Mass in place of the oration.[26] He instructed them further that a solemn service be held in all the churches of the archdiocese on November 28, 1918, at which the Church's official prayer of thanksgiving, the *Te Deum,* should be sung.[27] Written as early as AD 450, the words to one of Catholicism's most famous hymns speak of man's immortality, of Christ's divinity, and of his redemption of the dead:

> We praise Thee, O God: we
> acknowledge Thee to be the Lord.
> Thee, the Eternal Father, all
> the earth doth worship. . . .
>
> Thou, O Christ, art the King of glory.
> Thou art the Everlasting Son of the Father.
> Thou didst not abhor the Virgin's
> womb, when Thou tookest upon
> Thee human nature to deliver man.
>
> When Thou hadst overcome the
> sting of death, Thou didst open
> to believers the kingdom of heaven.
>
> Thou sittest at the right hand of
> God, in the glory of the Father.
> Thou, we believe, art the Judge to come.[28]

The American Protestant view of the war, and more especially of its postwar opportunities, are varied and diverse and defy simple categorization and analysis. There were almost as many "visions" as there were hundreds of denominations. While most, like Bishop Charles P. Anderson of the Protestant Episcopal Church, spoke in terms of gratitude, many others soon were speaking jingoistically, calling for immediate punishment and retribution.[29]

"*The Christian Century*, which was representative of a great portion of Christendom, believed in the thorough chastisement of Germany."[30] Likewise, the *Congregationalist* editorialized that "Germany is a criminal at the bar of justice."[31] Reverend Dr. S. Howard Young of Brooklyn called "retribution upon the war lords" as "divine," "the first world lesson to be derived from the German downfall."[32]

Meanwhile, Billy Sunday, "God's Grenadier" and by far the most popular patriot/evangelist of his day, saw the war as good against evil, God against Satan, "America and Christ, indissolubly linked, forging ahead in a glorious struggle."[33] Though some others shared his view, Billy characteristically always went a step or two further. "Hey, Jesus, you've gotta send a country like that to damnation," he once said. "I'll raise enough of an army myself to help beat the dust off the Devil's hordes."[34] He also saw the end of the war as a window, a God-given opportunity to revitalize the evangelical cause of Christian revivalism and of individual spiritual rebirth, a time to confront the anti-Christ of such foreign-inspired teachings as evolution, social Darwinism, higher criticism, and every other philosophical evil of the age.

Other, more moderate clergymen like the positive-minded Presbyterian Robert E. Speer saw a moral victory stemming out of the war, a new vision rising out of the ashes of Europe. "The war also has unmistakably set in the supreme place those moral and spiritual principles which constitute the message of the Church," he declared. "The war has shown that these values are supreme over personal loss and material interest. . . . We succeeded in the war whenever and wherever this was our spirit. . . . The war says that what Christ said is forever true."[35]

Rabbi Silverman, speaking in Chicago's Temple Beth-El synagogue, mirrored Speer's sentiments. "The world was nearer its millennium today than ever before," he is reported to have said. "War had brought mankind nearer to brotherhood than had centuries of religious teachings. . . . War had brought religion back to its original task of combating bigotry, fighting sin, and uplifting mankind."[36]

Both Reverend Speer and Henry Emerson Fosdick, professor of the Union Theological Seminary in New York, along with other leading religious leaders, welcomed the end of war as an opportunity to launch "the Church Peace Union," a new united religious order funded, in part, by Andrew Carnegie and his Carnegie Endowment for International Peace to unite multiple Protestant faiths marching under one grand united banner—"the new political heaven [to] regenerate earth," as Bishop Samuel

Fallows of the Reformed Episcopal Church liked to describe it. Though destined to failure because of oppressive debts, internal disagreements, and opposition from Protestant fundamentalism, for a brief moment this Interchurch World Movement of Protestants, Catholics, and Jewish leaders in America became "the principal voice of institutional religion on behalf of peace-keeping and peace-making" and appeared to hold enormous promise for church unity, social reform, and economic improvement.[37]

Fosdick, one of the most eloquent American Protestant statesmen of his time, had grudgingly supported America's entry into the war but came out of it a confirmed pacifist. Reflecting the utter disillusionment the war wrought on many religionists, Fosdick listed several elements in his vision of warning for the future: "There is nothing glamorous about war any more," "war is not a school for virtue any more," "there is no limit to the methods of killing in war any more," "there are no limits to the cost of war any more," "there is no possibility of sheltering any portion of the population from the direct effect of war any more," and "we cannot reconcile Christianity and war any more."[38] Every effort must be made to avoid such a future calamity. He, like many others, was bitterly disappointed by America's refusal to ratify the Versailles Peace Treaty and enter the League of Nations, which President Wilson had so arduously supported. As one commentary dryly remarked, "God won the war and the devil won the peace."[39]

JOSEPH F. SMITH'S VISIONS OF THE DEAD

Worn out by a long life of devoted Church service and worn down in sorrow due to the recent deaths of several members of his immediate family, Joseph F. Smith, though a loving soul, knew all about grief. "I lost my father when I was but a child," he once said. "I lost my mother, the sweetest soul that ever lived, when I was only a boy. I have buried one of the loveliest wives that ever blessed the lot of man, and I have buried thirteen of my more than forty children. . . . And it has seemed to me that the most promising, the most helpful, and, if possible, the sweetest and purest and the best have been the earliest called to rest."[40] Speaking of the loss of one of his former polygamist wives, Sarah E., and, shortly thereafter, of his daughter Zina, he further said: "I cannot yet dwell on the scenes of the recent past. Our hearts have been tried to the core. Not that the end of mortal life has come to two of the dearest souls on earth to me, so much as at the sufferings of our loved ones, which we were utterly powerless to relieve. Oh! How helpless is mortal man in the face of sickness unto death!"[41]

His daughter's death triggered four of the most revealing discourses ever given by a Latter-day Saint leader on the doctrines of death, the spirit world, and the Resurrection. As one noted scholar put it: "It is doubtful if in any given period of like duration in the entire history of The Church of Jesus Christ of Latter-day Saints so much detail as to the nature of the life after death has been given to any other prophet of this dispensation."[42] All were well received by the membership and extended hope and comfort to those who had lost loved ones or who might be asked to sacrifice family members in times of peace or of conflict. The war, still raging loud and cruel, served as a vivid backdrop to these emerging doctrines.

On April 6, 1916, with the battles of Verdun and the Somme very much dominating the daily news, he gave a talk entitled "In the Presence of the Divine" in which he spoke of the very thin veil separating the living from the dead. Speaking of Joseph Smith, Brigham Young, Wilford Woodruff, and his other predecessors, he preached the doctrine that the dead, those who have gone on before, "are as deeply interested in our welfare today, if not with greater capacity, with far more interest, behind the veil, than they were in the flesh. I believe they know more. . . . Although some may feel and think that it is a little extreme to take this view, yet I believe that it is true." He went on to say, "We cannot forget them; we do not cease to love them; we always hold them in our hearts, in memory, and thus we are associated and united to them by ties that we cannot break."[43]

President Smith taught that death was neither sleep nor annihilation; rather, death involved a change into another world where the spirits of those once here can be solicitous of our welfare, "can comprehend better than ever before, the weaknesses that are liable to mislead us into dark and forbidden paths."[44]

Two years later, speaking at a meeting in Salt Lake City in February 1918, he spoke additional words of comfort and consolation, particularly to those who had lost children or whose youthful sons were dying overseas. "The spirits of our children are immortal before they come to us," he began,

> and their spirits after bodily death are like they were before they came. They are as they would have appeared if they had lived in the flesh, to grow to maturity, or to develop their physical bodies to the full stature of their spirits. . . . [Furthermore,] Joseph Smith taught the doctrine that the infant child that was laid away in death would come up in the resurrection as a child; and, pointing to the mother of a lifeless child, he said to her: "You will have the joy, the pleasure and satisfaction of nurturing this child, after its resurrection, until it reaches the full

stature of its spirit.". . . . It speaks volumes of happiness, of joy and gratitude to my soul.[45]

Two months later, having recovered from illness sufficiently to speak at the April 1918 general conference of the Church, he gave a talk entitled "A Dream That Was a Reality." In it, he recounted a particularly poignant and unforgettable dream he had experienced sixty-five years earlier as a very young missionary in Hawaii, a dream-vision that dramatically influenced the rest of his life. He spoke of seeing his father, Hyrum, his mother, Mary, Joseph Smith, and several others who had ushered him into a mansion after he had bathed and cleansed himself. "That vision, that manifestation and witness that I enjoyed that time has made me what I am," he confessed. "When I woke up I felt as if I had been lifted out of a slum, out of despair, out of the wretched condition that I was in. . . . I know that that was reality, to show me my duty, to teach me something, and to impress upon me something that I cannot forget."[46]

Just weeks before, on January 23, his son Hyrum, a member of the Quorum of the Twelve, British Mission president, and then only forty-five years of age, died of a ruptured appendix. It was a devastating blow from which Joseph F. never fully recovered, compounded as it was with the further sorrowful news of the death of his daughter-in-law and Hyrum's wife, Ida Bowman Smith, just a few months thereafter. Wrote Talmage in behalf of the Twelve: "Our great concern has been over the effect the great bereavement will have upon President Joseph F. Smith, whose health has been far from perfect for months past. This afternoon he spent a little time in the office of the First Presidency, and we find him bearing up under the load with fortitude and resignation."[47] Sick and intermittently confined to bed rest for several months afterwards he rallied sufficiently to speak briefly in the October general conference of the Church, long enough to proclaim his particular message of peace to a war-weary world.[48]

He spoke of having lately received, while pondering on the biblical writings of the Apostle Peter, another, ultimately his final, vision of the dead. While meditating on these things, he said he "saw the hosts of the dead, both small and great," those who had died "firm in the hope of a glorious resurrection," waiting in a state of paradise for their ultimate redemption and resurrection. Suddenly, the "Son of God appeared, declaring liberty to the captives who had been faithful." Choosing not to go himself to the wicked and unfaithful dead who waited in the more nether realms of the spirit world, Christ mobilized a formidable missionary force among his most faithful followers, dispatching them to minister and teach the gospel of Jesus Christ to "all the spirits of men," those who had been less faithful and obedient in their mortal lives, including, as Peter writes, "those who were sometime disobedient" in the days of Noah and the great flood. In addition, he saw many of the ancients, including Adam and Eve and the prophets, involved in this spirit prison ministry of redemption. Likewise, "the faithful elders of this dispensation" and the "faithful daughters" of Eve were called to assist. His vision closed with the declaration that the dead "who repent will be redeemed, through obedience to the ordinances of the house of God . . . after they have paid the penalty of their transgressions."[49]

Whereas his earlier discourses have remained memorable sermons, this sixty-verse document was immediately sustained, in the words of James E. Talmage, as "the Word of the Lord" by his counselors in the First Presidency and by the Quorum of the Twelve.[50] For reasons not entirely clear, though widely read in the Church, the document was not formally accepted as canonized scripture until fifty-eight years later when, in 1976, President Spencer W. Kimball directed that it be added to the Pearl of Great Price.[51] Later, in June 1979, the First Presidency announced that the vision would become section 138 of the Doctrine and Covenants. Considered an indispensable contribution to a fuller understanding of temple work (especially in an age of very active temple construction), the performance of proxy ordinances for the dead, and the relationship between the living and the dead, it has been heralded as "central to the theology of the Latter-day Saints because it confirms and expands upon earlier prophetic insights concerning work of the dead."[52] Others have written elsewhere about the contributions of this document to Mormon temple work.[53]

Because this document is far more than a mere sermon to the faithful Latter-day Saint and because it is regarded as the word and will of the Lord—one of only two canonized revelations of the twentieth century—it bears careful scrutiny. And, as a wartime document, it may have other meanings and applications not plumbed before.

For instance, although a discourse on the dead, it owed nothing to spiritualism. It is a matter of record that public interest in the dead and in communicating with the dead peaked during and immediately following the war. In 1918 Arthur Conan Doyle of Sherlock Holmes fame published *New Revelation*, a book on the subject of psychical research and phenomena that bemoaned the decline in church attendance in England and of Christianity generally and proclaimed a new religion, a new revelation. He urged a belief not in the fall of man or in Christ's redemption as the basis of faith, but in the validity of "automatic writings," seances, and other expressions of spiritualism as a new universal religion of communicating with lost loved ones—or, as he put it, "the one provable thing connected with every religion, Christian or non-Christian, forming the common solid basis upon which each raises, if it must needs raise, that separate system which appeals to the varied types of mind."[54]

In contrast, President Smith's vision was very much Christ-centered, a reiteration of the Savior's atonement for a fallen world. Though he certainly believed that "we move and have our being in the presence of heavenly messengers and heavenly beings," and though the dead may even transcend the veil and appear unto loved ones if so authorized, he steered the Church away from any hint of spiritualism.[55] Latter-day Saints were to seek *after* the dead—that is, their spiritual welfare—rather than to seek the dead.

His revelation also reaffirmed the Christian belief in Adam and Eve and in a divine creation, for, in President Smith's words, he saw "Father Adam, the Ancient of Days, and father of all" as well as "our glorious Mother Eve" (Doctrine and Covenants 138:38–39). Though nothing is said specifically about evolution and the caustic, contemporary debates of the time over the origin of the species, these verses very simply restated the doctrines of the Church on this subject without argument or ambiguity.

Likewise, in an age of higher criticism with its attack on the authenticity and authority of the Bible, the revelation reestablished, for Latter-day Saints at least, a twentieth-century belief in the primacy, historicity, and authority of scripture, a belief in the writings of Peter, a belief in Noah and the flood not as allegory but as actual event, and, by extension, a renewed belief in the entire Old and New Testaments. For a Church oftentimes criticized for its belief in additional scripture, if nothing else, section 138 is a classic declaration of biblical authority for modern times.[56]

The vision may also be important for what it does not say. There is no discussion of peace treaties, no references to ecumenism or the interchurch movements of the times, no calls for social repentance and the social gospel. Neither pro war nor pacifist, it says nothing about cultural or nationalistic superiorities. The problem of evil is reduced to redeemable limits; and although man will always reap what he sows, there is still hope and redemption. Meanwhile, the Church retains its own mission as the gospel of Jesus Christ on the earth as preestablished in its restoration a century earlier.

Finally, the vision proclaimed God's intimate involvement in the affairs of humankind and his benevolent interest in his children. Steering the Church away from the yawning secularism that stood to envelope many other faiths in the postwar era, President Smith spoke confidently, above all, about Christ and his triumphant victory over sin and death.[57] To the utter waste and sheer terror of the just-concluded catastrophe, there was ultimate redemption. To those who had lost faith in God and in their fellowmen, there was certain restoration. To the soldier lost in battle, to the sailor drowned at sea, and to a prophet-leader mourning the deaths of his own family, there remained the reality of the Resurrection.

Richard E. Bennett is a professor of Church history and doctrine at Brigham Young University.

Richard E. Bennett, "'And I Saw the Hosts of the Dead, Both Small and Great': Joseph F. Smith, World War I, and His Visions of the Dead," *Religious Educator* 2, no. 1 (2001): 104–24.

NOTES

I thank my research assistant, Keith Erekson, for his valuable assistance in helping me prepare this work.

1. The definitive biography of President Joseph F. Smith remains to be written. Joseph Fielding Smith, one of his sons, wrote *Life of Joseph F. Smith, Sixth President of The Church of Jesus Christ of Latter-day Saints* (Salt Lake City: Deseret News Press, 1938; Deseret Book, 1969) in praise of his father. Since then, Francis M. Gibbons has written *Joseph F. Smith: Patriarch and Preacher, Prophet of God* (Salt Lake City: Deseret Book, 1984). See also Scott Kenney, "Joseph F. Smith," in *The Presidents of the Church*, ed. Leonard J. Arrington (Salt Lake City: Deseret Book, 1986), 179–211.

2. John McCrae, "In Flanders Fields," *One Hundred and One Famous Poems*, ed. Roy J. Cook (Chicago: Contemporary Books, 1958), 11. Lieutenant Colonel John McCrae, a member of the first Canadian contingent, died in France on January 28, 1918, after four years of service on the western front.

3. "Special Announcement" of the First Presidency, September 8, 1914, in *Messages of the First Presidency of The Church of Jesus Christ of Latter-day Saints*, ed. James R. Clark (Salt Lake City: Bookcraft, 1970), 4:311 (hereafter *MFP*).

4. Charles W. Penrose, "A Prayer for Peace," in Conference Report, October 1914, 9.

5. See Conference Report, April 1915, 3; and Conference Report, April 1916, 3.

6. Joseph F. Smith, in Conference Report, October 1914, 7.

7. Joseph F. Smith, in Conference Report, October 1914, 7.

8. Joseph F. Smith, in Conference Report, October 1914, 7

9. Joseph F. Smith, in Conference Report, October 1914, 8. In a letter to his son, Hyrum, then a mission president in Liverpool, England, President Smith said, "We still see from the papers that the war in Europe is going on, the whole thing is a sad comment upon the civilization and Christian spirit of the age." Joseph F. Smith to Hyrum Smith, November 7, 1914, Correspondence Files, Joseph F. Smith

Collection, Church Archives, The Church of Jesus Christ of Latter-day Saints, Salt Lake City (hereafter Church Archives).

10. Joseph F. Smith to Hyrum Smith, November 7, 1914.

11. From "A Christmas Greeting from the First Presidency," December 19, 1914, in *MFP*, 4:319. The prophecy alluded to, commonly referred to as the "Civil War Prophecy," spoke of the pending Civil War and its commencement in South Carolina. Later, the South would be compelled to call upon Great Britain for assistance. Great Britain, in turn, "shall also call upon other nations, in order to defend themselves against other nations, and thus war shall be poured out upon all nations" (Doctrine and Covenants 87:3).

12. From "Christmas Greeting from the First Presidency," in *MFP*, 4:325–26.

13. From "Christmas Greeting from the First Presidency," in *MFP*, 4:325–26

14. Journal of James E. Talmage, May 7 and 13, 1915, James E. Talmage Collection, L. Tom Perry Special Collections, Harold B. Lee Library, Brigham Young University. For a more thorough study of Elder Talmage's corresponding views of the war, see the author's "'How Long, Oh Lord, How Long?' James E. Talmage and the Great War," *Religious Educator* 3, no. 1 (2002): 87–102.

15. Joseph F. Smith, in Conference Report, April 1915, 6. Writing in an editorial of December 1915, he said much the same: "We pray that [America's] leaders may receive wisdom of our Father in Heaven, to so direct the affairs in their charge that we may continue in the enjoyment of peace and prosperity throughout the land." Joseph F. Smith to the editor of the *Liahona, The Elders' Journal*, 18 December 1915, Joseph F. Smith Papers, Church Archives.

16. Joseph F. Smith to his son, Hyrum Smith, February 19, 1916, Joseph F. Smith Papers, Church Historical Department.

17. Joseph F. Smith, in Conference Report, October 1916, 154.

18. Joseph F. Smith, in Conference Report, April 1917, 3–4.

19. The Church itself participated in the war effort by purchasing $850,000 in liberty bonds. In addition, it strongly encouraged its membership to participate in the bond drive with the result that the people of Utah far exceeded the state's quota of $6.5 million. One reason the Church was so eager to participate in the war effort was to shed the negative publicity cast upon it during and immediately following the Reed Smoot Senate hearing in Washington, DC. Elected in 1903, Smoot, a member of the Twelve Apostles, had been barred from taking his seat until 1907 because of acrimonious debates over plural marriage and Latter-day Saint loyalties. President Smith and many other prominent Church leaders traveled to Washington on several occasions to testify on behalf of the Church. In 1907 the First Presidency issued a special address to the world explaining the Church's stand on these and many other topics, including its loyalty to America. For a fine summary of the Reed Smoot hearings and their impact on the Church, see Thomas G. Alexander, *Mormonism in Transition: A History of the Latter-day Saints, 1890–1930* (Urbana: University of Illinois Press, 1986), 16–36. See also Kathleen Flake, *The Politics of Religious Identity: The Seating of Reed Smoot, Mormon Apostle* (Chapel Hill: University of North Carolina Press, 2004).

20. From a talk entitled "Status of Children in the Resurrection," May 1918, in *MFP*, 5:97.

21. Official word reached Salt Lake City very early in the morning of November 11, 1918. Despite the late hour and the curfews imposed because of the influenza epidemic, the city seemed to spring into life. In the words of James E. Talmage, "Bells

were tolled, whistles blown, and within an incredibly short time hundreds of automobiles were dashing about the streets, most of them having tin cans, sheet iron utensils and other racket-making appendages attached to the rear." Later in the day, "flags and bunting appeared in abundance everywhere, tons of confetti were thrown from the tops of high buildings, every available band was pressed into service, and during the afternoon and well on into the night dancing was indulged in on Main Street." Talmage enthusiastically concluded, "Such a day as this has never before been witnessed in the world's history." James E. Talmage Journal, November 11, 1918.

22. Randall Thomas Davidson, *The Testing of a Nation* (London: Macmillan, 1919), 159–60; from a sermon entitled "The Armistice," given November 10, 1918.

23. Davidson, *Testing of a Nation*, 176–77, 180; from a sermon entitled "The Day-spring," given December 29, 1918.

24. From "Quod Iam Diu," Encyclical of Pope Benedict XV on the Future Peace Conference, December 1, 1918, 182, in *The Papal Encyclicals, 1903–1939*, comp. Claudia Carlen (Wilmington, NC: McGrath, 1981), 1:153–54.

25. *Pastoral Letter of the Archbishops and Bishops of the United States Assembled in Conference at the Catholic University of America* (Washington, DC: National Catholic Welfare Council, 1920), 39–40.

26. *Chicago Daily Tribune,* November 11, 1918, 3.

27. See John Tracy Ellis, *The Life of James Cardinal Gibbons, Archbishop of Baltimore, 1834–1921* (Milwaukee: Bruce, 1952), 258.

28. "Te Deum," *The Catholic Encyclopedia for School and Home* (New York: McGraw-Hill, 1965), 10:563.

29. *Chicago Daily Tribune,* November 15, 1918, 4.

30. Ray H. Abrams, *Preachers Present Arms: The Role of the American Churches and Clergy in World War One and Two, with Some Observations on the War in Vietnam* (Scottsdale, PA: Herald, 1969), 232–33.

31. Abrams, *Preachers Present Arms,* 233.

32. *Chicago Daily Tribune,* 11 November 1918, 11.

33. Roger A. Bruns, *Preacher: Billy Sunday and Big-Time American Evangelism* (New York: Norton, 1922), 249.

34. Bruns, *Preacher,* 252.

35. R. E. Speer, *The New Opportunity of the Church* (New York: Macmillan, 1919), 48–49. As quoted in *A Documentary History of Religion in America Since 1865*, ed. Edwin S. Gaustad (Grand Rapids, Michigan: William B. Eerdmans, 1983), 148.

36. *Chicago Daily Tribune,* November 11, 1918. The editor of the *Methodist Review* called for the regeneration of the family and of motherhood and for reenshrining the teachings of Christ. "Without this light the world must stumble along in darkness. Is it not evident then that it is the bounden duty of the Church to seek a fresh Pentecost? The times, wild and disturbed as they are, are not unripe for a baptism of power from within the veil." "What the World Is Facing," *Methodist Review* 68, no. 4 (October 1919): 590.

37. Gaustad, *Documentary History of Religion,* 148. This interchurch vision continued to a lesser extent as the Federal Council of Churches, with Reverend Robert E. Speer playing an active part.

38. Henry Emerson Fosdick, "'Shall We End the War,' A Sermon Preached at the First Presbyterian Church, New York, June 5, 1921" (distributed through the Clearing House for the Limitation of Armament, New York), 3–12.

39. Eldon G. Ernst, *Moment of Truth for Protestant America: Interchurch Campaigns Following World War One*, Dissertation Series, no. 3 (n.p.: American Academy of Religion and Scholars, 1974), 139.

40. In *MFP*, 5:92.

41. Joseph F. Smith to Hyrum Smith, November 3, 1915, Joseph F. Smith Papers, Church Archives.

42. Editorial note by James R. Clark in *MFP*, 5:5.

43. In *MFP*, 5:6–7.

44. In *MFP*, 7.

45. From a discourse entitled "Status of Children in the Resurrection," in *MFP*, 5:94–95.

46. From a discourse entitled "A Dream That Was a Reality," in *MFP*, 5:100–101. This was not the first unique dream President Smith had of his beloved mother. On July 21, 1891, he had dreamed that his "precious mother came to live with him. It seemed that she had been gone for a long time." In this dream, "[I] fixed her up a room all for herself and made it as comfortable as I could. . . . This is the third time I have seemed to put [up] my mother since she left us." Joseph F. Smith to "My Dear Aunt Thompson," July 21, 1891, Letters of Joseph F. Smith, as cited in the Scott G. Kenney Collection, L. Tom Perry Special Collections, Harold B. Lee Library.

47. James E. Talmage Journal, January 25, 1918.

48. Because of his frail condition, President Smith did not actually read this document in conference but had it delivered in writing to the leadership of the Church shortly after the conference had concluded.

49. See Doctrine and Covenants 138 to read the vision in its entirety.

50. Wrote Elder Talmage in a journal entry for October 31, 1918: "Attended meeting of the First Presidency and the Twelve. Today President Smith, who is still confined to his home by illness, sent to the Brethren the account of a vision through which, as he states, were revealed to him important facts relating to the work of the disembodied Savior in the realm of departed spirits, and of the missionary work in progress on the other side of the veil. By united action the Council of the Twelve, with the Counselors in the First Presidency, and the Presiding Patriarch accepted and endorsed the revelation as the Word of the Lord. President Smith's signed statement will be published in the next issue (December) of the Improvement Era." James E. Talmage Journal, October 31, 1918.

51. From time to time, General Authorities referred to the vision before 1976. See, for example, Joseph L. Wirthlin, April 1945 general conference; Marion G. Romney, April 1964 general conference; Spencer W. Kimball, September 1966 general conference; and Boyd K. Packer, October 1975 general conference. For this information I am indebted to Robert L. Millet, "The Vision of the Redemption of the Dead," in *Hearken, O Ye People: Discourses on the Doctrine and Covenants* (Sandy, Utah: Randall Book, 1984), 268. Latter-day Saints accept the messages of their living prophets as scripture. "Whatsoever they shall speak when moved upon by the Holy Ghost shall be scripture, shall be the will of the Lord, shall be the mind of the Lord, shall be the word of the Lord, shall be the voice of the Lord, and the power of God unto salvation" (Doctrine and Covenants 68:4). However, there are degrees of scripture within the Church. Once Joseph F. Smith's vision had been presented to the Church membership and voted on and accepted as scripture, it shifted in significance from *scripture* to *canonized* scripture. As Robert L. Millet said, "Prior to 3 April 1976 it represented a theological document of inestimable worth to the Saints, one that deserved the study of those interested in spiritual things; on that date it was

circumscribed into the standard works, and thus its message—principles and doctrines—became binding upon the Latter-day Saints, the same as the revelations of Moses or Jesus or Alma or Joseph Smith. The Vision of the Redemption of the Dead became a part of the canon, the rule of faith and doctrine and practice—the written measure by which we discern truth from error" (Millet, "Vision of the Redemption of the Dead," in *Hearken O Ye People*, 265).

52. Millet, "Vision of the Redemption of the Dead," 259.

53. See Church Educational System, *The Doctrine and Covenants Student Manual* (Salt Lake City: The Church of Jesus Christ of Latter-day Saints, 1981), 356–61; see also Michael J. Preece, *Learning to Love the Doctrine & Covenants* (Salt Lake City: MJP Publishing, 1988), 409–13.

It should be noted in passing, however, that Joseph F. Smith's vision was not a sudden extension of his sickness or sorrows. For instance, as early as 1882 he had spoken of Christ's preaching in the spirit prison (*Gospel Doctrine—Selections from the Sermons and Writings of Joseph F. Smith* [Salt Lake City: Deseret Book, 1961], 437–38). Likewise, he had previously taught of ancient prophets and modern-day missionaries teaching to the spirits in prison (*Gospel Doctrine*, 430, 460). His funeral sermons are replete with this doctrine. For example, see his talk given in Logan, Utah, October 27, 1907, at the quarterly conference of the Logan Stake, typescript, 16, Papers of Joseph F. Smith, Church Archives. Although a careful analysis of President Smith's developing doctrines of death and the Resurrection remains to be done, what he said in October 1918 was entirely consistent with what he had been preaching for almost forty years.

54. Arthur Conan Doyle, *The New Revelation* (New York: George H. Doran, 1918), 52. Doyle visited Salt Lake City in May 1923, lecturing one night in the Salt Lake Tabernacle to more than five thousand people. Spiritualism was not an unknown phenomenon to the Latter-day Saints. Years before, the Godbeite movement in Salt Lake had proclaimed it a central part of their new religion, claiming former Apostle Amasa Lyman in the process. See Ronald W. Walker, *Wayward Saints: The Godbeites and Brigham Young* (Urbana: University of Illinois Press, 1998), 254–57.

55. Smith, *Gospel Doctrine*, 430. For more on this topic, see Michael W. Homer, "Spiritualism and Mormonism: Some Thoughts on Similarities and Differences," *Dialogue: A Journal of Mormon Thought* 27, no. 1 (spring 1994): 171–91.

56. Joseph F. Smith knew all about how decisive the debate over modernism and higher criticism could become. In 1913, after a series of prolonged hearings and debates, Brigham Young University dismissed four professors because of their tendency to accommodate the theory of evolution and to "de-mythologize" the Bible. For a full discussion of this controversy, see *Brigham Young University—The First One Hundred Years*, ed. Ernest L. Wilkinson, 4 vols. (Provo, UT: Brigham Young University Press, 1975), 1:412–32.

57. For more on the rising secularism after the war, see Alan D. Gilbert, *The Making of Post-Christian Britain: A History of the Secularization of Modern Society* (London: Longman Group, 1980) and Burnham P. Beckwith, *The Decline of U.S. Religious Faith 1912–1984 and the Effects of Education and Intelligence on Such Faith* (Palo Alto, California: P. A. Beckwith, 1985). According to one study, the decline in church attendance in England since World War I has been precipitous. Between 1885 and 1928, the proportion of the population in England of the age of fifteen and over who were Easter Day communicants in the Church of England never fell below 84 per 1,000. In 1925, it was 90 per 1,000. But since the early 1930s, that

number has steadily declined: by 1939 the proportion had dropped to 73 per 1,000, 63 per 1,000 by 1958, and 43 per 1,000 by 1973 (Alan Wilkinson, *The Church of England and the First World War* [London: SPCK, Holy Trinity Church, 1978], 292). In contrast, Latter-day Saint membership has grown from four hundred thousand to eleven million, and activity rates are higher now than ever before (see Rodney Stark, "The Basis of Mormon Success: A Theological Application," in *Latter-day Saint Social Life: Social Research on the LDS Church and Its Members,* ed. James T. Duke [Provo, Utah: Religious Studies Center, Brigham Young University, 1998]: 29–70).

Chapter Twenty-Three

Race, the Priesthood, and Temples

W. PAUL REEVE

A racially expansive vision of redemption through Jesus Christ for all of God's children marked the early decades of the Church's existence. One early leader, William Wines Phelps, wrote in 1835 that "all the families of the earth . . . should get redemption . . . in Christ Jesus," regardless of "whether they are descendants of Shem, Ham, or Japheth." Another publication declared that all people were "one in Christ Jesus . . . whether it was in Africa, Asia, or Europe." Apostle Parley P. Pratt similarly professed his intent to preach "to all people, kindred, tongues, and nations without any exception" and included "India's and Africa's sultry plains" in his vision of the global reach of the Latter-day Saint gospel message. More significantly, Joseph Smith Jr. received at least four revelations instructing him that "the gospel must be preached unto every creature, with signs following them that believe" (Doctrine and Covenants 58:64; see also 68:8; 84:62; 112:28). "Every creature" left no room for doubt; no one was to be excluded.[1]

This universal invitation initially included extending all of the unfolding ordinances of the Restoration to all members. To date there are no known statements made by Joseph Smith Jr. of a racial priesthood or temple restriction. In fact, there is incontrovertible evidence for the ordination of at least two Black men, Q. Walker Lewis and Elijah Able, during the Church's first two decades. Other men of Black African descent also received ordinations, including Able's son Moroni in 1871 and his grandson Elijah R. Ables in 1935, although the grandson passed as white to qualify.[2] However, racial restrictions developed under Brigham Young and were solidified over the course of the last half of the nineteenth century under subsequent leaders.

Brigham Young's rationale for the restriction was taught and preached as doctrine and centered on the biblical curse and "mark" that God placed on Cain for killing his brother Abel. Over time, other justifications tied to the premortal existence and the War in Heaven attempted to validate the practice, even though they were never used by Brigham Young. Some leaders also looked to the Book of Abraham and its passages regarding a pharaoh whose lineage was "cursed . . . as pertaining to the priesthood" (Abraham 1:26). Even though Joseph Smith produced the Book of Abraham, he never used it to justify a priesthood restriction, and neither did Brigham Young.[3]

The curse in the Book of Mormon of a "skin of blackness" (2 Nephi 5:21) was never used as a justification for withholding the priesthood or temple ordinances from Black Saints. Latter-day Saint leaders and followers alike understood the Book of Mormon curse to apply to Native Americans and viewed it as reversible. It was a vision of Indian redemption that placed white Latter-day Saints as agents in that process. In contrast, Brigham Young claimed the biblical curse of Cain was in God's hands only, something humankind could not influence or remove until God commanded it.[4]

WHITENESS IN AMERICAN HISTORY AND CULTURE

Being white in American history was considered the normal and natural condition of humankind. Anything less than white was viewed as a deterioration from normal, a situation that made such a person unfit for the blessings of democracy. Being white meant being socially respectable; it granted a person greater access to political, economic, and social power. Politicians equated whiteness with citizenship and fitness for self-rule. In 1790 Congress passed a naturalization act that limited citizenship to "free white persons," a decision that had a significant impact on race relations in the nineteenth century. Even Abraham Lincoln, the future "great emancipator," believed that as long as Blacks and white people coexisted, "there must be the position of superior and inferior," and he favored the "white race" in the "superior position." After the Civil War, as Southern whites reasserted white superiority, the Supreme Court affirmed their efforts when it ruled that separate-but-equal facilities were constitutional, a decision that legalized the segregation of most facets of American life.[5]

The founding decades of The Church of Jesus Christ of Latter-day Saints coincided with a period in which whiteness itself came under question. *Race* at the time was a word loosely used to refer to nationality as much as skin color. People spoke of an "Irish race," for example, and began to create a hierarchy of racial identities, with Anglo-Saxons at the top. A variety of less-white "races" were further down the list. Scots, Teutons, Welsh, Latin, Caucasian, Nordic, Celt, Slav, Alpine, Hebrew, Mediterranean, Iberic, and other such identifiers emerged to additionally blur racial categories.[6]

The Church was born in this era of splintering whiteness and did not escape its consequences. The Protestant majority in America was never quite certain how or where to situate Latter-day Saints within conflicting racial schemes, but they were nonetheless convinced that members of the upstart faith represented a racial decline. Many nineteenth-century social evolutionists believed in the development theory: all societies advanced across three stages of progress, from savagery to barbarism to civilization. As societies advanced, they left behind such practices as polygamy and adherence to authoritarian rule. In the minds of such thinkers, Latter-day Saints violated the development theory in practicing polygamy and theocracy, something that no true Anglo-Saxon would do. Latter-day Saints thereby represented a fearful racial descent into barbarism and savagery. Within this charged racial context, Latter-day Saints struggled to claim whiteness for themselves despite the fact that they were overwhelmingly white.[7] As legal scholar Ariel Gross argues, whiteness in the nineteenth century was measured in distance from blackness, and Latter-day Saints spent considerable effort attempting to become securely white at the expense of their own Black converts.[8]

RACIALIZATION OF LATTER-DAY SAINTS

The Saints' troubled sojourns in Ohio, Missouri, and Illinois were fraught with the perception that Latter-day Saints were too open and inviting to undesirable groups—Black people and Indians in particular. In 1830, the founding year of the Church, a former enslaved man named Peter became the first known African American to join the faith. Within a year of his conversion, the fact that the Latter-day Saints had a Black man worshipping with them made news in New York and Pennsylvania.[9] Edward Strutt Abdy, a British official on tour of the United States, noted that Ohio Latter-day Saints honored "the natural equality of mankind, without excepting the native Indians or the African race." Abdy feared, however, that it was an open attitude that may have gone too far for its time and place. He believed that the Latter-day Saint stance toward Indians and Black people was at least partly responsible for "the cruel persecution by which they have suffered." In his mind, the Book of Mormon ideal that "all are alike unto God," including "black and white" (2 Nephi 26:33), made it unlikely that the Saints would "remain unmolested in the State of Missouri."[10] Other outsiders tended to agree. They complained that Latter-day Saints were far too inclusive in the creation of their religious kingdom. They accepted "all nations and colours," they welcomed "all classes and characters," they included "aliens by birth" and people from "different parts of the world" as members of God's earthly family. Outsiders variously suggested that Latter-day Saints had "opened an asylum for rogues and vagabonds and free blacks," maintained "communion with the Indians," and walked out with "colored women." In short, Latter-day Saints were charged with creating racially and economically diverse transnational communities and congregations, a stark contrast to a national culture that favored the segregation and extermination of undesirable racial groups.[11]

Some Latter-day Saints recognized the ways in which outsiders denigrated them and called their whiteness into question. In 1840 Apostle Parley P. Pratt, for example, complained that during the Saints' expulsion from Missouri "most of the papers of the State" described them as "Mormons, in contradistinction to the appellation of citizens, whites, &c., as if we had been some savage tribe, or some colored race of foreigners." John Lowe Butler, another Latter-day Saint expelled from Missouri, recalled one Missourian who declared that "he did not consider the 'Mormons' had any more right to vote than the n[——]s." In Illinois, Apostle Heber C. Kimball acknowledged that Latter-day Saints were not "considered suitable to live among 'white folks'" and later declared, "We are not accounted as white people, and we don't want to live among them. I had rather live with the buffalo in the wilderness."[12]

The open announcement of polygamy in 1852 moved the concern among outsiders in a new direction, toward a growing fear of racial contamination. In the minds of outsiders, Latter-day Saint polygamy was not just destroying the traditional family—it was destroying the white race. A US Army doctor reported to Congress that polygamy was giving rise to a "new race," filthy, sunken, and degraded. One writer argued that polygamy placed "a mark of Cain" on Latter-day Saint women, while another said that the entire religion was "as degrading as old-fashioned negro slavery."[13] In general, outsiders conflated Latter-day Saints with Black people in a variety of ways. Their views were fluid and inconsistent, yet several themes emerged to suggest that outsiders sometimes viewed Latter-day Saints as racially suspect. Such depictions were designed to marginalize the Saints and justify discriminatory policies against them. As some outsiders described it, Latter-day Saint polygamy was a system of "white slavery," worse than the Black slavery that "existed in the South, and *far more filthy.*" Latter-day Saint men were sometimes depicted as violent or indolent slave drivers and Latter-day Saint women as their "white slaves."[14] In 1882 Alfred Trumble's *The Mysteries of Mormonism,* a sensationalized dime novel, captured this national theme in pictorial form in an illustration simply labeled "wives as slaves."[15]

More troubling to outsiders was the perception that polygamy was a system of unbridled interracial sex and marriage. One political cartoon depicted Brigham Young with two Black wives and degraded interracial off-spring. A parade in Indiana similarly featured a mock version of Brigham Young's family. It included six wives seated in Brigham Young's wagon, "white, black and piebald better-halves," a group of women unmistakably costumed to heighten national fears of race mixing and project them onto Latter-day Saints. The *New York Times* reported on two supposed "negro balls" in Salt Lake City where "negro men and women, and Mormon men and women, [were] all dancing on terms of perfect equality." The writer called it "the most disgusting of spectacles." Other cartoons and dime novels portrayed Latter-day Saint plural marriages as hotbeds of interracial sex, depictions deliberately designed to heighten American alarm over a perceived violation of racial boundaries and to portray Latter-day Saints as facilitators of racial contamination.[16]

Cartoons sometimes portrayed Latter-day Saint polygamous families as interracial, and unabashedly so. In September 1896, during the presidential race between Democrat William Jennings Bryan and Republican William McKinley, *Judge* magazine ran one such cartoon. The illustration was titled "The 16 to 1 Movement in Utah." It used a contentious issue in the campaign that year to make fun of polygamy. Bryan advocated freeing the nation's monetary system from the gold standard by allowing for the coinage of silver at a ratio of sixteen to one. In the *Judge* cartoon, however, sixteen to one took on new meaning in Utah: sixteen women to one man. The polygamist man carried a bag labeled "from Utah" and stood front and center of his sixteen wives, eight on either side. It was not merely the number of women to men, however, that made the cartoon significant. It was the interracial nature of the Latter-day Saint family it depicted. The sixteen wives were portrayed in a variety of shapes, sizes, and relative beauty, but it was the first wife holding the man's left arm that was meant to unsettle its audience. She was a Black woman boldly at the front of the other wives, a visual depiction of the racial corruption that outsiders worried was inherent in Latter-day Saint polygamy.[17]

THE PRIESTHOOD AND TEMPLE RESTRICTIONS BEGIN

At the same time that outsiders persistently criticized Latter-day Saints as facilitators of racial decline, Latter-day Saints moved in fits and starts across the course of the nineteenth century away from blackness toward whiteness. It is a mistake to try to pinpoint a moment, event, person, or line in the sand that divided Latter-day Saint history into a clear before and after. Rather, the policies and supporting teachings that Church leaders developed over the course of the nineteenth century increasingly solidified a rationale and gave rise to an accumulating precedent that each succeeding generation reinforced, so that by the late nineteenth century, Church leaders were unwilling to violate policies they mistakenly remembered beginning with Joseph Smith. By 1908, Joseph F. Smith solidified the priesthood and temple restrictions in place when he falsely remembered that his uncle, Joseph Smith Jr., started the racial limitations.[18] The new memory moving forward would be that of a white priesthood in place from the beginning, traceable from the founding prophet back to God, something with which no human could or should interfere.

Although Brigham Young's two speeches to the Utah territorial legislature in 1852 mark the first recorded articulations of a priesthood restriction by a Latter-day Saint prophet-president, it is a mistake to attribute the ban soley to seemingly inherent racism in Brigham Young. His own views evolved between 1847, when he first dealt with racial matters at Winter Quarters, and 1852, when he first publicly articulated a rationale for a priesthood restriction. In 1847, in an interview with William (Warner) McCary, a Black Latter-day Saint who married Lucy Stanton, a white Latter-day Saint, Brigham Young expressed an open position on race. McCary complained to Brigham Young regarding the way he was sometimes treated among the Saints and suggested that his skin color was a factor: "I am not a President, or a leader of the people," McCary lamented, but merely a "common brother," a fact that he said was true "because I am a little shade darker." In response, Brigham Young asserted that "we dont care about the color." He went on to suggest that color did not matter in priesthood ordination: "We have to repent & regain what we have lost," Brigham Young insisted, "we have one of the best Elders, an African in Lowell—a barber," he reported. Brigham Young here referred to Q. Walker Lewis, a barber, abolitionist, and leader in the Black community in Lowell, Massachusetts. Apostle William Smith, younger brother to Hyrum and Joseph Smith, had ordained Lewis an elder in 1843 or 1844. Brigham Young was fully aware of Lewis's status as a Black man and priesthood holder and favorably referred to that status in his interview with McCary. Brigham Young offered Lewis as evidence that even Black men were welcome and eligible for the priesthood in the restored Church.[19]

By December of 1847, however, Brigham Young's perspective had changed. Following his expedition to the Salt Lake Valley that summer, he returned to Winter Quarters. There he learned of McCary's interracial exploits in his absence. McCary had started his own splinter polygamous group predicated on white women being "sealed" to him in a sexualized ritual. When his exploits were discovered, he and his followers were excommunicated and McCary left the Church, never to return. Young was also greeted with news of the marriage of Enoch Lewis, Q. Walker Lewis's son, to Mary Matilda Webster, a white woman in the Lowell, Massachusetts, branch. In response, Brigham Young spoke forcefully against interracial marriage, even advocating capital punishment as a consequence. Like Joseph Smith before him, Brigham Young opposed racial mixing and made some of his most pointed statements on the subject. Yet none of the surviving minutes from the meetings that Brigham Young held that year raise priesthood as an issue negatively connected to race. It would be five more years before Brigham Young articulated his position on that subject.[20]

Brigham Young most fully elaborated his views in 1852 before an all–Latter-day Saint Utah territorial legislature as it contemplated a law to govern the Black enslaved people that Latter-day Saint converts from the South brought with them as they gathered to the Great Basin. Some of the enslaved people were also baptized Latter-day Saints. In fact, the very universalism of the gospel message in its first two decades created the circumstances for the restriction. Among those gathered to the Great Basin by 1852 were abolitionists and anti-abolitionists, Black slaves, white enslavers, and free Blacks. In casting a wide net, the Latter-day Saints had avoided the splits or schisms that divided the Methodists, Baptists, and Presbyterians over issues of race and slavery during the same period. The restored Church welcomed all comers into the gospel fold, "black and white, bond and free"

(2 Nephi 26:33). These various people brought their political and racial ideologies with them when they converted to The Church of Jesus Christ of Latter-day Saints, ideas that initially existed independently of their faith. In 1852, however, Brigham Young prepared to order his diverse group of followers according to prevailing racial ideas, white over Black and free over bound.[21]

Brigham Young tapped into long-standing biblical interpretations to draw on Noah's curse of Canaan, but more directly to link a racial priesthood ban to God's purported "mark/curse" on Cain for killing his brother Abel. "If there never was a prophet or apostle of Jesus Christ spoke it before, I tell you, this people that are commonly called Negroes are the children of old Cain. I know they are, I know they cannot bear rule in the priesthood."[22] In America, as scholar David M. Goldenberg demonstrates, the idea that Black people were descendants of Cain dated back to at least 1733 and in Europe to as early as the eleventh century, long before the Church's founding in 1830. It was an idea that infused American culture and permeated racialized understandings of who Black people were before the Church existed. In 1852 Brigham Young drew on these same centuries-old ideas to both justify Utah Territory's law legalizing "servitude" and to argue for a race-based priesthood curse.[23]

Brigham Young insisted that because Cain killed Abel, all of Cain's posterity would have to wait until all of Abel's posterity received the priesthood. Brigham Young suggested that "the Lord told Cain that he should not receive the blessings of the Priesthood, nor his seed, until the last of the posterity of Abel had received the Priesthood." It was an ambiguous declaration he and other Latter-day Saint leaders returned to time and again. It suggested a future period of redemption for Black people but only after the "last" of Abel's posterity received the priesthood. Brigham Young and other leaders failed to clarify what that meant, how one might know when the "last" of Abel's posterity was ordained, or even who Abel's posterity were. In Brigham Young's mind, Cain's murder of Abel was an effort on Cain's part to usurp Abel's place in the covenant chain of priesthood leading back to father Adam.[24]

Brigham Young's position was fraught with inconsistencies and significant departures from aspects of other foundational Latter-day Saint principles. An 1830 revelation to Joseph Smith included universal male ordination and stipulated that "*every* man" who embraced the priesthood "with singleness of heart may be ordained and sent forth" (Doctrine and Covenants 36:7; emphasis added). The Book of Mormon unambiguously posited that "all are alike unto God," "male and female, black and white, bond and free" (2 Nephi 26:33), and that all were invited to come unto Christ. The Book of Mormon declared a universal salvation, a gospel message for "every nation, kindred, tongue, and people." It rhetorically demanded, "Hath [the Lord] commanded any that they should not partake of his salvation?" and then answered, "Nay." It declared that "all men are privileged the one like unto the other, and none are forbidden" (vv. 13, 26–28). The Lord had established no limits to whom He invited to "partake of his salvation," even as the priesthood and temple restrictions created barriers to the fullness of that "salvation."

Brigham Young was also departing from his own earlier position on Q. Walker Lewis's ordination to the priesthood. And when he suggested that the priesthood was taken from Black people "by their own transgressions," he was further creating a race-based division to cloud Black redemption and make each generation after Cain responsible anew for the consequences of Cain's murder of Abel. Although Joseph Smith rejected long-standing Christian notions of original sin to argue that "men will be punished for their own sins and not for Adam's transgression," Brigham Young held millions of Black people responsible for the consequences of Cain's murder, something in which they obviously took no part.

By insinuation, Brigham Young's position removed the role of individual agency in the lives of Black people, a fundamental gospel tenet. It instead gave Cain's poor exercise of agency immitigable power over millions of his supposed descendants. To make matters worse, Brigham Young's position failed to distinguish exactly what it was that made Cain's murder of Abel worthy of a multigenerational curse when other biblical figures who also committed homicidal acts did not experience the same fate. As Brigham Young argued, it was the fractured human network that resulted from Cain's effort to usurp Abel's place in the great chain of being that most animated his articulation of a priesthood curse.[25]

Even though Brigham Young and other nineteenth-century leaders relied on the curse of Cain as the reason for the priesthood and temple restrictions, another explanation gained ground among some Latter-day Saints in the late nineteenth and early twentieth centuries. Because the curse of Cain so directly violated the role of individual agency in the lives of Black people, some Latter-day Saints turned to the premortal realm to solve the conundrum. In this rationale, Black people must have been neutral in the War in Heaven and thus were cursed with black skin and barred from the priesthood. In 1869 Brigham Young rejected the idea outright, but it did not disappear.[26] In 1907 Joseph Fielding Smith, then serving as assistant Church historian, argued that the teaching was "not the official position of the Church, merely the opinion of men."[27] In 1944 John A. Widtsoe also argued against neutrality when he said, "All who have been permitted to come upon this earth and take upon themselves bodies, accepted the plan of salvation." Nonetheless, he argued that because Black people themselves "did not commit Cain's sin," an explanation for the priesthood restriction had to involve something besides Cain's murder of Abel. "It is very probable," Widtsoe believed, "that in some way, unknown to us, the distinction harks back to the pre-existent state."[28]

By the 1960s, Joseph Fielding Smith slightly altered the idea, from "neutral" to "less valiant" and offered his own explanation. In his *Answers to Gospel Questions*, he claimed that some premortal spirits "were not valiant" in the War in Heaven. As a result of "their lack of obedience," Black people came to earth "under restrictions," including a denial of the priesthood.[29] The neutral/less valiant justifications grew over time to sometimes overshadow the curse-of-Cain explanation.

Brigham Young, nonetheless, tied the ban to Cain's murder of Abel and did not stray from that rationale throughout his life. It became the de facto position for the Church, especially as it hardened in practice and preaching across the course of the nineteenth century. Brigham Young also spoke out forcefully against interracial sex and marriage, something that marked him more American than uniquely Latter-day Saint. Although his bombast advocated capital punishment, an extreme position even in the nineteenth century, those views were never codified into Utah law but certainly shaped attitudes among Latter-day Saints regarding race mixing.[30]

Brigham Young's two speeches to the territorial legislature were never published. Even though Black priesthood ordination officially ended under Brigham Young, it was far from a universally understood idea. In 1879, two years after Brigham Young's death, Elijah Able, the sole remaining Black priesthood holder (Lewis had died in 1856), appealed to John Taylor for his remaining temple blessings: to receive the endowment and to be sealed to his wife. Able had received the washing and anointing ritual in the Kirtland Temple and was baptized as proxy for deceased relatives and friends at Nauvoo but was living in Cincinnati by the time the endowment and sealing rituals were introduced.

It is impossible to know what might have happened if Able had lived in Nauvoo during the introduction of temple rituals there. Surviving records, however, indicate that the Saints maintained an open racial vision to that date. At Nauvoo the Saints anticipated "people from every land and from every nation, the polished European, the degraded Hottentot, and the shivering Laplander" flowing to that city. They awaited "persons of all languages, and of every tongue, and of every color; who shall with us worship the Lord of Hosts in his holy temple, and offer up their orisons in his sanctuary."[31] In fact, in 1845 Sarah Ann Mode Hofheintz, the daughter of a Black man and a white woman, received her anointing and endowment rituals in the Nauvoo Temple before the exodus west, although she had likely passed as white to do so.[32] By 1879, however, the space for full Black participation was no longer as expansive, and Abel's appeal for his temple blessings prompted a further contraction.

John Taylor presided over an investigation into Able's priesthood. Taylor's inquiry indicates that as late as 1879, the priesthood and temple restrictions were still not unambiguously in place; otherwise, why the need to investigate? Able claimed that Ambrose Palmer, presiding elder at New Portage, Ohio, had ordained him an elder on January 25, 1836, and that Joseph Smith himself sanctioned his ordination, and Able produced certificates to verify his claims.[33] John Taylor nonetheless concluded that Able's ordination was something of an exception, which was left to stand because it happened before the Lord had fully made his will known on racial matters through Brigham Young. John Taylor was unwilling to violate the precedent established by Brigham Young, even though that precedent violated the open racial pattern established under Joseph Smith. John Taylor allowed Able's priesthood to stand but denied him access to the temple. Able did not waver in his faith, though, and died in 1884 after serving a third mission for the Church. His obituary, published in the *Deseret News*, noted that he passed of "old age and debility, consequent upon exposure while laboring in the ministry in Ohio" and concluded that "he died in full faith of the Gospel." It also substantiated his priesthood ordinations as an integral part of his identity.[34]

With Able dead, Jane Manning James, another faithful Black pioneer, took up the cause. She repeatedly appealed for temple privileges, including permission to receive her endowment and to be sealed to Q. Walker Lewis. She was just as repeatedly denied. The curse of Cain was used to justify her exclusion. Although Church leaders did allow her to perform baptisms for dead relatives and friends and to be "attached" via proxy as a servant to Joseph and Emma Smith, she was barred from further temple access.[35]

Between the 1879 investigation led by John Taylor and 1908, when Joseph F. Smith solidified the bans, Latter-day Saint leaders adopted an increasingly conservative stance on Black priesthood and temple admission. They responded to incoming inquiries by relying on distant memories and accumulating historical precedent. Sometimes they attributed the bans to Brigham Young and other times they mistakenly remembered them beginning with Joseph Smith.[36] George Q. Cannon also began to refer to the Book of Abraham as a justification for the bans. As finally articulated sometime before early 1907, leaders put a firm "one drop" rule in place: "The descendants of Ham may receive baptism and confirmation but no one known to have in his veins negro blood, (it matters not how remote a degree) can either have the Priesthood in any degree or the blessings of the Temple of God; no matter how otherwise worthy he may be."[37] Race, not personal worthiness, thus became the basis for the restrictions.

Then in 1908, President Joseph F. Smith solidified this decision when he recalled that Elijah Able was ordained to the priesthood "in the days of the Prophet Joseph" but suggested that his "ordination was declared null and void by the Prophet himself." Four years earlier, Joseph F. Smith had implied that Able's ordination was a mistake that "was never corrected," but now he claimed that the Church's founder had in fact corrected that mistake although he offered no evidence to substantiate his claim. Adding to the discrepancy, in 1879 and 1895 he had defended Able's priesthood as valid, even reminding leaders that Able was ordained to the priesthood "at Kirtland under the direction of the Prophet Joseph Smith." Now, in 1908, Joseph F. Smith insisted otherwise and then recalled that Able applied for his endowment and asked to be sealed to his wife and children, but "notwithstanding the fact that he was a staunch member of the Church, Presidents Young, Taylor, and Woodruff all denied him the blessings of the House of the Lord." Joseph F. Smith also deliberately curtailed missionary efforts among Black people, a decision that ensured a white identity for the Church moving forward.[38]

This new memory became so entrenched among leaders in the twentieth century that by 1949 the First Presidency declared that the restriction was "always" in place: "The attitude of the Church with reference to Negroes remains as it has always stood. It is not a matter of the declaration of a policy but of direct commandment from the Lord." The "doctrine of the Church" on priesthood and race was in place "from the days of its organization," it professed. The First Presidency said nothing of the original Black priesthood holders, an indication of how thoroughly reconstructed memory had come to replace verifiable facts.[39]

Even though President David O. McKay pushed for reform on racial matters, he was convinced that it would take a revelation to overturn the ban. Hugh B. Brown, his counselor in the First Presidency, believed otherwise. Brown reasoned that because there was no revelation that began the bans, no revelation was needed to end them. McKay's position held sway, especially as McKay claimed he did not receive a divine mandate to move forward.[40] As early as 1963, however, Apostle Spencer W. Kimball signaled an open attitude for change: "The doctrine or policy has not varied in my memory," Kimball acknowledged. "I know it could. I know the Lord could change his policy and release the ban and forgive the possible error which brought about the deprivation."[41] That forgiveness ultimately came with Kimball at the helm in 1978.[42]

UNDERSTANDING THE PRIESTHOOD AND TEMPLE BANS

Apostle Bruce R. McConkie, a man responsible for some of the Church's justifications for a racial ban, denounced his own statements within months of the 1978 revelation. He asked a Latter-day Saint audience at Brigham Young University to "forget everything that I have said, or what President Brigham Young or George Q. Cannon, or whomsoever [sic] has said in days past that is contrary to the present revelation. We spoke with a limited understanding and without the light and knowledge that now has come into the world."[43] It was a statement that suggested that prior teachings on race were devoid of the "light and knowledge" that revelation represents to Latter-day Saints.

Even still, it is a difficult question with which some Saints continue to grapple: How could race-based priesthood and temple restrictions creep into the Church and last for so long? Was Brigham Young speaking for himself in 1852 when he announced the priesthood ban to the territorial legislature or for God? If for himself, why would God permit him to do so? If for God, why implement a restriction that violated scriptural notions of equality? Some have suggested that while the explanations for the bans are invalid, the bans themselves were inspired for purposes known only to God. In an American culture that so thoroughly privileged whiteness, the priesthood and temple restrictions brought Latter-day Saints into conformity with the national mainstream. In this explanation, Brigham Young's and later leaders' implementation of the restrictions over time were bound by surrounding cultural norms, a violation of which may have produced significant disdain and additional turmoil for the nineteenth-century Church. This interpretation is problematic because if God or his prophets were somehow bound by cultural norms, the introduction of polygamy into an American society that so thoroughly abhorred it would have never taken place. Joseph Smith claimed, "No unhallowed hand can stop the work from progressing,"[44] yet this explanation suggests that treating Black people equally could have done so.

Others view the priesthood and temple restrictions as perhaps a trial for both white and Black Latter-day Saints, or a way in which they were forced to confront the prejudices of their day, be it the 1850s or the 1950s. In this version, race becomes a calling, not a curse. Perhaps it was and is a test that forces Latter-day Saints to search their hearts to see if they might summon the courage and strength to rise above differences and embrace commonalities centered on the worship of Jesus Christ. Could white Latter-day Saints transcend cultural norms and the privileges of being white in America, both before and after 1978, to welcome Black people into the gospel fold, into the priesthood, into the temple, and into their hearts? Could Black Latter-day Saints embrace a gospel message, both before and after 1978, that views them as children of God but that historically was burdened with teachings that they were cursed, less valiant, or neutral children of that same God? If God stands at the helm of his Church and directs his kingdom, what were his purposes and how does one square them with scriptural messages of universal salvation?

Ezra Taft Benson, speaking as an Apostle in 1975, offered an overarching principle that is broadly applicable to the historical development of the priesthood and temple bans. Benson was not speaking specifically about race, but his guiding philosophy might be useful in approaching the issue.

> If you see some individuals in the Church doing things that disturb you, or you feel the Church is not doing things the way you think they could or should be done, the following principles might be helpful: God has to work through mortals of varying degrees of spiritual progress. Sometimes he temporarily grants to men their unwise requests in order that they might learn from their own sad experiences. Some refer to this as the "Samuel principle." The children of Israel wanted a king like all the other nations. The prophet Samuel was displeased and prayed to the Lord about it. The Lord responded by saying, Samuel, "they have not rejected thee, but they have rejected me, that I should not reign over them." The Lord told Samuel to warn the people of the consequences if they had a king. Samuel gave them the warning. But

they still insisted on their king. So God gave them a king and let them suffer. They learned the hard way. God wanted it to be otherwise, but within certain bounds he grants unto men according to their desires.[45]

President Benson's Samuel principle suggests a viable way of looking at the race question in the Church, but first let us consider other examples. This concept applies to the lost 116 manuscript pages of the Book of Mormon as well. God let Joseph Smith give those pages to Martin Harris and then let him learn from "his own sad experience." The Lord called Joseph Smith to repentance in Doctrine and Covenants 3:6–7: "And behold, how oft you have transgressed the commandments and the laws of God, and have gone on in the persuasions of men. For, behold, you should not have feared man more than God."

Even the Prophet is susceptible to "the persuasions of men." Later, Joseph Smith organized the Kirtland Safety Society Anti-Banking Institution. He and other leaders did so after being denied a bank charter by the state of Ohio. They inserted the prefix *anti-* before the word *banking* and opened the doors for business. Many Saints at the time believed the Prophet gave them assurances of the bank's success. Instead, the bank failed within a few months. Some Latter-day Saints lost their money and their faith. It was a factor in the disillusionment of many Saints, so much so that by June of 1837, Heber C. Kimball claimed that not twenty men in Kirtland believed Joseph Smith was a prophet. Parley and Orson Pratt, David Patten, Frederick G. Williams, Warren Parrish, David Whitmer, and Lyman Johnson all dissented. Why did God not stop Joseph Smith from founding the bank? God knew it would fail before it was founded. Why not simply tell Joseph Smith not to start the bank and save the Church from all of the turmoil that followed?[46]

Again, it seems that God let Joseph Smith and the Saints learn from their sad experiences. Perhaps the same principle is applicable to the development of the priesthood and temple bans. Were Church leaders susceptible to the "persuasions of men"? Did they borrow from then-current political and "scientific" ideas about race that dominated nineteenth-century American thought? In what ways did the racialization of Latter-day Saints at the hands of outsiders have an impact on events on the inside?

While I don't believe that God instigated the priesthood and temple restrictions, I do believe he let them happen, just as he let the children of Israel have a king, let Joseph Smith give Martin Harris the 116 pages of manuscript, and let Joseph Smith open an "anti-banking institution." As

President Benson said, "Sometimes [God] temporarily grants to men their unwise requests in order that they might learn from their own sad experiences."[47] In the end it makes me wonder what we are to learn from our racial history, and have we learned it? It should force us to stare the myth of a micromanager God squarely in the face and allow ample room for women and men with divine callings to fall short of the divine. My work as a historian has habituated me to messy history, something I expect just as much of religious people reaching toward heaven as I do of American history in general. As the American Historical Association puts it, "Multiple, conflicting perspectives are among the truths of history."[48]

As a twenty-first-century Latter-day Saint, I am not bound by Church leaders' past teachings on race any more than I am bound as an American by Thomas Jefferson's views on race. Past Church leaders speak for me on matters of race only as far as they point me toward a universal redemption through Christ. For all of the emphasis that outsiders place on a perceived blind obedience to authority among Latter-day Saints, they fail to give equal weight to the democratizing impact of personal revelation, a central tenet of the faith from its beginnings. Even Brigham Young, sometimes depicted as an extreme authoritarian, counseled Latter-day Saints to avoid blind faith: "Let every man and woman know by the whispering of the spirit of God to themselves whether their leaders are walking in the path the Lord dictates or not. This has been my exhortation continually."[49]

While one may indeed find Latter-day Saints today who hold racists views, they do so in direct violation of Church standards, specifically a 2006 call to repentance by Church President Gordon B. Hinckley: "How can any man holding the Melchizedek Priesthood arrogantly assume that he is eligible for the priesthood whereas another who lives a righteous life but whose skin is of a different color is ineligible?" Speaking to the men of the Church, he further admonished, "Brethren, there is no basis for racial hatred among the priesthood of this Church. If any within the sound of my voice is inclined to indulge in this, then let him go before the Lord and ask for forgiveness and be no more involved in such."[50]

The 1978 Official Declaration is the only revelation in the Latter-day Saint canon on priesthood and race. It returned the Church to its universalistic roots and reintegrated its priesthood and temples. It confirmed the biblical standard that God is "no respecter of persons" (Acts 10:34) and the Book of Mormon principle that "all are alike unto God." The Church in the twenty-first century no longer teaches that black skin is a curse, that Black people are descendants of Cain or Ham, that Blacks were less valiant or neutral or rejected the priesthood in the premortal existence, that mixed-race marriages are a sin or culturally undesirable, that Black people or any other race or ethnicity are inferior in any way to white people, or that the priesthood and temple restrictions were revelations from God. It does, however, emphatically endorse the admonition of President Gordon B. Hinckley, "Let us all recognize that each of us is a son or daughter of our Father in Heaven, who loves all of His children."[51]

W. Paul Reeve is Simmons Chair of Mormon Studies in the History Department at the University of Utah.

W. Paul Reeve, "Race, the Priesthood, and Temples," in *A Reason for Faith: Navigating LDS Doctrine and Church History*, ed. Laura H. Hales (Provo, UT: Religious Studies Center, Brigham Young University; Salt Lake City: Deseret Book, 2016), 159–78.

NOTES

1. See "The Gospel, No. 5," *Latter Day Saints' Messenger and Advocate*, Kirtland, Ohio, February 1835; "The Ancient Order of Things," *Latter Day Saints' Messenger and Advocate*, September 1835; Parley P. Pratt, *A Voice of Warning and Instruction to All People, Containing a Declaration of the Faith and Doctrine of the Church of the Latter Day Saints, Commonly Called Mormons* (New York: W. Sandford, 1837), 140; and Parley P. Pratt, *The Millennium and Other Poems: To Which Is Annexed a Treatise on the Regeneration and Eternal Duration of Matter* (New York: W. Molineux, 1840), 58.

2. An online database, http://centuryofblackmormons.org, documents all known people of Black African descent baptized into the faith between 1830 and 1930 and includes evidence of those ordained to the priesthood. Joseph T. Ball was another person of Black African ancestry who was ordained to the priesthood but who passed as white. The database will include additional examples and thus demonstrate the impossibility of policing racial boundaries.

3. For explanations on the Book of Abraham and race, see Alma Allred, "The Traditions of Their Fathers: Myth versus Reality in LDS Scriptural Writings," in *Black and Mormon*, ed. Newell G. Bringhurst and Darron T. Smith (Urbana: University of Illinois Press, 2004), 34–49; Richard Lyman Bushman, *Joseph Smith: Rough Stone Rolling* (New York: Alfred A. Knopf, 2005), 285–89; Hugh Nibley and Michael Rhodes, *One Eternal Round* (Salt Lake City: Deseret Book; Provo, UT: FARMS, 2010), 162; and Hugh Nibley, *Abraham in Egypt*, ed. Gary P. Gillum (Provo, UT: FARMS; Salt Lake City: Deseret Book, 2000), 360–61, 428, 528.

4. For a thorough exploration of these events, see W. Paul Reeve, *Religion of a Different Color: Race and the Mormon Struggle for Whiteness* (New York: Oxford University Press, 2015), chaps. 4–7 and conclusion.

5. "An Act to Establish an Uniform Rule of Naturalization," 1st Cong., March 26, 1790, Sess. II, chap. 3, 1 stat 103; Congressional Globe, 30th Cong., 1st Sess.

(Washington, DC: Blair and Rives, 1848), 53–56, 96–100; *Political Debates Between Hon. Abraham Lincoln and Hon. Stephen A. Douglas, in the Celebrated Campaign of 1858, in Illinois* (Columbus, OH: Follett, Foster and Company, 1860), 136; and Scott v. Sandford, 60 U.S. 393 (1857), 407.

6. See Matthew Frye Jacobsen, *Whiteness of a Different Color: European Immigrants and the Alchemy of Race* (Cambridge, MA: Harvard University Press, 1998), 37–38, 41; Matthew Frye Jacobson, *Barbarian Virtues: The United States Encounters Foreign Peoples at Home and Abroad, 1876–1917* (New York: Hill and Wang, 2000), 140–49; and Nell Irvin Painter, *The History of White People* (2010; repr., New York: W. W. Norton, 2011), 132–50.

7. See David R. Roediger, *Working Toward Whiteness: How America's Immigrants Became White* (New York: Basic Books, 2005), 12; and Reeve, *Religion of a Different Color*, introduction and chap. 1.

8. See Patricia J. Williams, *The Alchemy of Race and Rights* (Cambridge, MA: Harvard University Press, 1991); Patricia J. Williams, *Seeing a Color-Blind Future: The Paradox of Race* (New York: Noonday Press, 1997); Ariela J. Gross, *What Blood Won't Tell: A History of Race on Trial in America* (Cambridge, MA: Harvard University Press, 2008), 138–39; and Reeve, *Religion of a Different Color*, chaps. 4–7.

9. See "Fanaticism," *Albany Evening Journal* (Albany, NY), February 16, 1831, 3; "Mormonites," *The Sun* (Philadelphia, PA), August 18, 1831, 1; "Mormonism," *Boston Recorder*, October 10, 1832, 161; and Mark Lyman Staker, *Hearken, O Ye People: The Historical Setting of Joseph Smith's Ohio Revelations* (Salt Lake City: Greg Kofford Books, 2009), 64–65. See also Matthew McBride, "Peter," https://exhibits .lib.utah.edu/s/century-of-black-mormons/page/peter.

10. E. S. Abdy, *Journal of a Residence and Tour in the United States of North America, From April, 1833, to October, 1834*, 3 vols. (London: John Murray, 1835), 1:324–25; 3:40–42, 54–59.

11. Simon G. Whitten (La Harpe, Illinois) to Mary B. Whitten (Parsonsfield, Maine), June 22, 1844, Mormon File, HM 31520, box 13, Huntington Library, San Marino, CA; Captain Frederick Marryat, *Monsieur Violet: His Travels and Adventures among the Snake Indians and Wild Tribes of the Great Western Prairies* (London: Thomas Hodgson, 1849), 275; "To His Excellency, Daniel Dunklin, Governor of the State of Missouri," *Evening and the Morning Star* (Kirtland, OH), December 1833, 114; To the Citizens of Howard County, October 7, 1838, in *Document Containing the Correspondence, Orders, &C. in Relation to the Disturbances with the Mormons; and the Evidence Given Before The Hon. Austin A. King* (Fayette, MO: Office of the Boon's Lick Democrat, 1841), 40; and Abraham Owen Smoot, diary, May 28, 1836, MSS 896, vol. 1, L. Tom Perry Special Collections, Harold B. Lee Library, Brigham Young University, Provo, UT. I am indebted to Jonathan Stapley for this reference.

12. Parley P. Pratt, *Late Persecution of the Church of Jesus Christ of Latter-day Saints. Ten Thousand American Citizens Robbed, Plundered, and Banished; Others Imprisoned, and Others Martyred for their Religion. With a Sketch of their Rise, Progress and Doctrine* (New York: J. W. Harrison, 1840), 59; William G. Hartley, *My Best for the Kingdom: History and Autobiography of John Lowe Butler, a Mormon Frontiersman* (Salt Lake City: Aspen Books, 1993), 389; "Speech Delivered by Heber C. Kimball," *Times and Seasons*, July 15, 1845, 969–71; and "Conference Minutes," *Times and Seasons*, November 1, 1845, 1012.

13. Reeve, *Religion of a Different Color*, chap. 1; US Senate, "Statistical Report on the Sickness and Morality in the Army of the United States, compiled from the Records of the Surgeon General's Office; Embracing a Period of Five Years from January 1, 1855, to January, 1860," Senate Executive Document 52, 36th Congress, 1st session, 301–2; Jennie Anderson Froiseth, ed., *The Women of Mormonism; or the Story of Polygamy as Told by the Victims Themselves* (Chicago: A. G. Nettleton & Co., 1881), iv, 25; and "The Old Mormons Likely to Give Way," *Chicago Daily Tribune*, March 10, 1873, 7.

14. William Jarman, *U. S. A. Uncle Sam's Abscess, or Hell Upon Earth for U. S. Uncle Sam* (Exeter, England: H. Leduc's Steam Printing Works, 1884), 6; emphasis in original.

15. Alfred Trumble, *The Mysteries of Mormonism* (New York: Police Gazette, 1882).

16. See Reeve, *Religion of a Different Color*, chap. 6; *Frank Leslie's Budget of Fun* (New York, NY), January 1872, 16; "Immense Meeting in Indianapolis," *New York Times*, July 21, 1856, 2; and "Later From Utah," *New York Times*, February 7, 1859, 1.

17. See Zim, "The 16 to 1 Movement in Utah," *The Judge*, September 12, 1896, 176; and Reeve, *Religion of a Different Color*, chap. 6.

18. See George A. Smith Family Papers, MS 36, box 78, folder 7, August 26, 1908, Manuscripts Division, Special Collections, J. Willard Marriott Library, University of Utah, Salt Lake City.

19. See Reeve, *Religion of a Different Color*, chaps. 4 and 5; Church Historian's Office, General Church Minutes, 1839–1877, CR 100 318, box 1, folder 52, March 26, 1847, Church History Library, The Church of Jesus Christ of Latter-day Saints, Salt Lake City (hereafter CHL); spelling standardized.

20. See Reeve, *Religion of a Different Color*, 128–39; William W. Major (Elk Horn), to Brigham Young, June 16, 1847, Brigham Young Collection, CR1234/1, box 21, folder 8, reel 30, CHL; Nelson W. Whipple, autobiography and journal, microfilm, manuscript, MS 9995, 30–31, CHL; General Church Minutes, CR100–318, box 1, folder 59, 3 December 1847, 6–7, CHL; William I. Appleby, autobiography and journal, MS 1401, folder 1, May 19, 1847, 170–71; December 3, 1847, 203–4, CHL; William I. Appleby, Batavia, New York, letter to Brigham Young, June 2, 1847, Brigham Young Collection, CR1234/1, box 21, folder 5, reel 30, CHL.

21. See Reeve, *Religion of a Different Color*, 122–23, chap. 5.

22. Brigham Young, February 5, 1852, a speech before a Joint Session of the Territorial Legislature, Papers of George D. Watt, MS 4534, box 1, folder 3, CHL, transcribed by LaJean Purcell Carruth; and Richard S. Van Wagoner, *The Complete Discourses of Brigham Young* (Salt Lake City: Smith-Pettit Foundation, 2009), 1:468–72.

23. See David M. Goldenberg, *The Curse of Ham: Race and Slavery in Early Judaism, Christianity, and Islam* (Princeton, NJ: Princeton University Press, 2003), 178–82; see, for example, David Walker, *Walker's Appeal, in Four Articles; Together with a Preamble, to the Coloured Citizens of the World, but in Particular, and Very Expressly, to Those of the United States of America, Written in Boston, State of Massachusetts, September 28, 1829* (Boston: David Walker, 1830), 68.

24. Young, February 5, 1852; Reeve, *Religion of a Different Color*, 145–46, 152–61.

25. See Reeve, *Religion of a Different Color*, 155–57; "Church History," *Times and Seasons*, March 1, 1842; and Royal Skousen, *The Book of Mormon: The Earliest Text* (New Haven, CT: Yale University Press, 2009), 137.

26. See Scott G. Kenney, ed., *Wilford Woodruff's Journal* (Midvale, UT: Signature Books, 1984), 6:511 (December 25, 1869). For Orson Pratt and B. H. Roberts's use of the

idea, see "The Pre-Existence of Man," *The Seer* (Washington, DC), April 1853; and B. H. Roberts, "To the Youth of Israel," *Contributor*, May 1885.

27. Joseph F. Smith Jr. letter to Alfred M. Nelson, January 13, 1907, microfilm, MS 14591, CHL.

28. John A. Widtsoe, "Were Negroes Neutrals in Heaven?," *Improvement Era*, June 1944, 385.

29. See Joseph Fielding Smith, *Answers to Gospel Questions*, 5 vols. (Salt Lake City: Deseret Book, 1966), 5:163–64.

30. See Reeve, *Religion of a Different Color*, 158–59; and Young, February 5, 1852.

31. Reeve, *Religion of a Different Color*, 195–201; *The Joseph Smith Papers, Journals*, 1:152; and "Report from the Presidency," *Times and Seasons*, October 1840, 188.

32. See W. Paul Reeve, "Sarah Ann Mode Hofheintz," https://exhibits.lib.utah.edu/s/century-of-black-mormons/page/hofheintz-sarah-ann-mode.

33. Joseph F. Smith, Notes on Elijah Able, undated [likely ca. 1879], CHL.

34. Reeve, *Religion of a Different Color*, 195–200; L. John Nuttall, diary, vol. 1 (December 1876–March 1884), typescript, 290–93, L. Tom Perry Collection; Council Meeting, June 4, 1879, Lester E. Bush Papers, MS 685, box 10, folder 3, Special Collections, J. Willard Marriott Library; and "Deaths," *Deseret News*, December 31, 1884, 800.

35. See Reeve, *Religion of a Different Color*, 200–10.

36. See George A. Smith Family Papers, MS 36, box 78, folder 7; December 15, 1897; March 11, 1900; August 18, 1900; January 2, 1902; and August 16, 1908, Manuscripts Division, Special Collections, J. Willard Marriott Library.

37. George A. Smith Family Papers, extract from George F. Richards record of decisions by the Council of the First Presidency and the Twelve Apostles (no date given, but the next decision in order is dated February 8, 1907), J. Willard Marriott Library.

38. See Reeve, *Religion of a Different Color*, 208–10; Joseph F. Smith, Notes on Elijah Able, undated [likely ca. 1879], CHL; George A. Smith Family Papers, Council Minutes, August 22, 1895; August 26, 1908, J. Willard Marriott Library; for the "never corrected" instance, see David McKay (Huntsville, UT) to John R. Winder (Salt Lake City), March 14, 1904, Joseph F. Smith, Stake Correspondence, CR 1/191, box 12, folder 17, CHL.

39. Reeve, *Religion of a Different Color*, 255–56; and First Presidency Statement, August 17, 1949, in Lester E. Bush Jr. and Armand L. Mauss, eds., *Neither White nor Black: Mormon Scholars Confront the Race Issue in a Universal Church* (Midvale, UT: Signature Books, 1984), 221.

40. See Edward L. Kimball, "Spencer W. Kimball and the Revelation on Priesthood," *BYU Studies* 47, no. 2 (2008): 21–22, 27; Gregory A. Prince and William Robert Wright, *David O. McKay and the Rise of Modern Mormonism* (Salt Lake City: University of Utah Press, 2005), chap. 4; D. Michael Quinn, *The Mormon Hierarchy: Extensions of Power* (Salt Lake City: Signature Books, 1997), 13–14; and Matthew L. Harris, "Mormonism's Problematic Racial Past and the Evolution of the Divine-Curse Doctrine," *John Whitmer Historical Association Journal* 33 (Spring/Summer 2013), 106–7; and Reeve, *Religion of a Different Color*, 259–60.

41. Edward L. Kimball, ed., *The Teachings of Spencer W. Kimball: Twelfth President of The Church of Jesus Christ of Latter-day Saints* (Salt Lake City: Bookcraft, 1982), 448–49.

42. See Kimball, "Spencer W. Kimball and the Revelation on Priesthood."

43. See Bruce R. McConkie, "All Are Alike unto God," August 18, 1978, Second Annual Church Educational System Religious Educators' Symposium, Brigham Young University, Provo, UT.

44. Joseph Smith, "Church History," *Times and Seasons* 3 (March 1, 1842): 706–10; and *The Joseph Smith Papers*, http://josephsmithpapers.org/.

45. Ezra Taft Benson, "Jesus Christ—Gifts and Expectations," *New Era*, May 1975, 16. See also 1 Samuel 8.

46. See Larry T. Wimmer, "Kirtland Economy," in *Encyclopedia of Mormonism*, ed. Daniel H. Ludlow (New York: Macmillan, 1992), 2:792–93; and Staker, *Hearken, O Ye People*, 391–548.

47. Ezra Taft Benson, "Jesus Christ—Gifts and Expectations," *New Era*, May 1975, 16.

48. American Historical Association, "Statement on Standards of Professional Conduct," http://historians.org/pubs/Free/ProfessionalStandards.cfm.

49. Brigham Young, "Remarks," *Deseret News*, February 12, 1862, 257.

50. Gordon B. Hinckley, "The Need for Greater Kindness," *Ensign*, May 2006, 58–61.

51. Hinckley, "Need for Greater Kindness," 58.

Selected RSC Publications on Church History in Salt Lake City and Beyond, 1847–Present

GENERAL READING

Baugh, Alexander L., and Susan Easton Black, eds. *Banner of the Gospel: Wilford Woodruff* (2010).

Freeman, Robert C., ed. *Nineteenth-Century Saints at War* (2007).

Goodman, Michael A., and Mauro Properzi, eds. *The Worldwide Church: Mormonism as a Global Religion* (2016).

Holzapfel, Richard Neitzel, and David M. Whitchurch, eds. *My Dear Sister: Letters between Joseph F. Smith and His Sister Martha Ann Smith Harris* (2018).

Manscill, Craig K., Brian D. Reeves, Guy L. Dorius, and J. B. Haws, eds. *Joseph F. Smith: Reflections on the Man and His Times* (2013).

Neilson, Reid L., and Fred E. Woods, eds. *Go Ye into All the World: The Growth and Development of Mormon Missionary Work* (2012).

Neilson, Reid L., and Wayne D. Crosby, eds. *Lengthening Our Stride: Globalization of the Church* (2018).

Whittaker, David J., and Arnold K. Garr, eds. *A Firm Foundation: Church Organization and Administration* (2011).

Woodger, Mary Jane, ed. *Champion of Liberty: John Taylor* (2009).

THE PIONEER TRAIL AND SETTLING OF THE WEST

Bennett, Richard E., ed. *The Journey West: The Mormon Pioneer Journals of Horace K. Whitney with Insights from Helen Mar Kimball Whitney* (2018).

Clayton, Roberta Flake, Catherine H. Ellis, and David F. Boone. *Pioneer Women of Arizona* (2017).

Esplin, Scott C., Richard E. Bennett, Susan Easton Black, and Craig K. Manscill, eds. *Far Away in the West: Reflections on the Mormon Pioneer Trail* (2015).

Esplin, Scott C., and Kenneth L. Alford, eds. *Salt Lake City: The Place Which God Prepared* (2011).

Mason, Patrick Q., and Thomas A. Wayment. "Discussing Difficult Topics: The Mountain Meadows Massacre." *Religious Educator* 18, no. 2 (2017): 148–61.

Merrill, Timothy G. "Remembering the Pioneer Legacy." *Religious Educator* 11, no. 2 (2010): 163–71.

INTERNATIONAL EXPANSION

Chou, Po Nien (Felipe), and Petra Cho. *Voice of the Saints in Taiwan: A History of the Latter-day Saints in Taiwan* (2017).

Freeman, Robert C., and Richard Neitzel Holzapfel, eds. *Regional Studies in Latter-day Saint Church History: The British Isles* (2007).

Neilson, Reid L., Steven C. Harper, Craig K. Manscill, and Mary Jane Woodger, eds. *Regional Studies in Latter-day Saint Church History: The Pacific Isles* (2008).

Prete, Roy A., and Carma T. Prete, eds. *Canadian Mormons: History of the Church of Jesus Christ of Latter-day Saints* (2017).

Top, Brent L., and Donald Q. Cannon, eds. *Regional Studies in Latter-day Saint Church History: Europe* (2003).

Toronto, James A., Eric R Dursteler, and Michael W. Homer. *Mormons in the Piazza: History of the Latter-day Saints in Italy* (2017).

Underwood, Grant, ed. *Pioneers in the Pacific: Memory, History, and Cultural Identity among the Latter-day Saint* (2005).

PRIESTHOOD AND TEMPLE BLESSINGS FOR ALL

Bennett, Richard E. "'That Every Man Might Speak in the Name of God the Lord': A Study of Official Declaration 2." *Religious Educator* 4, no. 2 (2003): 41–56.

LeBaron, E. Dale. "Revelation on the Priesthood, Thirty-Five Years Later." *Religious Educator* 14, no. 3 (2013): 121–35.

Reeve, W. Paul, and Thomas A. Wayment. "Discussing Difficult Topics: Race and the Priesthood." *Religious Educator* 17, no. 3 (2016): 126–43.

Woodger, Mary Jane. "Revelation Attitudes: The Coming Forth of Official Declaration 2." *Religious Educator* 3, no. 2 (2002): 185–200.

Index

H